I0831114

Wooden Churches in Eastern Europe

Siegfried von Quast

Wooden Churches in Eastern Europe

Geleitwort/Preface
Rudolf Moser

Edition Axel Menges

ISBN 978-3-86905-036-2

Druck und Bindearbeiten/Printing and binding: Graspo CZ, a.s., Zlín, Tschechische Republik/Czech Republic

Lektorat/Editorial work: Dorothea Duwe
Buchgestaltung/Book design: Axel Menges

Inhalt

Contents

Rudolf Moser

Über meinen Freund Siegfried von Quast

Siegfried von Quast verbrachte seine frühen Jugendjahre auf Schloß und Landgut Radensleben (Neuruppin). Das in seinem Konzept von Karl Friedrich Schinkel, einem Freund der Familie, beeinflußte Schloß seiner Eltern prägte früh sein Empfinden für maßstabsgerechte, anspruchsvolle Architektur. Im Jahr 1945 floh die Familie angesichts der vorrückenden russischen Armee nach Murnau in Bayern, wo der Vater, Wilfried von Quast, das 1909 von Emanuel von Seidl erbaute ehemalige Kavalierhaus des Schlosses Seeleiten, ein schönes, großzügiges Gebäude in einem Park, erwarb. Auch dort erfolgte wieder eine sein Raumvorstellungsvermögen fördernde Beeinflussung durch die in ihrer Massenentwicklung und ihren Details vorbildliche Architektur des Hauses mit wohlproportionierten Innenräumen und artikuliertem Landschaftsbezug.

Diese Prägungen sowie seine sich schon früh zeigende gestalterische Begabung, gepaart mit weitreichenden geistigen Interressen, veranlaßten ihn zunächst, ein Studium der Philosophie, Germanistik und Kunstgeschichte aufzunehmen, dem schließlich ein Studium der Architektur an der Technischen Hochschule in München folgte. Dort war sein wichtigster Lehrer Hans Döllgast. Dieser lehrte, aktuelle Architekturmoden ausschließend, das aus der tradierten Architektur erfahrbare Wissen um Konstruktion und Gestaltung in zeitgemäße Orientierungs- und Realisierungsmöglichkeiten umzusetzen. Positive Beeinflussung erfuhr von Quast auch durch das geistige und kulturelle Klima in München und an der dortigen Universität. Seine enge Freundschaft mit den Assistenten des Physikers Werner Heisenberg verschaffte ihm Zugang zu naturwissenschaftlichen Gesprächszirkeln und damit eine geistige Horizonterweiterung. Von Quast, aus preußischem Uradel, war dem bayrischen Brauchtum so zugetan, daß er sich mit Freuden deren Ritualen hingab. Er beherrschte den bayrischen Dialekt vollkommen.

Nach dem Vordiplom setzte er sein Studium an der Technischen Hochschule in Karlsruhe bei Egon Eiermann fort. Hier glänzte er schon bald durch klare Charakterisierung, Gliederung und Durchführung von Entwurfsaufgaben und zu beurteilenden Entwürfen. Er war fähig, aus dem Stand einen Entwurf oder ein Gebäude treffend und umfassend zu beschreiben und zu beurteilen. Auch ich studierte in Karlsruhe, und wir wurden bald Freunde. Wir spürten die damalige Spannung und die Kontroversen zwischen den bestehenden Architekturgestaltungsrichtungen und versuchten uns in anderen Gestaltungsansätzen und Entwurfstheorien – meist konträr zu den Gestaltungslinien von Ludwig Mies van der Rohe, Walter Gropius, Richard Neutra und auch Eiermann. Ganz besonders begeisterte uns die »Raumsatz-Entwurfstheorie« von Wolfgang Th. Otto, der bei Theodor Fischer Architektur studiert und lange bei Frank Lloyd Wright in Taliesin gearbeitet hatte. Otto erteilte mir die Ehre, mit ihm zusammen in Zürich sein Buch *Der Raumsatz* zu entwickeln. Ich schenkte das Buch Eiermann, der mich in sein Entwurfsteam aufgenommen hatte und mir sogar ein Honorar zahlte. Ich durfte den Wettbewerbsentwurf für eine Kirche in Mühlheim an der Ruhr erarbeiten, dem ich die Raumsatz-Theorie zugrundelegte und der mit dem ersten Preis ausgezeichnet wurde. Eiermann zeigte diesen Entwurf in seiner Präsentation seines Lebenswerks in der Zeitschrift *L'Architecture d'aujourdhui*, weigerte sich aber zum Ärger aller Beteiligten, die Kirche auch zu bauen. Der Entwurf entspreche nicht seinem gestalterischen Glaubensbekenntnis. Wir haben uns auch mit den Arbeiten von Hans Scharoun, Jörn Utzon und dem anthroposophischen Entwurfsansatz von Rolf Gutbrod, der später mein väterlicher Freund und Berater wurde, auseinandergesetzt. Dank handwerklicher Vorbildung interessierten uns zudem traditionelle Baumethoden, vor allem Holzkonstruktionen, die ja heute wieder an Aktualität gewonnen haben.

Nach seinem Diplom bei Eiermann stellte sich für von Quast die Frage, ob nun der Sprung in die Praxis folgen oder er sein bisher erworbenes Wissen weiter vertiefen sollte. Japans historische und zeitgenössische Architektur war damals das Traumziel vieler junger Architekten. Von Quast entschied sich, die rational-karge Architektur Japans vor Ort zu erkunden, lernte in kürzester Zeit japanisch und fuhr als Hilfsheizer auf einem Dampfer nach Japan. Dort arbeitete er in einem Architekturbüro, das parallel die spezielle japanische Architekturphotographie pflegte. Nach zwei Jahren kehrte er zurück nach Deutschland und begann seine Karriere als Architekturphotograph.

Er war fähig, komplexe gestalterische Zusammenhänge, die die Erscheinung und das Wesen eines Gebäudes ausmachen, zu erkennen und in seine Photographien umzusetzen, was ihn bald zu einem der gefragtesten Architekturphotographen Deutschlands machte. Die Bauzeitschrift *Bauwelt* buchte ihn, wann immer er verfügbar war. Auch für andere Printmedien war er tätig. So wurde er unter anderem mit einem viel beachteten Photo- und Gesprächstreffen mit dem Philosophen Martin Heidegger in dessen Hütte im Schwarzwald beauftragt.

Später widmete er sich vermehrt eigenen Themen, darunter Gebäude der Gründerzeit, Eisenbahnanlagen, Kriegerdenkmale, Barockengel und Industriebauten. Jedes dieser umfangreich behandelten Themen wäre eine eigene Veröffentlichung wert. Sein Interesse kulminierte schließlich in einem umfassenden Studium der von der Baugeschichte bisher kaum beachteten Holzkirchen in Osteuropa.

Von Quast folgte durch seine Arbeit zu den Holzkirchen auch einer Familientradition. Sein Urgroßvater, Alexander Ferdinand von Quast, studierte Architektur bei Schinkel und war später dessen Freund und Förderer. Er wurde von dem kunstaffinen König Friedrich Wilhelm IV. von Preußen 1843 zum ersten Konservator der Baudenkmale im preußischen Staat berufen. In dieser Rolle rettete er unzählige bedeutende Gebäude, darunter das Holstentor in Lübeck – und begründete damit den Denkmalschutz in Deutschland. Seit 1987 verleiht das Land Berlin die Ferdinand-von-Quast-Medaille an Personen und Institutionen, die sich in besonderem Maße für den Denkmalschutz einsetzen.

Rudolf Moser

About my friend Siegfried von Quast

Siegfried von Quast spent his early youth at Radensleben Castle and Manor (Neuruppin). His parents' castle, which was influenced in its concept by Karl Friedrich Schinkel, a friend of the family, had an early influence on his sense of scale-appropriate, sophisticated architecture. In 1945, faced with the advancing Russian army, the family fled to Murnau in Bavaria, where the father, Wilfried von Quast, bought the former cavalier house of Schloß Seeleiten, built by Emanuel von Seidl in 1909, a beautiful, spacious building in a park. There, too, his spatial imagination was again influenced by the building's exemplary architecture in its mass development and details, with well-proportioned interior rooms and articulated reference to the landscape.

These influences, as well as his early talent for design, coupled with wide-ranging intellectual interests, initially prompted him to take up studies in philosophy, German literature, and art history, which was eventually followed by studies in architecture at the Technische Hochschule in Munich. His most important teacher there was Hans Döllgast. He taught him to exclude current architectural fashions and to translate the knowledge of construction and design gained from traditional architecture into contemporary possibilities for orientation and realisation. Von Quast was also positively influenced by the intellectual and cultural climate in Munich and at the university there. His close friendship with the assistants of the physicist Werner Heisenberg gave him access to natural-science discussion circles and thus broadened his intellectual horizons. Von Quast, from Prussian nobility, was so fond of Bavarian customs that he enjoyed their rituals. He had a perfect command of the Bavarian dialect.

After his intermediate diploma, he continued his studies at the Technische Hochschule in Karlsruhe under Egon Eiermann. Here he soon shone with his clear characterisation, structuring and execution of design tasks and designs to be assessed. He was able to describe and assess a design or a building accurately and comprehensively from a standing start. I also studied in Karlsruhe and we soon became friends. We sensed the tension and controversy between the existing architectural design trends of the time and tried our hand at other design approaches and design theories – mostly contrary to the design lines of Ludwig Mies van der Rohe, Walter Gropius, Richard Neutra and also Eiermann. We were particularly enthusiastic about the »Raumsatz design theory« by Wolfgang Th. Otto, who studied architecture with Theodor Fischer and worked for a long time with Frank Lloyd Wright in Taliesin. Otto gave me the honour of working with him in Zurich on his book *Der Raumsatz*. I gave the book to Egon Eiermann, who included me in his design team and even paid me a fee. I was allowed to work on the competition design for a church in Mühlheim an der Ruhr, which I based on the »Raumsatz« theory and which was awarded first prize. Eiermann showed this design in his presentation of his life's work in the magazine *L'Architecture d'aujourdhui*, but to the annoyance of everyone involved, he refused to build the church. In his view, the design would not be in line with his design creed. We also studied the works of Hans Scharoun, Jörn Utzon and the anthroposophical design approach of Rolf Gutbrod, who later became my fatherly friend and advisor. Thanks to our training as a craftsman, we were also interested in traditional building methods, especially wooden constructions, which have gained in relevance again today.

After receiving his diploma from Eiermann, von Quast asked himself whether he should now take the leap into practice or continue to deepen the knowledge he had acquired so far. Japan's historical and contemporary architecture was the dream destination of many young architects at the time. Von Quast decided to explore Japan's rational-sparse architecture on site, learned Japanese in no time and went to Japan as an assistant stoker on a steamer. There he worked in an architectural office, which in parallel cultivated the special Japanese architectural photography. After two years, he returned to Germany and began his career as an architectural photographer.

He was able to identify complex design relationships that make up the appearance and essence of a building and translate them into his photographs, which soon made him one of the most sought-after architectural photographers in Germany. The building magazine *Bauwelt* booked him whenever he was available. He also worked for other print media. Among other things, he was commissioned to photograph and talk with the philosopher Martin Heidegger in his hut in the Black Forest, which attracted a great deal of attention.

Later he devoted himself increasingly to his own topics, including buildings of the Gründerzeit, railway facilities, war memorials, baroque angels and industrial buildings. Each of these extensively treated subjects would be worth its own publication. His interest finally culminated in a comprehensive study of the wooden churches in Eastern Europe, which had hitherto received little attention in the history of architecture.

Von Quast's work on wooden churches also followed a family tradition. His great-grandfather, Alexander Ferdinand von Quast, studied architecture with Schinkel and was later his friend and patron. He was appointed the first curator of architectural monuments in the Prussian state by the art-loving King Friedrich Wilhelm IV of Prussia in 1843. In this role, he saved countless important buildings, including the Holsten Gate in Lübeck – and thus founded the protection of historical monuments in Germany. Since 1987, the state of Berlin has awarded the Ferdinand von Quast Medal to individuals and institutions, who have made a special contribution to the protection of historical monuments.

Siegfried von Quast

Aus der Einführung zu dem geplanten, aber nicht mehr realisierten Buch über die Holzkirchen in Osteuropa

Bis jetzt führten mich in den vergangenen 15 Jahren 18 Studienreisen in die Karpaten: nach Mähren, Schlesien, Kleinpolen, Oberungarn, Transkarpatien, Transsilvanien (Siebenbürgen), in die Moldau und in die Walachei – heute Gebiete von Tschechien, Polen, der Slowakei, der Ukraine, von Rumänien und Ungarn – um einem Phänomen der anonymen, der Volksarchitektur zu begegnen: den Holzkirchen.

Der hufeisenförmige Karpatenbogen beginnt nördlich von Preßburg mit den Kleinen Karpaten und umfaßt die Beskiden mit den Tatras, der Fatra, den Bieszczady, den Wald- und Ostkarpaten bis hin zu den Südkarpaten und endet, wieder in Donaunähe, mit dem Banater Gebirge. Es sind meist waldreiche Mittelgebirge mit dazwischen herausragenden Hochgebirgen. Hier in den armen, abseits gelegenen Gegenden gibt es noch zahlreiche Holzkirchen – christliche Sakralbauten.

Wie überall im abendländischen und morgenländischen Europa, wo Tausende von Dorfkirchen Wahrzeichen des christlichen Glaubens sind, signalisieren die Kuppeln und Türme, die Hoheitszeichen dieser Holzkirchen: »Hier ist der Himmel – hier ist unser Gott, hier ist das himmlische Jerusalem«, gleich wie in den gewaltigen Kathedralen und übermächtigen Klöstern im Westen.

Aus dem Westen wandert der pfeilspitze gotische Glockenturm bis nach Transsilvanien und die Kuppel aus dem weitesten Südosten der christlichen Kultur nach Galizien und in die Moldau. Aus steinernen Bauformen werden hölzerne. Die Kuppel selbst kehrt schließlich mit dem Barock zurück in den Osten, bis in die Ukraine und nach Rußland.

Allen diesen Bauten gemeinsam ist, daß hier mit vorhandenem Material, dem Holz, und bescheidensten Mitteln, Gotteshäuser, Mittelpunkte in den Dörfern, mit viel Gefühl und Liebe gebaut wurden. Die Konstruktionen in Holz sind in alter Tradition von Wohn- und Wirtschaftsbauten der bäuerlichen Bevölkerung abgeleitet worden. Deren Architektur mit ihren typologischen Formen kam wohl als Idee in diese Abgeschiedenheit. »Die Idee von einer Kirche als Bauwerk« wurde mitgebracht von Geistlichen und wandernden Handwerksmeistern aus den fruchtbareren Ebenen und den reichen, großen Bergbau- und Handelstädten.

Die ältesten Kirchen wurden bereits im 15. Jahrhundert erbaut, die meisten der jetzt noch erhaltenen im 18. und 19. Jahrhundert, und etliche entstehen noch heute. Viele wurden in den beiden Weltkriegen zerstört, viele fielen ethnischen Säuberungsmaßnahmen nach 1945 zum Opfer, manche verfielen in der Sowjetzeit, andere verbrannten durch Blitz oder Kurzschluß, nicht wenige aber wichen ganz einfach schon seit dem 19. Jahrhundert den »repräsentativeren« Steinkirchen. Aber viele Kirchen sind noch vorhanden, sind konsekriert, und Gläubige versammeln sich in ihnen. Fast alle stehen in den verschiedenen Karpatenländern unter Denkmalschutz, viele wurden in jüngster Zeit auch liebevoll restauriert. Dennoch sind einige in einem schlechten Zustand.

Mehr als nach dem bauhistorischen Wert stellt sich hier die Frage nach der ästhetischen Beurteilung dieser kleinen Bauwerke. Es ist kein raffinierter und baugeschichtlich ableitbarer und beweisbarer Formenkanon großer Architektur, was uns so begeistert. Es sind im Grunde auch keine handwerklich übertrieben ausgeklügelten Konstruktionen, dennoch sind sie in ihrer einfachen Art sicher und schön. Zu ihrem ästhetischen Reiz gehören aber auch das oberflächenverwitterte Material, verformte Baukörper, Farbimprovisationen, neuerdings ornamentiertes Blech, im Inneren Wandmalereien, Altar- und Ikonostase-Ausstattungen aus Renaissance und Barock, vor allem aber ihre Lage im Dorf, meist isoliert, oft erhöht, umgeben von alten Bäumen, Einfriedungen und Gräbern ohne Friedhofsordnung.

In den verschiedenen Gegenden der Karpaten finden wir sehr unterschiedliche Grundriß- und Aufbautypen. Durch die Karpaten verläuft die alte Kulturgrenze zwischen Rom und Byzanz, also zwischen West- und Ostkirche, und so gibt es unter den Bauwerken der beiden großen Kulturräume entsprechende Unterschiede, aber auch wechselseitige Einflüsse, wozu besonders beigetragen haben mag, daß es in der Zeit, in der die meisten Holzkirchen gebaut wurden, in den Karpaten keine nationalstaatlichen Grenzen in der heutigen Form gab. Die meisten Regionen waren Jahrhunderte lang unter polnischer und ungarischer, später österreichischer Herrschaft.

Allen gemeinsam ist eben die Holzbauweise, und zwar wurden mit Ausnahme der protestantischen Holzkirchen, die zum Teil in Fachwerkkonstruktion errichtet wurden, alle anderen in Blockbauweise erstellt. Die Glockentürme – frei stehend oder mit den Baukörpern verbunden – wurden in reiner oder mit dem Blockbau kombinierter Ständerbauweise konstruiert. Das Material ist meist Nadelholz. Für die Schwellenkränze, auch für andere Bauteile, manchmal sogar für Schindeln, wurde kostbares Eichenholz verwendet. Es wurden die verschiedensten Eckverbindungen – Verkämmungen und Verblattungen – zur Anwendung gebracht. Die Konstruktionen von Kuppel- und Pyramidenbekrönungen, aus Blockverbänden aufgeschichtet bis unter die oberste Dachhaut im Wechsel vom quadratischen zum achteckigen Grundriß, sind sehr kunstvoll. Um die Kirchen vor schädlicher Witterung zu schützen, wurden die Blockwände, wie natürlich die Dächer und Dachhäute verschindelt, die Wände auch verbrettert, es wurden auch Vor- und Flugdächer angebracht. Sie schaffen den unglaublich differenzierten Reiz der Baukörper. Heute mußten oft aus Not Schindeldächer durch Blechdächer ersetzt werden, sie werden aber seit einiger Zeit liebevoll ornamentiert, und damit wurde ein neues Stilelement geschaffen.

Die Schönheit dieser Kirchen, sei sie von diesen einzigartigen Holzkuppeln der galizischen Kirchen oder die oft von vier Scharwachttürmchen umstellten, gotischen Himmelsnadeln in Transsilvanien getragen, aber auch von den verborgenen Wandmalereien, von den sich in den winzigen Gotteshäusern auftürmenden Ikonostasen sowie den prachtvollen Barockaltären und Triumphbögen in den katholischen Kirchen, muß nicht den Vergleich mit der sakralen Holzarchitektur in anderen Teilen Europas, in Skandinavien oder Rußland, scheuen.

Siegfried von Quast

From the introduction to the planned, but no longer realised book on the wooden churches in Eastern Europe

So far, 18 study trips in the past 15 years have taken me to the Carpathians: to Moravia, Silesia, Lesser Poland, Upper Hungary, Transcarpathia, Transsylvania, Moldavia and Wallachia – today areas of Tchechia, Poland, Slovakia, Ukraine, Romania and Hungary – to encounter a phenomenon of anonymous, folk architecture: wooden churches.

The horseshoe-shaped Carpathian arc begins north of Bratislava with the Little Carpathians and includes the Beskids with the Tatras, the Fatra, the Bieszczady, the Forest and Eastern Carpathians up to the Southern Carpathians and ends, again near the Danube, with the Banat Mountains. These are mostly forested low mountain ranges with prominent high mountains. Here, in the poor, remote areas, there are still numerous wooden churches – Christian sacred buildings.

As everywhere in western and eastern Europe, where thousands of village churches are emblems of the Christian faith, the domes and towers, the emblems of these wooden churches, signalise »Here is heaven – here is our God, here is the heavenly Jerusalem«, just like those of the mighty cathedrals and overpowering monasteries in the West.

From the West, the arrowhead Gothic bell tower travels as far as Transsylvania, and the dome from the far southeast of Christian culture travels to Galicia and Moldavia. Stone building forms become wooden ones. The dome itself finally returned with the Baroque to the East, as far as in the Ukraine and Russia.

What all these buildings have in common is that with the available material, wood, and the most modest means, places of worship, centres in the villages, were built with much feeling and love. The constructions in wood were derived in an old tradition from the dwellings and farm buildings of the peasant population. Their architecture, the typological forms probably penetrated into this seclusion as an idea. »The idea of a church as a building« was brought with them by clergymen and wandering master craftsmen from the more fertile plains and the rich, large mining and trading towns.

The oldest churches were built as early as in the 15th century, most of those still standing were built in the 18th and 19th centuries, and quite a few are still being built today. Many were destroyed in the two World Wars, many fell victim to ethnic cleansing after 1945, some fell into disrepair during the Soviet era, others were burnt down by lightning or short circuits, and quite a few simply gave way to the more »representative« stone churches as early as the 19th century. But many churches are still standing, consecrated, and believers gather in them. In fact, almost all of them in the various Carpathian countries are protected monuments, and not a few been lovingly restored in recent times. Nevertheless, some are in a poor condition.

More than the architectural-historical value, the question arises here of the aesthetic assessment of these small buildings. It is not a refined canon of forms of great architecture that can be derived and proven from the history of architecture that inspires us so much. Basically, they are not overly sophisticated constructions in terms of craftsmanship, they are safe and beautiful in their simplicity. Their aesthetic appeal, however, also includes the surface-weathered material, deformed structures, colour improvisations, recently ornamented sheet metal, inside wall paintings, altar and iconostasis furnishings derived from Renaissance and Baroque periods, but above all their location in the village, mostly isolated, often elevated, surrounded by old trees, enclosures and graves without cemetery order.

In the different regions of the Carpathians we find very different types of floor plans and structures. The old cultural border between Rome and Byzantium, i.e. between the Western and Eastern Churches, runs through the Carpathians, and so there are corresponding differences between the buildings of the two great cultural areas, but also mutual influences, to which the fact that there were no national borders in the Carpathians in their present form at the time when most wooden churches were built may have contributed in particular. Most of the regions were under Polish and Hungarian and later Austrian rule for centuries.

What they all have in common is the wooden construction method. With the exception of the Protestant wooden churches, which were partly built as half-timbered structures, all the others were built as log structures. The bell towers – free-standing or connected to the building structures – were constructed in pure or combined post and beam construction. The material is mostly coniferous wood. Precious oak was used for the sill rings, also for other components, sometimes even for shingles. A wide variety of corner joints – hammering and lathing – were used. The constructions of dome and pyramid crowns, piled up from blocks to under the uppermost roof skin, alternating from a square to an octagonal floor plan, are very artistic. In order to protect the churches from damaging weather, the block walls, as well as the roofs and roof skins, were shingled, the walls were also boarded up, and porches and flying roofs were attached. They create the incredibly differentiated charm of the buildings. Today, shingle roofs often had to be replaced by tin roofs out of necessity, but they have been lovingly ornamented for some time, and thus a new stylistic element has been created.

The beauty of these churches, be it emphasised by the unique wooden domes of the Galician churches or the Gothic celestial needles in Transsylvania, often surrounded by four little watchtowers, but also by the hidden wall paintings, the iconostases towering in the tiny houses of worship and the magnificent Baroque altars and triumphal arches in the Catholic churches, need not fear comparison with the sacred wooden architecture in other parts of Europe, in Scandinavia or Russia.

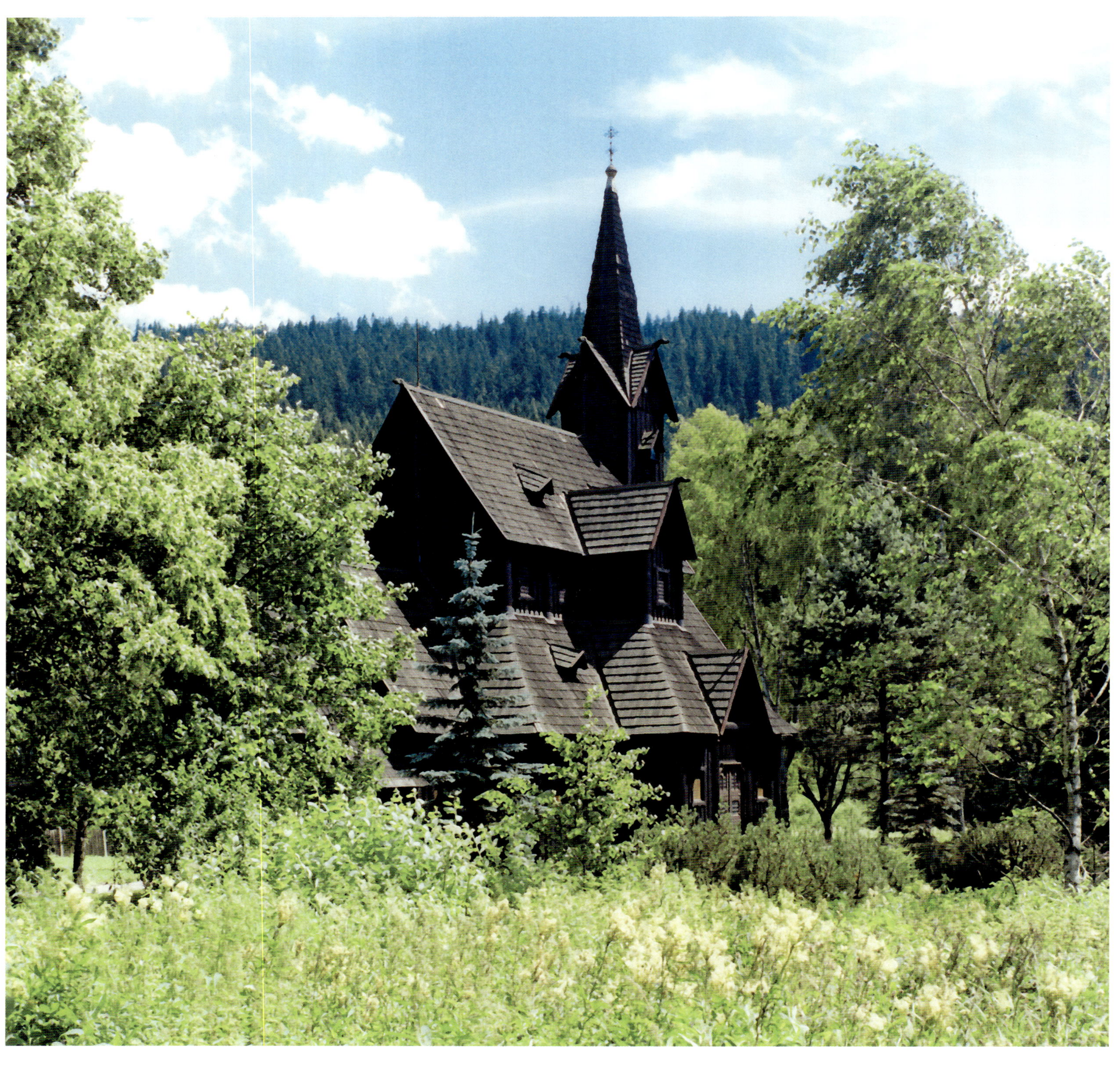

Bílá
Moravskoslezský kraj, Tschechien
Friedrichskirche, nach Kardinal Friedrich
Egon von Fürstenberg benannt
1873/74
Architekt: A. Kybasta

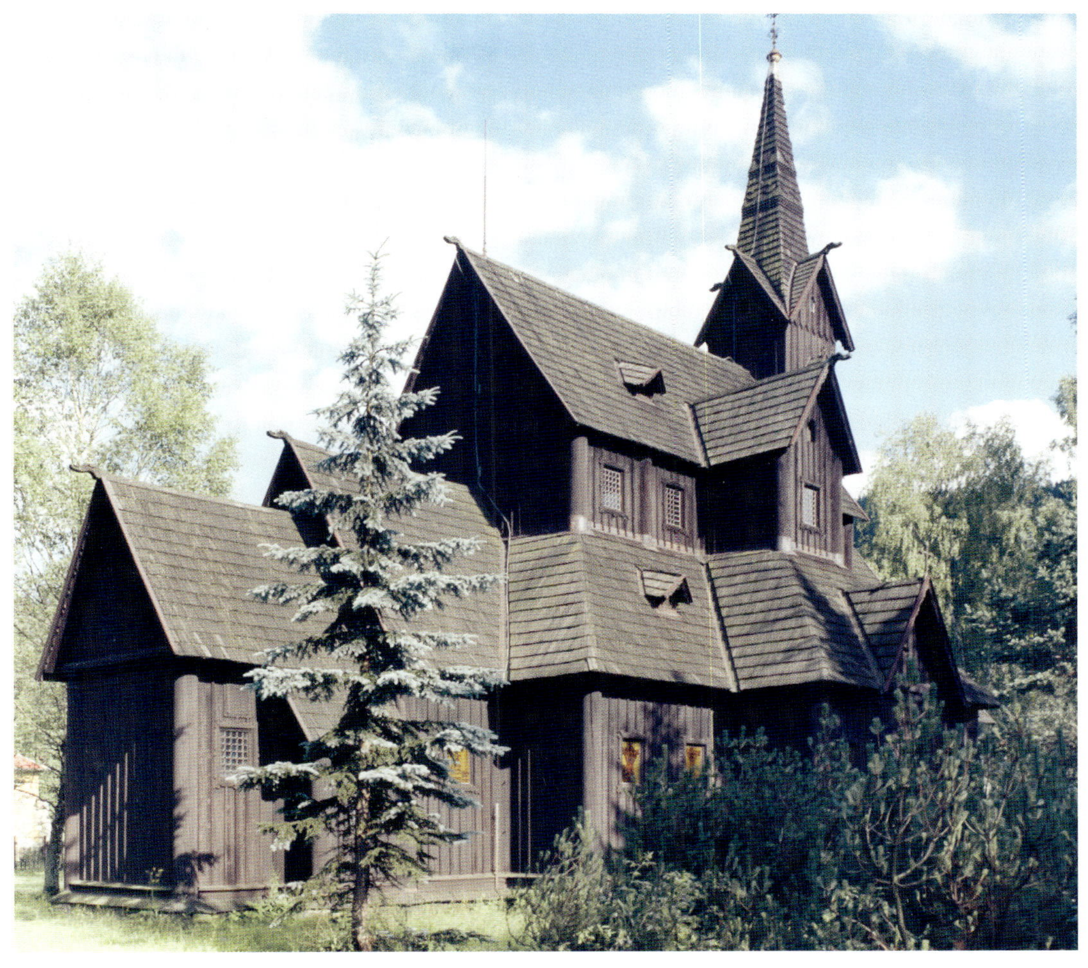

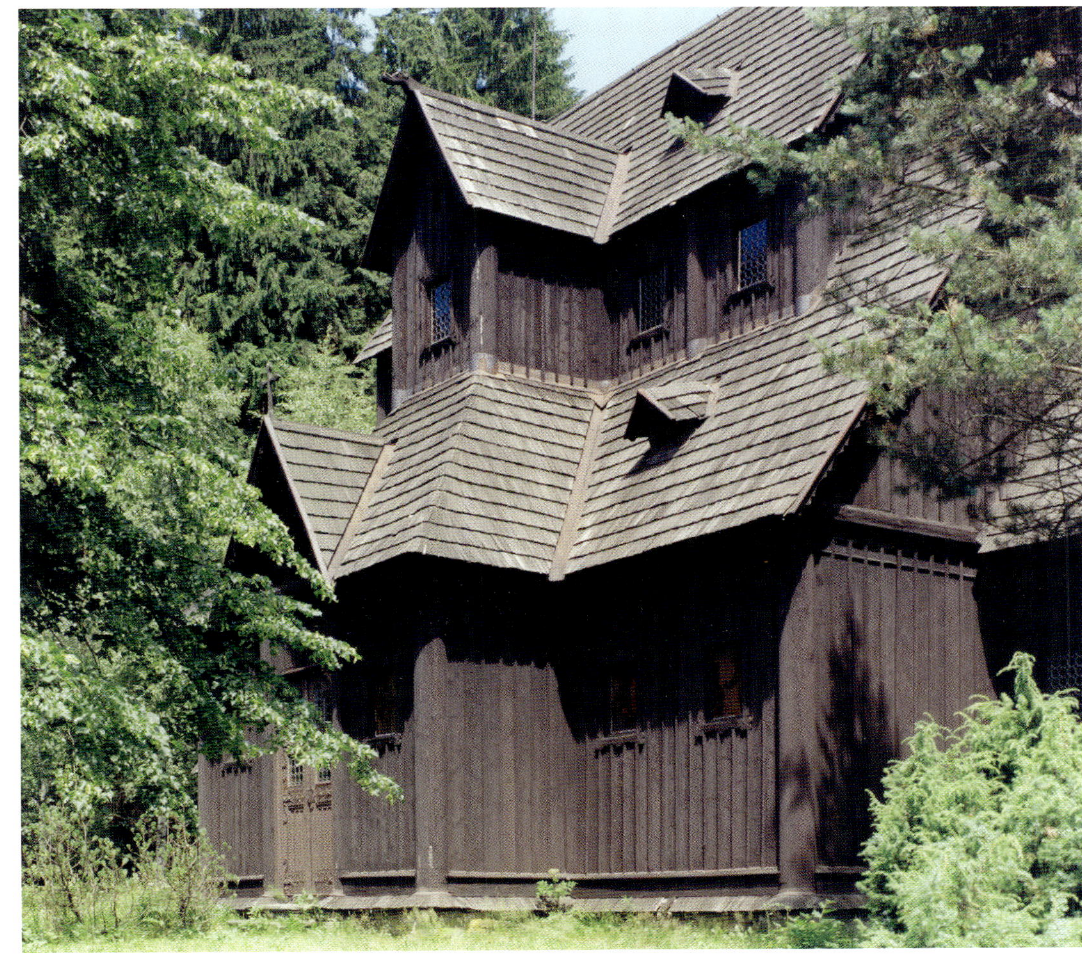

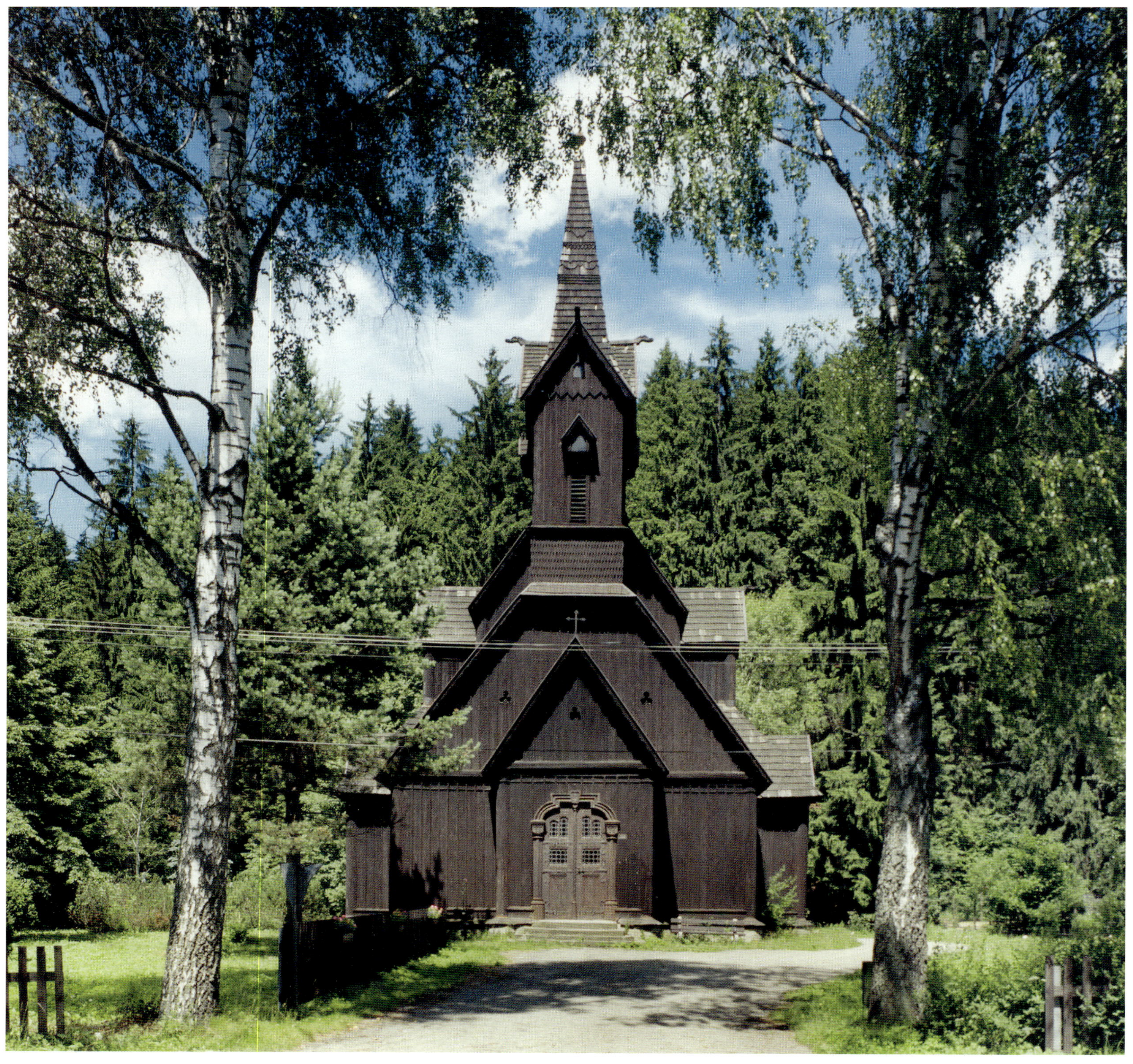

Bílá
Moravskoslezský kraj, Tschechien
Friedrichskirche, nach Kardinal Friedrich
Egon von Fürstenberg benannt
1873/74
Architekt: A. Kybasta

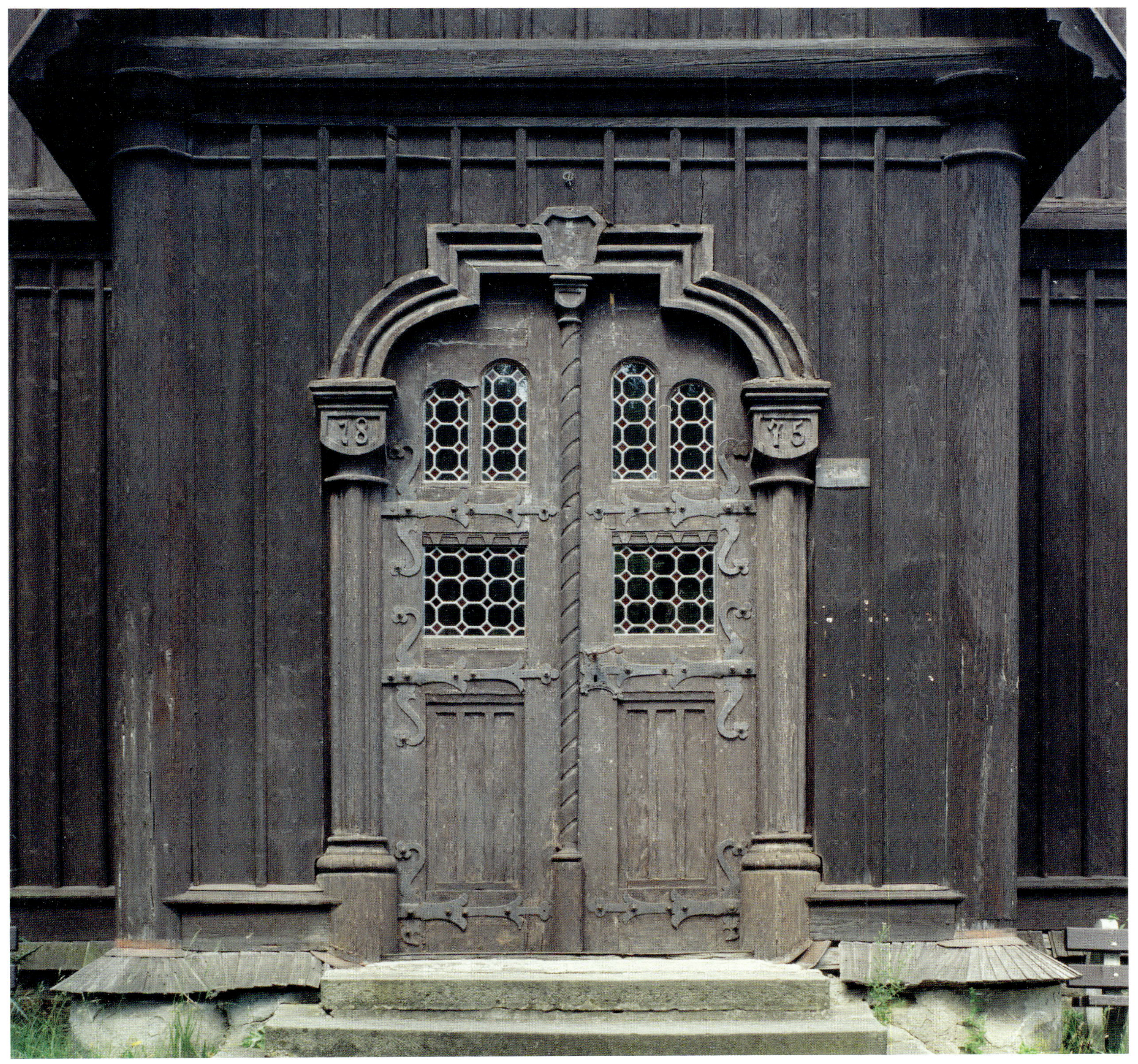

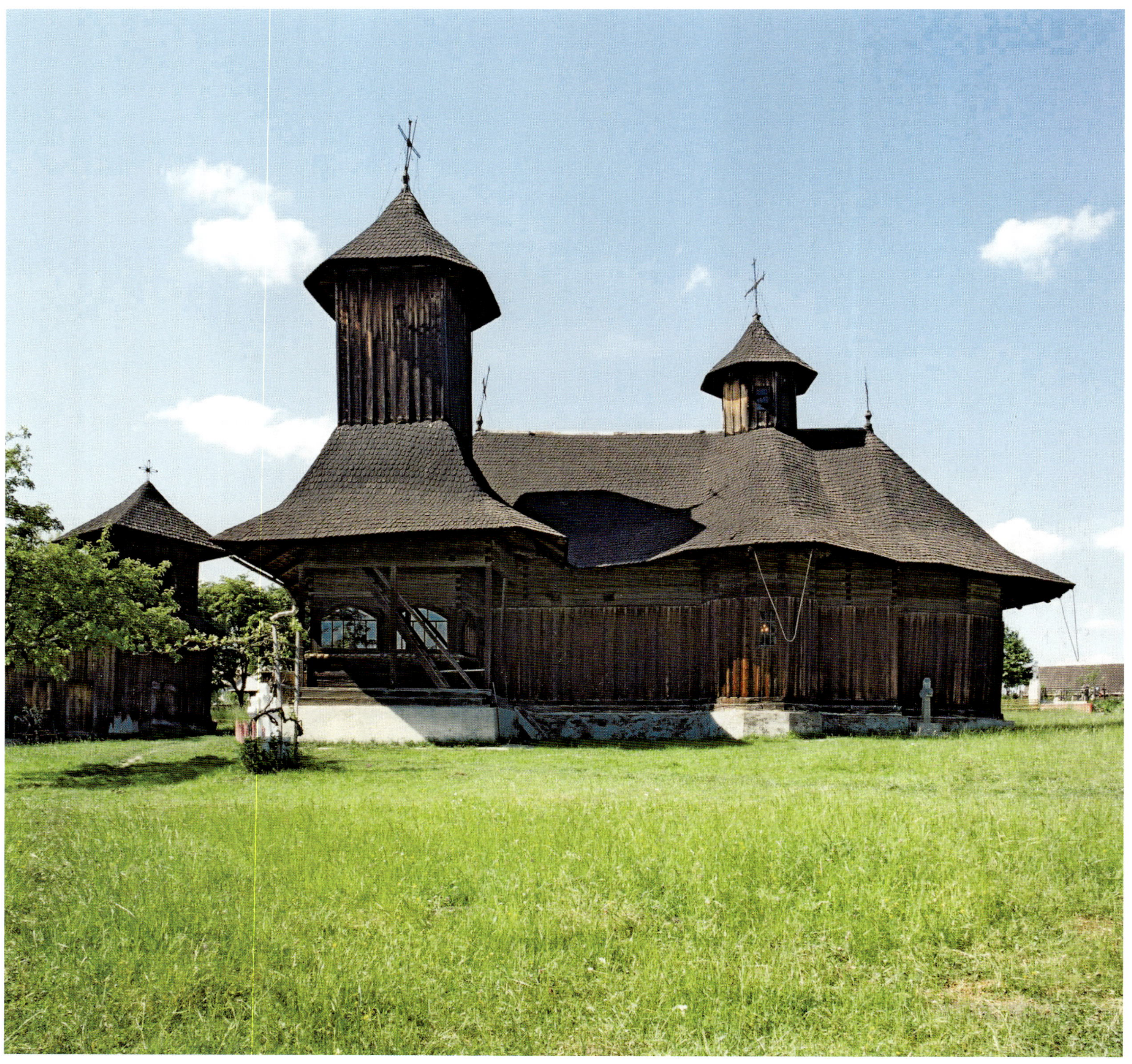

Botoșana
Suceava, Rumänien
Sankt Demetrius
1810

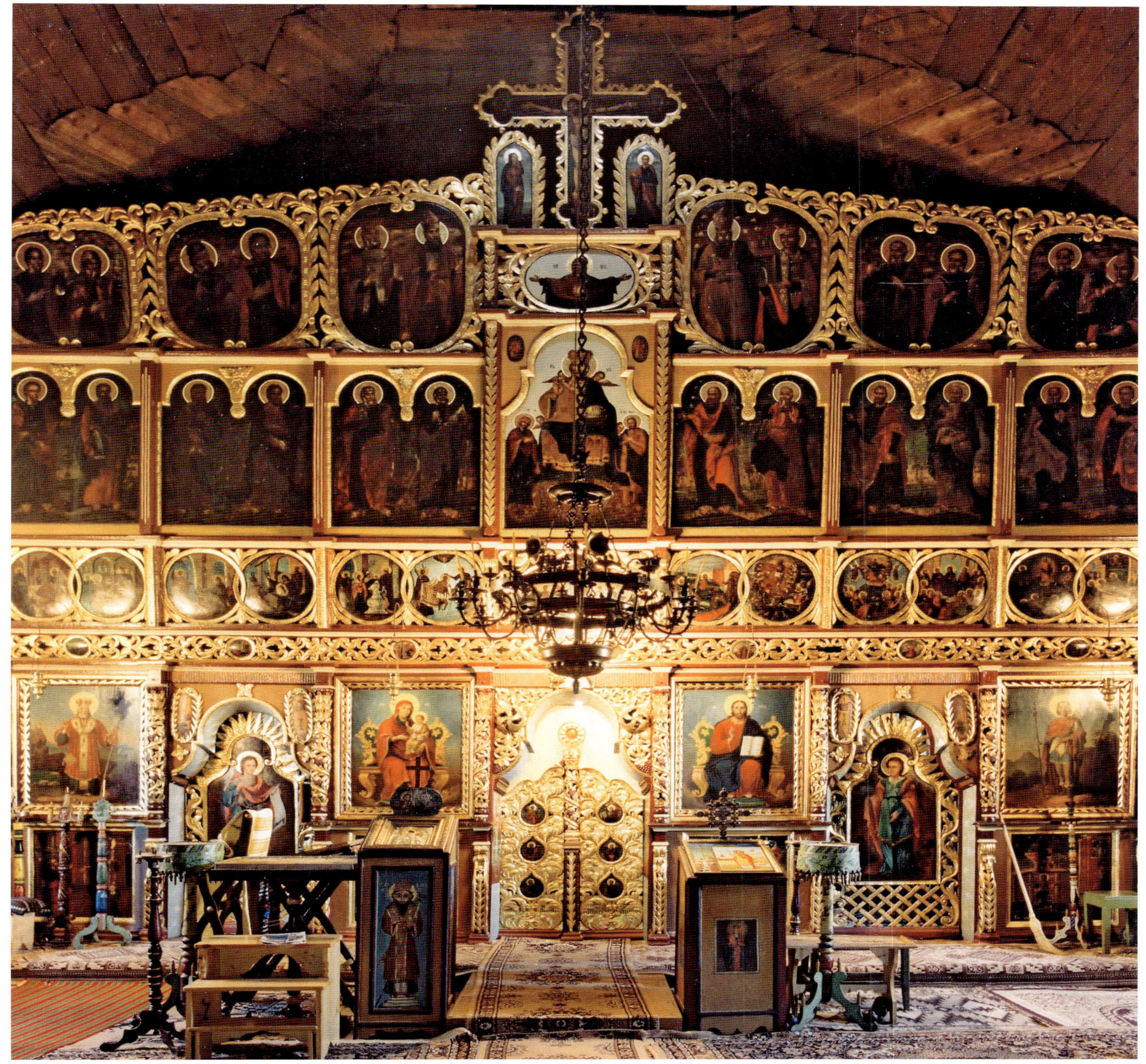

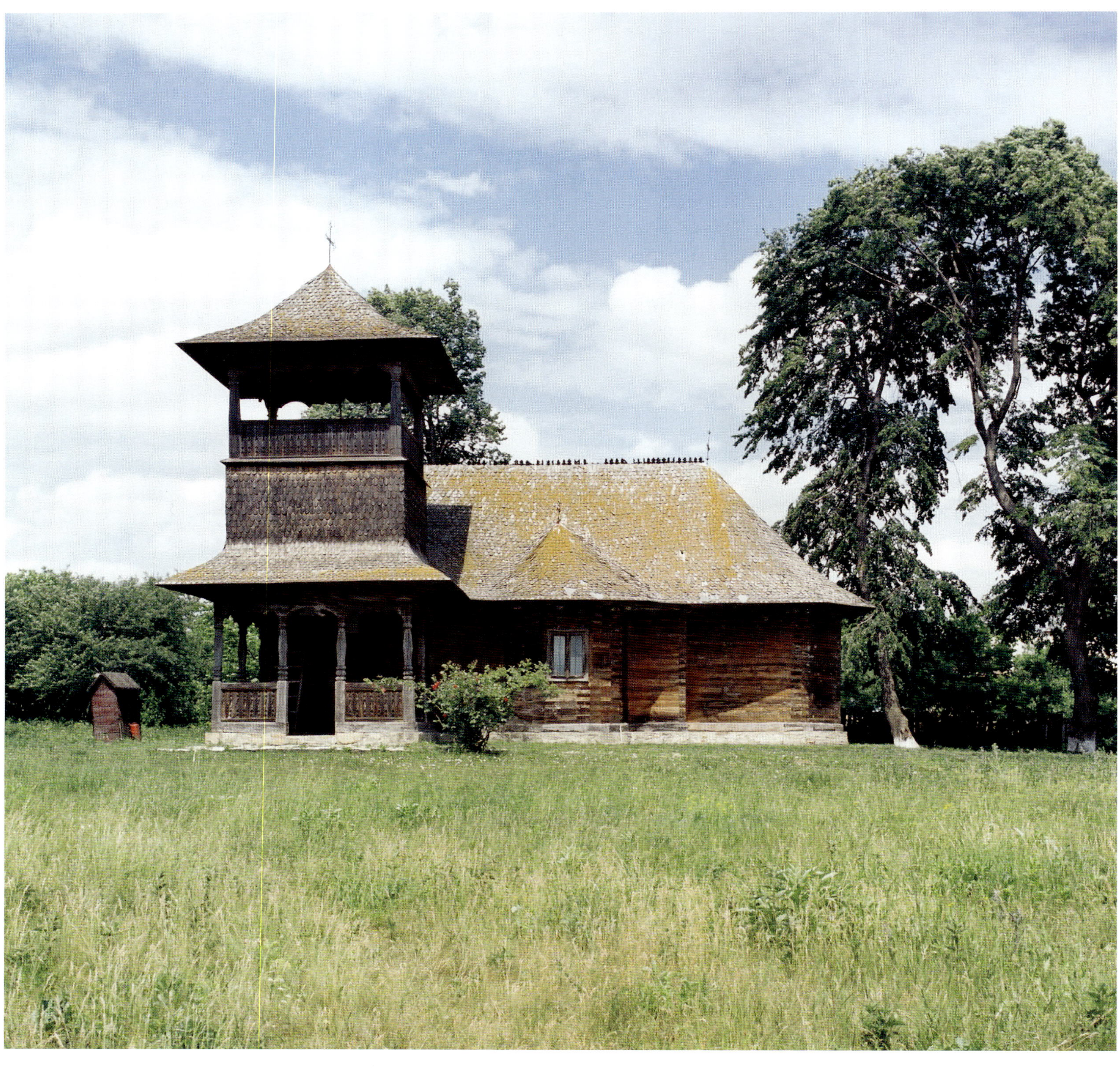

Brăești
Botoșani, Rumänien
Entschlafen der Gottesmutter
1745

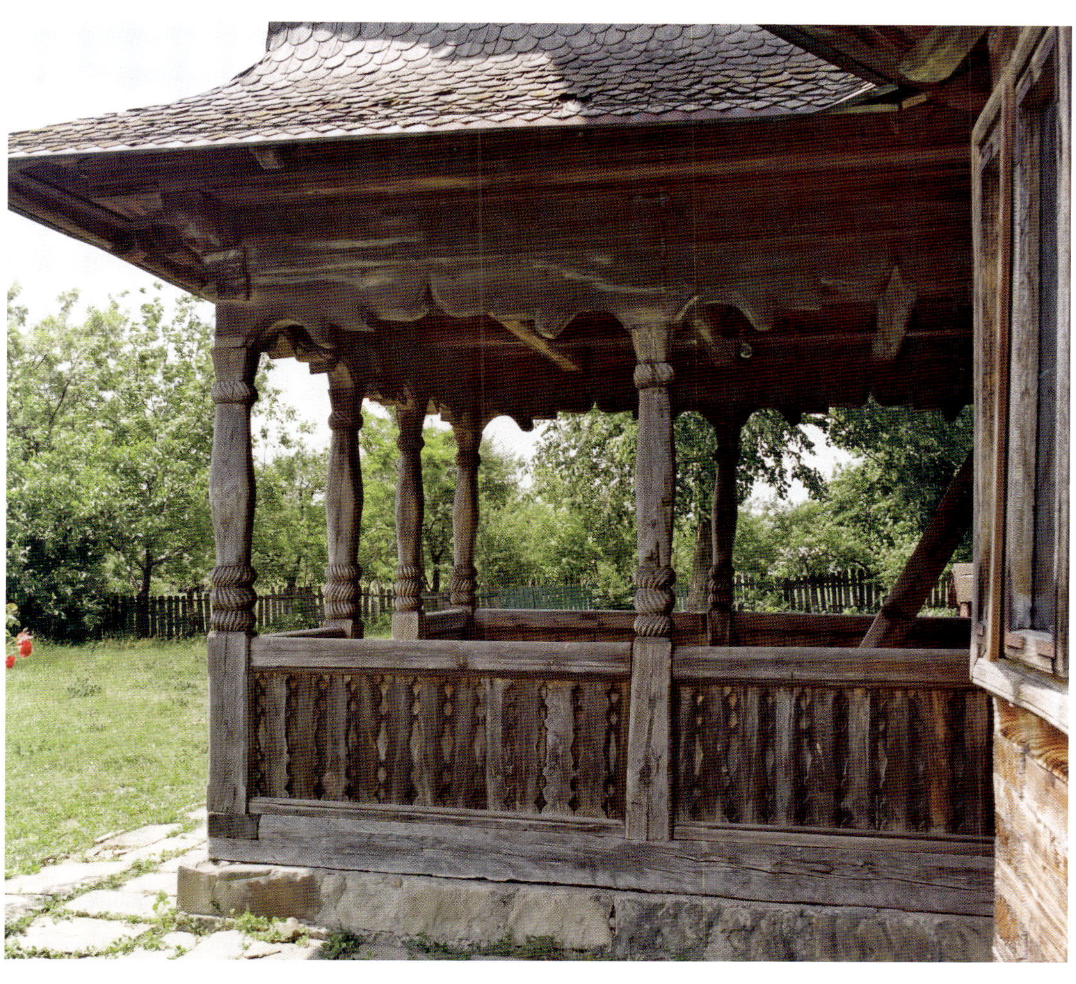

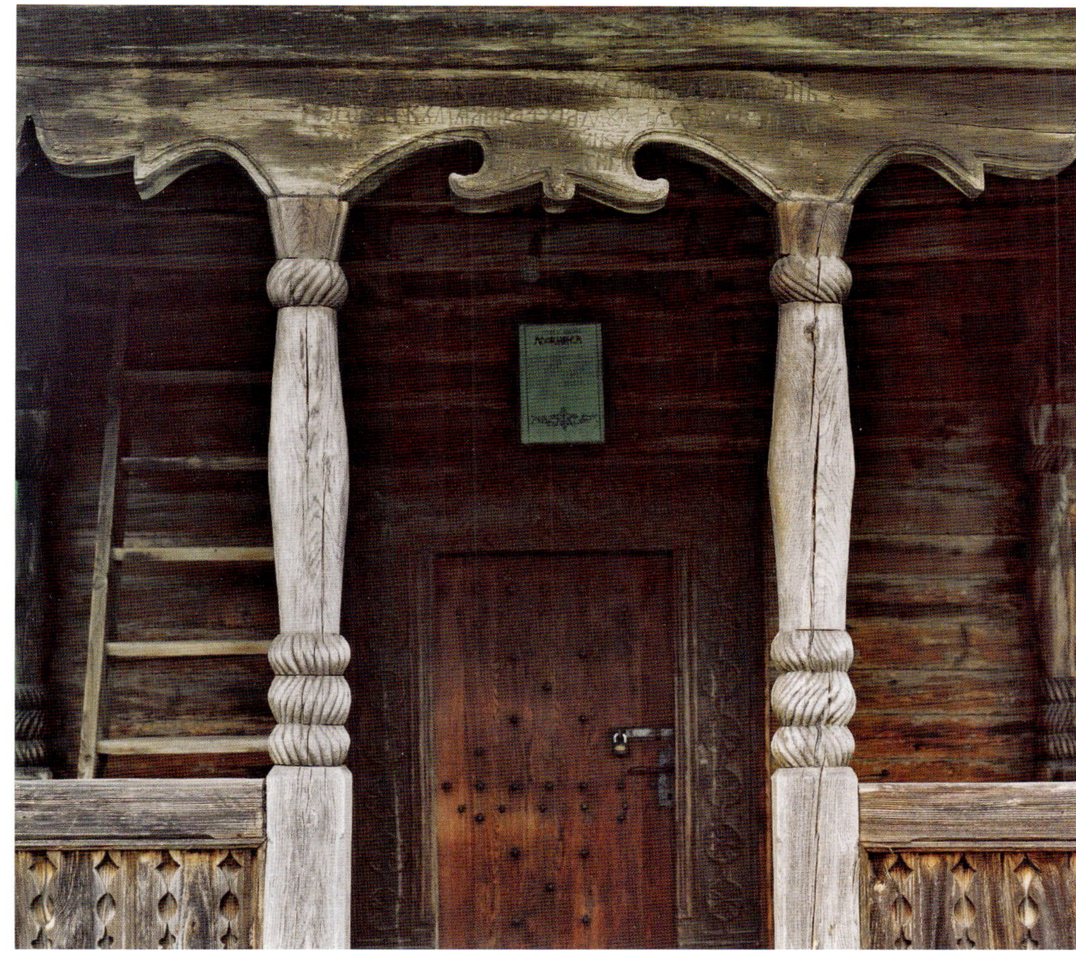

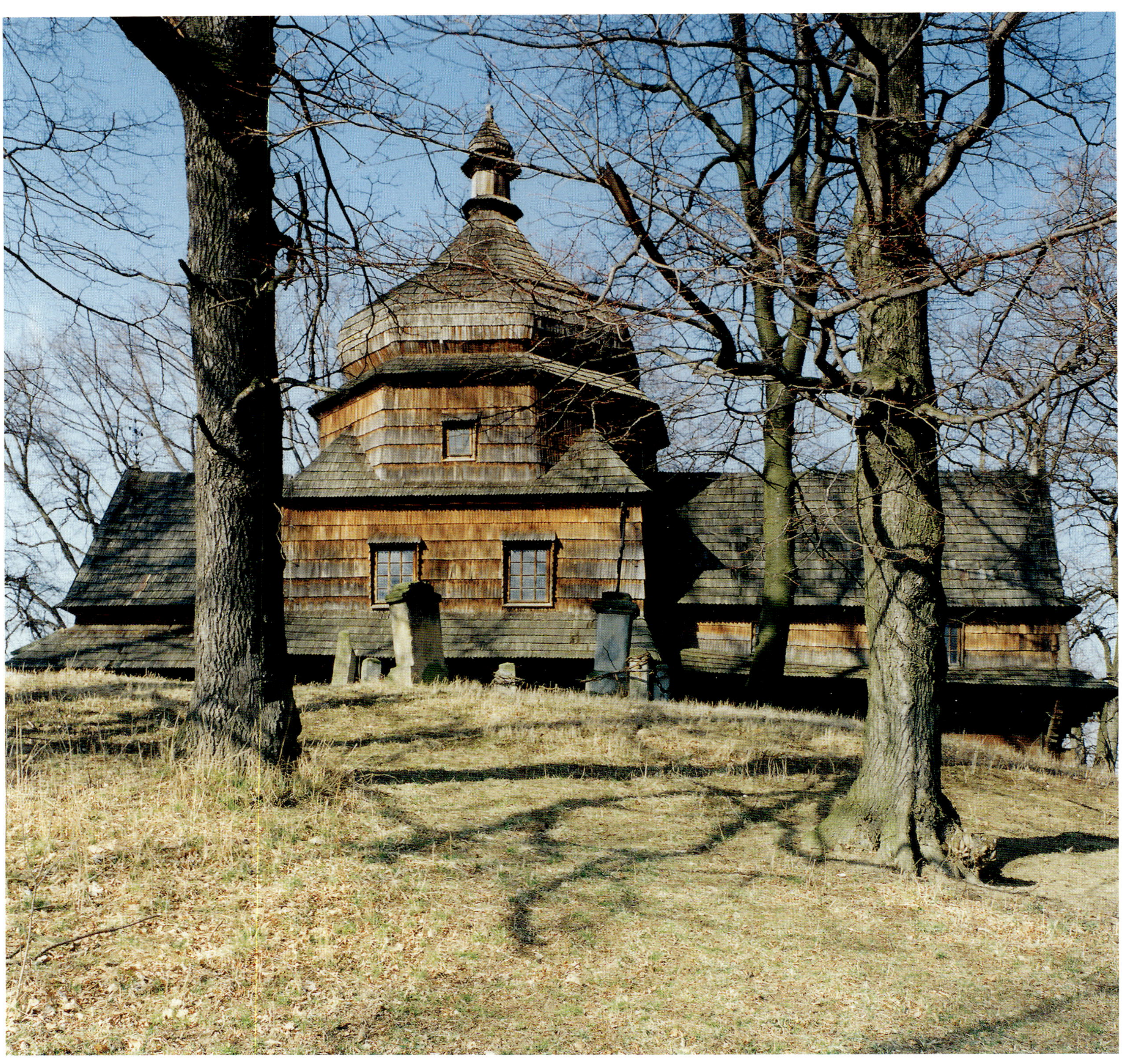

Czerteż
Sanok, Polen
Verklärung Christi
1742

Colești
Bihor, Rumänien
Hll. Erzengel
18. Jh.

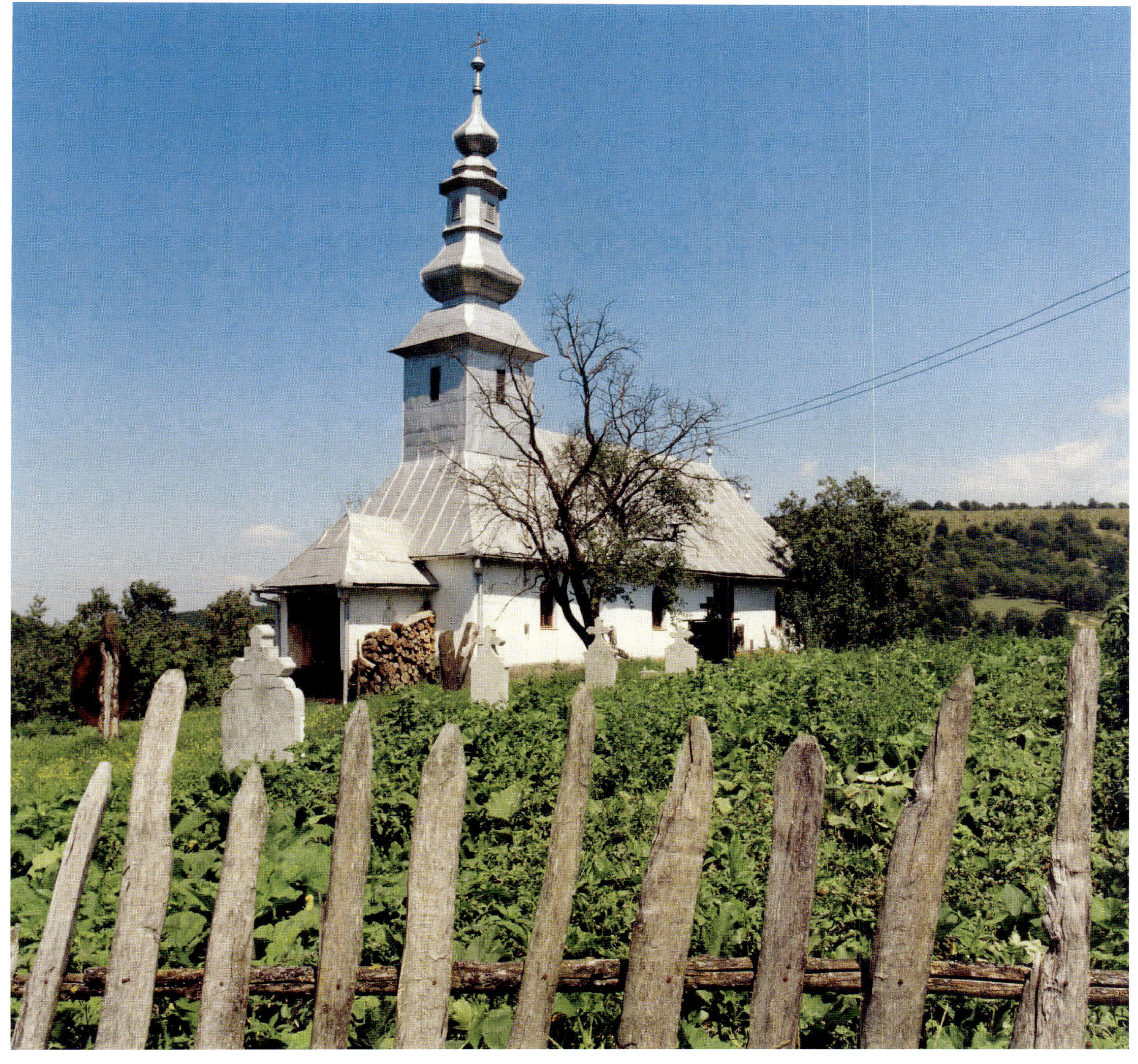

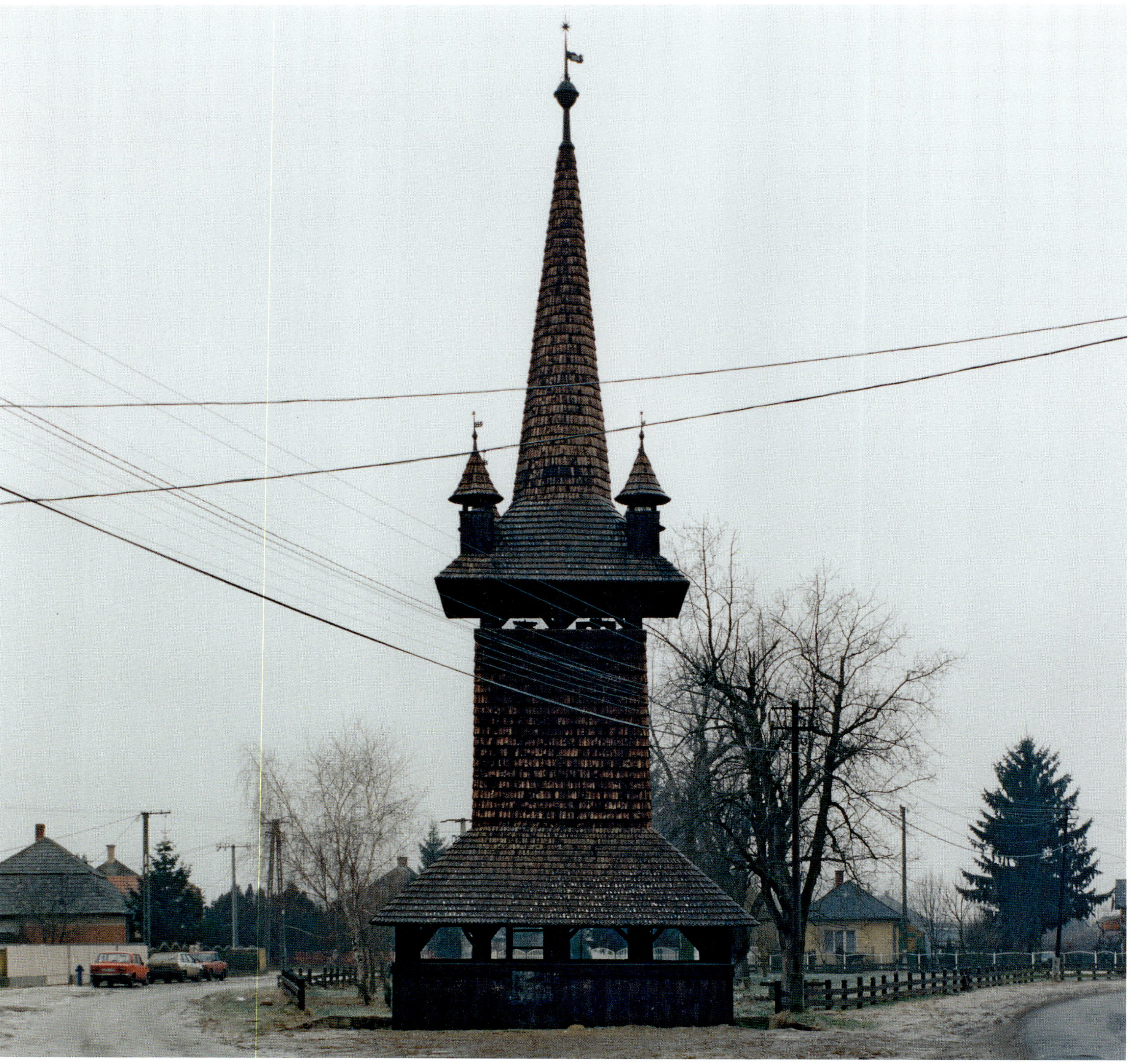

Gemzse
Szabolcs-Szatmár-Bereg, Ungarn
1889

Hervartov
Prešov, Slowakei
1500

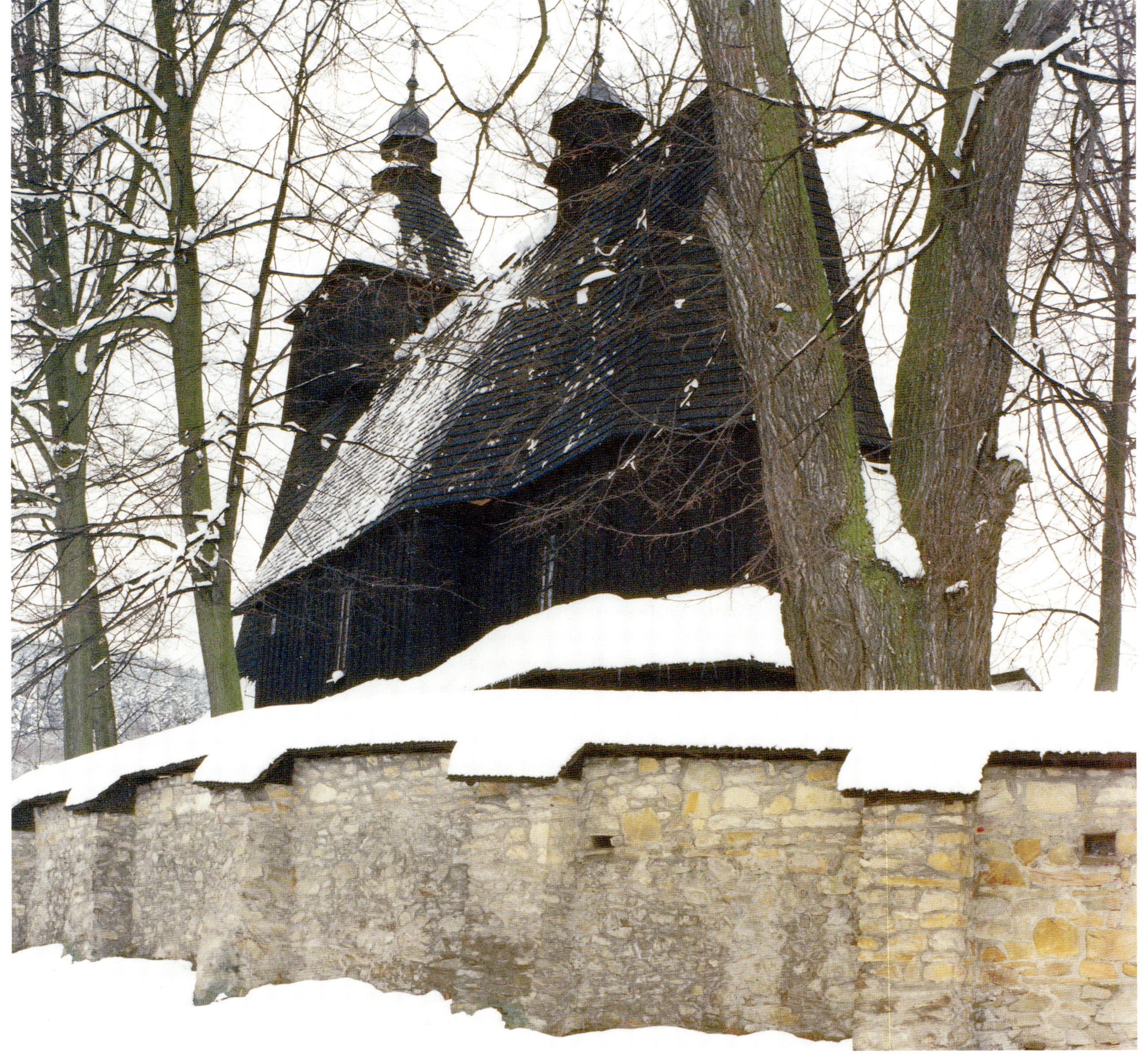

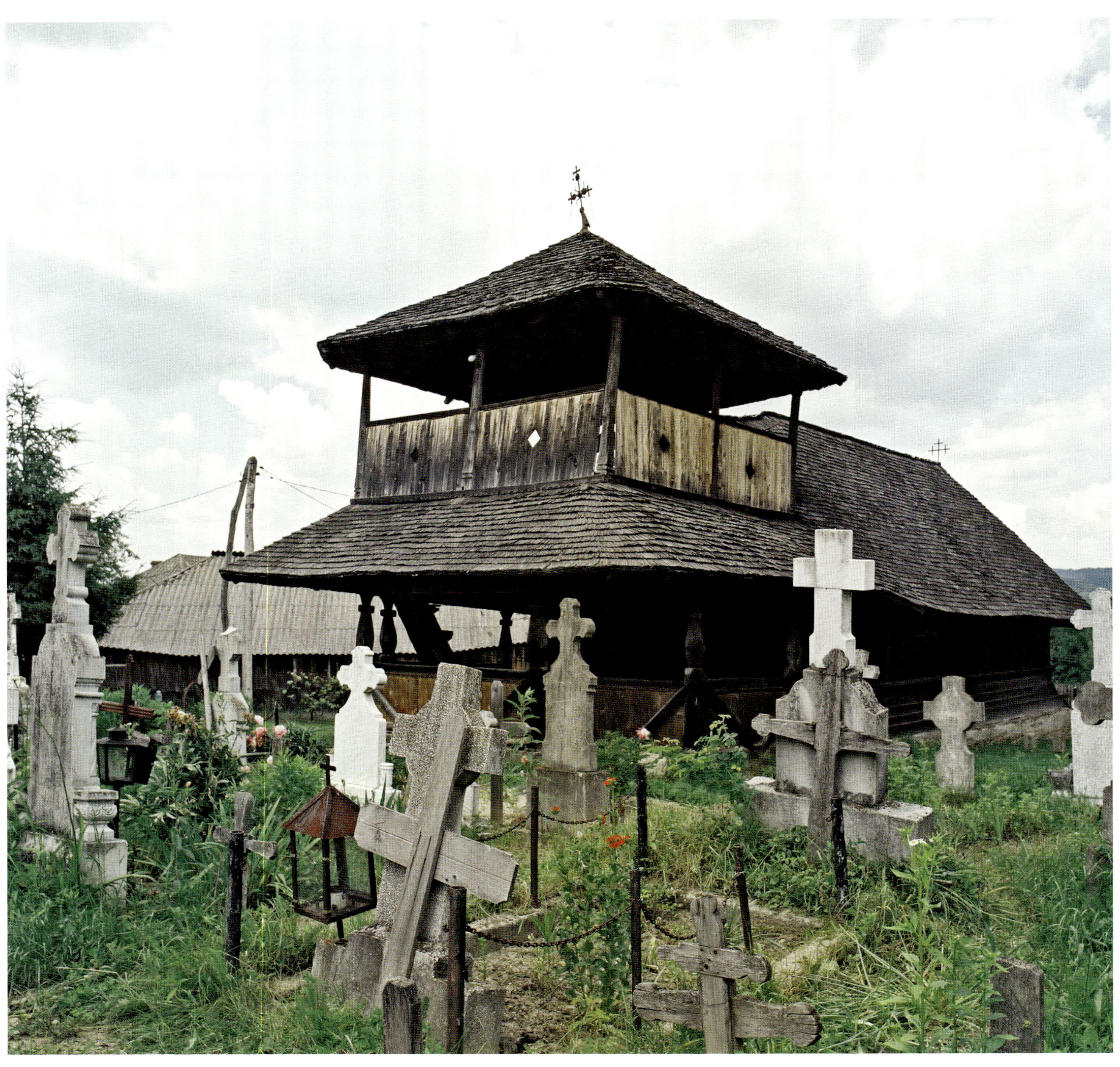

Jupânești
Gorj, Rumänien
1742

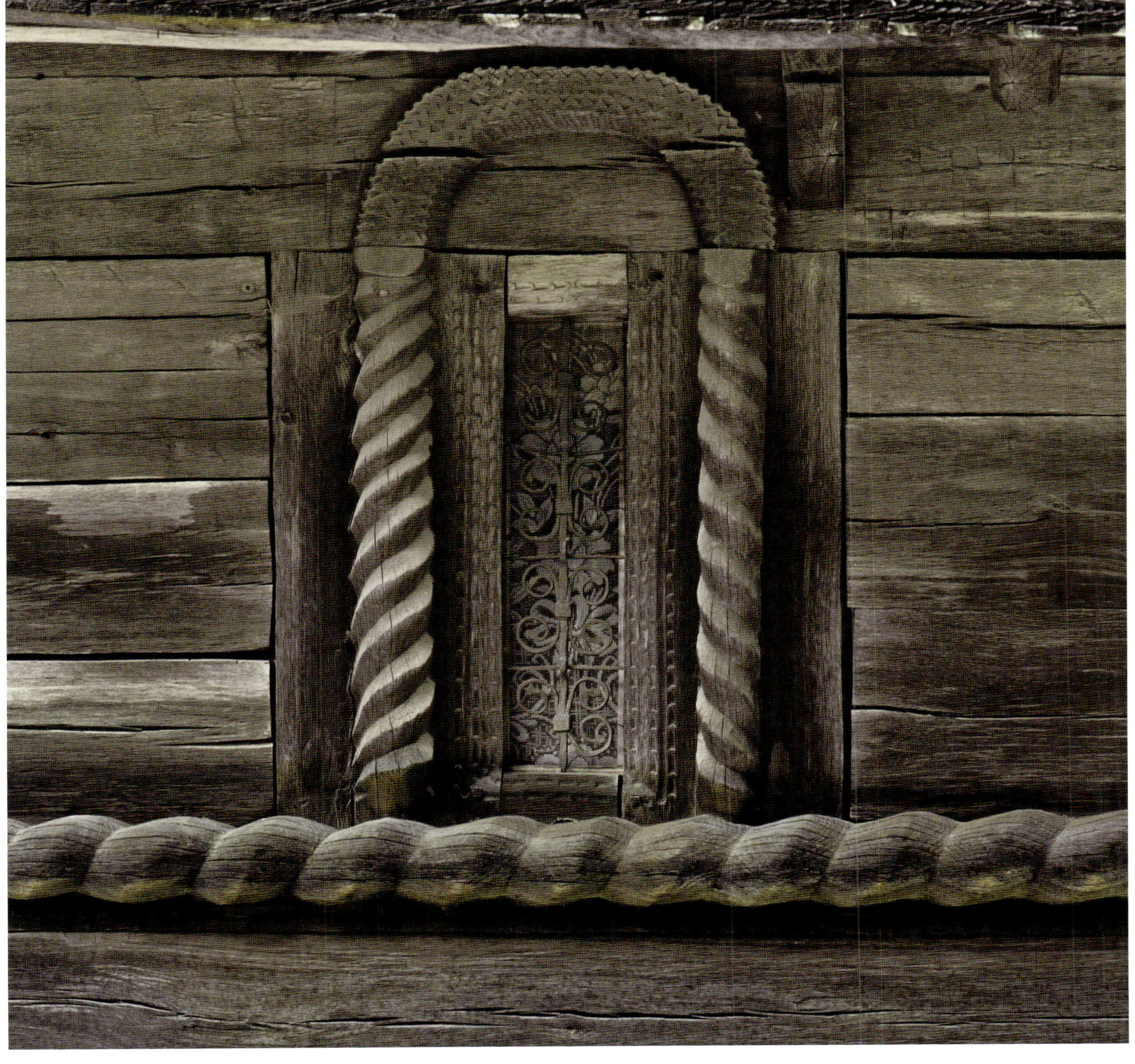

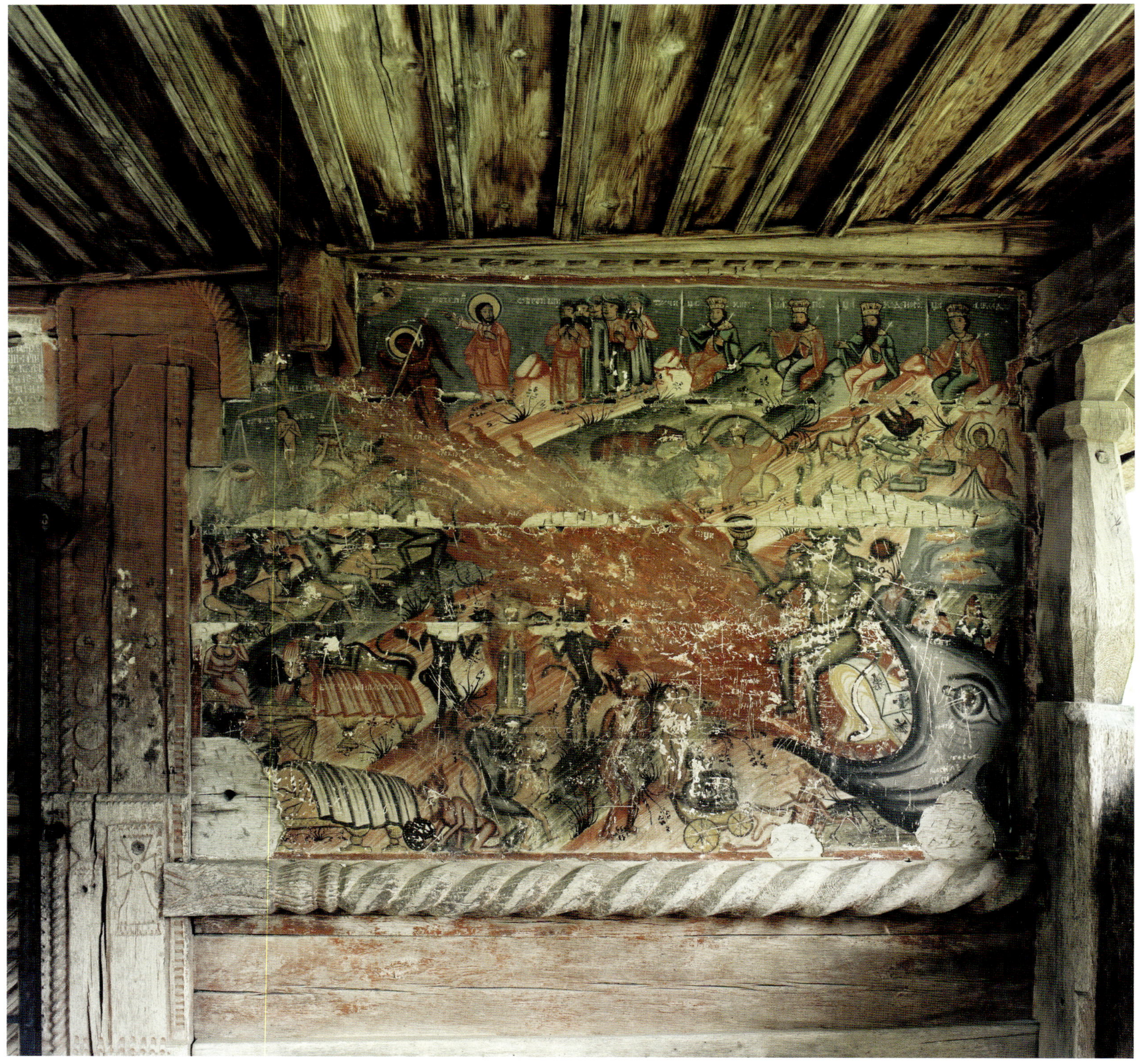

Jupânești
Gorj, Rumänien
1742

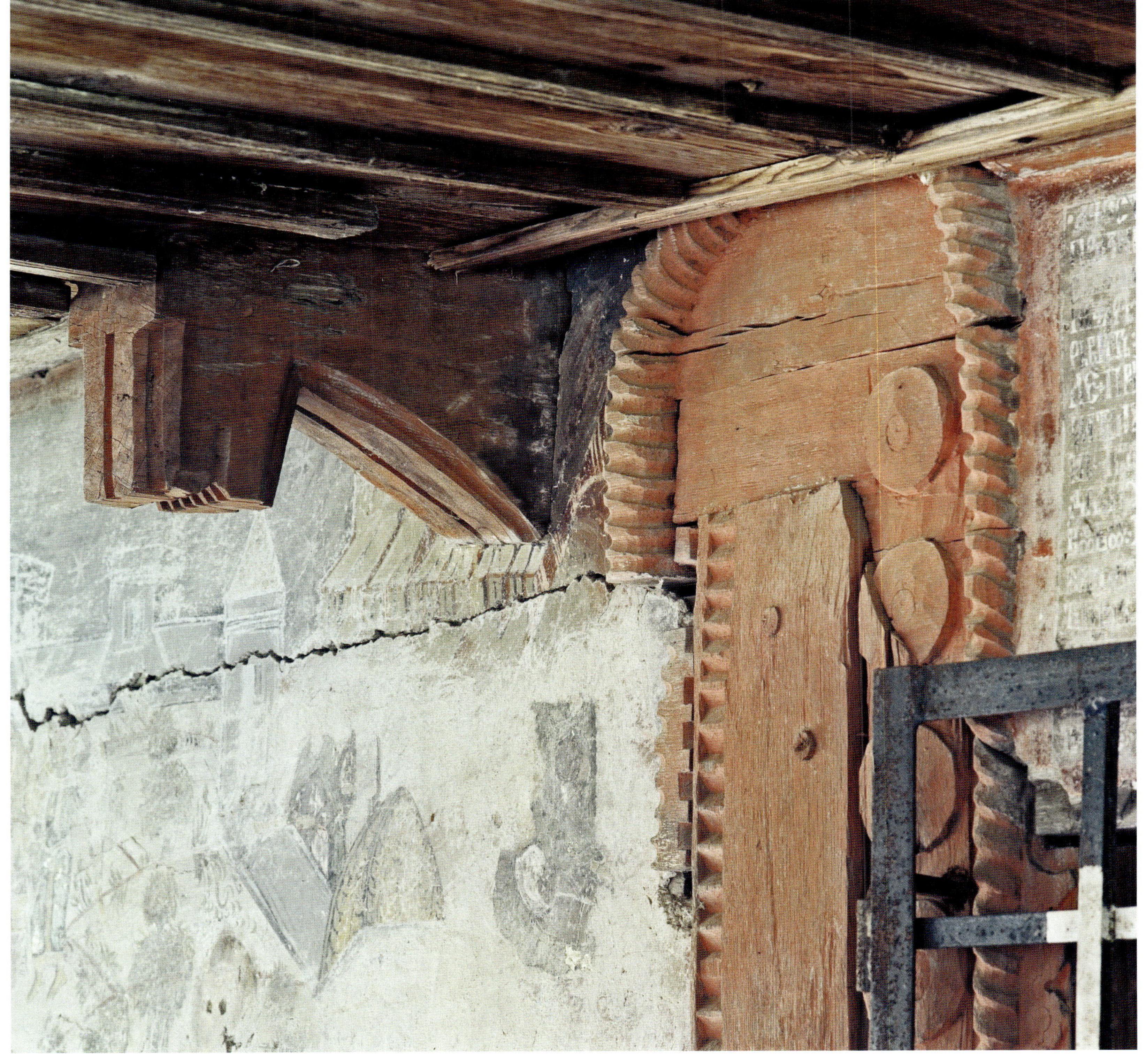

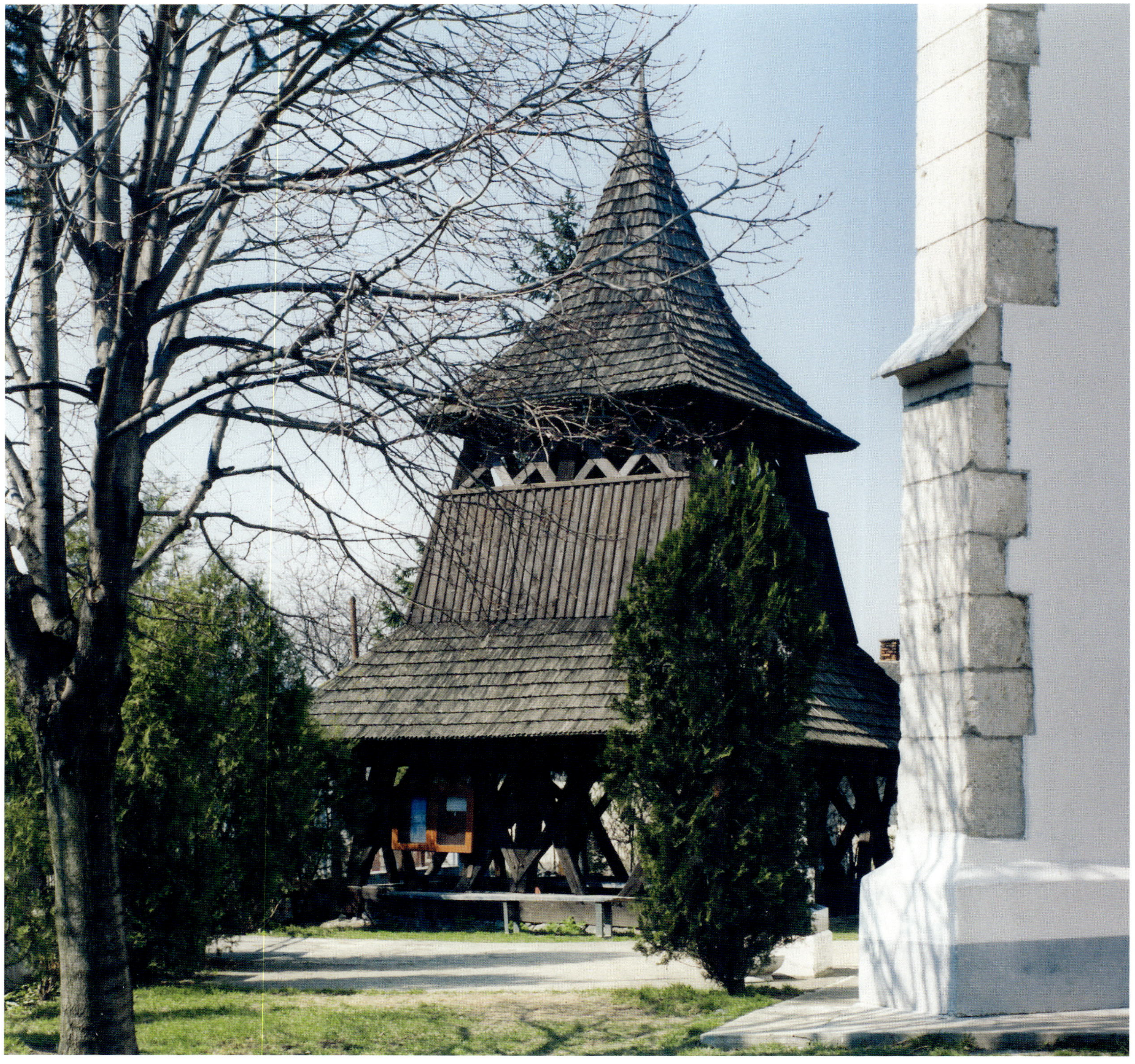

Malé Ozorovce
Košice, Slowakei
Anfang 15. Jh.
Glockenturm 1619

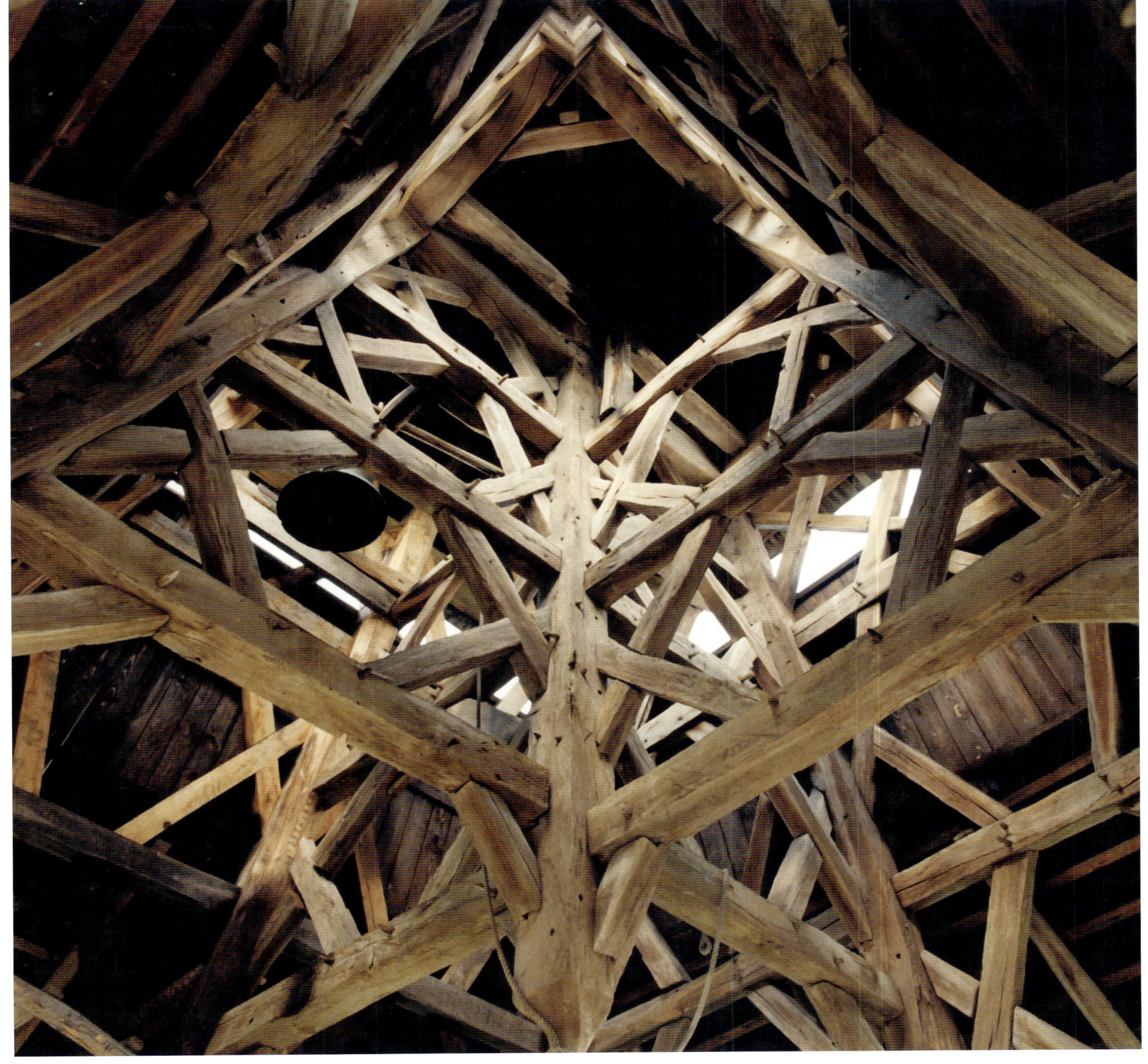

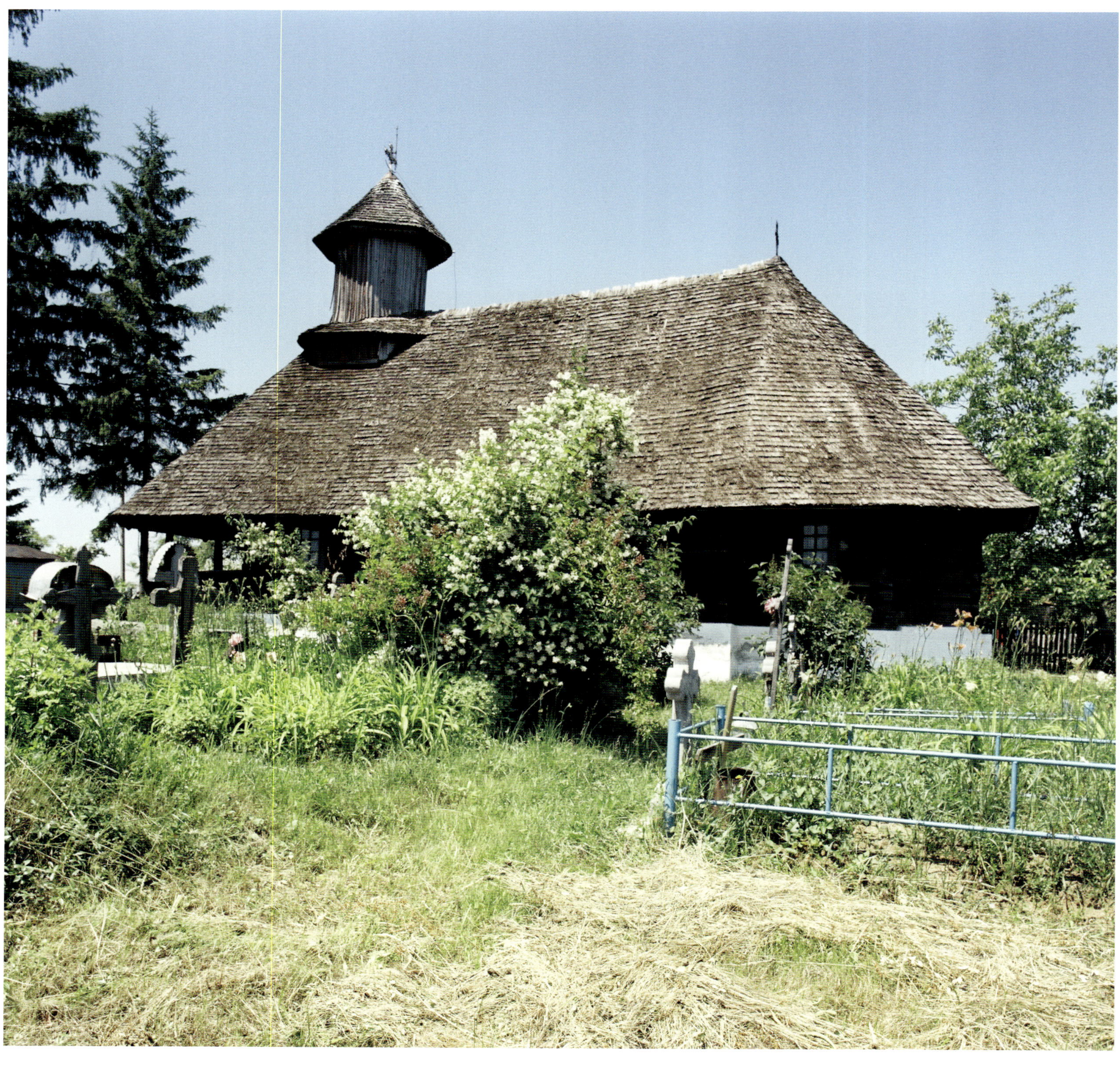

Morărești
Argeș, Rumänien
1832

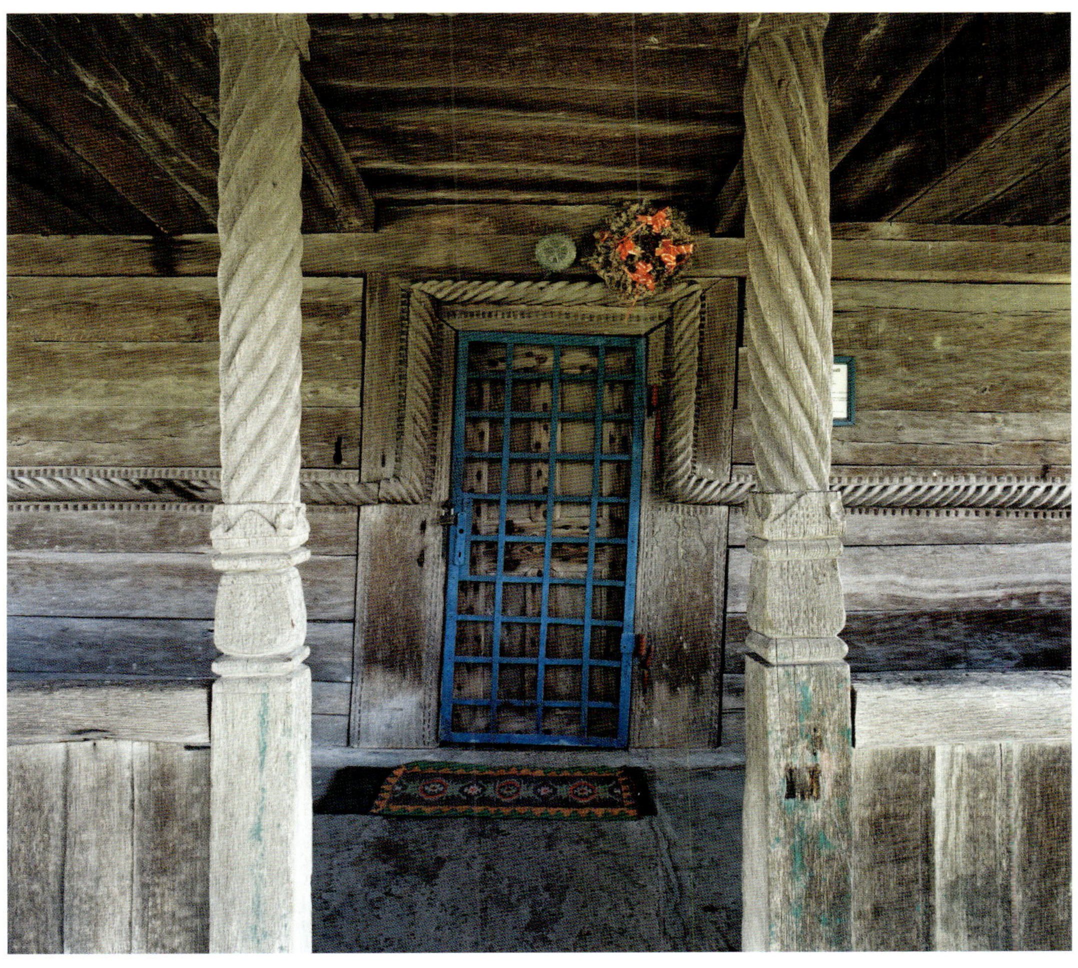

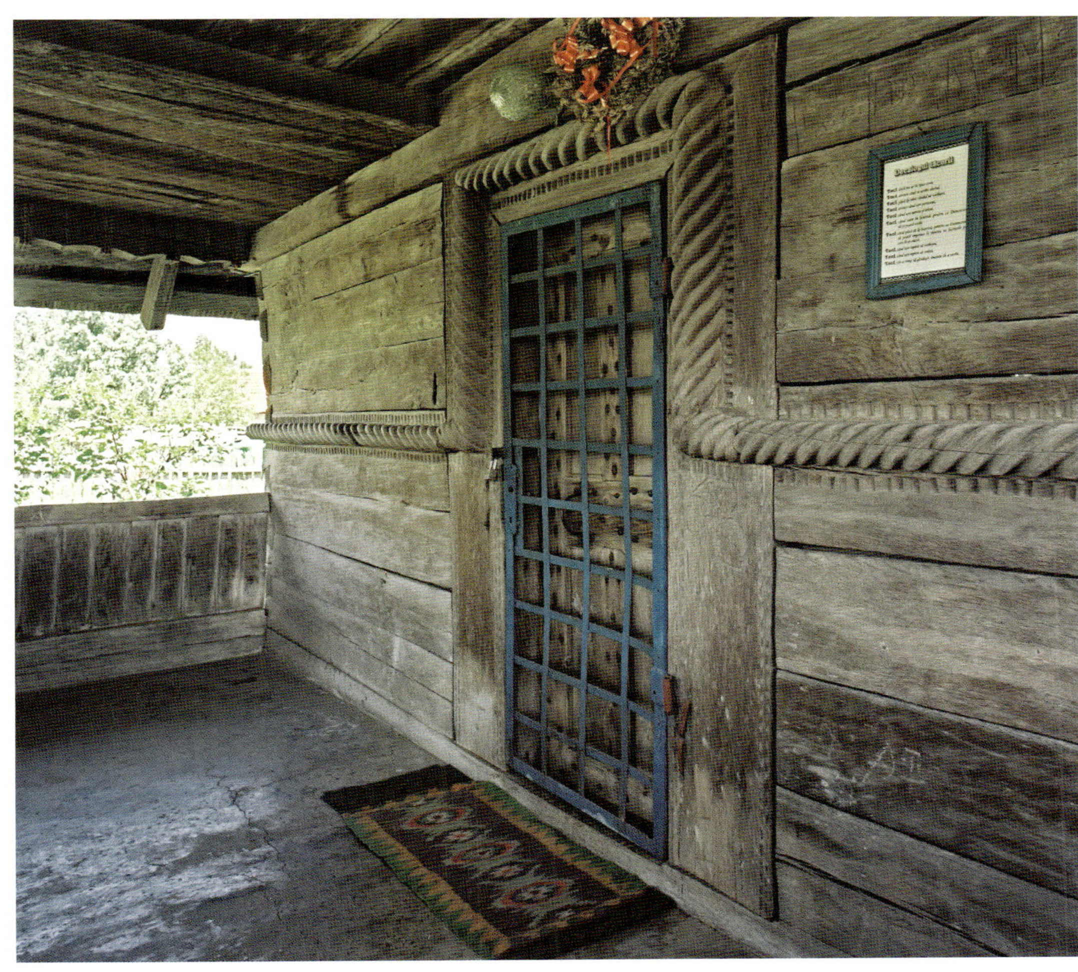

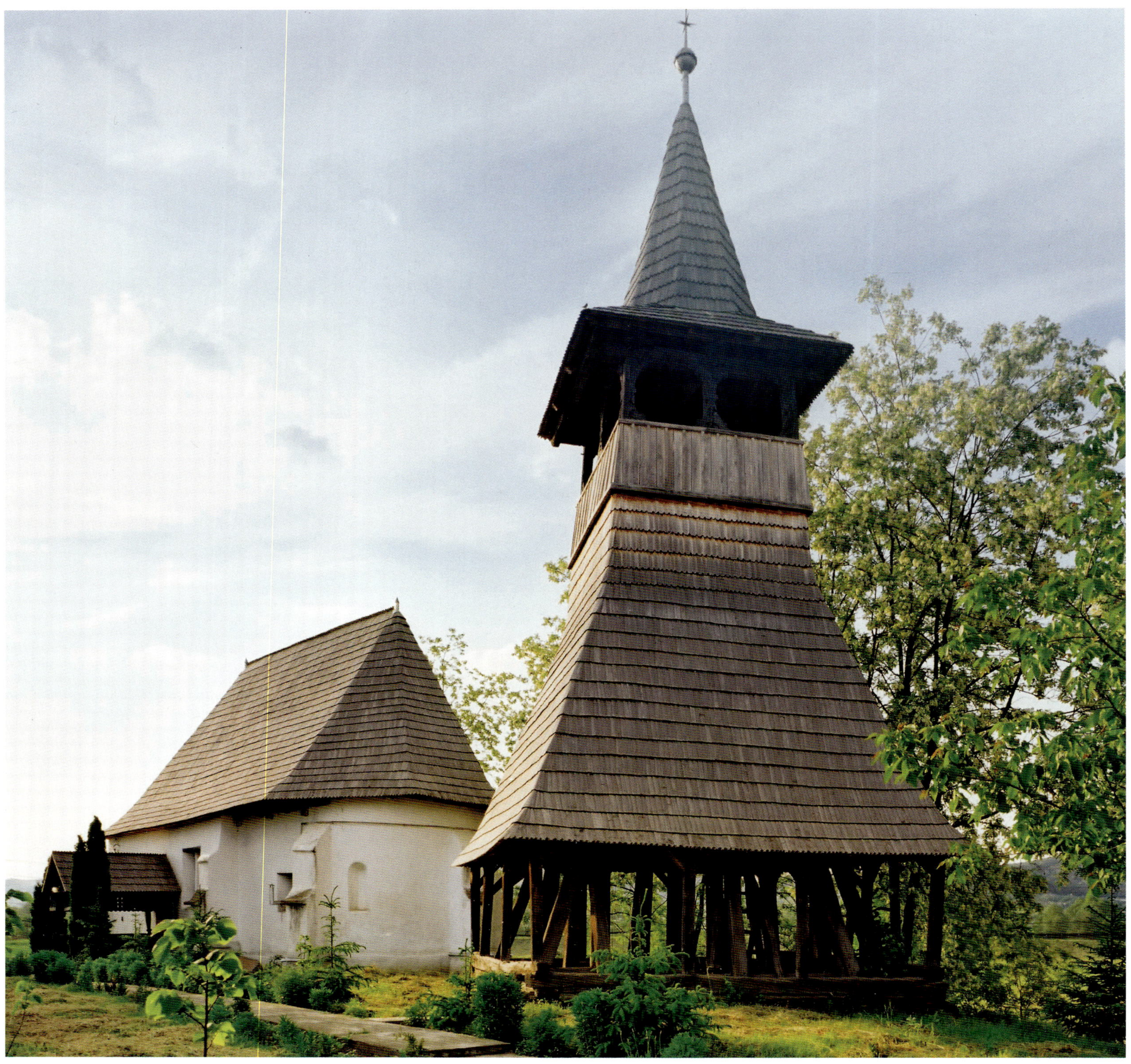

Agrişteu (Bălăuşeri)
Mureş, Rumänien

Deleni (Băgaciu)
Mureş, Rumänien

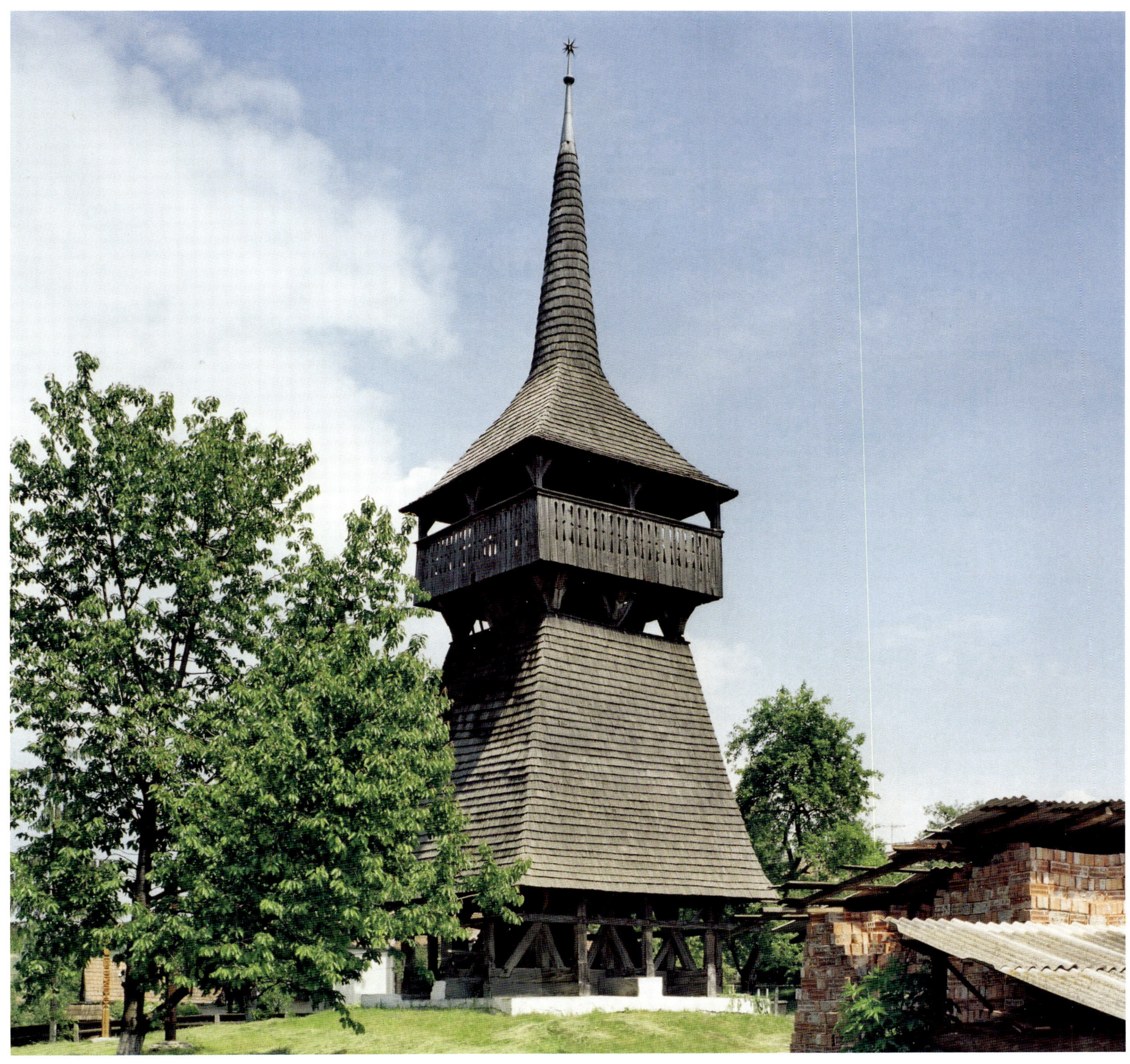

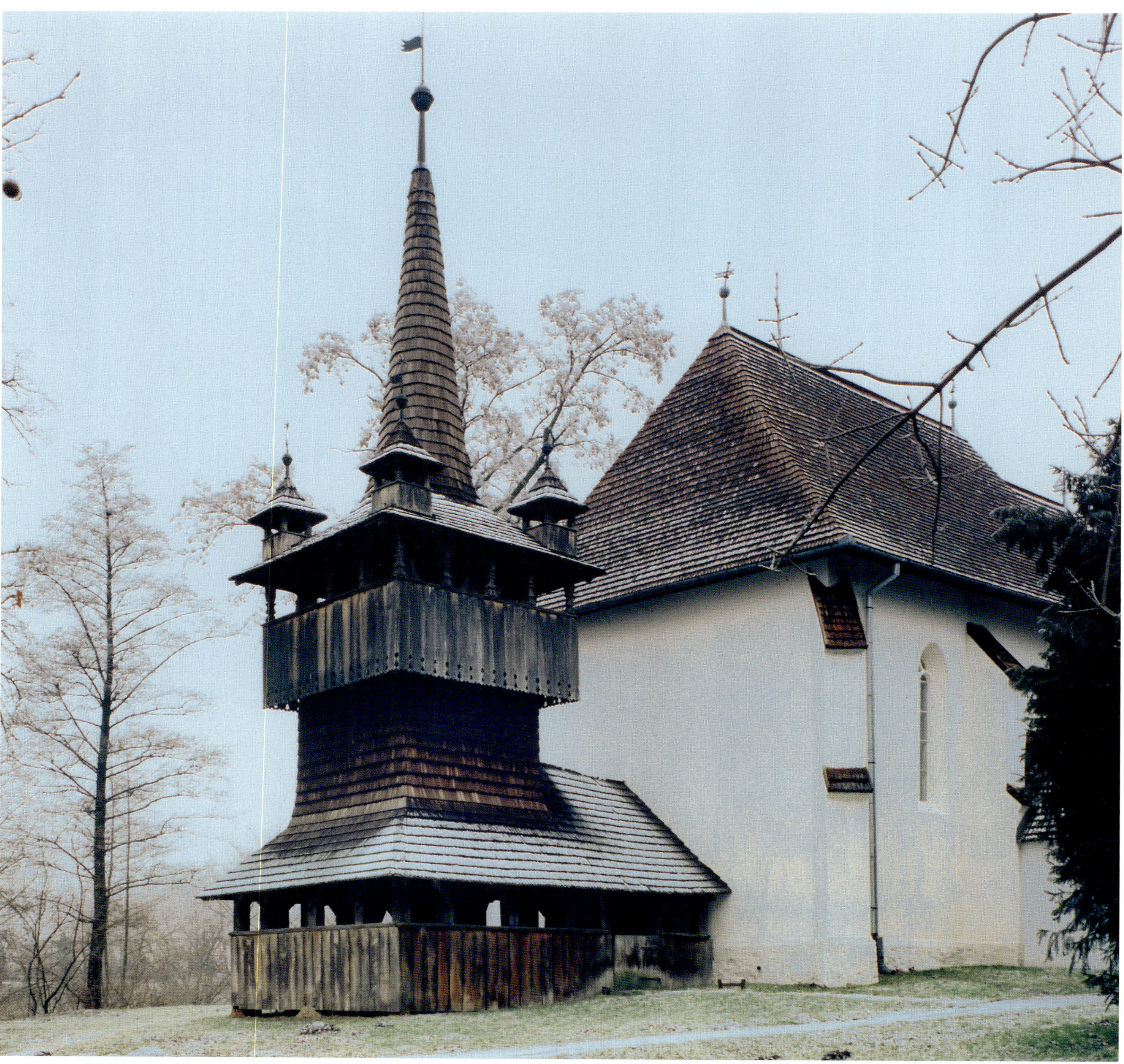

Nagyszekeres
Szabolcs-Szatmar-Bereg, Ungarn
1819 und 1836

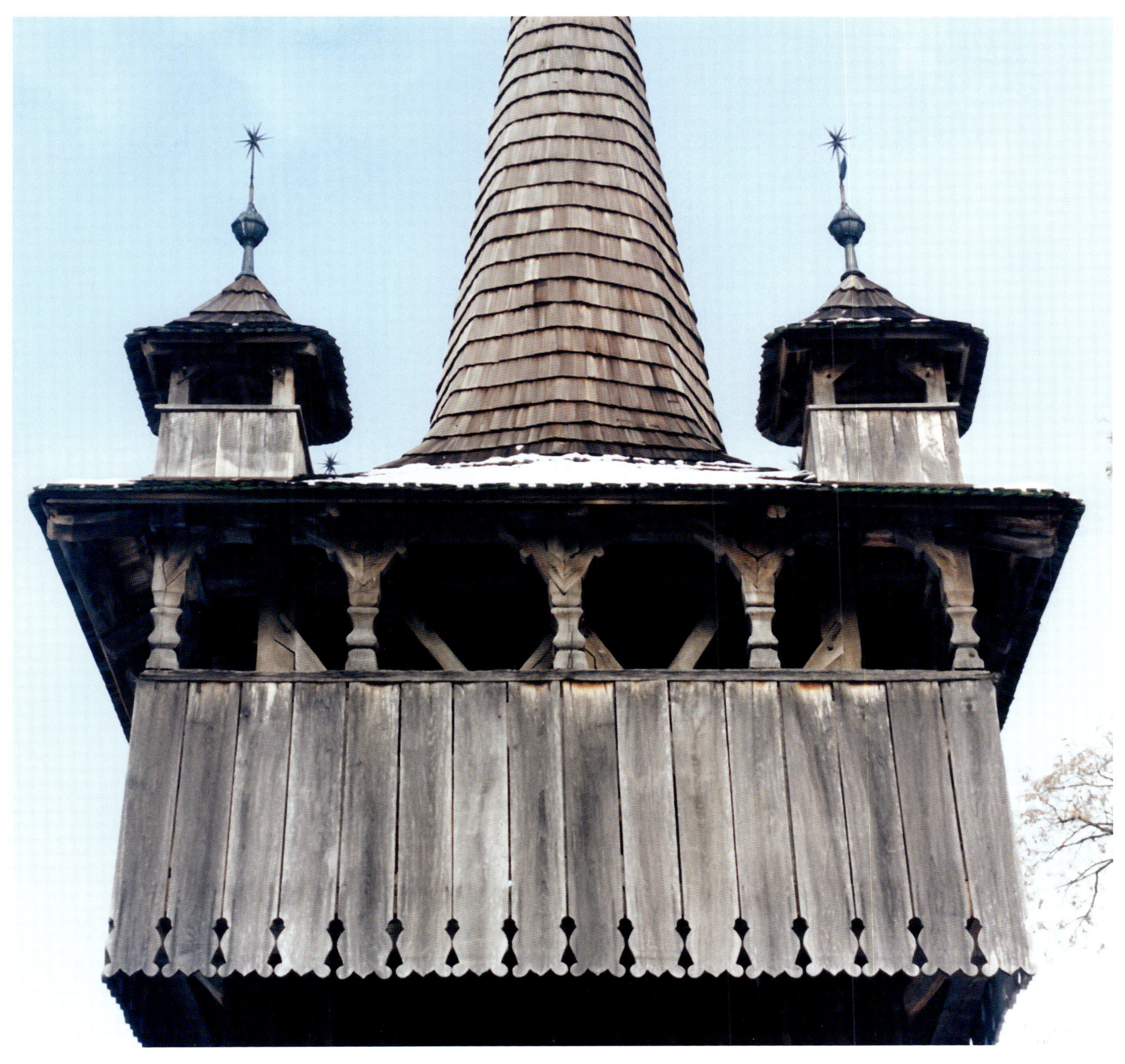

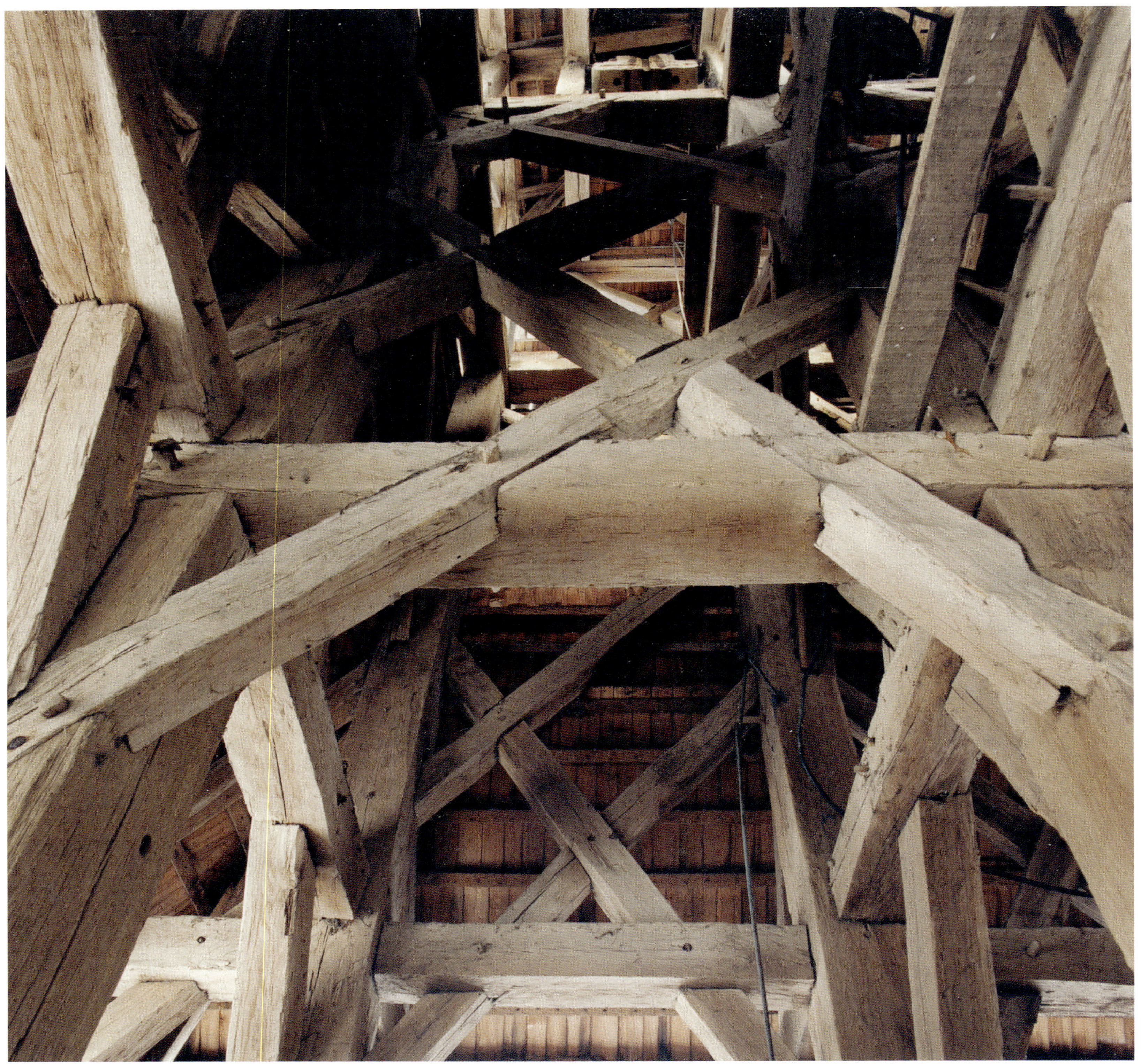

Nagyszekeres
Szabolcs-Szatmar-Bereg, Ungarn
1819 und 1836

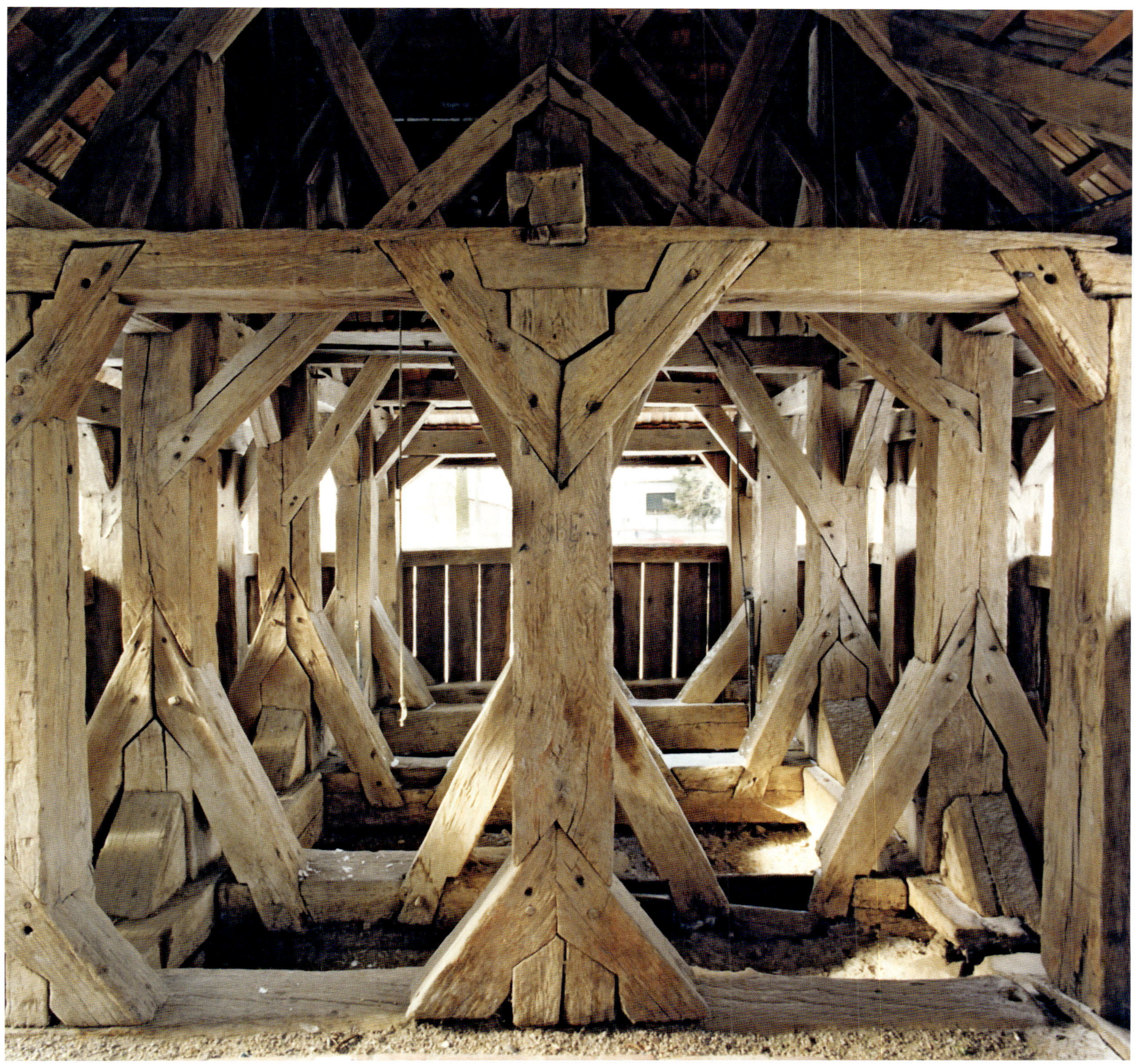

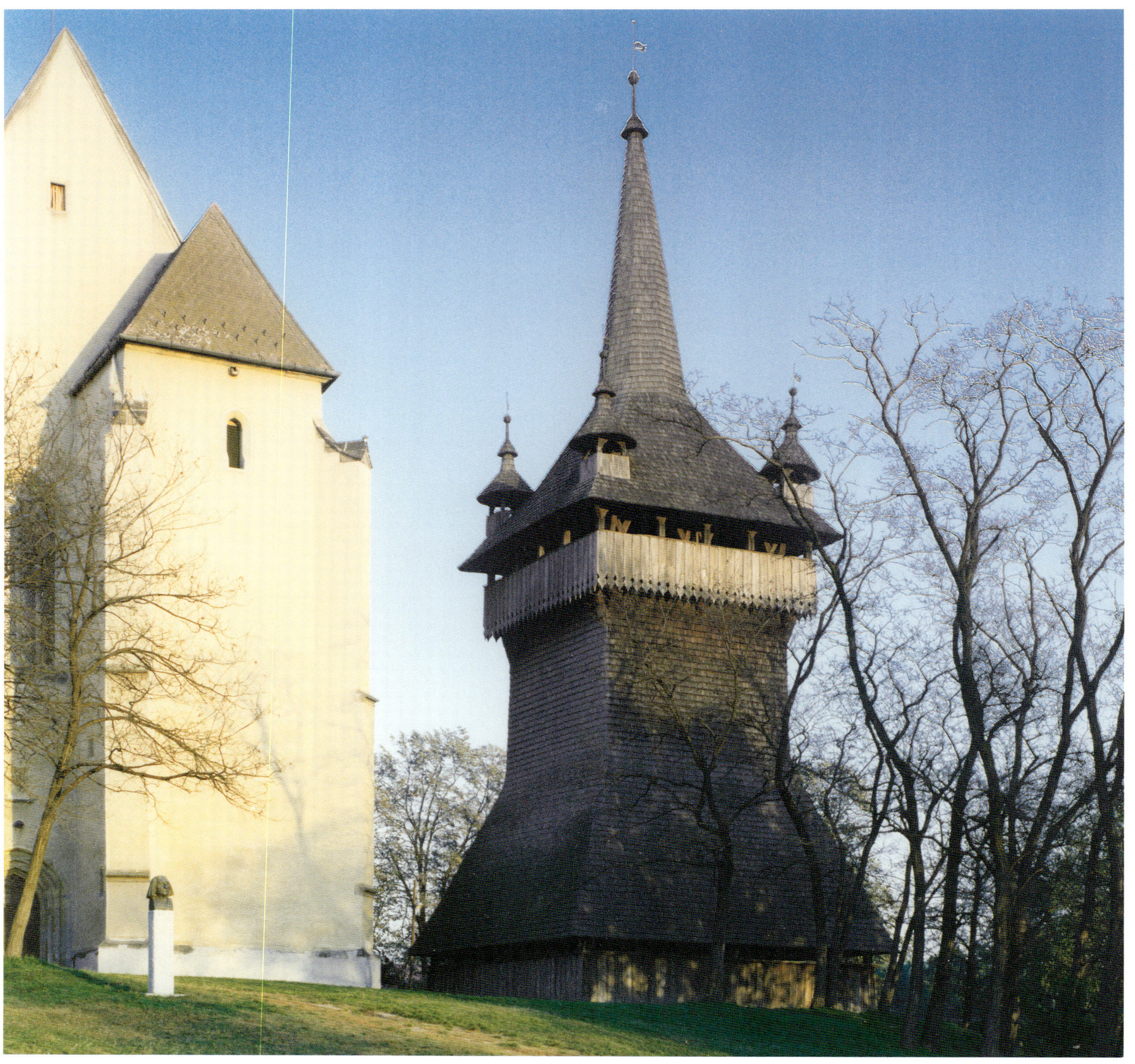

Nyírbátor
Szabolcs-Szatmár-Bereg, Ungarn
Ende 15. Jh.
Glockenturm 1640

Păușa
Bihor, Rumänien
St. Nikolaus
1730

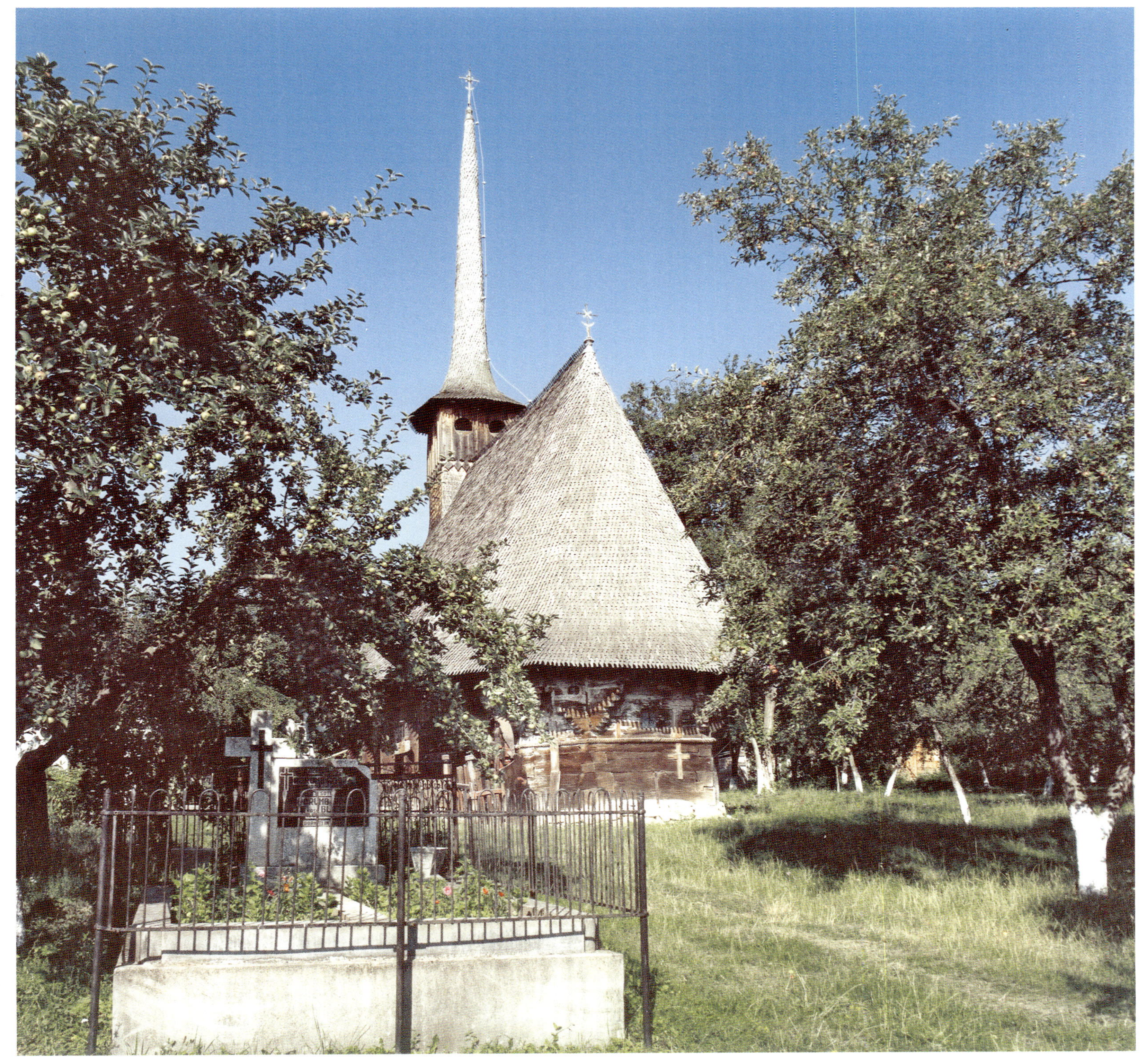

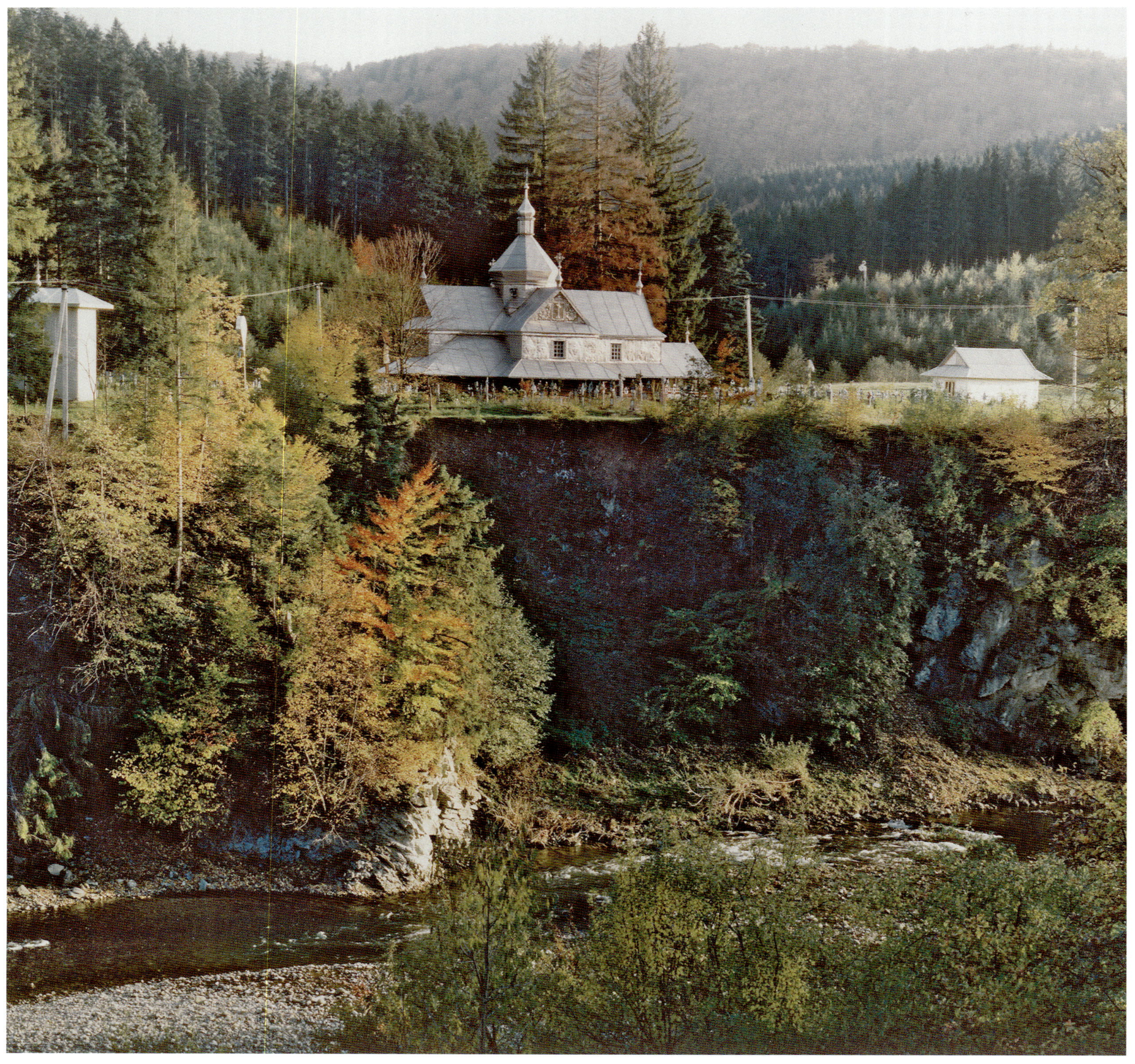

Pistyn
Ivano-Frankivsk, Ukraine
Entschlafen der Gottesmutter
1858

Poarta Sălajului
Sălaj, Rumänien
Hll. Erzengel
1670

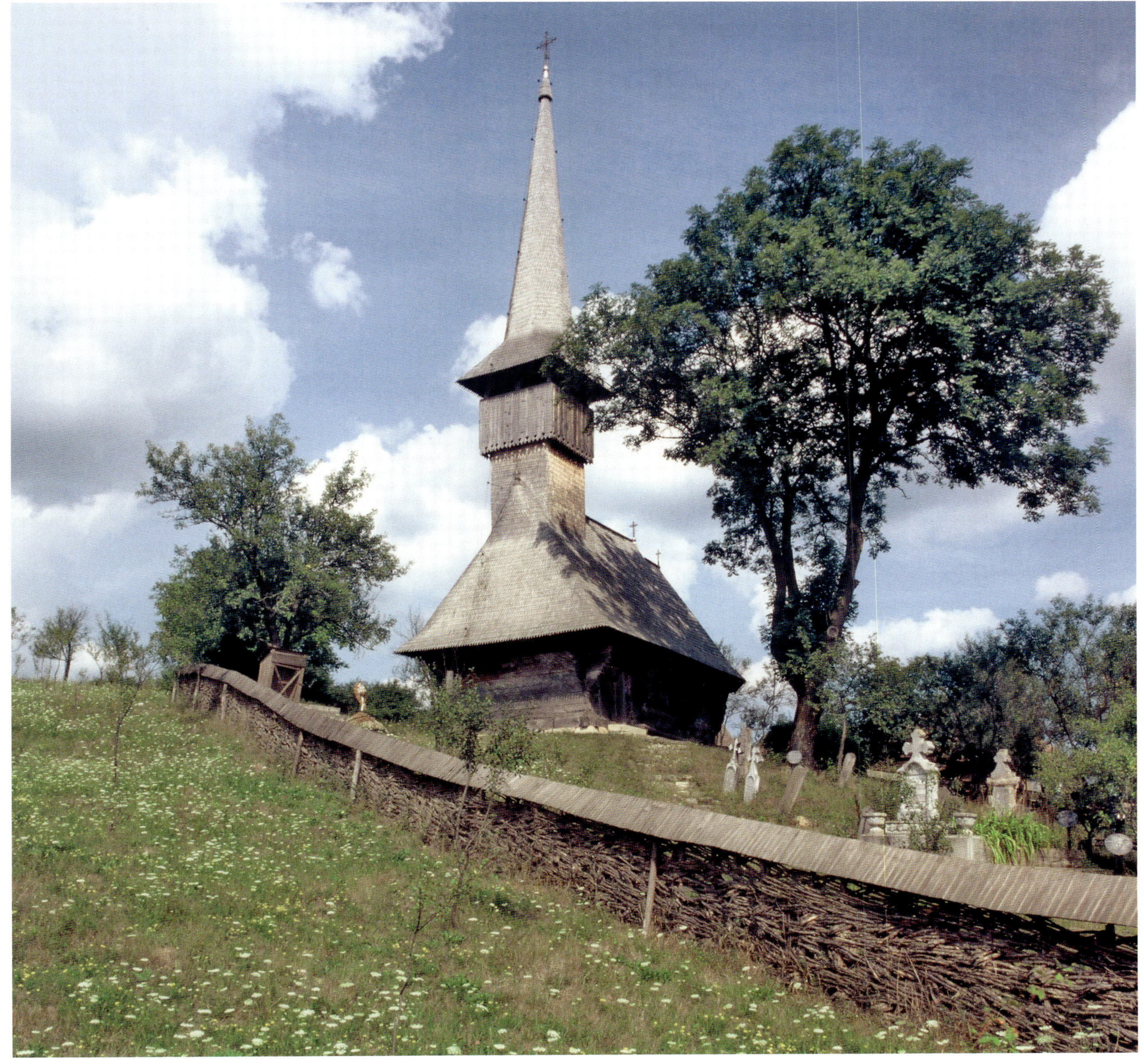

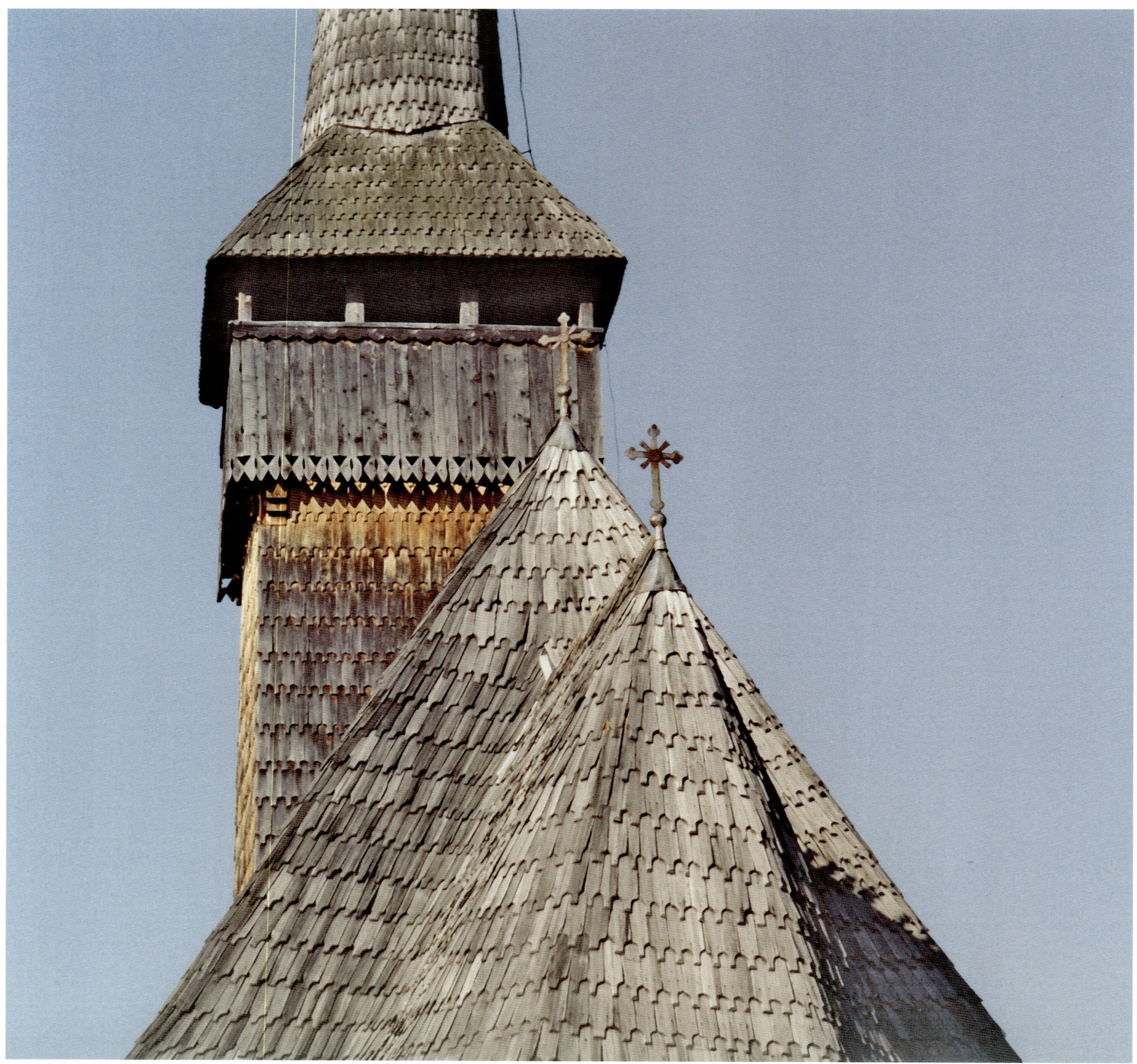

Rozavlea
Maramureş, Rumänien
1716

Rusky Potok
Prešov, Slowakei
Erzengel Michael
18. Jh.

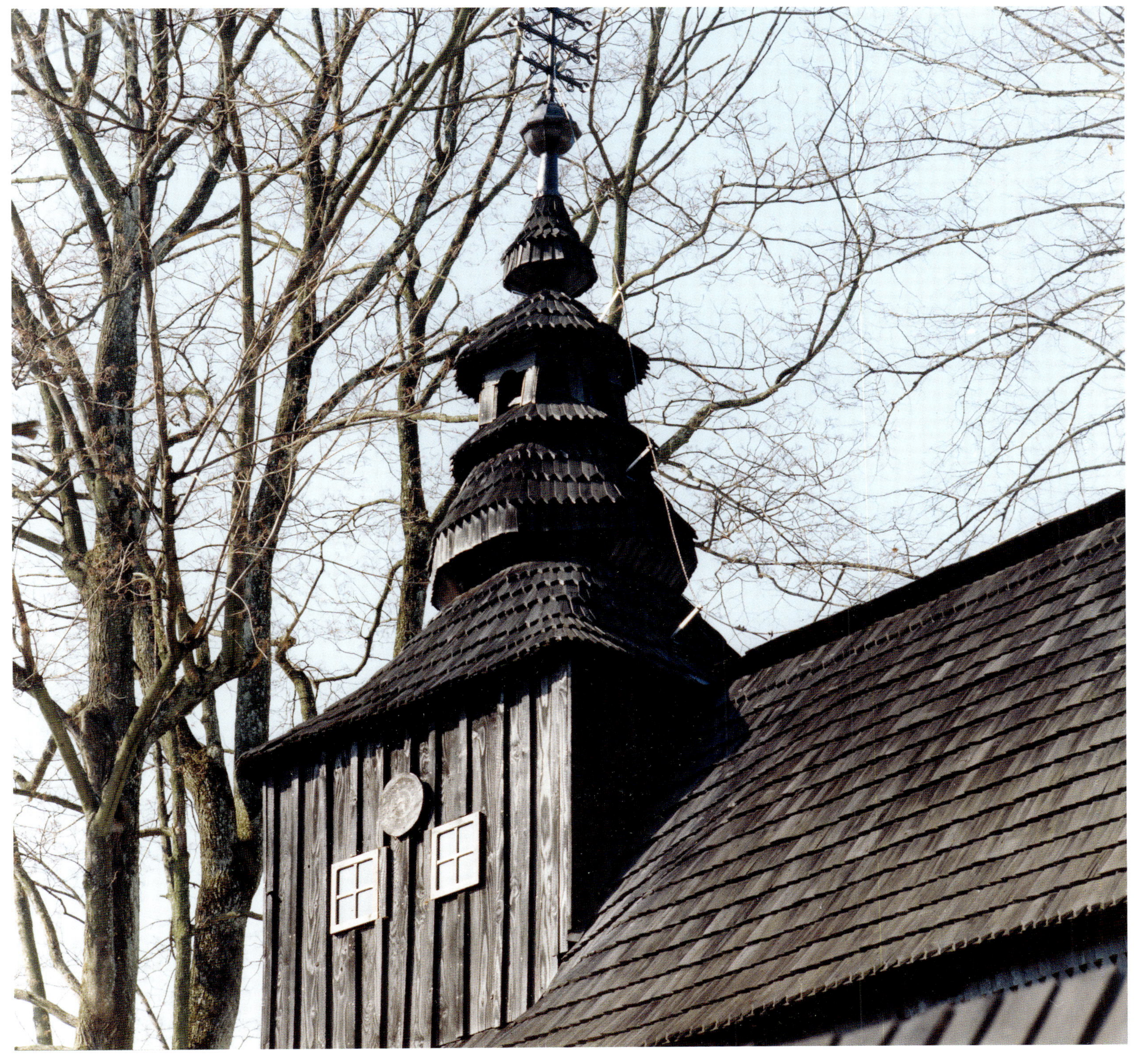

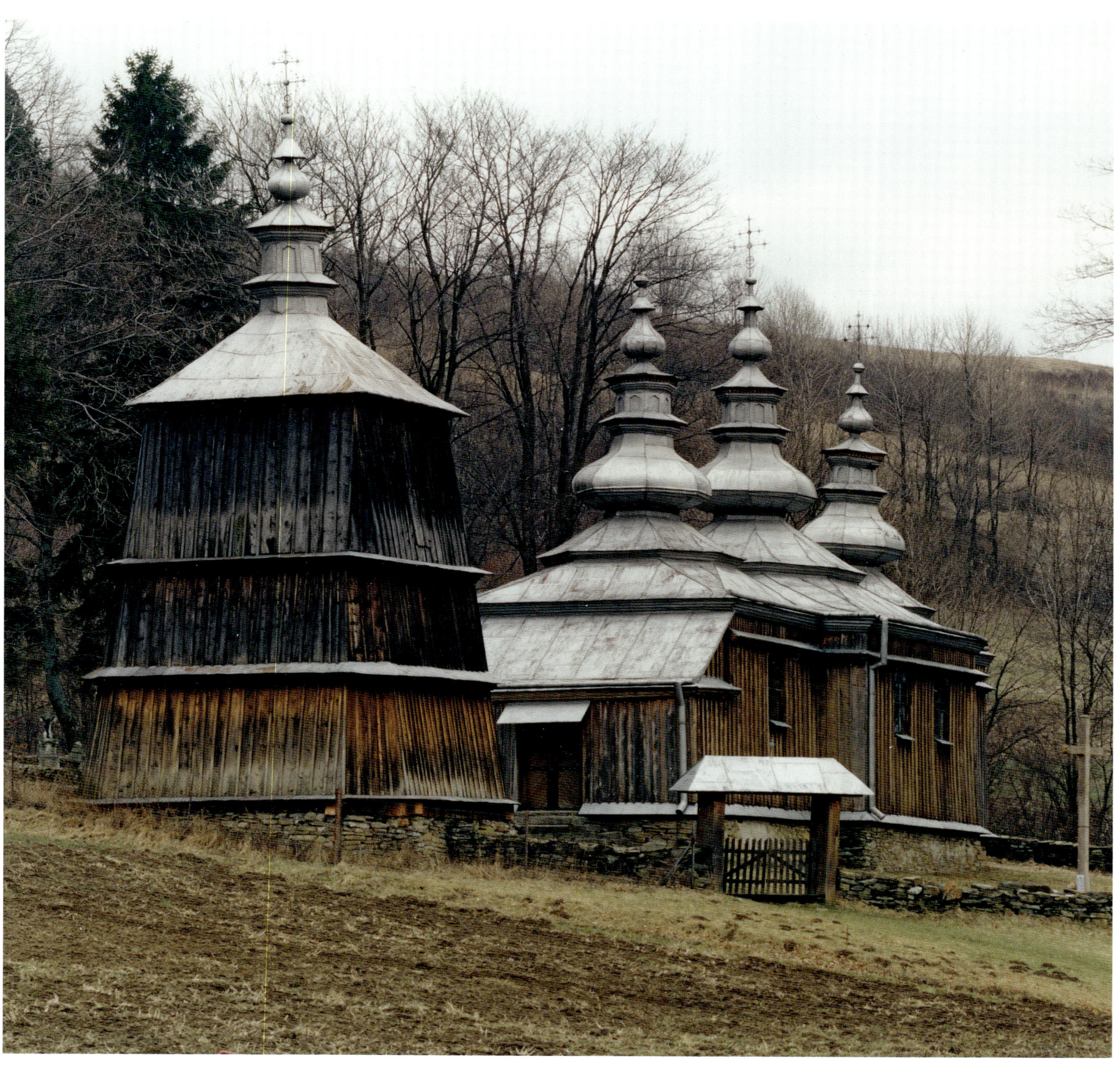

Rzepedź
Sanok, Polen
Hl. Nikolaus
1826

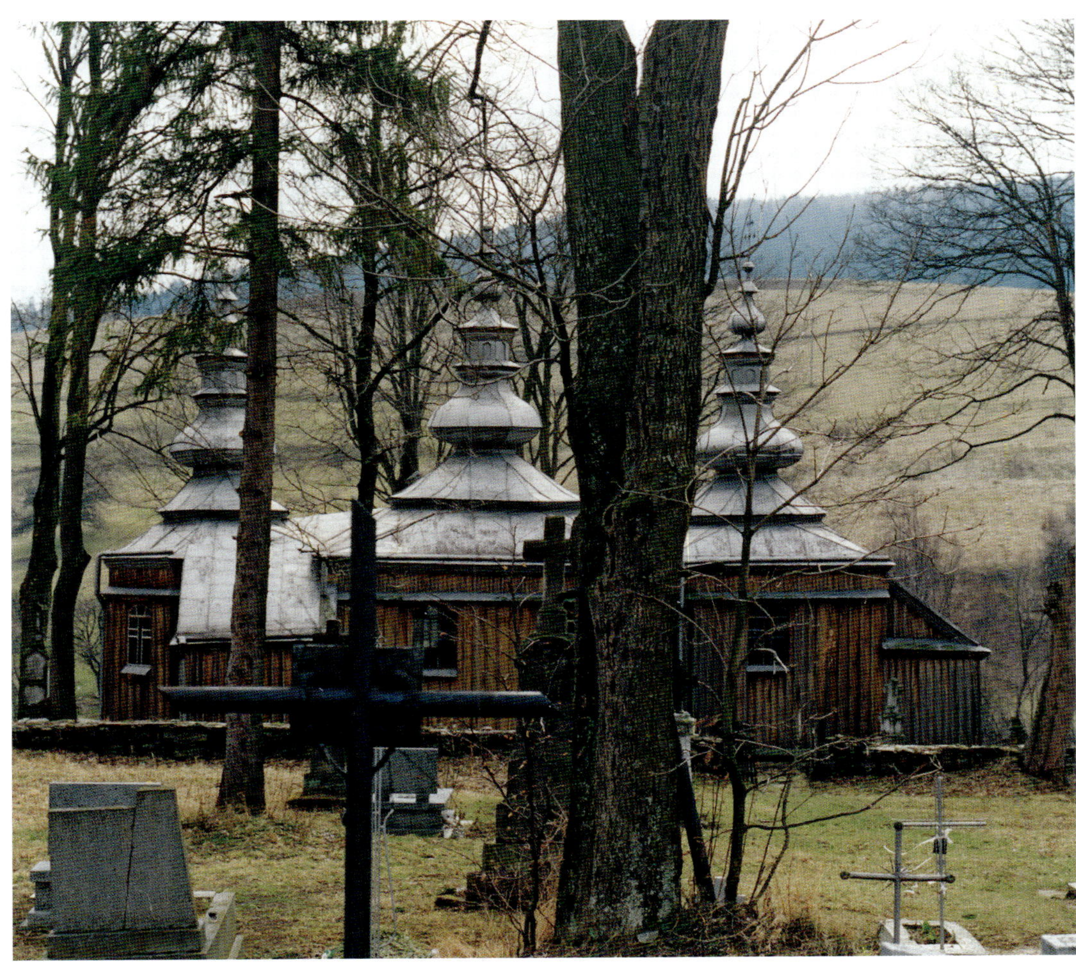

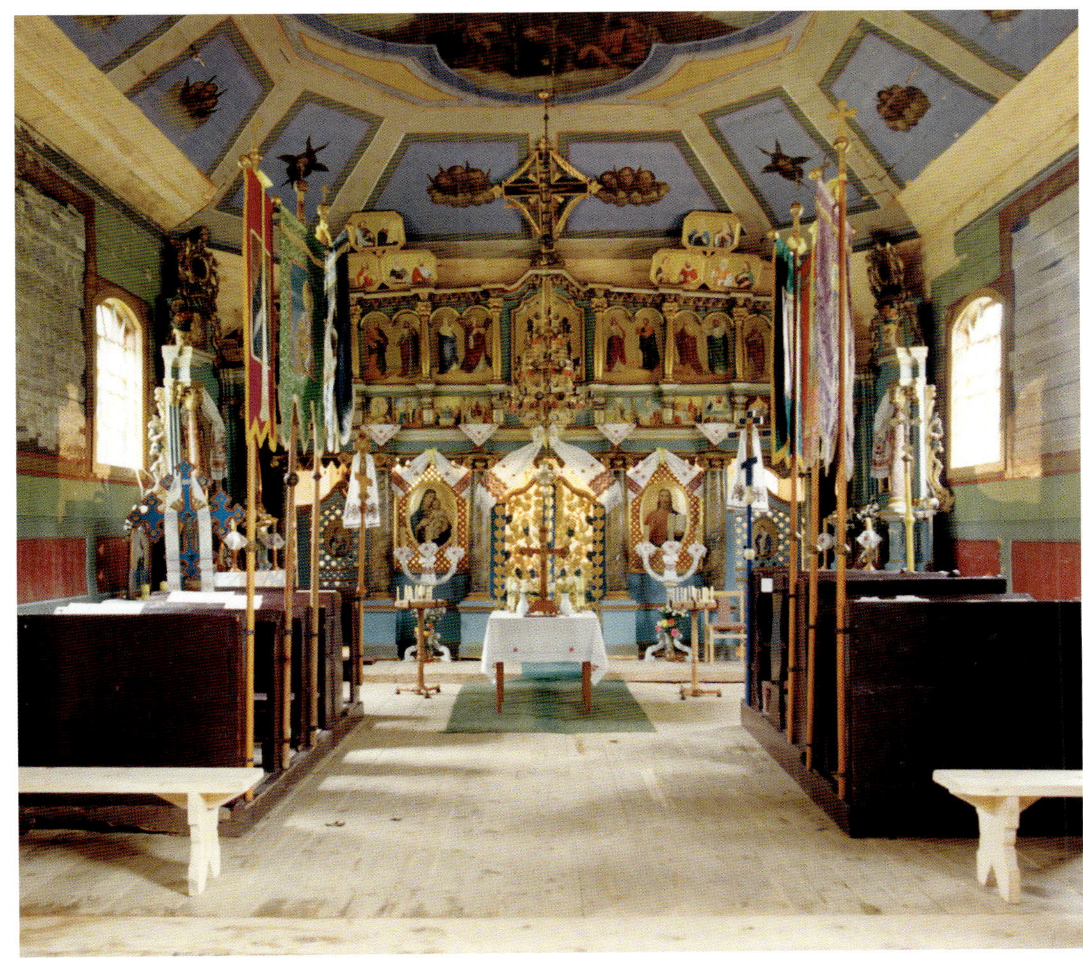

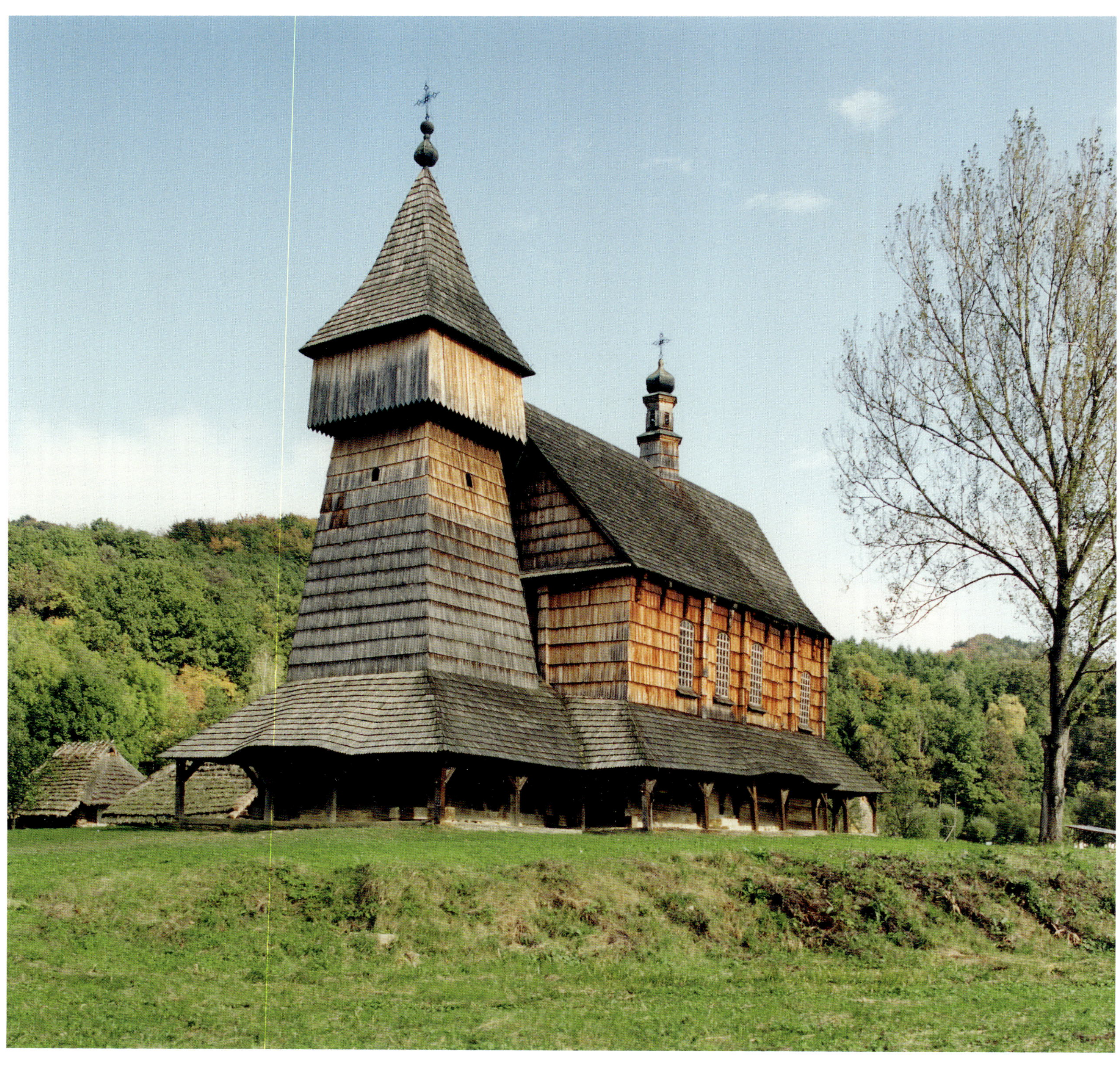

Sanok
Sanok, Polen
transloz. aus Bączal Dolny, Jasło, Polen
St. Nikolaus
1667

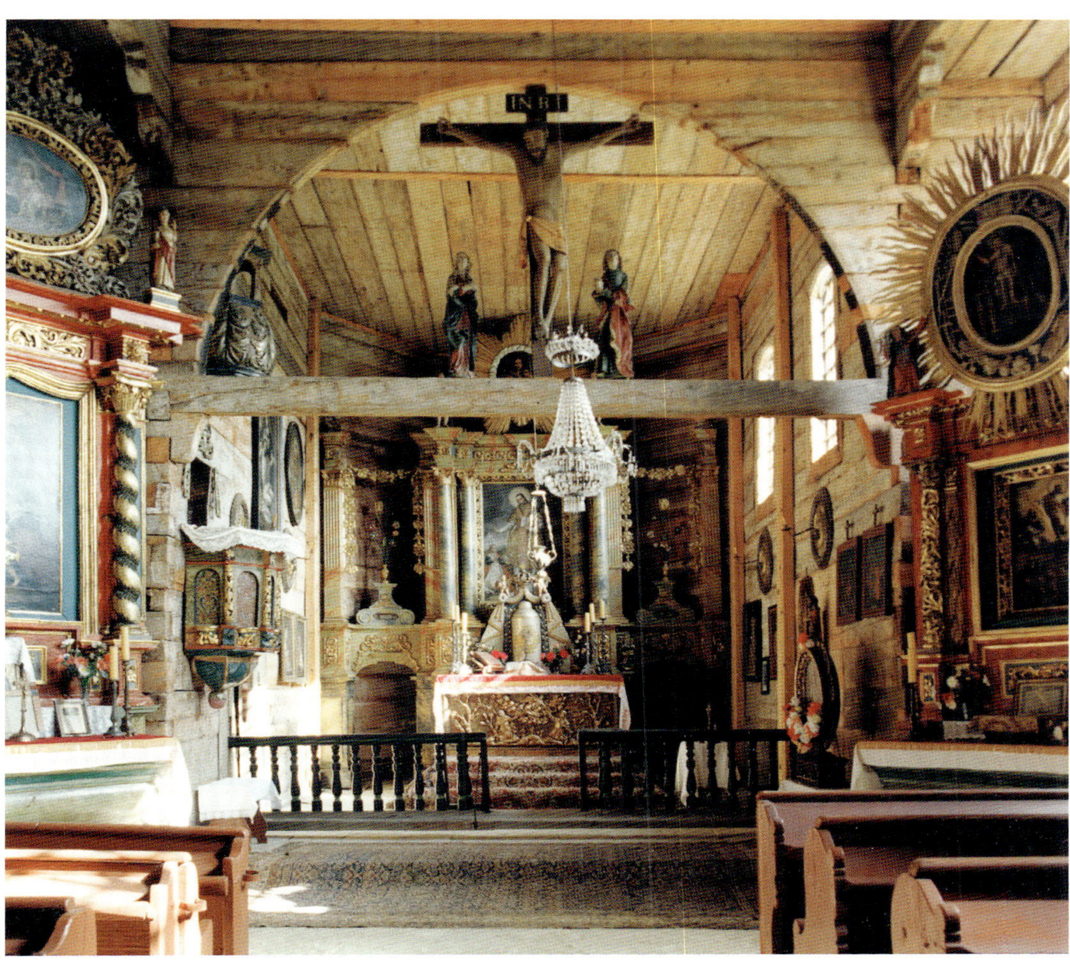

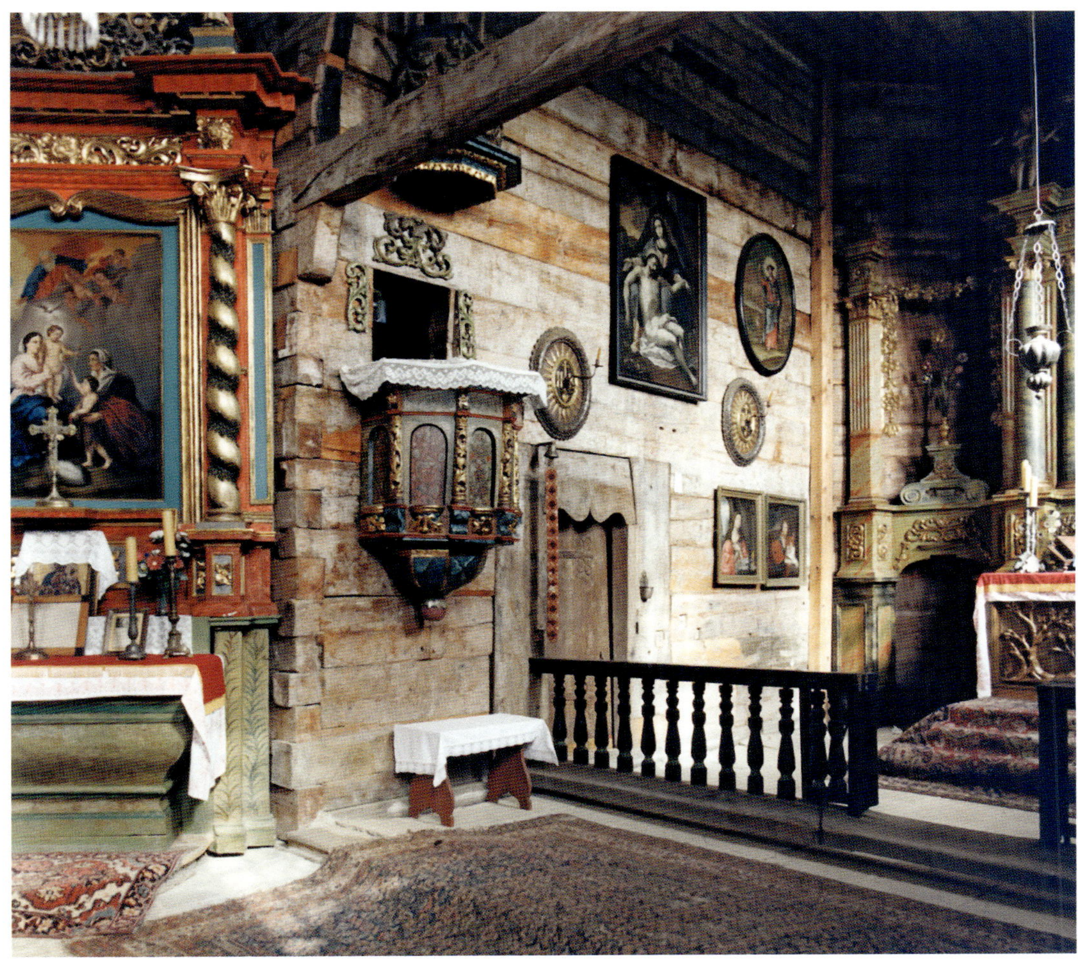

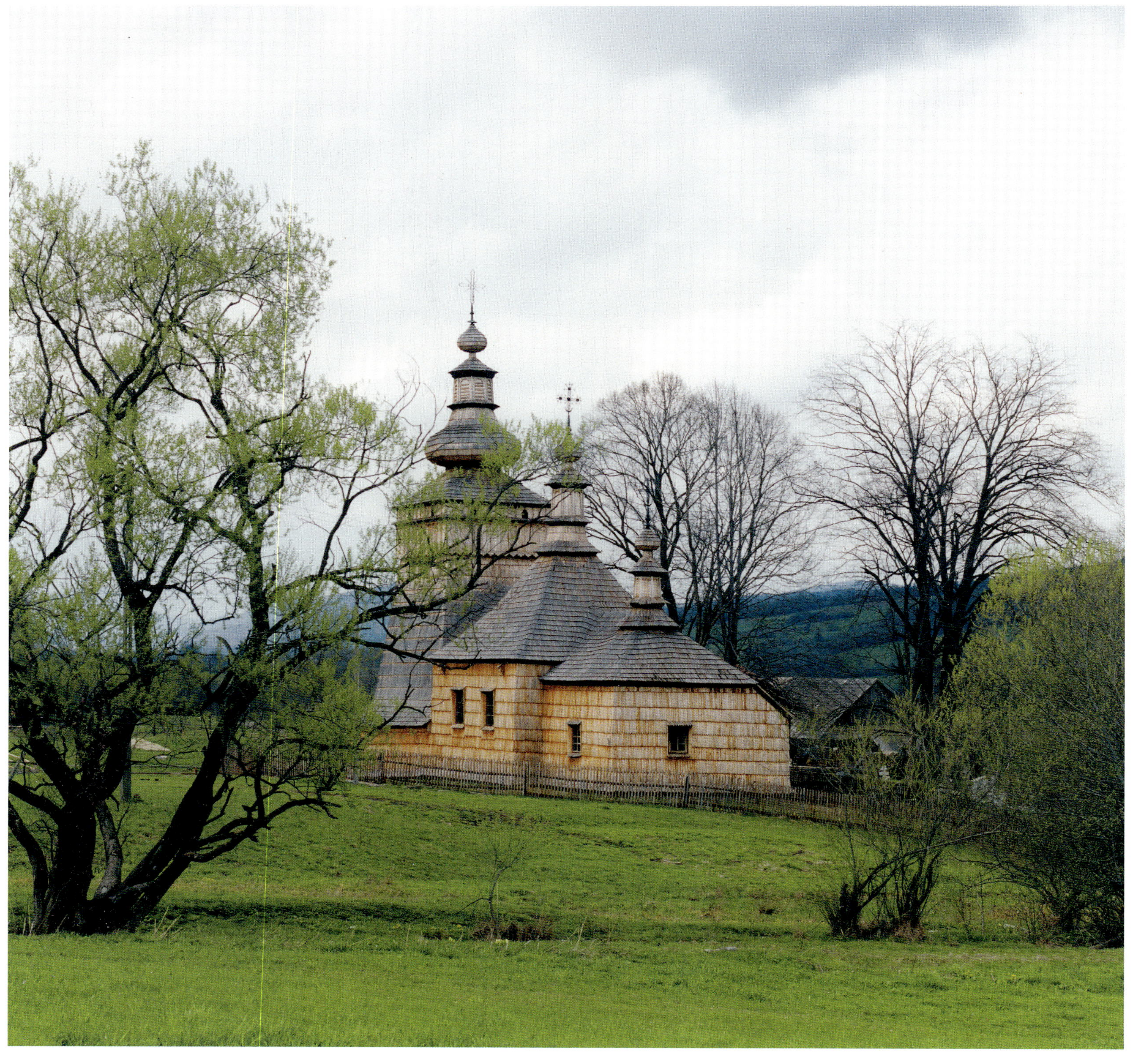

Skwirtne
Gorlice, Polen
Hll. Cosmas und Damian
1837

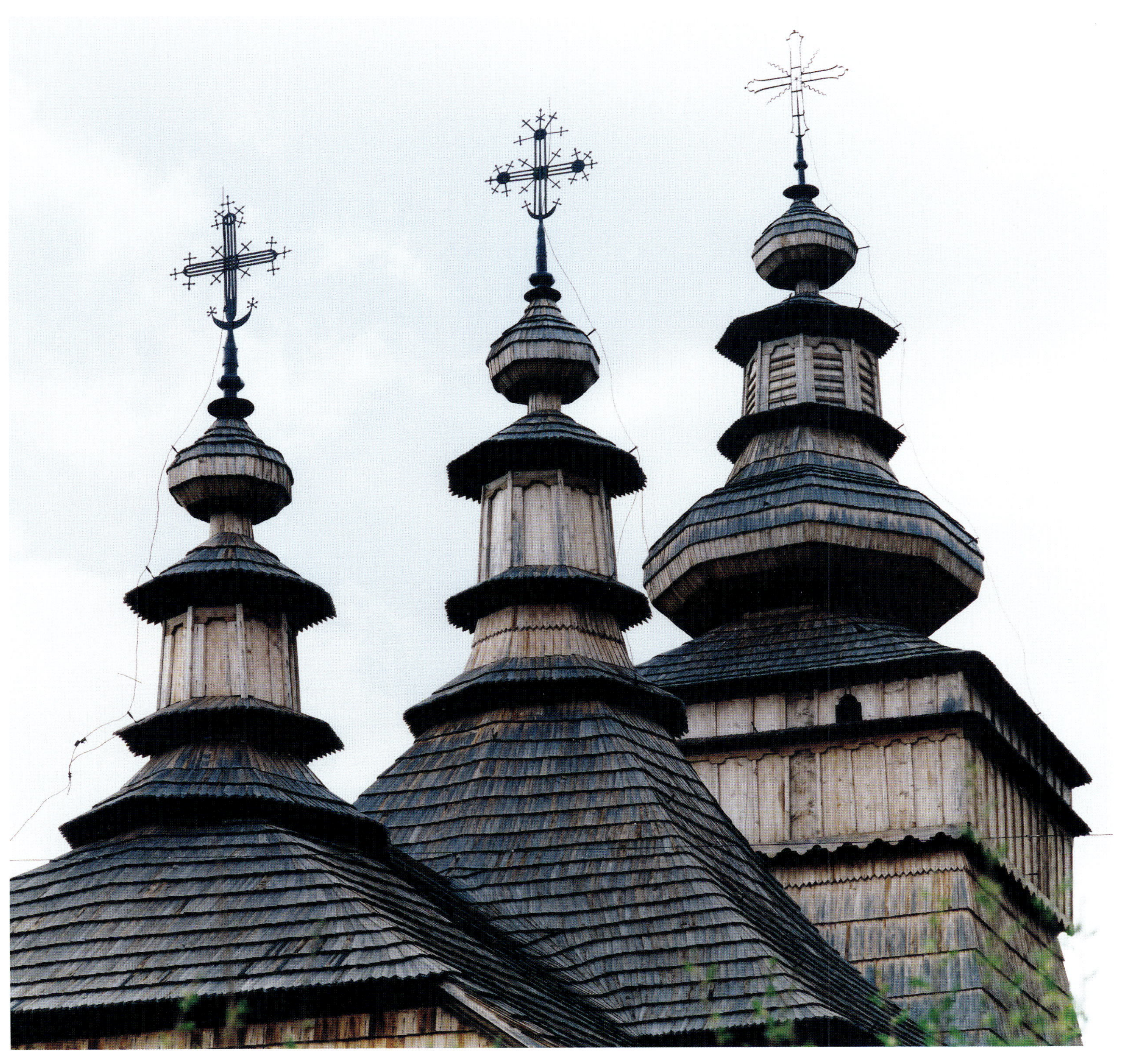

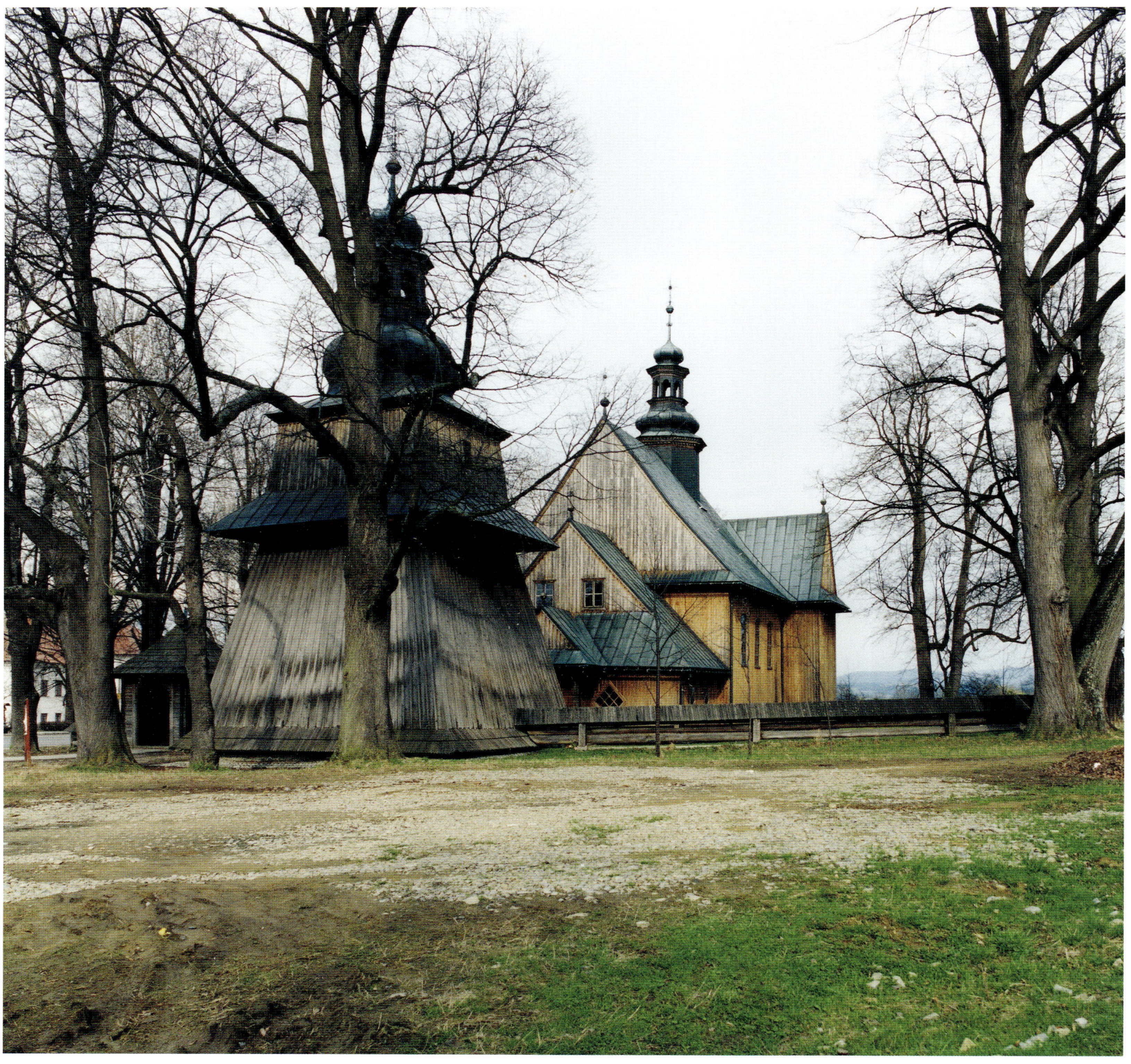

Spytkowice
Wadowice, Polen
Gottesmutter

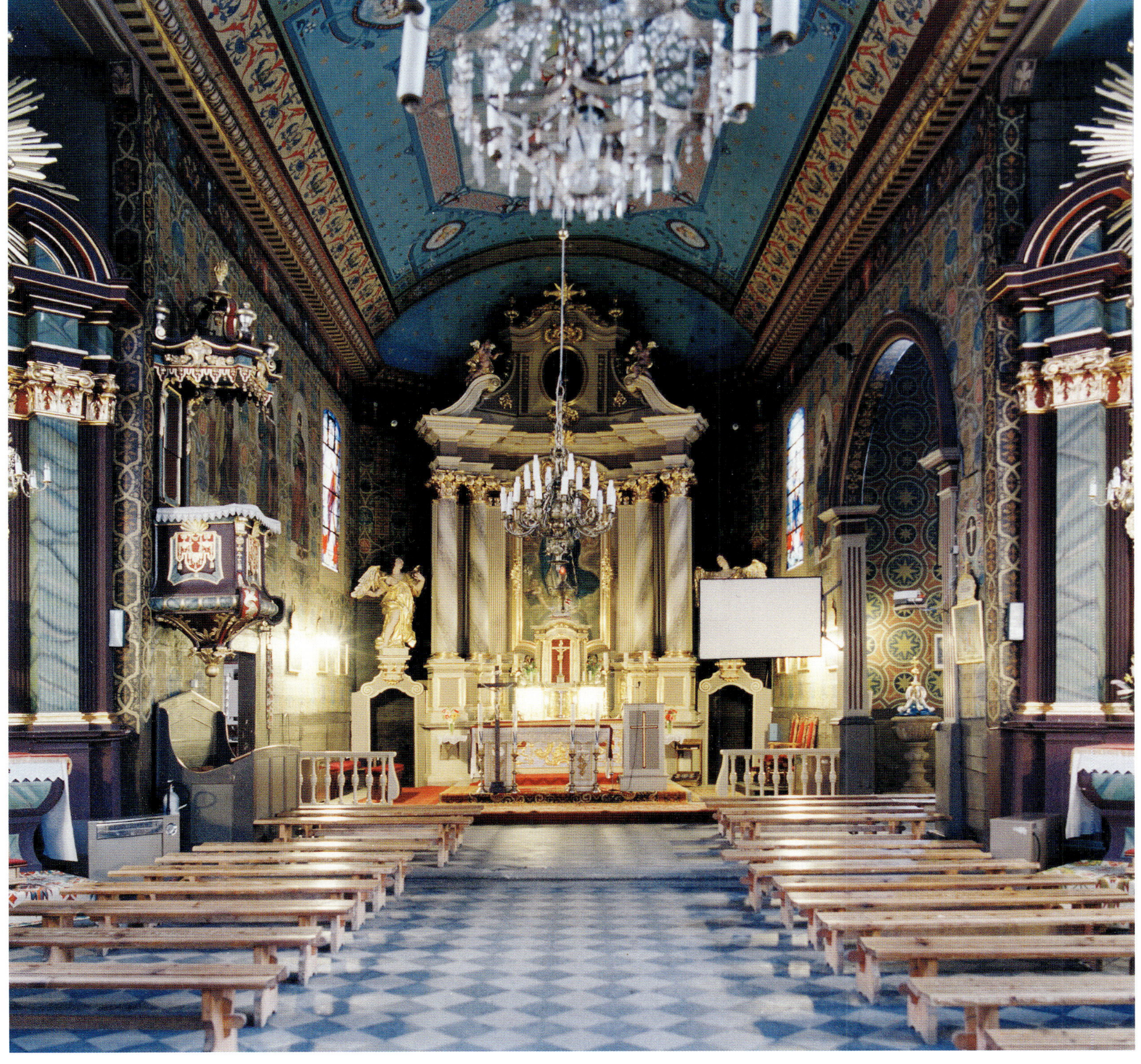

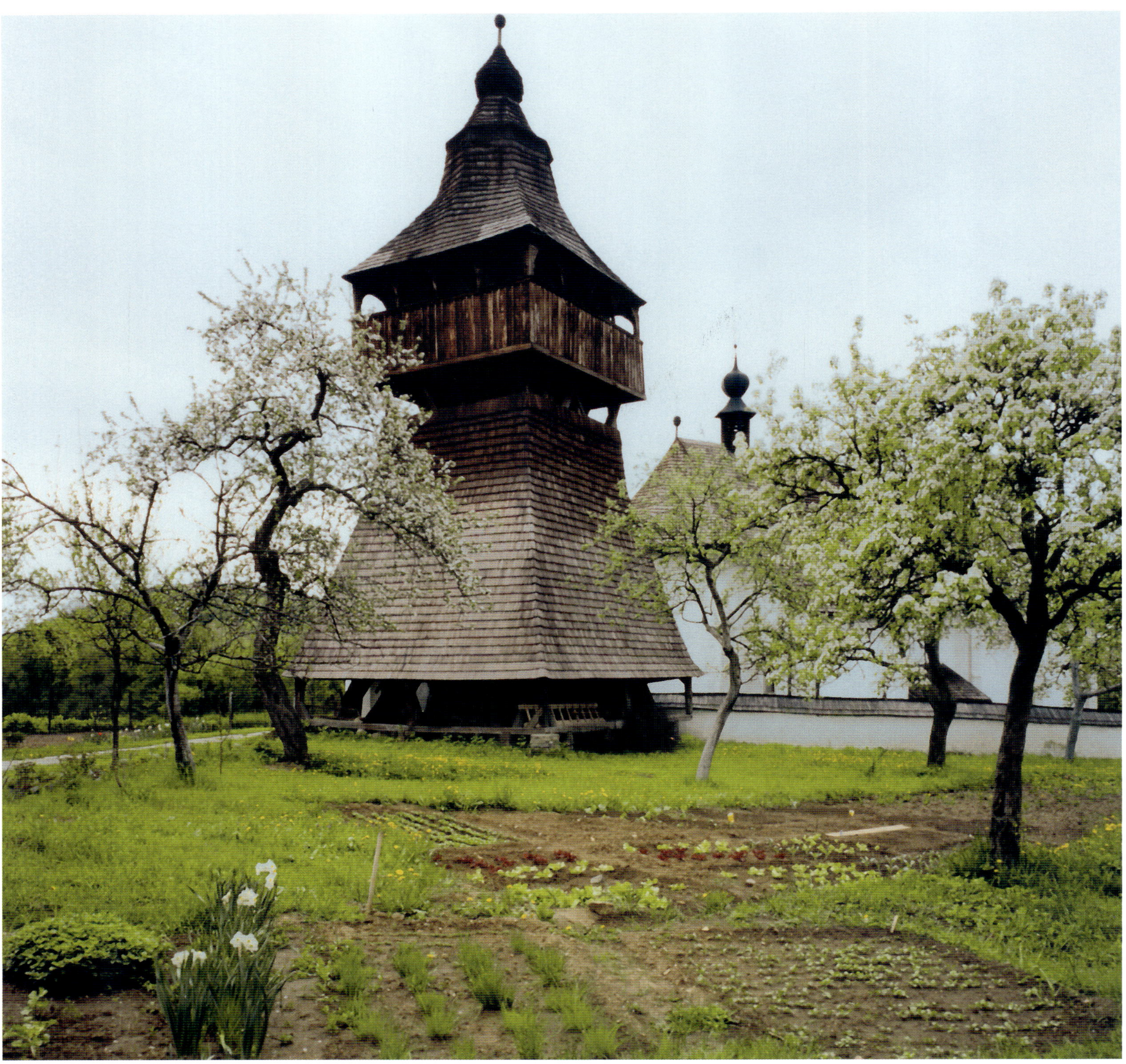

Stará Halič
Lučenec, Slowakei
um 1300
Glockedntutm 1673

Svidník
Prešov, Slowakei
transloz. aus Nová Polianka, Prešov
Hl. Paraskeva
1766

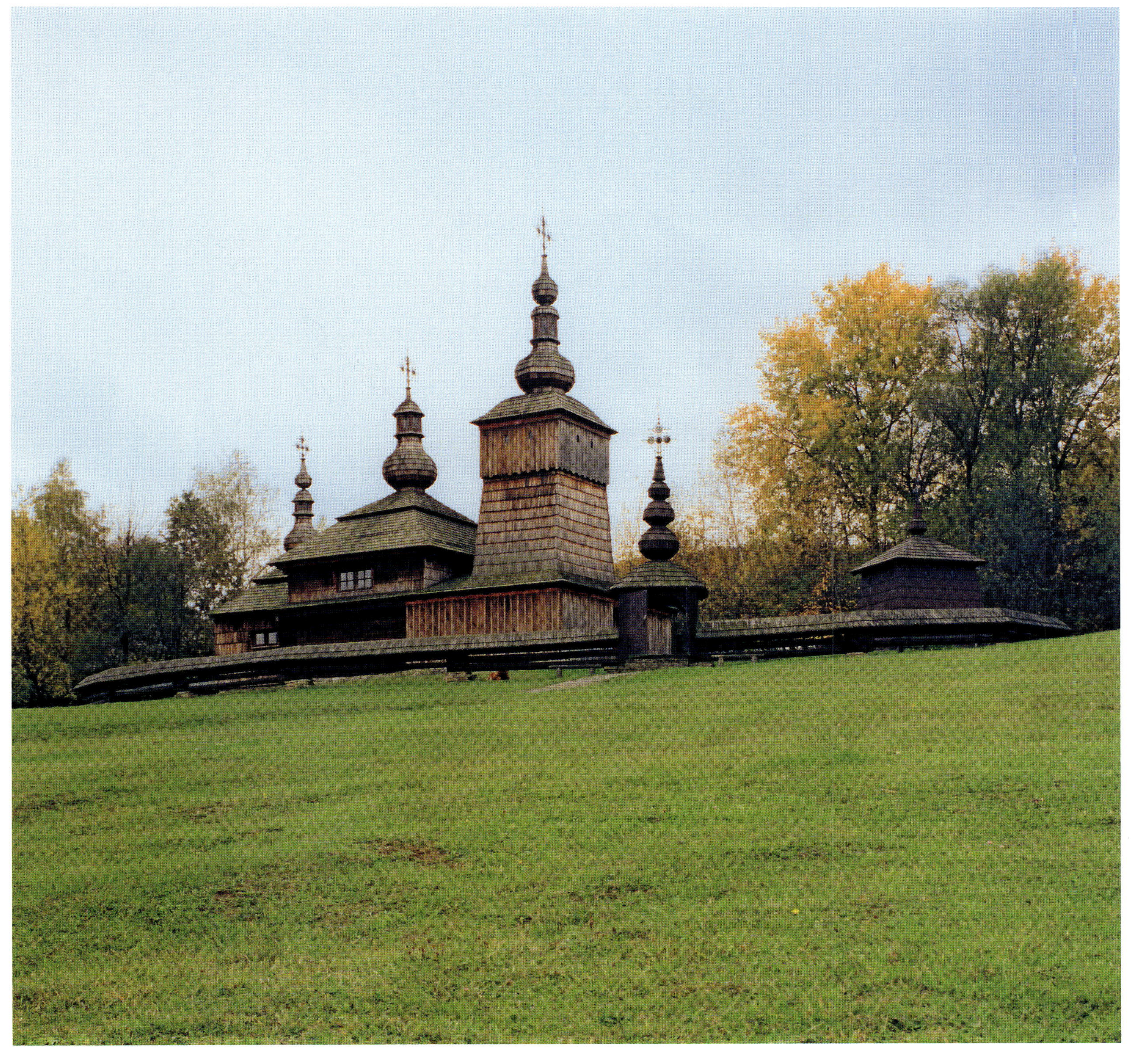

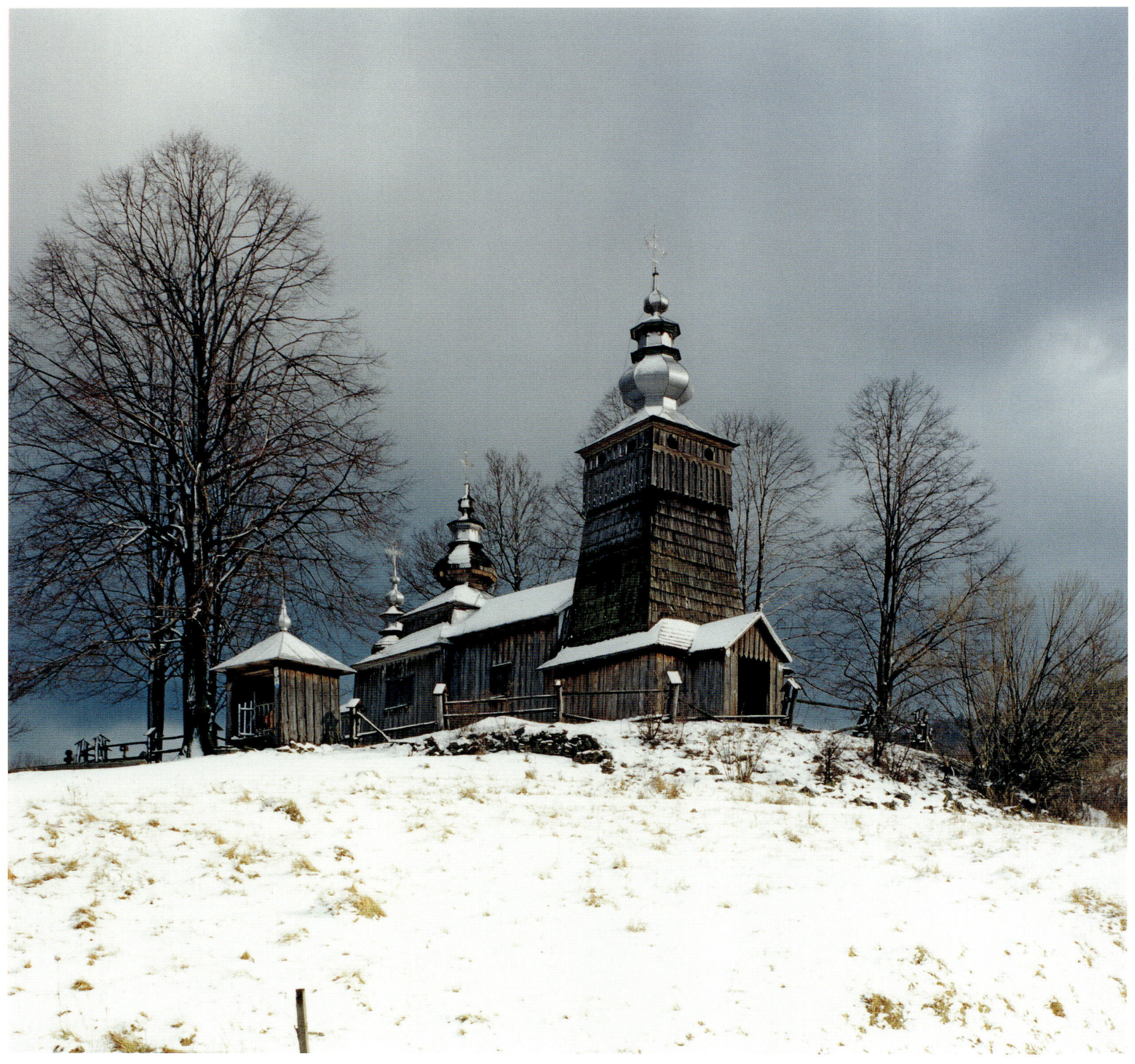

Świątkowa Mała
Jasło, Polen
Erzengel Michael
1757

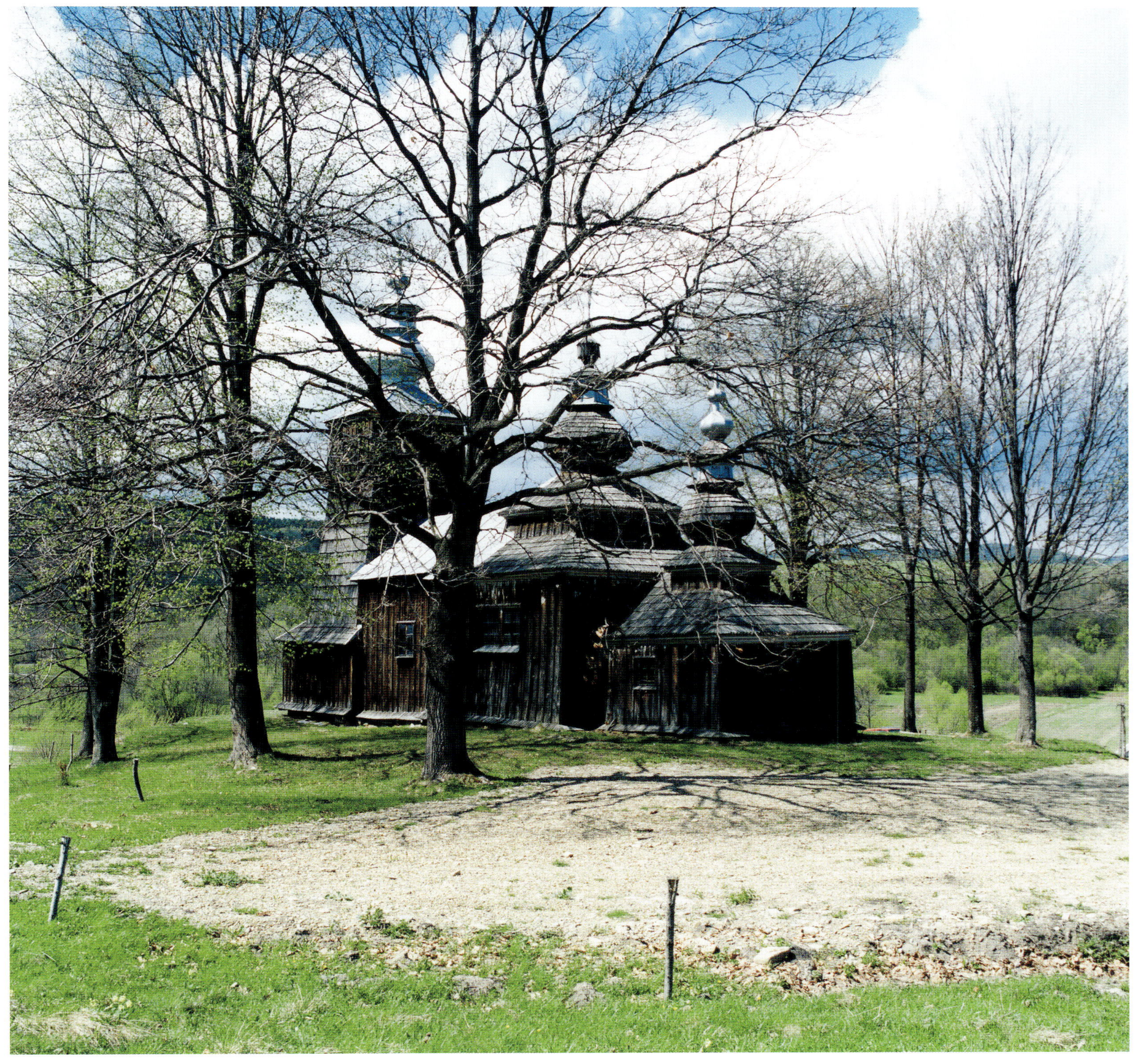

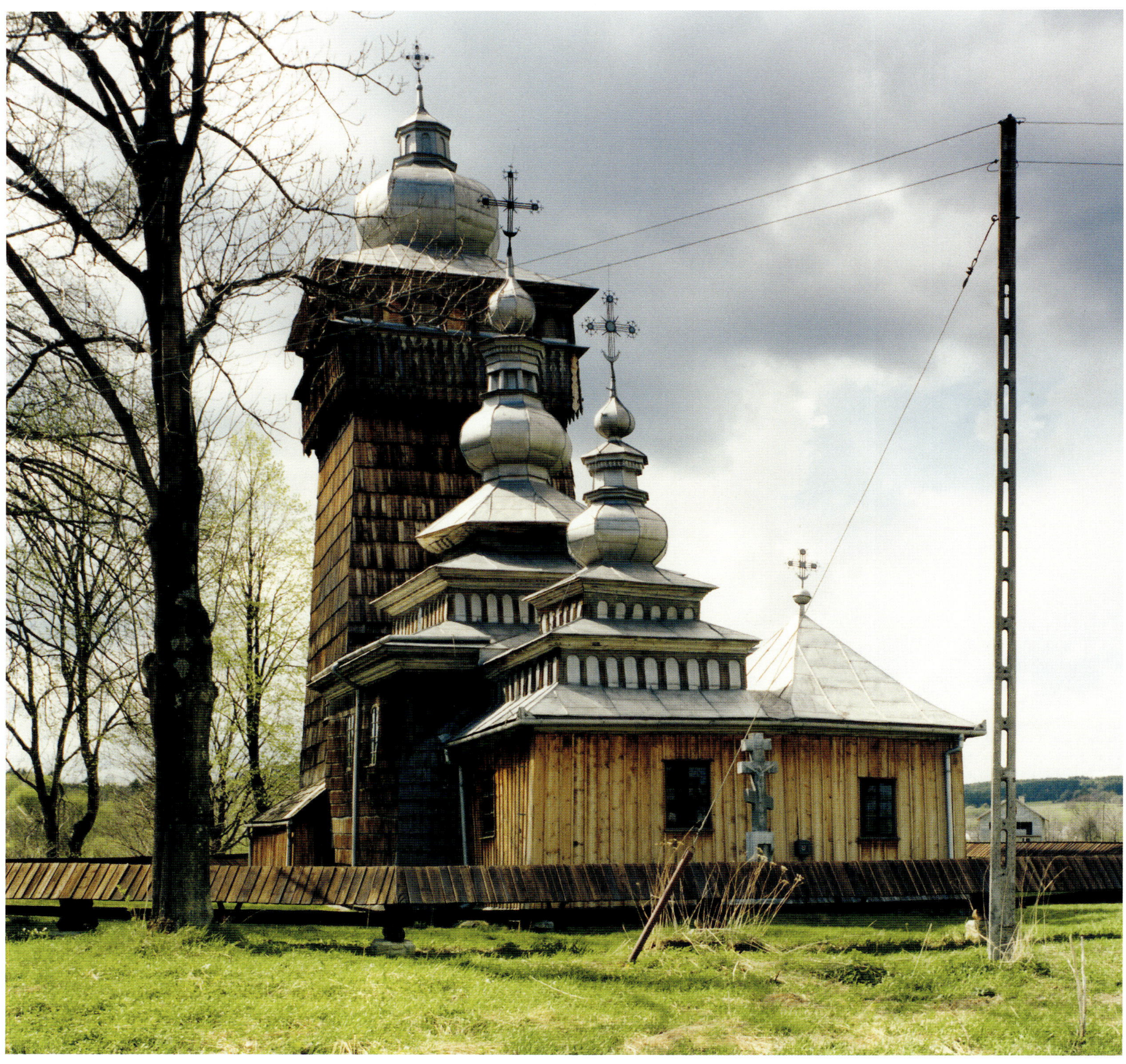

Świątkowa Wielka
Jasło, Polen
Erzengel Michael
1757

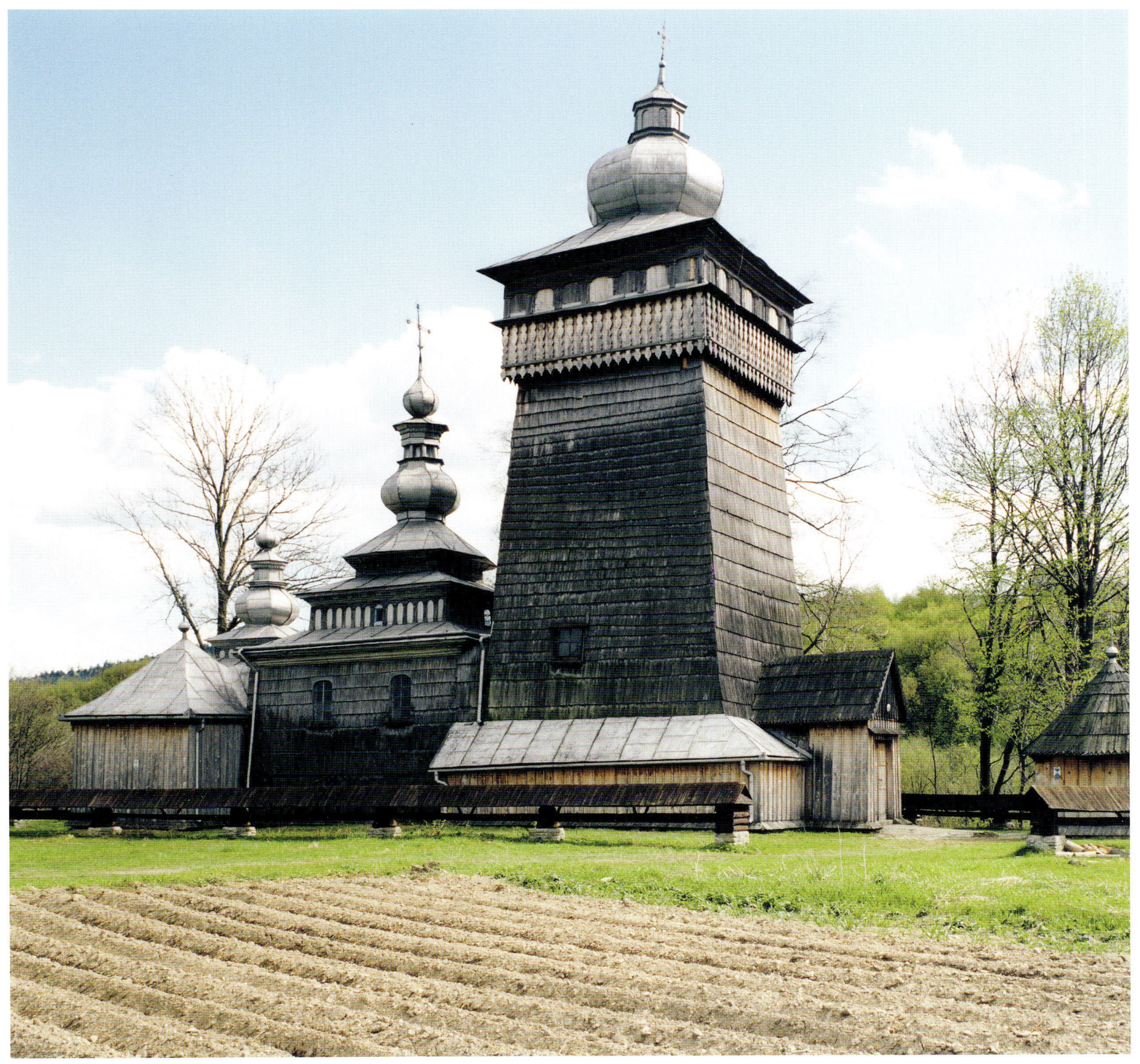

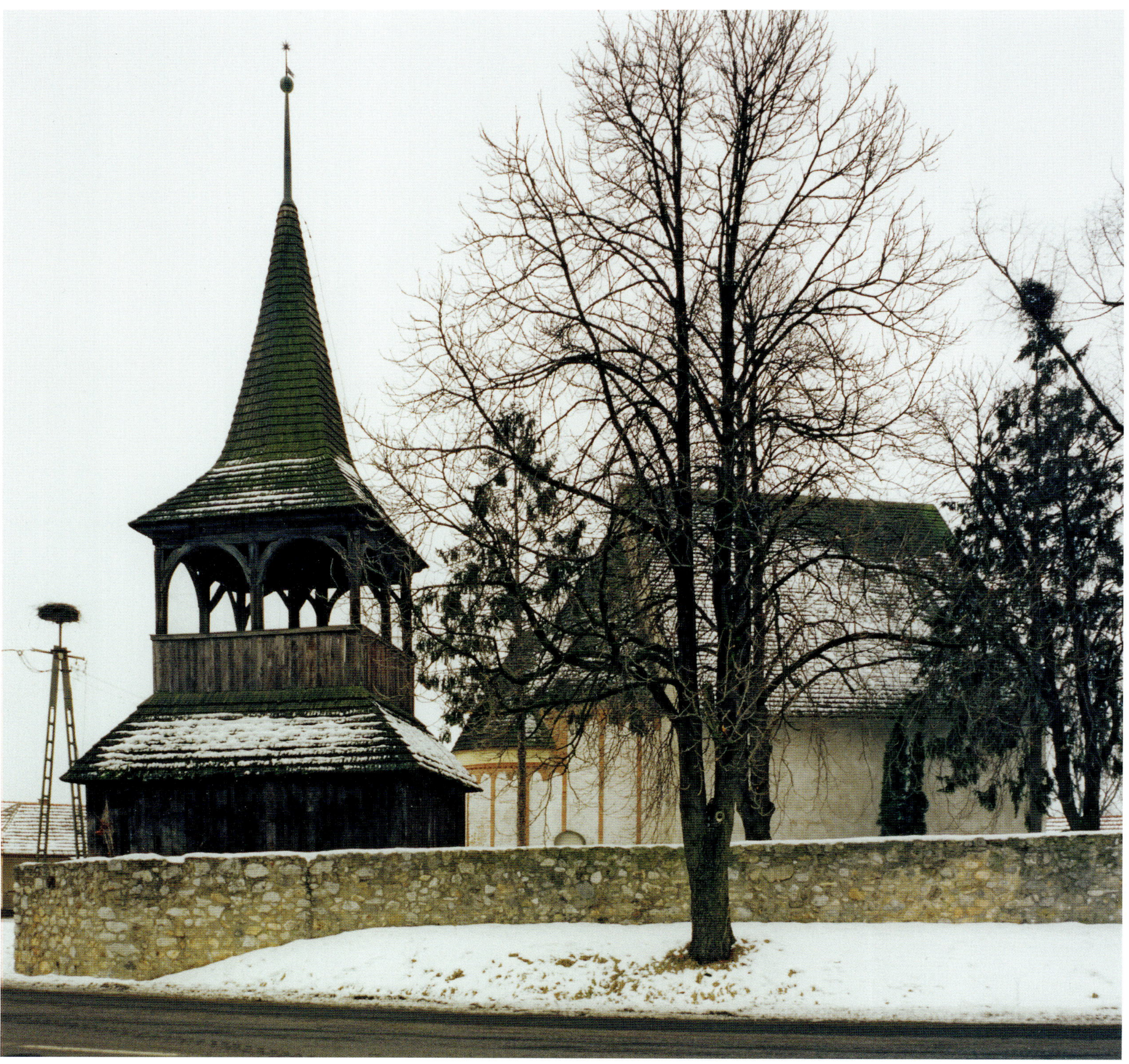

Szalonna
Borsod-Abaúj-Zemplén, Ungarn
1765

Szczawne
Sanok, Polen
Entschlafen der Gottesmutter
1888

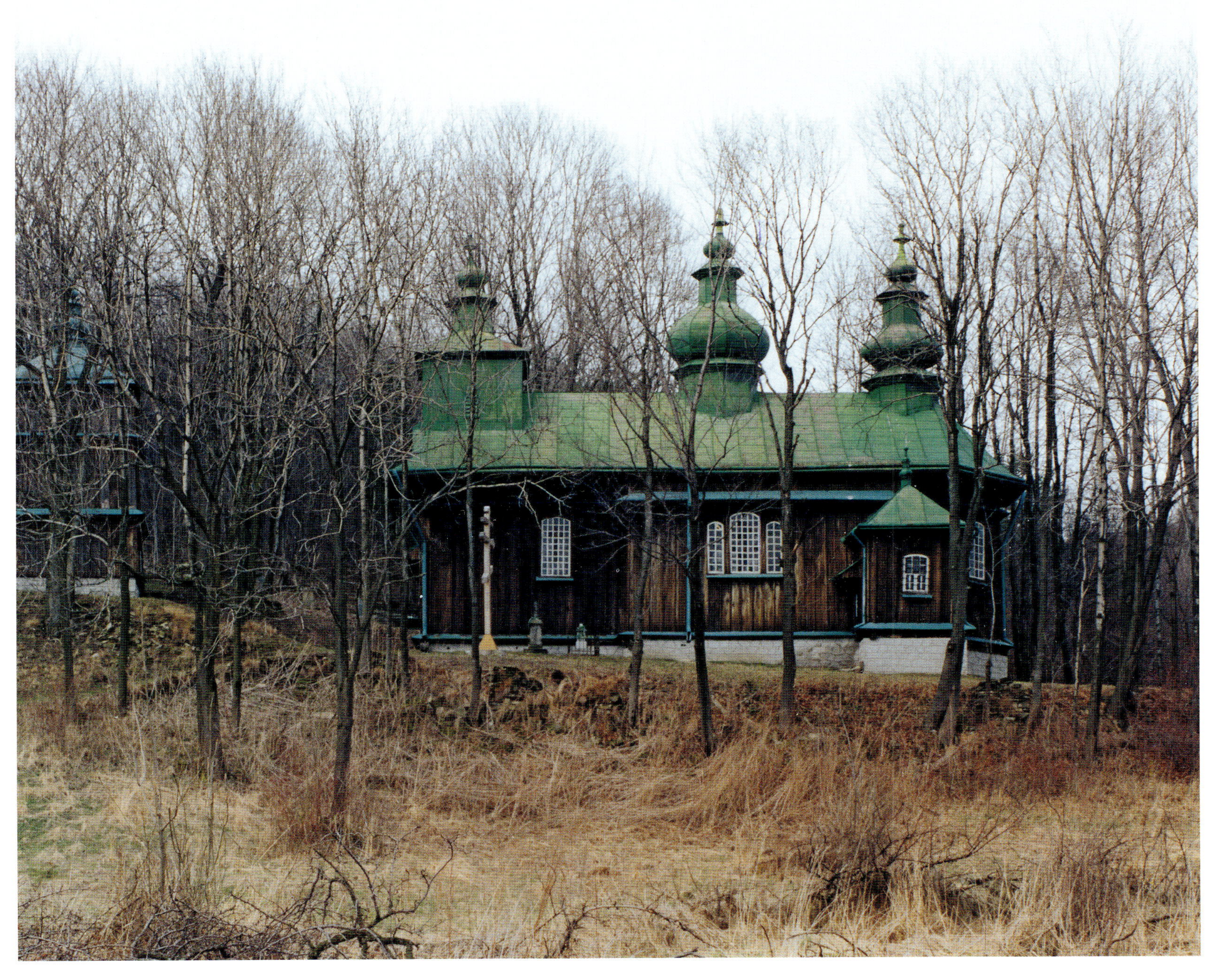

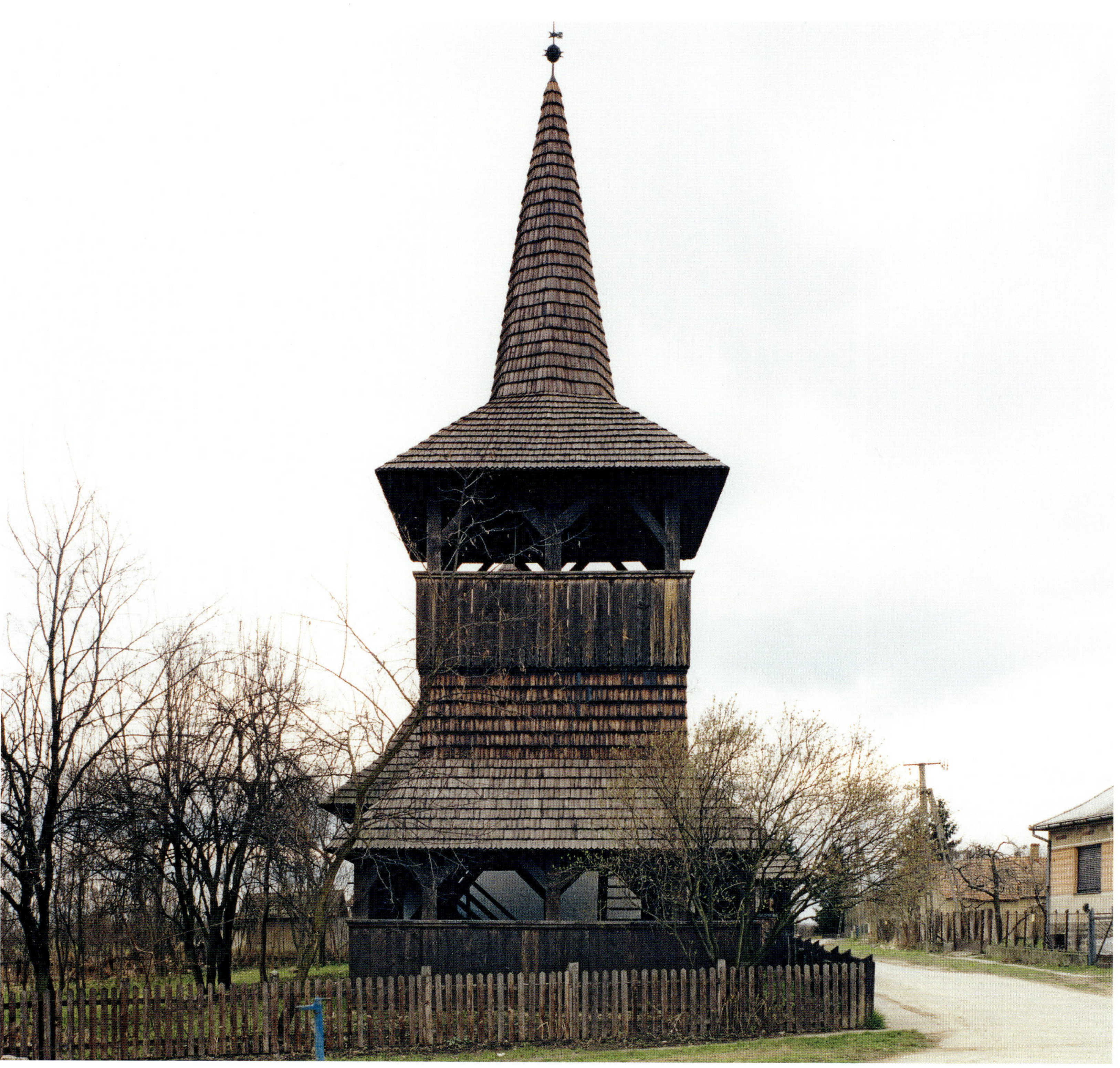

Tákos
Szabolcs-Szatmár-Bereg, Ungarn
18. Jh.

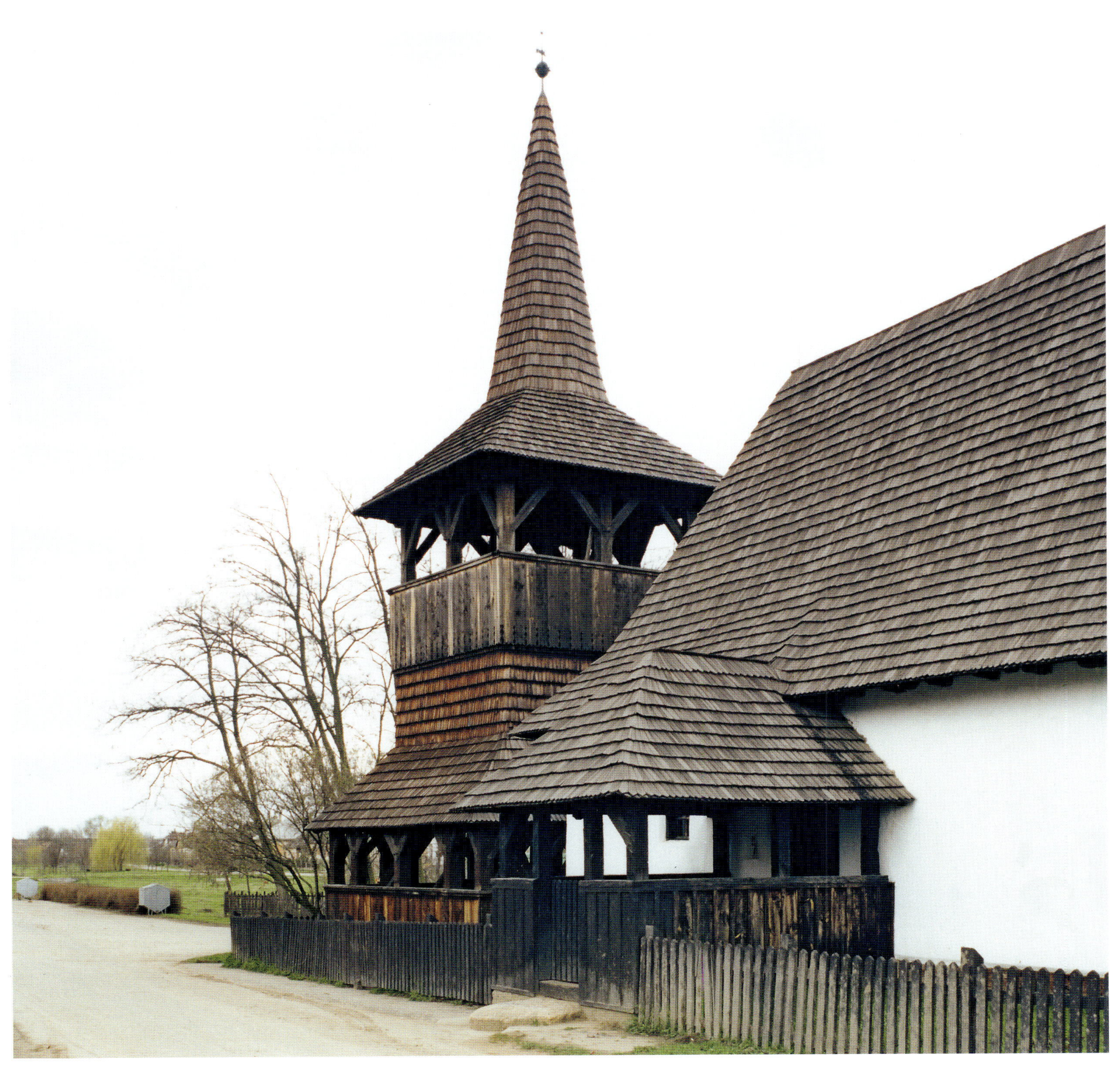

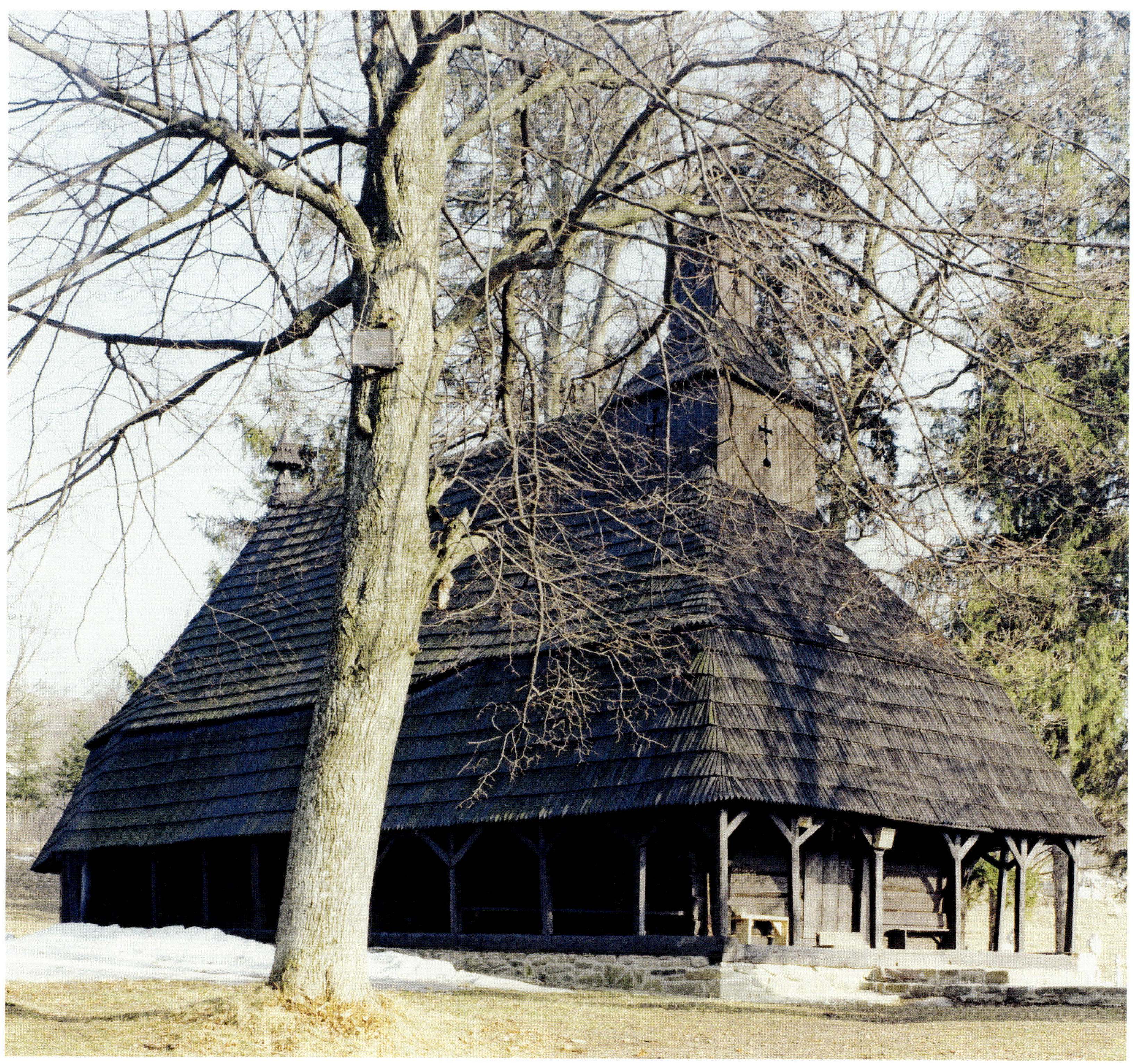

Topol'a
Prešov, Slowakei
Erzengel Michael
1700

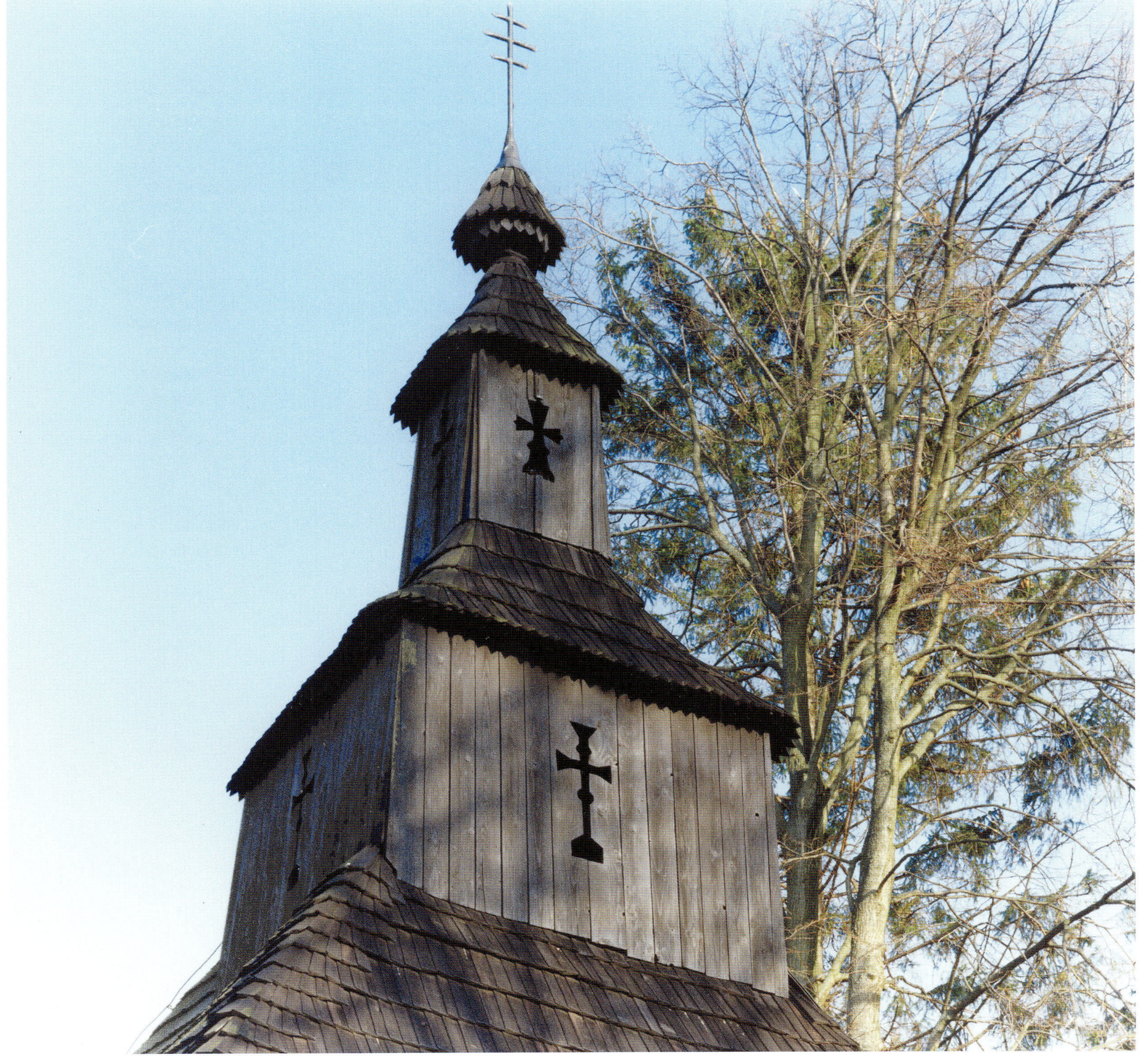

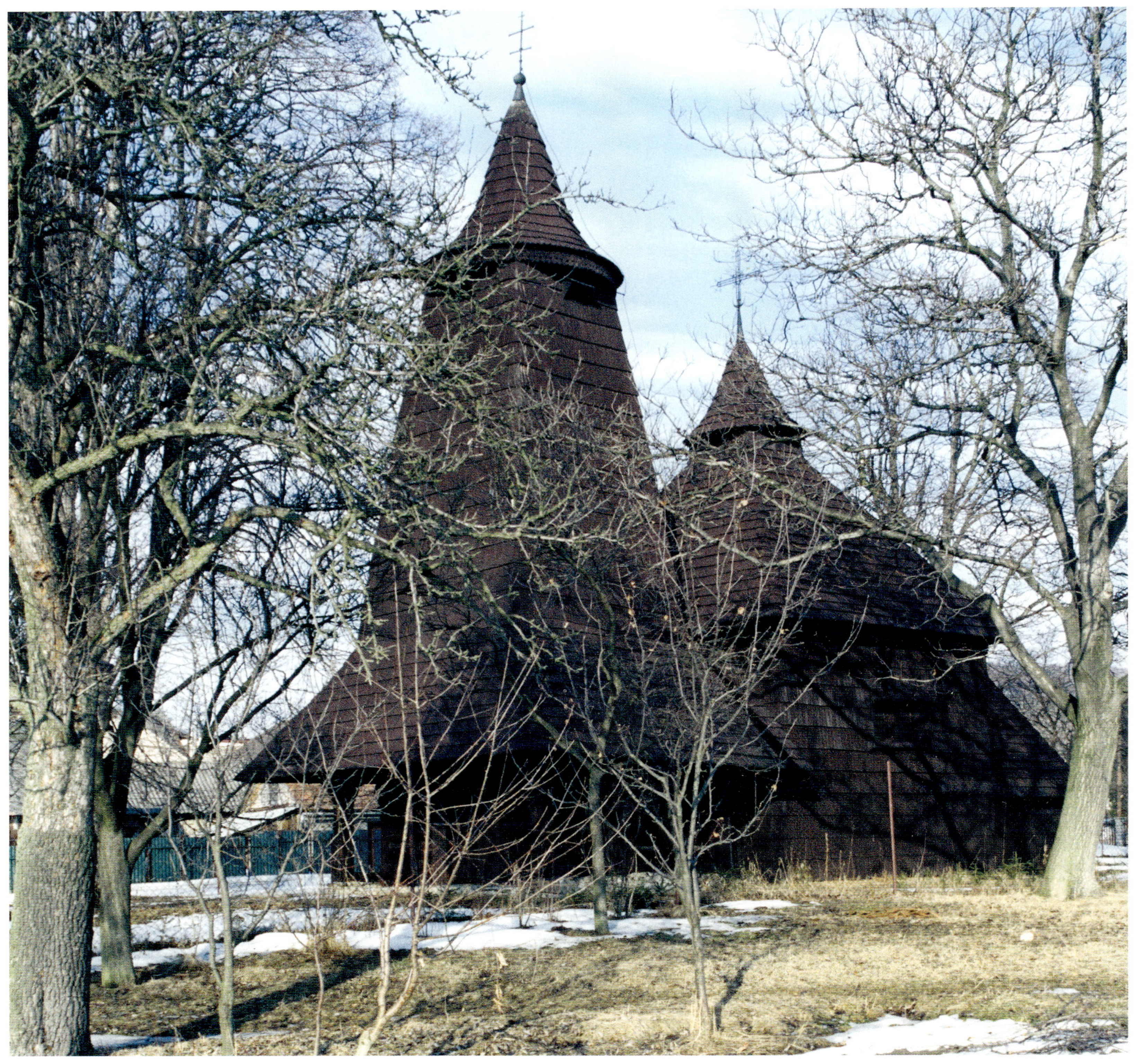

Tročany
Prešov, Slowakei
Ev. Lukas
1739

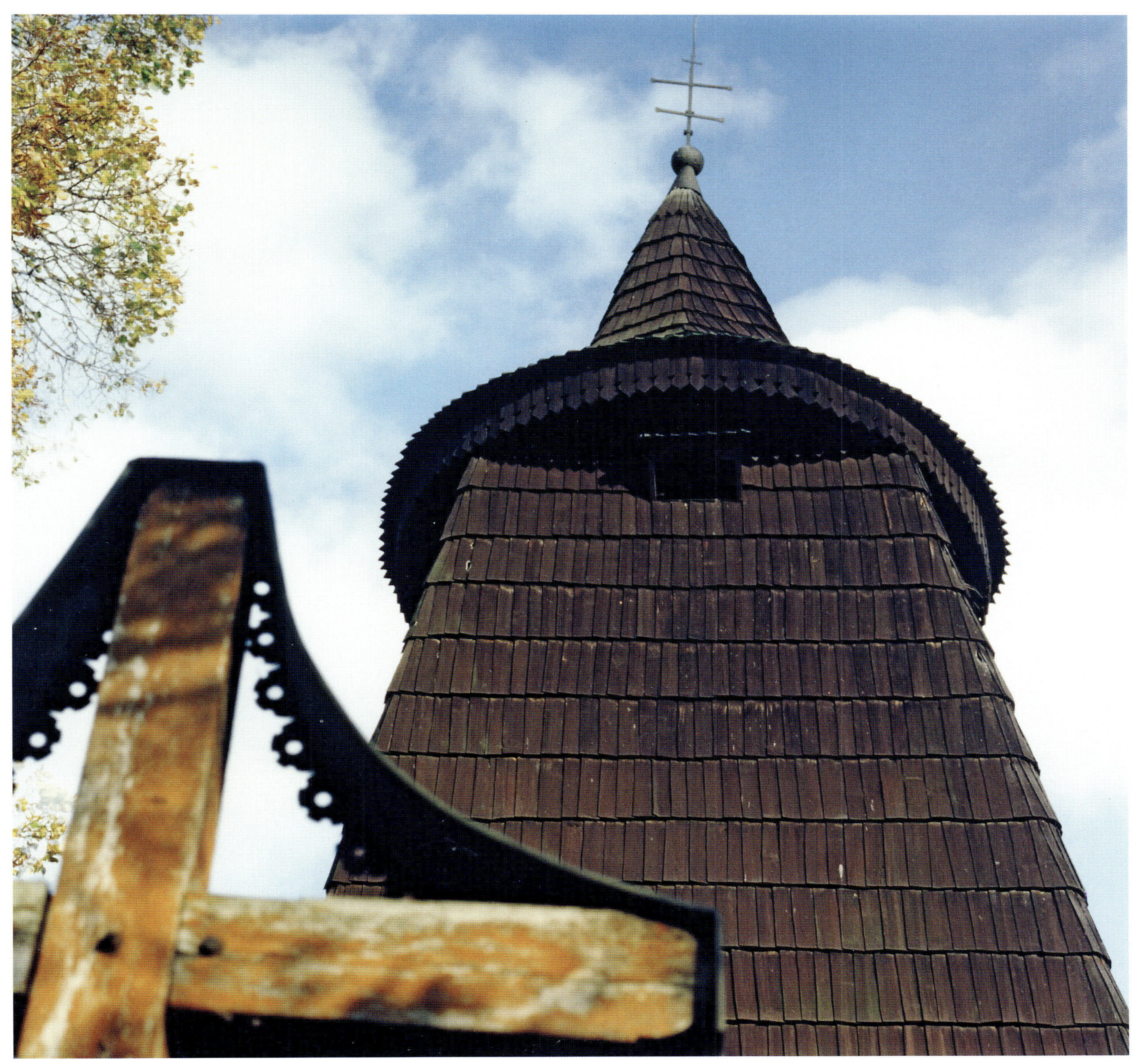

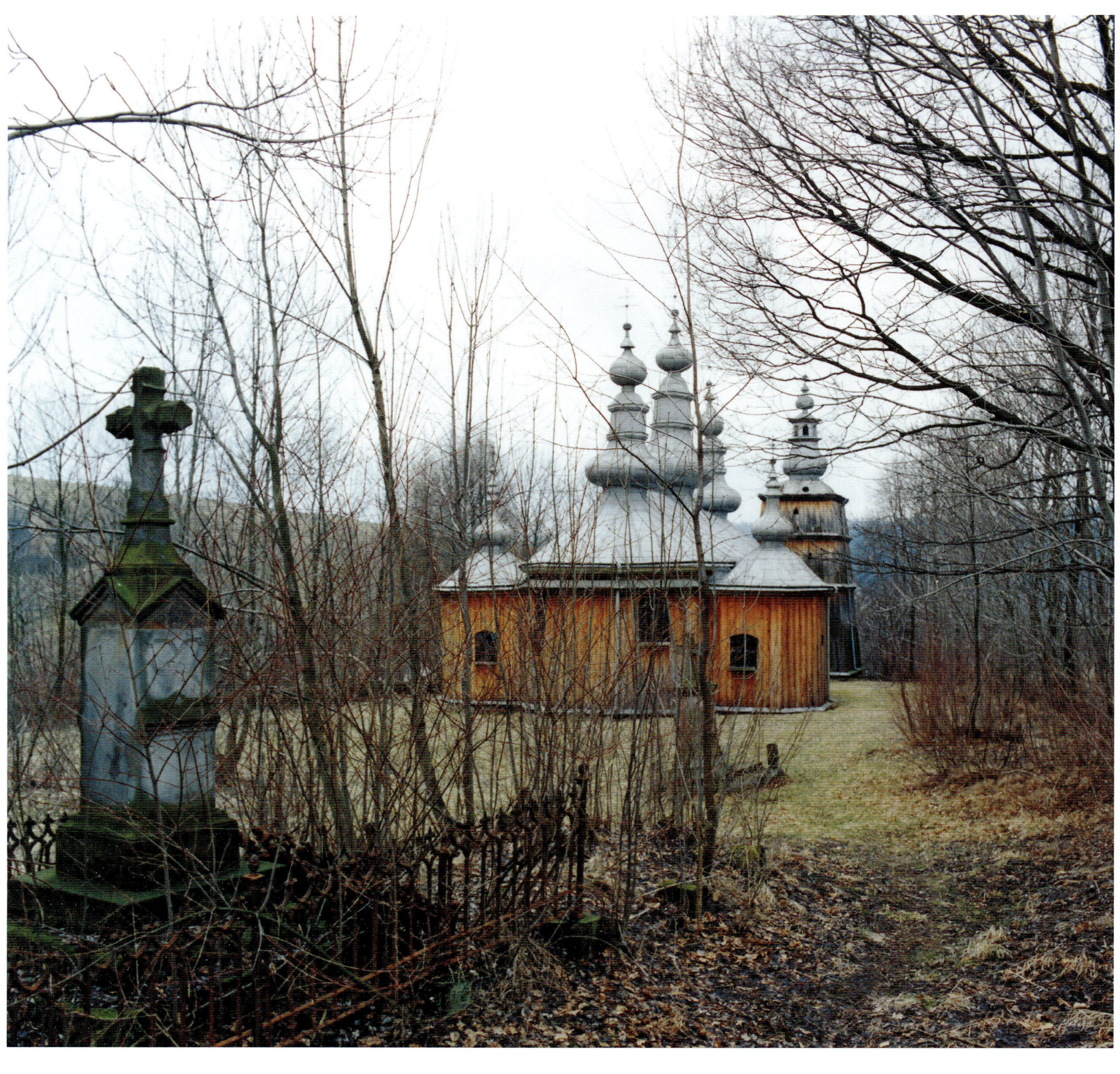

Turzańsk
Sanok, Polen
Erzengel Michael
1801

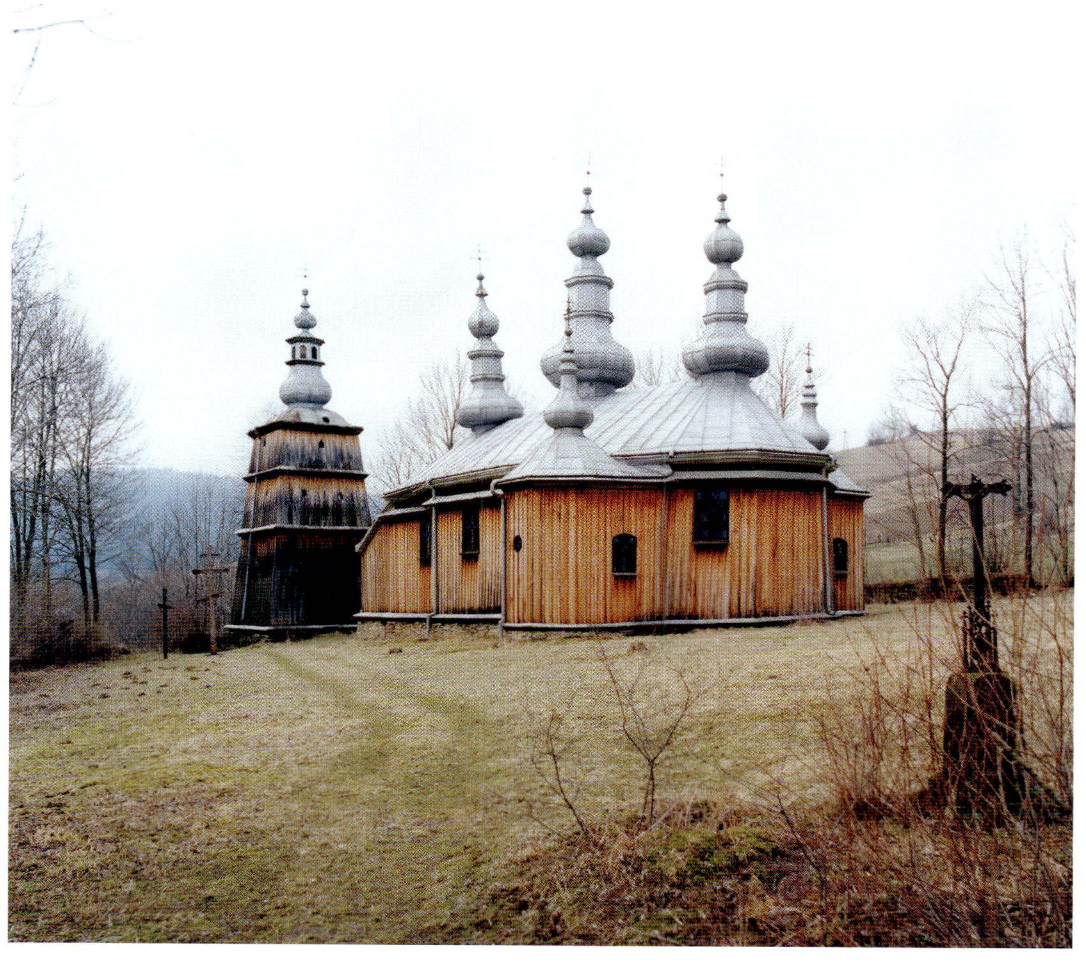

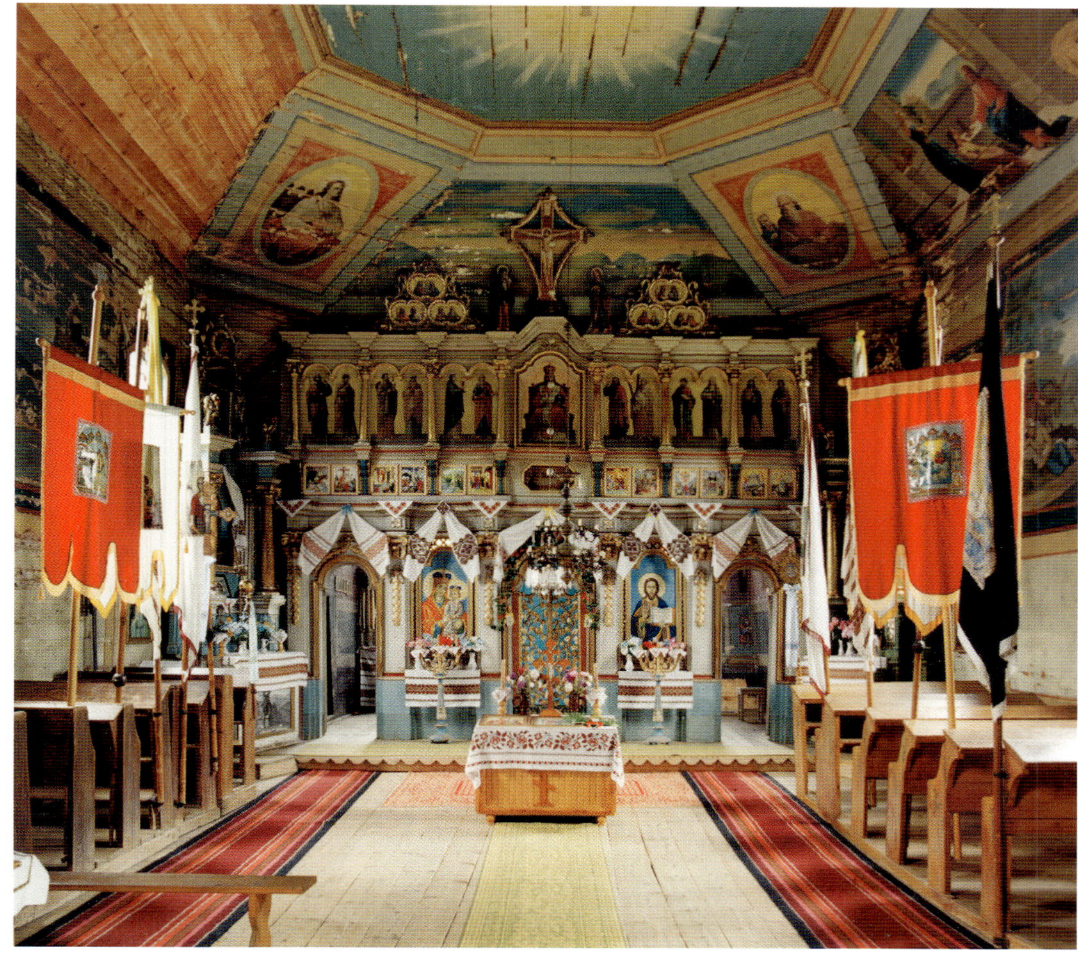

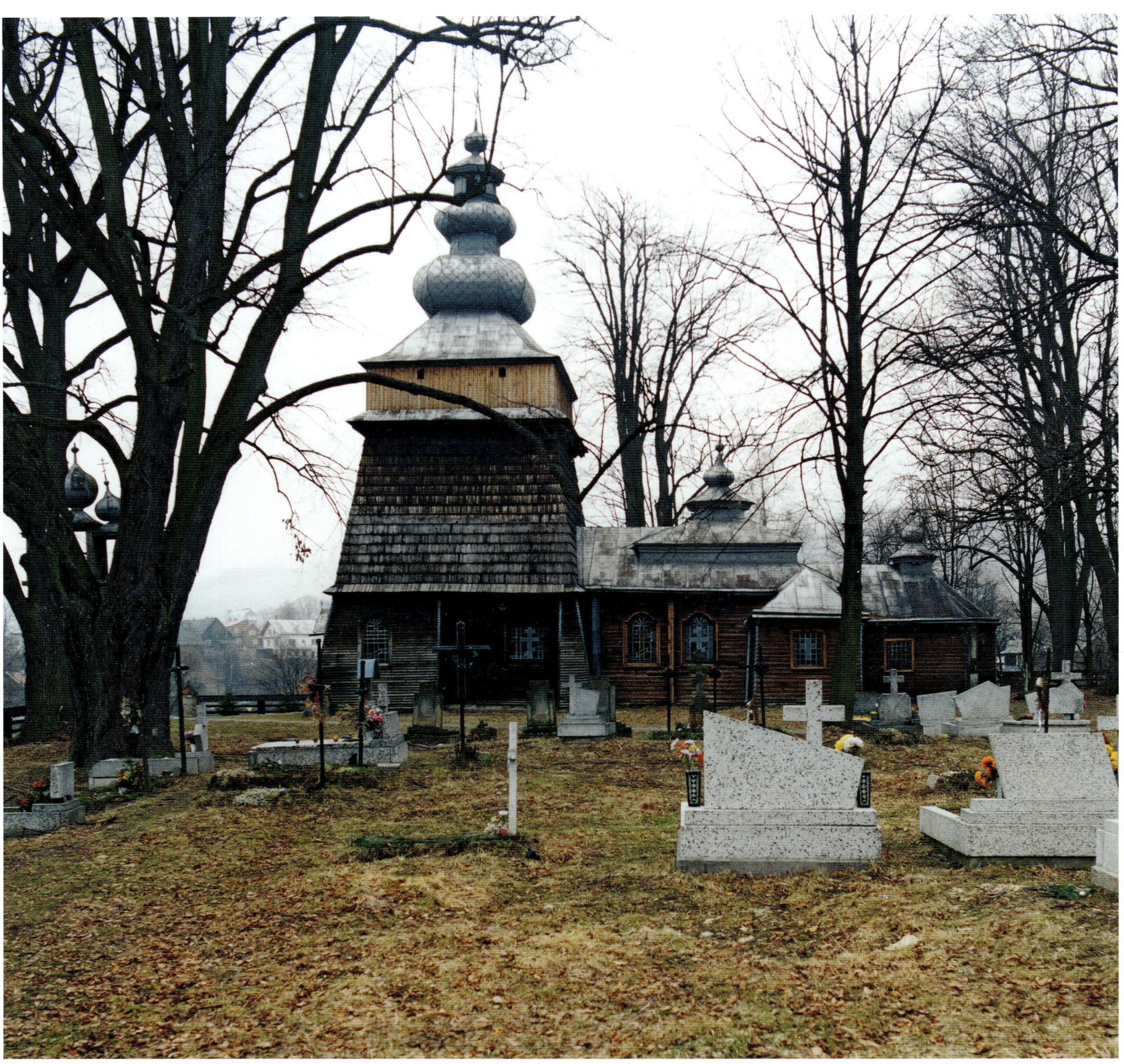

Tylicz
Nowy Sącz, Polen
Hll. Cosmas und Damian
1742

Tyshiv
Zakarpatska, Ukraine
Entschlafen der Gottesmutter
1898

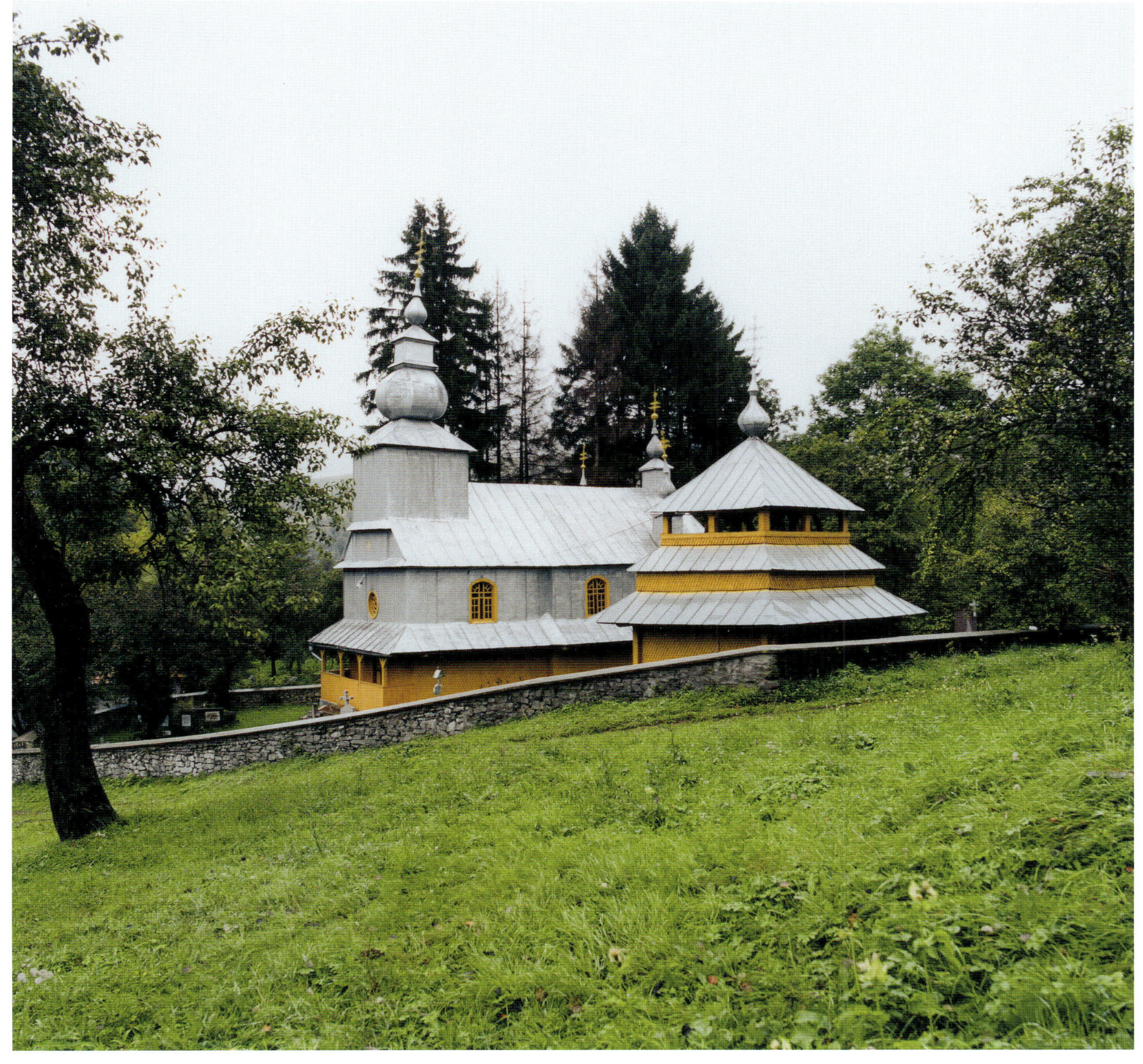

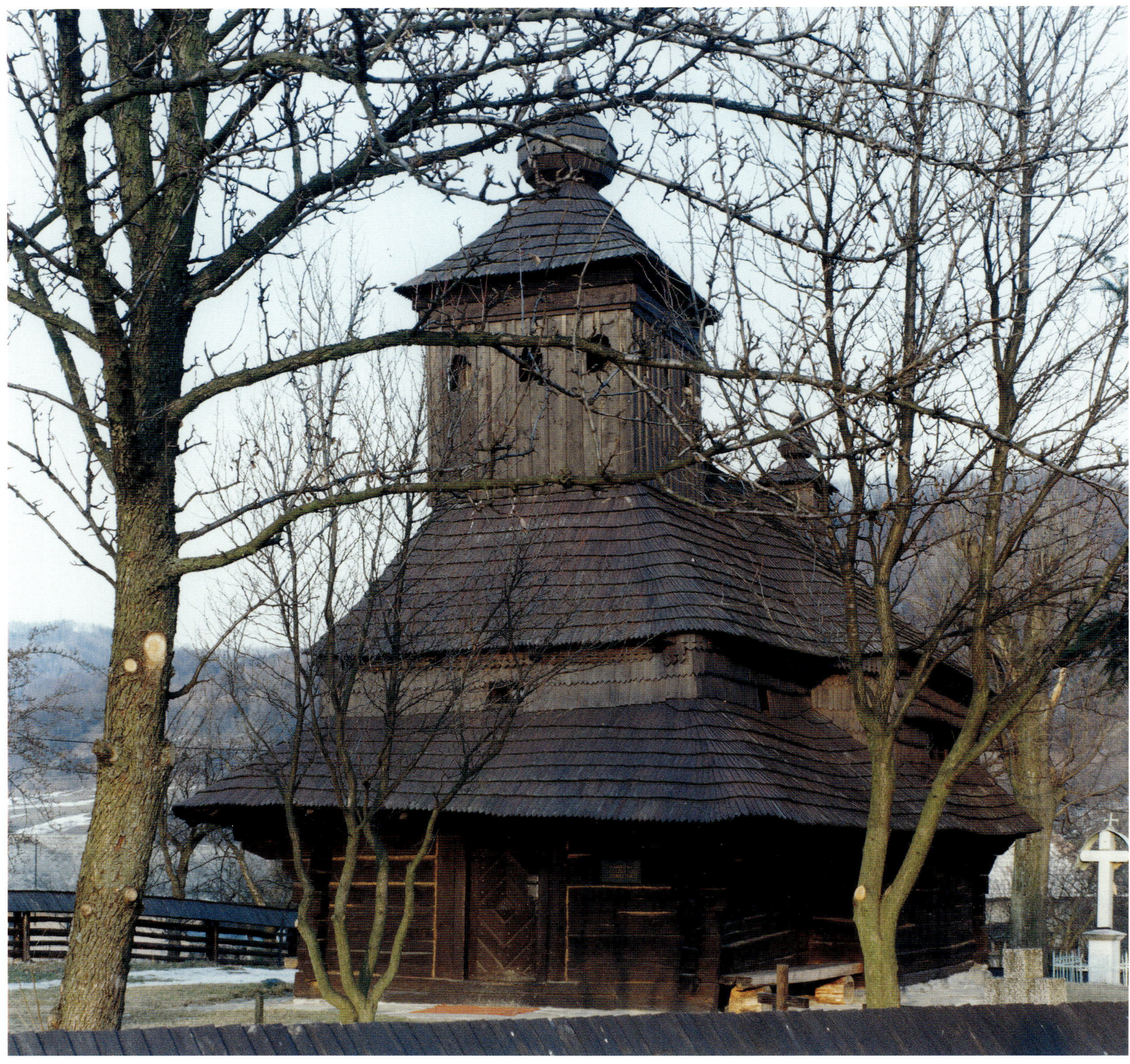

Uličské Krivé
Prešov, Slowakei
Erzengel Michael
18 Jh.

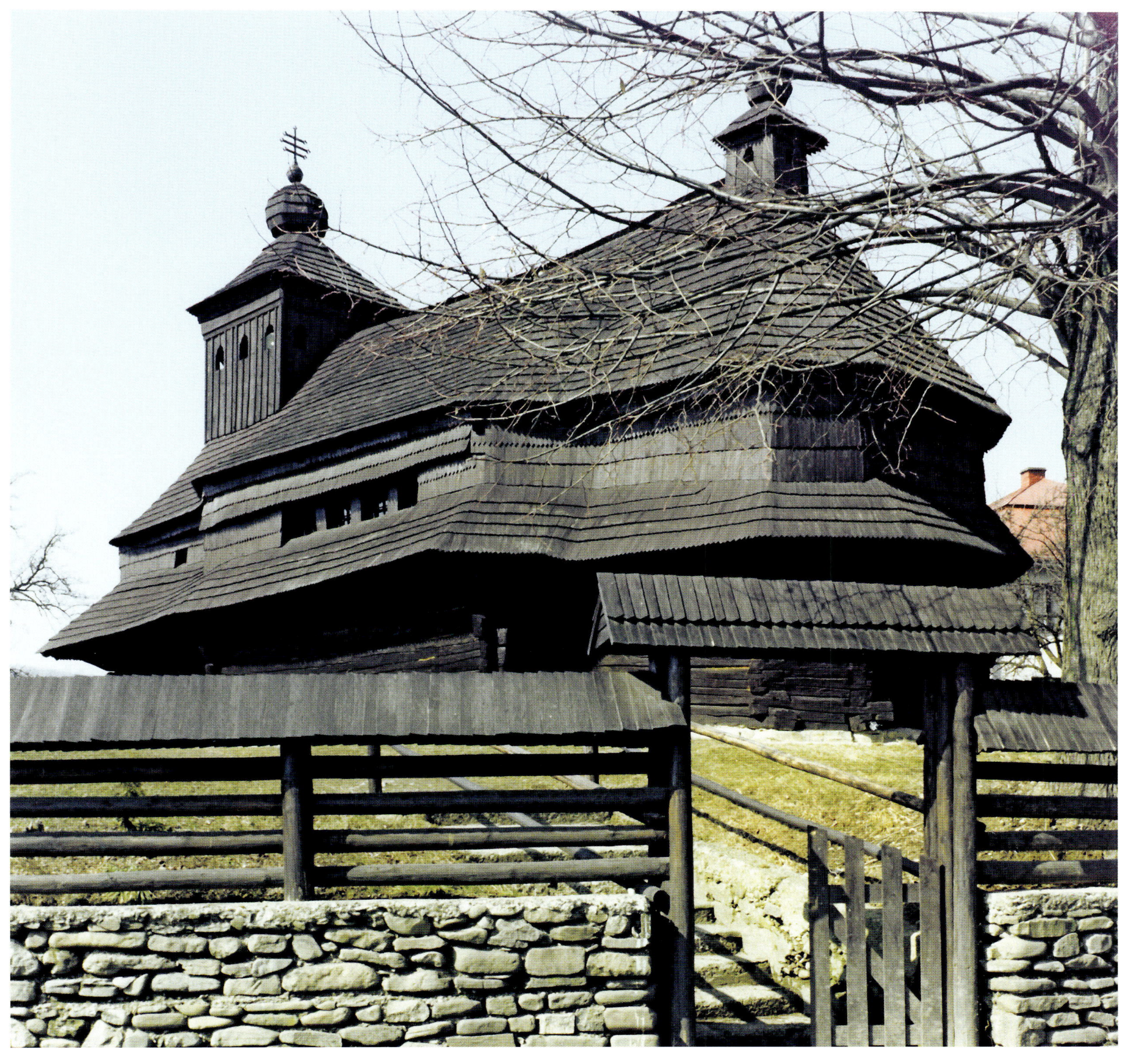

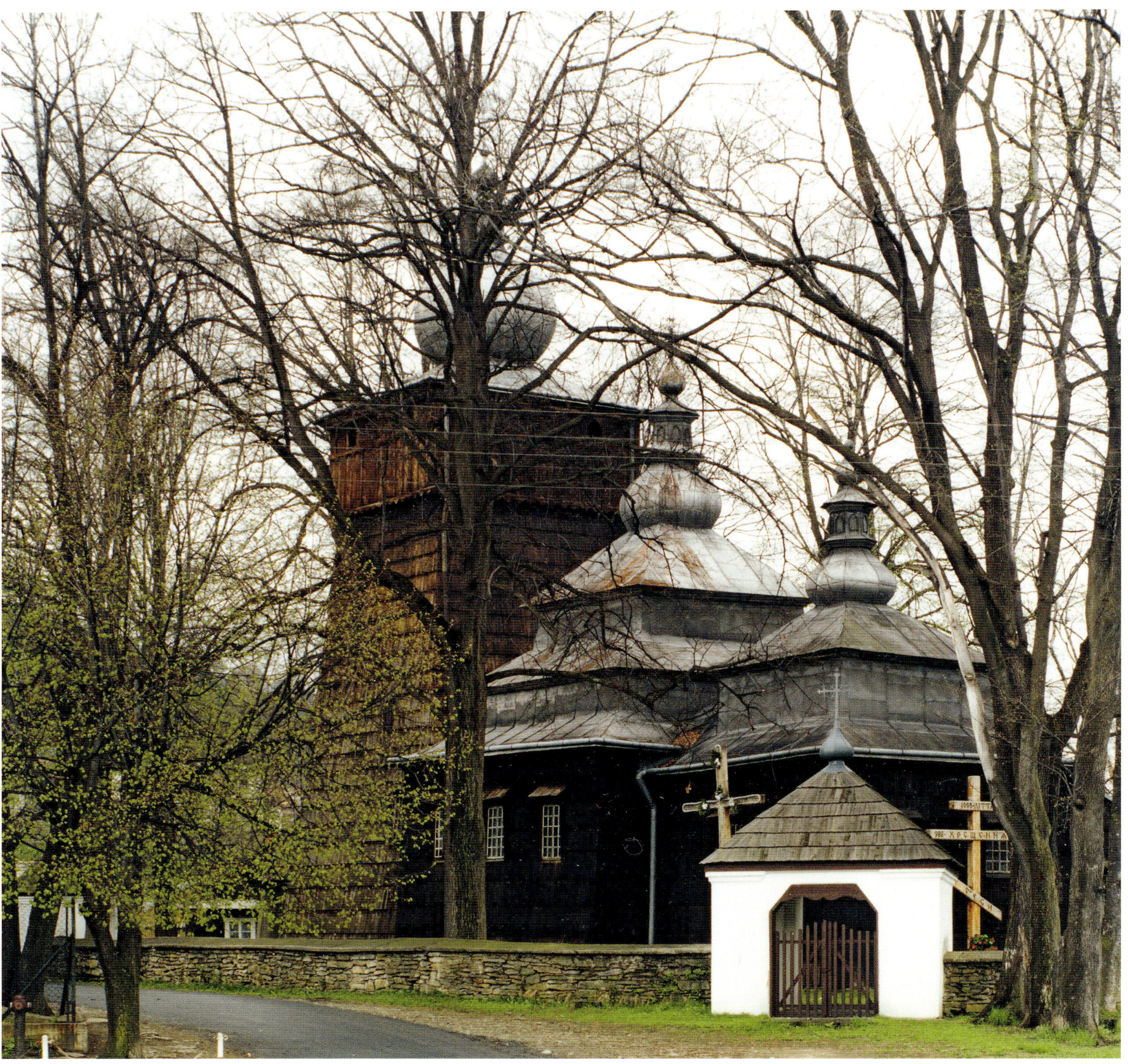

Uście Gorlickie
Gorlice, Polen
Hl. Paraskeva
1786

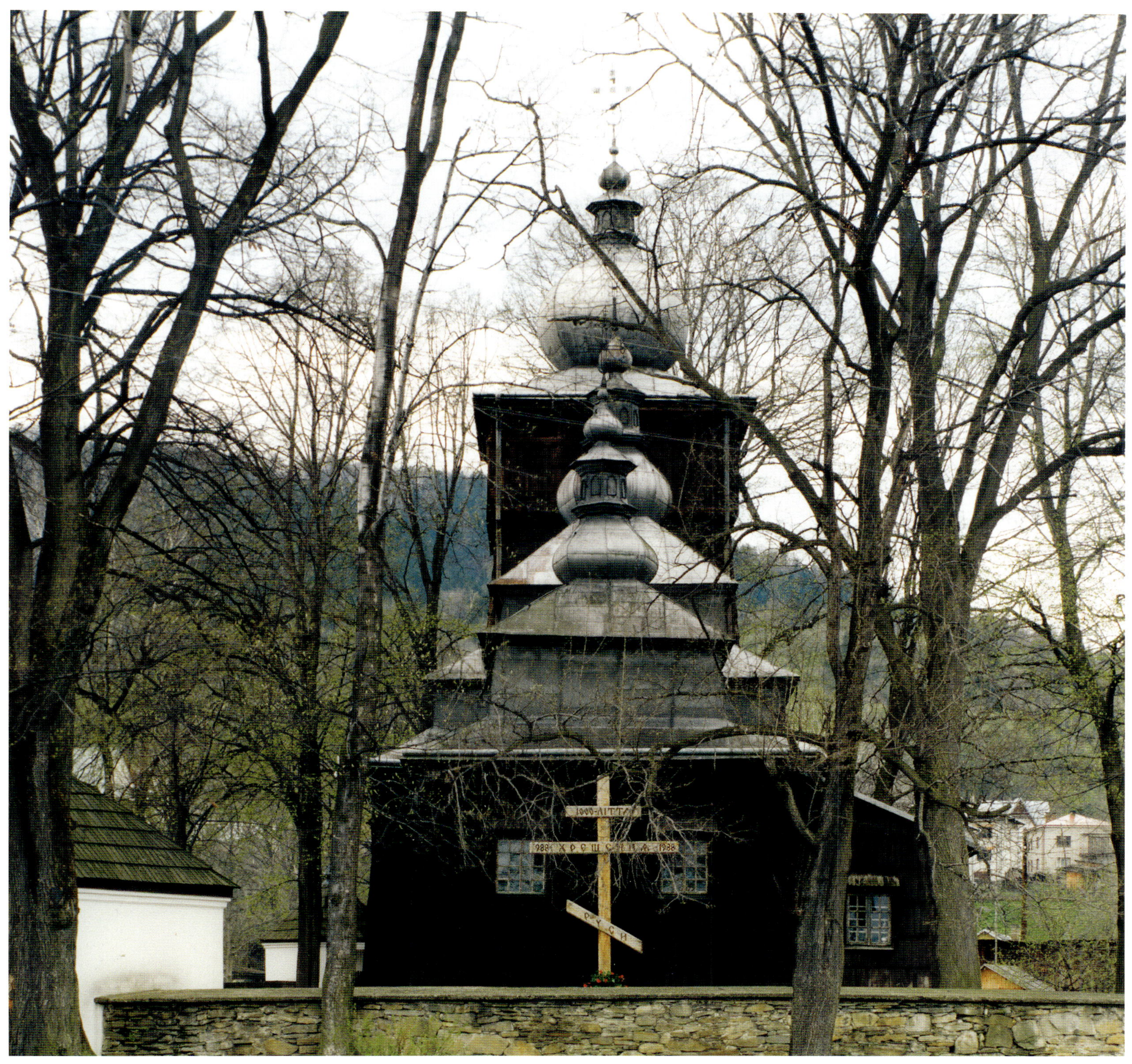

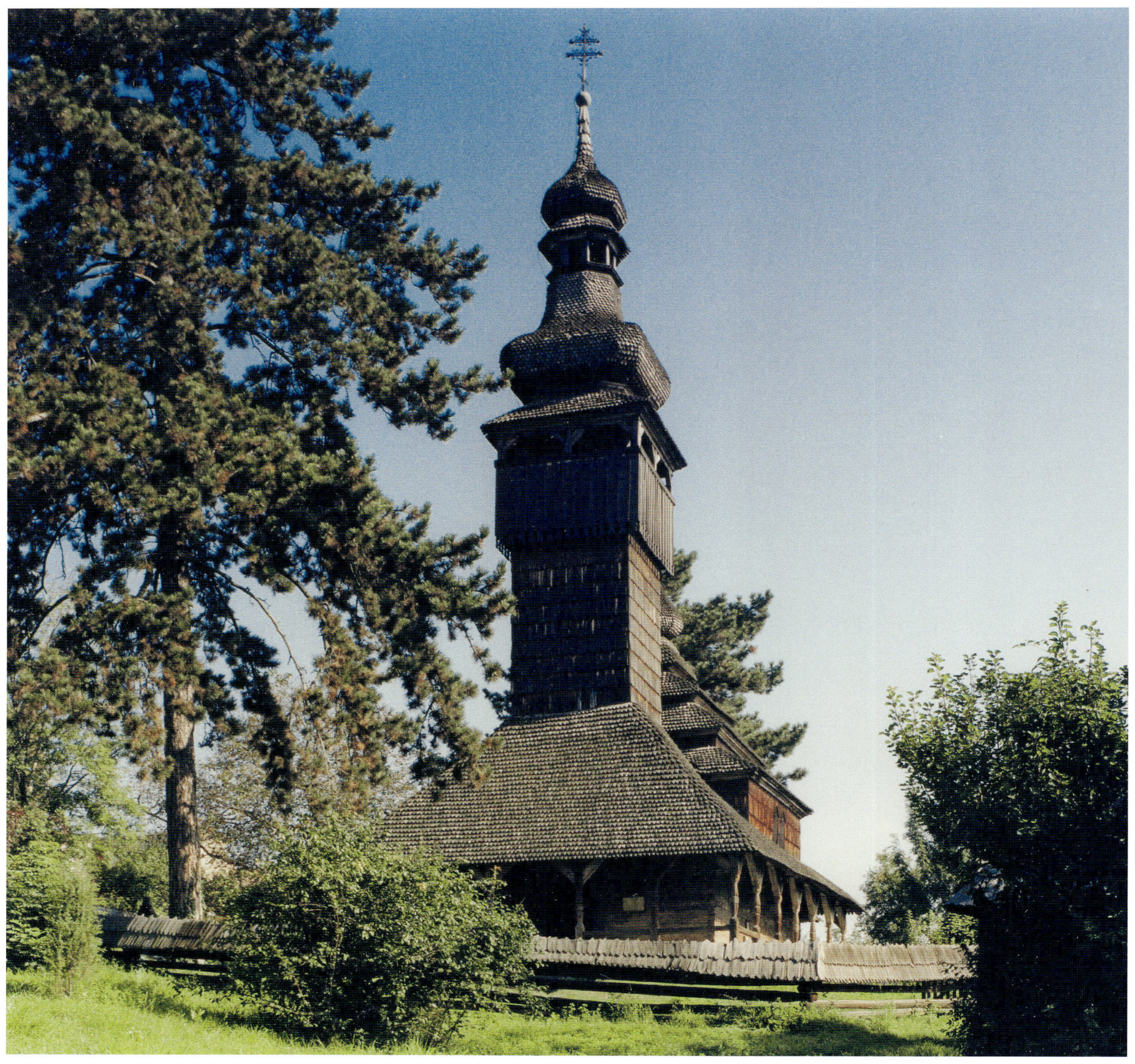

Uzhhorod
Zakarpattia, Ukraine
transloz. aus Shelestovo, Kharkivs'ka, Ukraine
1777

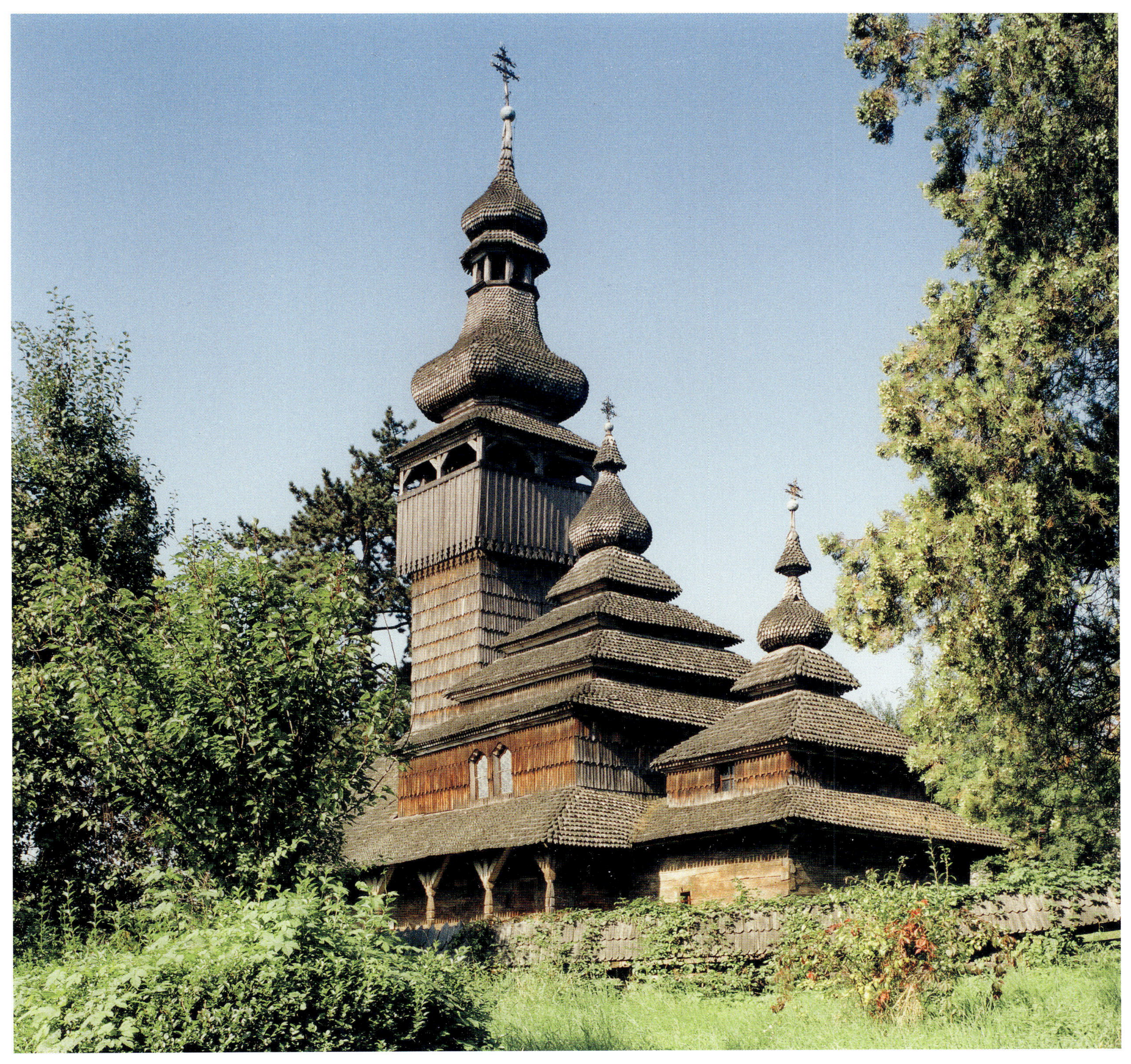

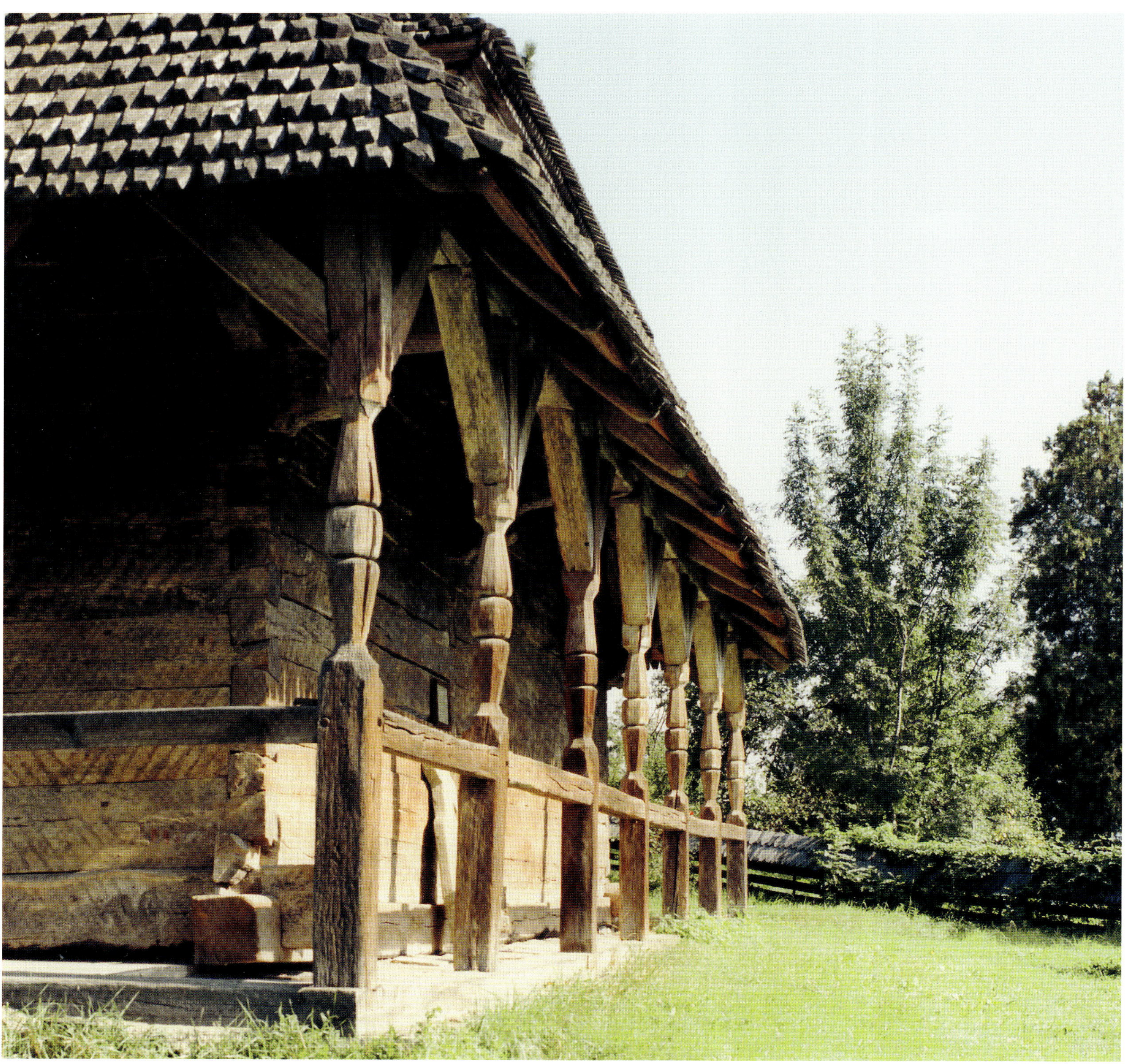

Uzhhorod
Zakarpattia, Ukraine
transloz. aus Shelestovo, Kharkivs'ka, Ukraine
1777

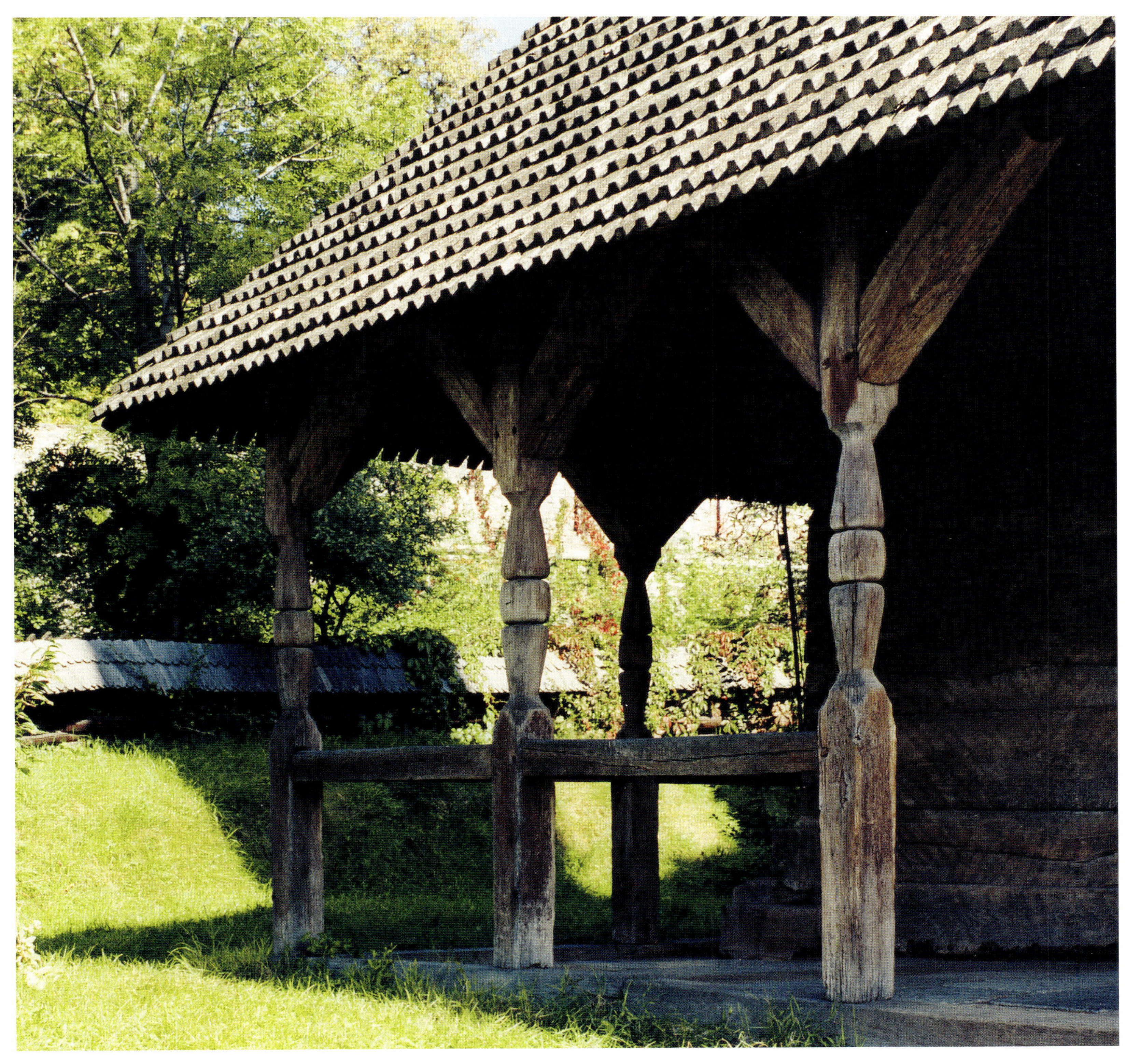

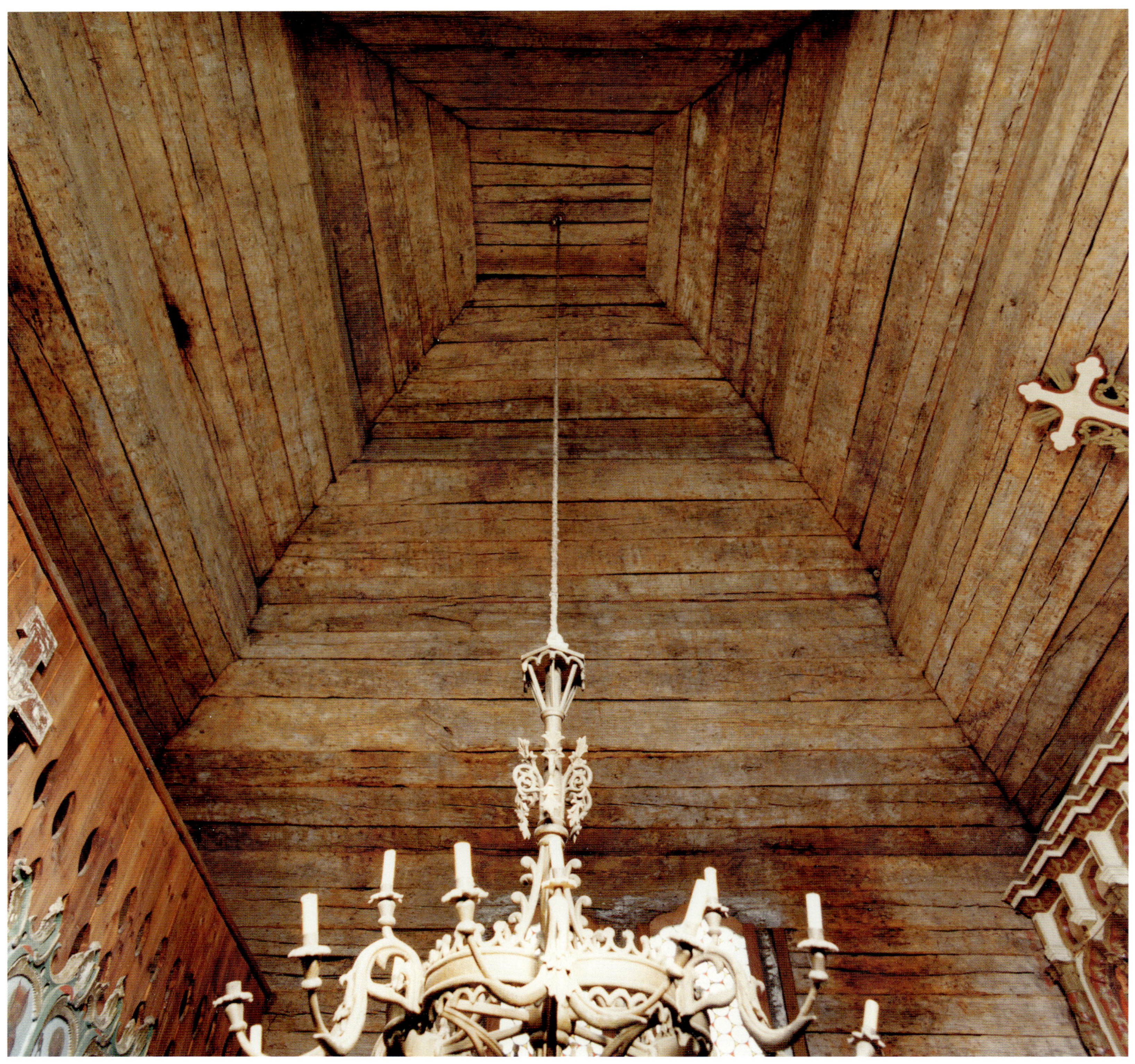

Uzhhorod
Zakarpattia, Ukraine
transloz. aus Shelestovo, Kharkivs'ka, Ukraine
1777

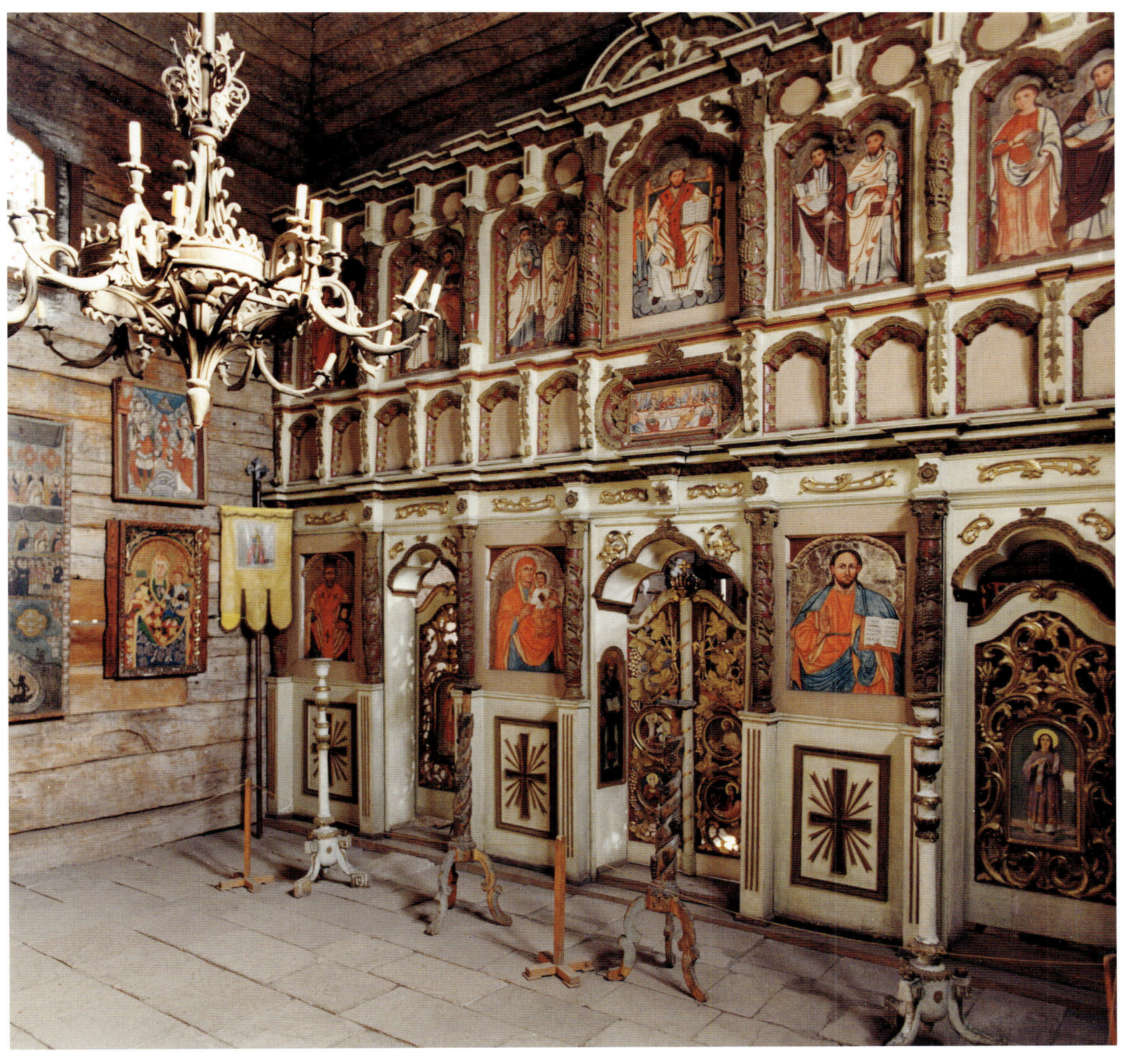

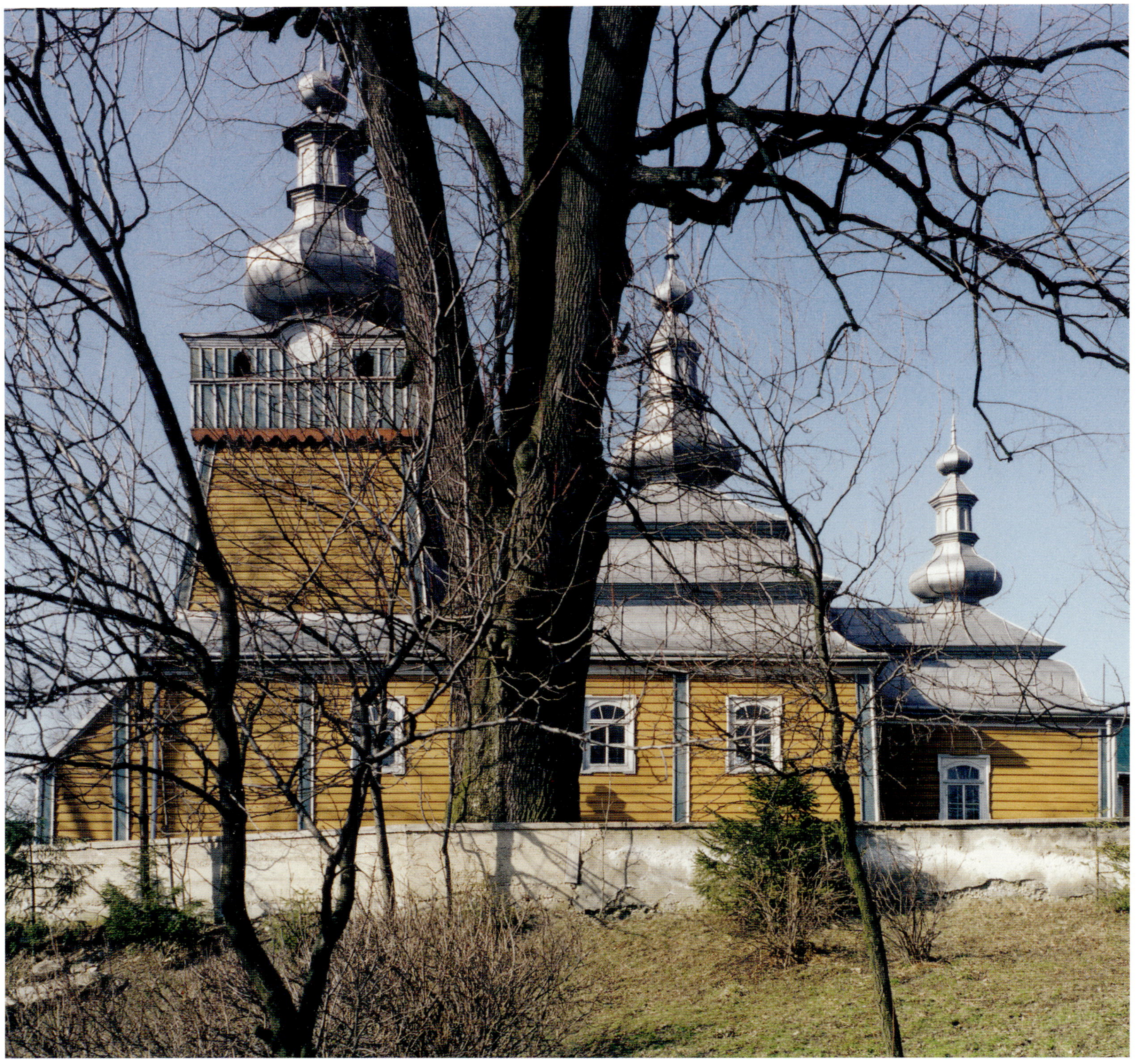

Wysowa-Zdrój
Gorlice, Polen
Erzengel Michael
1779

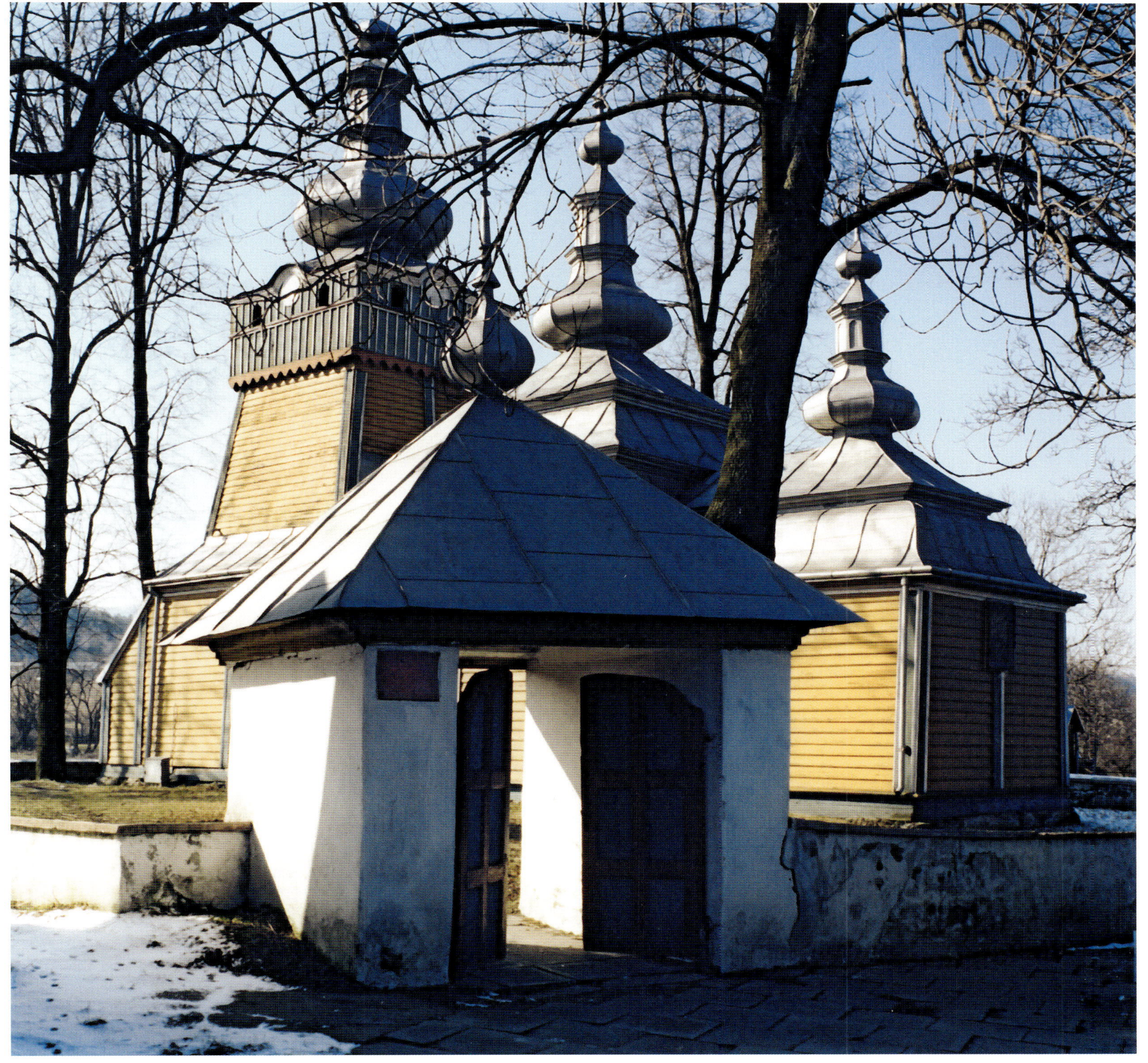

streets of new york

teNeues | MENDO

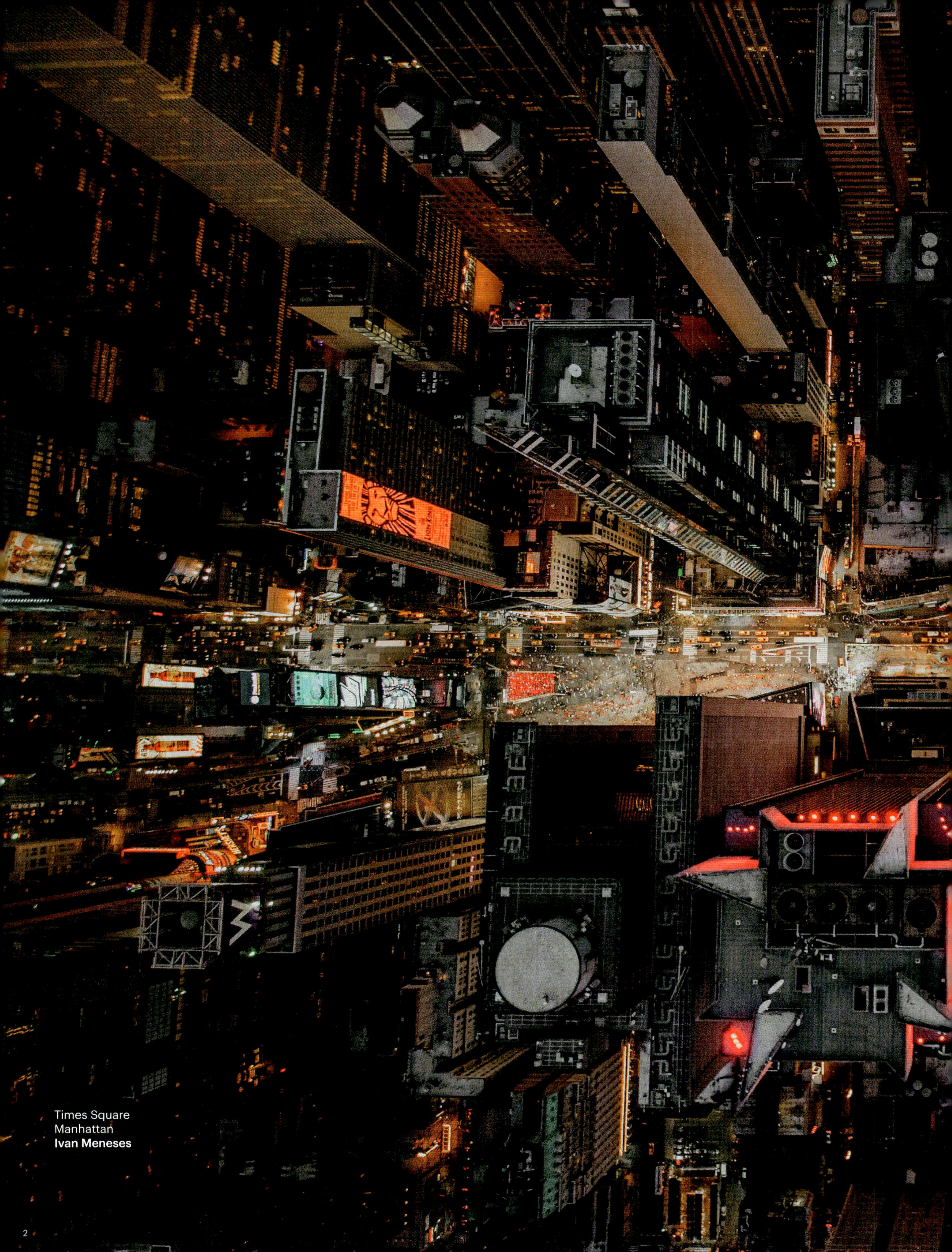

Times Square
Manhattan
Ivan Meneses

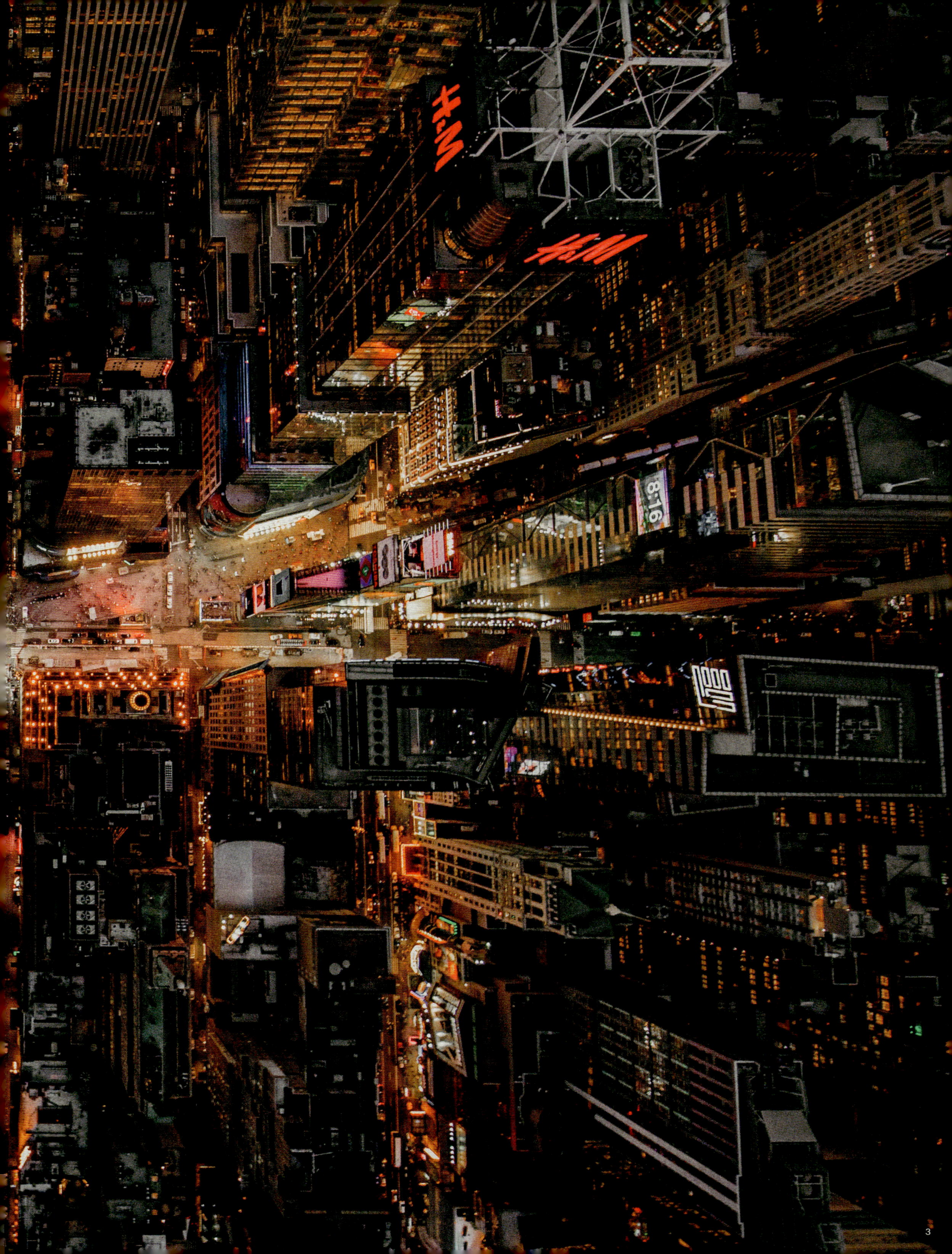
H&M
H&M
8:16

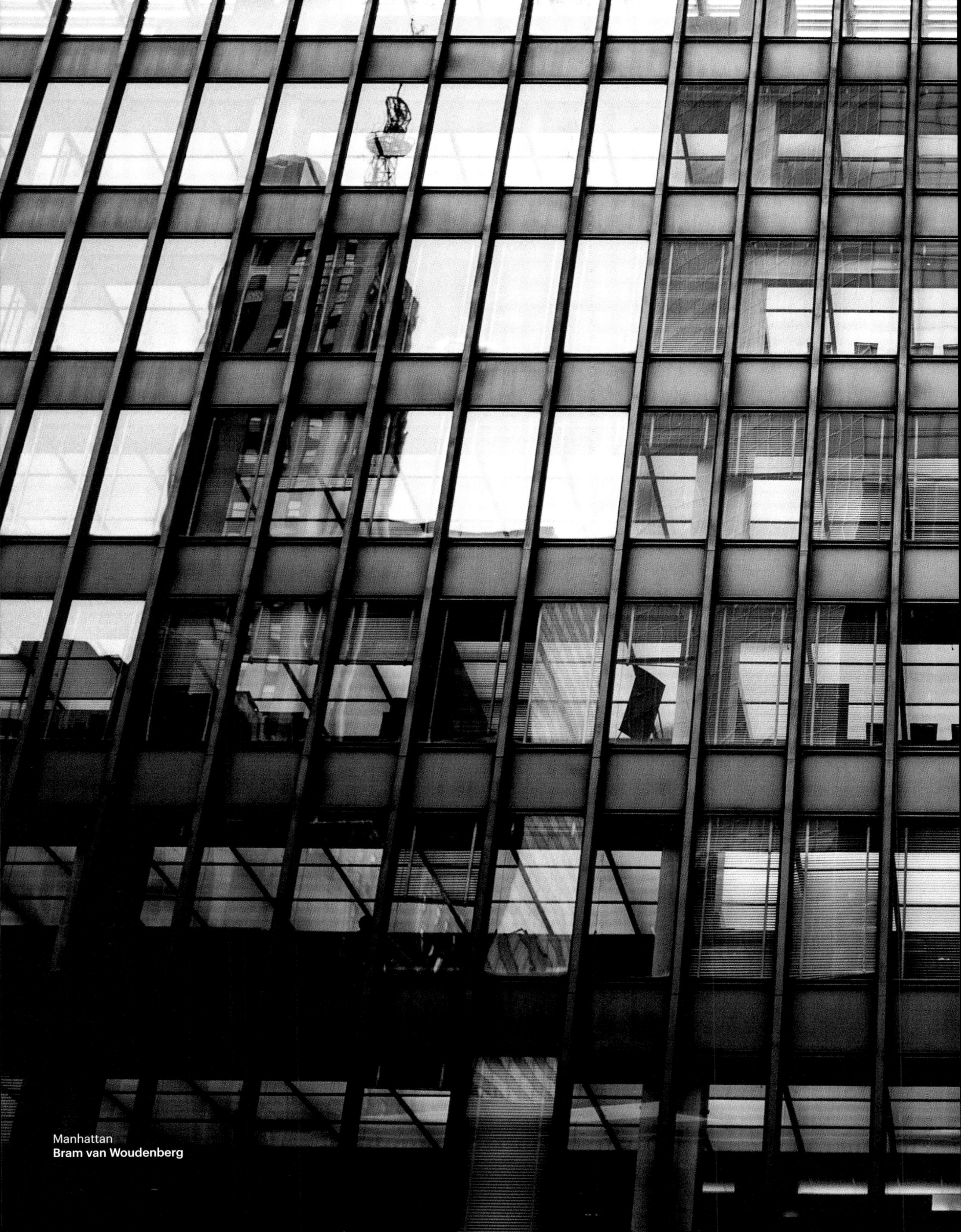

Manhattan
Bram van Woudenberg

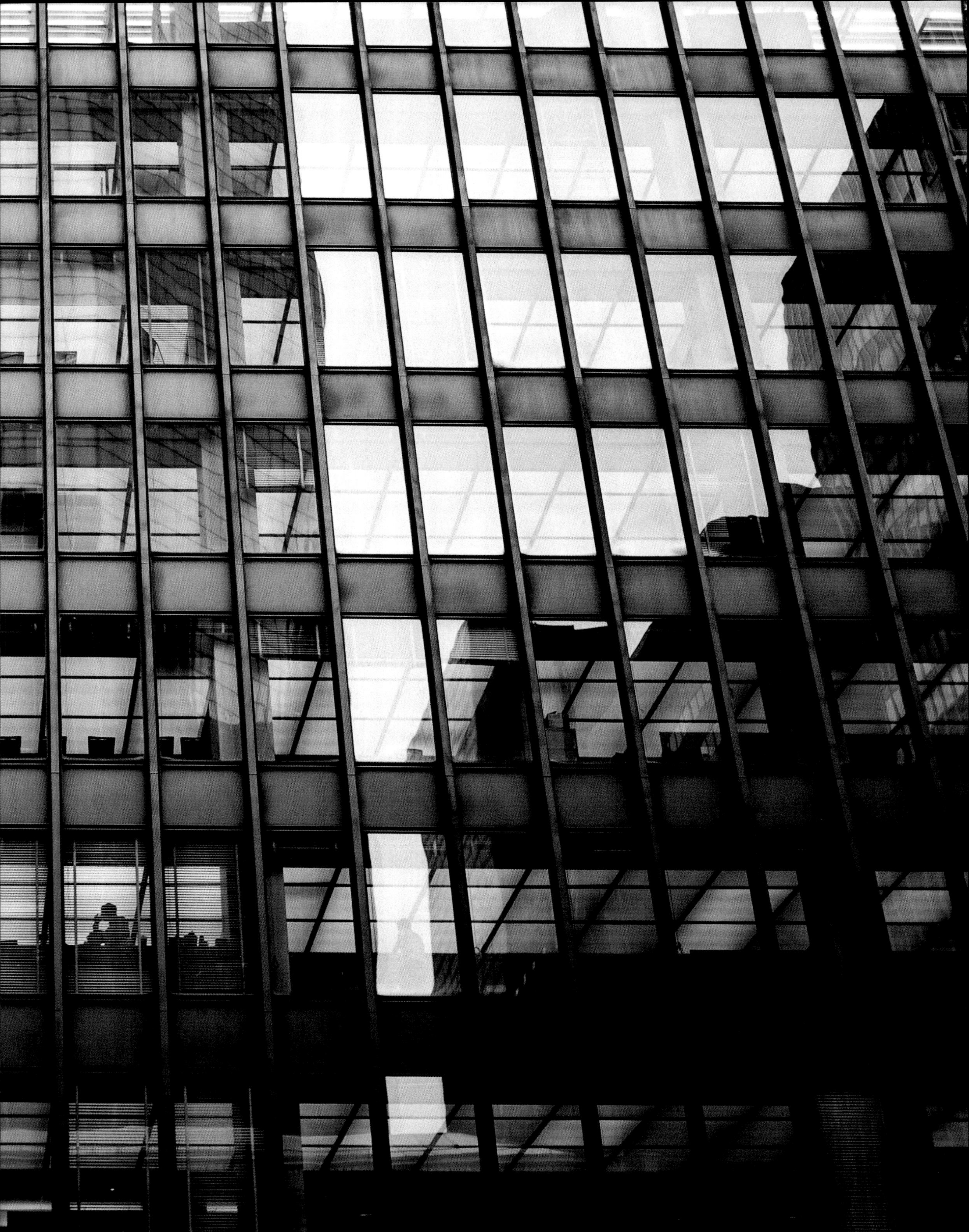

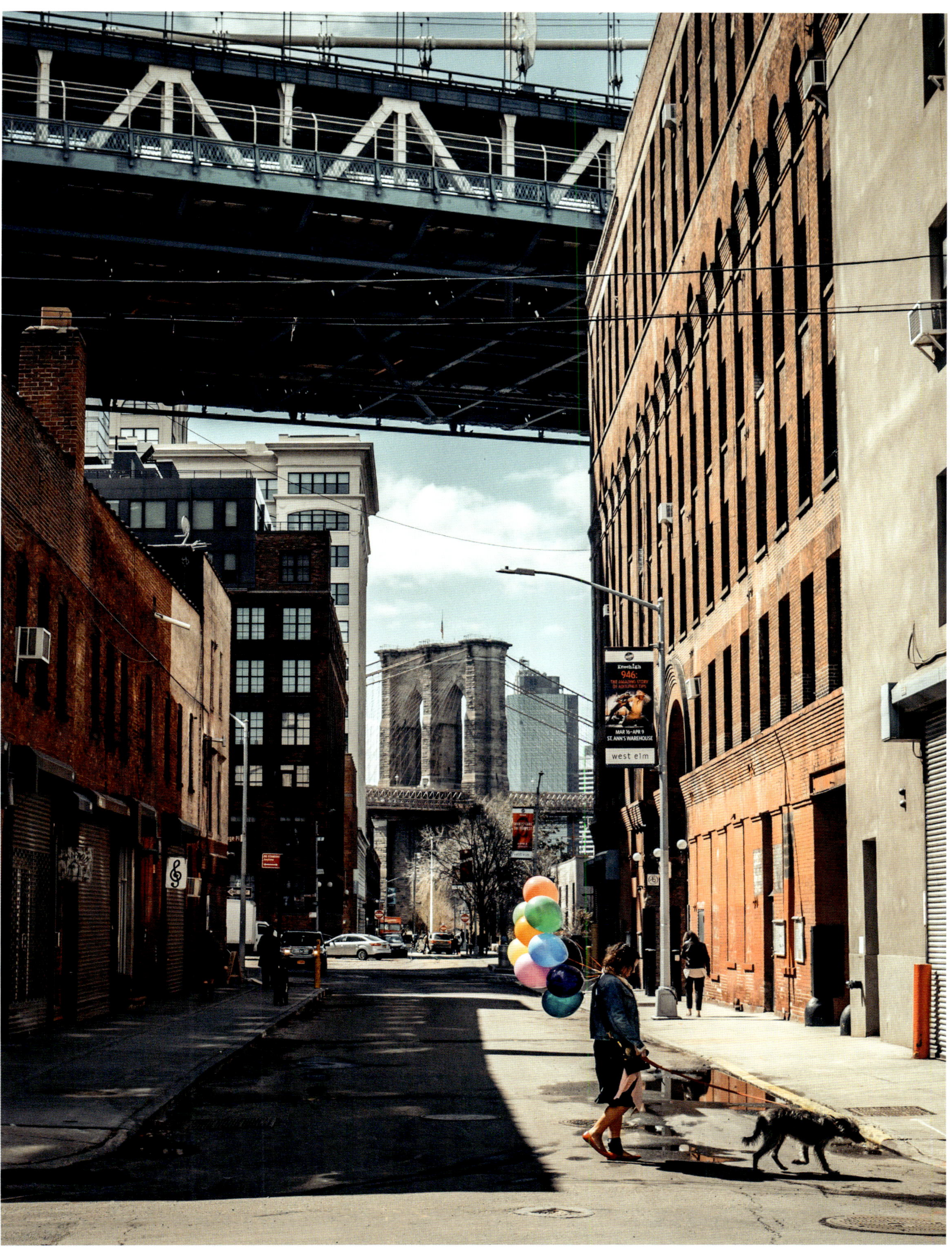
Kneehigh
946:
MAR 16–APR 9
ST. ANN'S WAREHOUSE
west elm

In New York City, there is a constant influx of newcomers who bring interesting perspectives and unique voices.

—Wesley Verhoeve

Dumbo, Brooklyn
Stijn Hoekstra

Frantic, eclectic energy

Words Joost Bastmeijer
IG handle @joostbastmeijer

I vividly remember the first time I looked up at Manhattan's massive skyscrapers: quite a sight for a teenager from Amsterdam, a city with barely any high-rise buildings. I was in a yellow taxi cab with my parents and my brother. Coming from Newark Airport, we could only catch a glimpse of Manhattan, which increased the sudden awe we experienced when we exited the Lincoln Tunnel, instantly driving in Hell's Kitchen. I remember pressing my face against the cold window, trying to figure out at what point the buildings vanished into the snowing clouds.

Every visit to New York City since that first family trip has been a totally different, but just as otherworldly, experience. There's something addicting about this modern-day Rome or Cairo—with Yankee Stadium, the New York Stock Exchange, and Madison Square Garden as contemporary Colosseums, and the skyscrapers as the twenty-first-century equivalent of the pyramids. Because of the dynamic, movie set–like environment, you can feel Western culture being molded and shaped from up close.

New York feels like a distant friend, a rare feeling that I have only have experienced with a few other places in the world. Amsterdam, my hometown, certainly is one of those places. I'd say that "Old" and "New Amsterdam" have a lot of similarities. Both cities have an amazing ethnic diversity, a unique social fabric that shapes its society. Like Amsterdam, New York City keeps on evolving, reinventing itself thanks to the constant influx of newcomers. In the subway, you can see a cross-section of the people who fashion New York into whatever the city is going to be next. The eclectic energy is just as frantic as the city's famous jazz scene. Each street corner has a different flavor to it, a melody if you will, but all of them pulse with the rhythm of the city. Living in such a vast metropolis encourages a mentality of survival of the fittest—a healthy competition for some, a murderous and exhausting rat race for others.

On the streets of New York, photographers are moving with and between the leaders in fashion, art, design, and commerce. New York City has nurtured and raised some of the world's best-known photographers, like Richard Avedon, William Klein, Vivian Maier, Alfred Eisenstaedt, and Diane Arbus. There's no place in the world that is as hard to capture, because every inch of it has already been captured before—by these famous photographers and many others.

Looking for new voices in photography, I spent weeks scrolling through online portfolios and Instagram accounts, putting together a selection of observers, stealthily moving artists who roam the streets of the city, hiding behind their cameras, trying to blend in. Through the eyes of the next generation's photographers, you can see how they look at New York City and find new stories to tell. Some explore lesser-known boroughs like the Bronx and Harlem; others discover new angles and perspectives in Manhattan and Brooklyn. After having seen thousands of pictures from all kinds of photographers, we bundled the best, most iconic pictures that scream New York. It's a selection of the best shots per featured photographer, which doesn't say you shouldn't look them up on Instagram. From architecture to nature, from aerial helicopter shots to reflections in puddles, from iPhone shots to DSLR photos, and from Brooklyn brownstones to hip SoHo apartment complexes, *Streets of New York* has it all.

All that makes this a quintessential New York book, filled with perfect New York City moments. Captured by a range of photographers of all ages, ranks, lineages, and origins, this book is more than just the streets itself. *Streets of New York* shows the striking people on those streets and the city they built around them. And although you never know where the streets are taking the people who walk them, this book succeeds in bringing you to those streets. New York is almost tangible.

Central Park, Manhattan
Ivan Meneses

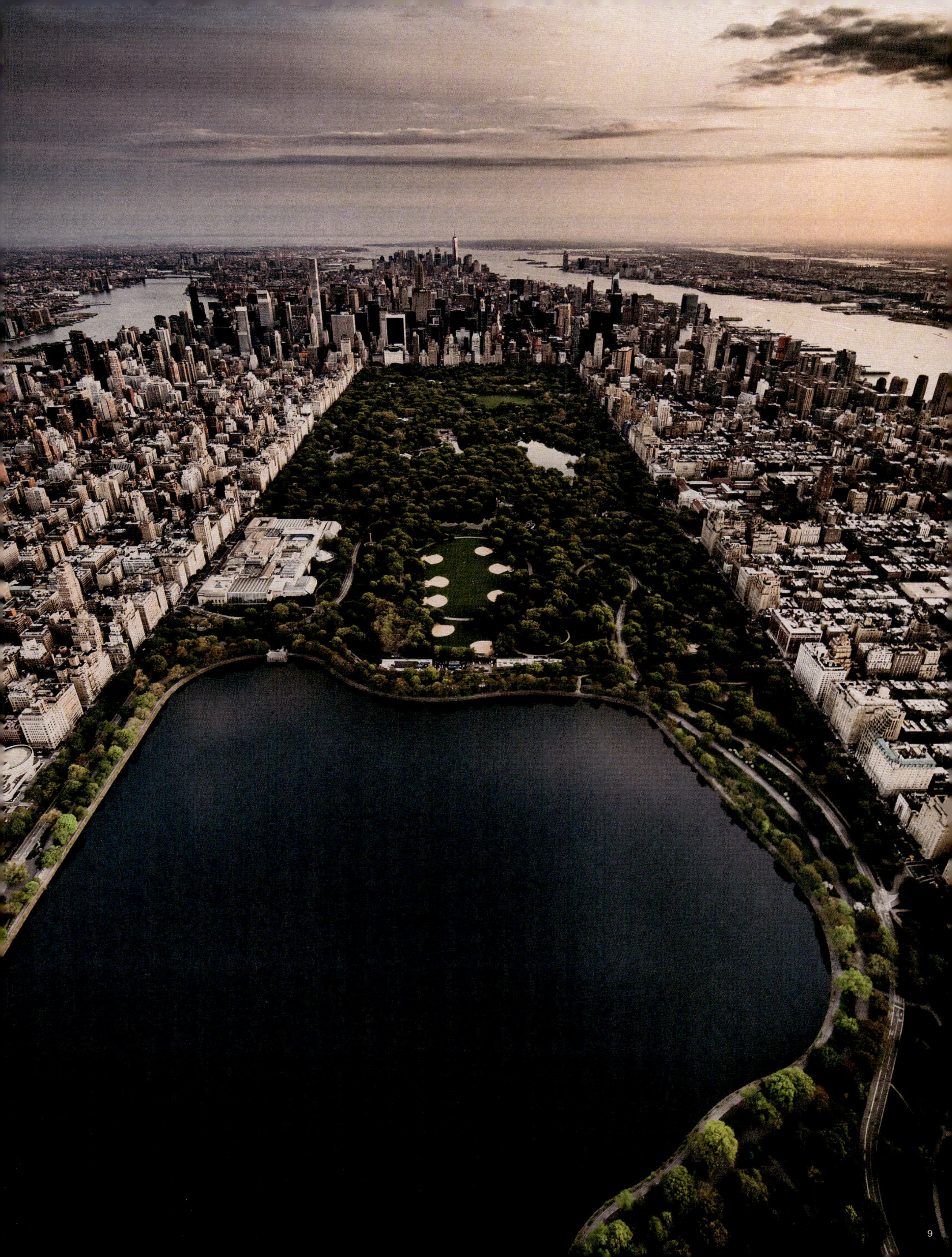

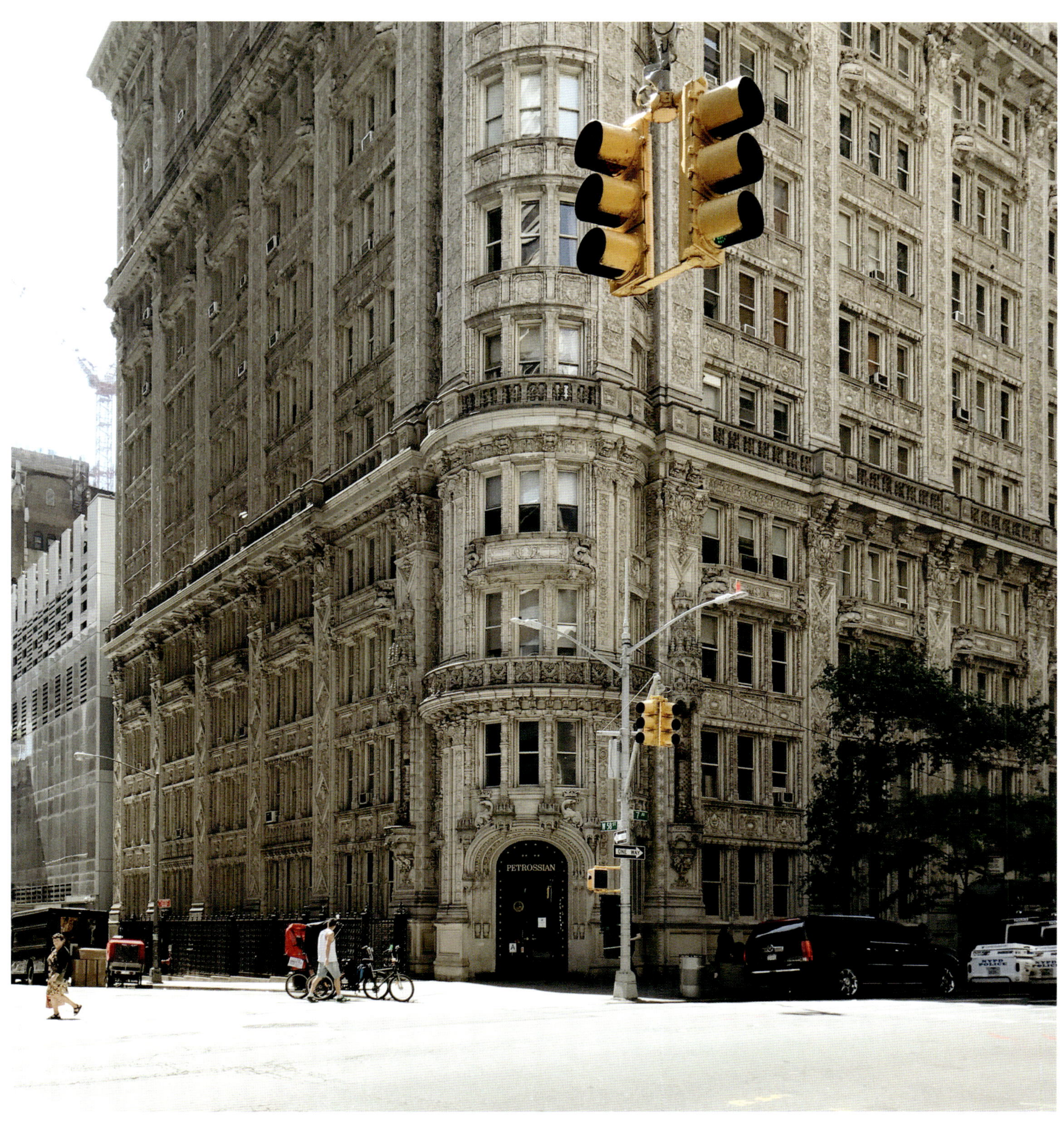

The Alwyn Court
Midtown, Manhattan
Patrick Janelle

Fiebrige, eklektische Energie

Text von Joost Bastmeijer
IG handle @joostbastmeijer

Ich erinnere mich noch lebhaft daran, wie ich zum ersten Mal zu den wuchtigen Wolkenkratzern von Manhattan aufschaute: Was für ein Anblick für einen Teenager aus Amsterdam, eine Stadt, in der es kaum Hochhäuser gibt! Ich saß mit meinen Eltern und meinem Bruder in einem der gelben Taxis. Während der Fahrt vom Flughafen Newark hatten wir nur einen kurzen Blick auf Manhattan erhascht – das verstärkte die plötzliche Ehrfurcht, die uns erfasste, als wir den Lincoln Tunnel verließen und sofort in Hell's Kitchen landeten. Ich weiß noch genau, wie ich mein Gesicht ans kalte Fenster presste und festzustellen versuchte, an welchem Punkt die Gebäude in die Schneewolken verschwanden.

Seit jenem ersten Familienausflug waren alle Besuche in New York City vollkommen unterschiedliche, aber ebenso unwirkliche Erfahrungen. Dieses Rom oder Kairo der Moderne hat etwas Suchterregendes – mit dem Yankee Stadium, der New Yorker Börse und dem Madison Square Garden als neuzeitliche Kolosseen und den Wolkenkratzern als Pyramiden des 21. Jahrhunderts. In dieser dynamischen, wie ein Filmset anmutenden Umgebung kann man aus der Nähe spüren, wie die westliche Kultur geformt und gestaltet wird.

New York fühlt sich an wie ein weit entfernt lebender Freund, ein seltenes Gefühl, das ich nur an wenigen anderen Orten der Welt empfunden habe. Amsterdam, meine Heimatstadt, gehört auf jeden Fall zu diesen Orten. Meiner Meinung nach haben das alte Amsterdam und „New Amsterdam" viele Gemeinsamkeiten. Beide Städte haben eine erstaunliche ethnische Vielfalt, ein einzigartiges soziales Gefüge, das ihre Gesellschaft prägt. Wie Amsterdam entwickelt sich New York City immer weiter und erfindet sich selbst neu, dank eines konstanten Zustroms von Neuankömmlingen. In der Subway sieht man einen Querschnitt jener Menschen, die dabei sind, New York in die Stadt zu verwandeln, die es demnächst sein wird. Die eklektische Energie ist ebenso fiebrig wie die berühmte Jazzszene New Yorks. Jede Straßenecke hat ihren eigenen Charakter, eine Melodie, wenn man so will, aber sie alle pulsieren im Rhythmus der Stadt. Das Leben in einer so riesigen Metropole fördert eine „survival of the fittest"-Mentalität – für manche bedeutet das gesunde Konkurrenz, für andere ein mörderisches, erbarmungsloses Wettrennen.

Auf den Straßen New Yorks bewegen sich Fotografen inmitten der führenden Vertreter von Mode, Kunst, Design und Wirtschaft. New York City hat einige der bekanntesten Fotografen der Welt wachsen und gedeihen lassen, darunter Richard Avedon, William Klein, Vivian Maier, Alfred Eisenstaedt und Diane Arbus. Kein Ort der Welt ist so schwierig einzufangen, weil jeder Zentimeter schon dokumentiert worden ist – von diesen berühmten Fotografen und vielen anderen.

Auf der Suche nach neuen Stimmen in der Fotografie habe ich Wochen damit verbracht, Online-Portfolios und Instagram-Accounts zu durchforsten und eine Auswahl von Beobachtern zusammenzustellen, von Künstlern, die sich heimlich durch die Straßen der Stadt bewegen, versteckt hinter ihren Kameras, im Versuch, sich unsichtbar zu machen. Durch die Augen dieser Fotografen der nächsten Generation erleben wir, wie sie New York City betrachten, neue Geschichten finden und erzählen. Einige erkunden weniger bekannte Stadtbezirke wie die Bronx oder Harlem; andere entdecken neue Blickwinkel und Perspektiven in Manhattan und Brooklyn. Nachdem wir Tausende von Fotografien gesehen hatten, fassten wir die besten zusammen – jene Bildikonen, die „New York!" schreien. Entstanden ist eine Auswahl der schönsten Aufnahmen der vertretenen Fotografen, was aber nicht heißt, dass Sie ihnen nicht auf Instagram folgen sollten! Von Architektur bis Natur, von Luftaufnahmen aus dem Helikopter bis zu Spiegelungen in Pfützen, von iPhone-Schnappschüssen bis zu digitalen Spiegelreflexfotos, von Ziegelhäusern in Brooklyn bis zu hippen Apartmentgebäuden in SoHo – *Streets of New York* zeigt alles: Alles, was diesen Band zum Standardwerk über New York macht, gefüllt mit perfekten New-York-Momenten.

Mit Bildern einer Vielzahl von Fotografen aller Altersgruppen, Karrierestufen, Abstammungen und Herkunftsorte, enthält dieses Buch mehr als nur die Straßen als solche. *Streets of New York* zeigt die erstaunlichen Menschen auf diesen Straßen, und die Stadt, die sie sich erbaut haben. Und obwohl man nie wissen wird, wohin die Straßen New Yorks ihre Passanten führen, schafft es dieses Buch, uns auf diese Straßen zu versetzen. New York wird beinahe greifbar.

Une énergie éclectique et frénétique

Mot par Joost Bastmeijer
IG handle @joostbastmeijer

Je me souviens avec netteté de la première fois où j'ai levé les yeux et découvert les impressionnants gratte-ciels de Manhattan : quel spectacle pour un adolescent venu d'Amsterdam, ville qui ne possède quasiment aucun bâtiment de grande hauteur. Nous étions, mon frère, mes parents et moi-même, dans un taxi jaune. Comme nous arrivions de l'aéroport de Newark, nous ne pouvions qu'entrapercevoir Manhattan, ce qui a rendu d'autant plus intense l'émerveillement que nous avons éprouvé lorsque nous avons émergé du Lincoln Tunnel avant de plonger aussitôt dans le quartier de Hell's Kitchen. Je me rappelle avoir pressé mon visage contre la vitre froide pour tenter de distinguer l'instant où les immeubles disparaissaient dans les nuages lourds de neige.

Depuis ce premier voyage familial, chaque séjour à New York s'est révélé être une expérience entièrement différente mais de nature tout aussi mystique. Cette Rome, ou ce Caire, du XXIème siècle possède une dimension addictive – avec son Yankee Stadium, son New York Exchange ou encore Madison Square Garden qui se dressent tels des Colisées modernes, avec ses gratte-ciels qui sont l'équivalent contemporain des pyramides. Cet environnement dynamique, semblable à un décor de cinéma, nous donne le sentiment d'assister de près à la création, à la formation de la culture occidentale.

New York évoque un ami lointain, sensation rare que je n'ai ressentie qu'en quelques autres lieux dans le monde. Assurément, Amsterdam, ma ville natale, en fait partie. Il me semble que l' « Ancienne » et la « Nouvelle » Amsterdam présentent de nombreuses similitudes. Les deux villes se caractérisent par une étonnante diversité ethnique, un tissu social unique. Tout comme Amsterdam, New York ne cesse d'évoluer, de se réinventer grâce au flux ininterrompu de nouveaux-venus. Le métro offre un échantillon de tous ceux qui façonnent New York, font de la ville ce qu'elle est appelée à devenir. L'éclectique énergie qui l'habite est tout aussi frénétique que son célèbre monde du jazz. Le moindre coin de rue offre une saveur – une mélodie si vous préférez – différente, et tous cependant, bougent en accord avec le rythme de la ville. Vivre dans une aussi vaste métropole induit un état d'esprit qui est celui de la « survie du plus apte » – compétition saine aux yeux de certains, foire d'empoigne épuisante et meurtrière pour d'autres.

Sur les trottoirs de New York, les photographes croisent ou accompagnent tous ceux qui décident de la mode, de l'art, du design, du commerce. La ville a nourri et élevé certains des plus célèbres photographes au monde, à l'exemple de Richard Avedon, William Klein, Vivian Meier, d'Alfred Eisenstaedt ou encore, de Diane Arbus. Il n'est nul autre lieu sur cette planète qui ne soit aussi difficile à saisir en ce que le moindre centimètre carré y a déjà été capturé – par ces photographes connus ou par de nombreux autres.

En quête de voix nouvelles dans le domaine de la photographie, j'ai passé de nombreuses semaines à consulter des portfolios ou des comptes Instagram, à choisir et réunir ces observateurs, ces artistes qui, dissimulés derrière leur appareil, vagabondent discrètement dans ces rues où ils tentent de se fondre. Au travers du regard que porte cette future génération de photographes, nous découvrons la façon dont ils perçoivent New York, les histoires nouvelles qu'ils racontent.
Certains explorent des quartiers moins familiers comme le Bronx ou Harlem ; d'autres abordent Manhattan ou Brooklyn selon des perspectives ou des angles inédits. Après avoir observé des milliers d'images, prises par des photographes de toutes sortes, nous avons rassemblé celles qui évoquaient New York de la façon la plus parfaite et la plus emblématique qui soit. Pour chaque photographe, nous avons sélectionné les meilleurs clichés, ce qui ne vous empêche pas de les chercher sur Instagram. De l'architecture à la nature, des vues aériennes prises en hélicoptère aux reflets dans les flaques, des images prises avec un iPhone à celles capturés au moyen d'un appareil numérique, des édifices en briques de Brooklyn aux immeubles branchés de SoHo, *Streets of New York* englobe tout – tout ce qui en fait un ouvrage essentiel sur cette ville, riche en instants parfaitement new yorkais.

Composé par un ensemble de photographes de tous âges et rangs sociaux, de toute ascendance ou origine, ce livre ne montre pas seulement les rues de New York. Il dévoile les saisissants personnages qui arpentent la ville qu'ils sont en train de bâtir. Il réussit à vous entraîner jusque dans ces rues, quoique nul ne sache où celles-ci emmènent les passants qui les empruntent. New York en devient quasiment palpable.

Manhattan
Jones Crow

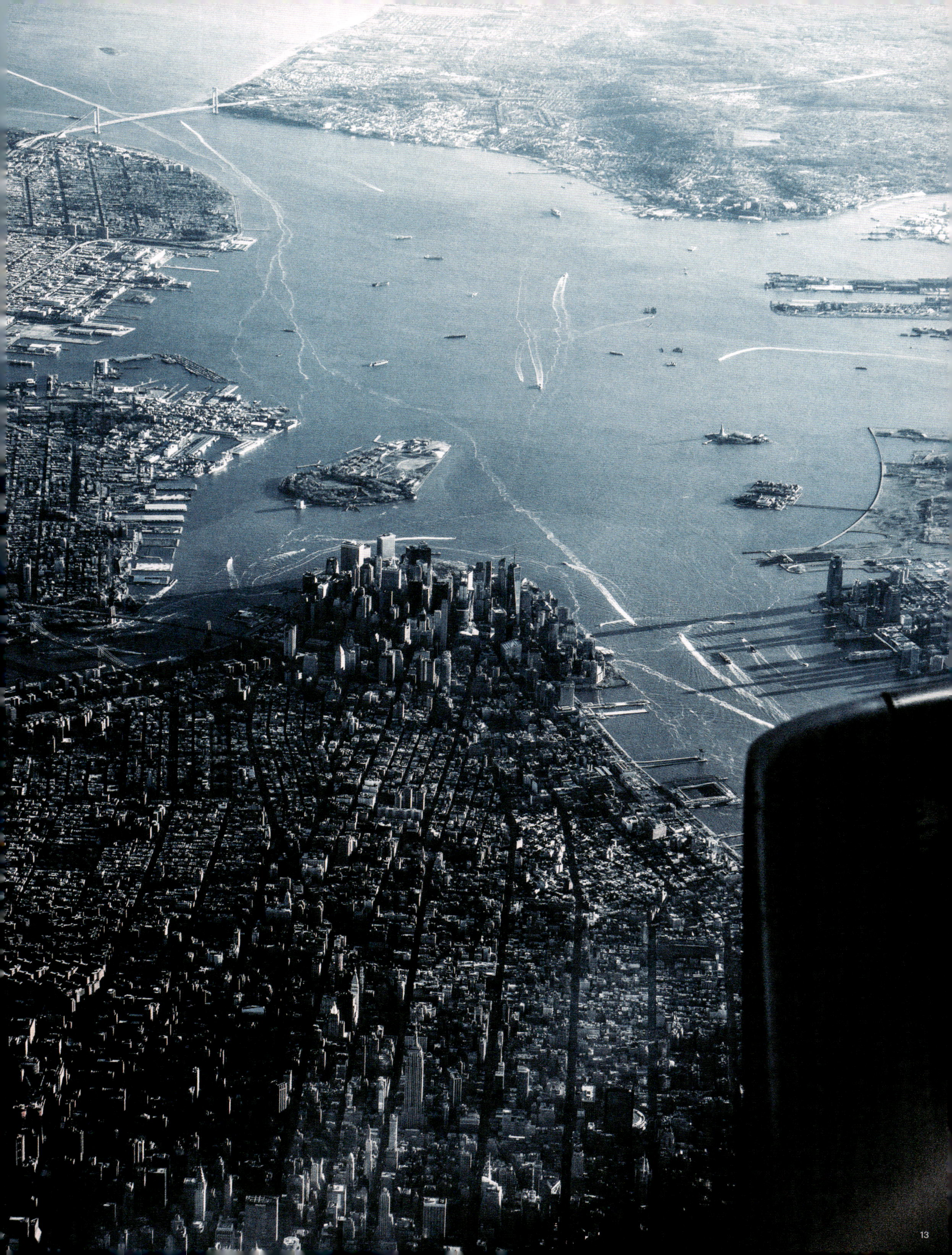

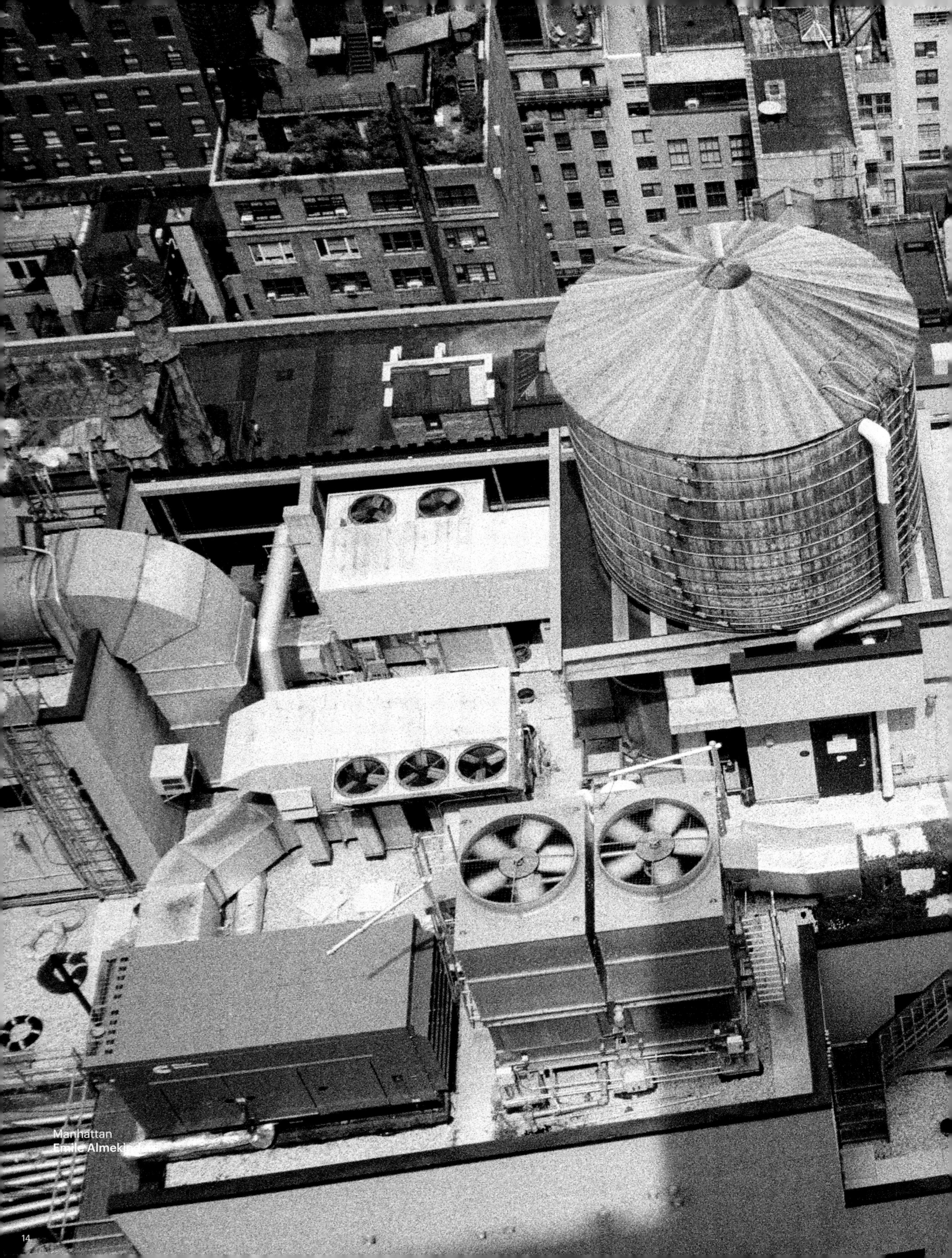

Manhattan
Emile Almekinders

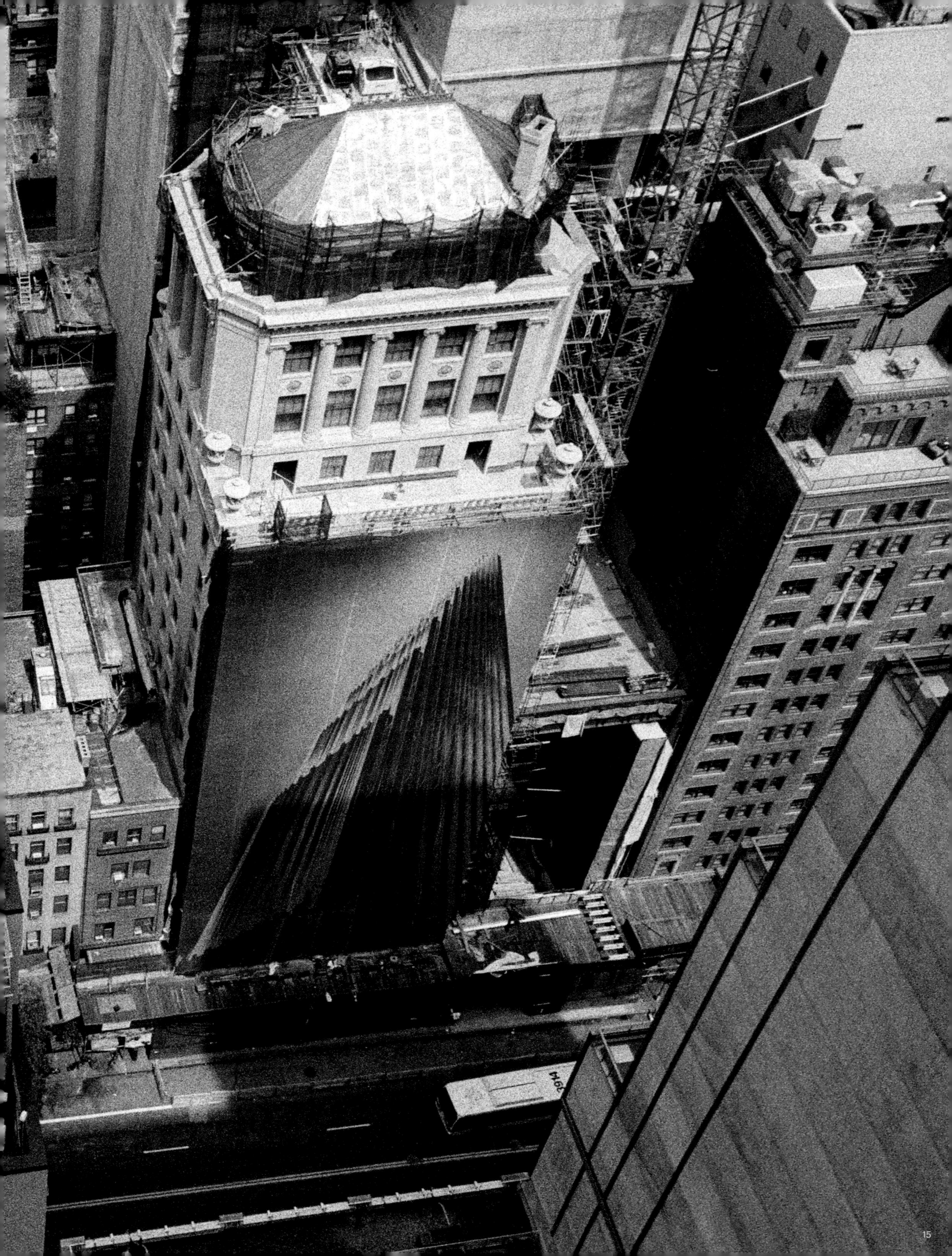

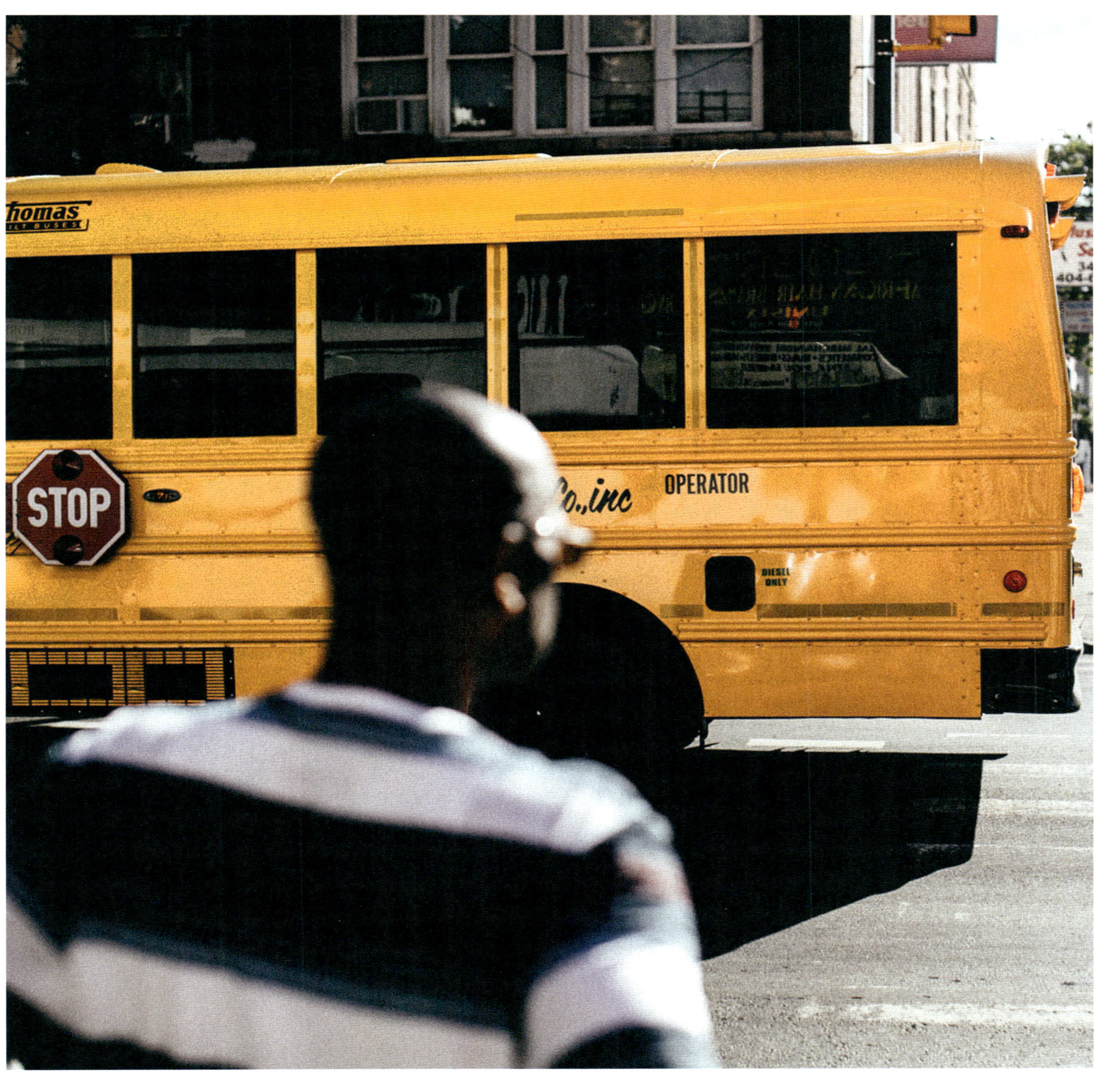

Brooklyn
Demilade Balogun

Flatbush, Brooklyn
Demilade Balogun –

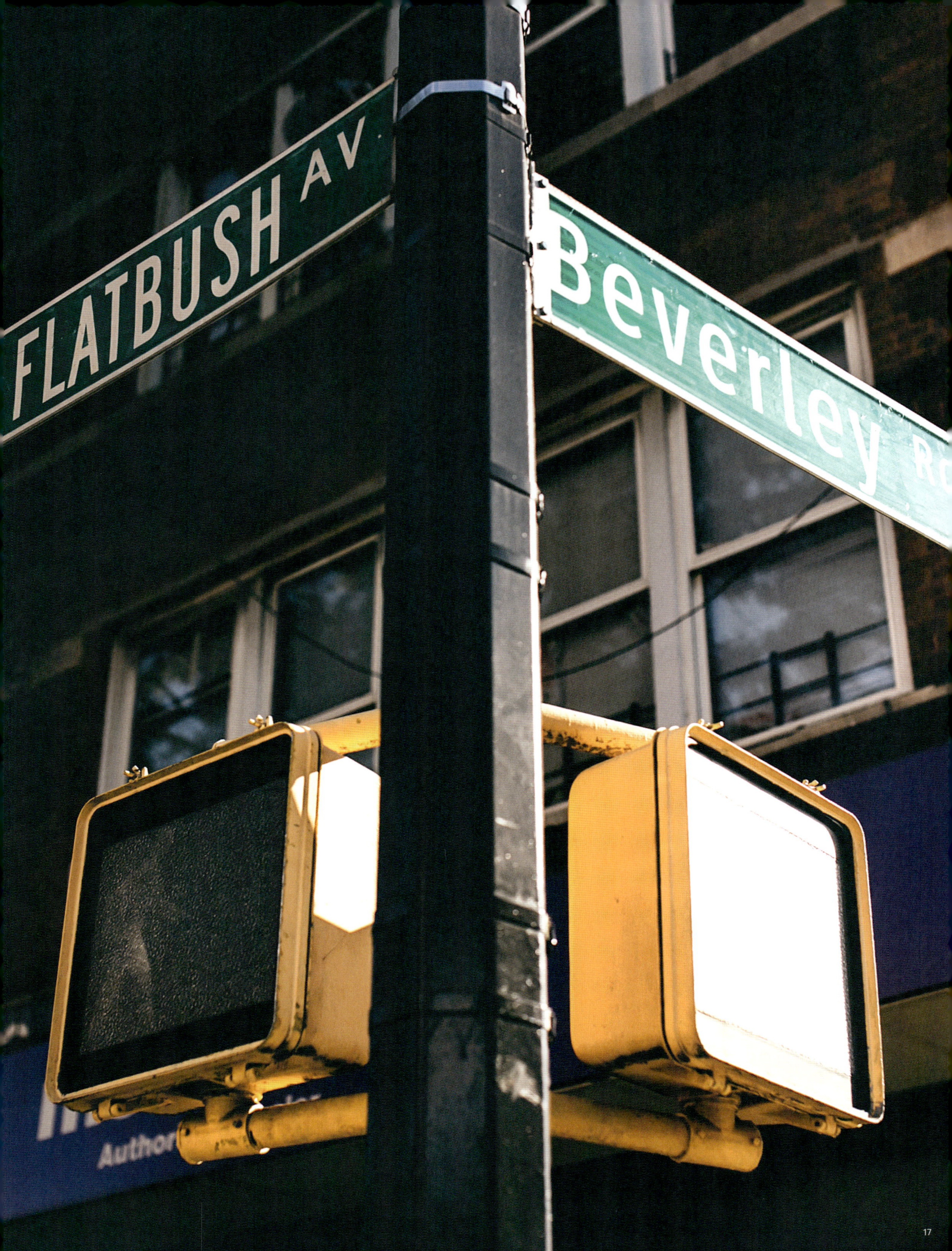
FLATBUSH AV
Beverley

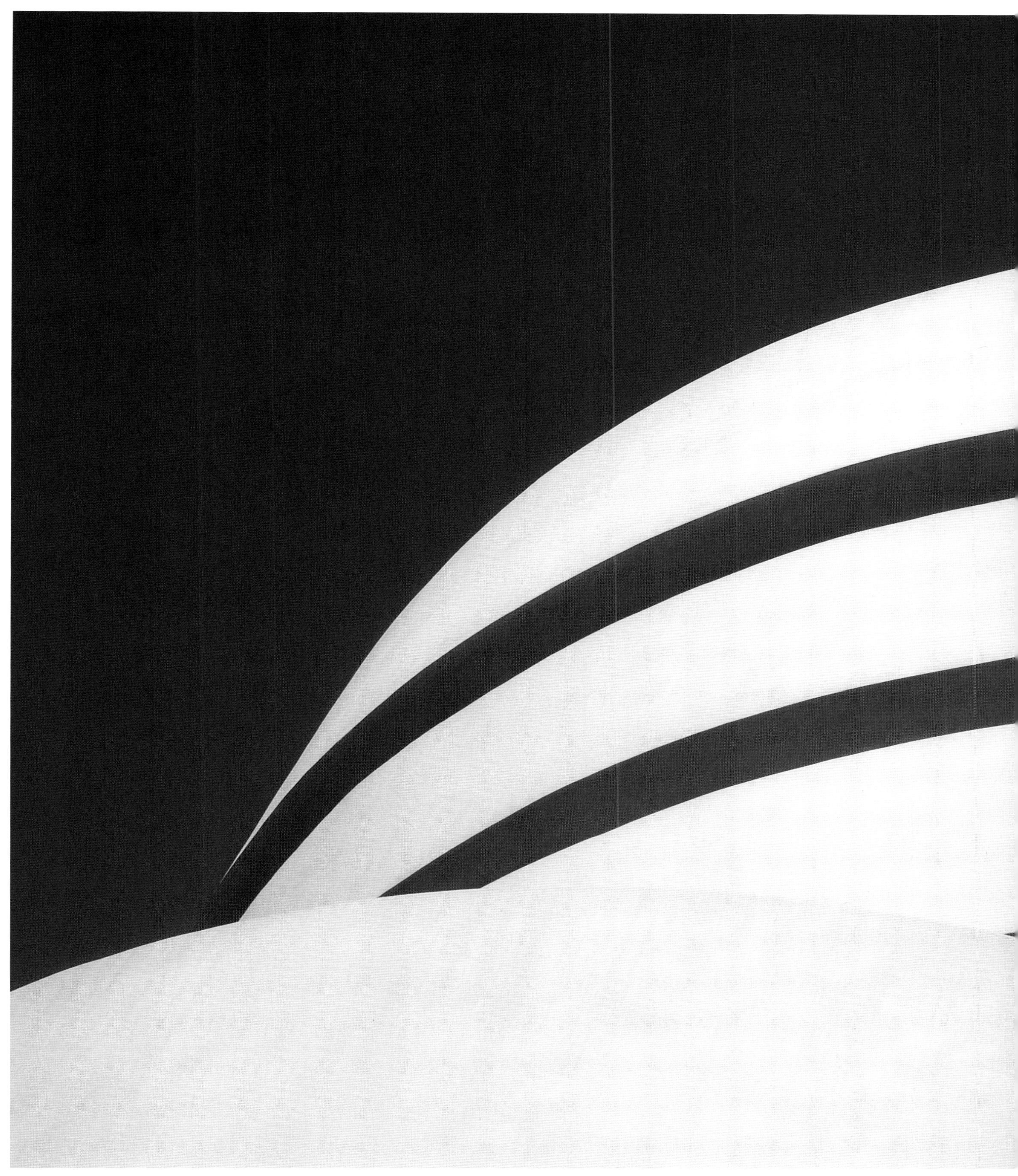

The Solomon R. Guggenheim Museum
Upper East Side, Manhattan
Jared Blake

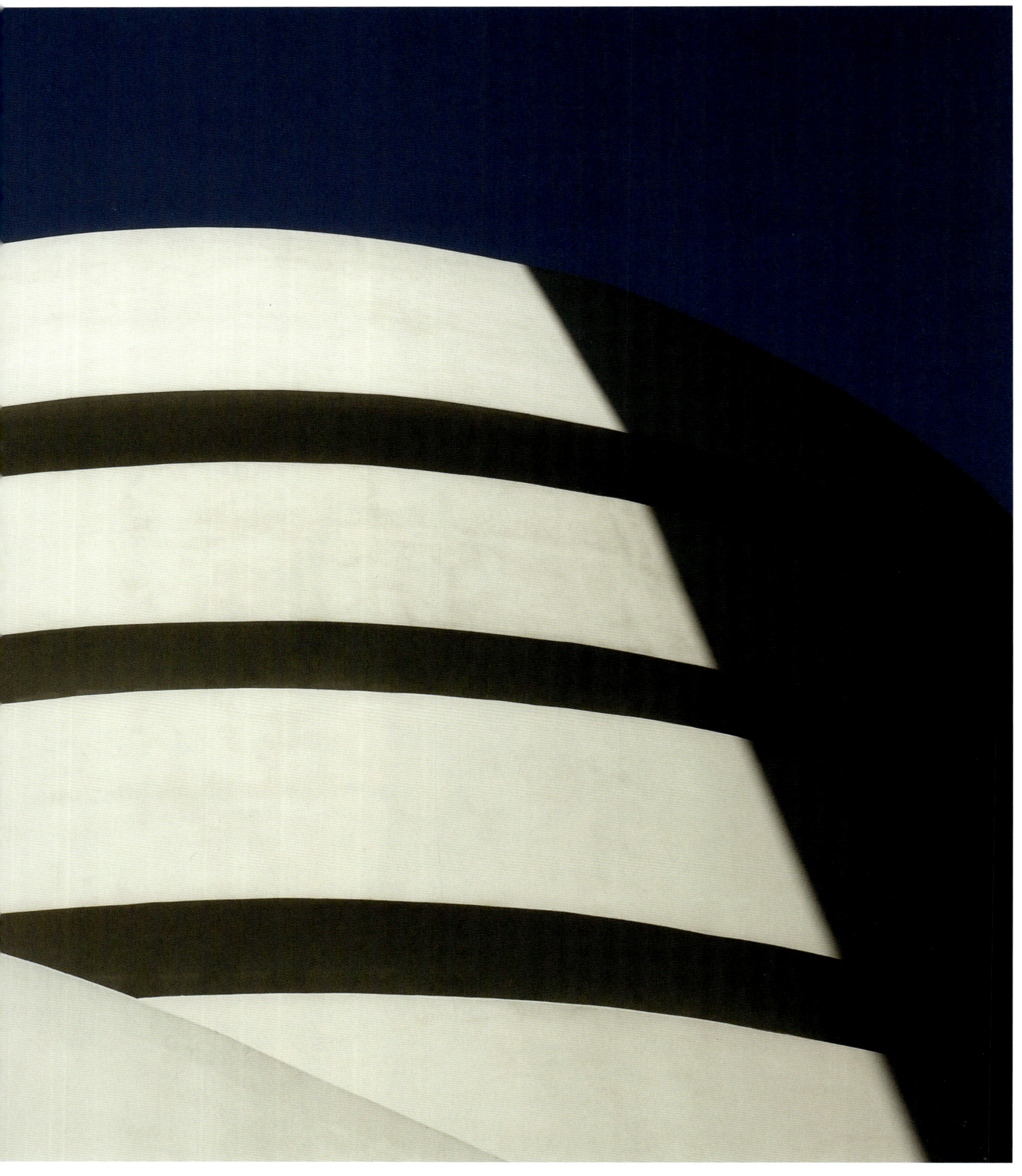

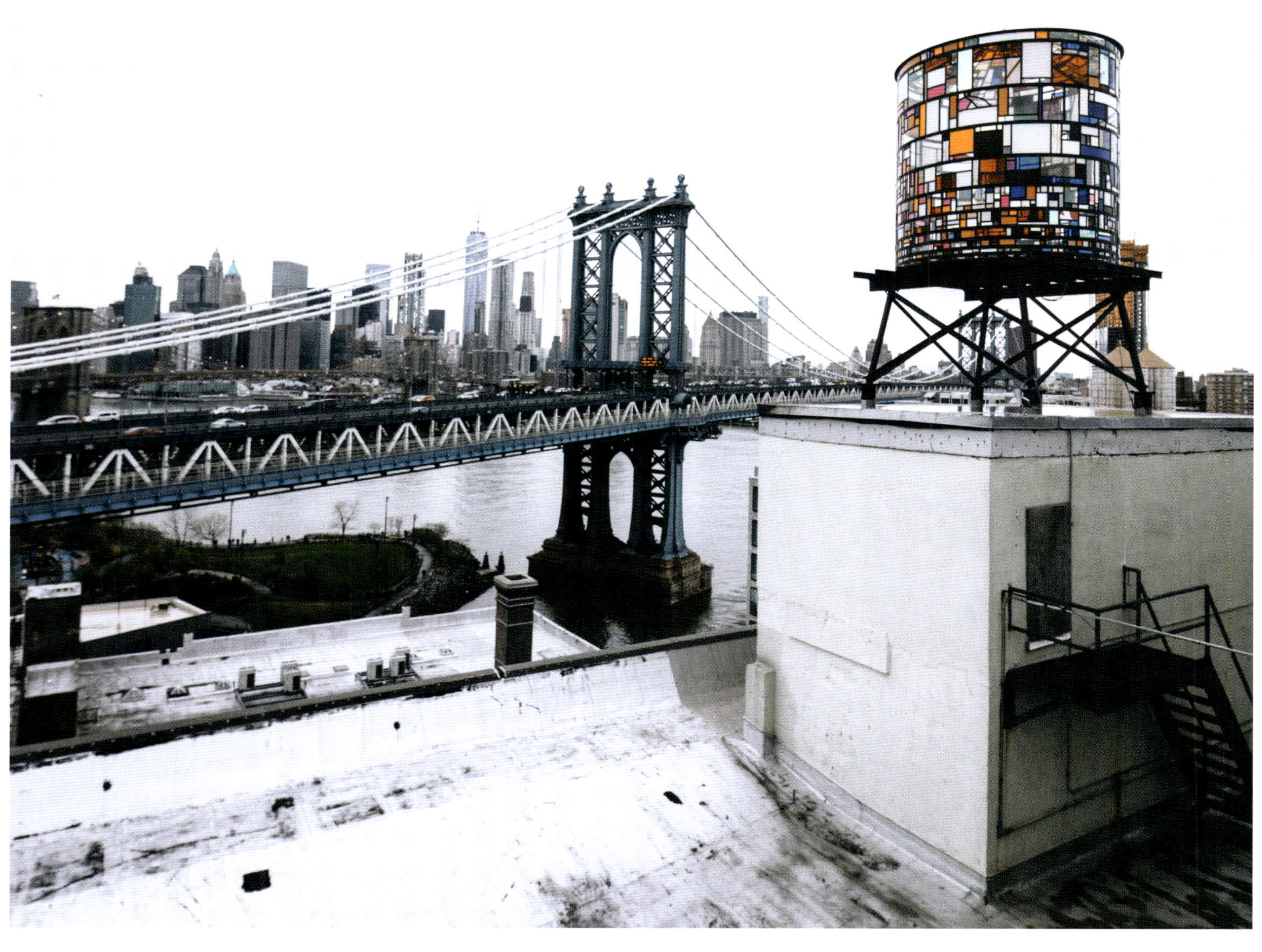

Tom Fruin's Watertower
Dumbo, Brooklyn
Alexis Le Bagousse

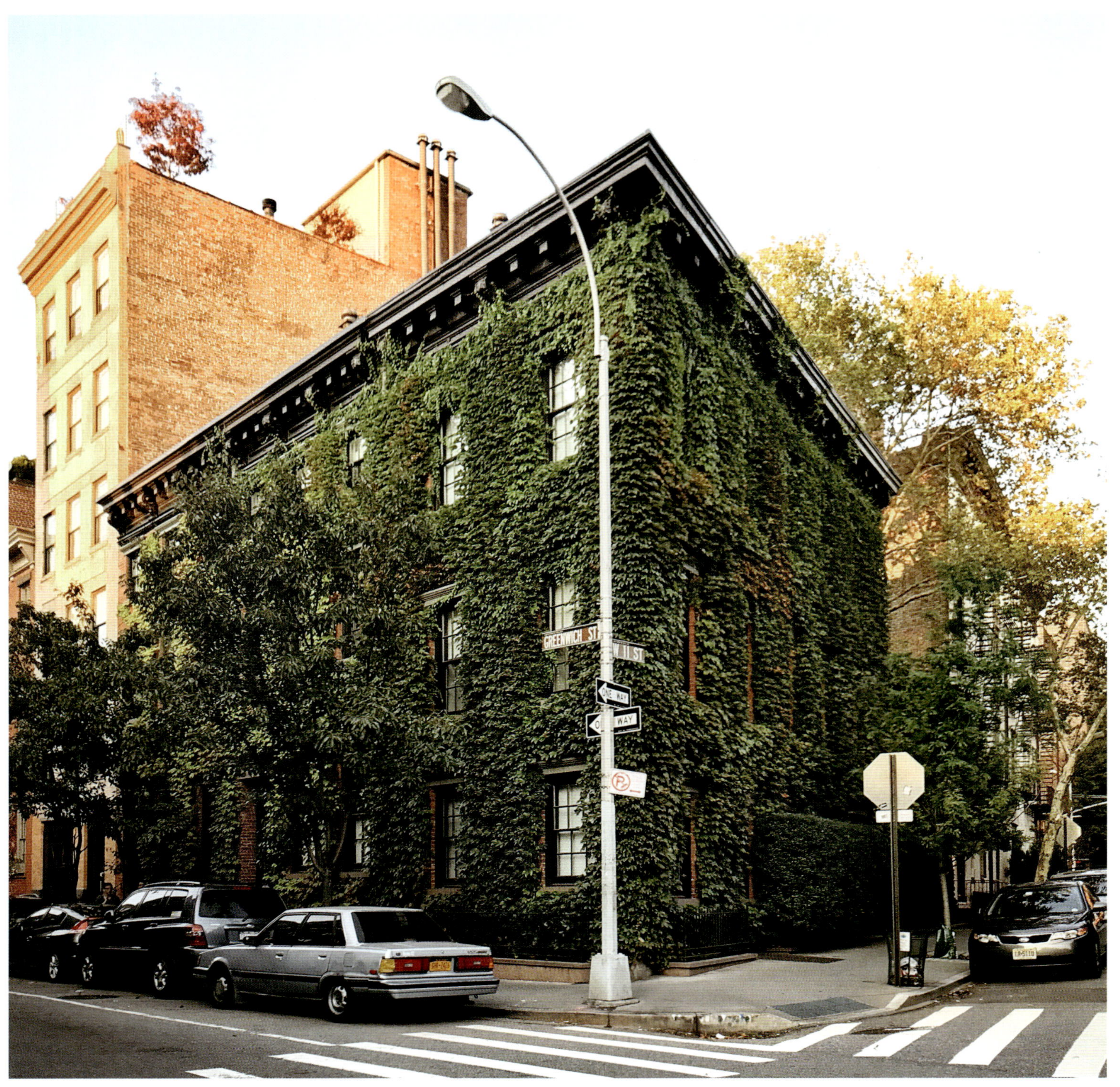

Greenwich Village, Manhattan
Patrick Janelle

Wil Suárez

hometown The Bronx, New York, USA
IG handle @wsuarez

"My love for the city comes from always being able to find something new." Photographer Wil Suárez has lived in New York City for twenty-eight years after leaving Puerto Rico. "There's always a new street, a new window, a new hue, a new day." Ever since he moved to the Bronx district, he's been a shy observer in an at-times overwhelming city. "The truth is, I had always been shooting photos in some sense since I was a child, I just never realized it." When Wil was in high school, 9/11 happened. "Living in a post 9/11 world has made us all more aware of our limited time here. I believe that's helped influence my outlook on photography and being in the moment."

"Growing up in New York, basketball and skateboarding were the two sports I gravitated to the most. I grew up skateboarding and watching kids play basketball all around me. They were the social fabric of some neighborhoods here," Wil says about his photos involving sports. "They're dynamic, intense, and draw parallels. Skateboarding is an individual endeavor while basketball mainly relies on a team effort. But basketball can be played one-on-one, which makes it all the more interesting. One-on-one combat, which is where I relate it to skateboarding. In skateboarding it's you versus an obstacle: one-on-one." Having lived in the Bronx for so long definitely influenced Wil's eye and photography, he finds. "My background allows me to identify with many cultures, while also feeling able to just blend in and become part of the background." Sometimes though, photographing a city like New York can be tough. "The hardest part is wanting to capture it all. But lately I've grown comfortable with potentially 'losing a moment' by telling myself I'll get another chance, somehow, somewhere—I'll have another shot."

„Ich liebe diese Stadt, weil man hier immer etwas Neues entdecken kann." Der Fotograf Wil Suárez lebt in New York City, seit er vor 28 Jahren Puerto Rico verlassen hat. „Es gibt immer eine neue Straße, ein neues Fenster, einen neuen Farbton, einen neuen Tag." Seit seiner Ankunft in der Bronx lebt er als schüchterner Beobachter in einer manchmal einschüchternden Stadt. „Tatsächlich habe ich schon seit meiner Kindheit in gewissem Sinne immer Fotos gemacht, ich habe es nur nicht gemerkt." Wil ging noch zur Highschool, als die Anschläge vom 11. September stattfanden. „In einer Welt nach 9/11 zu leben, hat uns allen deutlicher bewusst gemacht, dass unsere Zeit hier endlich ist. Ich glaube, das hat meinen Blick auf die Fotografie und den gegenwärtigen Moment beeinflusst", erinnert sich Wil.

„Da ich in New York aufgewachsen bin, sind Basketball und Skateboardfahren die beiden Sportarten, zu denen ich mich am meisten hingezogen fühlte. Ich bin damit groß geworden, Skateboard zu fahren und überall Jugendliche Basketball spielen zu sehen. Das war der soziale Kitt in einigen Stadtvierteln hier", erklärt Wil seine Sportfotografien. „Beide Disziplinen sind dynamisch, anstrengend und zeigen einige Parallelen. Skateboarding ist ein Individualsport, Basketball lebt vor allem von der Teamleistung. Aber Basketball kann man auch eins gegen eins spielen, das macht es sogar noch interessanter. Der Kampf Mann gegen Mann, da sehe ich die Beziehung zum Skateboarding. Auf dem Skateboard trittst du gegen ein Hindernis an: eins gegen eins." Schon so lange in der Bronx zu leben, hat nach Wils eigener Einschätzung auch seinen Blick und seine Fotografie eindeutig geprägt: „Dank meiner Vorgeschichte kann ich mich mit vielen Kulturen identifizieren, aber gleichzeitig auch gut integrieren und einfach mit dem Hintergrund verschmelzen." Manchmal könne es allerdings anstrengend sein, eine Stadt wie New York zu fotografieren: „Die größte Schwierigkeit ist, dass man alles einfangen will. Aber in letzter Zeit habe ich mich mit dem Gedanken angefreundet, möglicherweise einen Moment zu verpassen, indem ich mir sage, dass ich eine zweite Chance bekommen werde, irgendwo, irgendwie, versuche ich es noch einmal."

« L'amour que j'éprouve pour cette ville tient à toutes les choses nouvelles que je peux sans cesse y découvrir ». Il y a vingt-huit ans, Wil Suárez quitte Porto Rico pour New York. « Il peut s'agir d'une nouvelle rue, une nouvelle fenêtre, une nouvelle nuance, une nouvelle journée ». Dès l'instant où il emménage dans le Bronx, le photographe se fait l'observateur discret d'une ville parfois envahissante. « En vérité, depuis l'enfance, je prends des photographies, sous une forme ou une autre. Simplement, je ne m'en étais jamais rendu compte ». Au moment du 11 septembre, Wil est au lycée. « Vivre dans le monde de l'après 11 septembre nous a permis d'avoir une plus grande conscience des limites du temps que nous passons ici. Cela a, je crois, influencé ma conception de la photographie tout en m'aidant à être présent dans l'instant. (...).

J'ai grandi à New York où le basket et le skate sont les deux sports qui m'ont le plus attiré. J'ai grandi en faisant du skate et en observant les gamins qui, autour de moi, jouaient au basket. Ils créaient le tissu social d'un certain nombre de quartiers ici », affirme Wil lorsqu'il évoque ses clichés sur le sport. « Ils sont dynamiques, intenses, ils établissent des parallèles. Faire du skate est un engagement individuel, alors que le basket repose essentiellement sur l'effort d'une équipe. Mais on peut jouer à deux au basket, ce qui rend ce sport d'autant plus intéressant. Un combat particulier, ce qui, à mon sens, le relie au skate. Avec le skate, c'est vous versus un obstacle : un duel ». Le fait d'avoir si longtemps vécu dans le Bronx a indéniablement marqué le regard de Wil et sa photographie, estime-t-il. « Grâce à mon histoire, je peux m'identifier à plusieurs cultures tout en me sentant capable de simplement m'y intégrer et de faire partie de cette histoire ». Parfois, cependant, photographier une ville telle que New York peut s'avérer difficile. « Le plus dur, c'est de chercher à la capter dans sa totalité. Mais récemment, j'ai commencé à me sentir plus à l'aise avec le fait de 'manquer un instant', en me disant qu'une autre occasion se présenterait, sous une autre forme, ailleurs – que je prendrai un autre cliché ».

New York City Subway
Wil Suárez

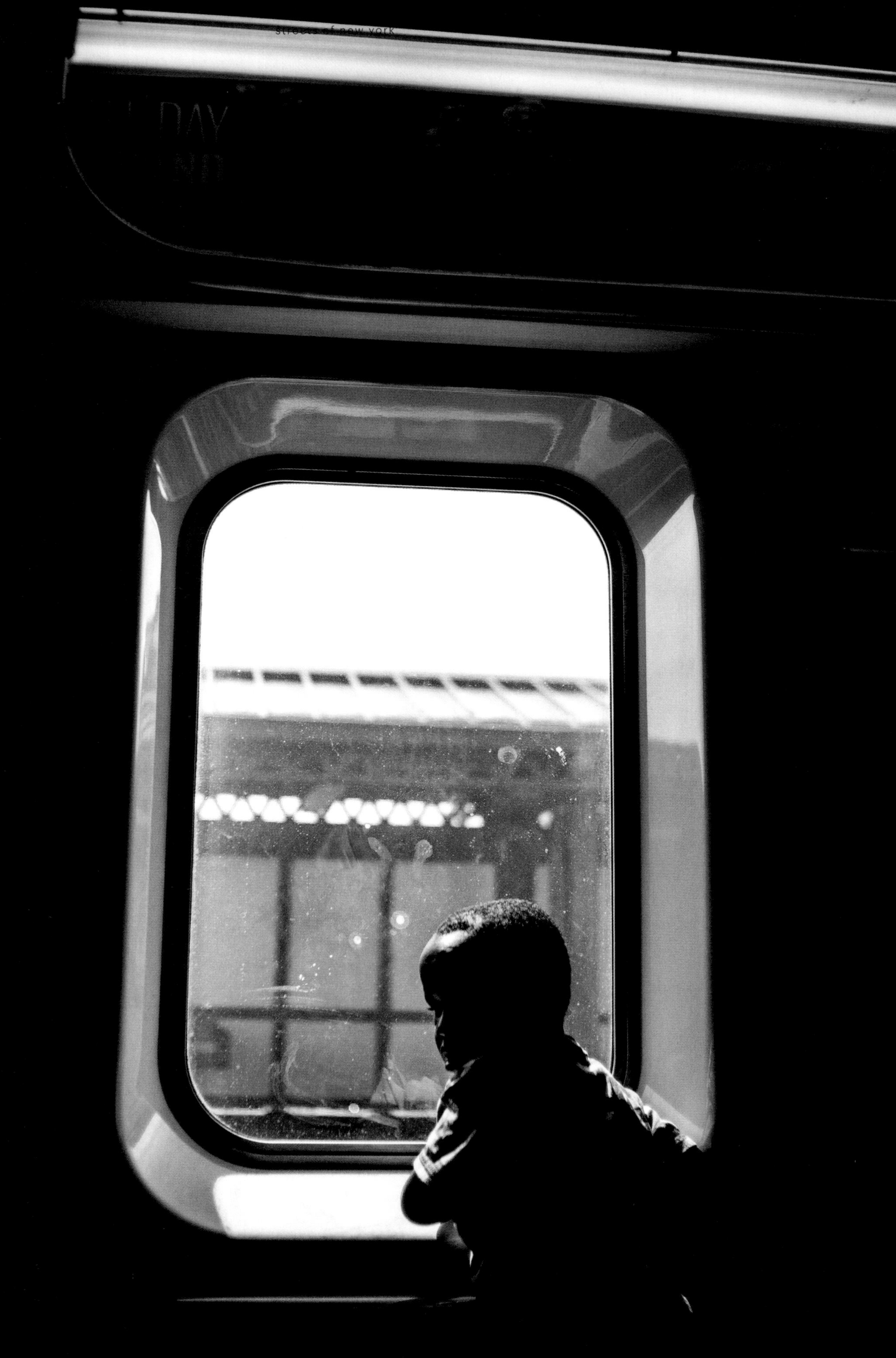

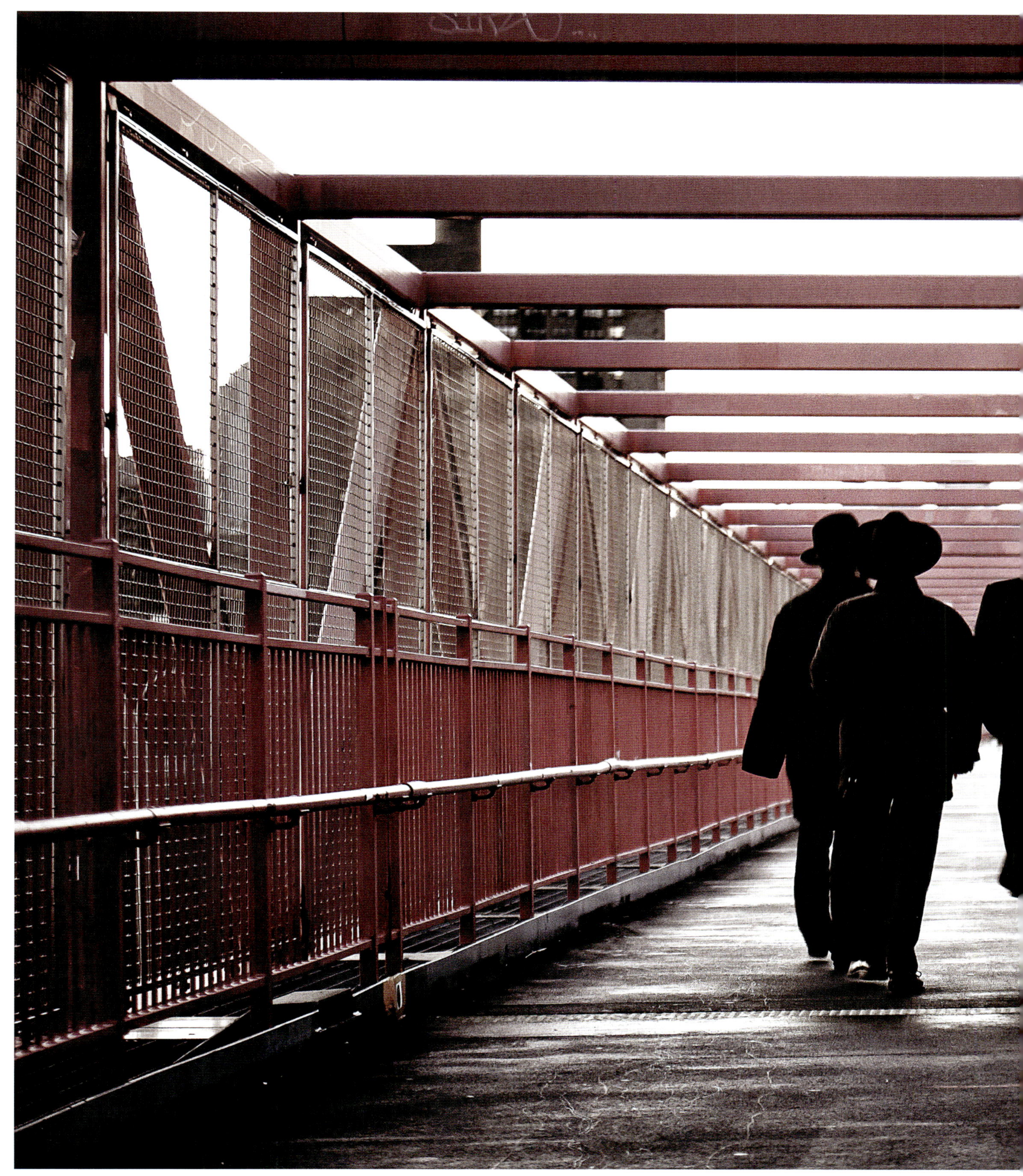

The Williamsburg Bridge
Williamsburg, Brooklyn
Bram van Woudenberg

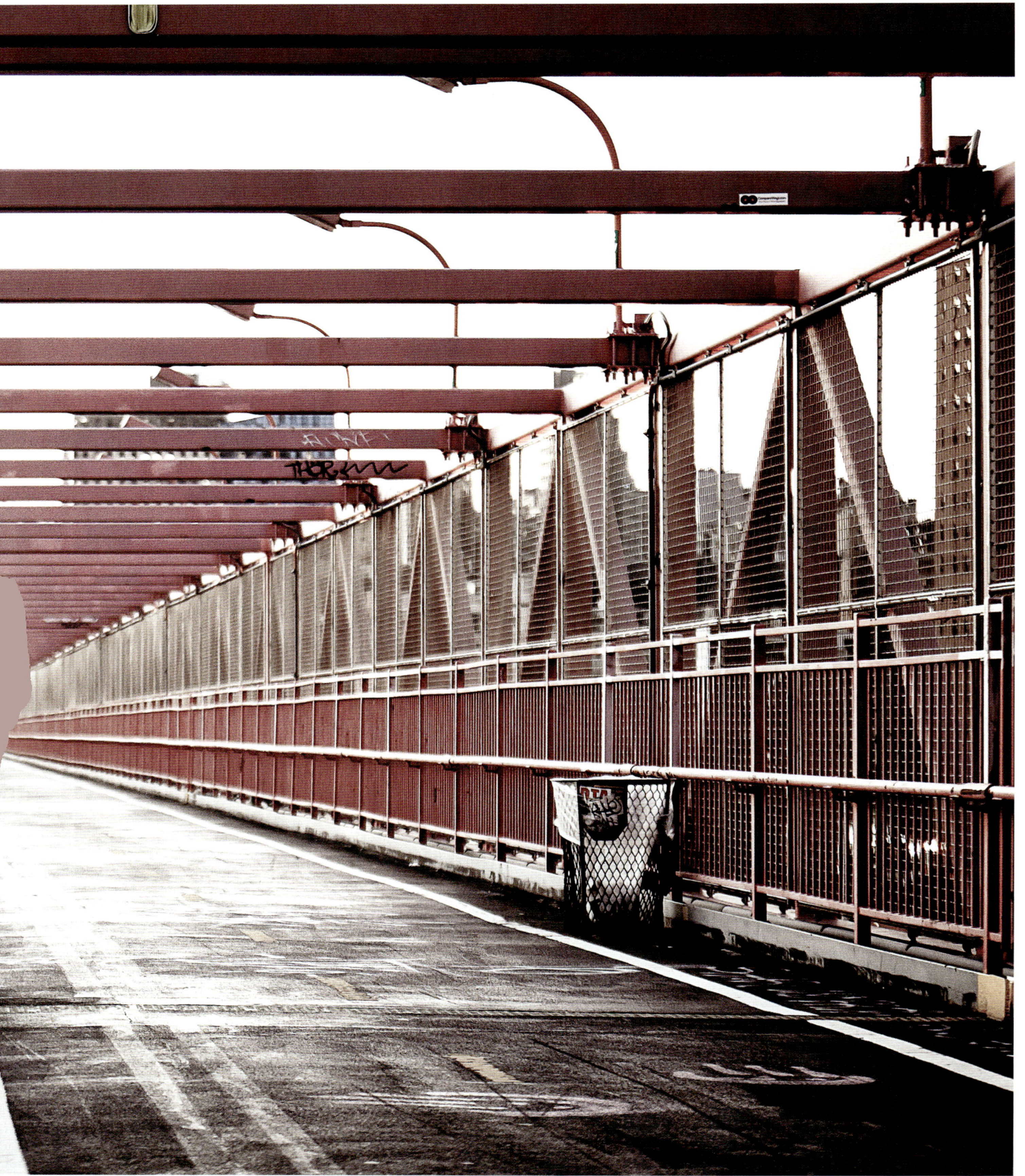

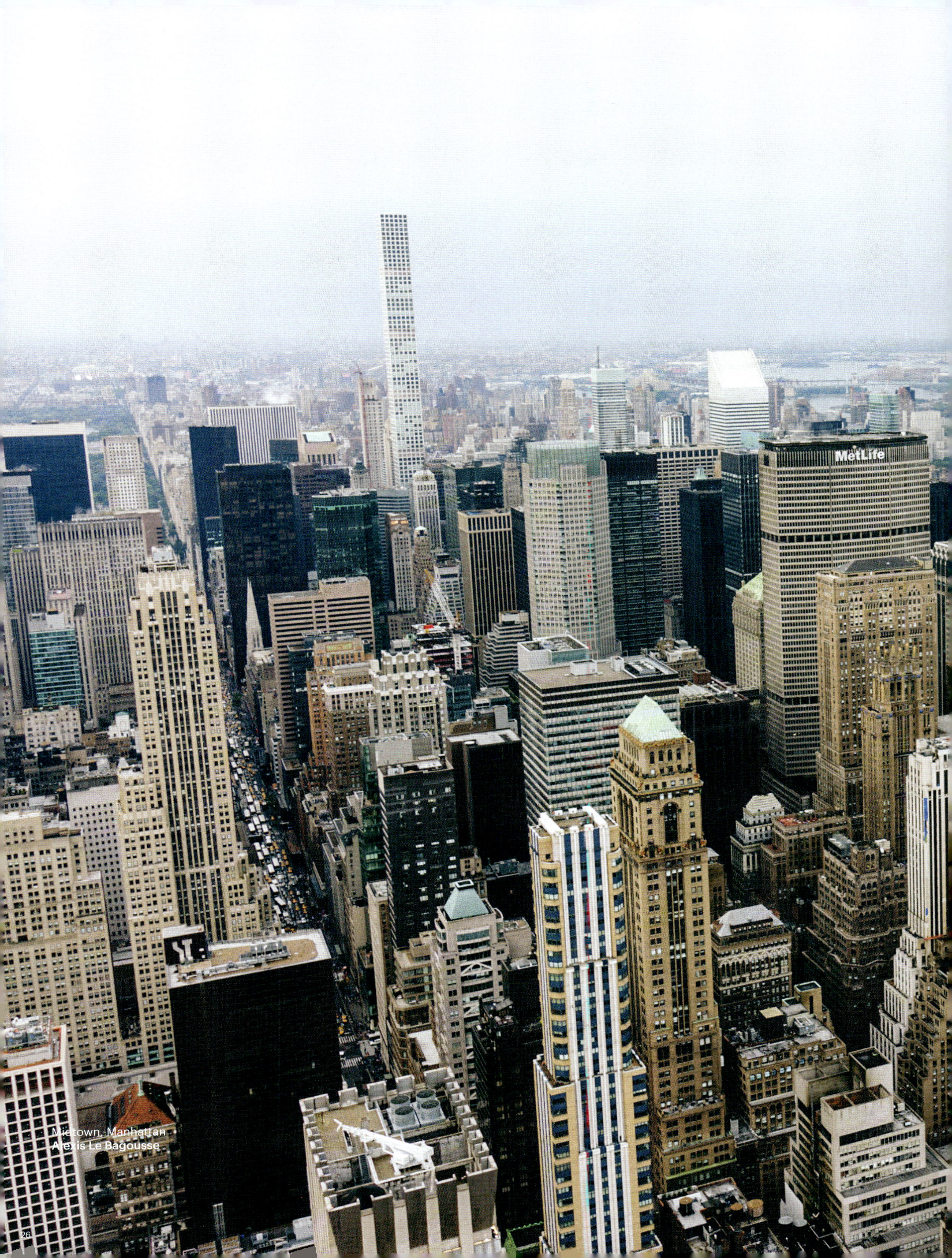

Midtown, Manhattan
Alexis Le Bagousse

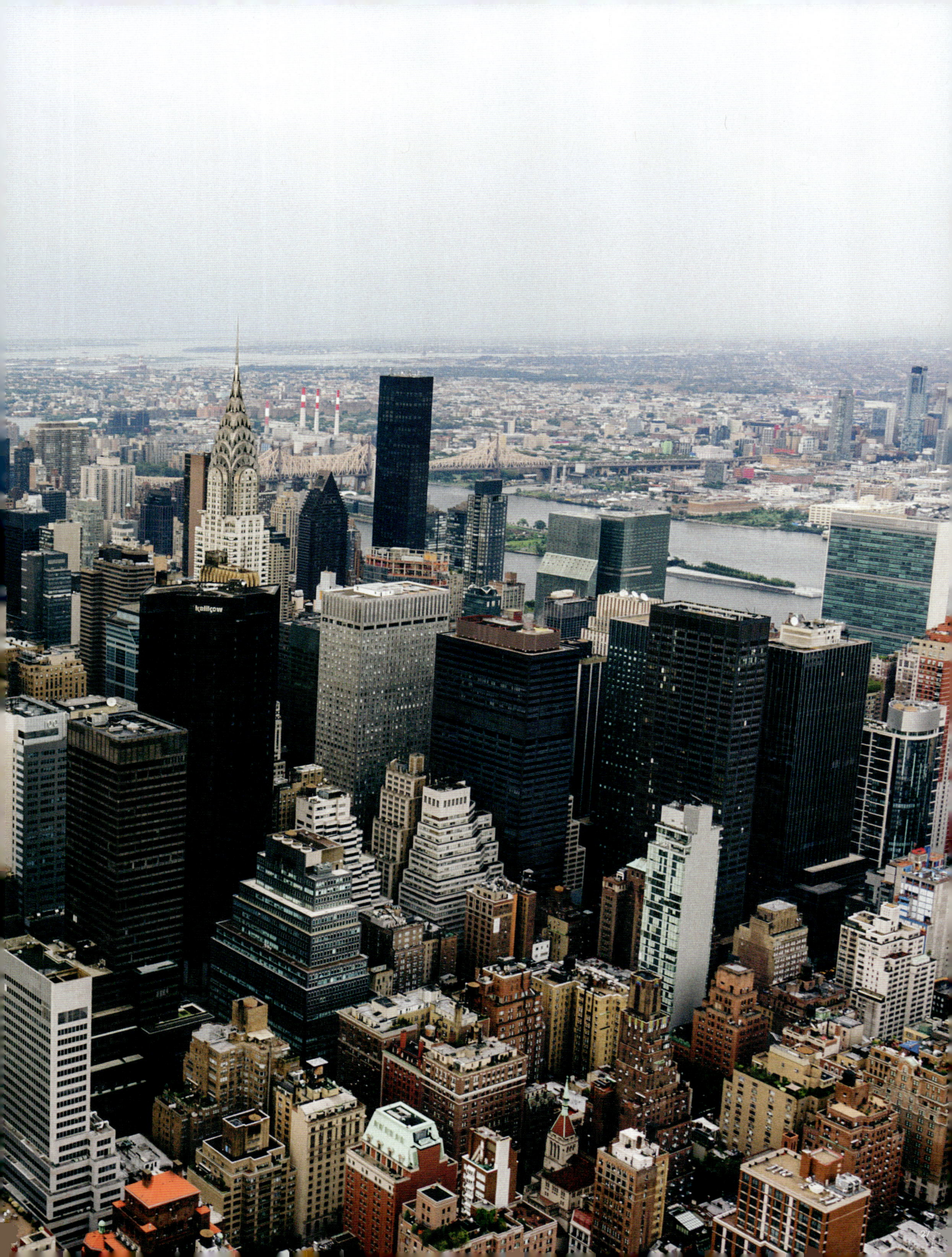
kalikow

Sometimes perfect moments only last a few seconds. You have to be ready for when they come.

—Casey Tang

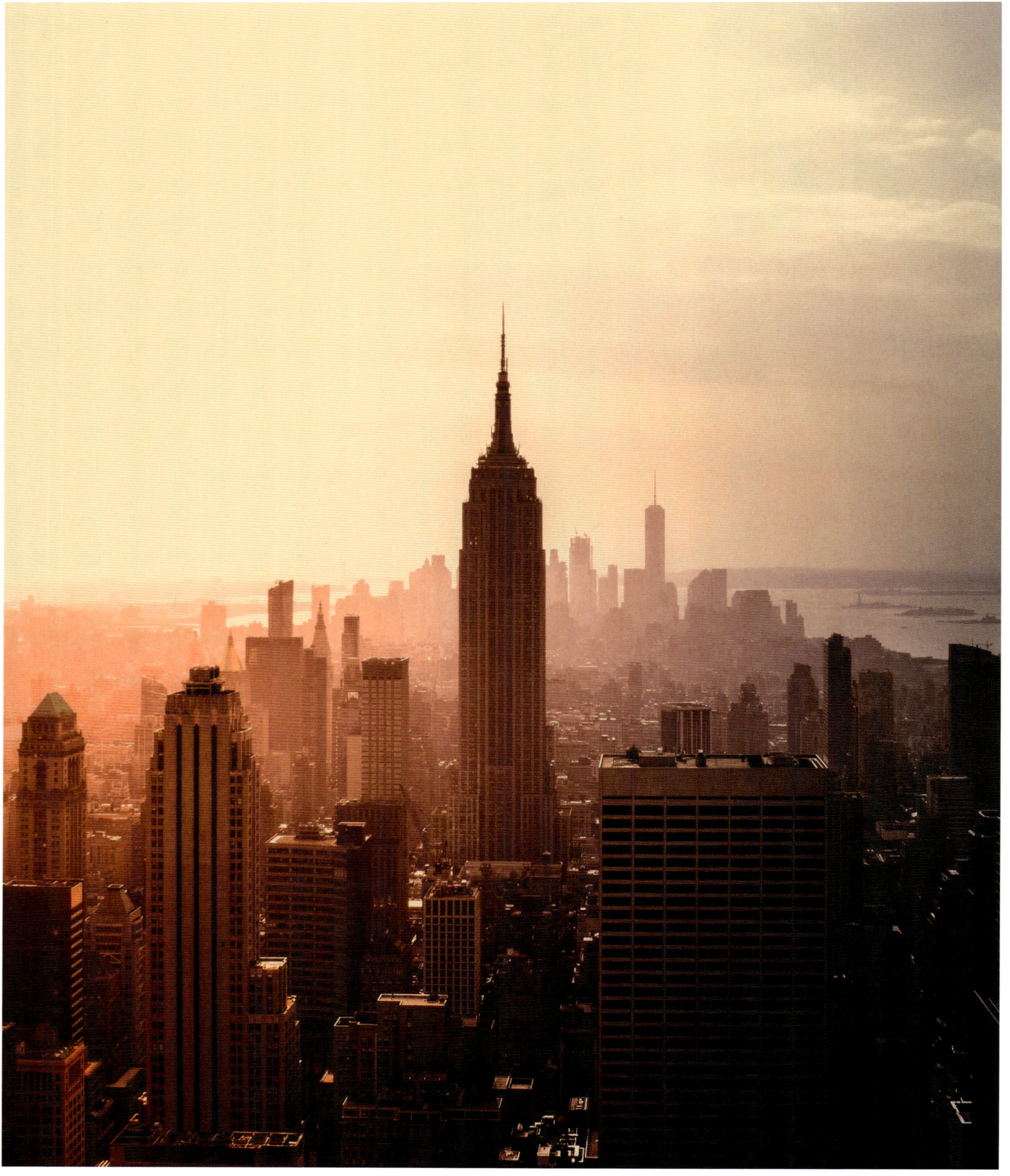

The Empire State Building
Manhattan
Casey Tang

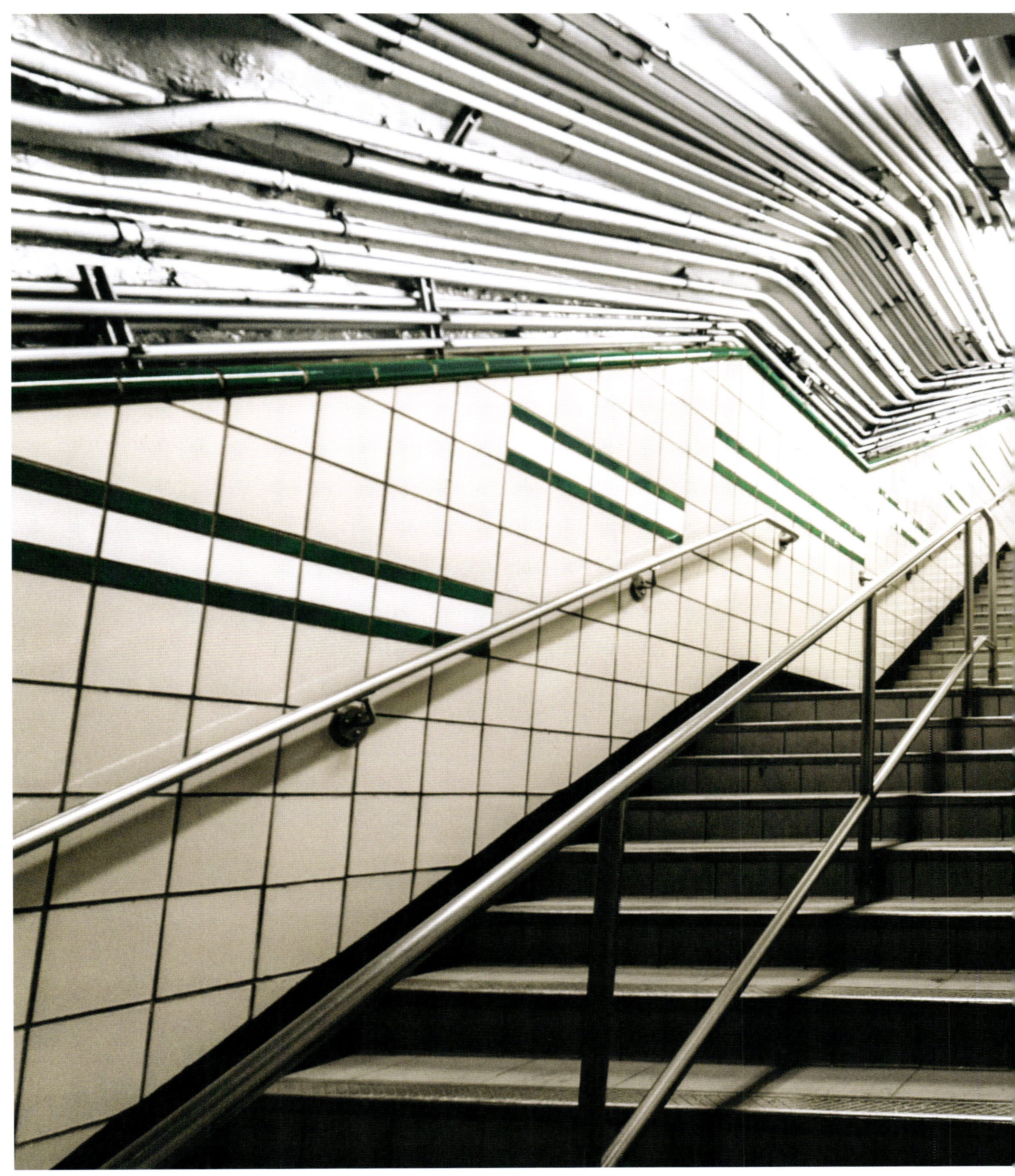

Christopher Street Station
Greenwich Village, Manhattan
Alexis Le Bagousse

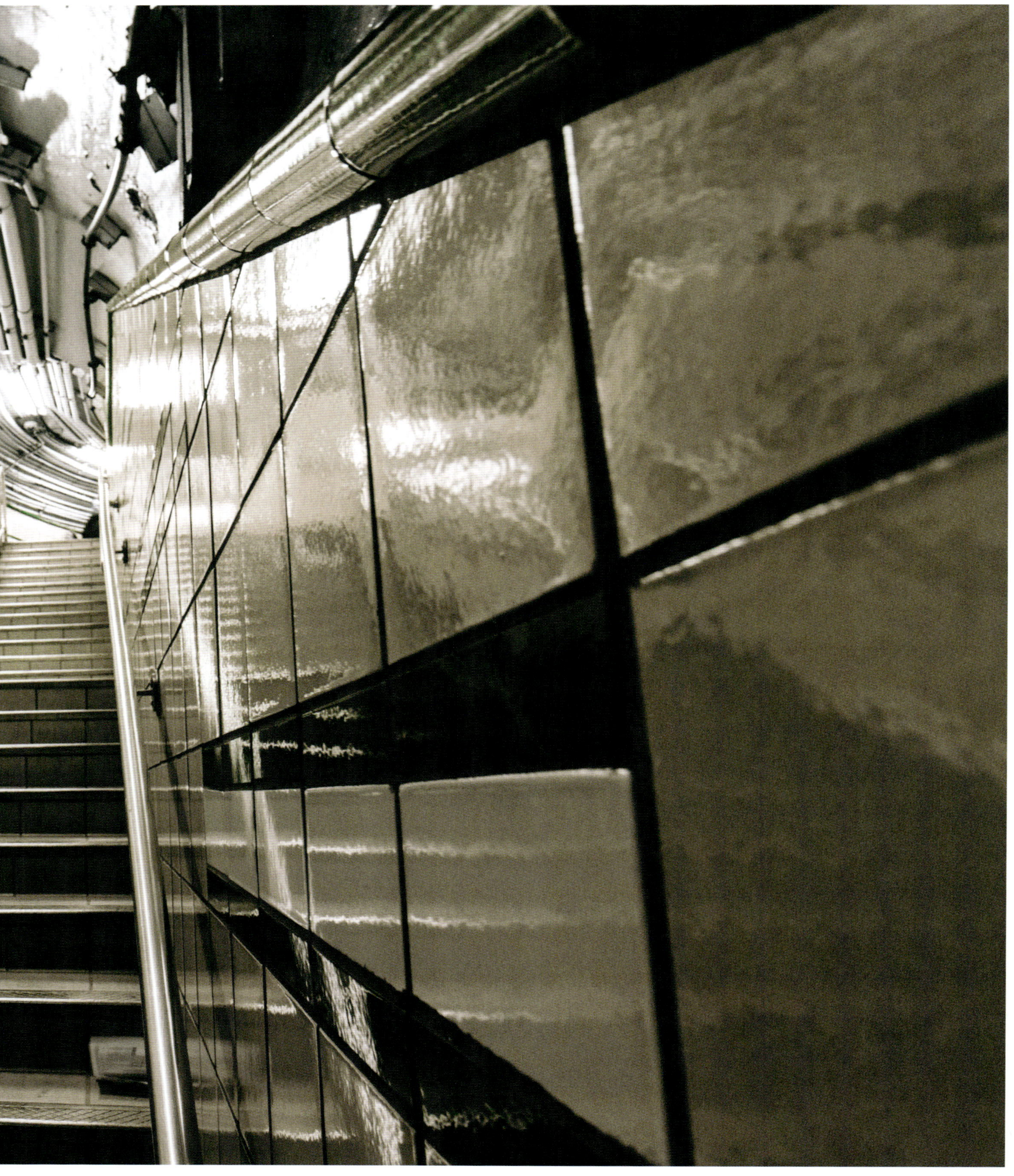

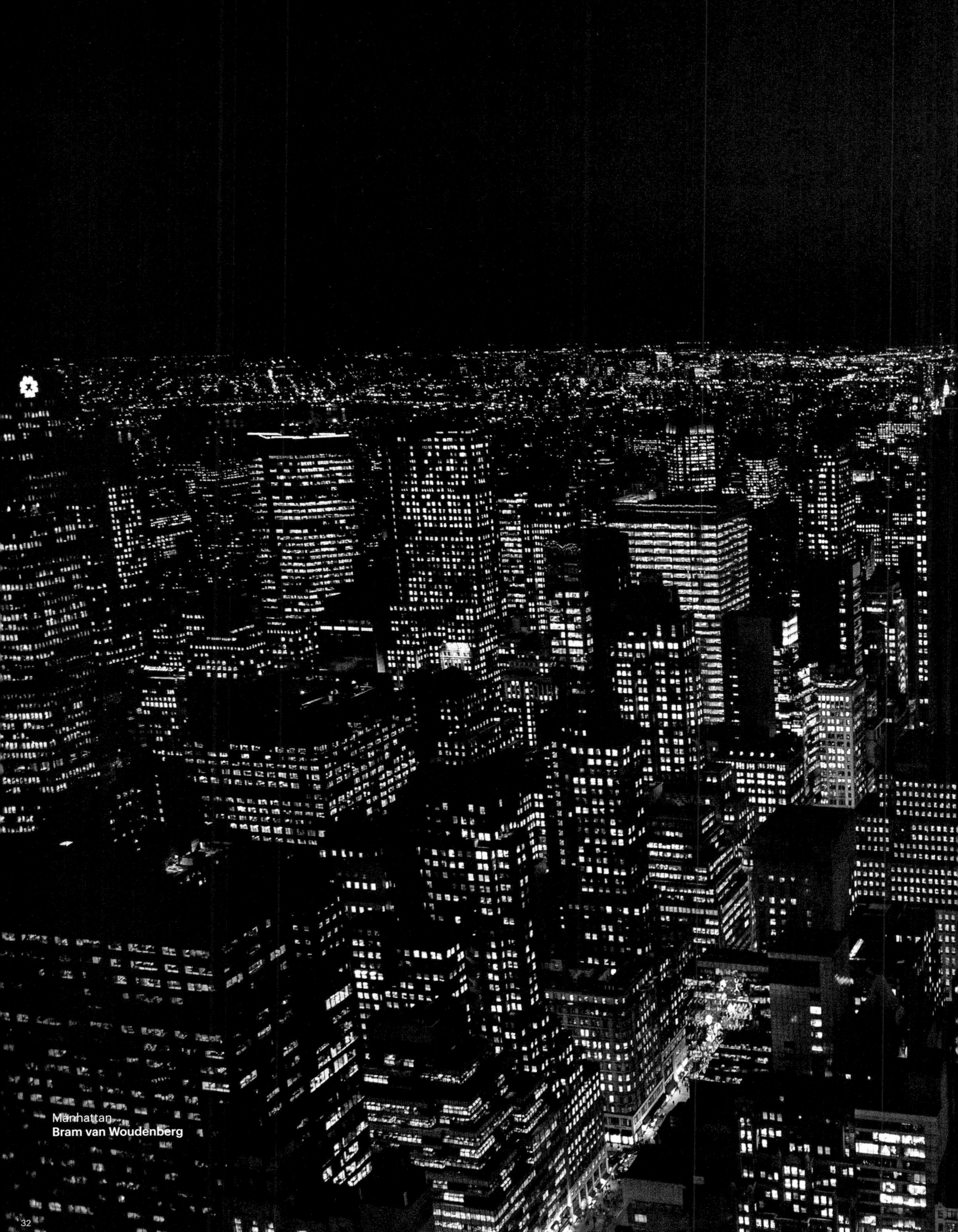

Manhattan
Bram van Woudenberg

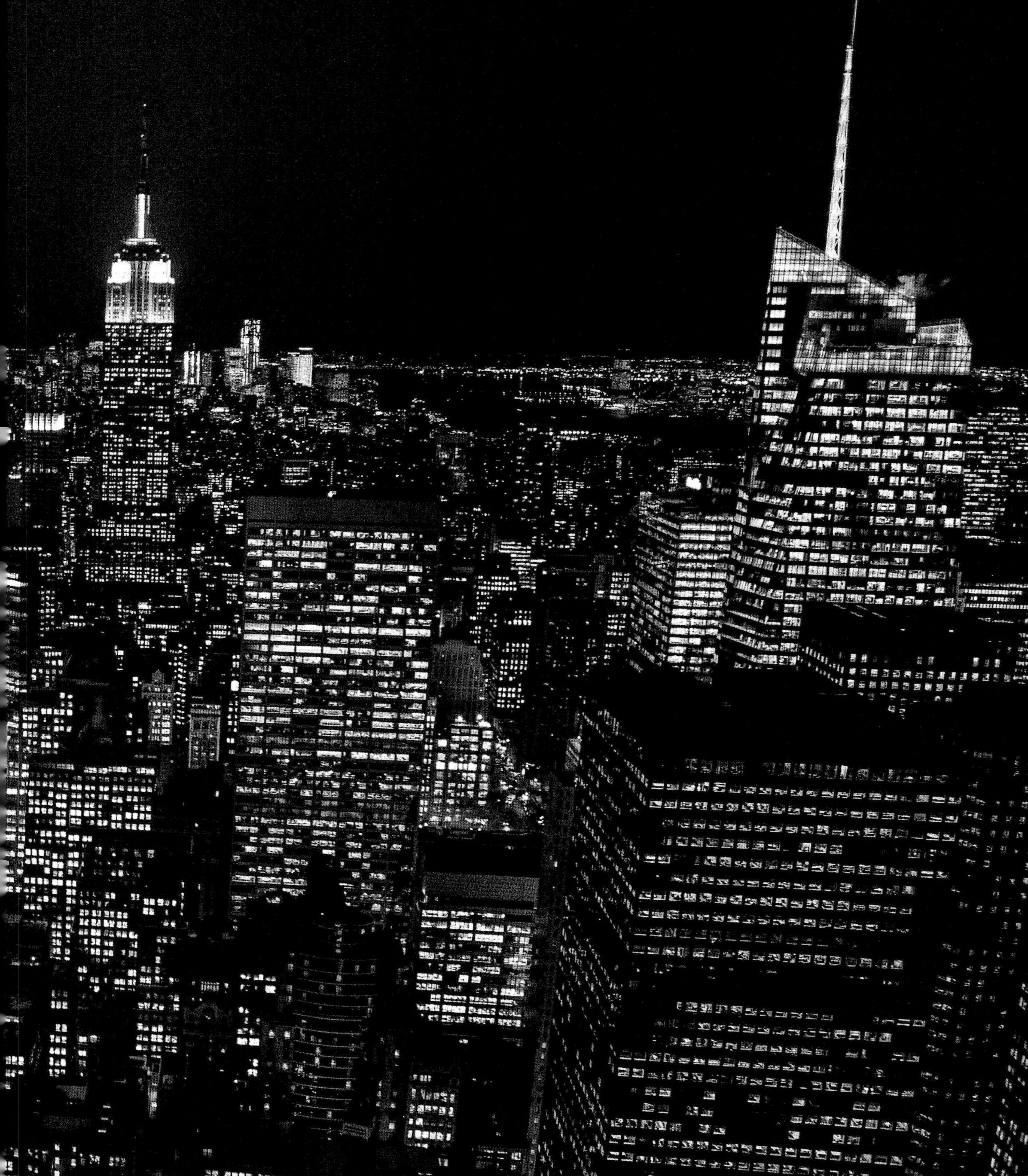

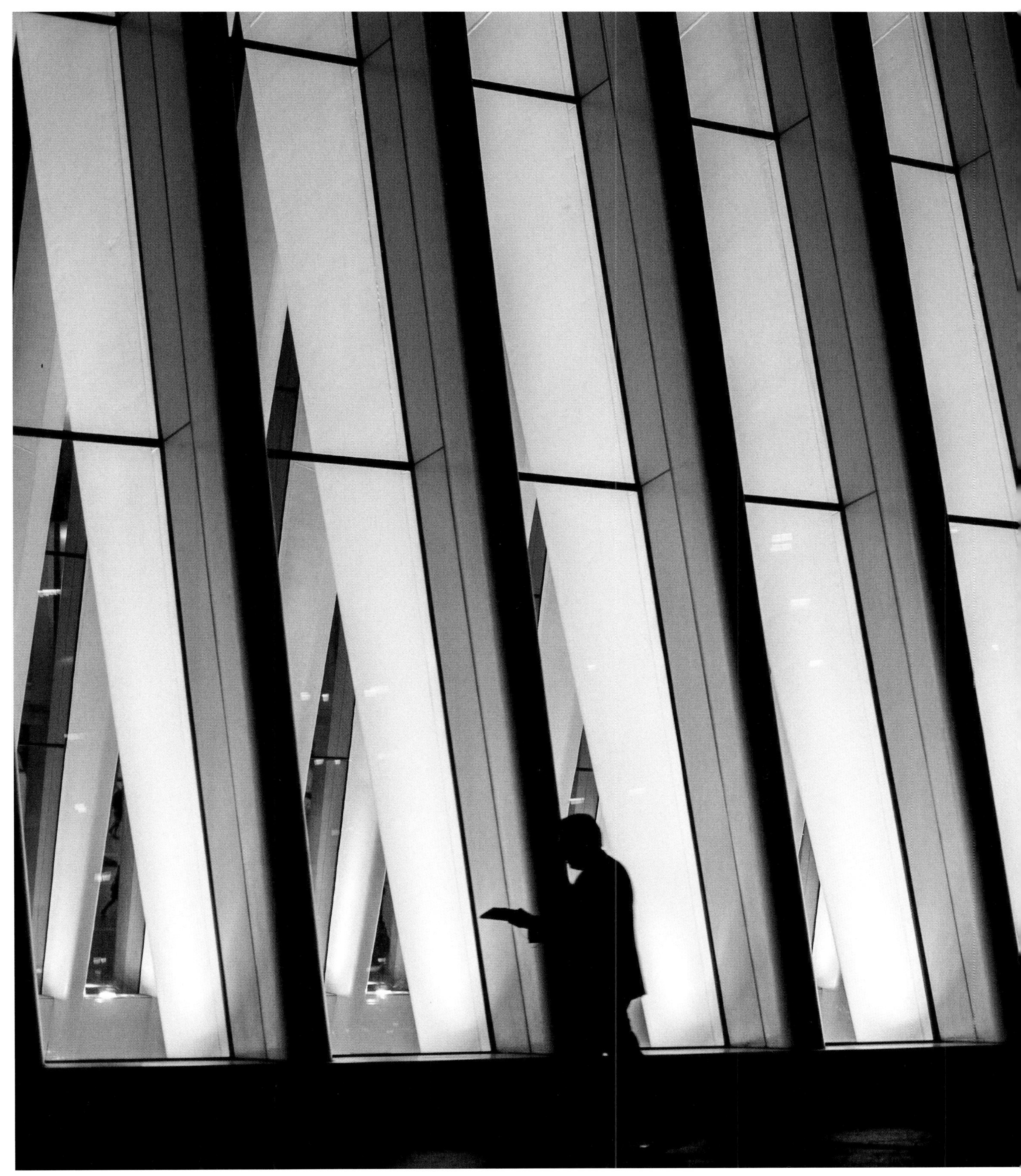

Financial District, Manhattan
Bram van Woudenberg

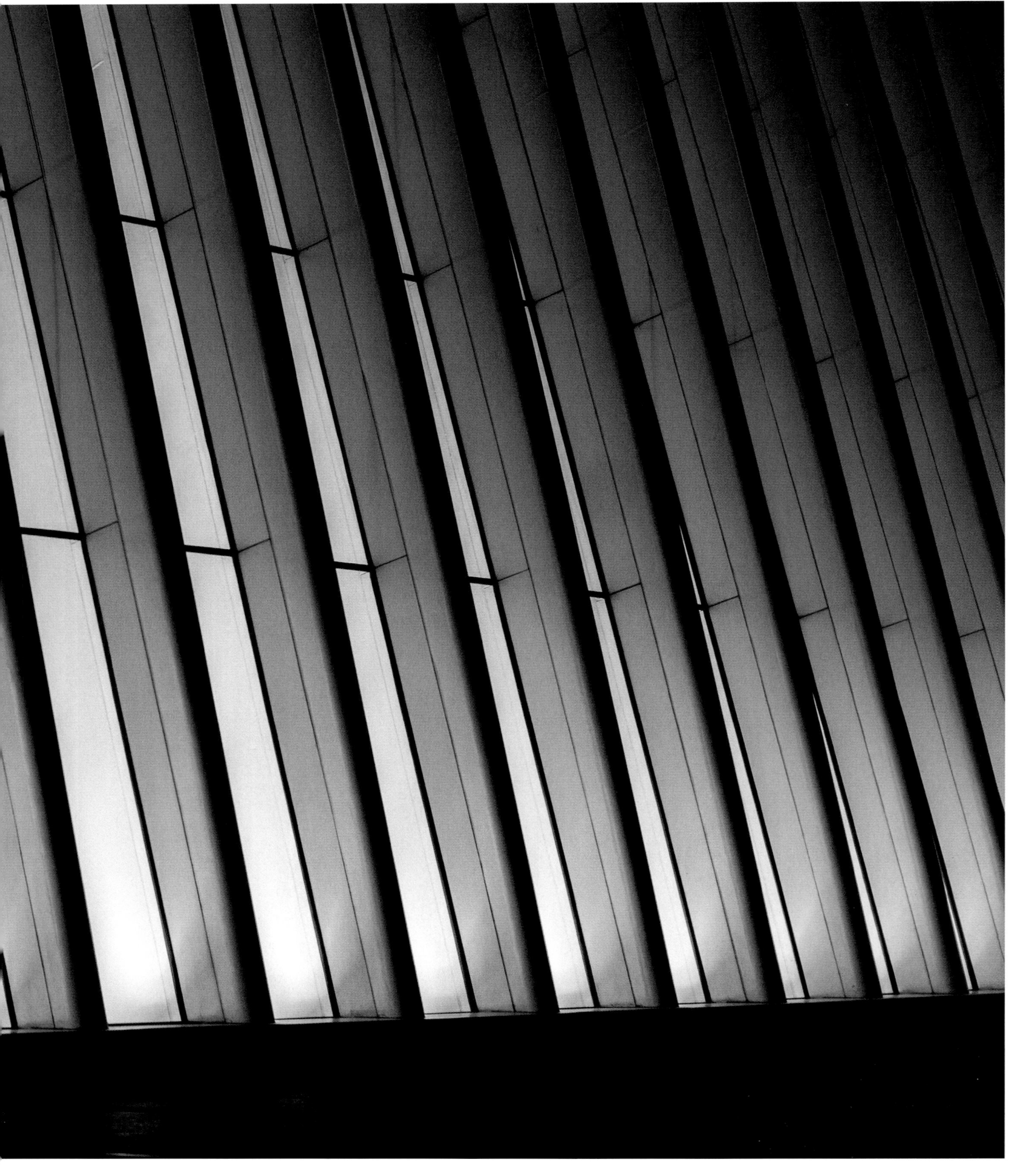

Financial District, Manhattan
Casey Tang –

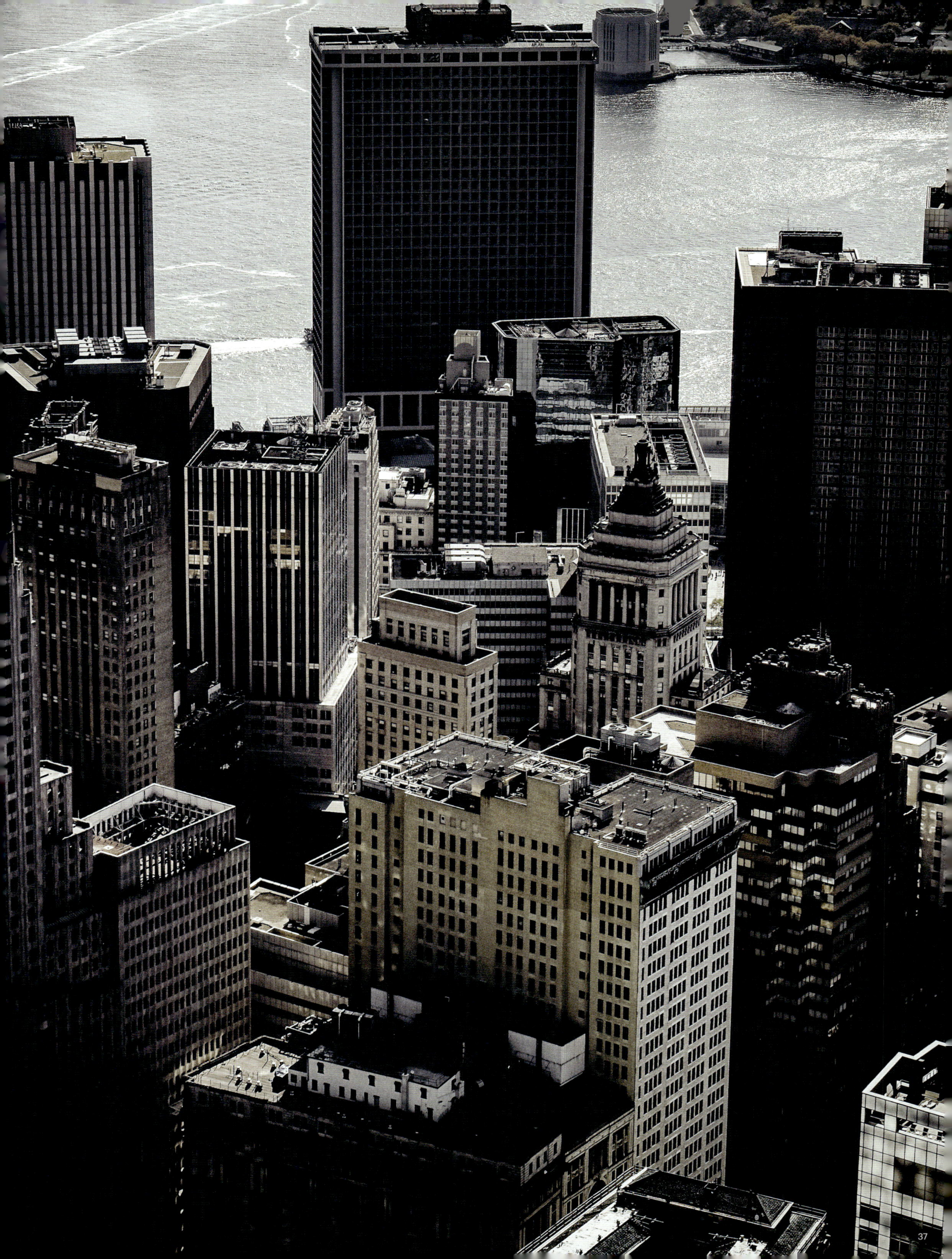

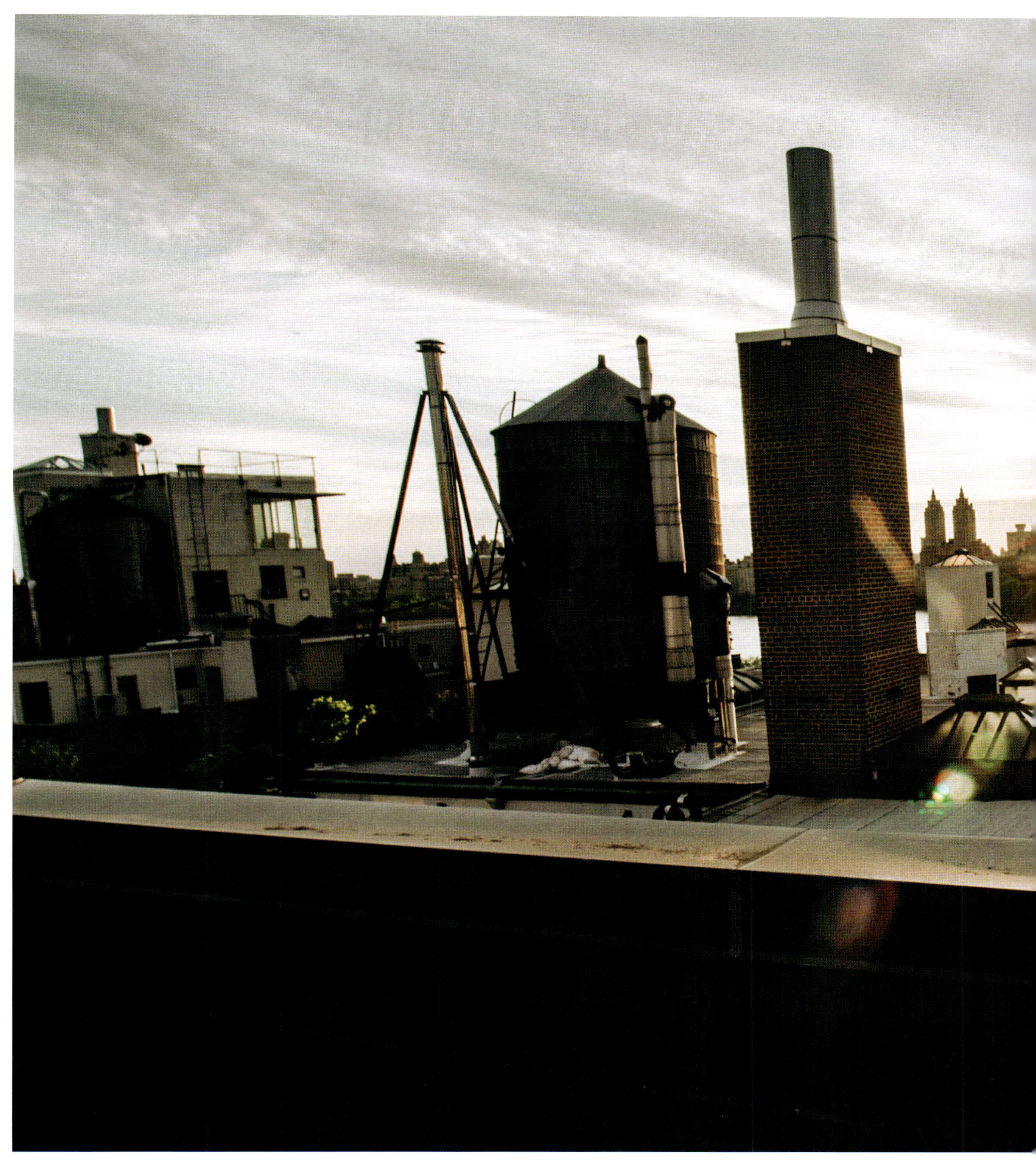

Central Park
Upper East Side, Manhattan
Alexis Le Bagousse

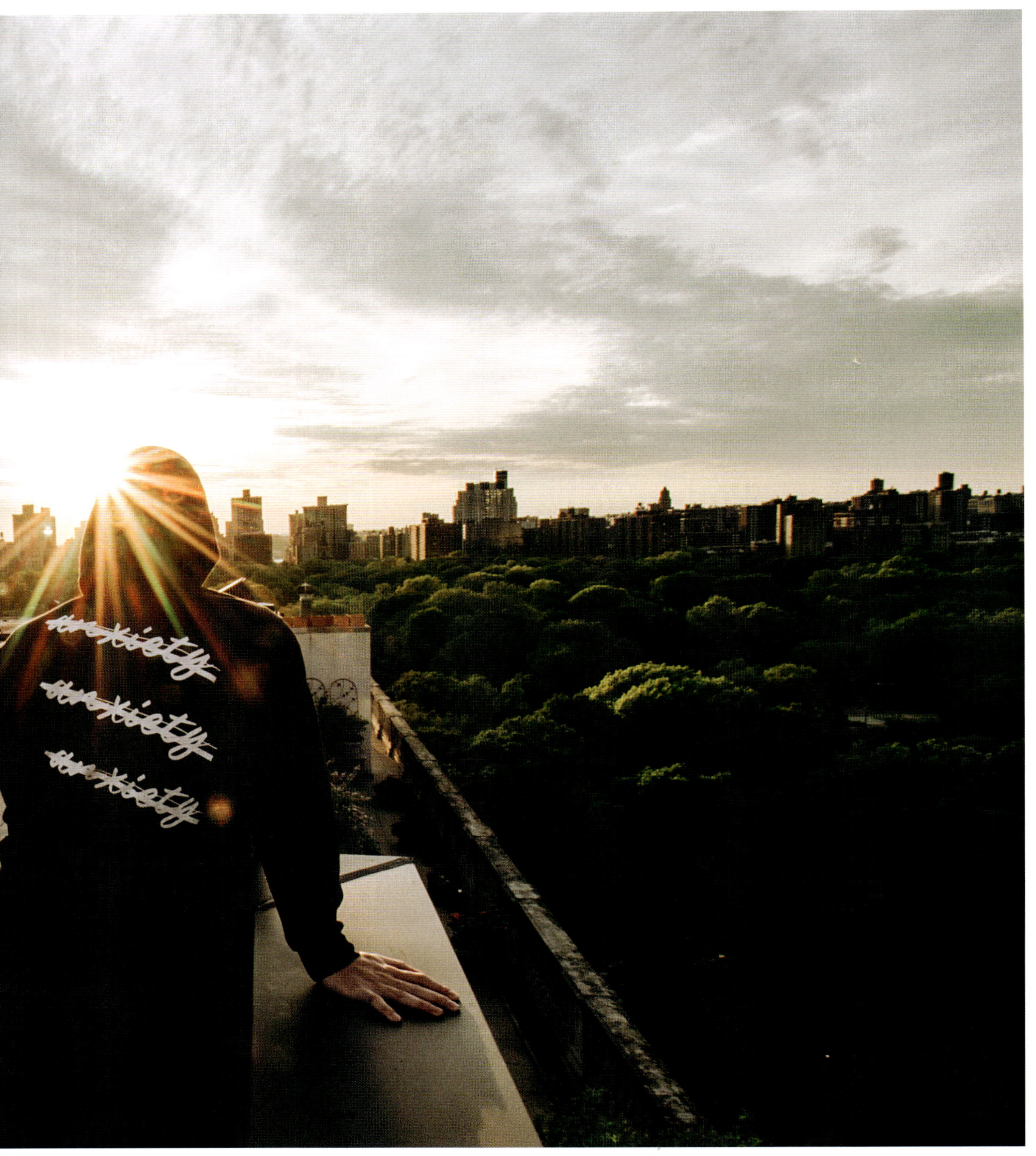

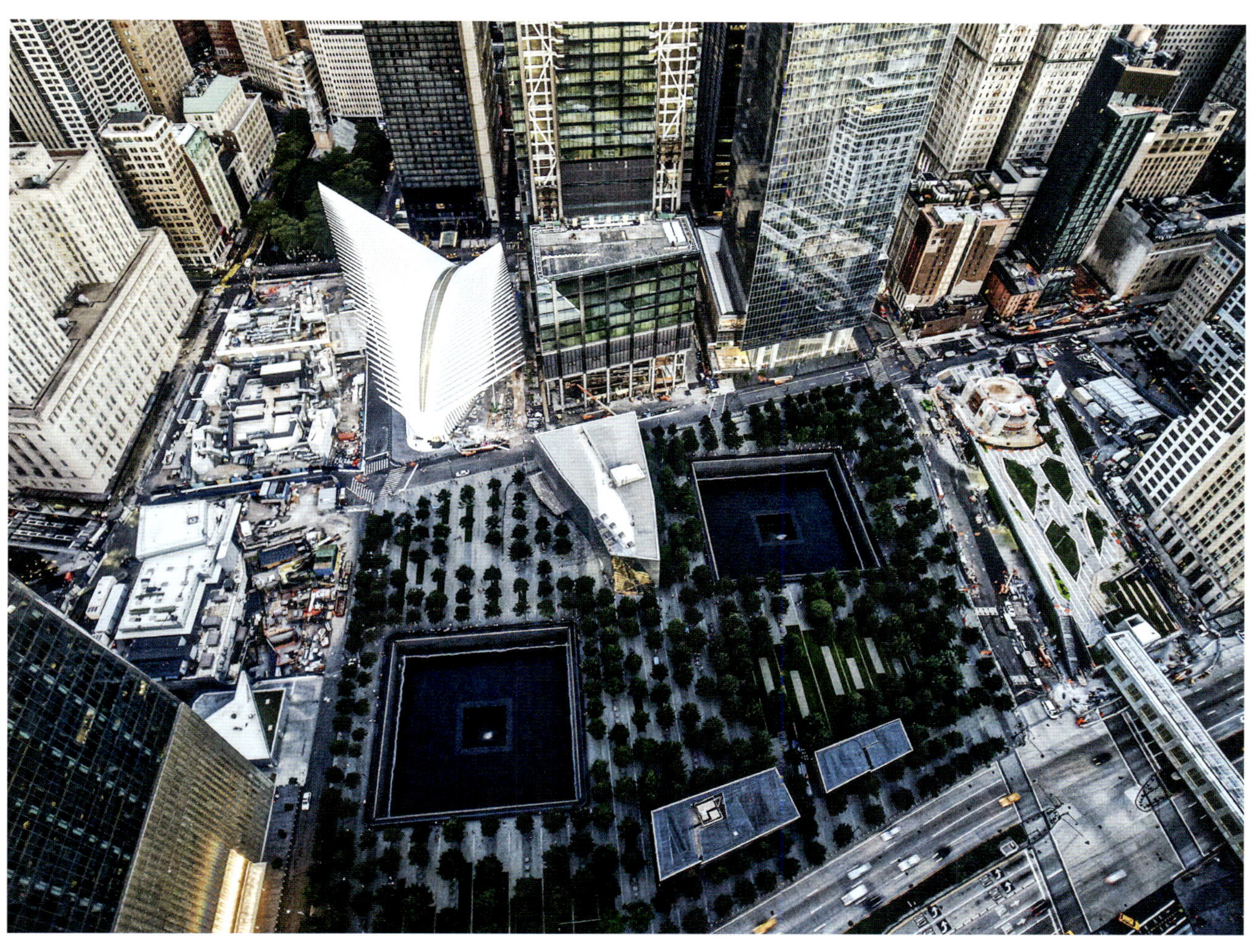

The Oculus
World Trade Center, Manhattan
Bryan Dumas

The Oculus
World Trade Center, Manhattan
Wesley Verhoeve →

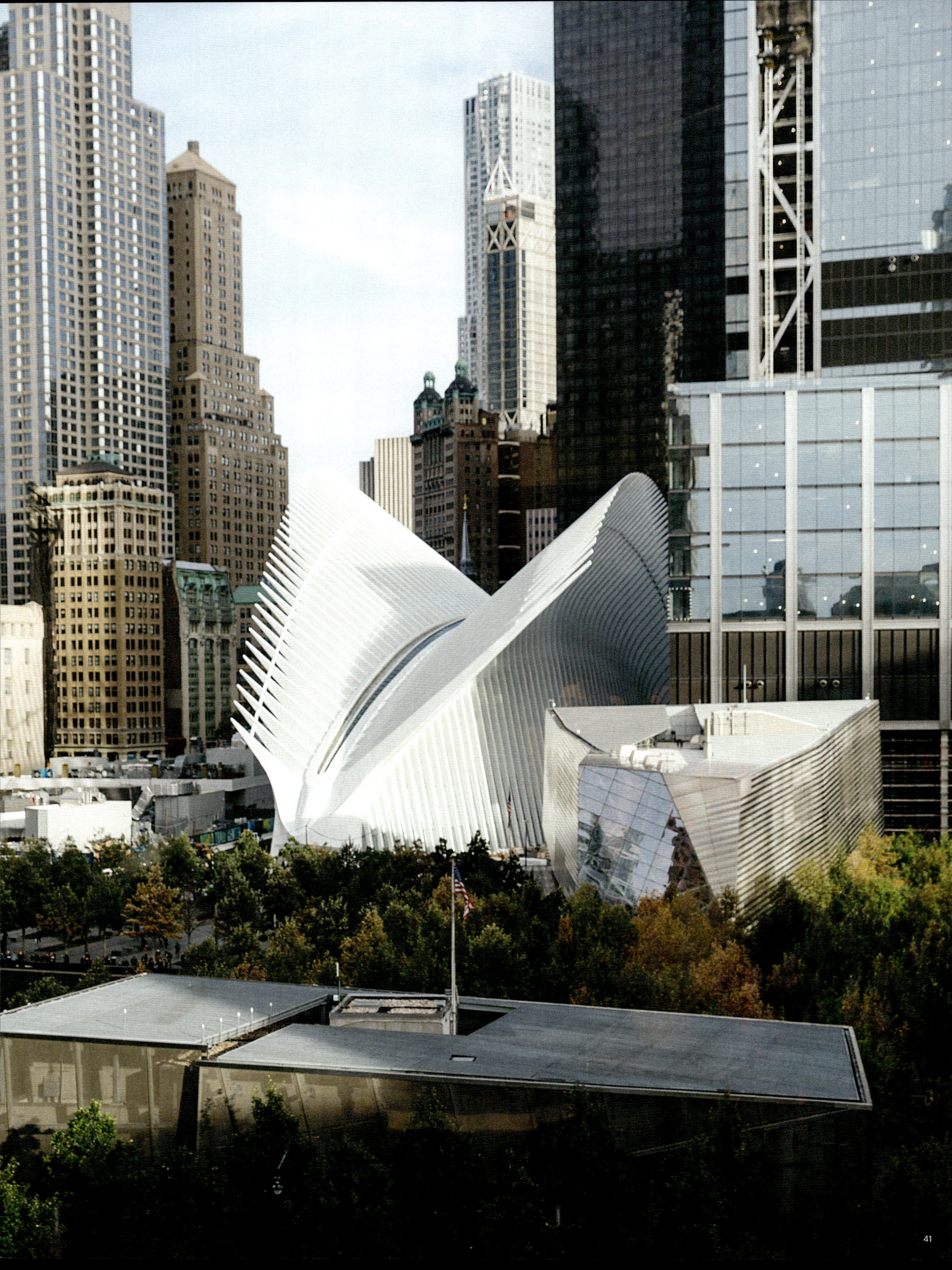

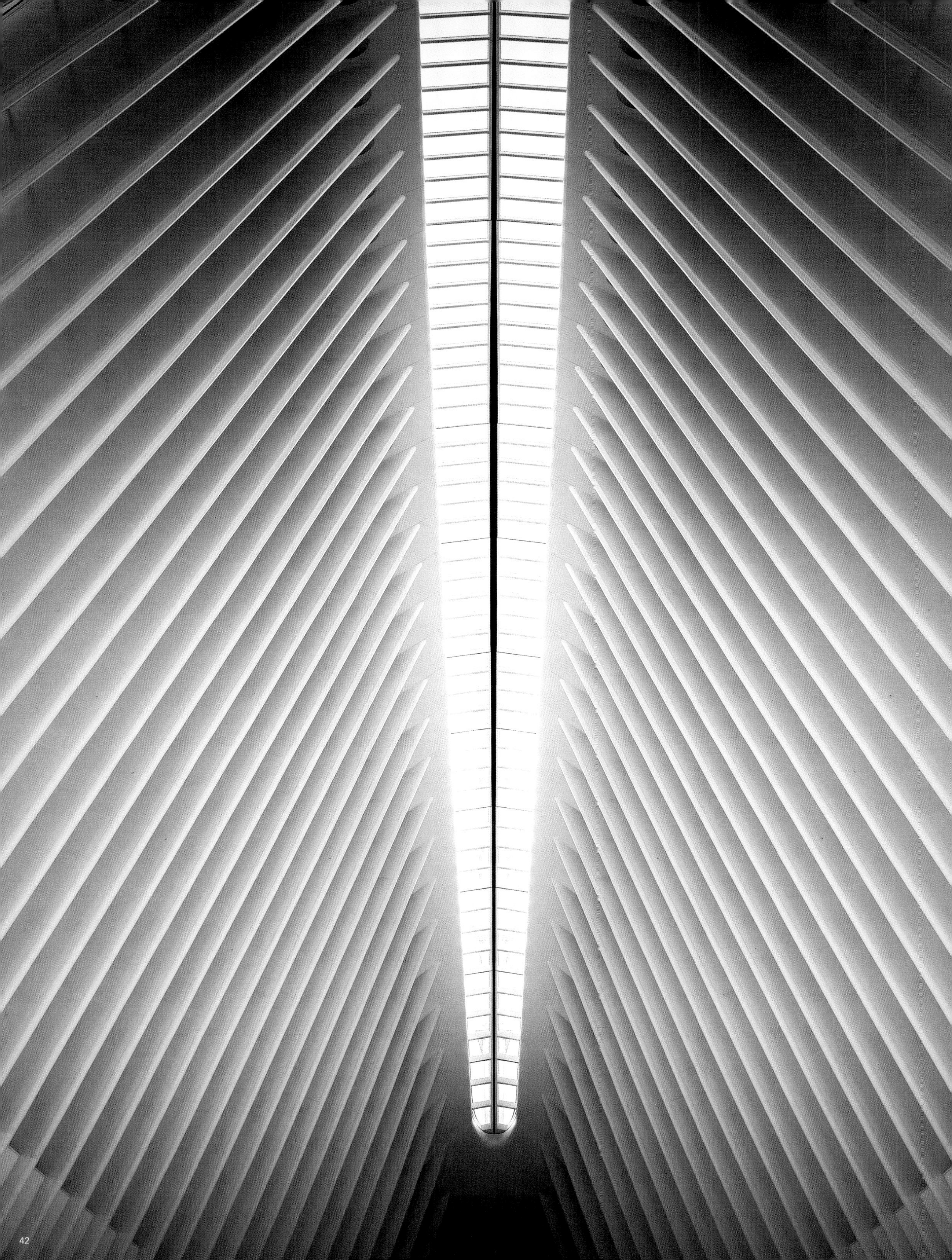

The Oculus
World Trade Center, Manhattan
Jason Peterson

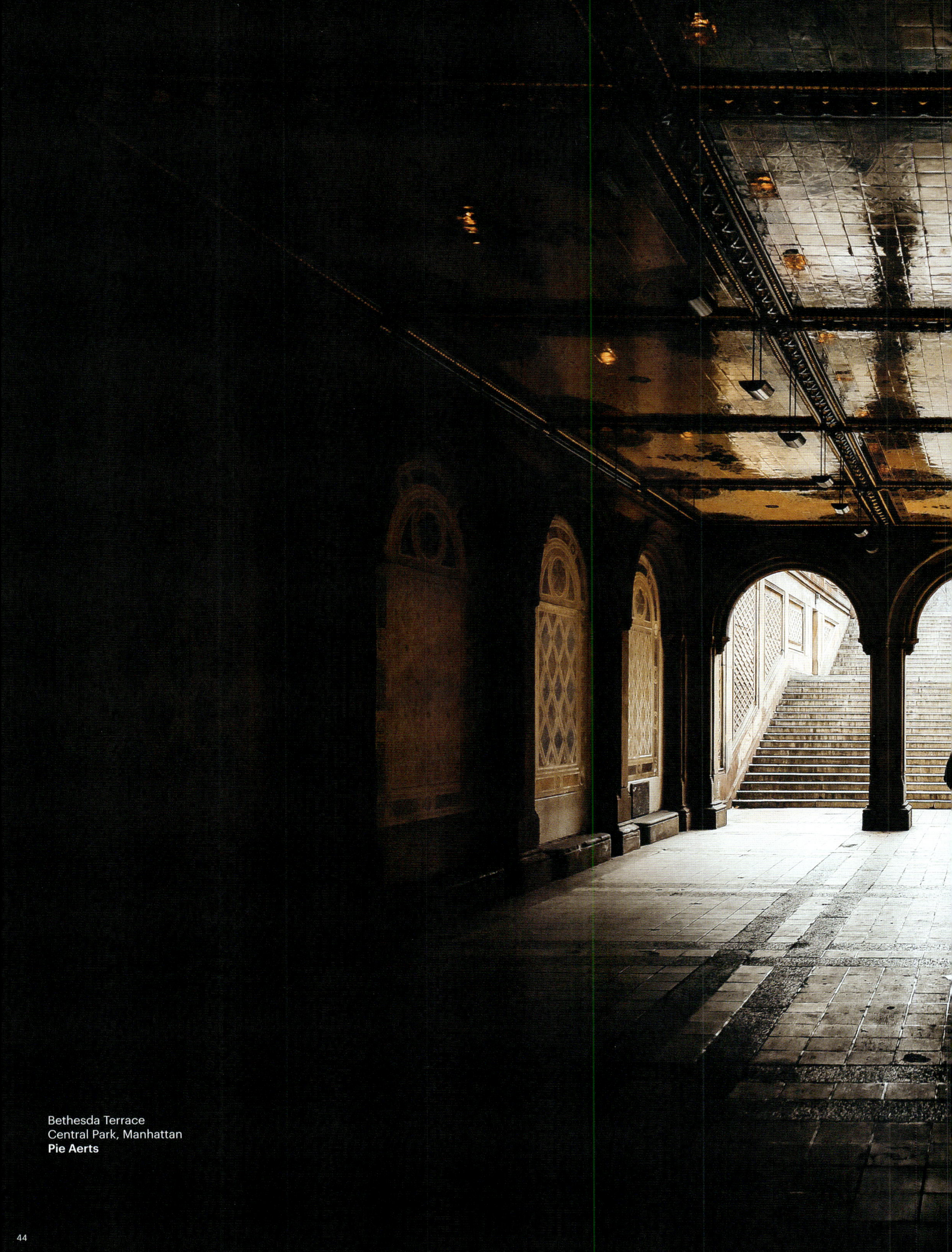

Bethesda Terrace
Central Park, Manhattan
Pie Aerts

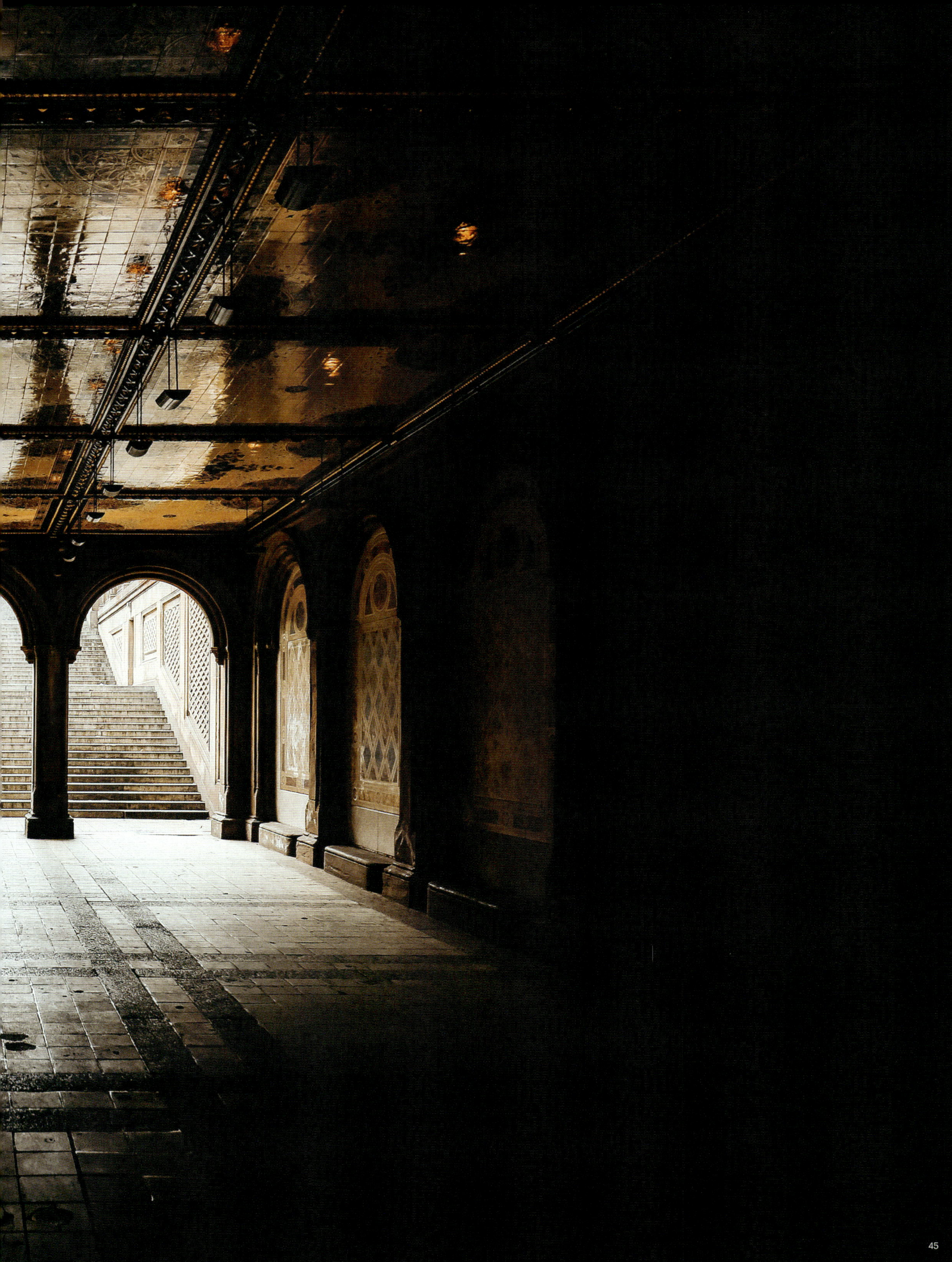

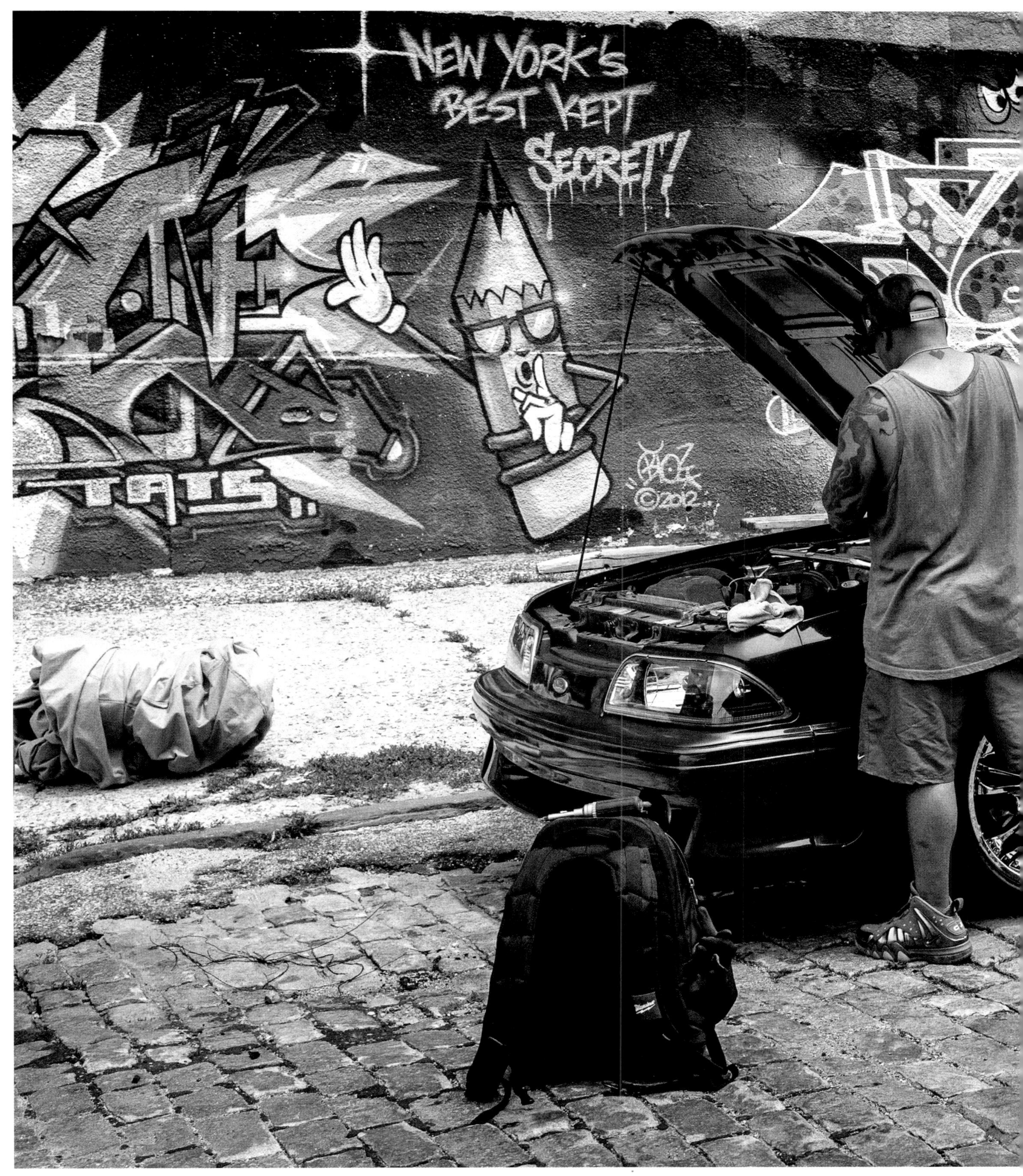

Greenpoint, Brooklyn
Bram van Woudenberg

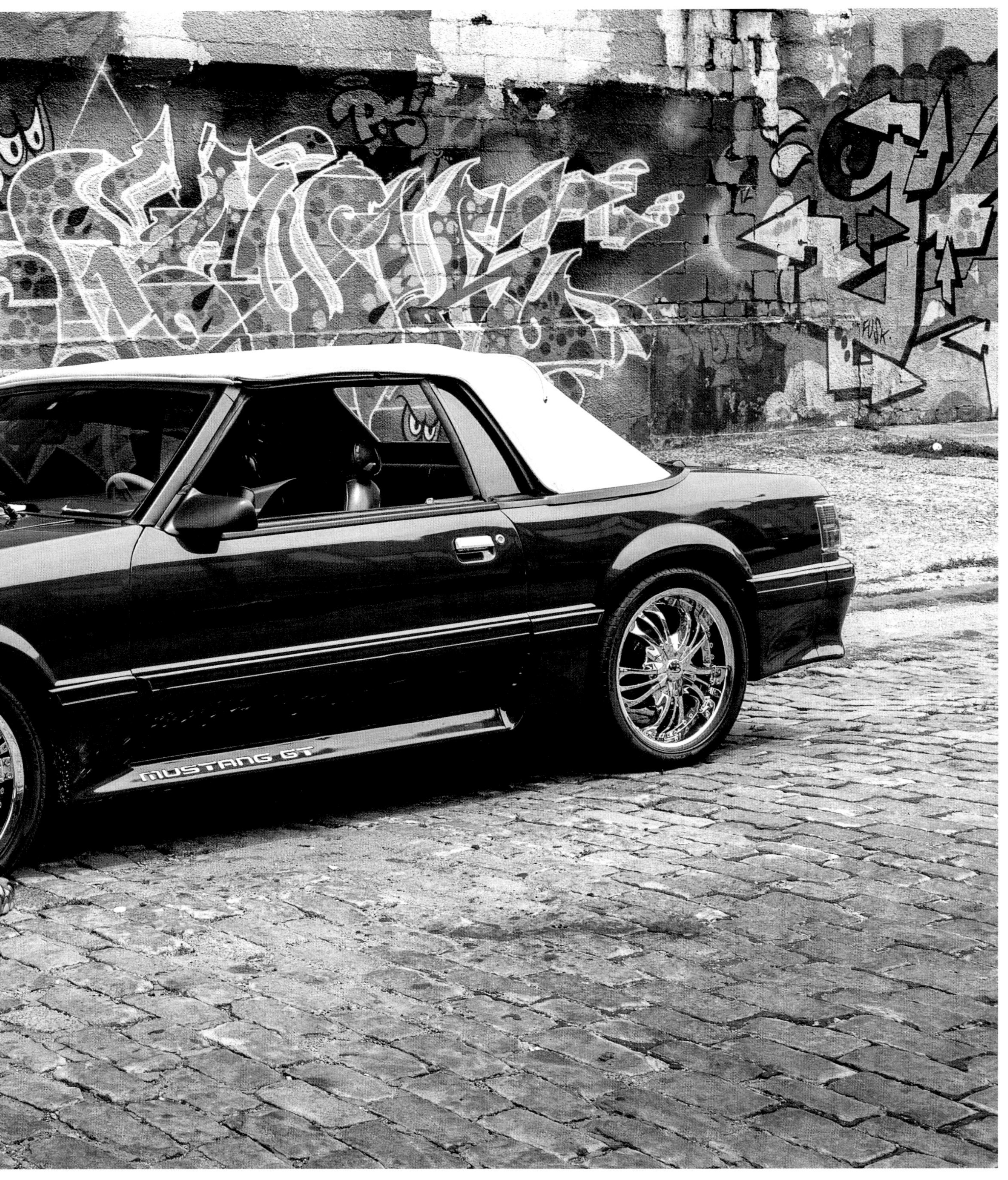
MUSTANG GT

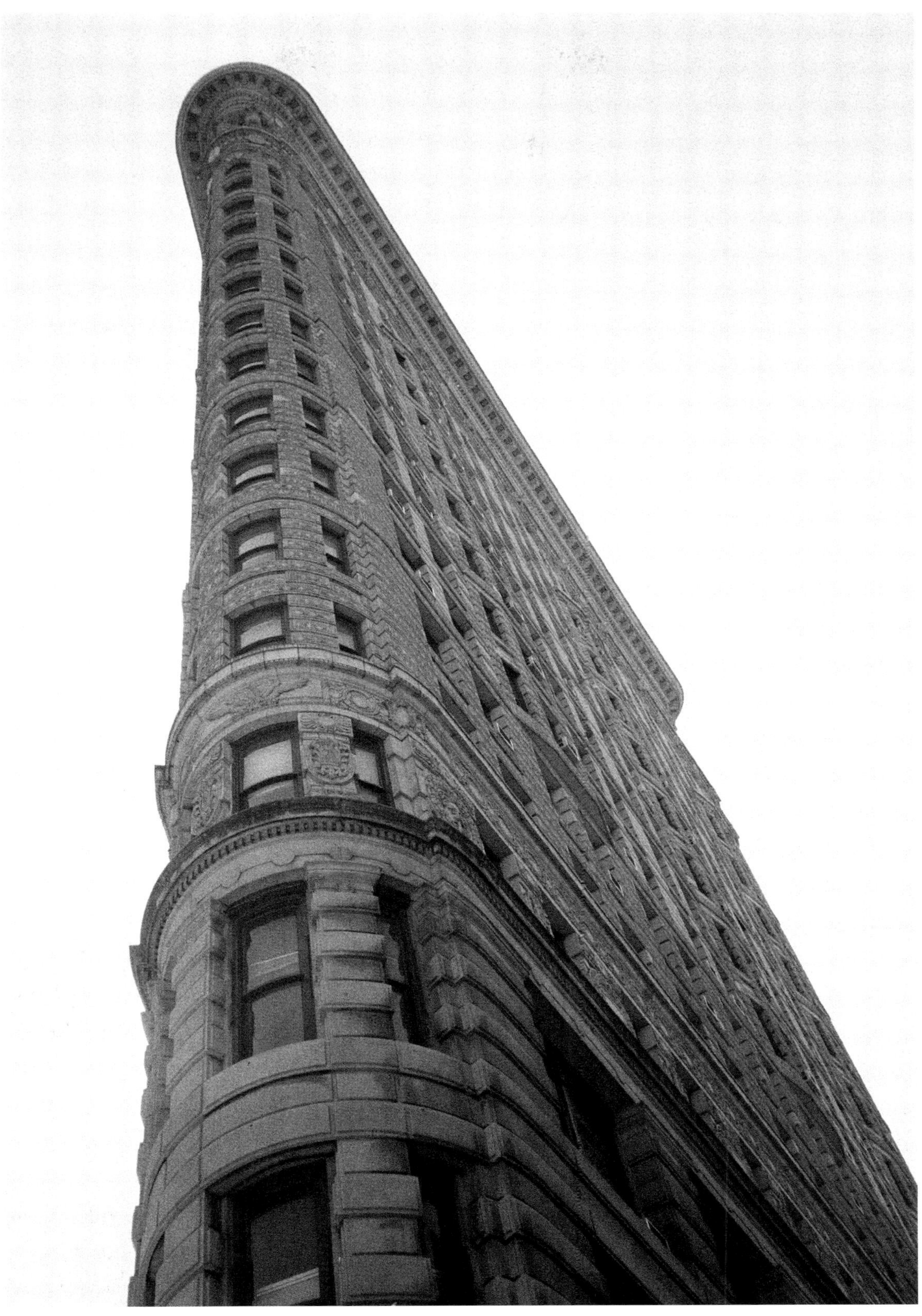

The Flatiron Building
Flatiron District, Manhattan
Emile Almekinders

Manhattan
Emile Almekinders –

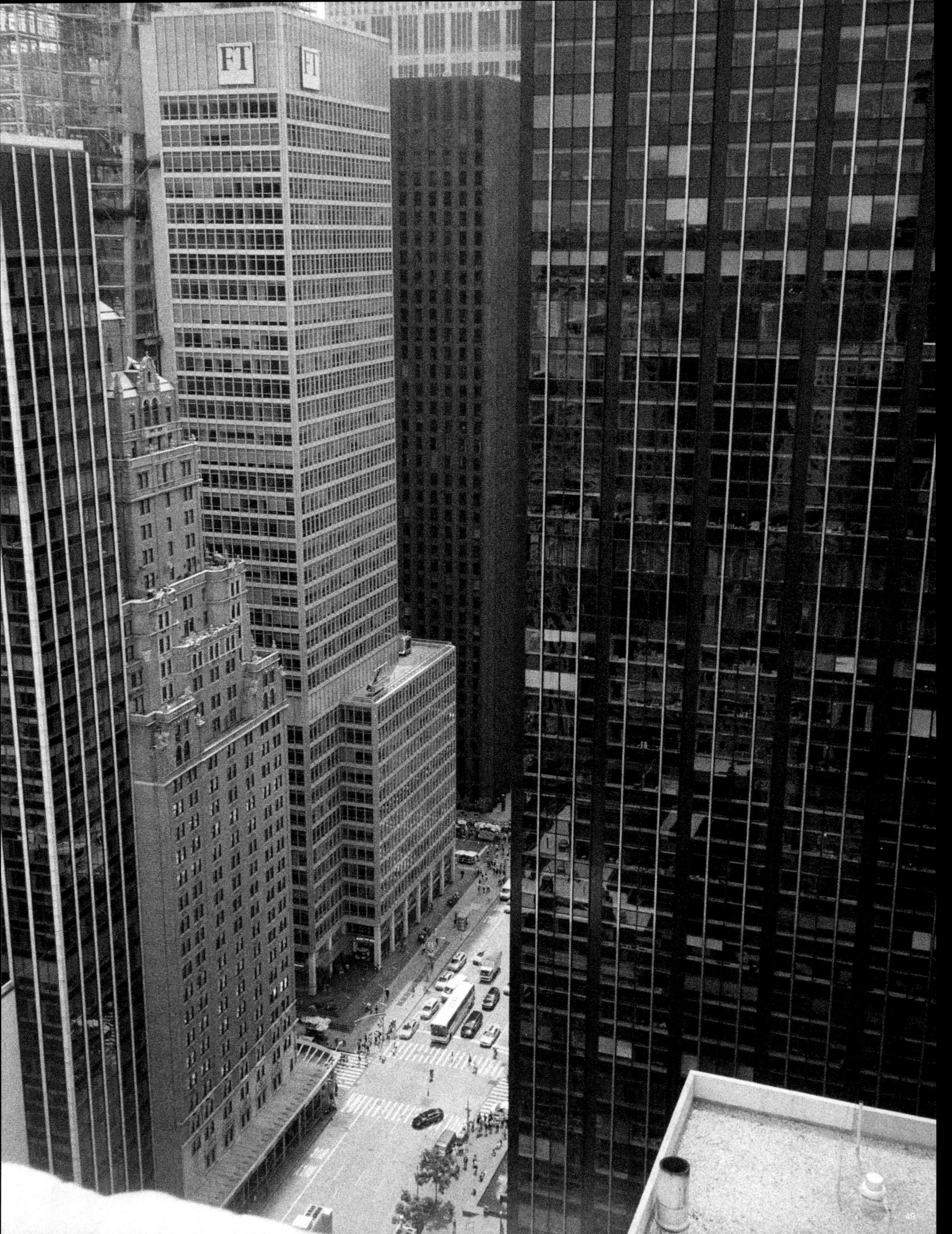
FT
FT

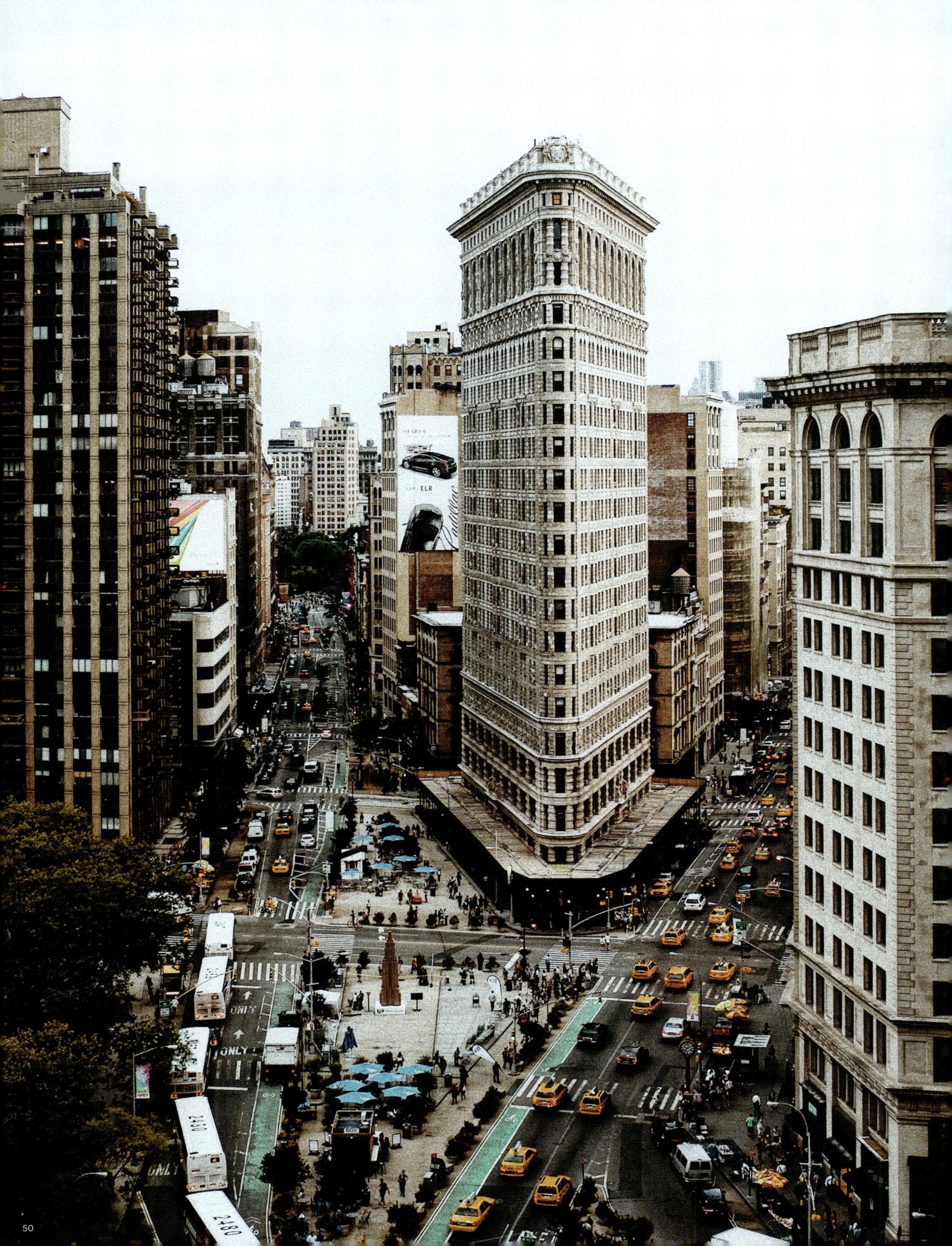
ONLY
ONLY
2430
2480

My love for the city comes from always being able to find something new.

—Wil Suárez

The Flatiron Building
Flatiron District, Manhattan
Nazly Kasim

Theater District, Manhattan
Jennifer Bin

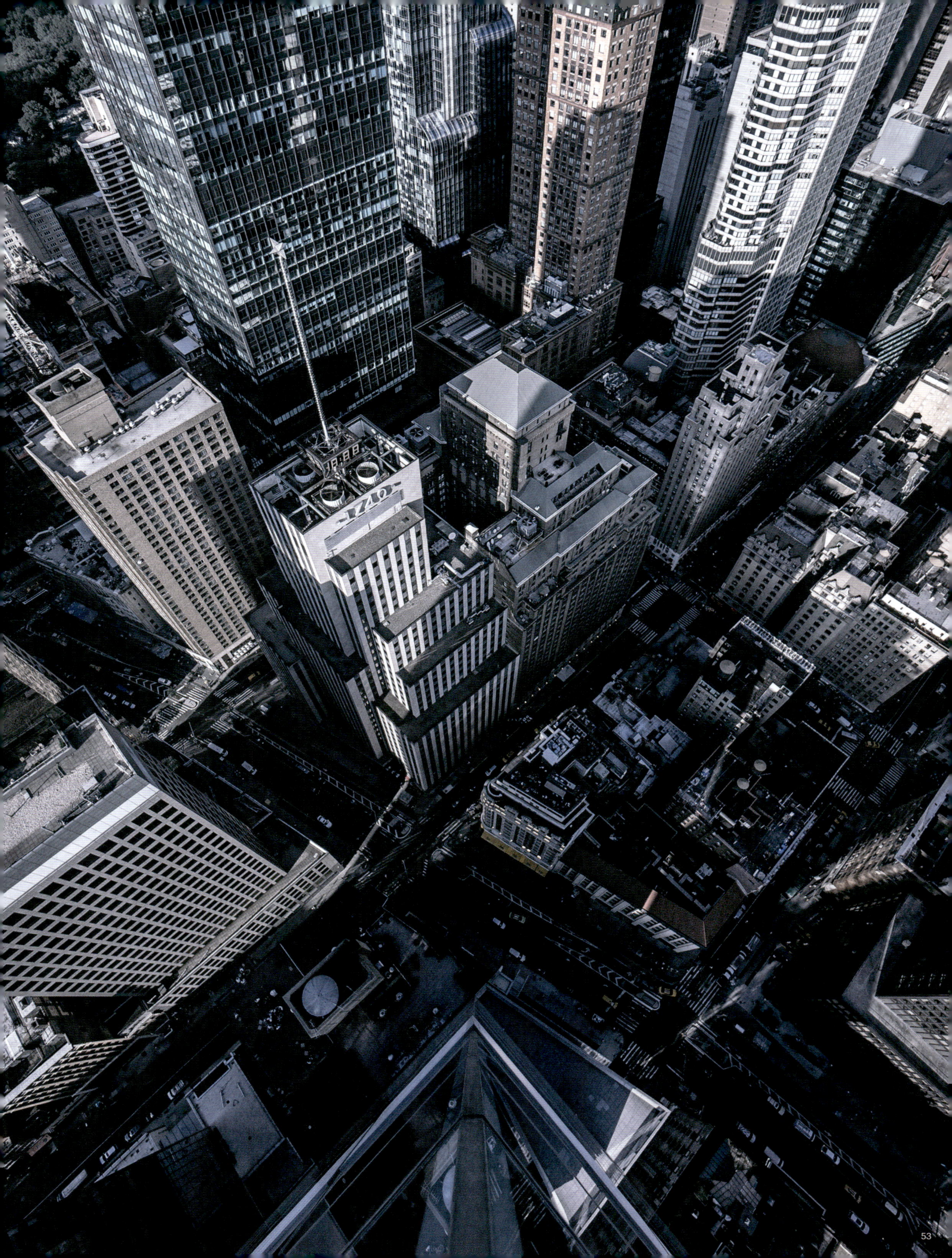

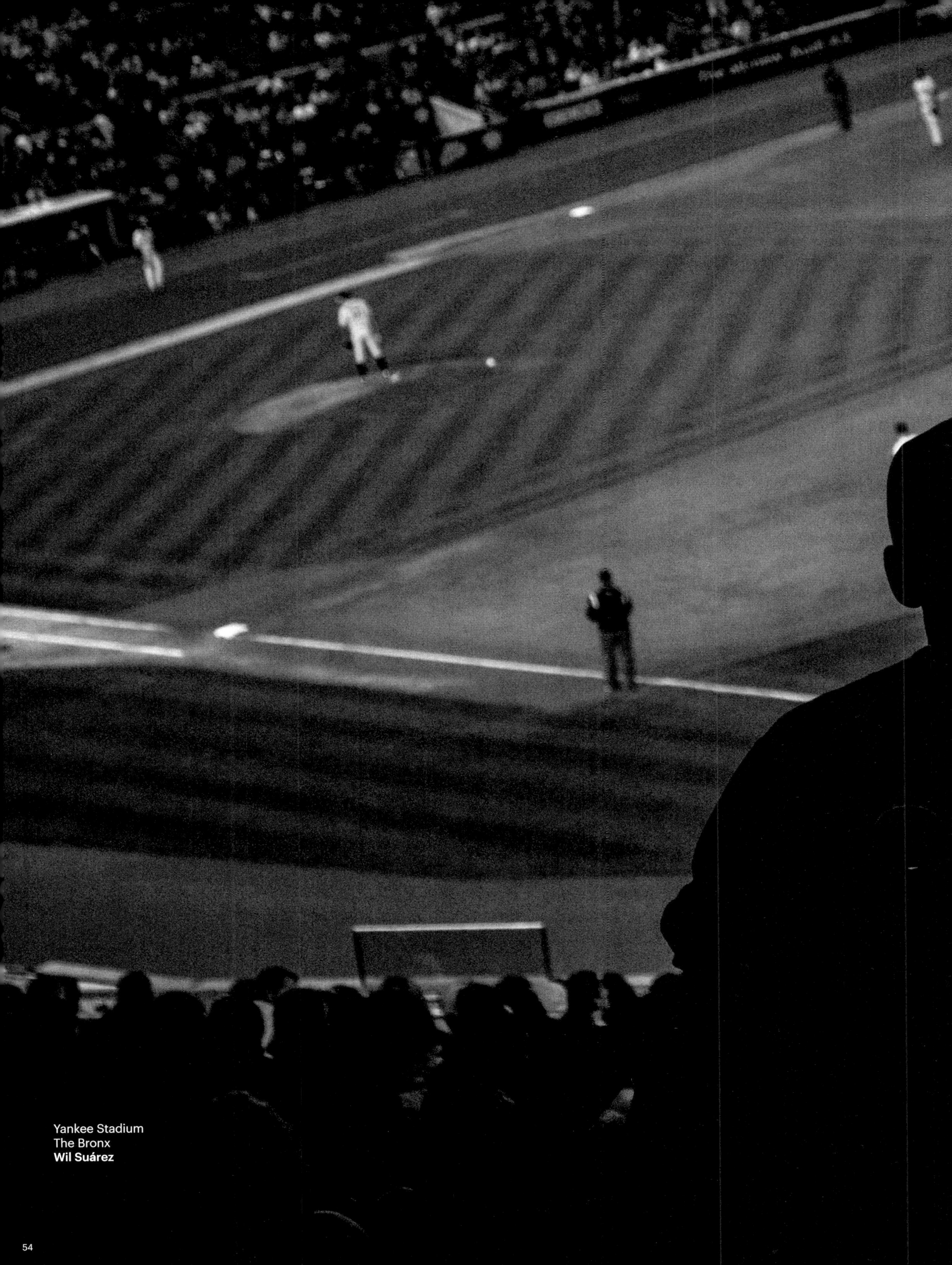

Yankee Stadium
The Bronx
Wil Suárez

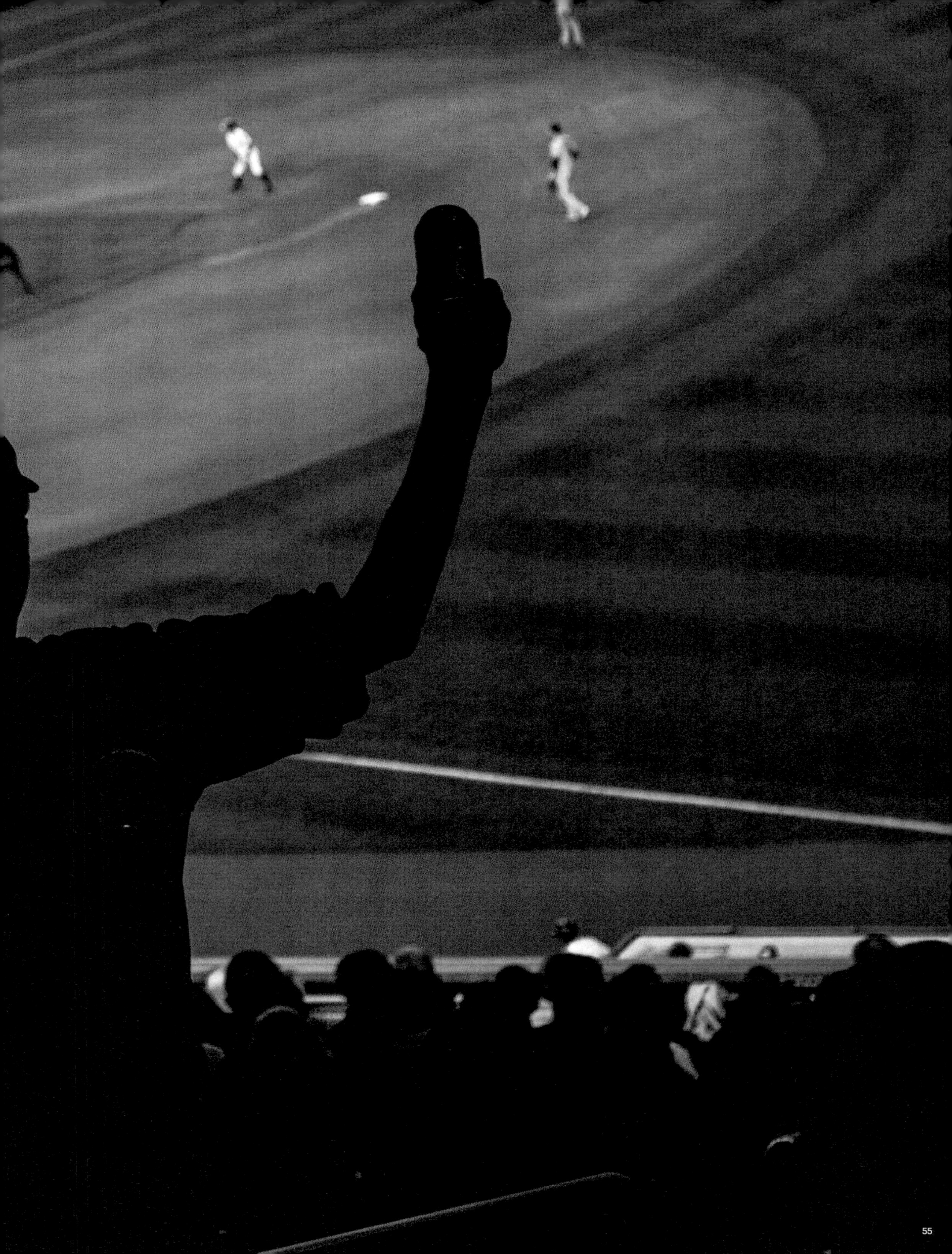

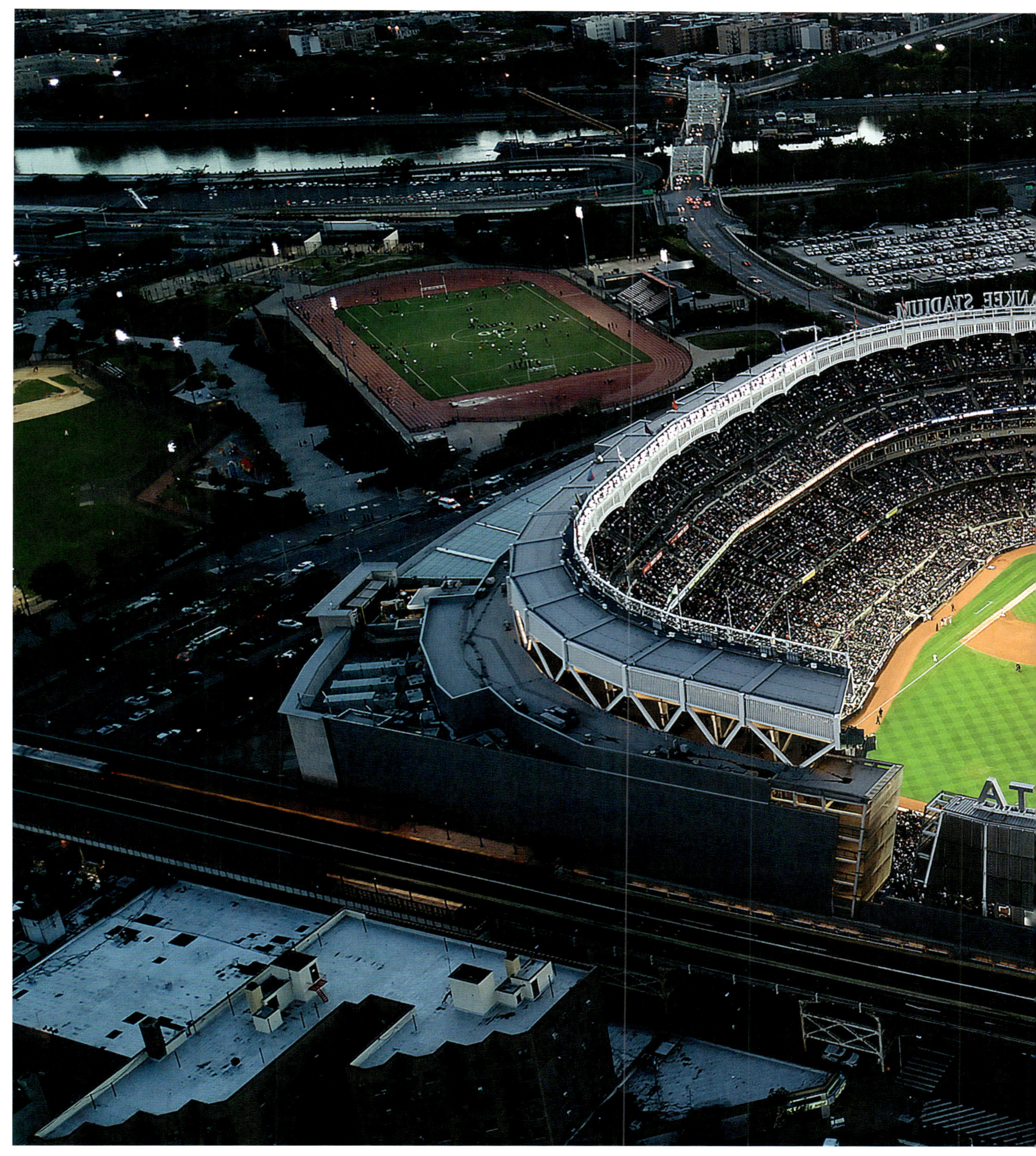

Yankee Stadium
The Bronx
Alex Rivera

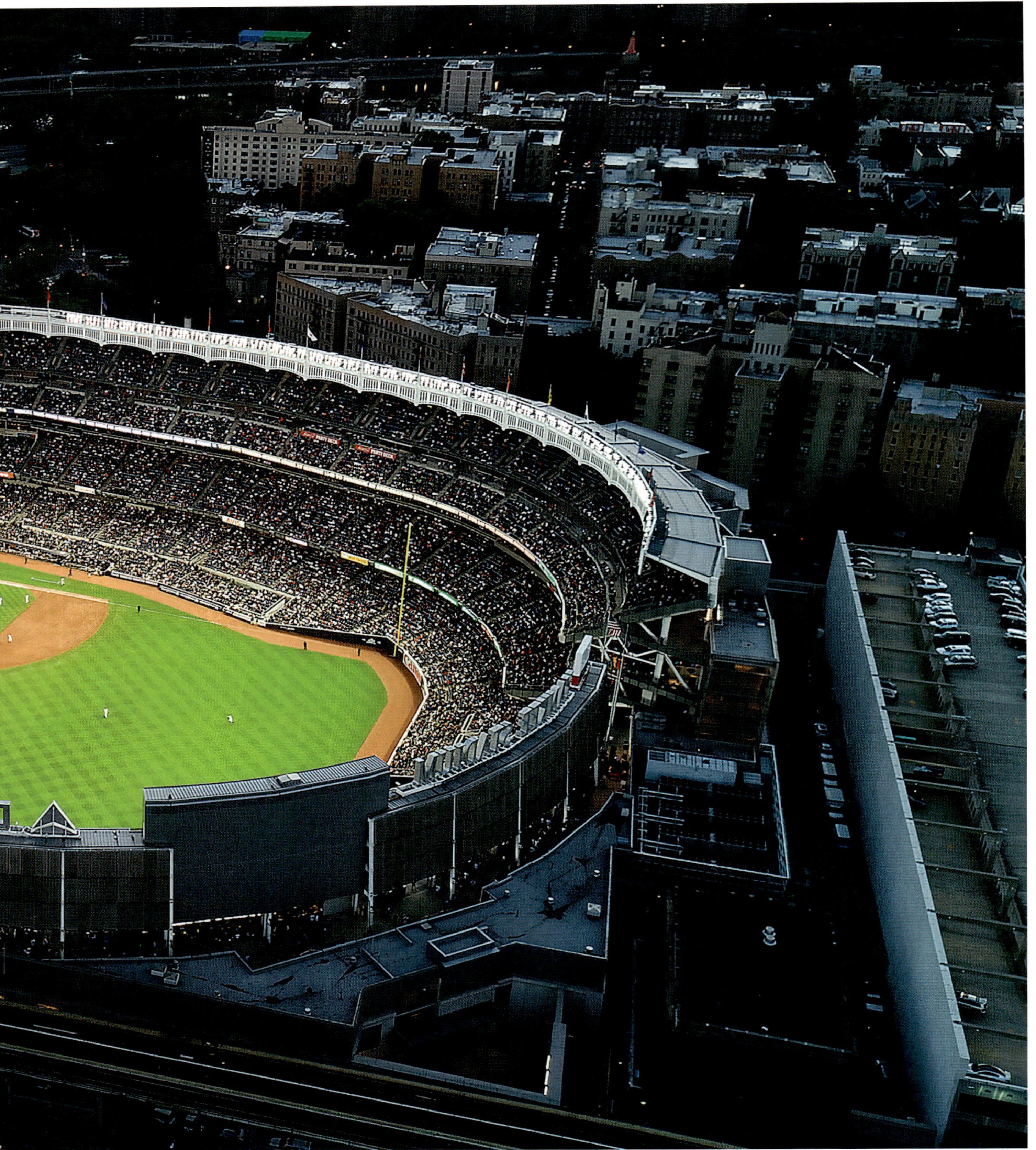

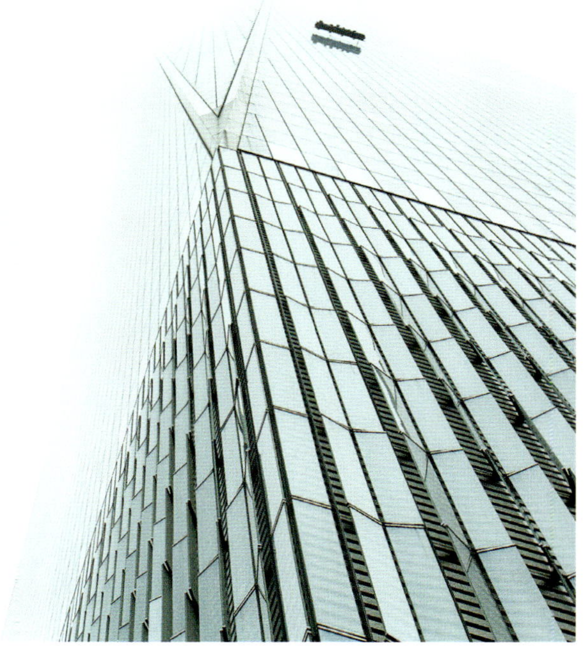

Financial District, Manhattan
Bram van Woudenberg

The Fulton Center
Financial District, Manhattan
Bram van Woudenberg —

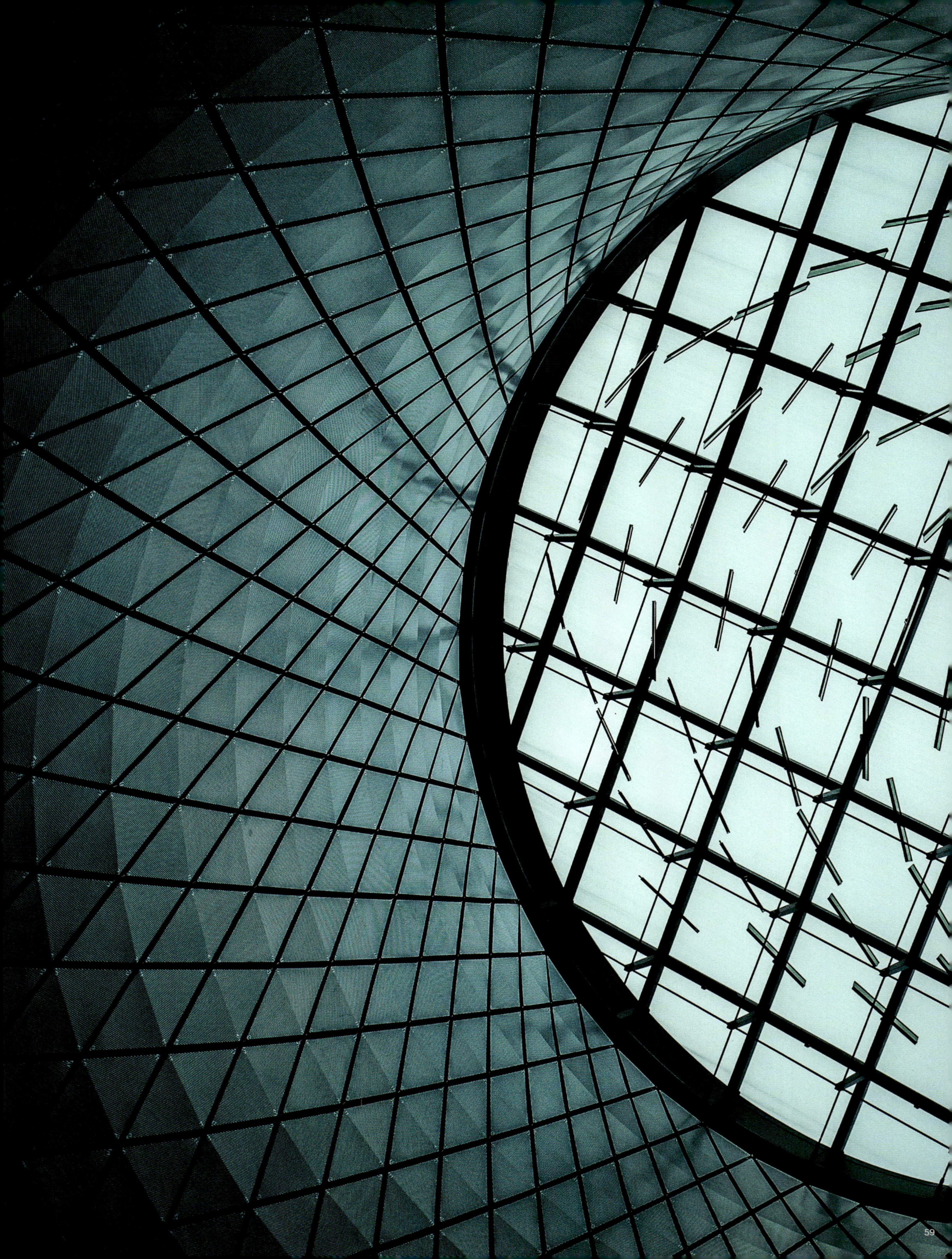

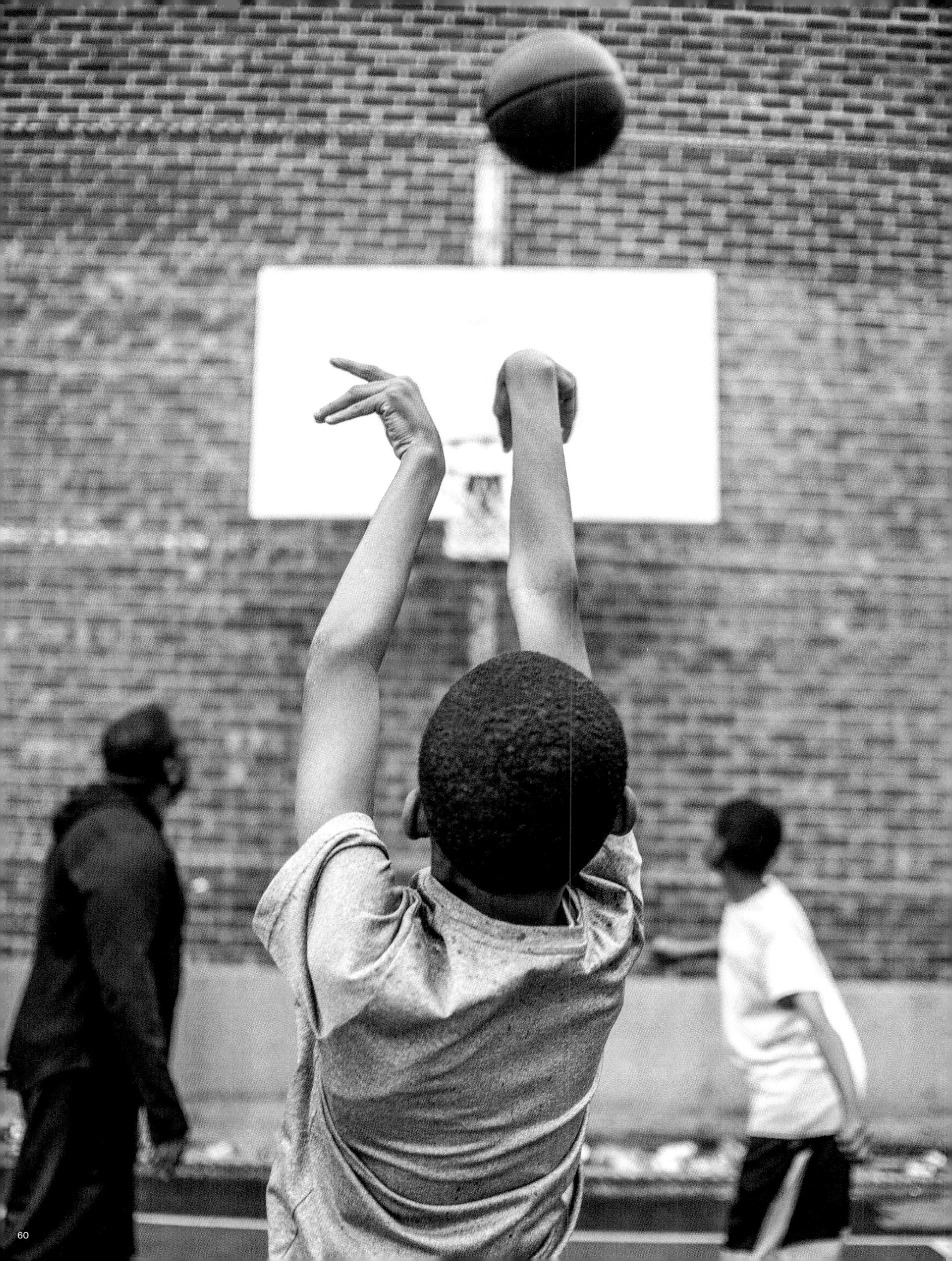

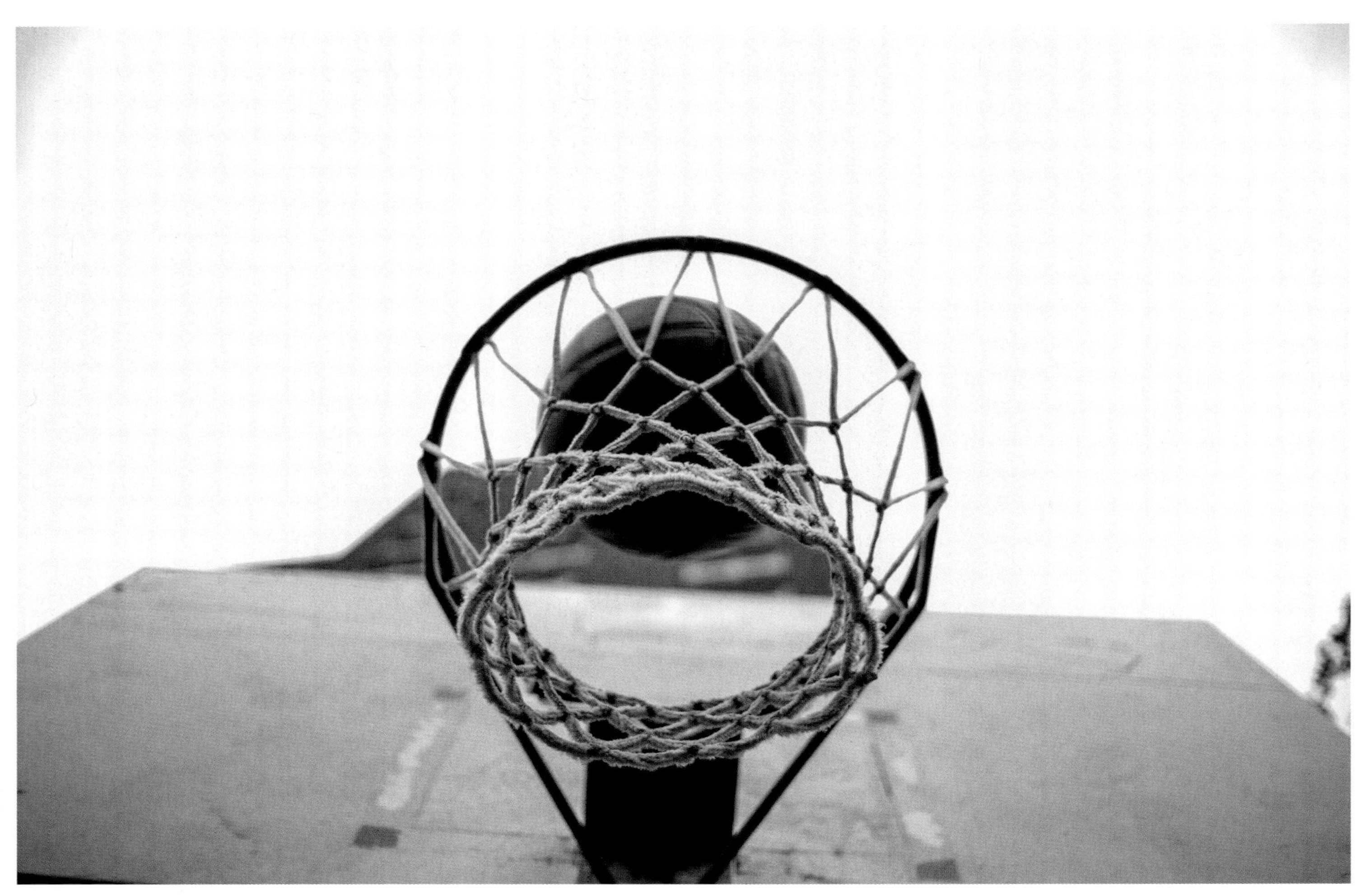

Public School 187 Basketball Court
Fort George, Manhattan
Wil Suárez

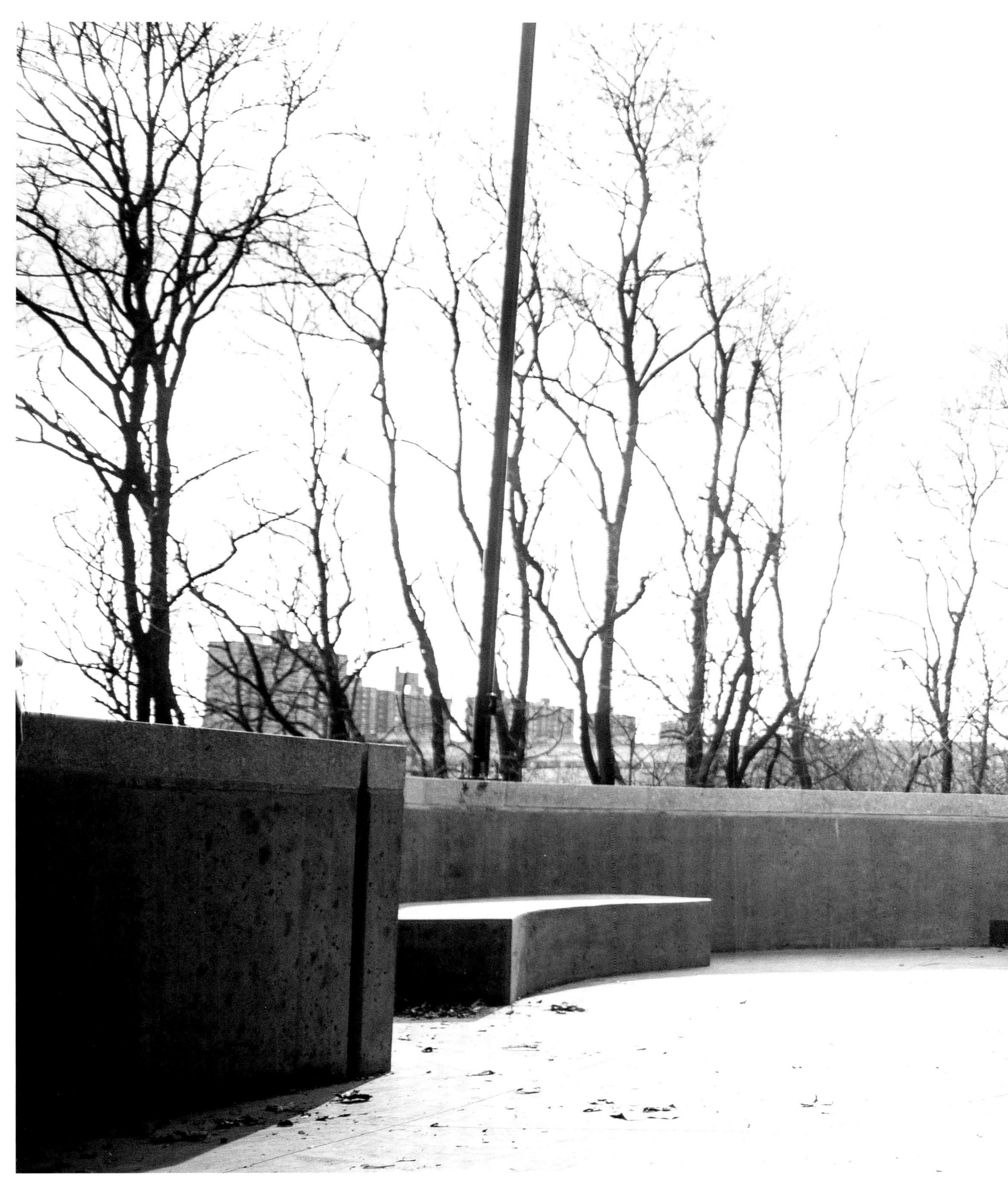

Hamilton Bridge Skatepark
Washington Heights, Manhattan
Wil Suárez

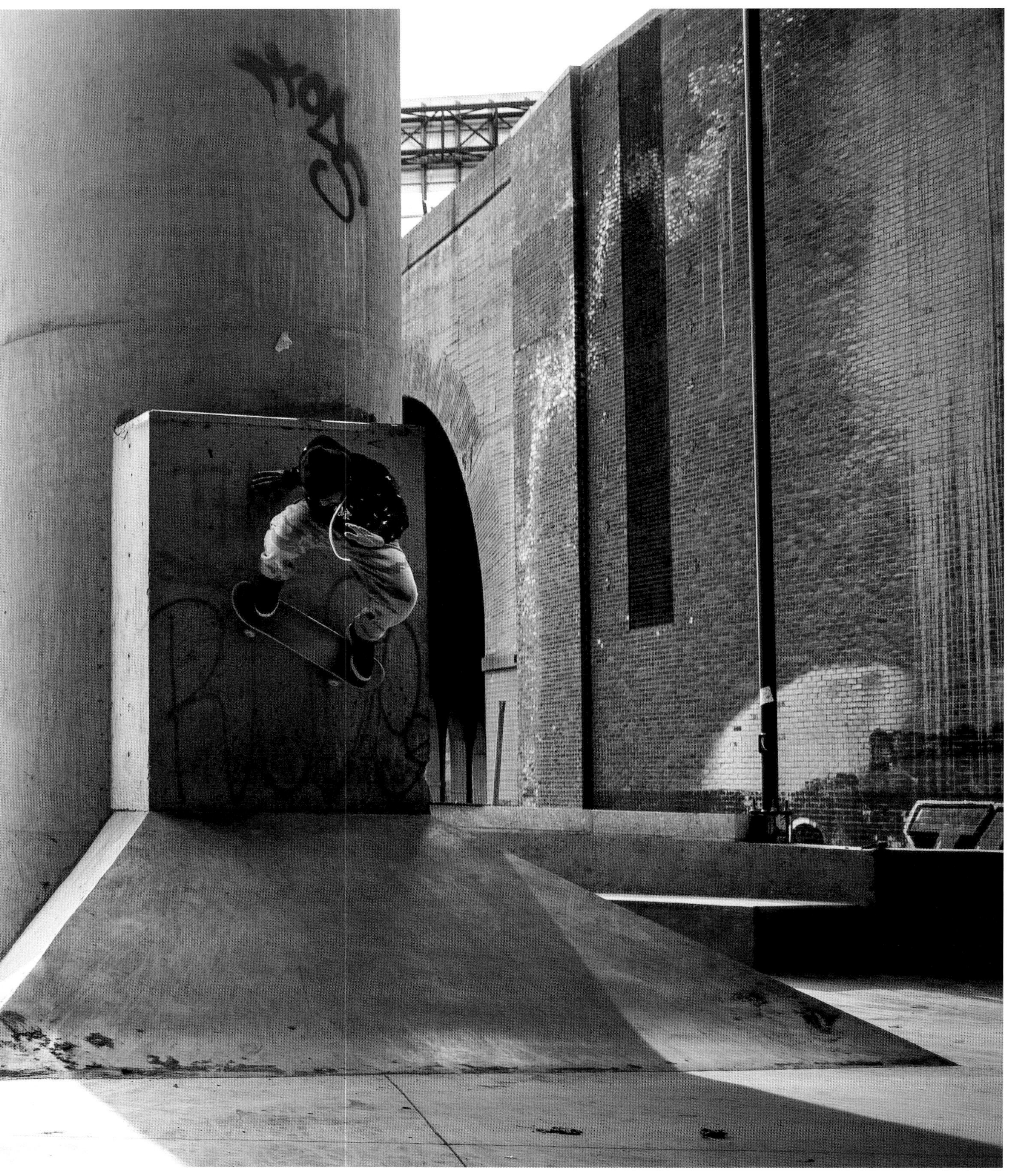

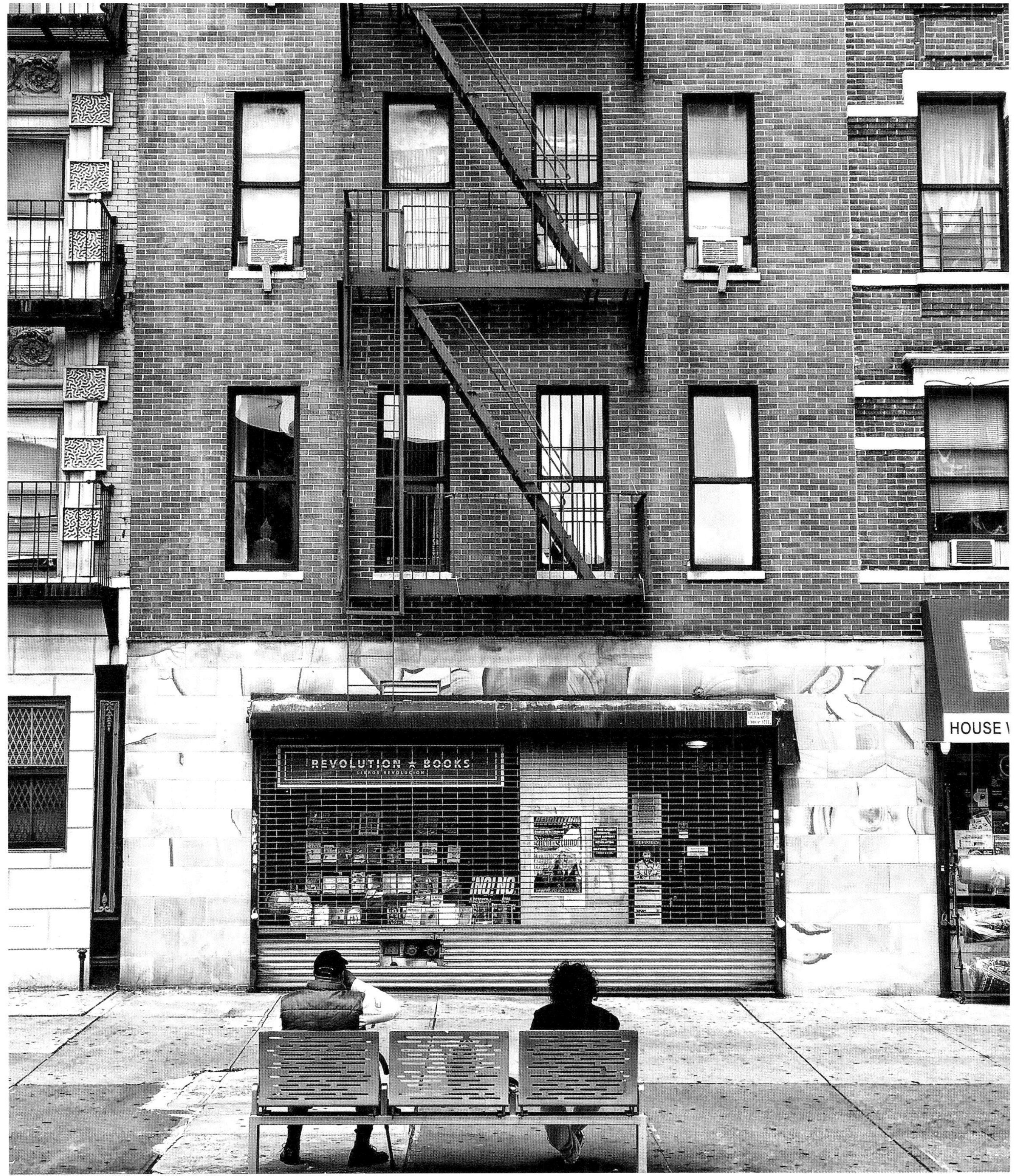

Revolution Books
Harlem, Manhattan
Michael Young

Manhattan
Miklas Manneke -

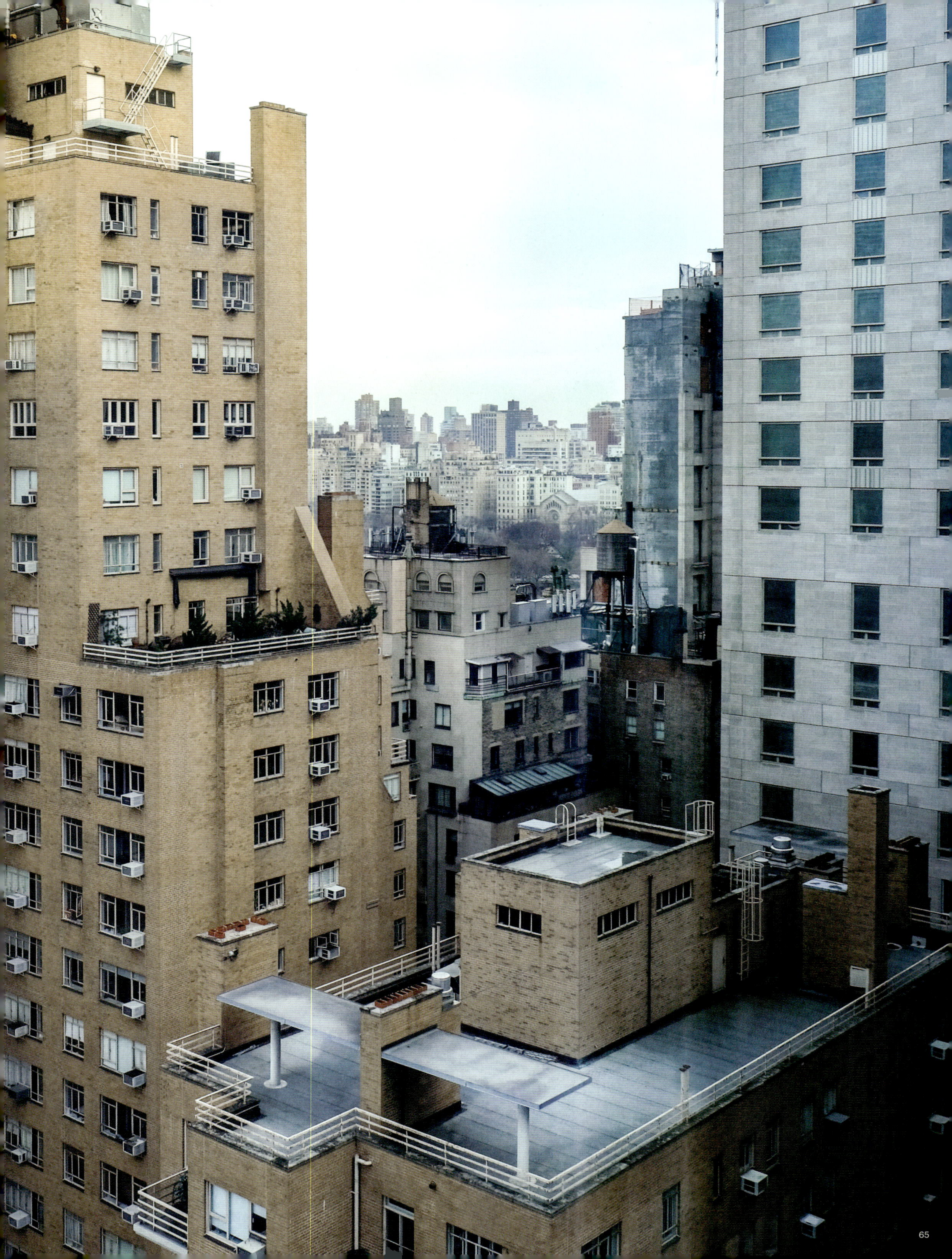

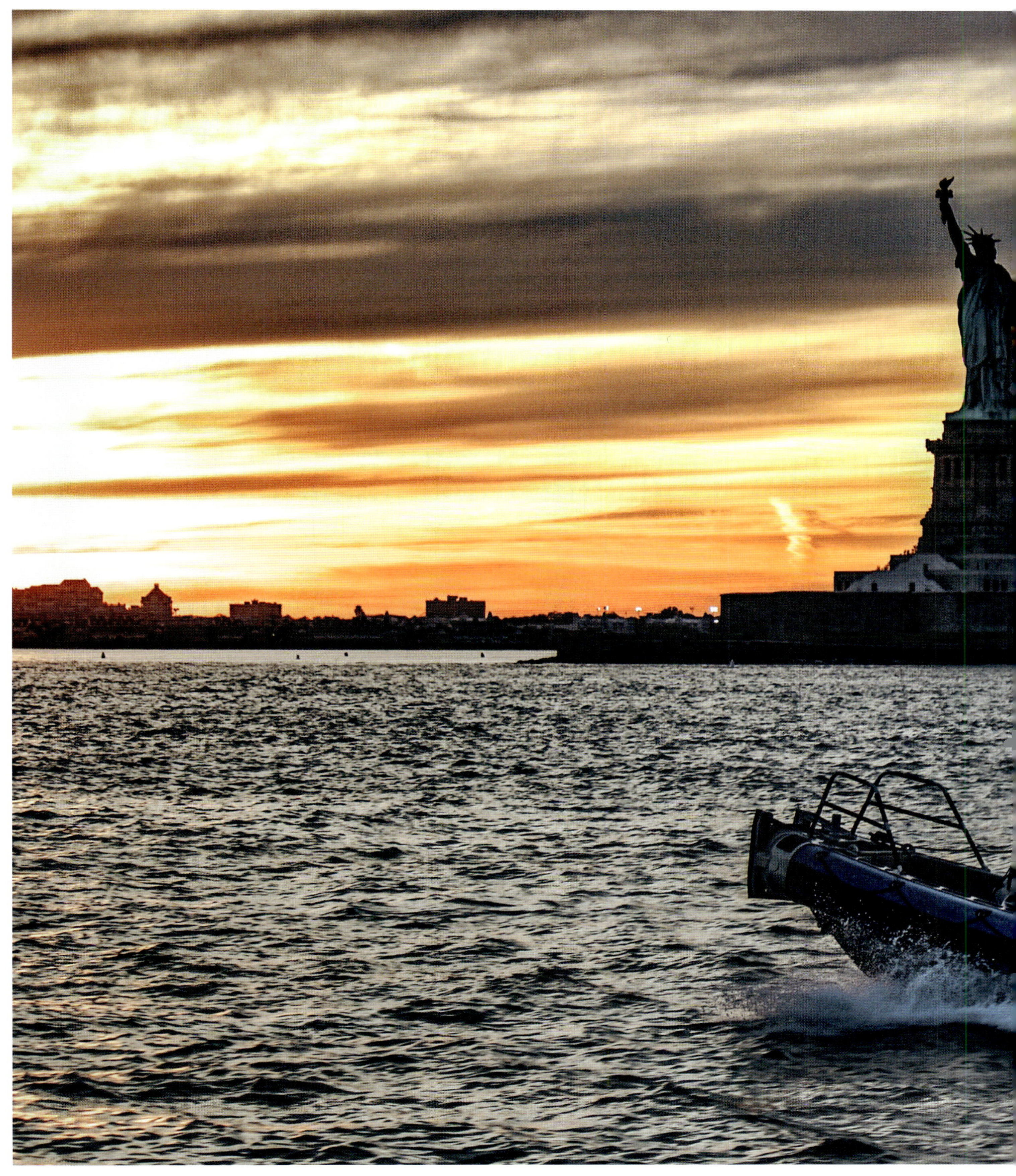

The Statue of Liberty
Liberty Island
Bryan Dumas

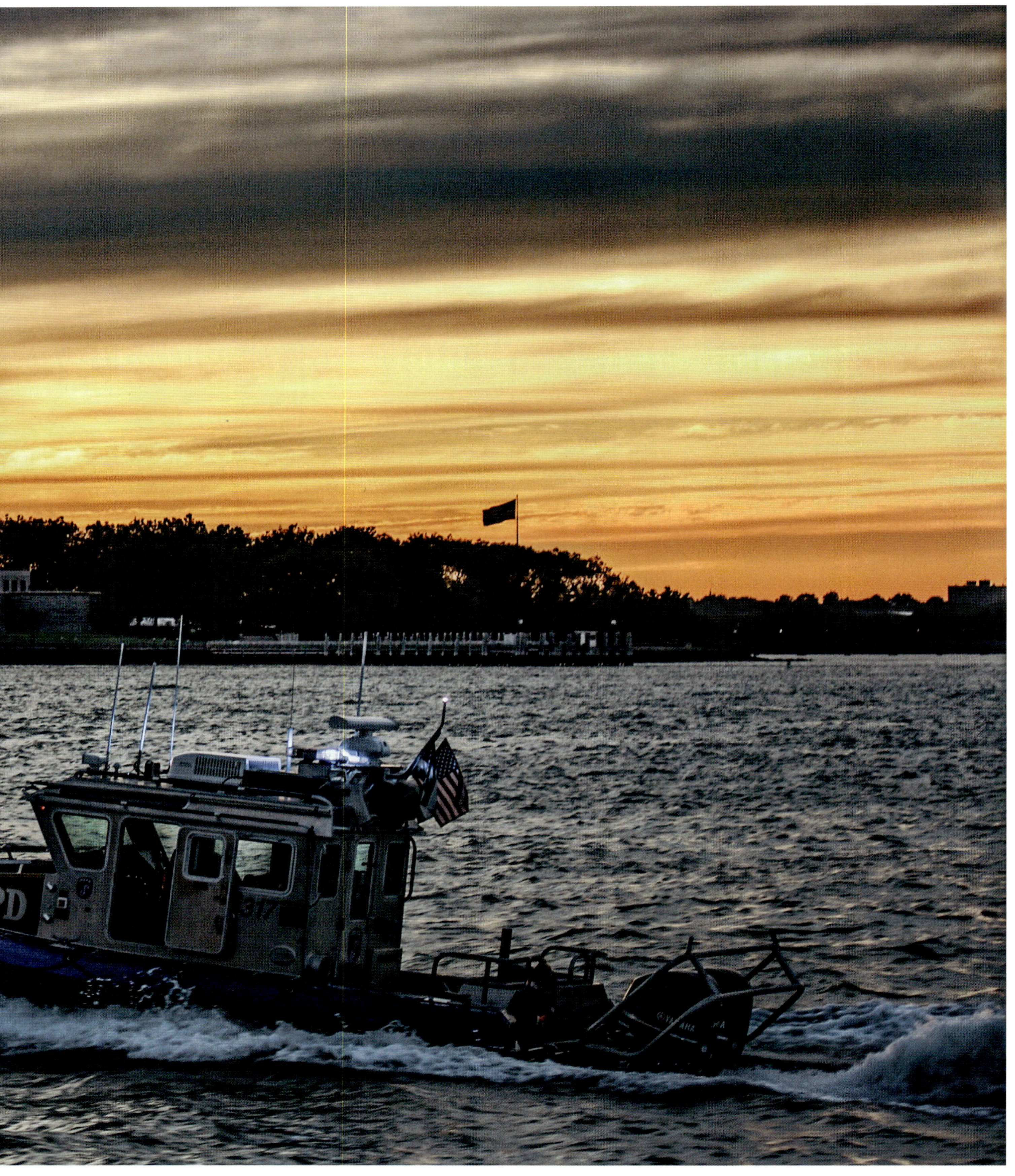

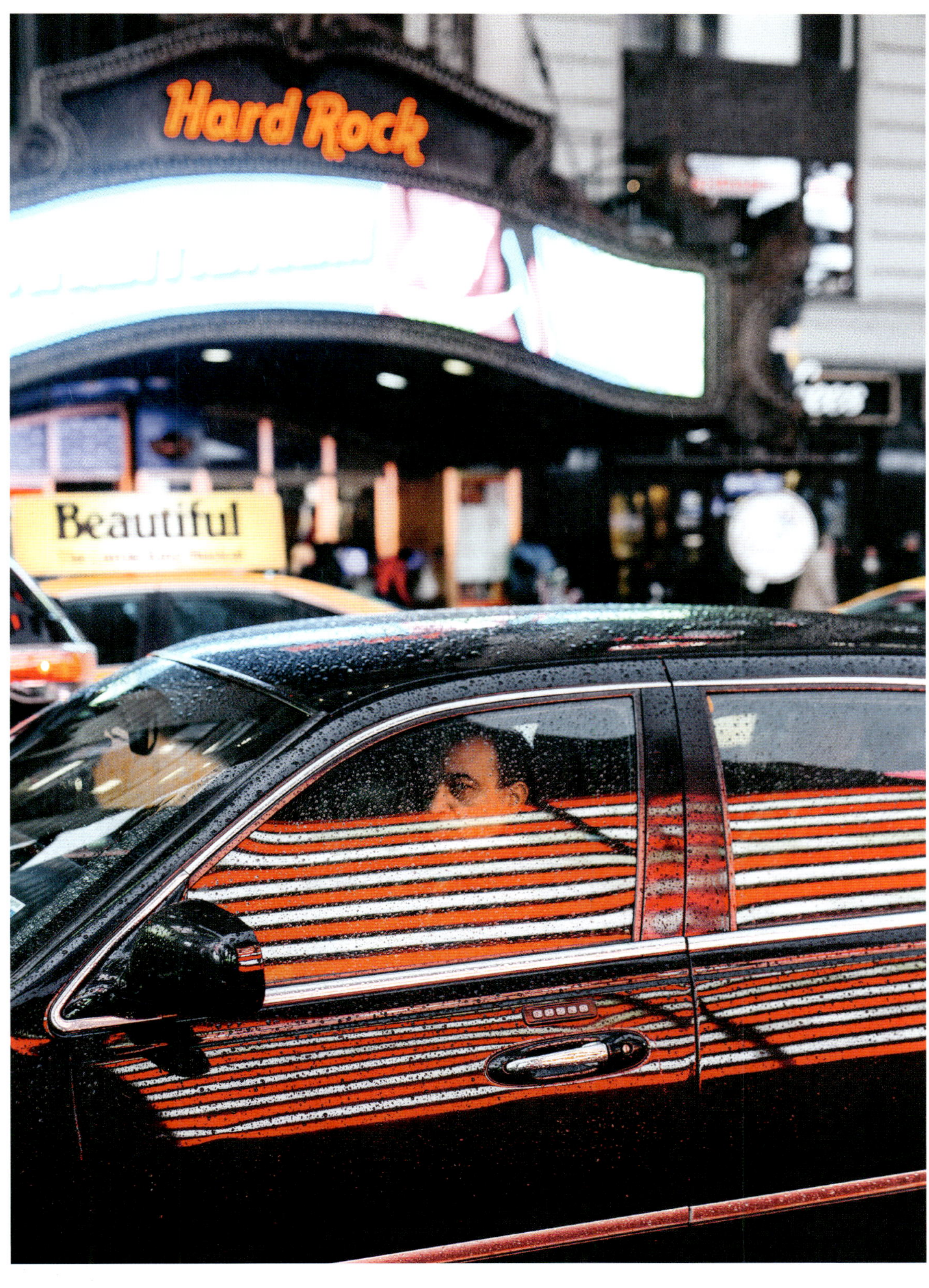

Hard Rock Café
Theater District, Manhattan
Ollie Nordh

Trump Mask
Manhattan
Ollie Nordh –

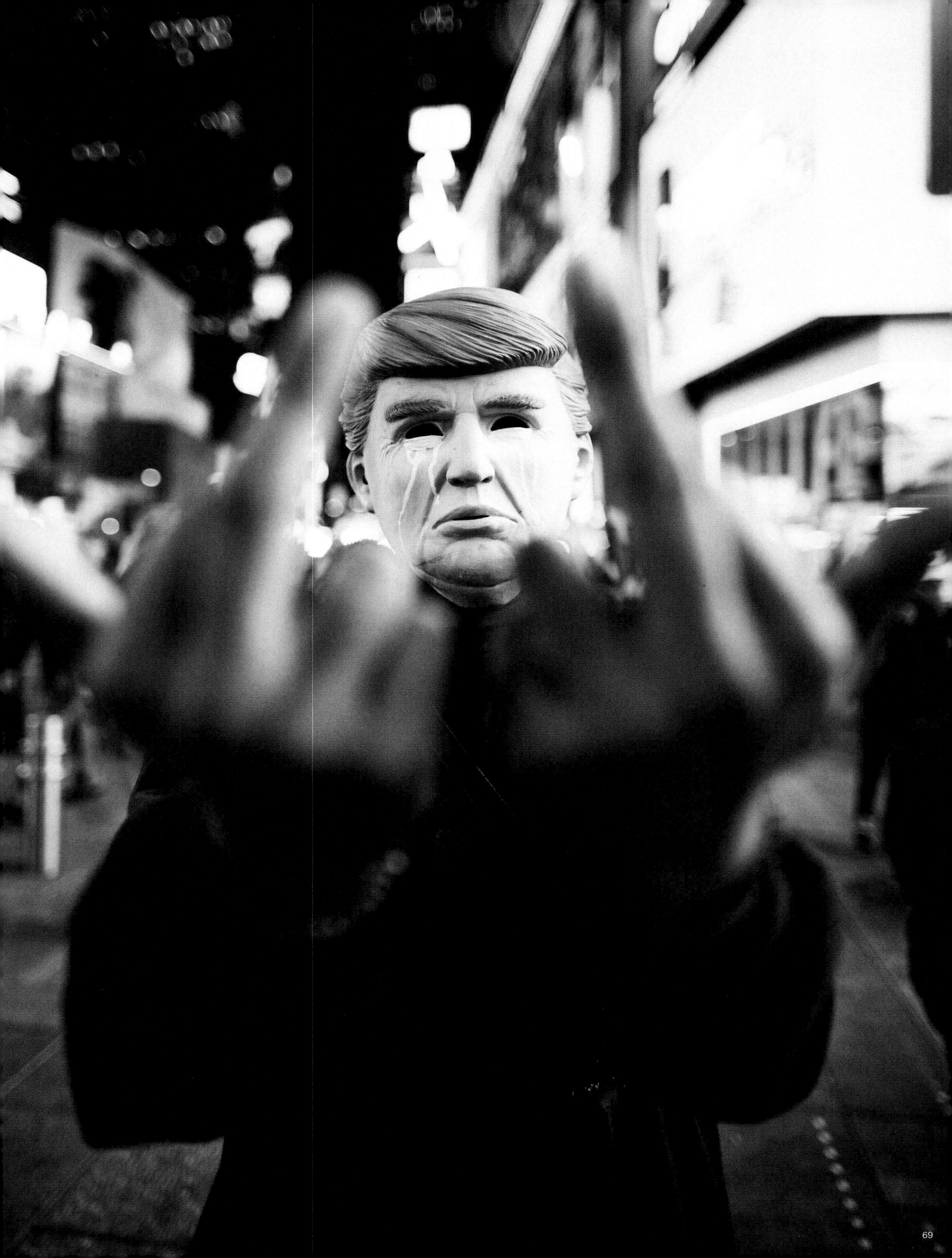

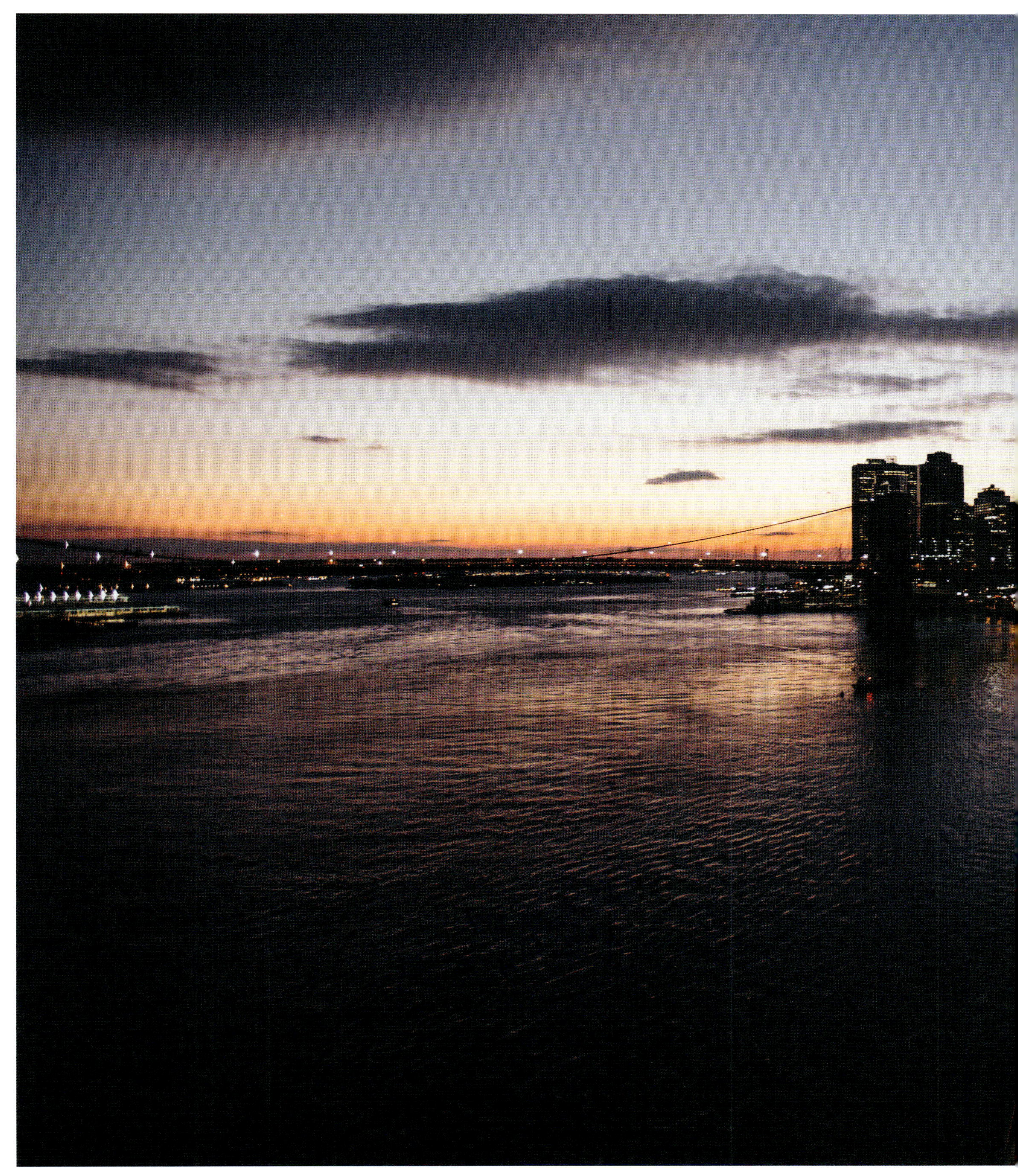

Two Bridges, Manhattan
Pie Aerts

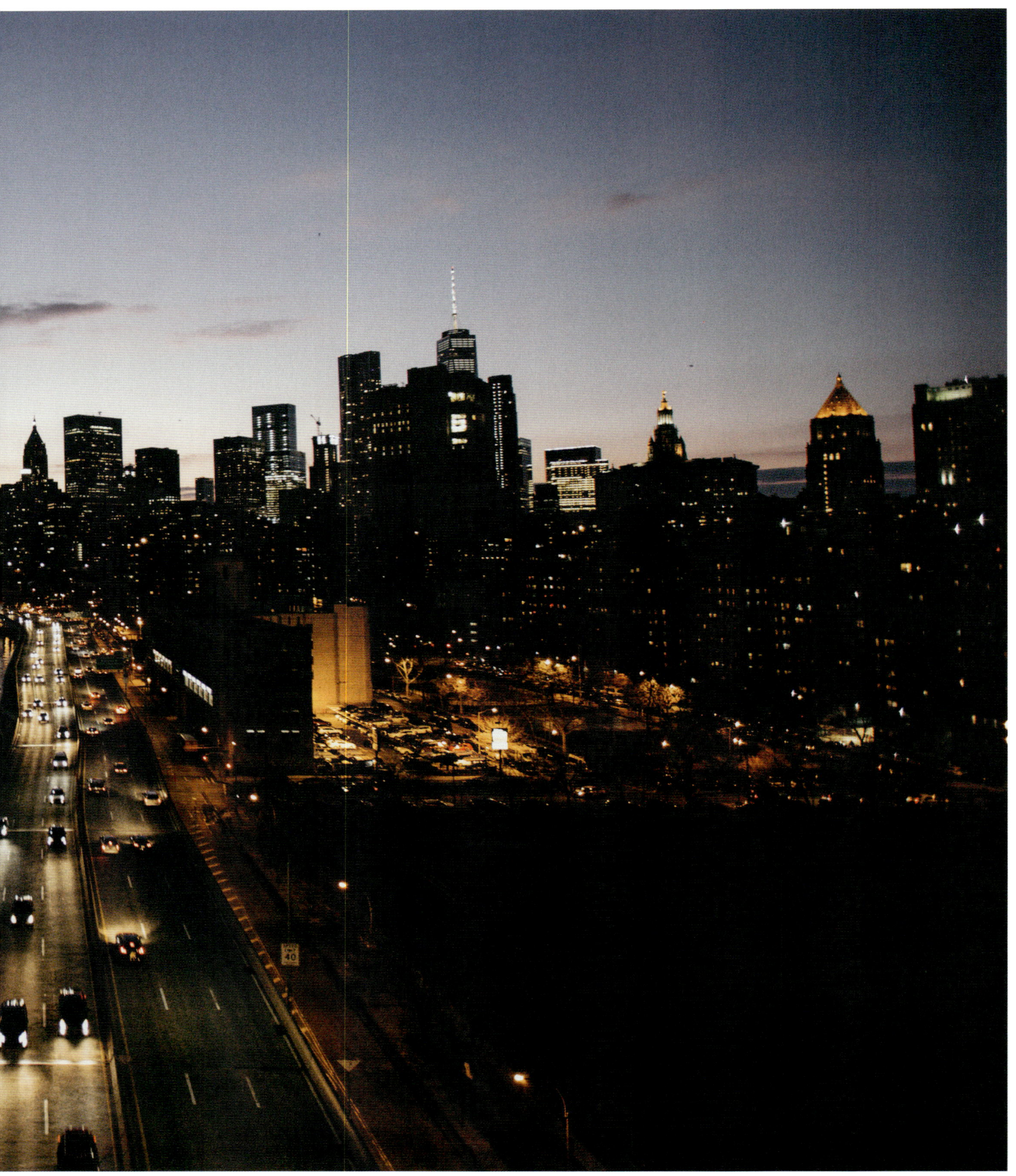

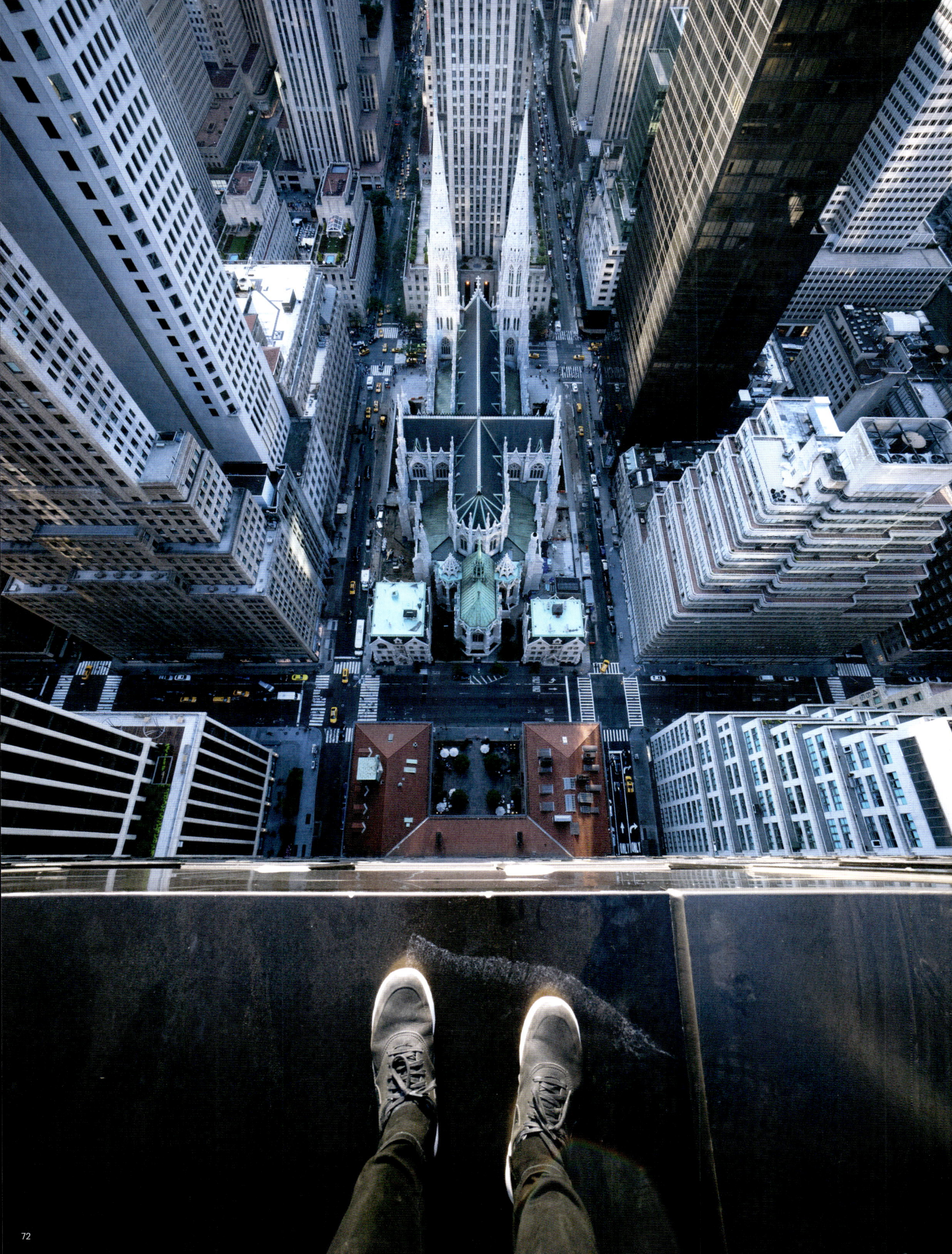

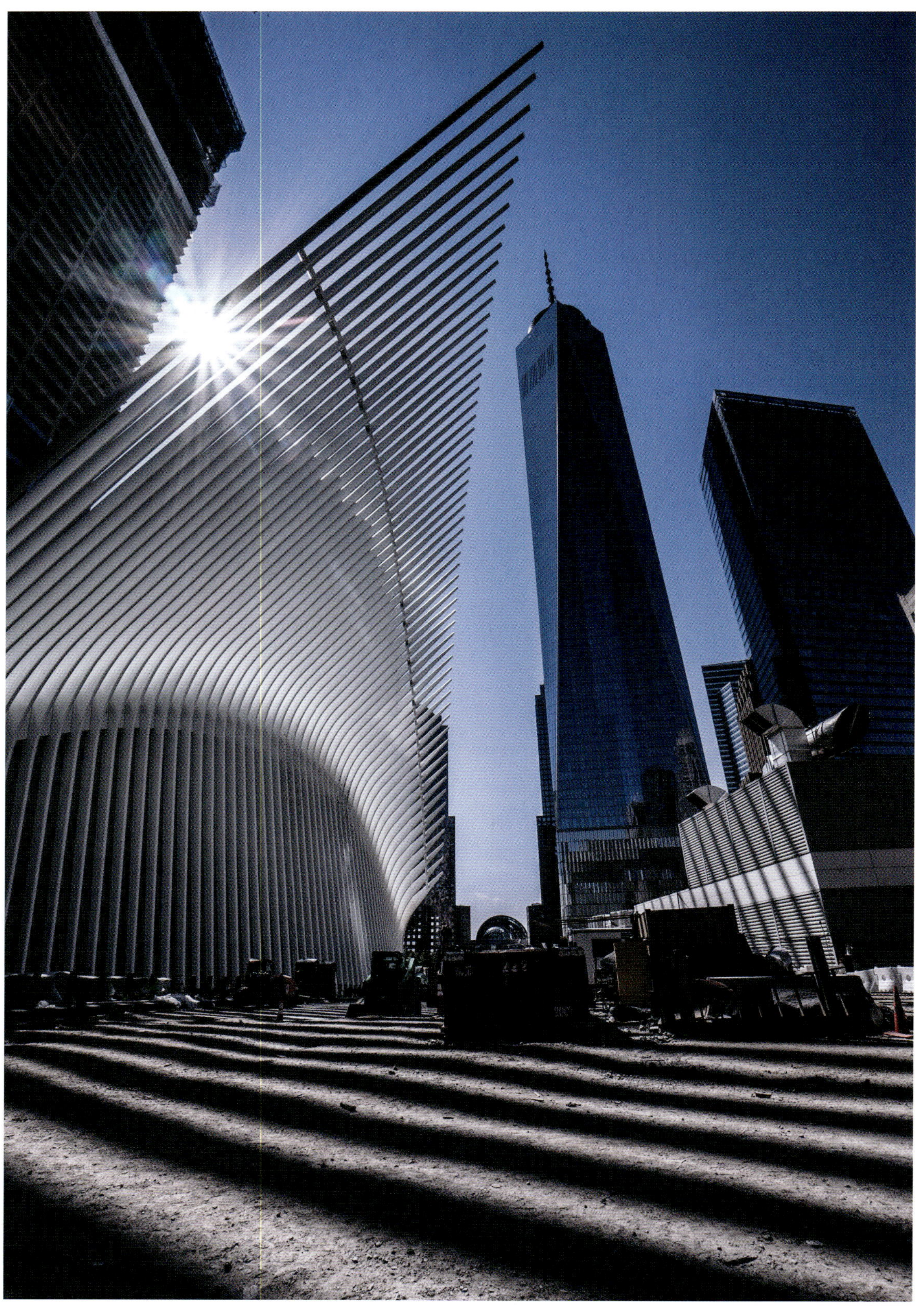

Saint Patrick's Cathedral
Midtown East, Manhattan
– **Jennifer Bin**

The Oculus & One World Trade Center
Financial District, Manhattan
Jennifer Bin

There's no place in the world that is as hard to capture, because every inch of it has already been captured before.

—Joost Bastmeijer

Manhattan
Charissa Fay

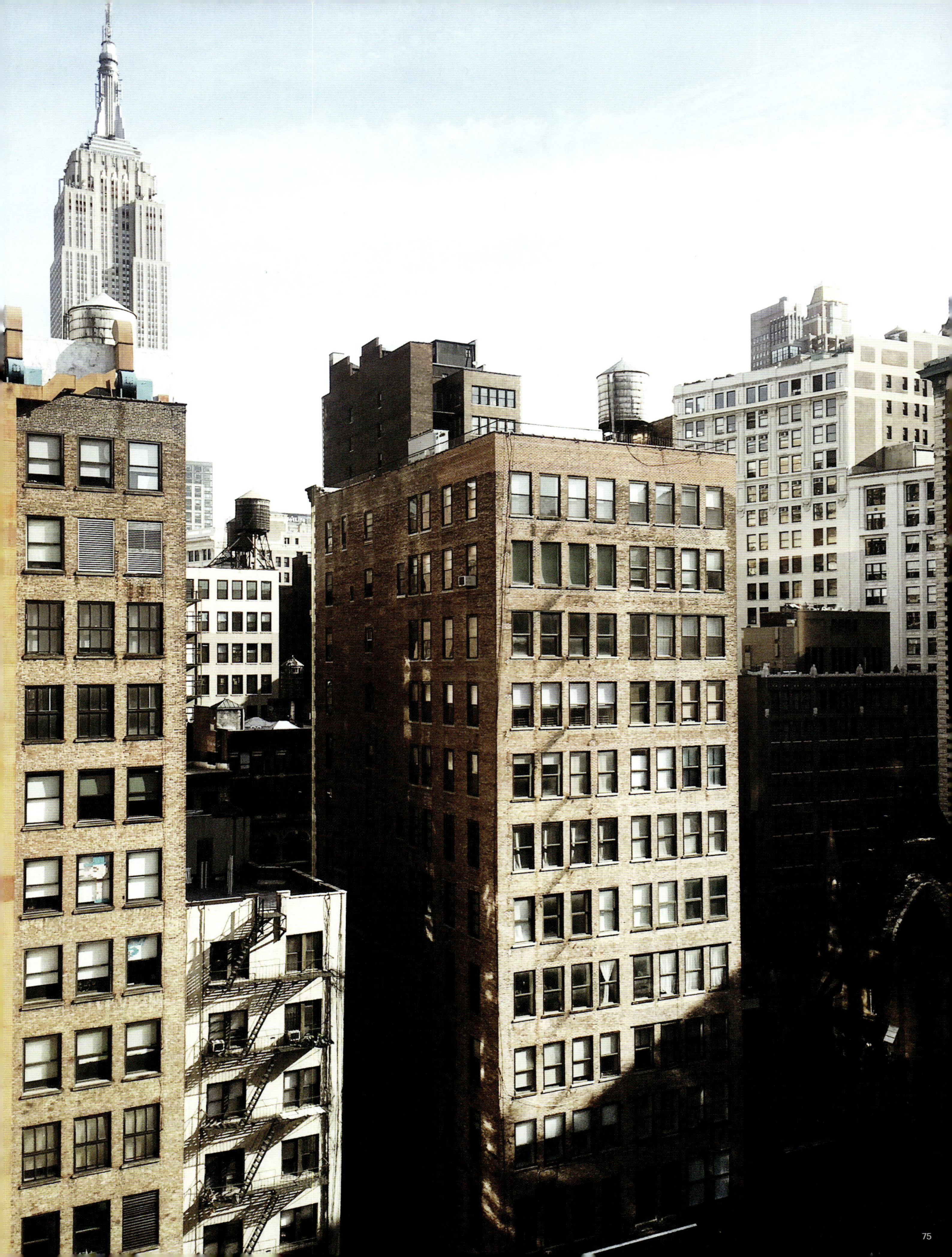

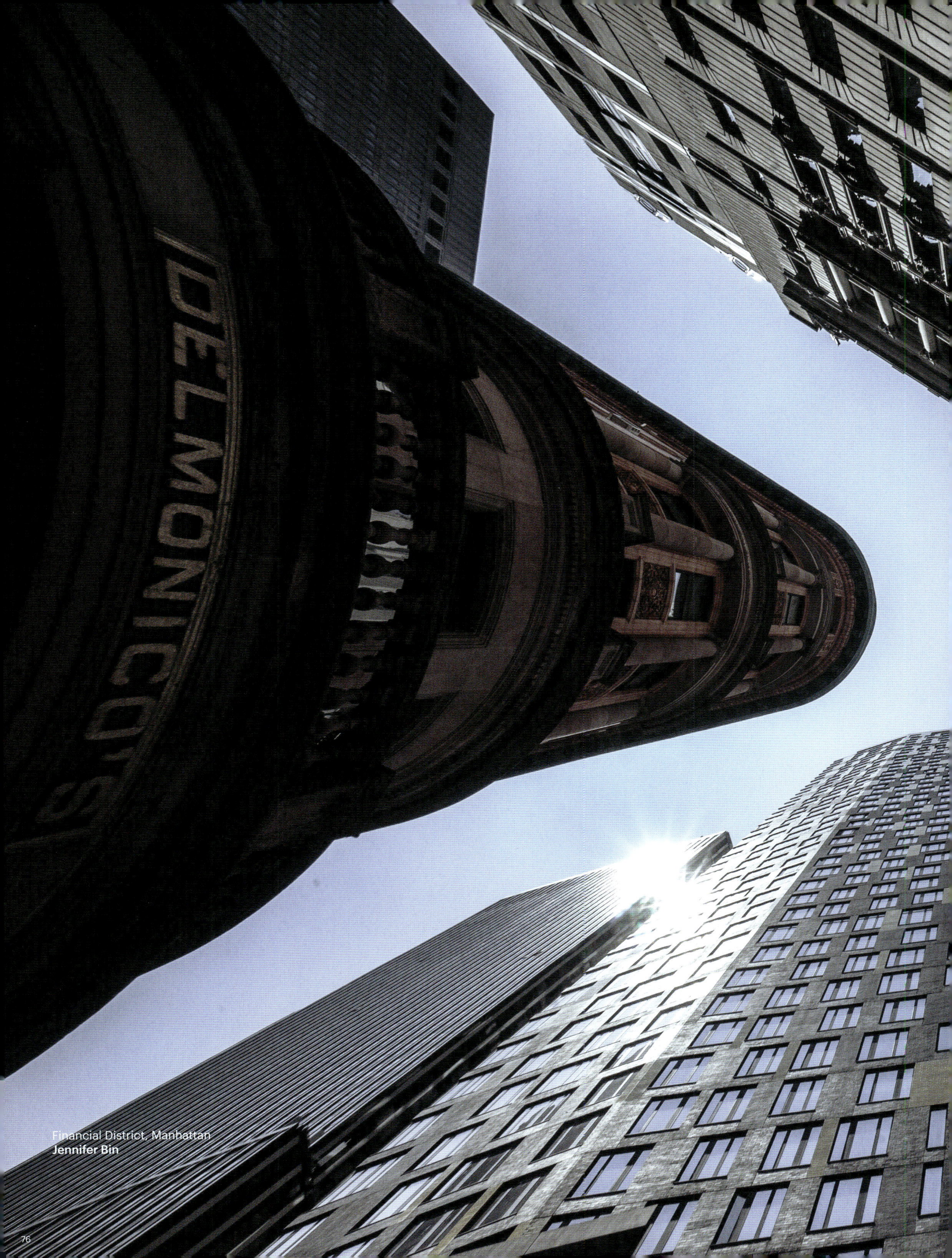

Financial District, Manhattan
Jennifer Bin

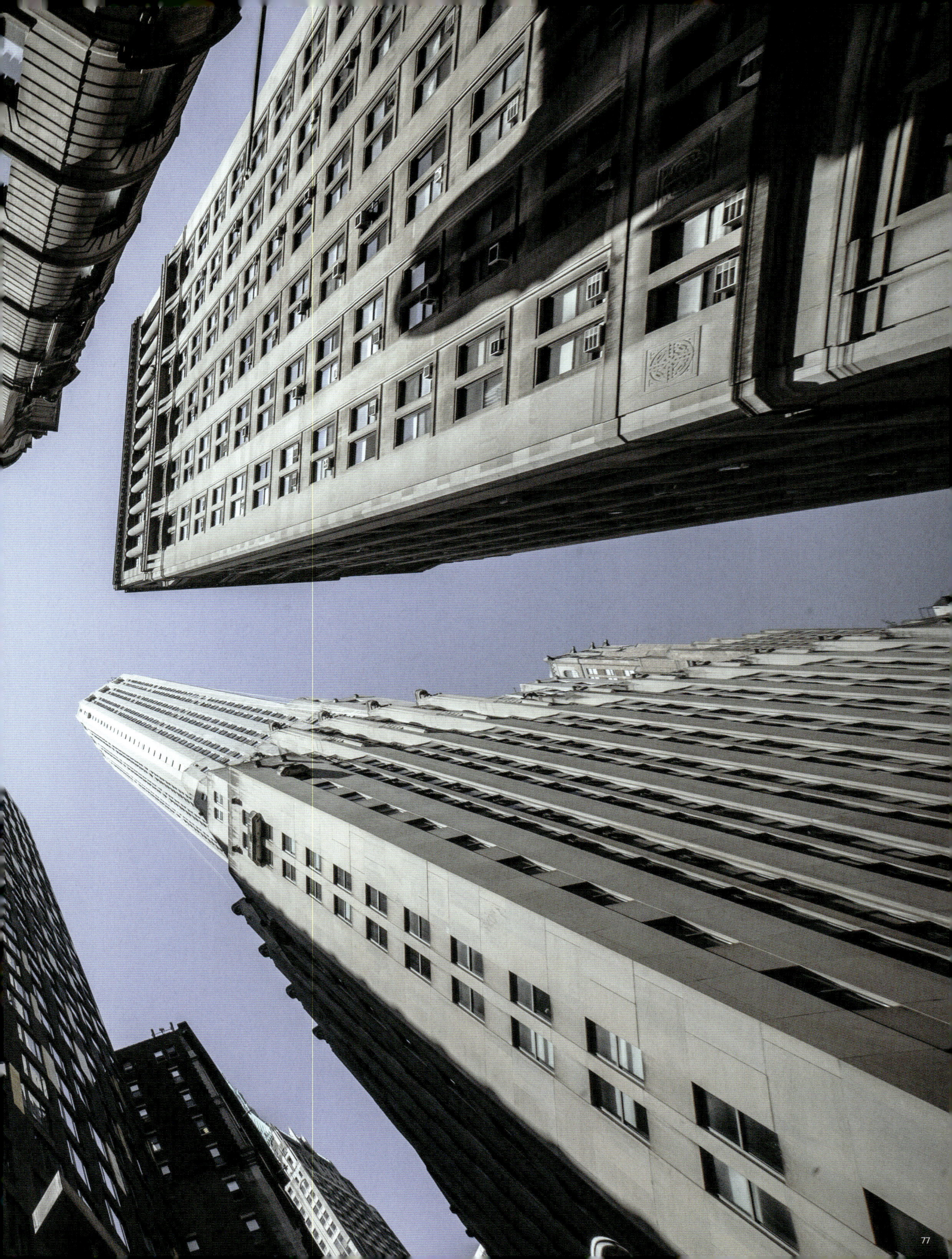

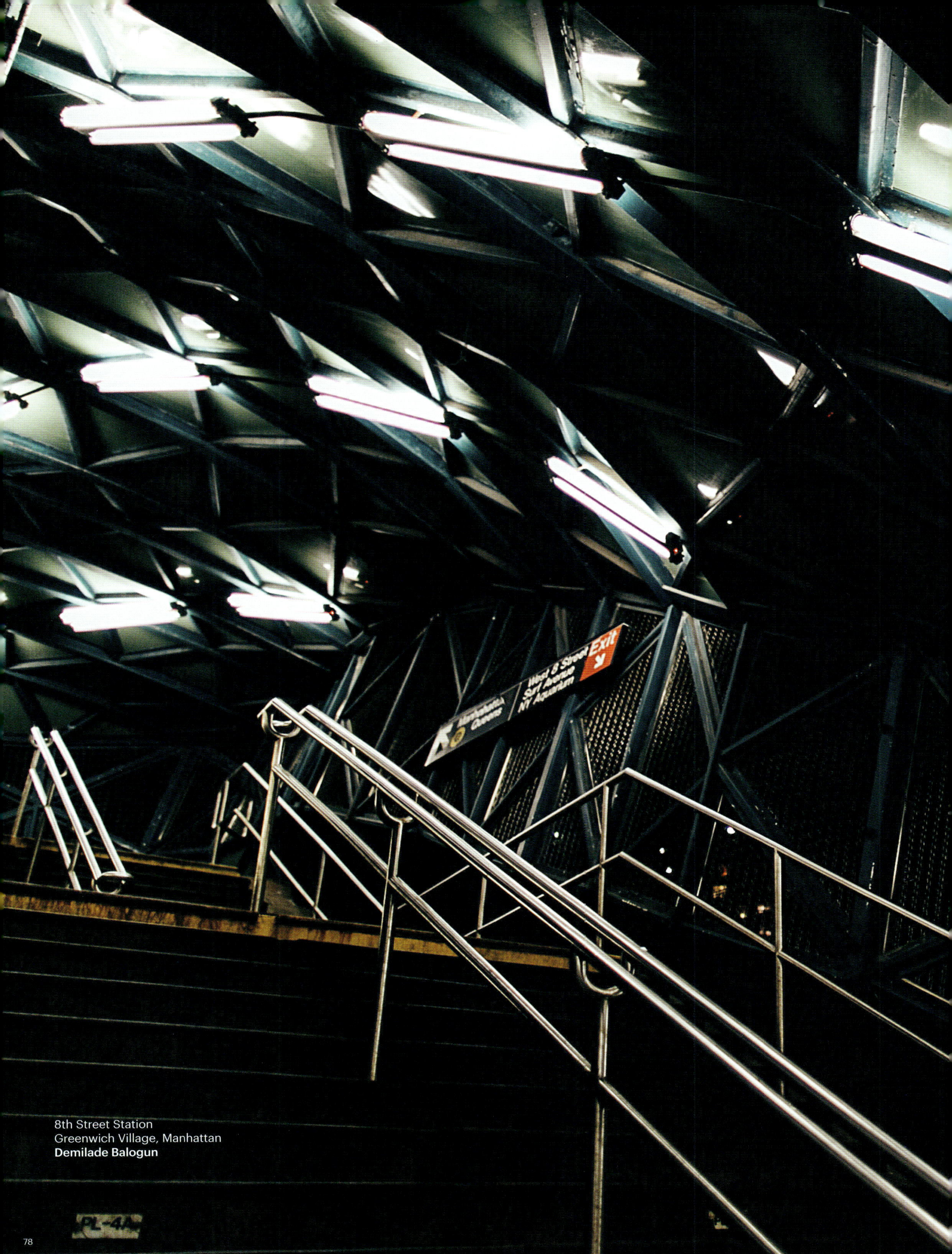

8th Street Station
Greenwich Village, Manhattan
Demilade Balogun

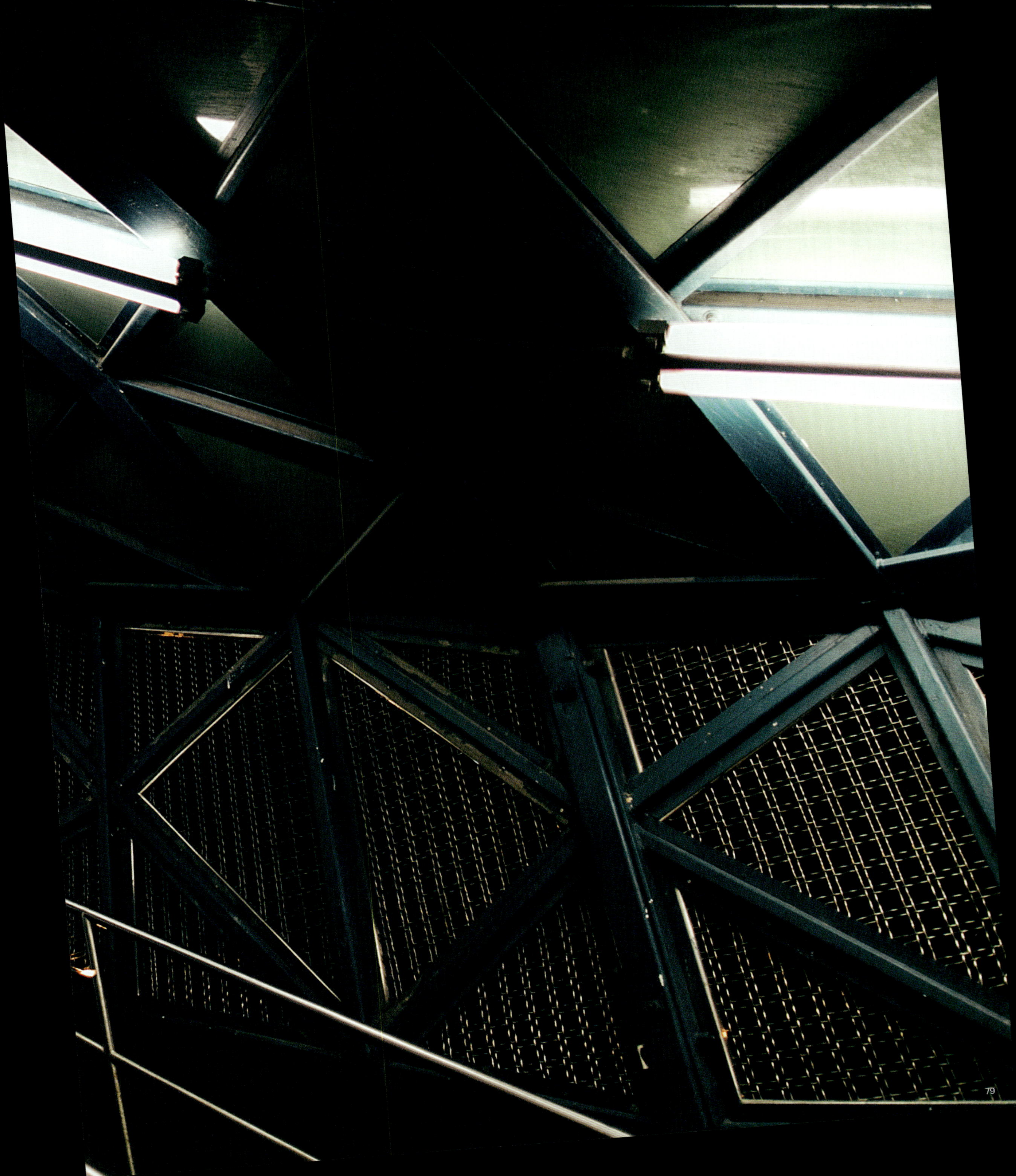

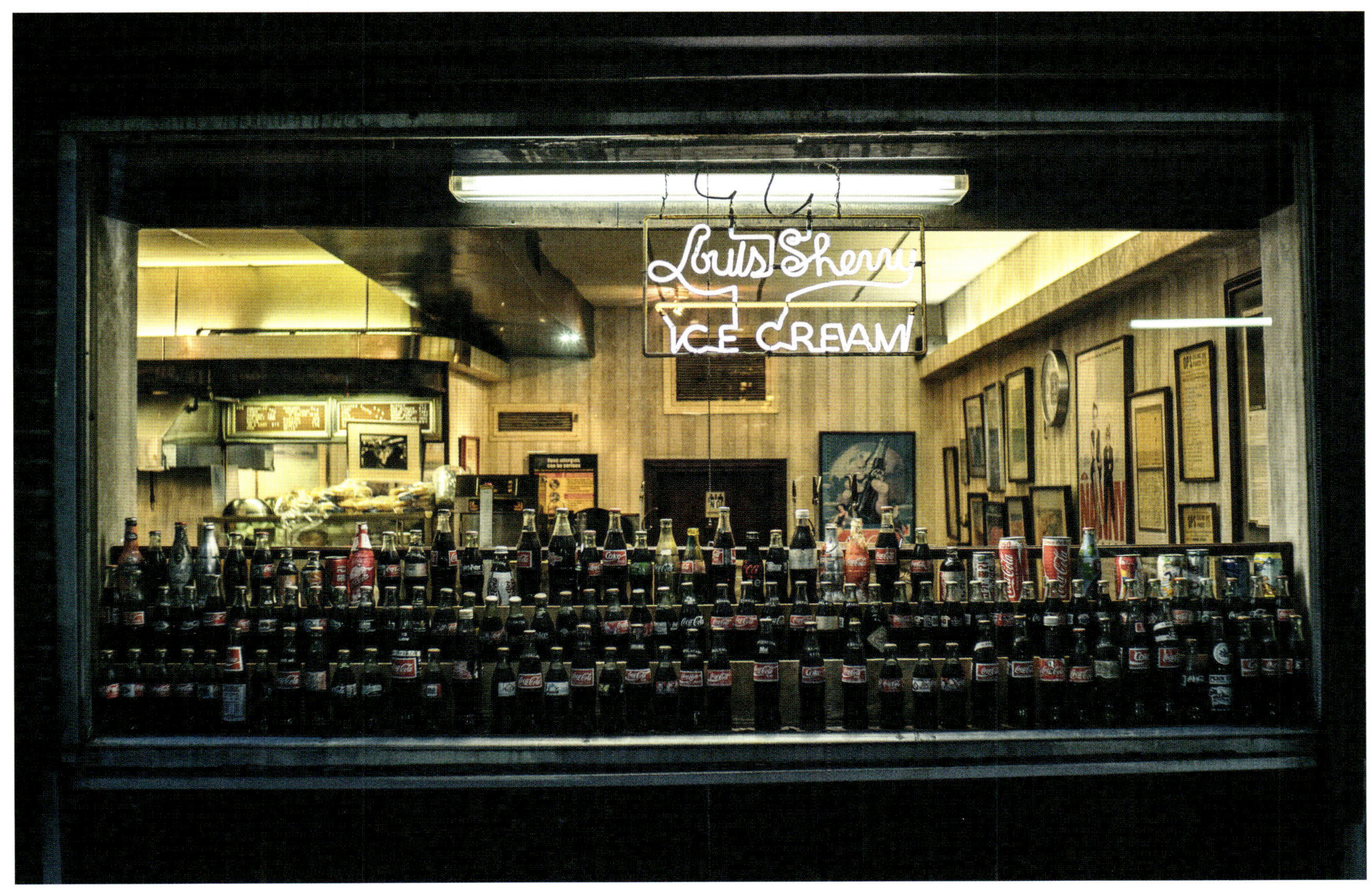

Upper East Side, Manhattan
Bram van Woudenberg

The Laundromat That Never Sleeps
Williamsburg, Brooklyn
Bram van Woudenberg →

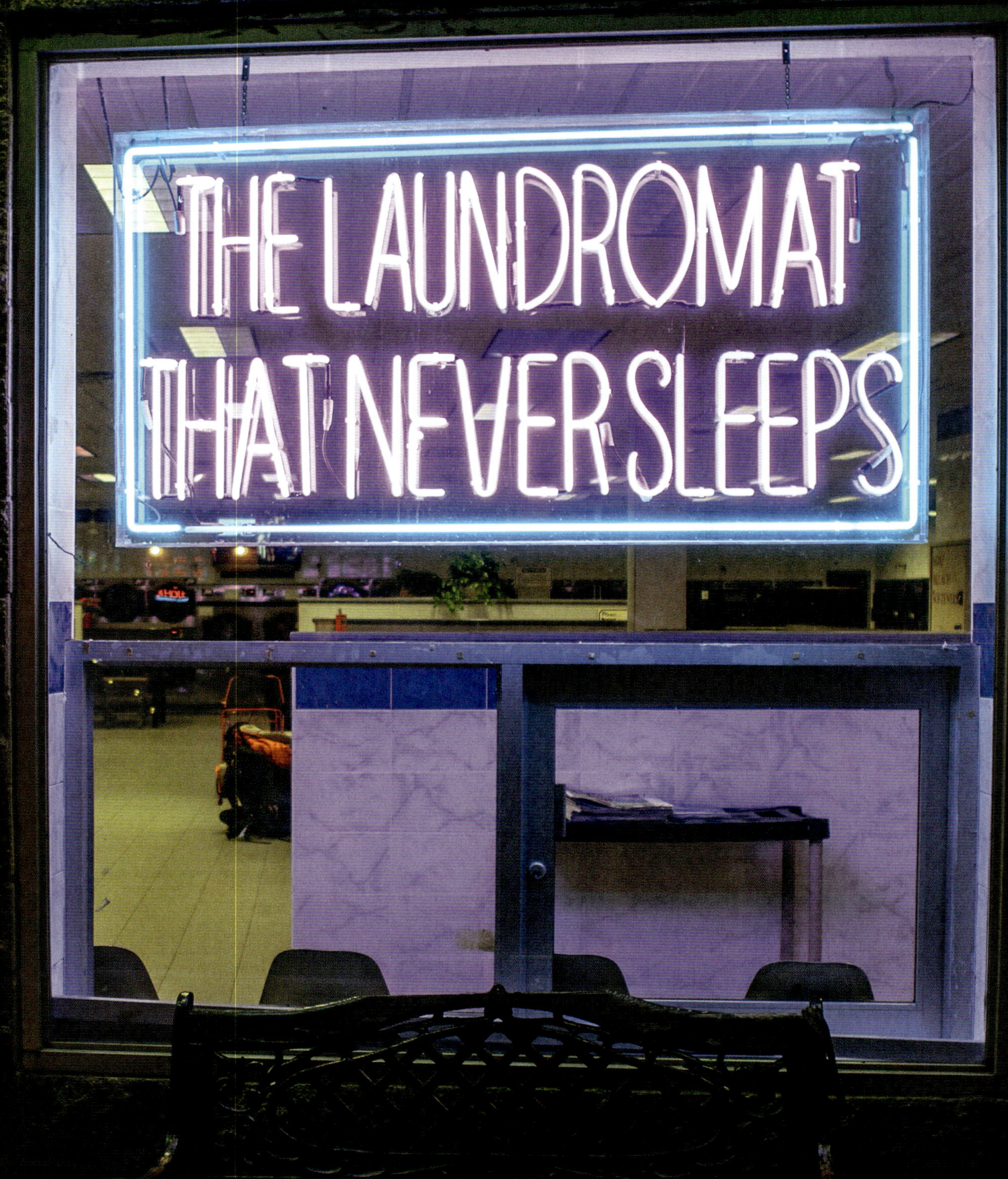
THE LAUNDROMAT
THAT NEVER SLEEPS

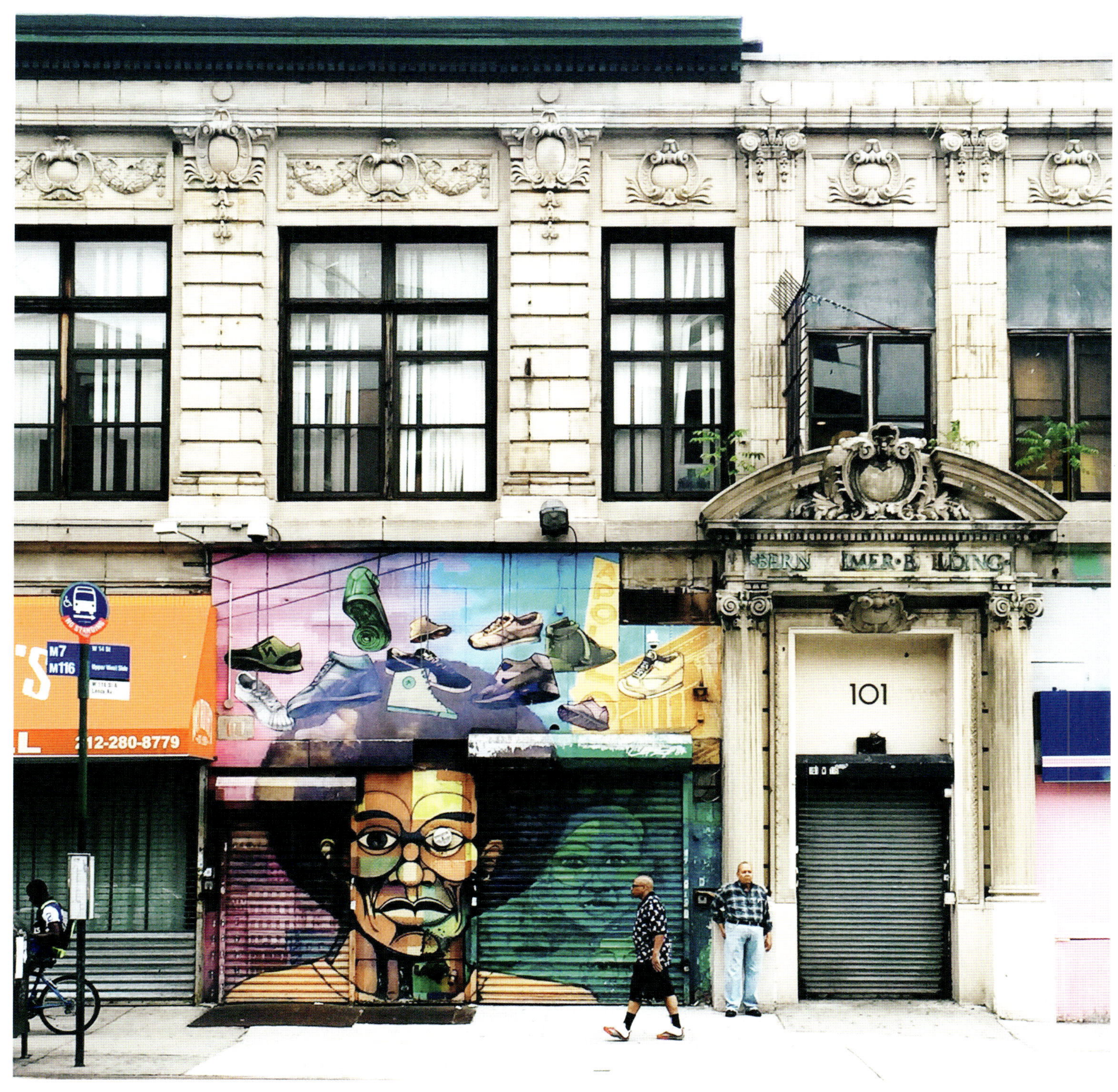

Harlem, Manhattan
Dondre Green

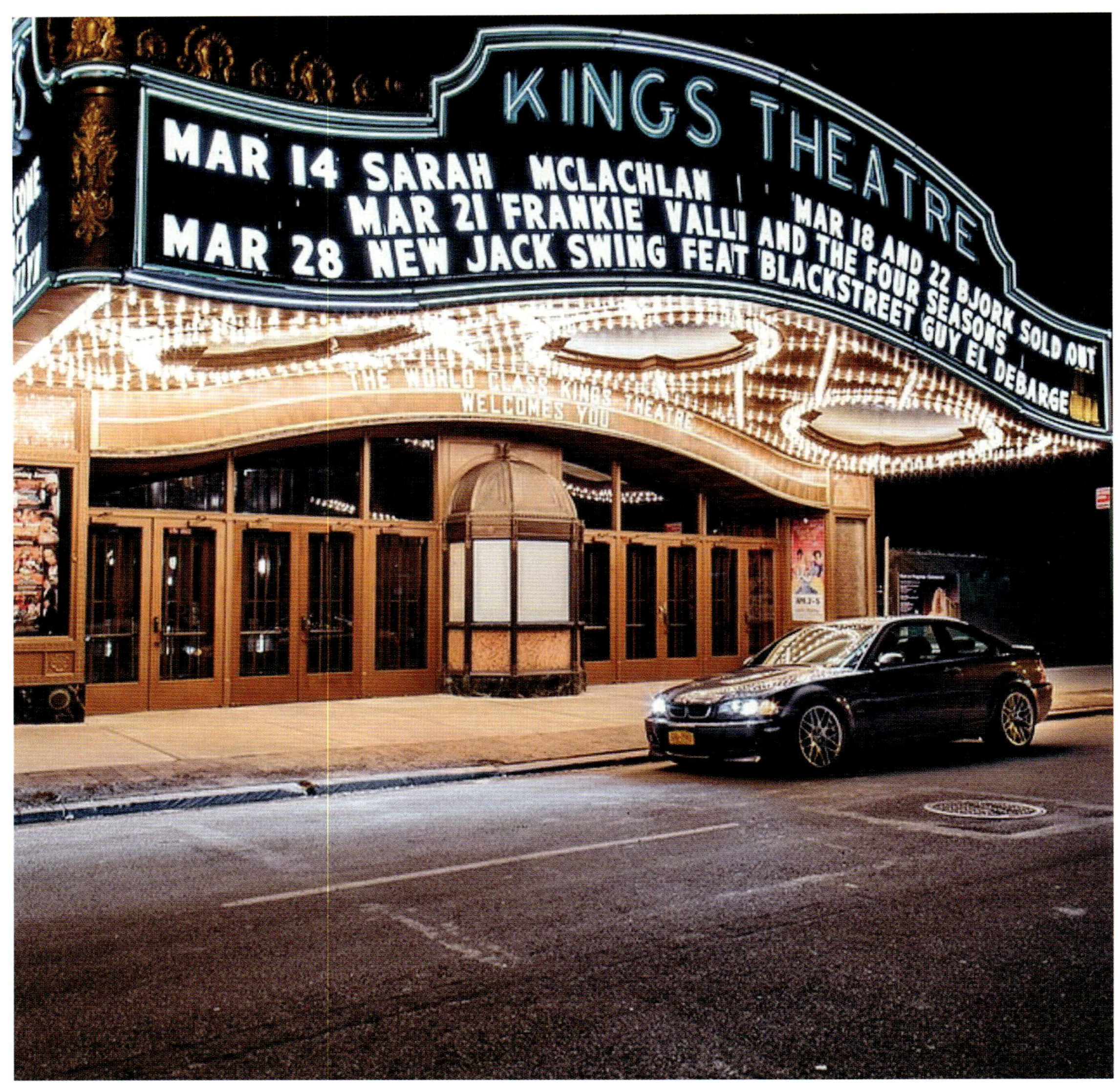

Kings Theatre
Flatbush, Brooklyn
Demilade Balogun

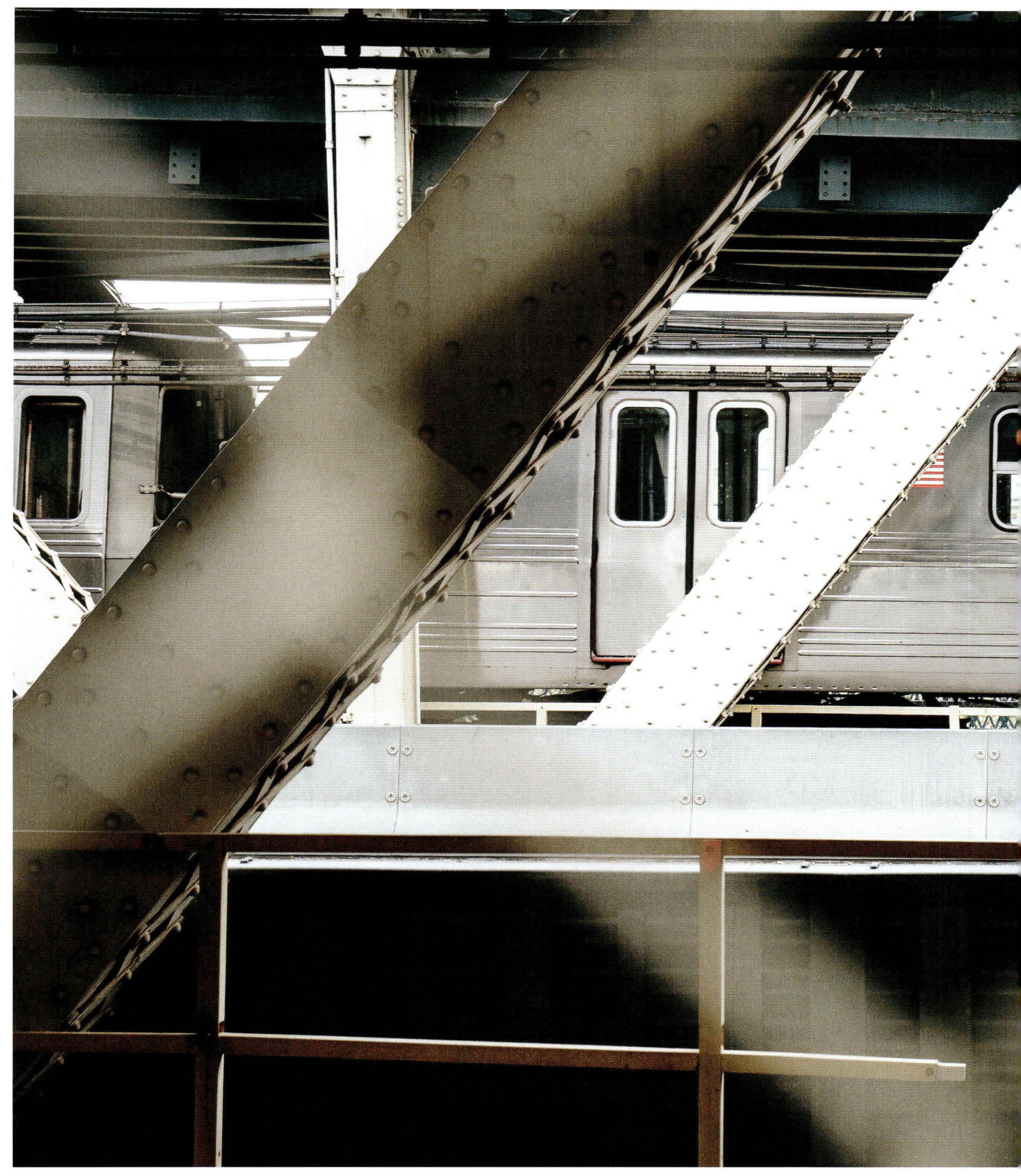

New York City Subway
Eelco Roos

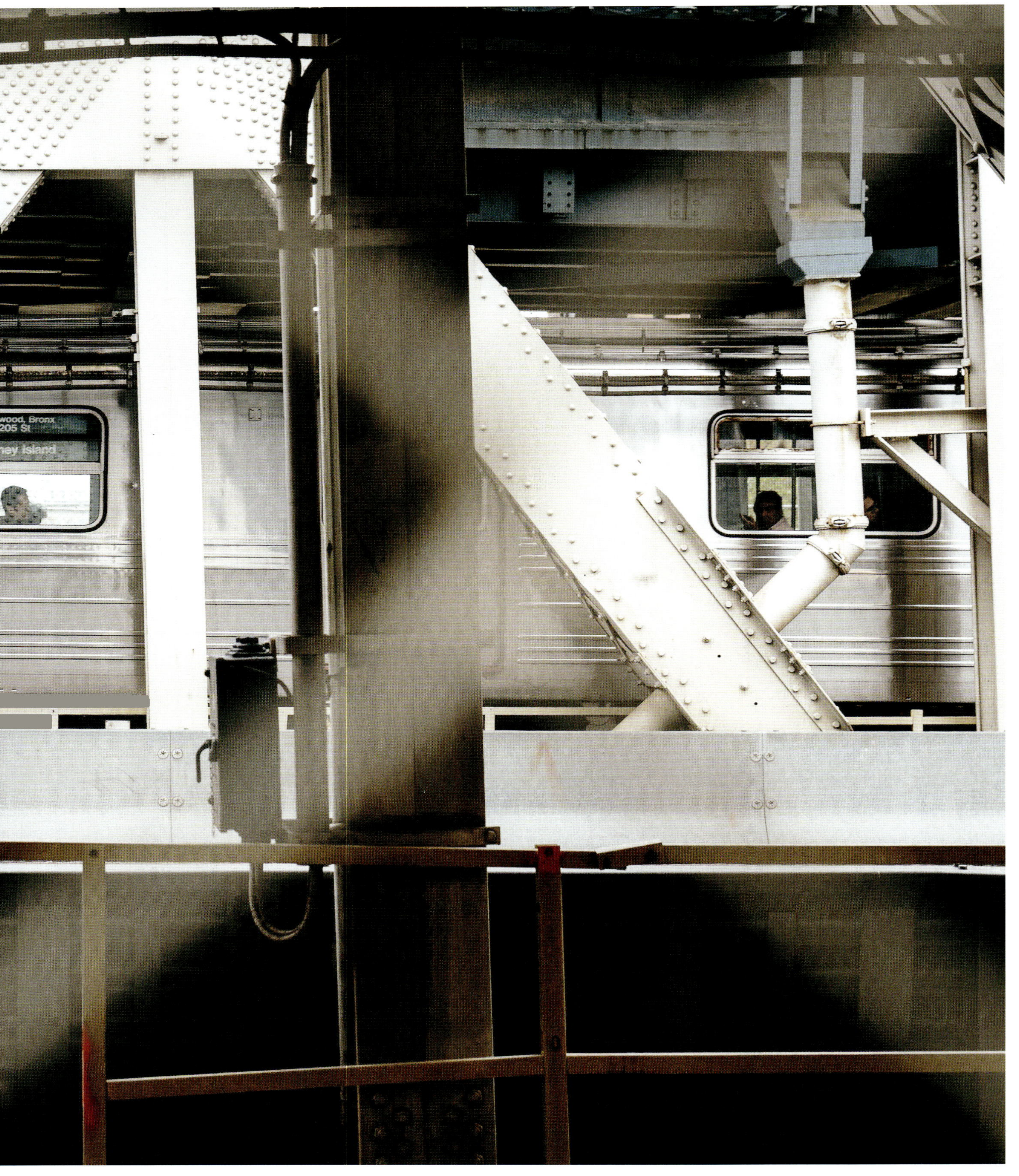
wood, Bronx
205 St
ney Island

Edgar Santana

hometown The Bronx, New York, USA
IG handle @esantana

"Born and raised in the Bronx, I have an incredible relationship with New York; it has treated me great. I am proud to be where I'm from and I express that gratitude in my photos." Photographer Edgar Santana "wants to show what everyone else is missing," he says. "But, I only show the positive side of the life here. No need to focus on the negative. I showcase the beauty of the people, the streets, and the classic cars."

Edgar started taking pictures when he was a teen. "I would use disposable cameras because my parents were afraid I would lose an expensive one." Nowadays, he still prefers a small camera. He shoots on his iPhone, before he uploads his photos on social media. "I've gotten many opportunities through Instagram," Edgar explains. "I've sold photos, I've been reposted numerous times by several major social media outlets and it has given me the opportunity to meet people in my community that love my borough as much as I do." But social media has its downside, too. "Online, everyone is a photographer now," says Edgar. "Ten years ago, you didn't see that. People are followers and post what everyone is posting. It gets tiring seeing the same stuff all the time."

Because most people know Brooklyn and Manhattan, Edgar solely posts pictures taken in the Bronx. "It's the last true borough and I want to showcase that, to those that don't live here." He recommends a trip to Hunts Point, in South Bronx. "Spending a day there will truly overwhelm you. It's an industrial area, so lots of interesting areas, cars, people, street corners. I live in the absolute best city in the world; it's hard not to love it. The love comes from the streets that inspire me every single day."

„In der Bronx geboren und aufgewachsen, habe ich eine unglaubliche Beziehung zu New York, und die Stadt hat mich großartig behandelt. Ich bin stolz auf meine Herkunft und drücke diese Dankbarkeit in meinen Fotos aus." Der Fotograf Edgar Santana will „zeigen, was alle anderen verpassen", erzählt er. „Aber ich zeige nur die positive Seite des Lebens hier. Man muss den Fokus nicht auf das Negative lenken. Ich präsentiere die Schönheit der Menschen, der Straßen und der klassischen Autos."

Edgar fing als Teenager an, Fotos zu machen. „Ich benutzte Einwegkameras, weil meine Eltern Angst hatten, ich könnte eine teure verlieren." Noch heute verwendet er am liebsten eine kleine Kamera. Er fotografiert mit seinem iPhone und veröffentlicht die Bilder dann über soziale Medien im Internet. „Instagram bietet mir viele Möglichkeiten", erklärt Edgar. „Ich habe Fotos verkauft, meine Bilder sind schon oft auf wichtigen Social-Media-Plattformen weiterverbreitet worden und ich habe die Gelegenheit, Menschen in meiner Umgebung kennenzulernen, die mein Stadtviertel ebenso sehr lieben wie ich." Aber soziale Netzwerke haben auch ihre Nachteile. „Im Internet ist heutzutage jeder ein Fotograf", sagt Edgar. „Das war vor zehn Jahren noch nicht so. Die Leute sind Mitläufer, sie posten das, was alle anderen posten. Es ist ermüdend, ständig das gleiche Zeug zu sehen."

Weil die meisten Menschen Brooklyn und Manhattan kennen, veröffentlicht Edgar ausschließlich Bilder, die in der Bronx aufgenommen wurden. „Sie ist der letzte echte Stadtbezirk, und genau das will ich denjenigen zeigen, die nicht hier leben." Er empfiehlt einen Ausflug nach Hunts Point in die South Bronx. „Sie werden es wirklich überwältigend finden, einen Tag dort zu verbringen. Es ist ein Industriegebiet, deshalb gibt es jede Menge interessante Gegenden, Autos, Leute und Straßenecken. Ich lebe in der absolut besten Stadt der Welt; es ist schwer, sie nicht zu lieben. Diese Liebe stammt von den Straßen, die mich tagtäglich inspirieren."

« Comme je suis né et que j'ai grandi dans le Bronx, j'ai une relation incroyable avec New York ; la ville m'a beaucoup donné. Je suis fier de ce lieu d'où je viens, et j'exprime cette gratitude au travers de mes images ». Le photographe Edgar Santana affirme vouloir « montrer à tous les autres ce qu'ils ratent », avant d'ajouter : « mais je ne révèle que l'aspect positif de la vie ici. Pas besoin de se focaliser sur ce qui est négatif. Je mets en valeur la beauté des personnes, des rues et des voitures typiques ».

Edgar commence à photographier alors qu'il est adolescent. « J'utilisais des appareils jetables parce que mes parents craignaient que je ne perde un matériel coûteux ». Aujourd'hui encore, il préfère travailler avec un petit appareil et se sert de son iPhone dont il télécharge ensuite les images sur les réseaux sociaux. « Instagram m'a offert beaucoup d'opportunités », explique Edgar. « J'ai vendu des photographies, été reposté de très nombreuses fois par plusieurs grands sites, et j'ai eu la possibilité de rencontrer des membres de ma communauté qui aimaient autant que moi mon quartier ». Les réseaux sociaux, toutefois, ont aussi leur revers. « Sur le Net aujourd'hui, tout le monde est photographe », déclare Edgar. « C'est quelque chose qu'on ne voyait pas il y a dix ans. Les internautes suivent et postent ce que tout le monde poste. Cela devient fatigant de voir tout le temps la même chose ».

Parce que Brooklyn et Manhattan sont connus de la plupart, Edgar ne poste que des images prises dans le Bronx. « C'est le dernier vrai quartier, ce que je tiens à montrer à tous ceux qui n'y vivent pas ». Son conseil, c'est de se rendre à Hunts Point, dans le Bronx. « Y passer une journée, vous submergera complètement. C'est une zone industrielle, avec donc beaucoup de sites intéressants, de voitures, de personnes, de coins de rue. Je vis dans la plus formidable ville du monde ; difficile de ne pas l'aimer. Un amour qui vient de ces rues, lesquelles m'inspirent chaque jour qui passe ».

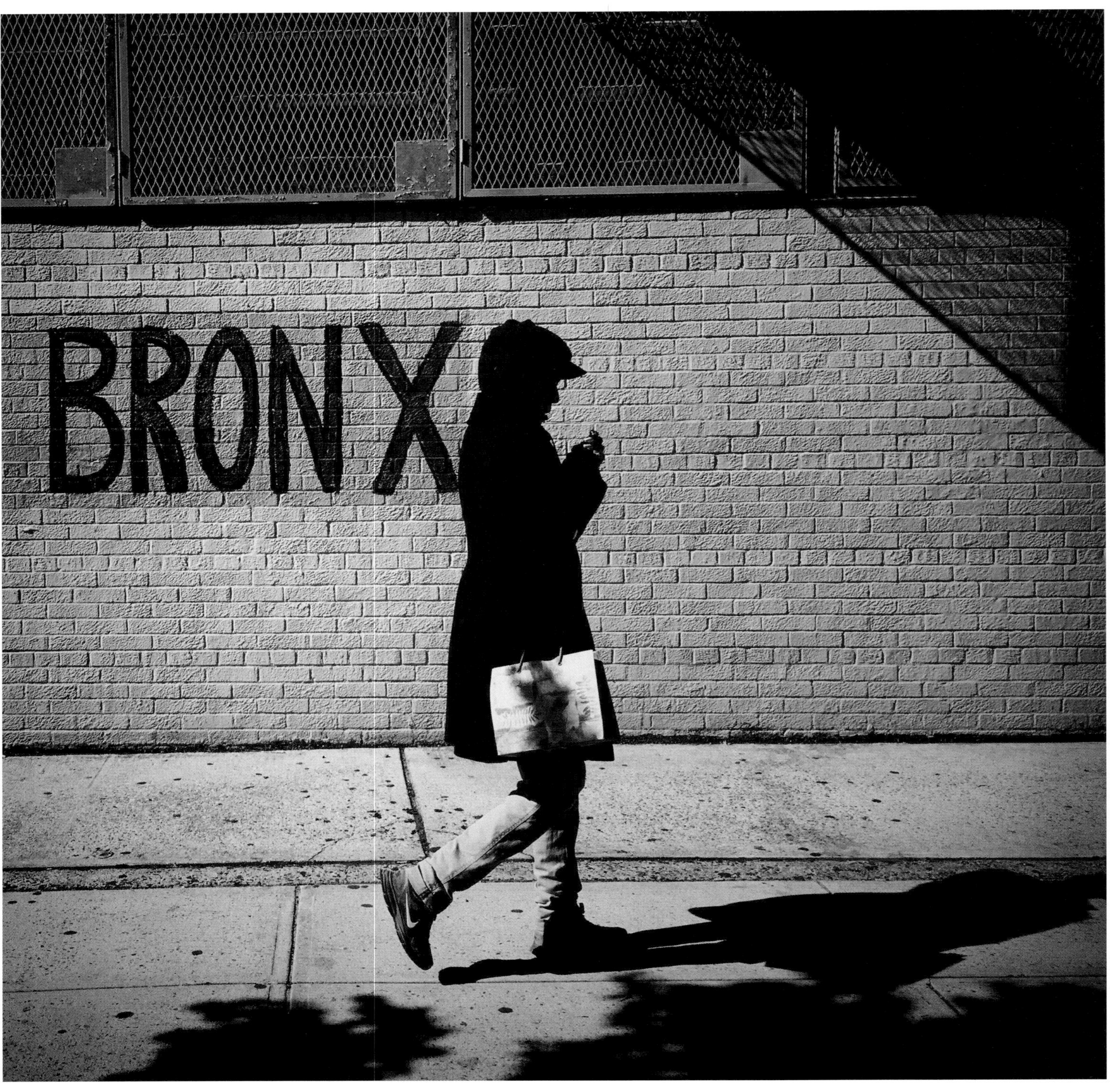

The Bronx
Edgar Santana

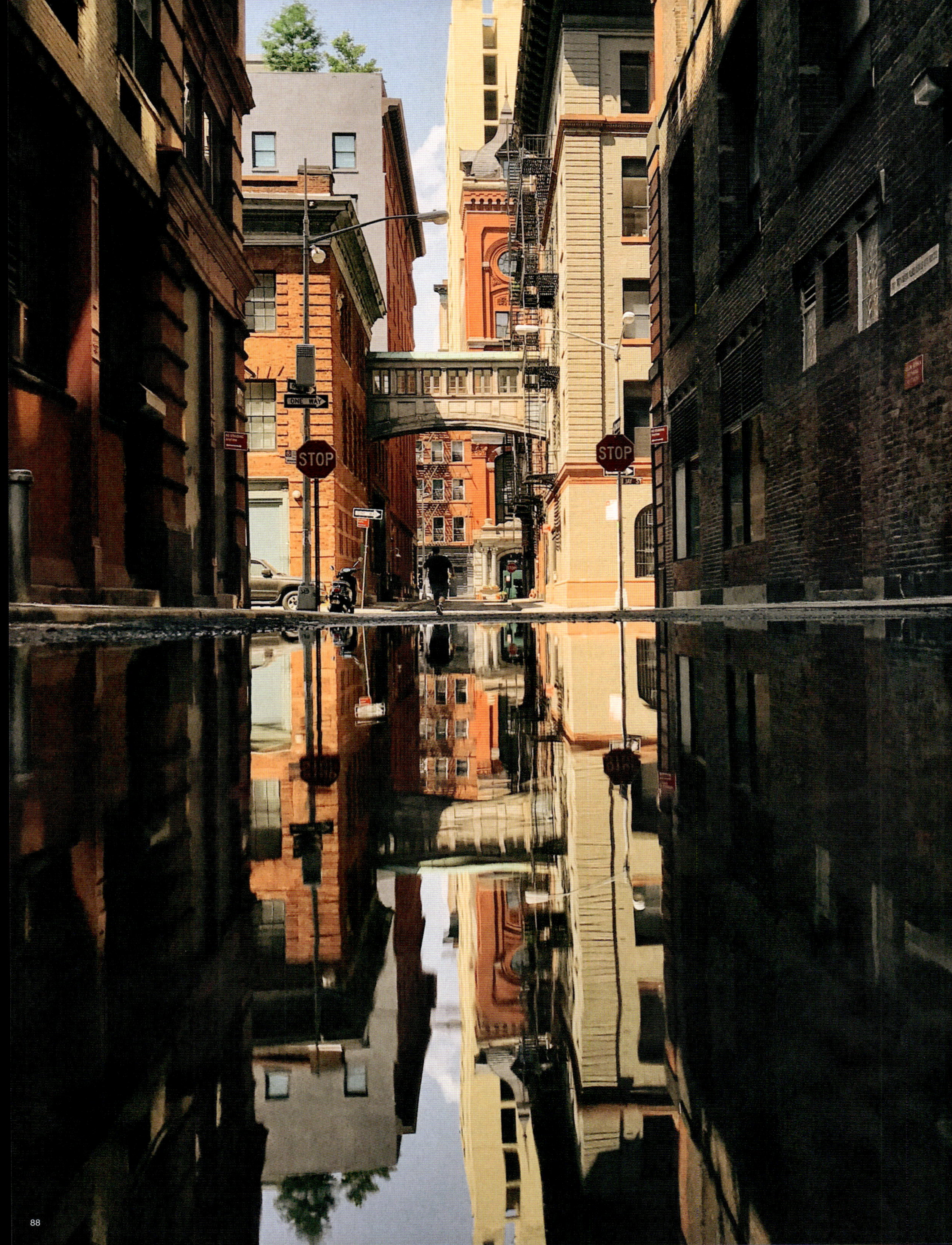
ONE WAY
STOP
STOP

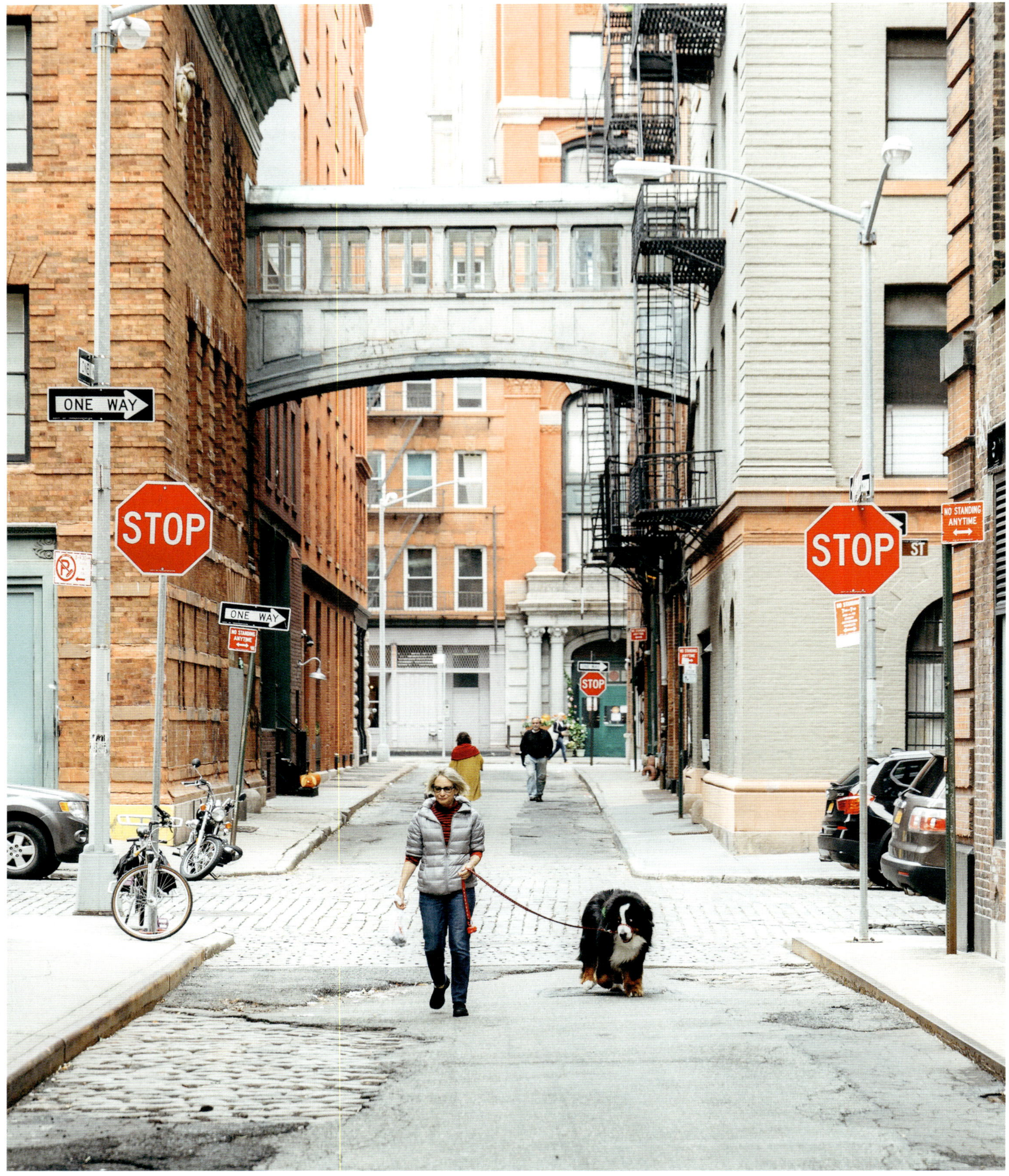

Staple Street Skybridge
Tribeca, Manhattan
Lucas Hornsby

Staple Street Skybridge
Tribeca, Manhattan
Eelco Roos

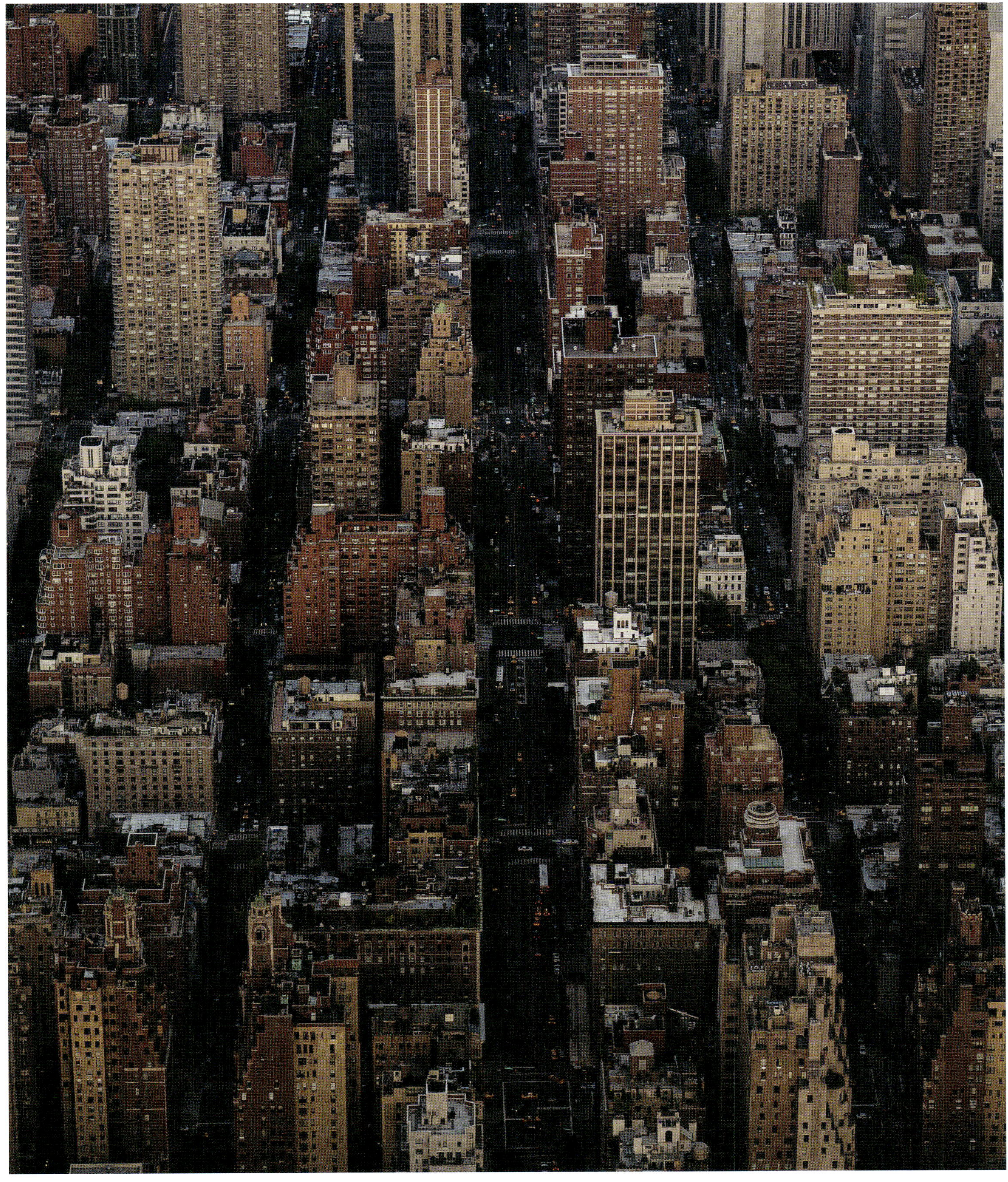

Manhattan
Ivan Meneses

Beekman ‾ower
City Hall, Manhattan
Ivan Meneses –

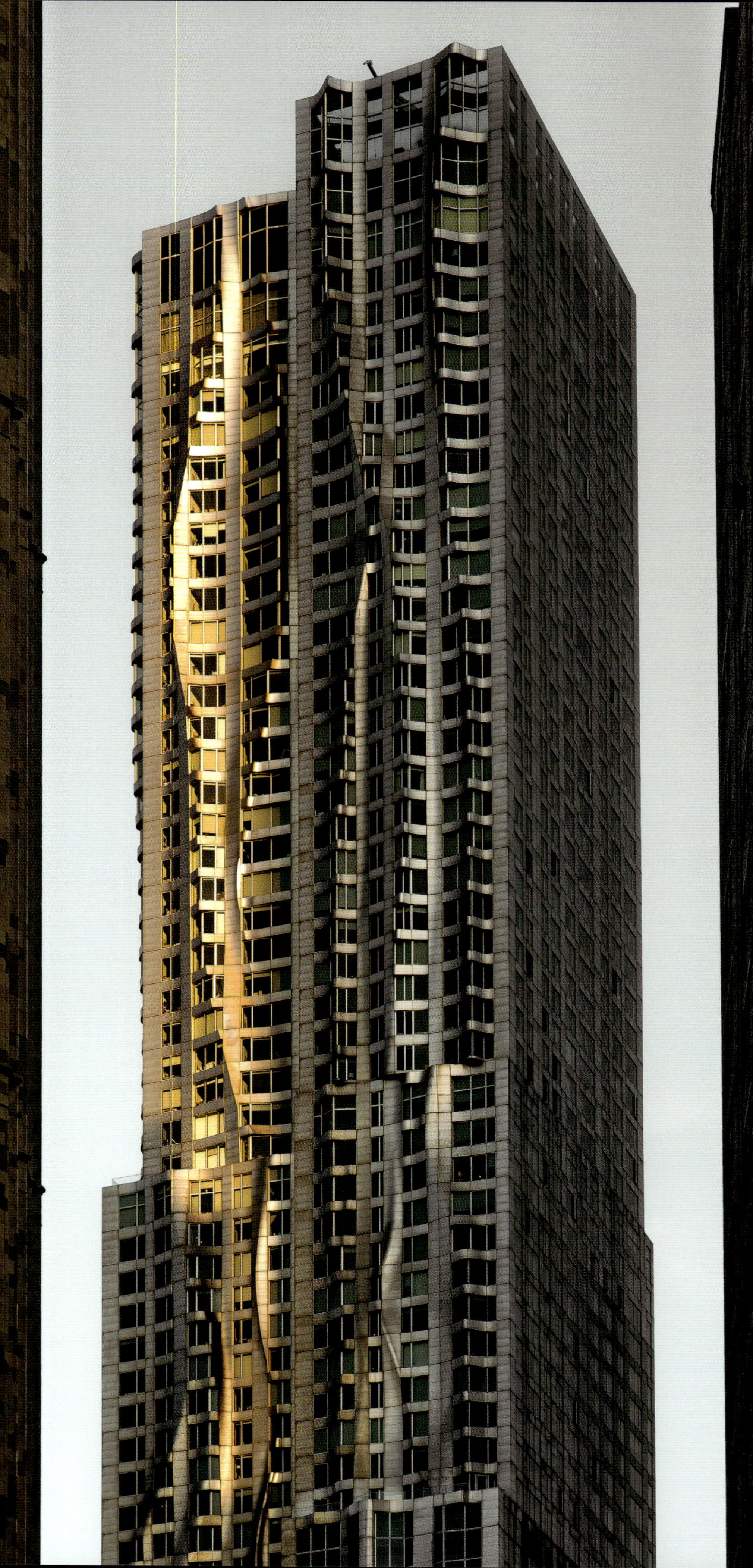

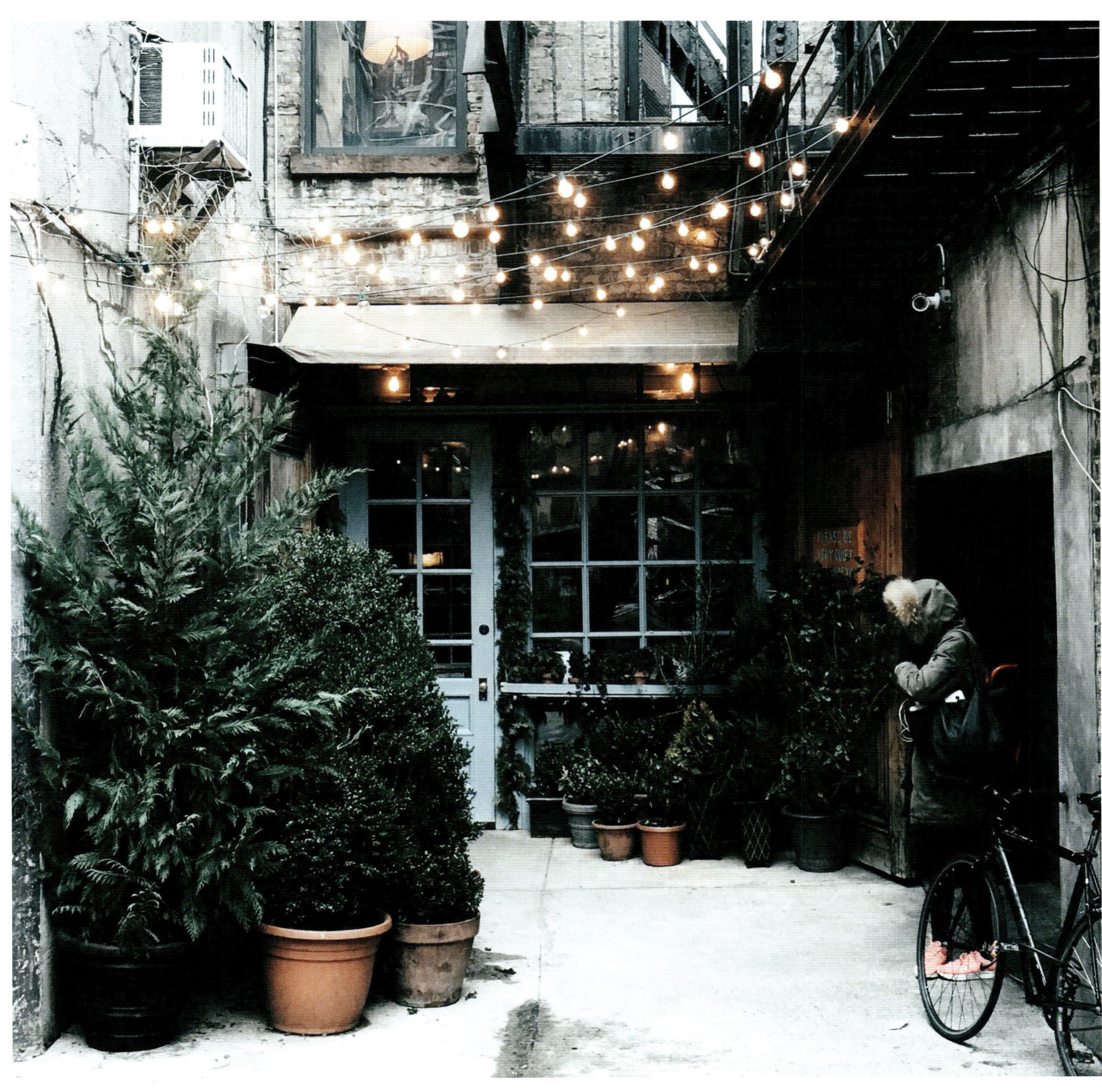

Freemans
Lower East Side, Manhattan
Peter Wu

Bavaria Bierhaus
Financial District, Manhattan
Jayson Cassidy -

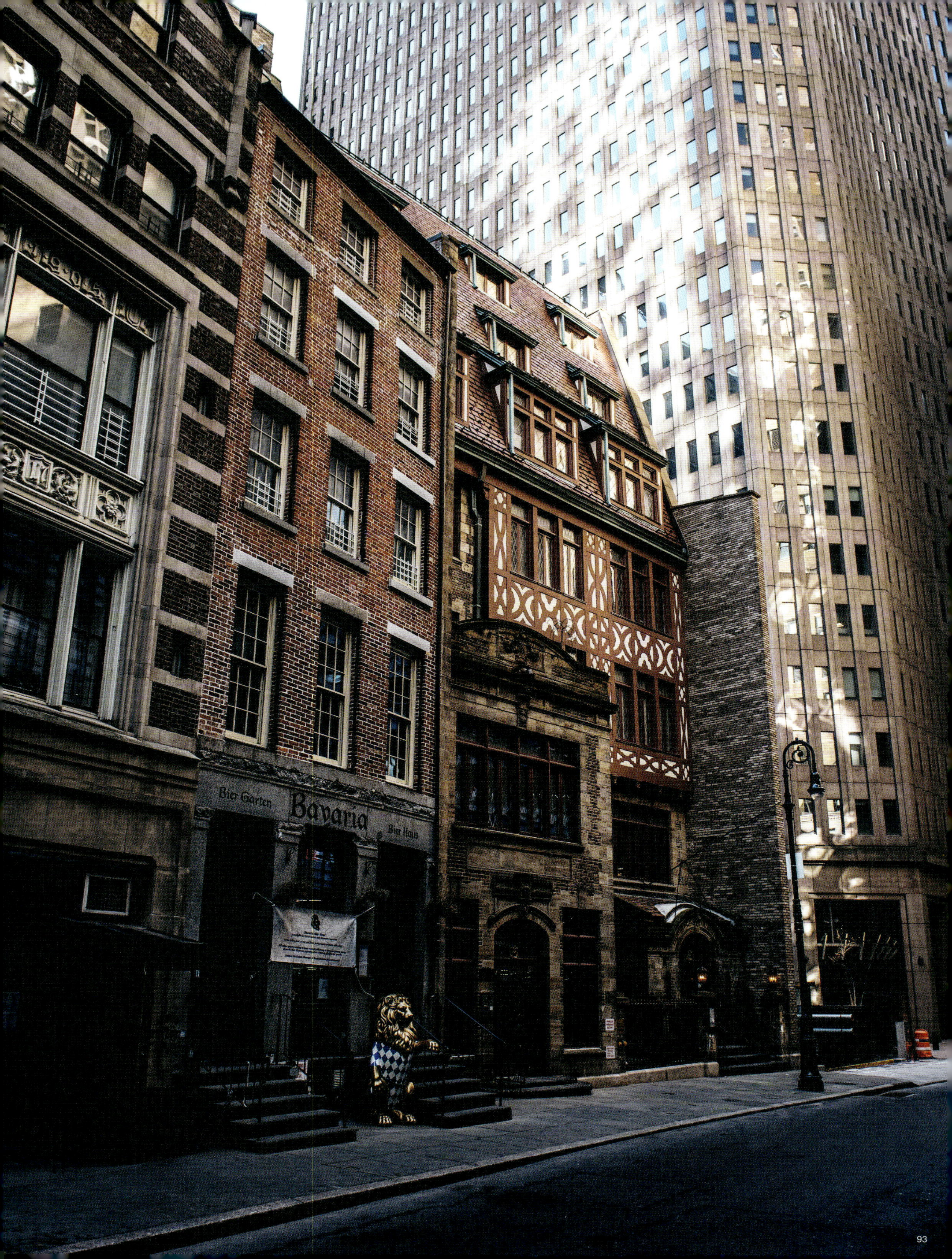
Bier Garten
Bavaria
Bier Haus

I want the viewer to feel a bit of thrill when they see my photos, so I usually try to convey a sense of scale and vastness. It usually takes a little imagination and some risk.

—Casey Tang

Midtown, Manhattan
Casey Tang

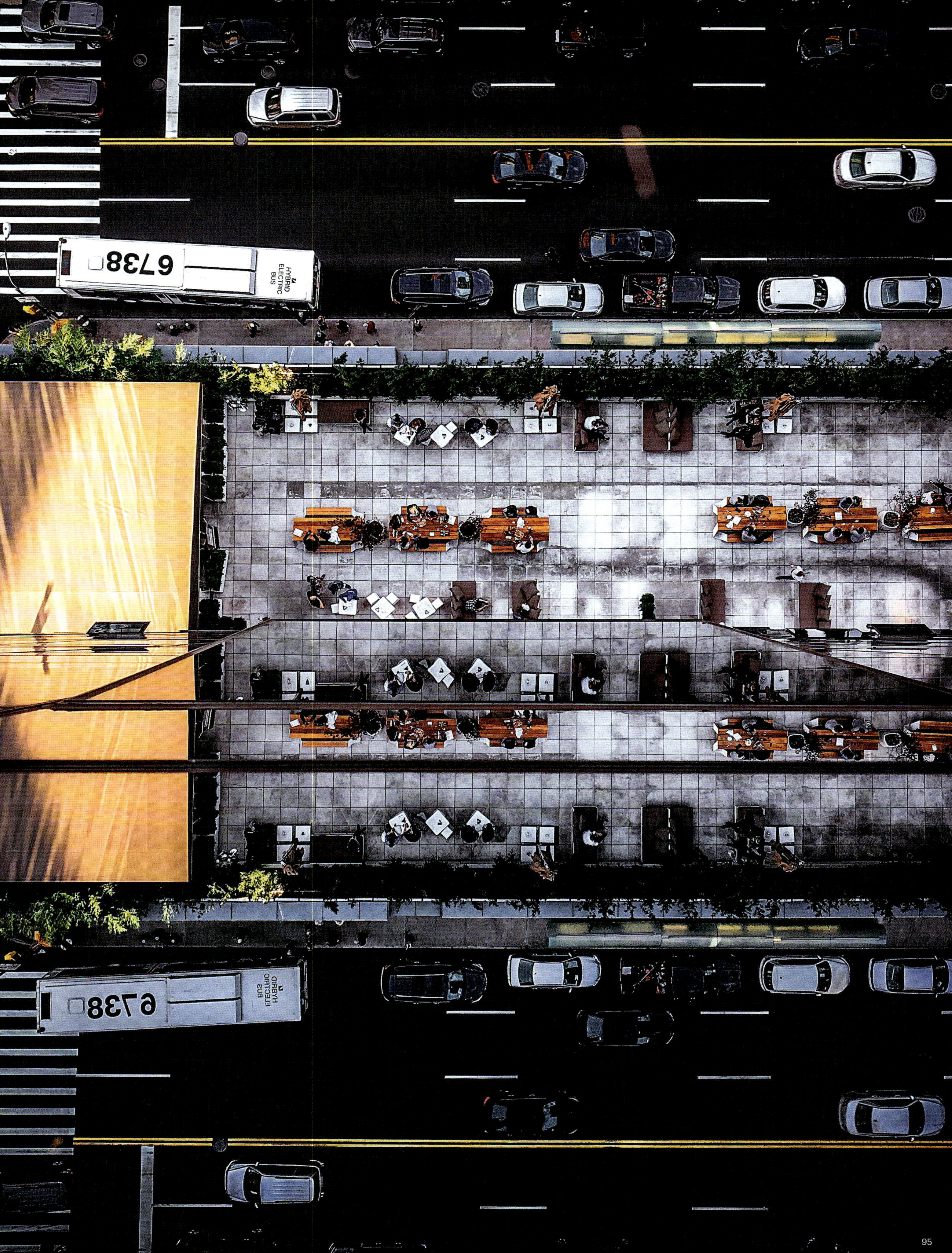
6738
HYBRID ELECTRIC BUS

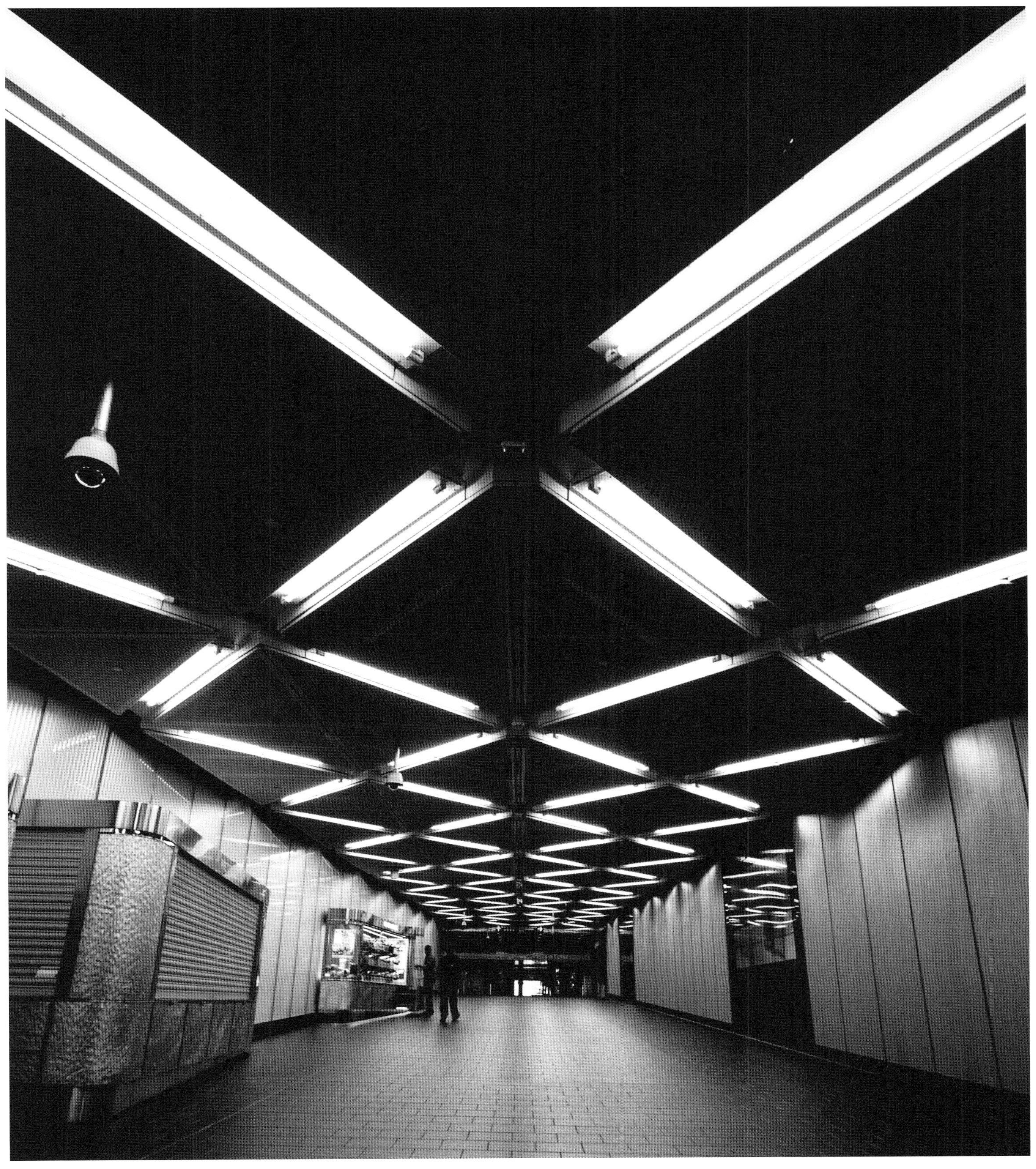

Fulton Street Subway Station
Financial District, Manhattan
Alexis Le Bagousse

PUBLIC Hotel Lobby
Lower East Side, Manhattan
Alexis Le Bagousse

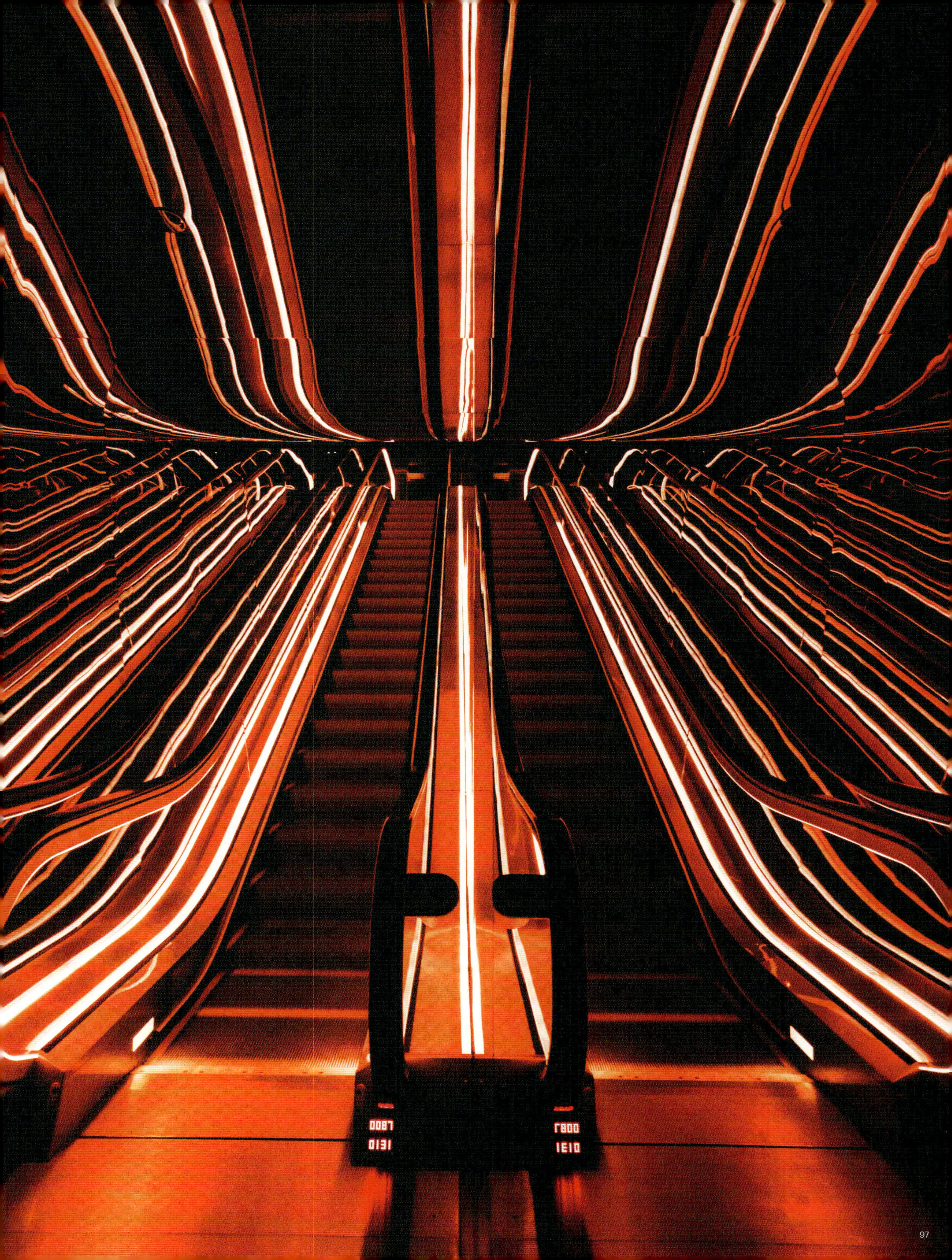

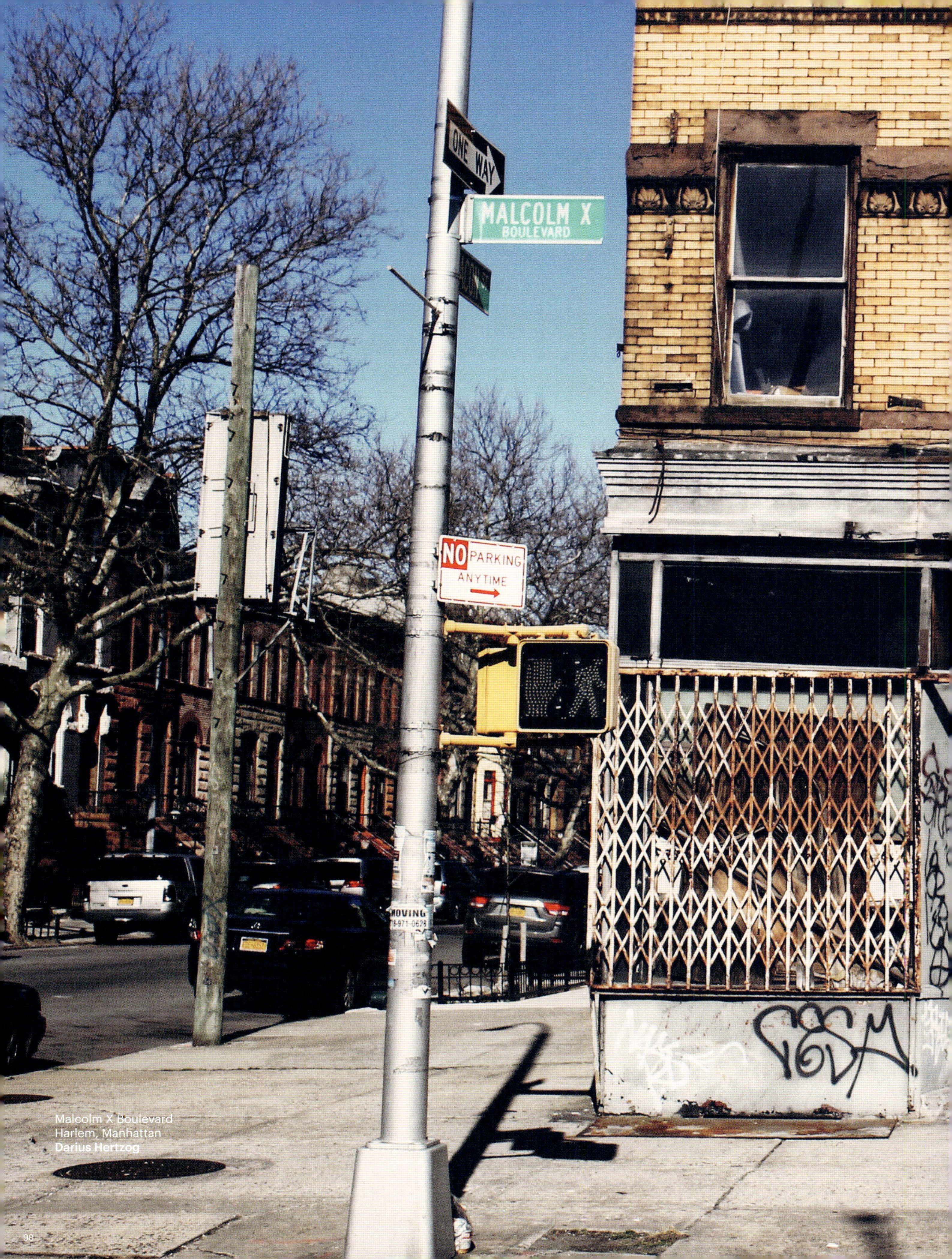

Malcolm X Boulevard
Harlem, Manhattan
Darius Hertzog

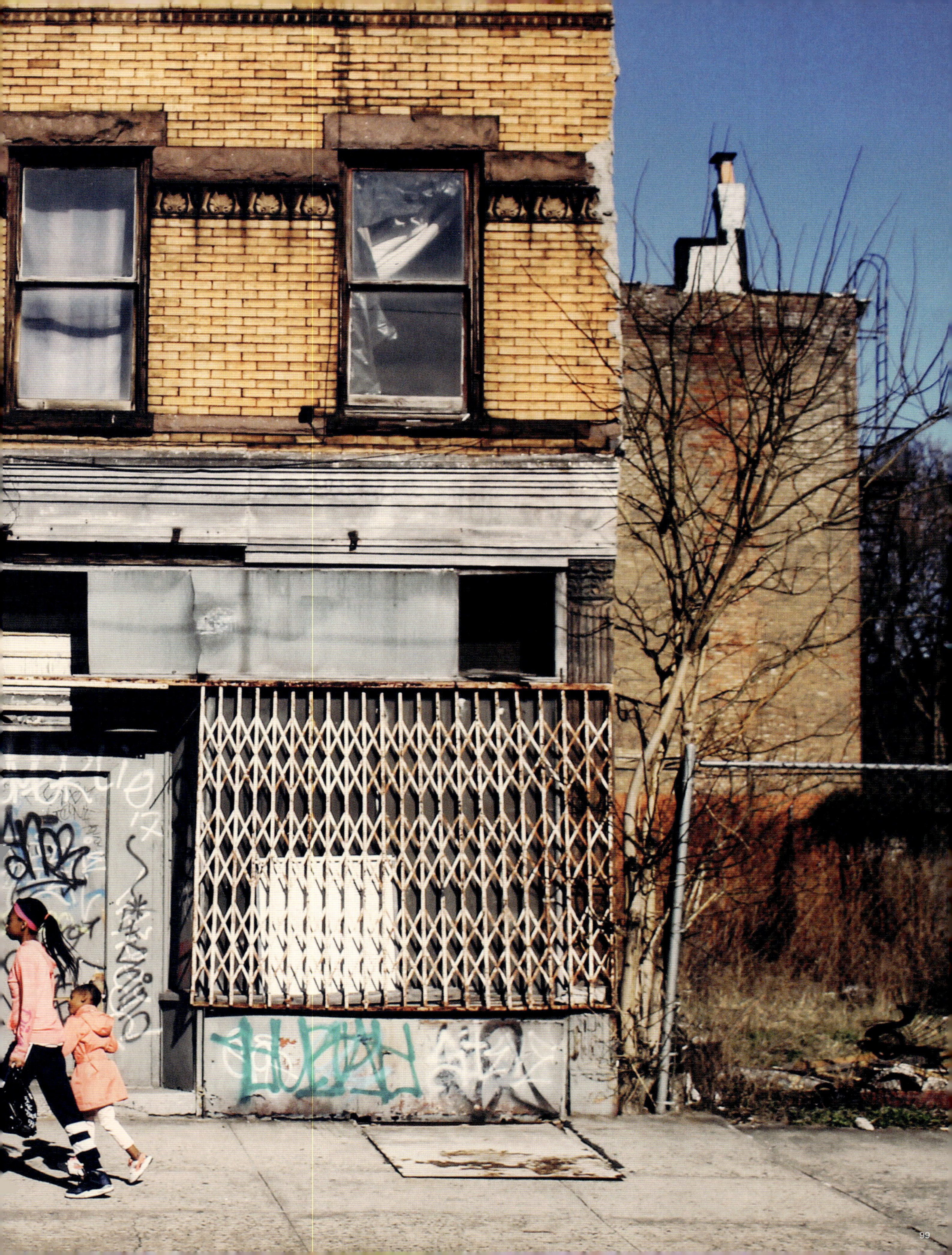

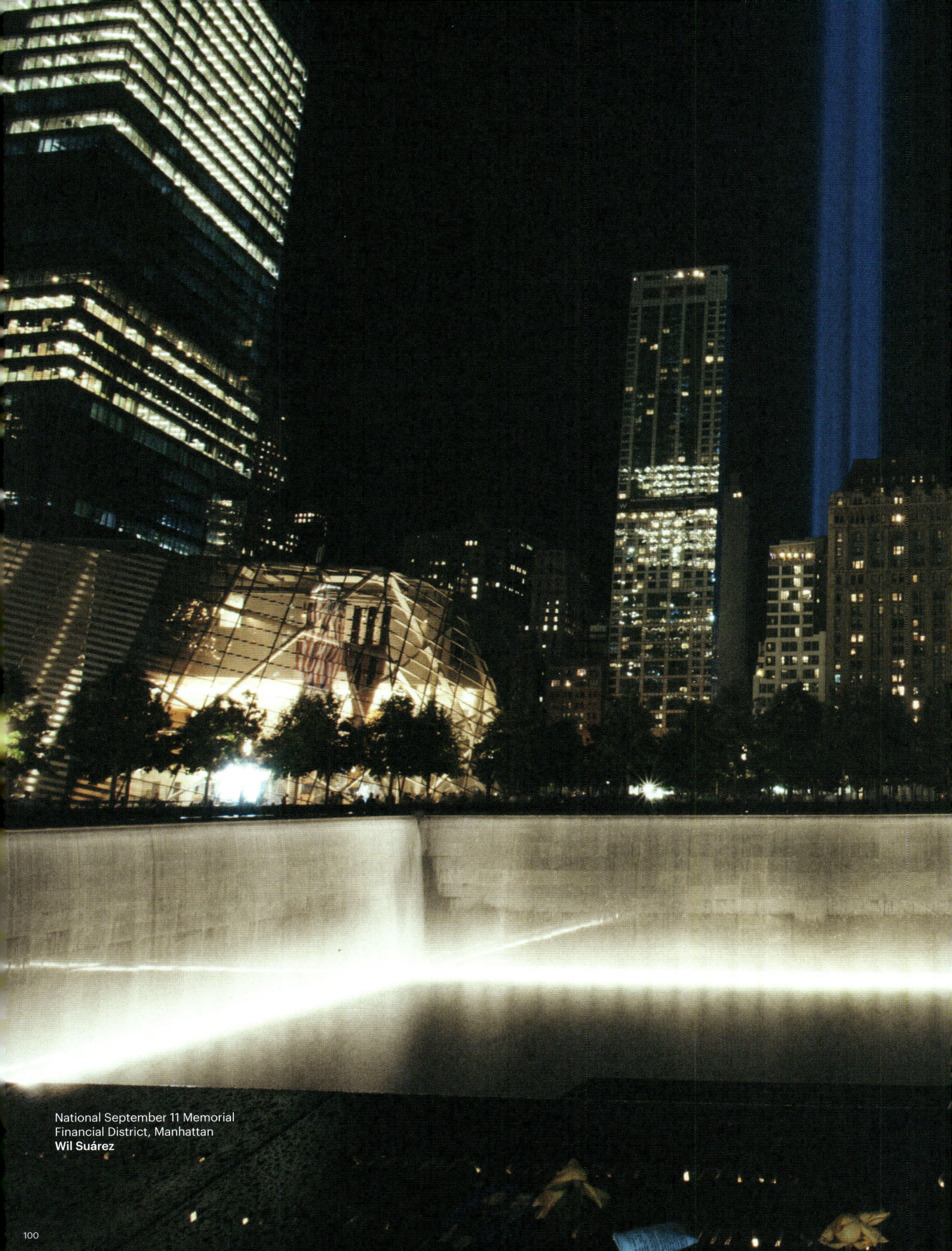

National September 11 Memorial
Financial District, Manhattan
Wil Suárez

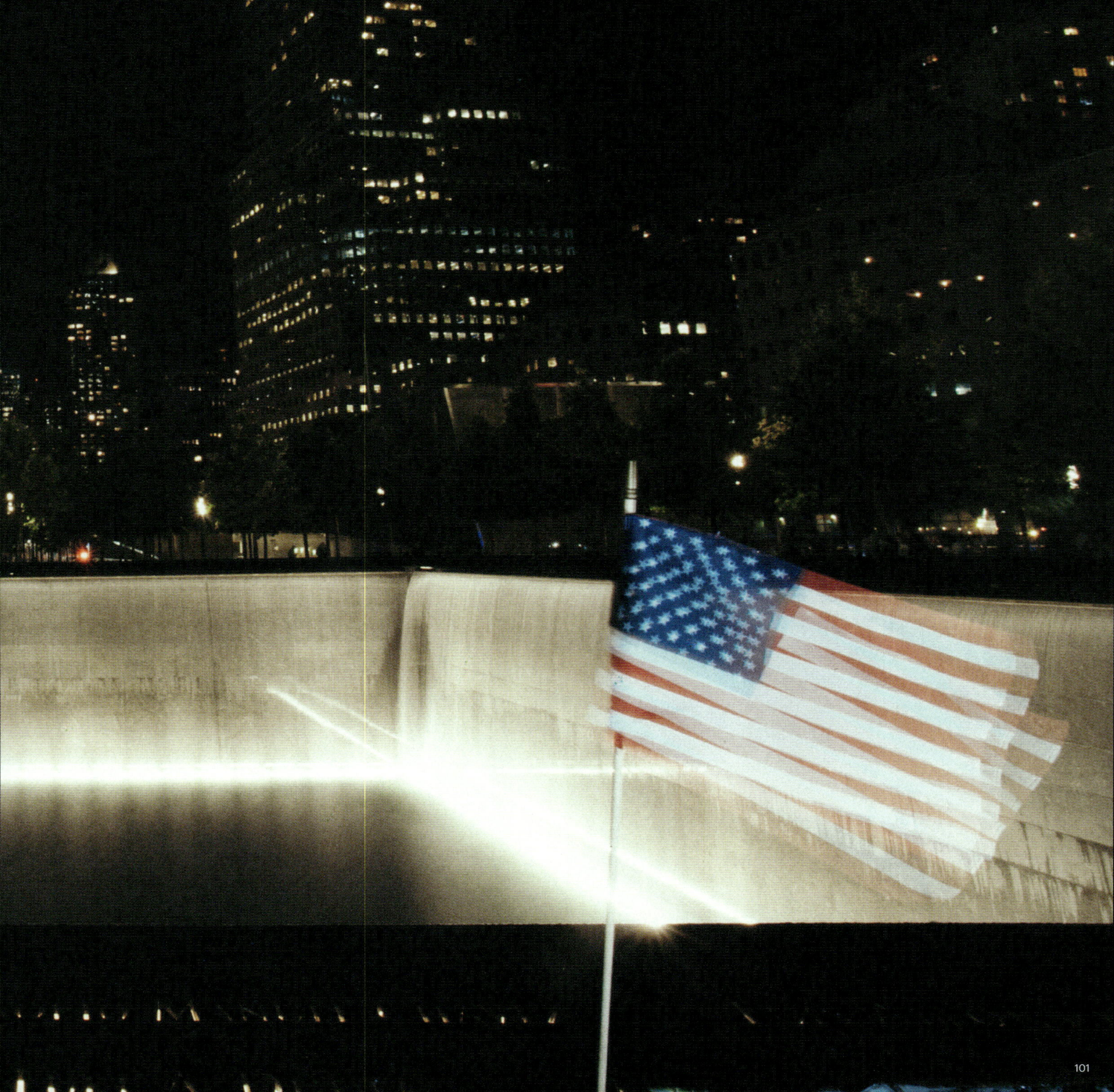

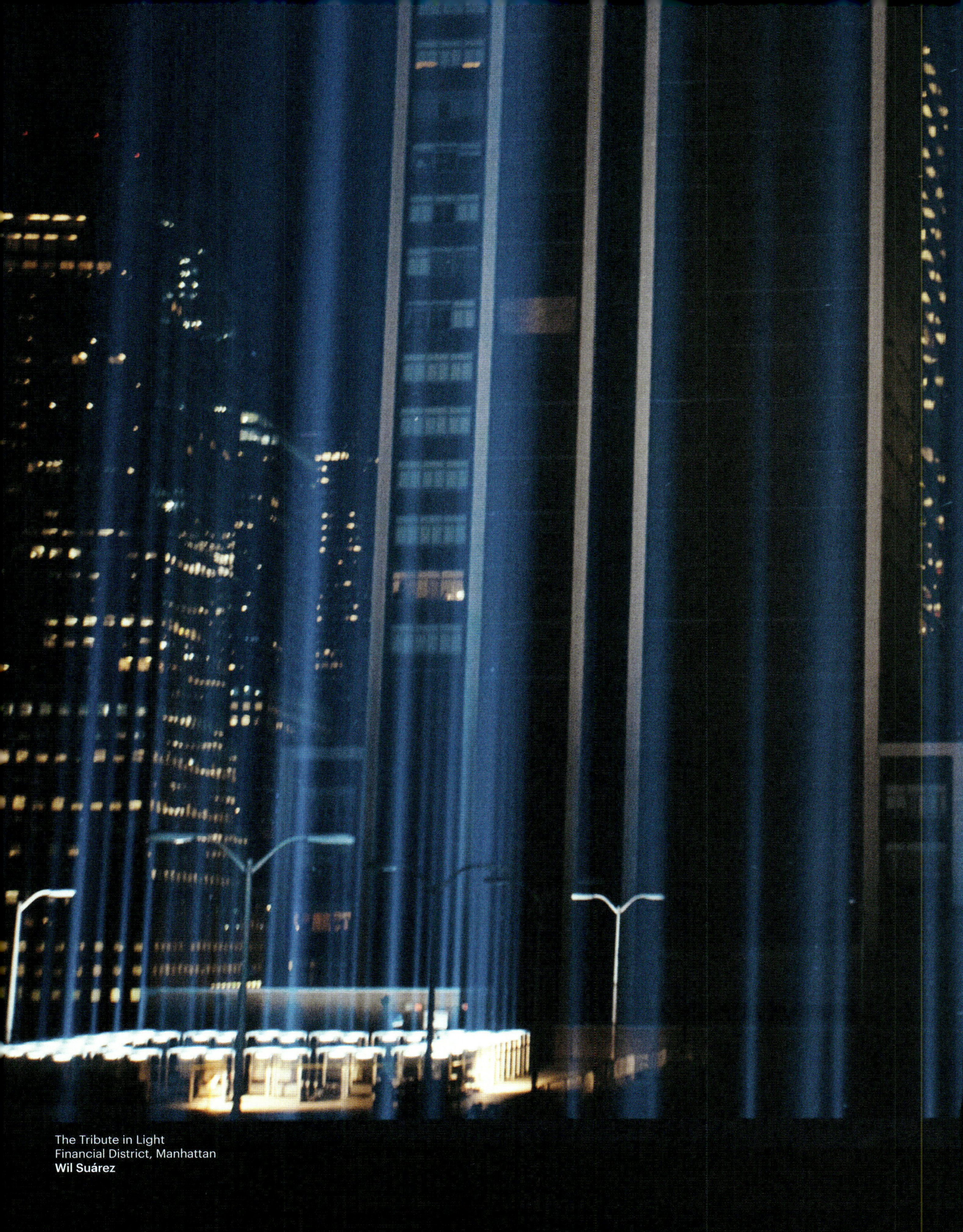

The Tribute in Light
Financial District, Manhattan
Wil Suárez

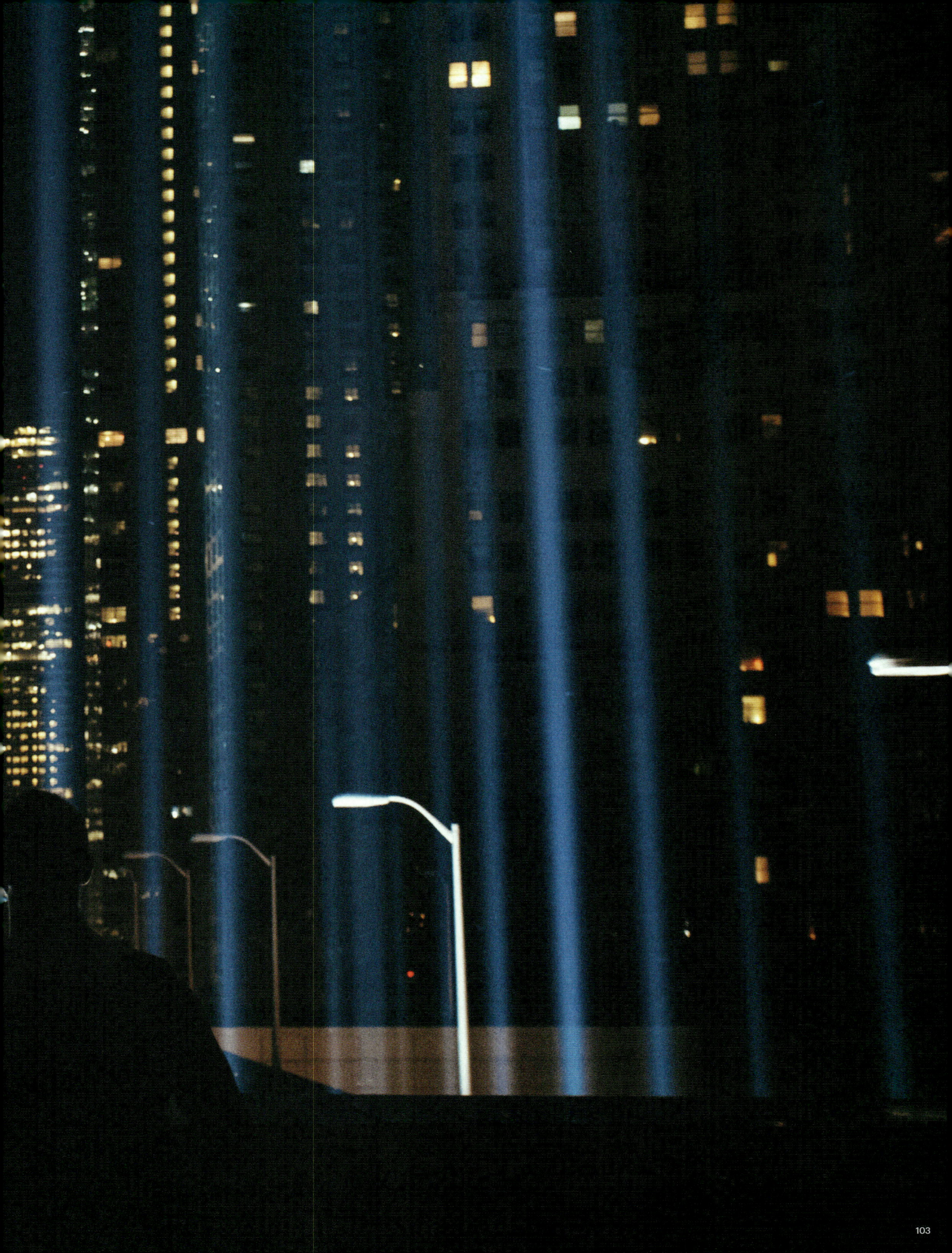

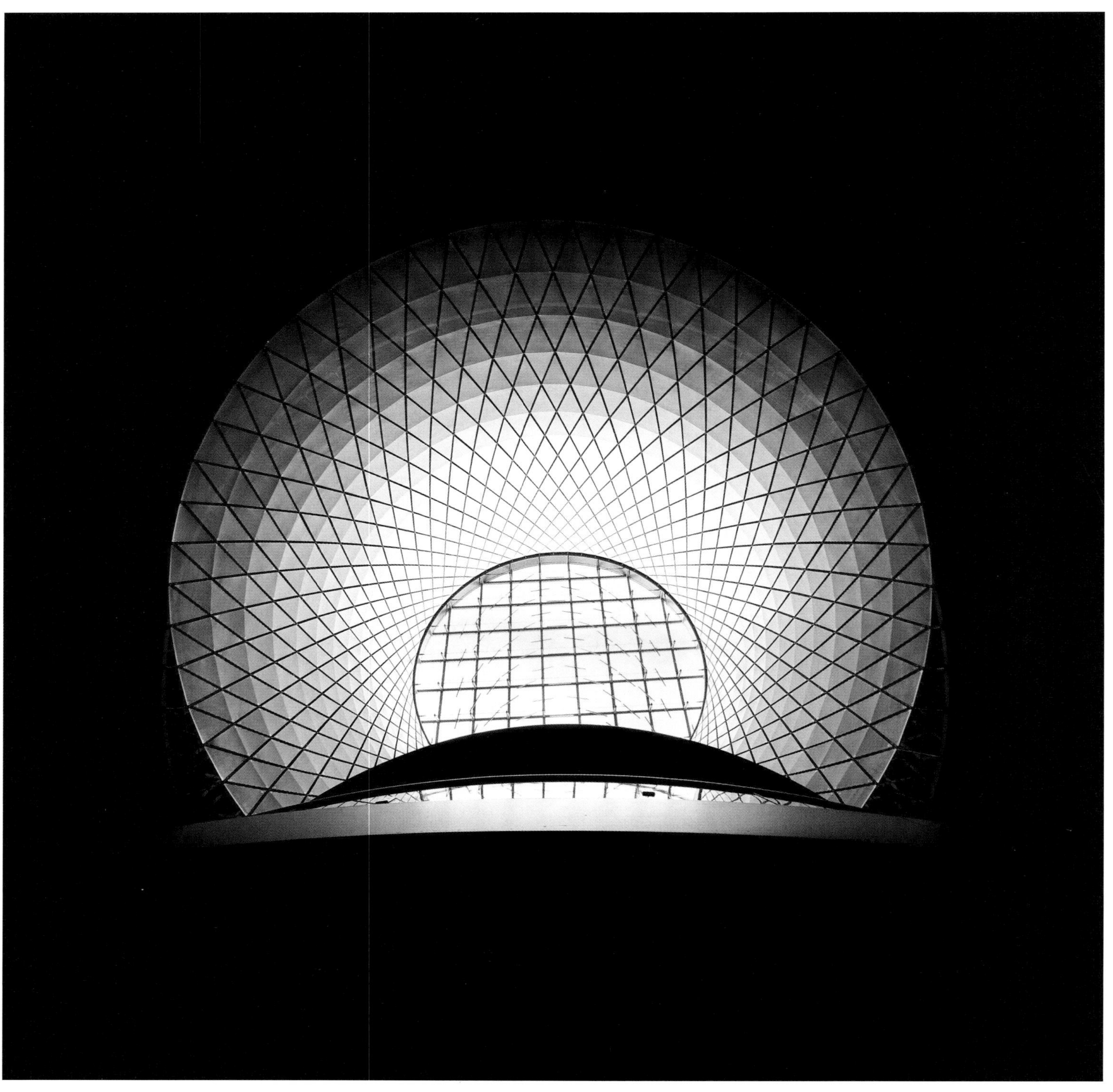

The Fulton Center
Financial District, Manhattan
Jason Peterson

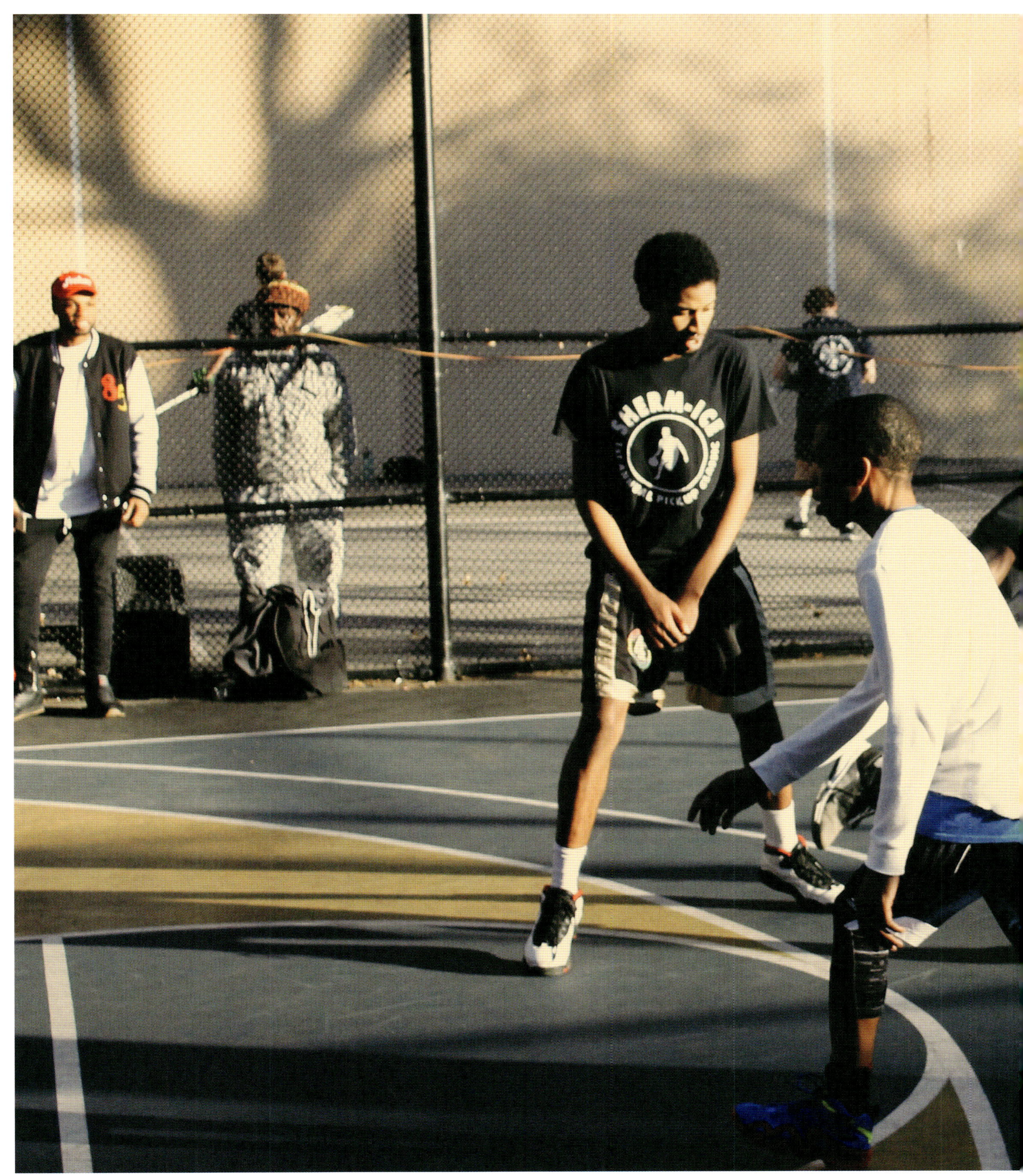

"The Cage," aka West Fourth Street Courts
Greenwich Village, Manhattan
Darius Hertzog

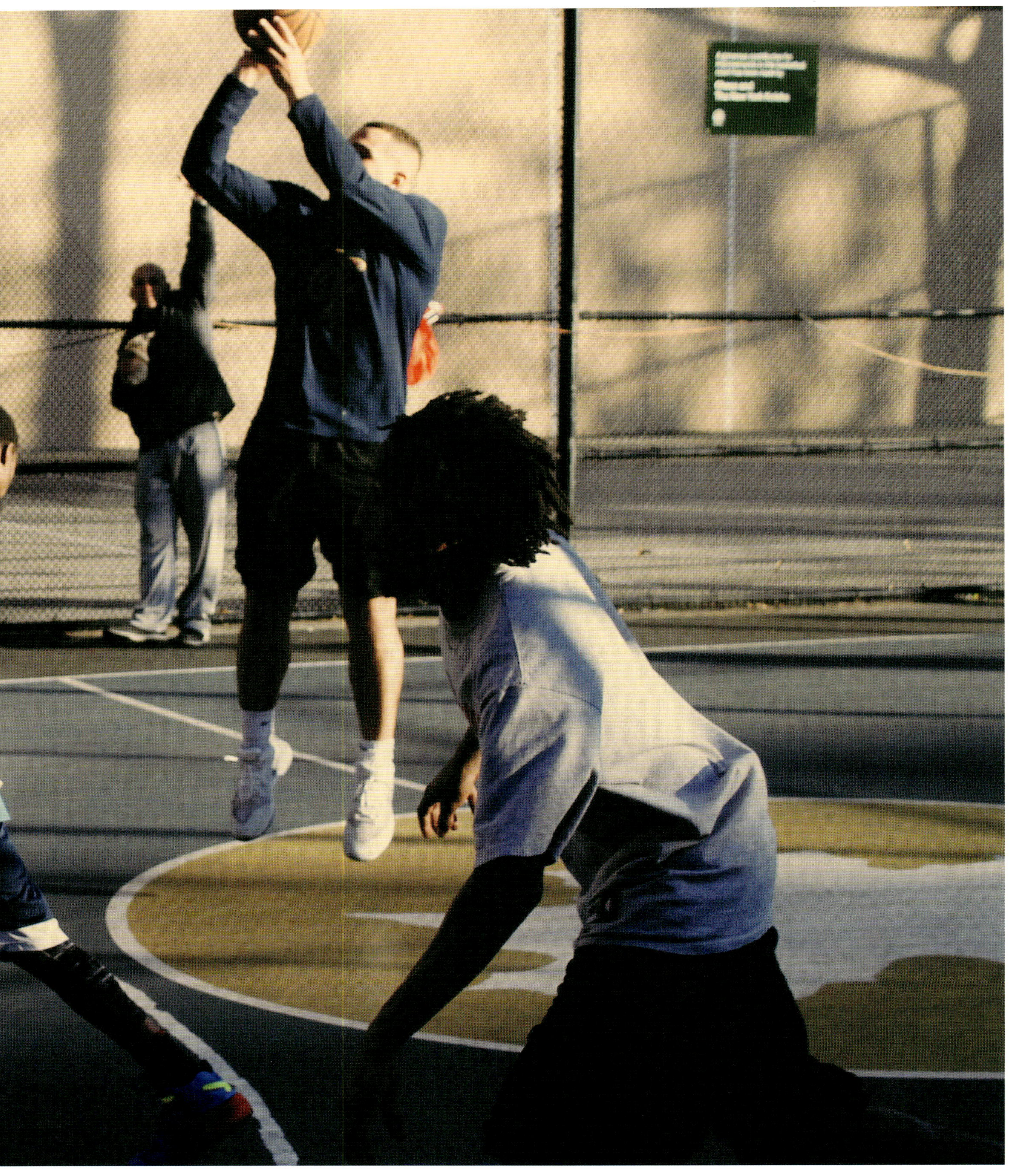

Upper West Side, Manhattan
Lucas Hornsby

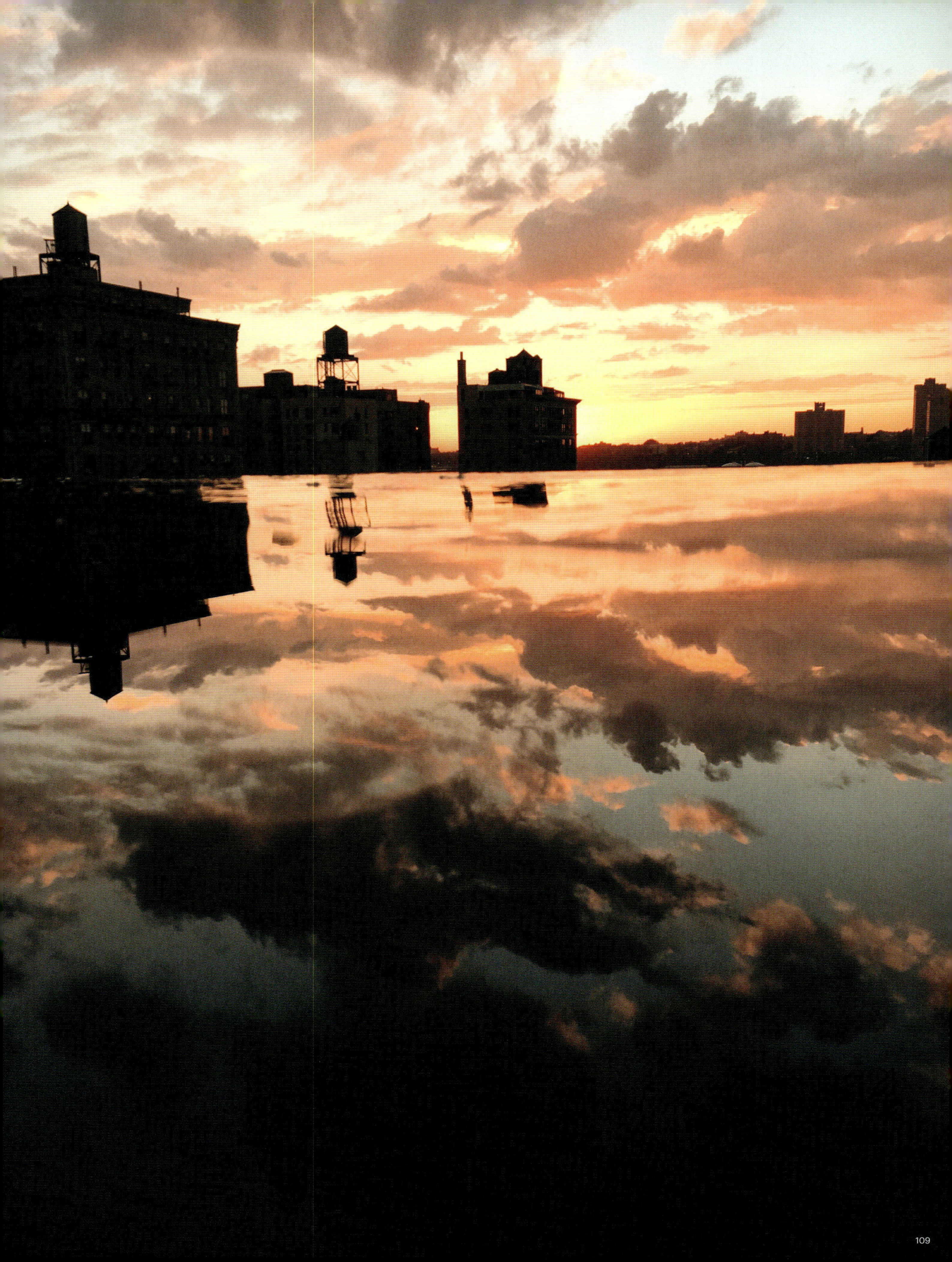

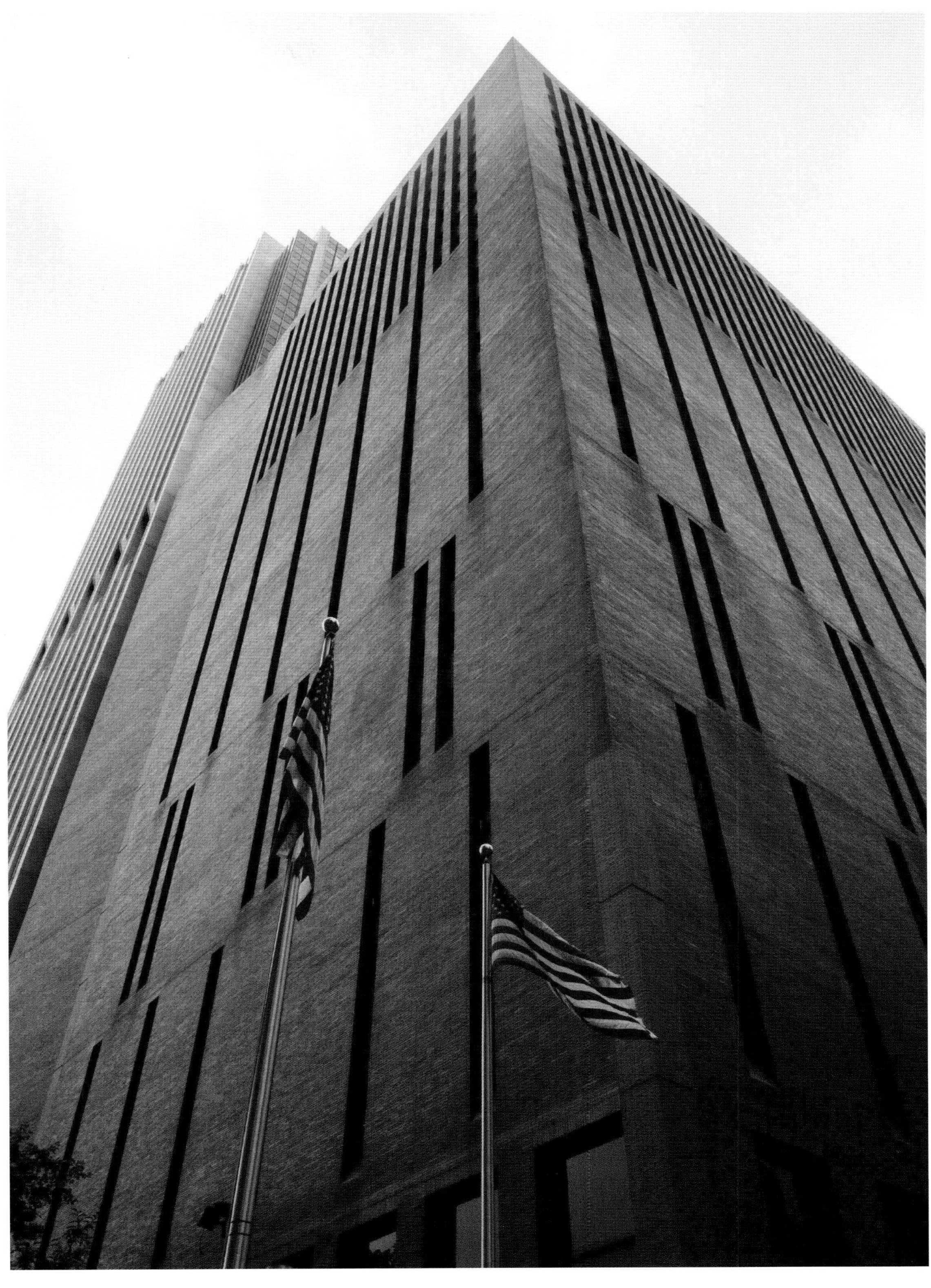

Vietnam Veterans Memorial Plaza
Financial District, Manhattan
Mikel van den Boogaard

New Museum
Bowery, Manhattan
Mikel van den Boogaard

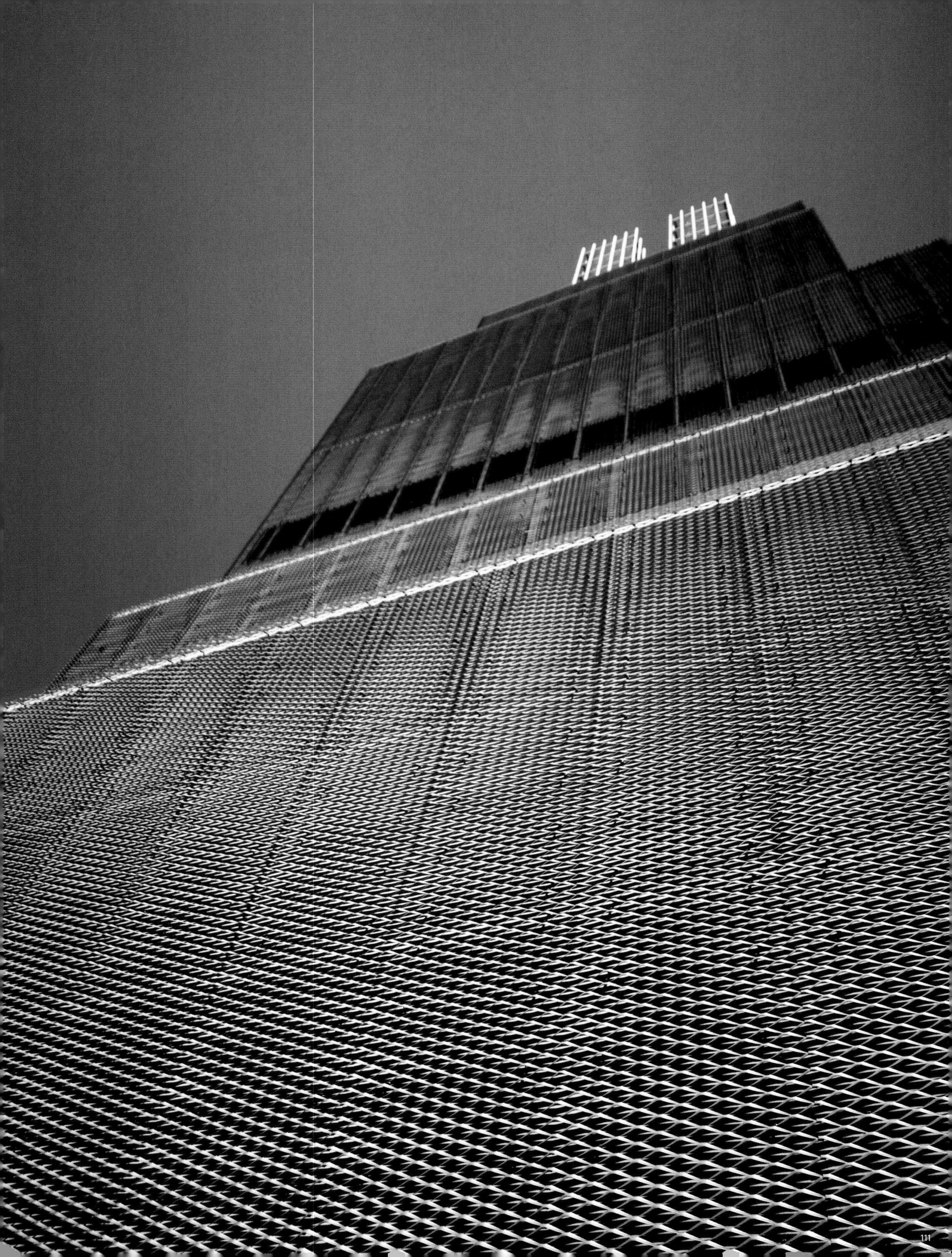

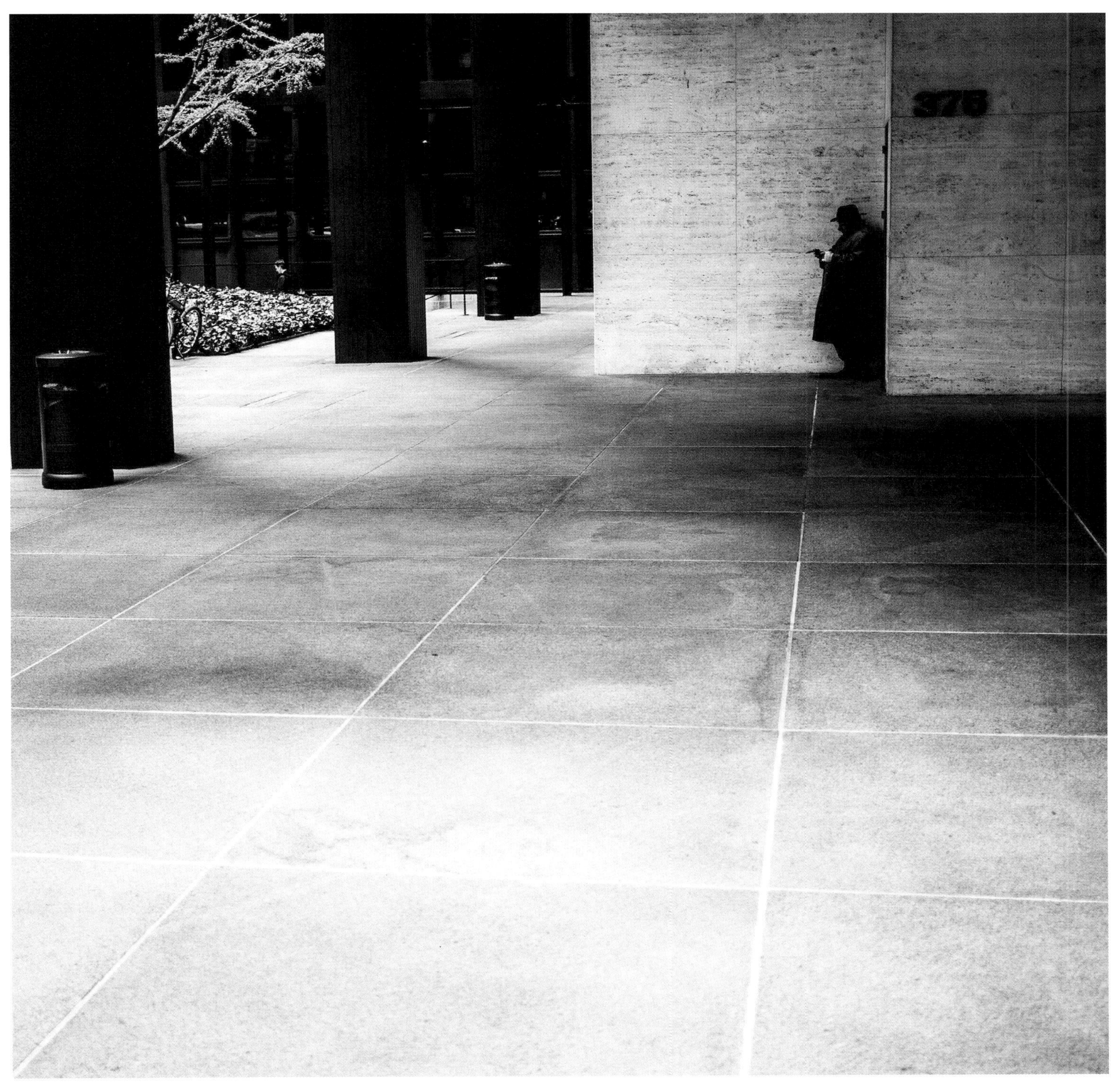

Theater District, Manhattan
Bram van Woudenberg

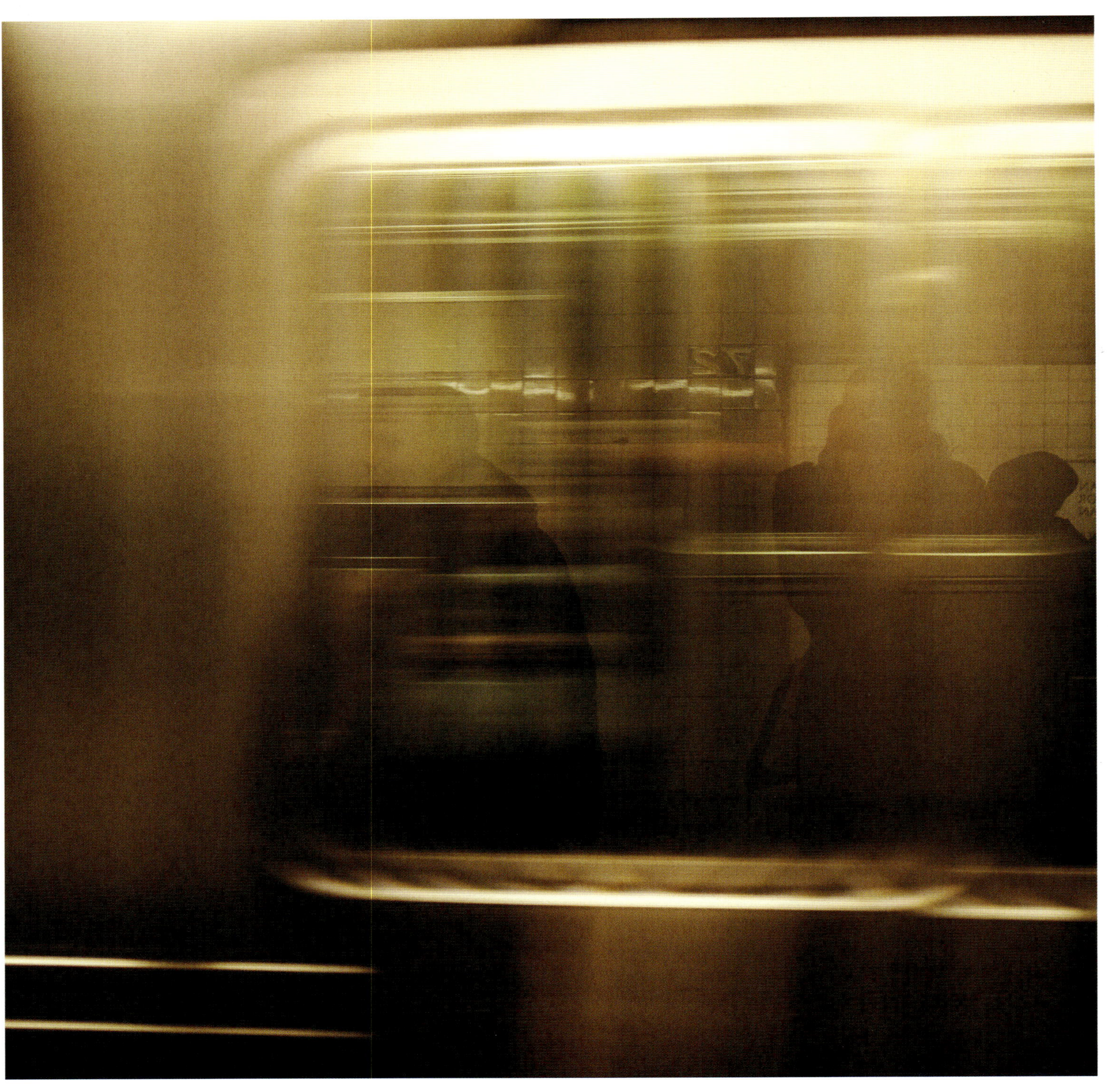

72nd Street Subway Station
Manhattan
Bram van Woudenberg

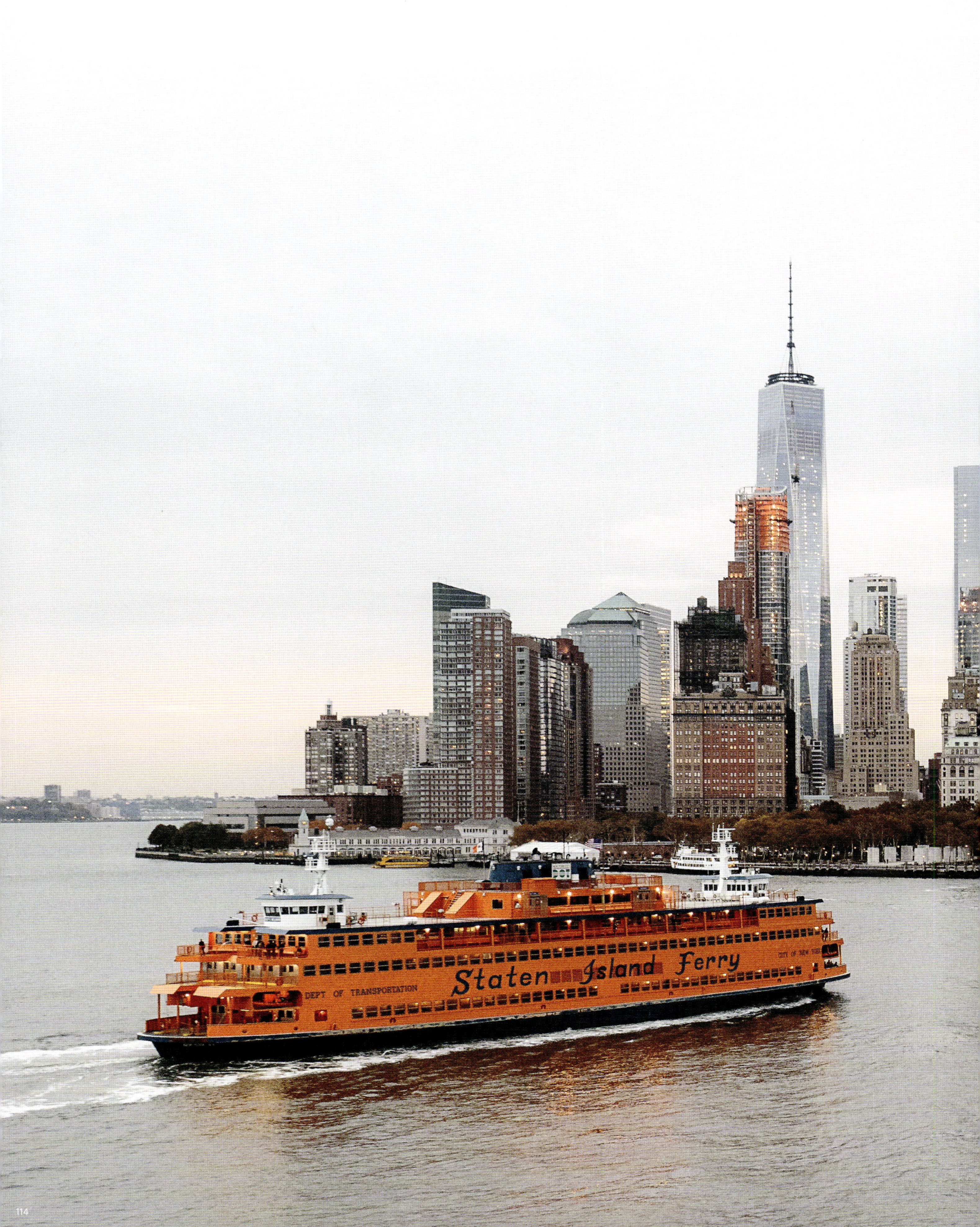
Staten Island Ferry
DEPT OF TRANSPORTATION

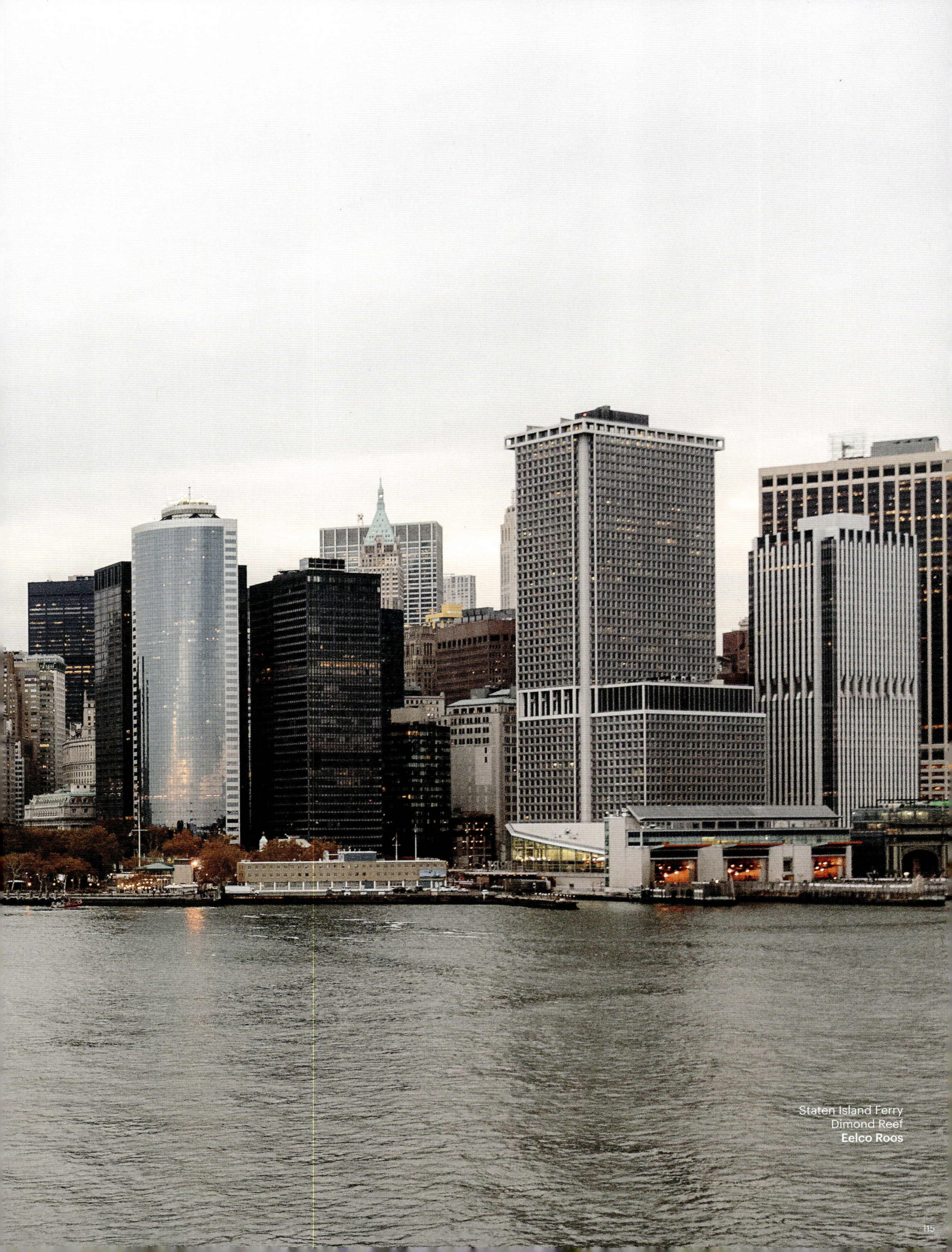

Staten Island Ferry
Dimond Reef
Eelco Roos

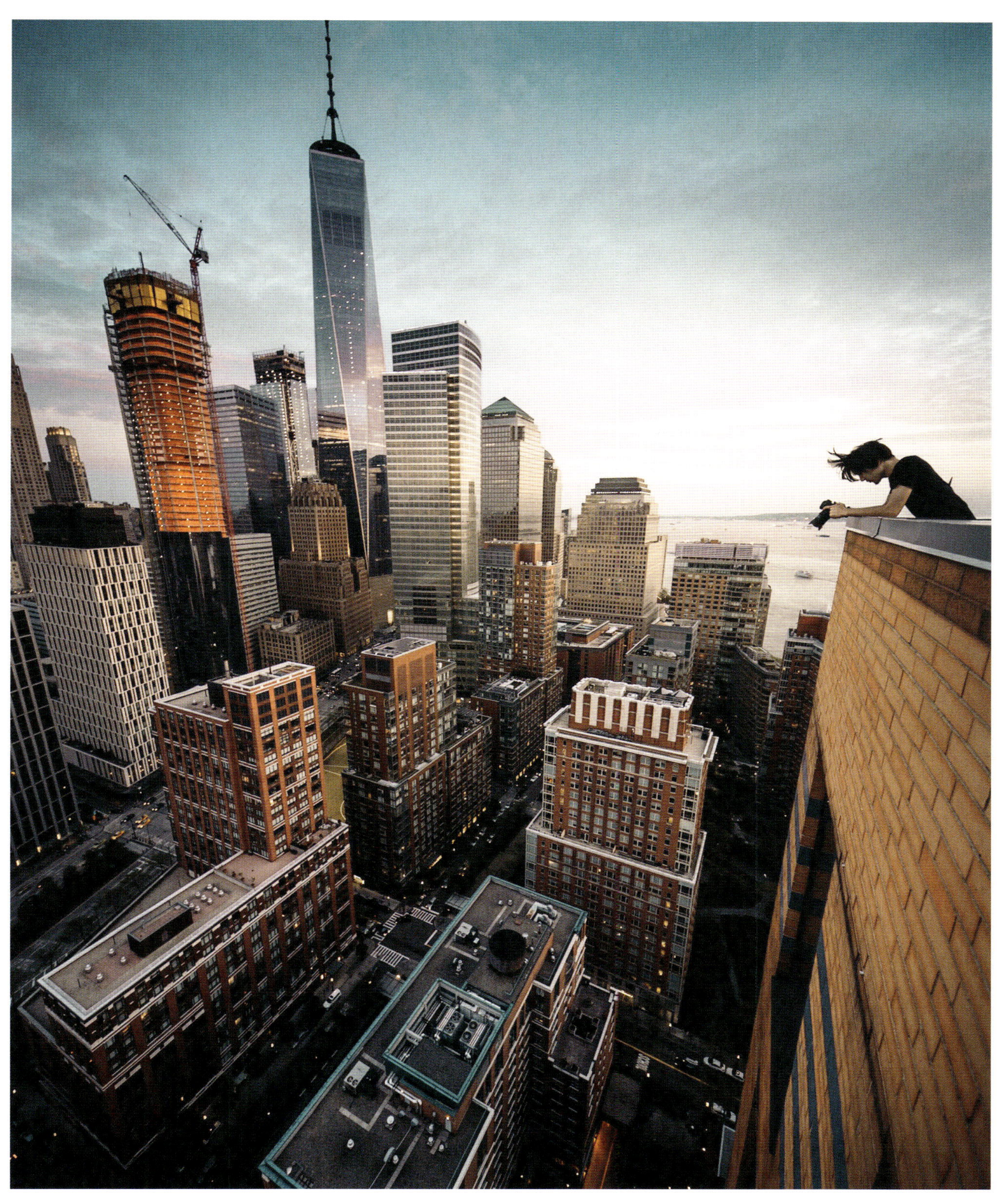

Financial District, Manhattan
Ivan Wong

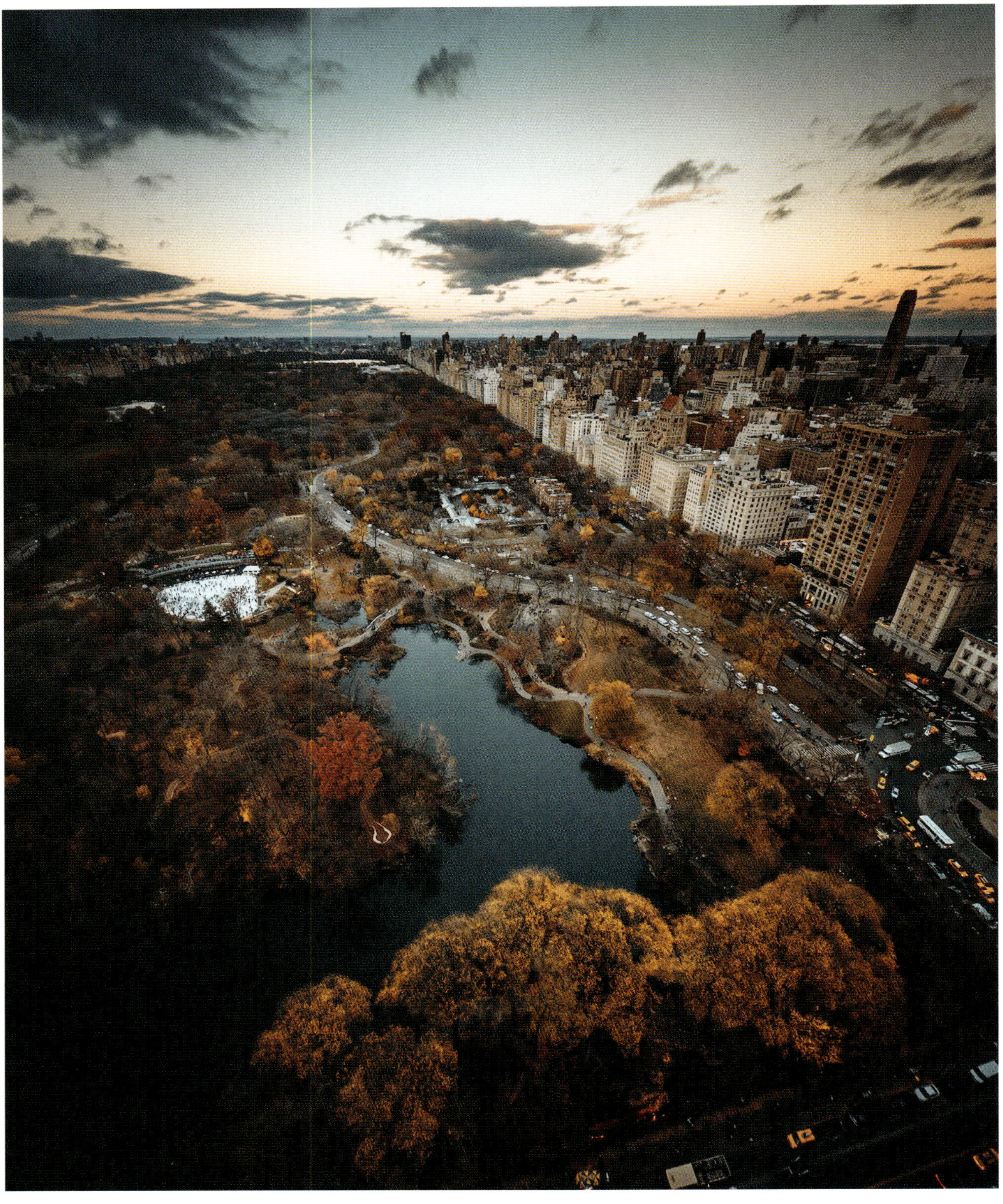

Central Park, Manhattan
Ivan Wong

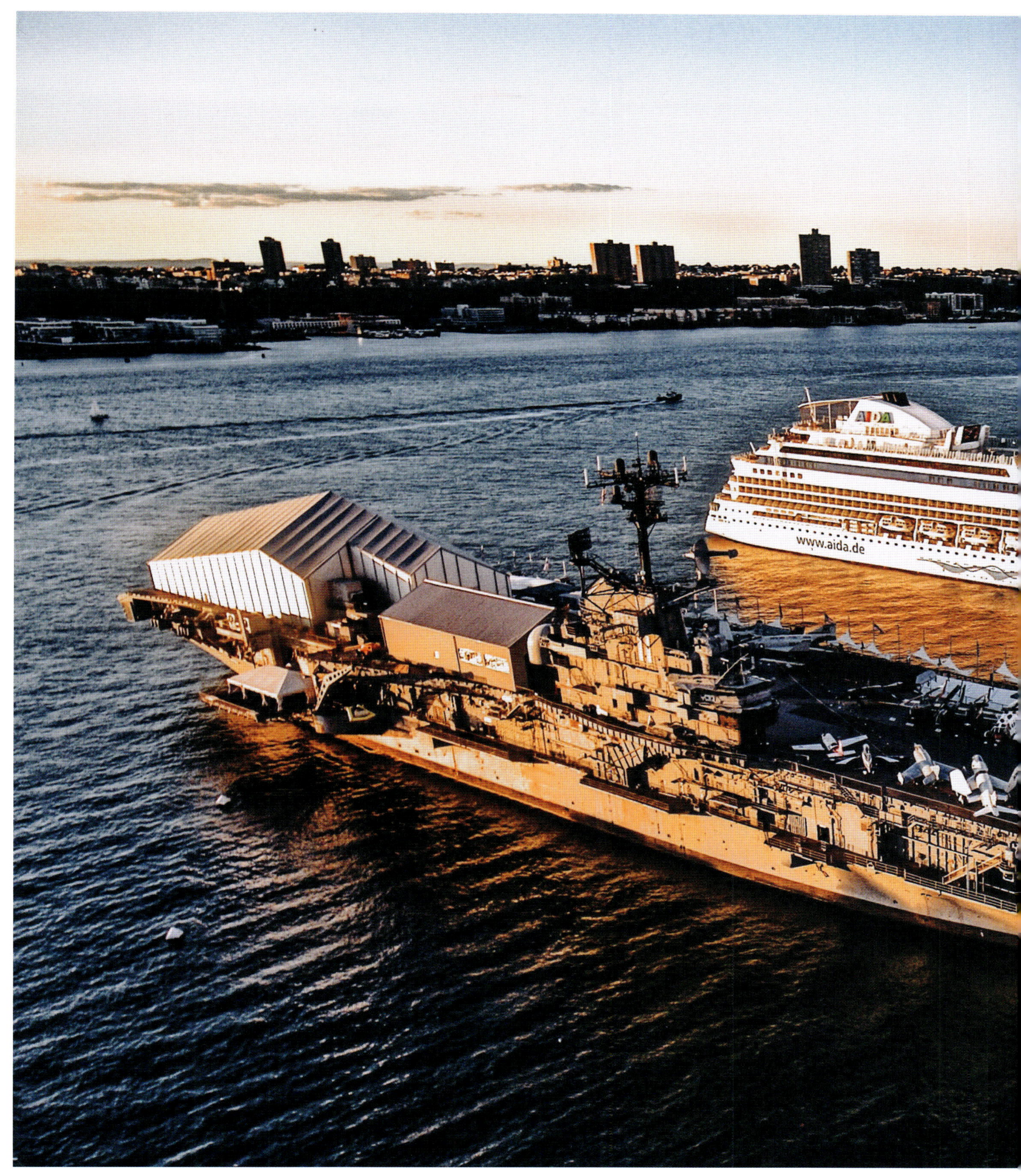

New York City Piers
Hell's Kitchen, Manhattan
Bryan Dumas

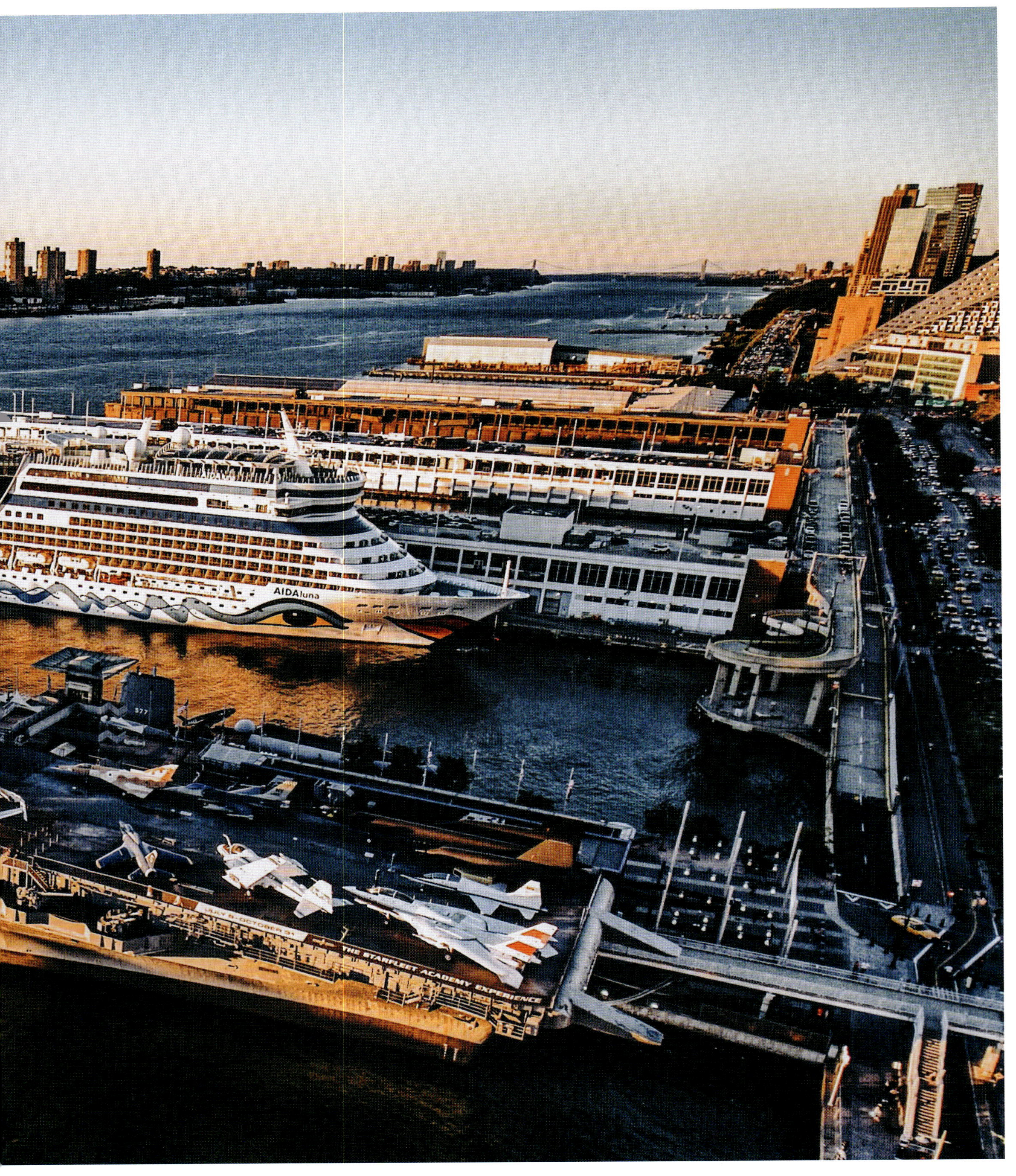
AIDAluna
577
THE STARFLEET ACADEMY EXPERIENCE

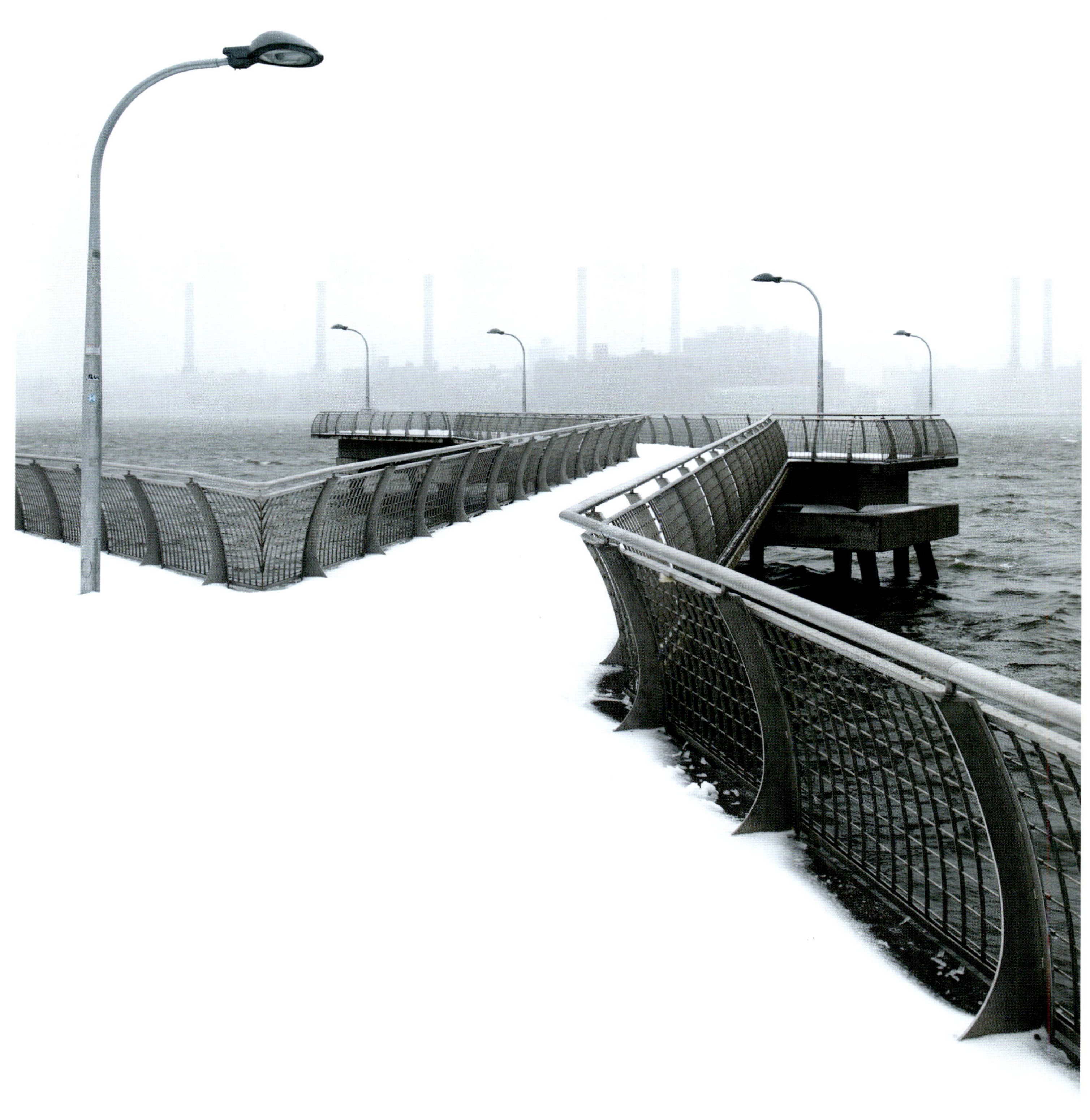

Greenpoint
Brooklyn
Wesley Verhoeve

Josie Robertson Plaza
Lincoln Square, Manhattan
Wesley Verhoeve —

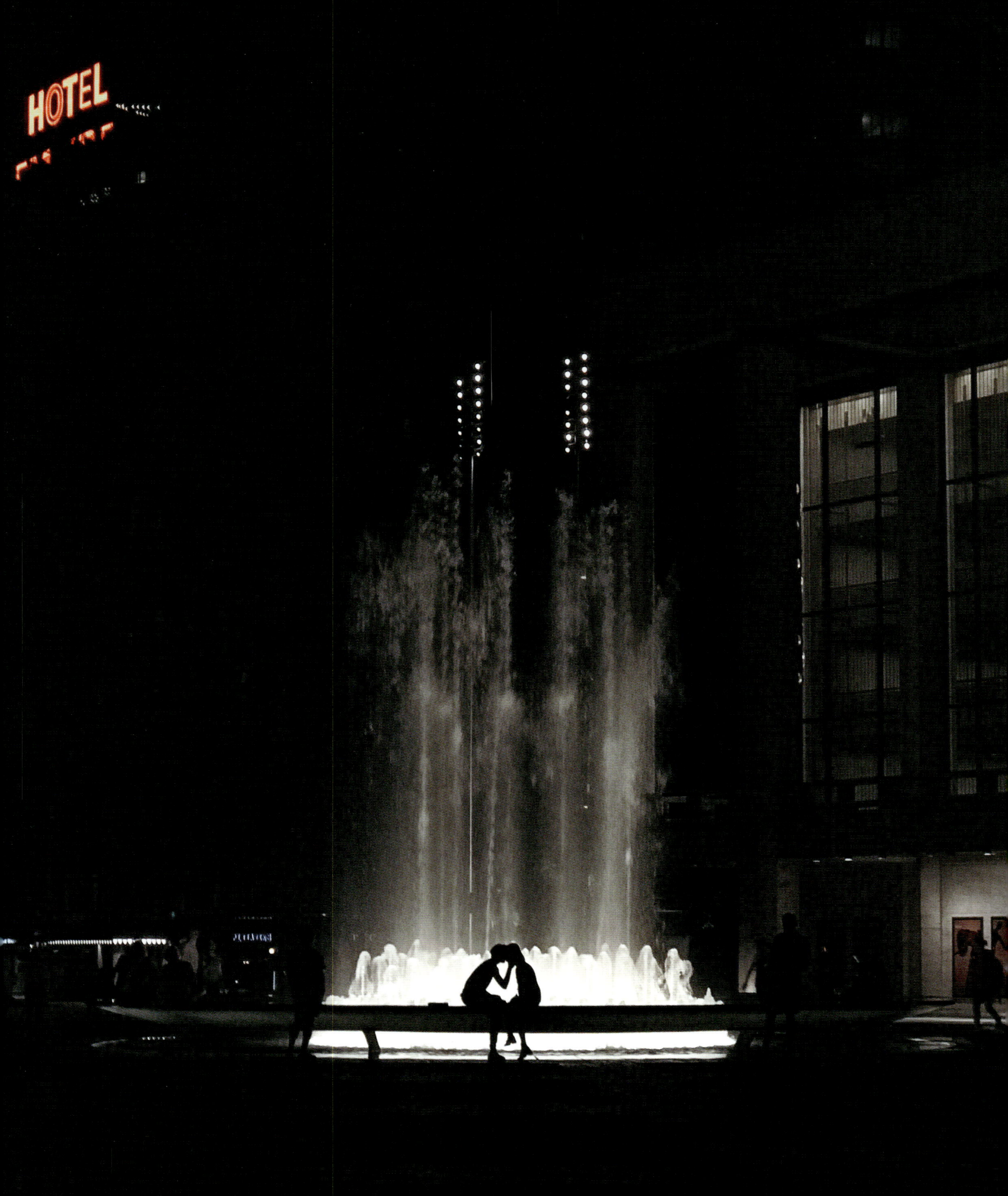
HOTEL

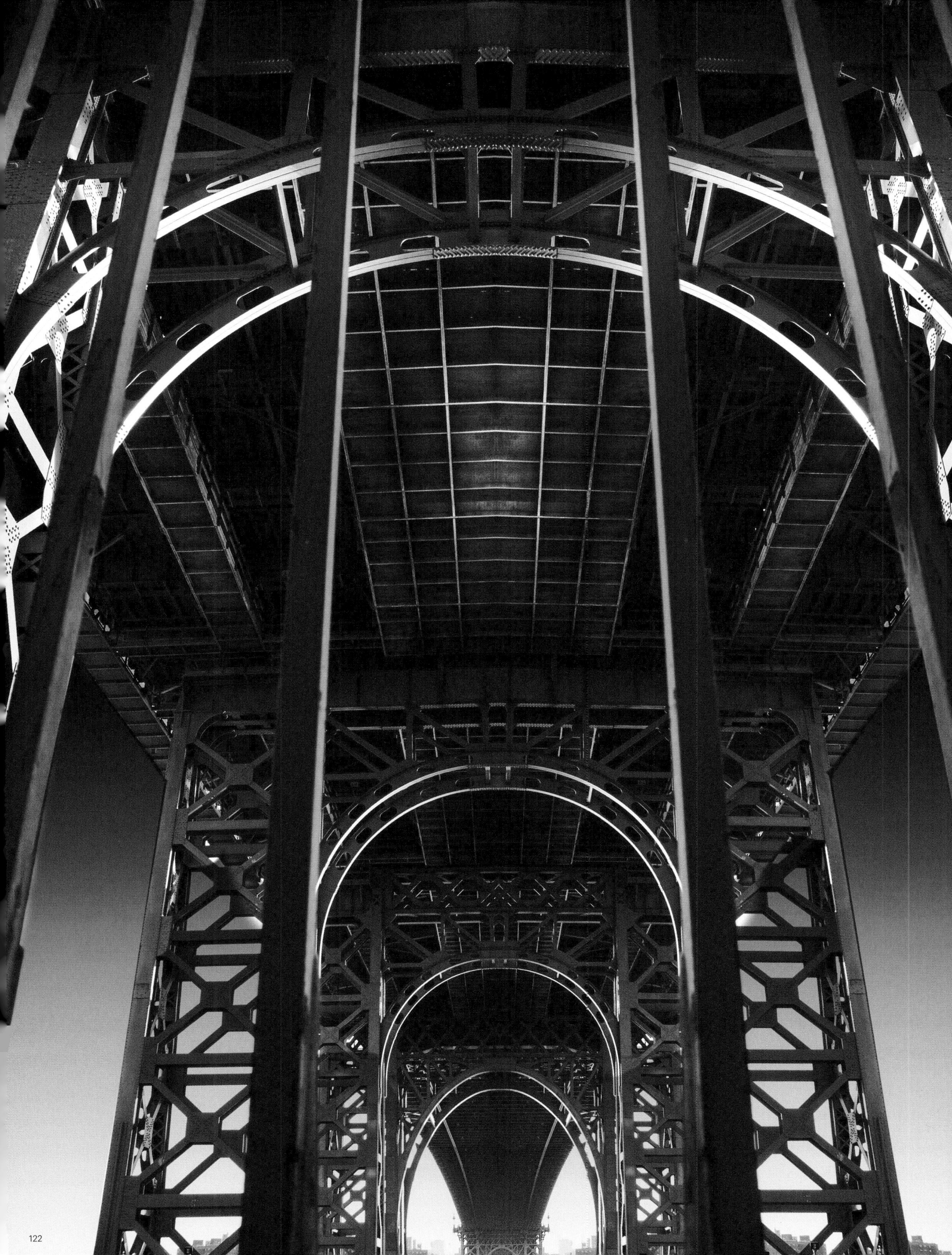

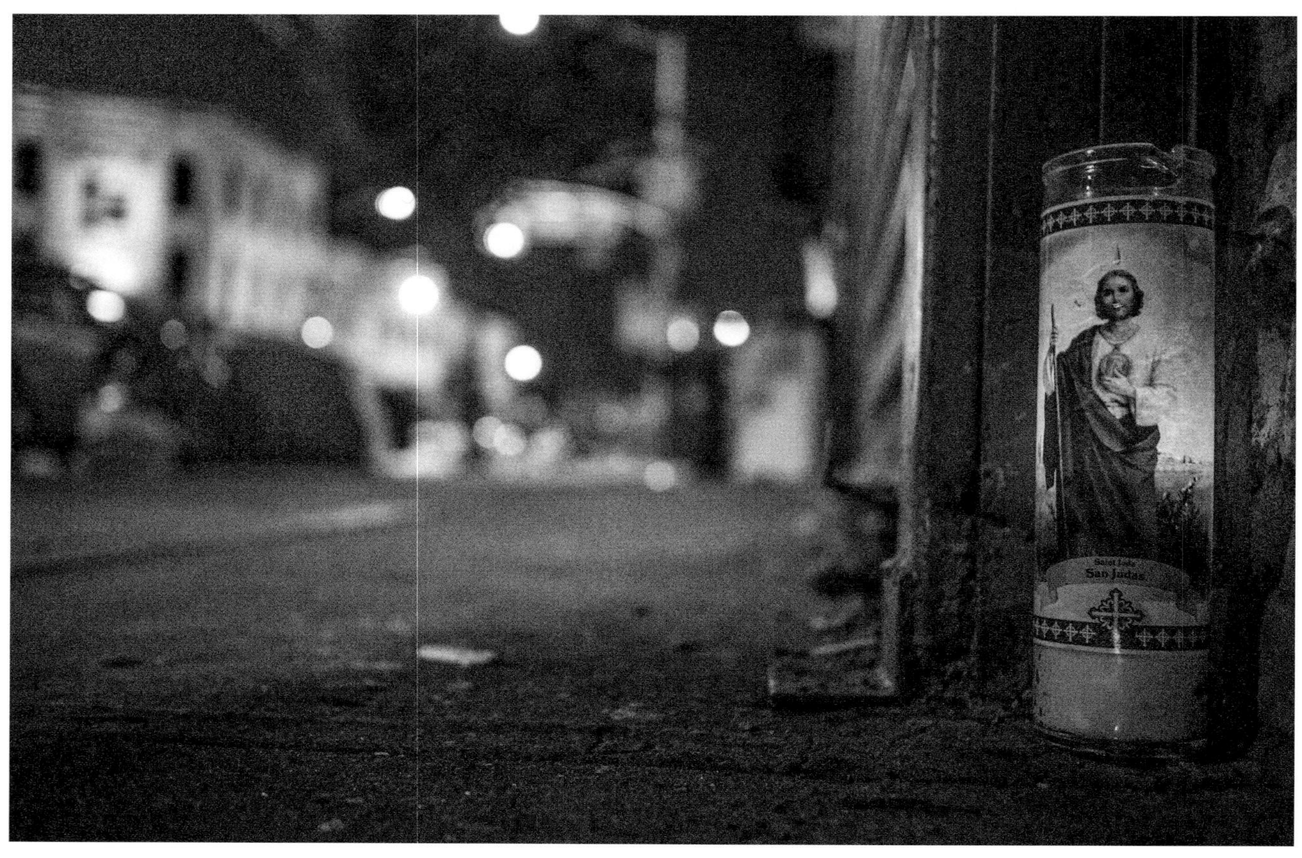

The Williamsburg Bridge
Manhattan
Jason Peterson

Bushwick, Brooklyn
Wil Suárez

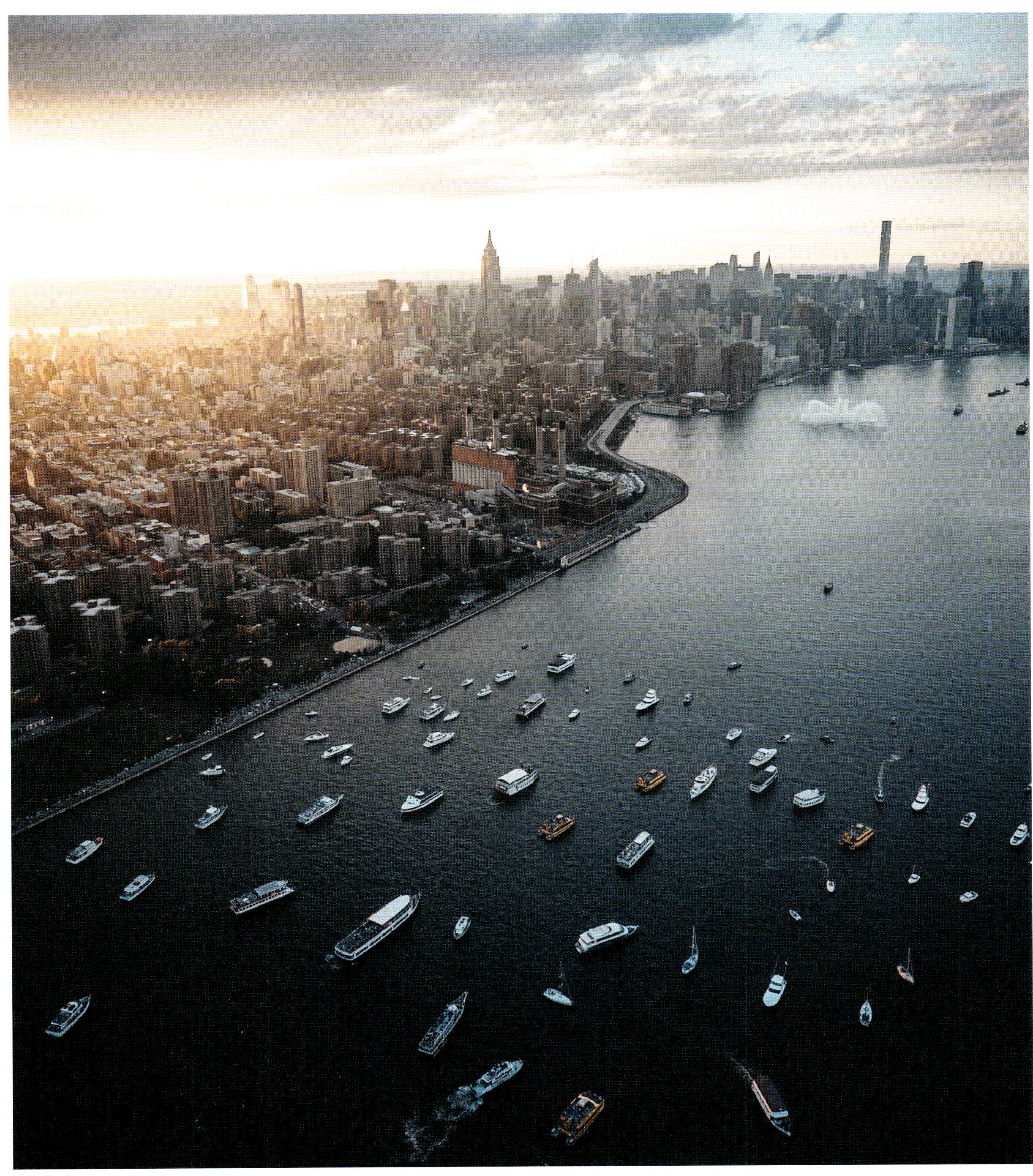

East River
Manhattan
Ivan Wong

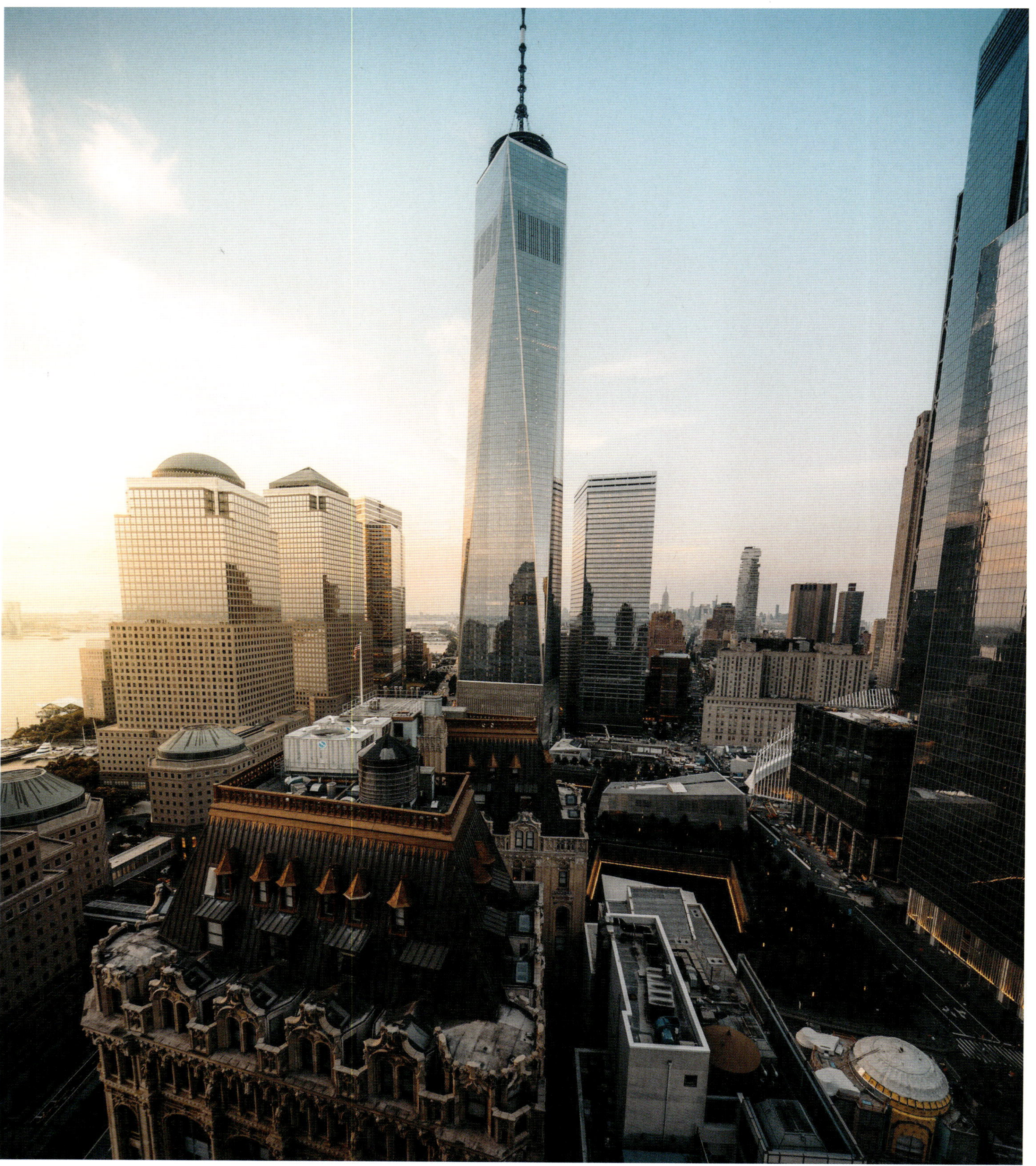

One World Trade Center
Financial District, Manhattan
Ivan Wong

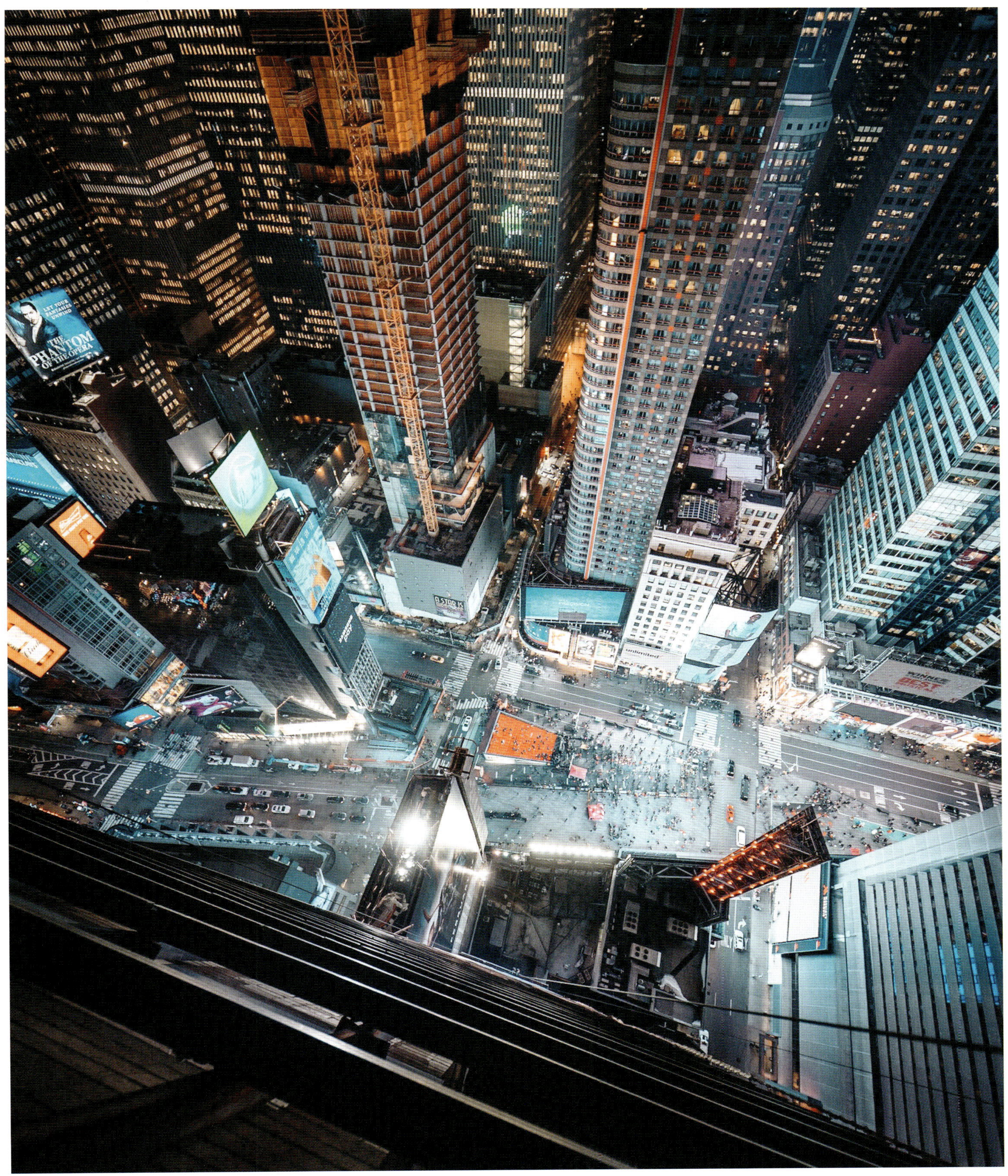

Times Square
Manhattan
Ivan Wong

Times Square
Manhattan
Ivan Meneses

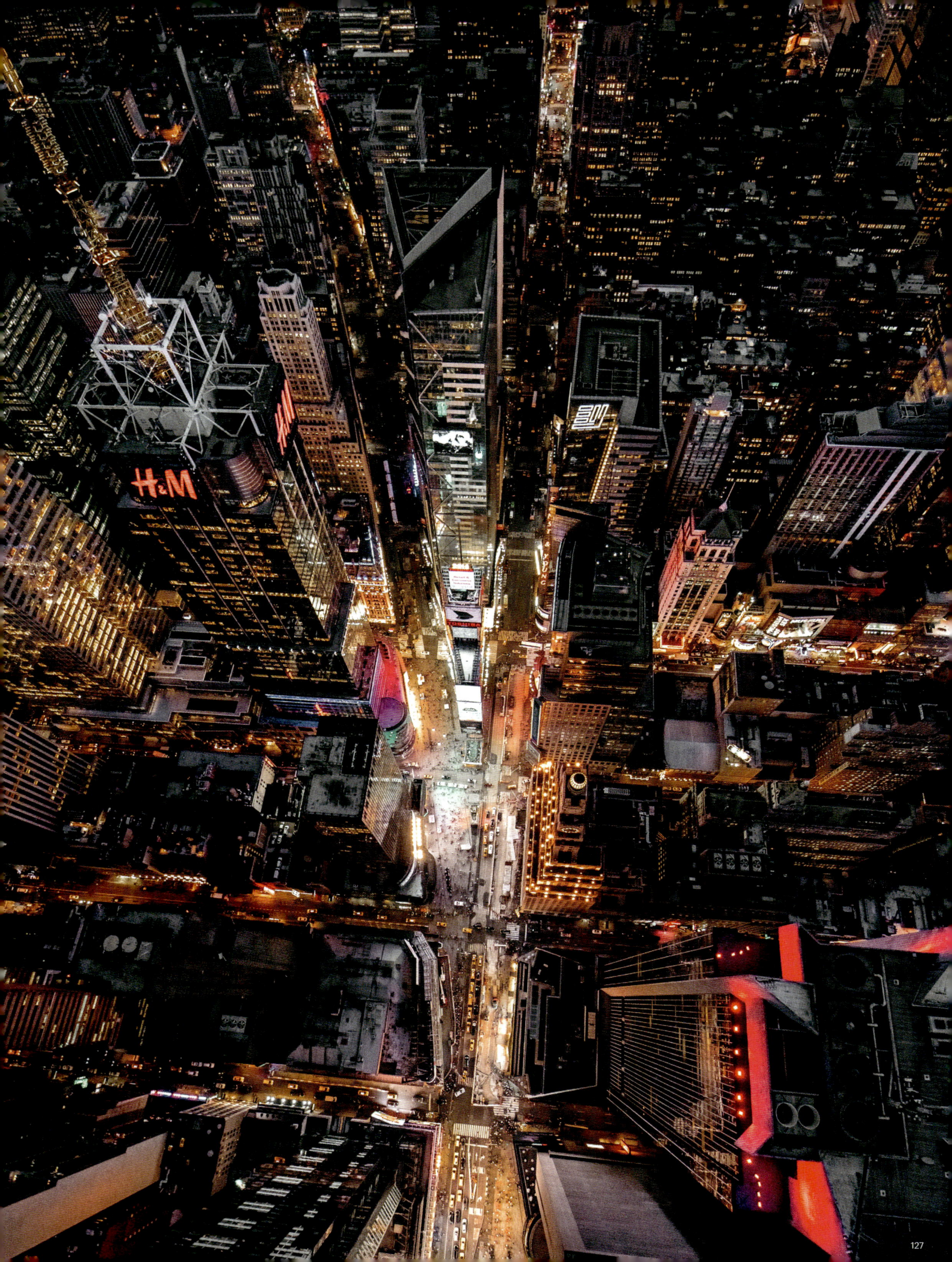
H&M

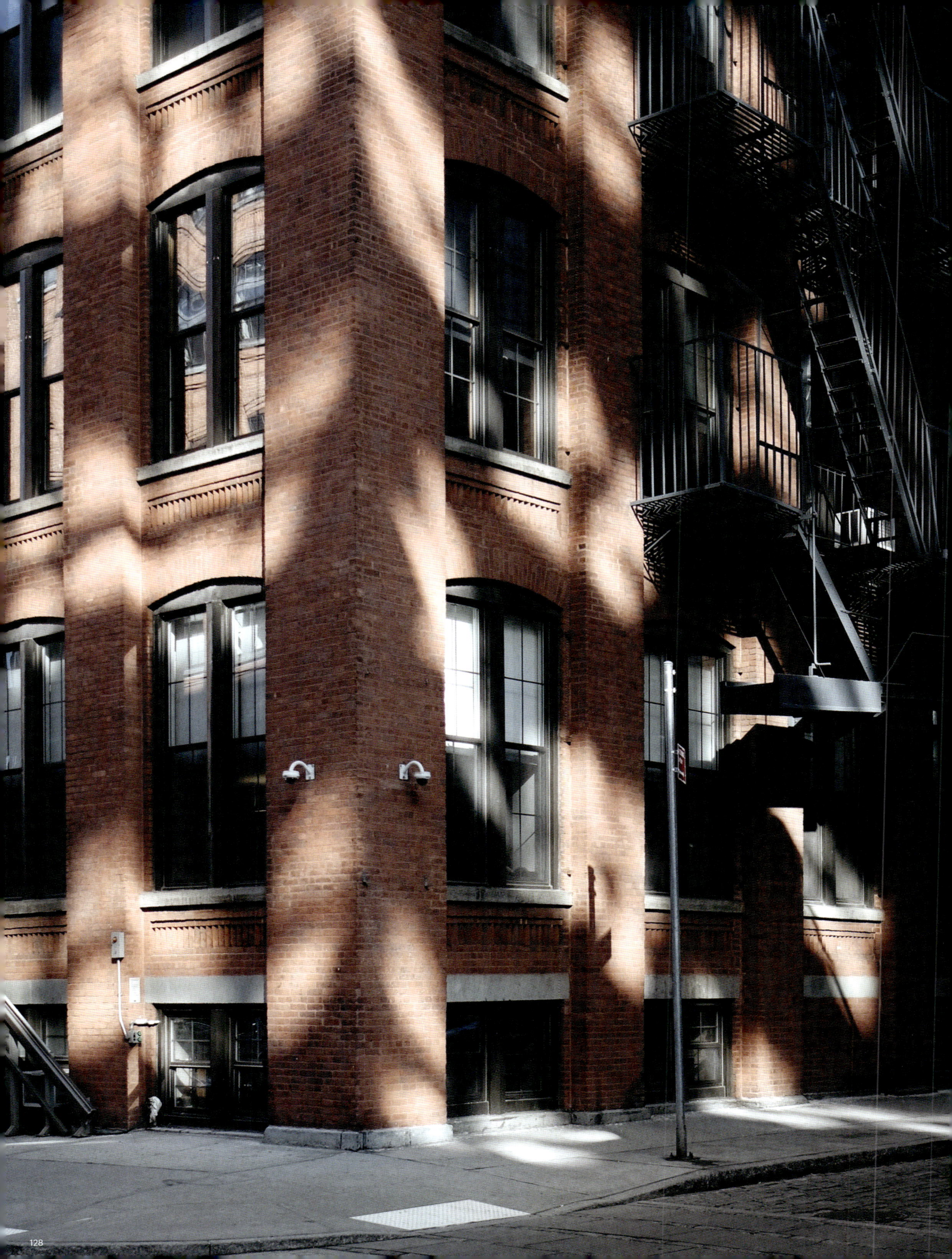

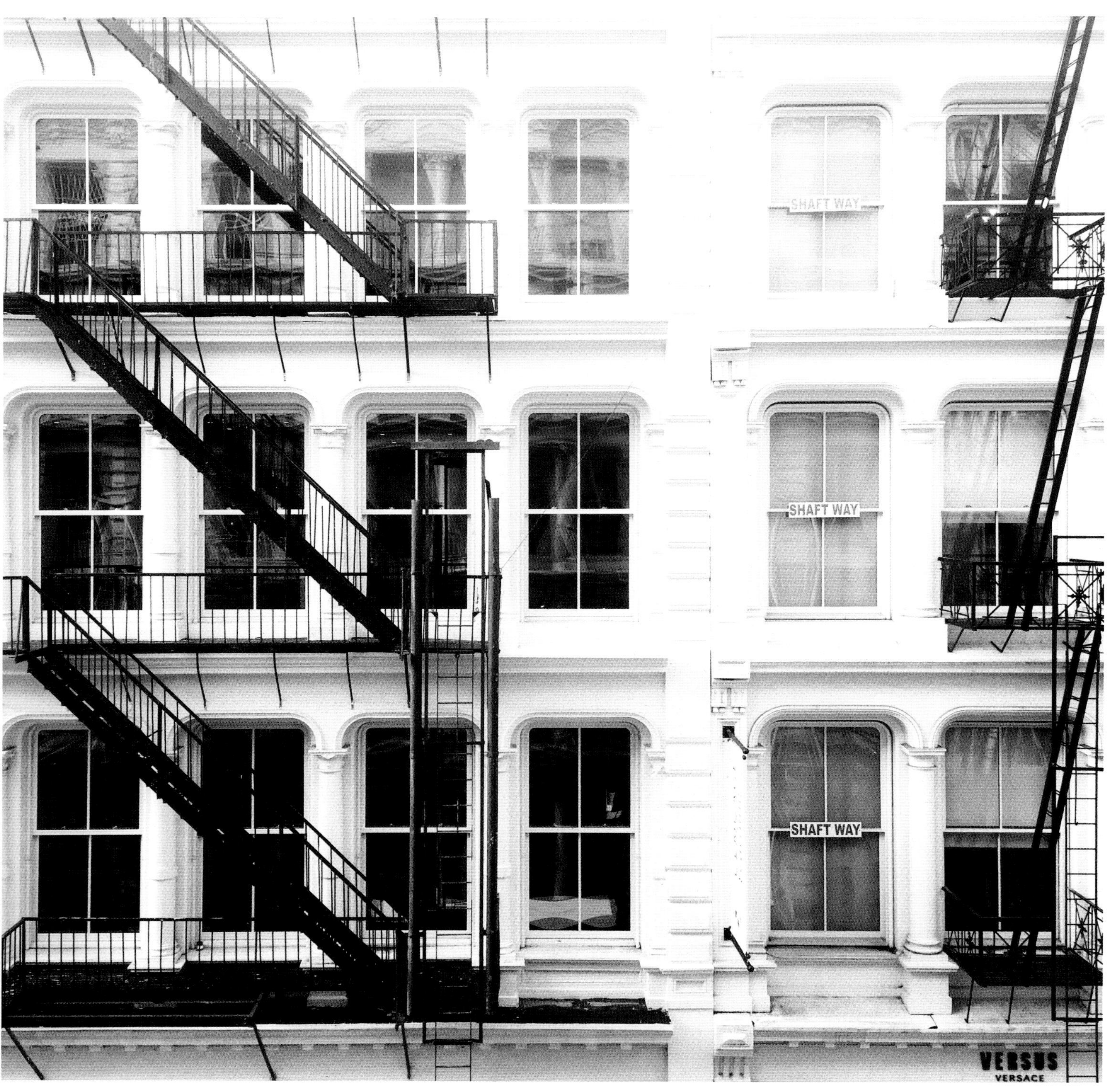

Dumbo, Brooklyn
Peter Wu

The Apartment by The Line
SoHo, Manhattan
Peter Wu

Bram van Woudenberg

hometown Amsterdam, The Netherlands
IG handle @bramvanwoudenberg

As a true Dutchman in New York, Bram van Woudenberg rides the streets of New York by bike. Often without a specific destination, he lets sounds or traffic lights guide his way through the city. "I'll stop at certain places to shoot that shot that has been waiting," he says. "When friends visit our home in Bed-Stuy, I take them for a bike ride to the East River Park. Through the Jewish neighborhood in South Williamsburg, Green Point—all of the different neighborhoods in Brooklyn. I show them the big melting pot of the world, all living apart together."

Bram works on New York City movie sets, as a gaffer: "I talk with the director of photography (DOP) about lighting a certain scene." He then makes a lighting plan, translating the wishes to logistics. Obviously, there's no photography without light, and Bram applies his lighting knowledge to his photography work. "Unconsciously, I take the lighting situation into account. What is the ideal lighting setup, under the circumstances? Working with great DOPs taught me a lot about framing and using available light." "I want to show the little things that otherwise might go unnoticed. Little stories that happen every day," Bram says. That's why he'd also like to take more portraits. "Without invading someone's privacy, I want to take a picture of someone, without him or her being aware of the camera. That's a challenge. I always say that I need an invisibility coat, so people can't see that I'm taking a picture."

There's one more reason why he likes photography: "I find it hard to let things go. Quite literally. I want a memory of the things we see and do in life."

Als echter Holländer fährt Bram van Woudenberg mit dem Fahrrad durch die Straßen New Yorks. Oft hat er kein klares Ziel, sondern lässt sich von Geräuschen oder Ampeln durch die Stadt leiten. „An bestimmten Stellen halte ich an, um ein Foto zu schießen, das auf mich gewartet hat", erzählt er. „Wenn Freunde bei uns in Bed-Stuy zu Besuch sind, nehme ich sie auf eine Fahrradtour zum East River Park mit. Durch das jüdische Viertel in South Williamsburg, durch Green Point – die ganzen unterschiedlichen Stadtviertel von Brooklyn. Ich zeige ihnen den großen Schmelztiegel der Welt, wo alle für sich und doch zusammenleben."

Bram arbeitet als Chefbeleuchter auf Filmsets in New York City: „Ich spreche mit dem leitenden Kameramann darüber, wie eine bestimmte Szene beleuchtet werden soll." Dann macht er einen Beleuchtungsplan und übersetzt die Wünsche in die technische Praxis. Selbstverständlich gibt es auch keine Fotografie ohne Licht, und Bram wendet sein Fachwissen auch auf seine fotografische Arbeit an: „Unbewusst berücksichtige ich die Lichtsituation: Was ist unter den gegebenen Umständen die ideale Beleuchtung? Bei der Arbeit mit großen Kameraleuten habe ich viel darüber gelernt, wie man Bildausschnitte wählt und vorhandenes Licht nutzt. Ich will die kleinen Dinge zeigen, die sonst vielleicht unbemerkt bleiben. Kleine Geschichten, die jeden Tag passieren", sagt Bram. Deshalb würde er auch gerne mehr Porträts aufnehmen. „Ich möchte Bilder von Menschen machen, ohne in ihre Privatsphäre einzudringen, ohne dass sie sich dessen bewusst sind. Das ist eine Herausforderung. Ich sage immer, ich brauche einen Tarnumhang, damit die Leute nicht sehen, dass ich sie ablichte."

Es gibt noch einen Grund, warum er das Fotografieren mag: „Mir fällt es schwer, Dinge loszulassen. Ganz buchstäblich. Ich möchte eine bleibende Erinnerung an all die Dinge, die wir im Leben sehen und tun."

En véritable Hollandais de New York, Bram van Woudenberg parcourt les rues de la ville en vélo. N'ayant souvent aucun but, il laisse les sons ou les feux rouges guider son périple dans la ville. « Je m'arrête en certains lieux pour y photographier ce qui attend de l'être », explique-t-il. « Lorsque des amis viennent chez nous, à Bed-Stuy, je les emmène en vélo jusqu'à East River Park. Nous traversons le quartier juif de South Williamsburg, Green Point – chacun des différents quartiers de Brooklyn. Je leur montre ce vaste melting pot international où tous vivent ensemble séparément ».

Bram est éclairagiste et travaille sur des tournages à New York : « Je parle avec le directeur de la photographie de la façon d'éclairer telle scène », avant d'établir ensuite un plan qui traduise les désirs en logistique. Clairement, il n'existe pas de photographie sans lumière, et Bram applique à son travail photographique le savoir qu'il possède en matière d'éclairage. « Inconsciemment, je tiens compte de la lumière présente. Quel est l'éclairage idéal pour telle situation donnée ? Le fait d'avoir collaboré avec de grands directeurs de la photographie m'a beaucoup appris quant au cadrage ou à l'exploitation de la lumière disponible. (…). Je veux montrer ces petites choses qui, autrement, passeraient inaperçues. Ces petites histoires qui se produisent chaque jour », affirme Bram. Raison pour laquelle il souhaiterait réaliser plus de portraits. « J'aimerais photographier une personne, sans faire intrusion dans son intimité, ni qu'elle soit consciente de l'appareil. C'est un défi. Je dis toujours que j'ai besoin d'une cape d'invisibilité, afin que nul ne voie que je suis en train de prendre une photo ».

Il est une autre raison à son amour de la photographie : « C'est difficile, je trouve, de renoncer aux choses. Assez littéralement. Je tiens à conserver le souvenir de ce que nous voyons et accomplissons dans la vie ».

Manhattan
Bram van Woudenberg

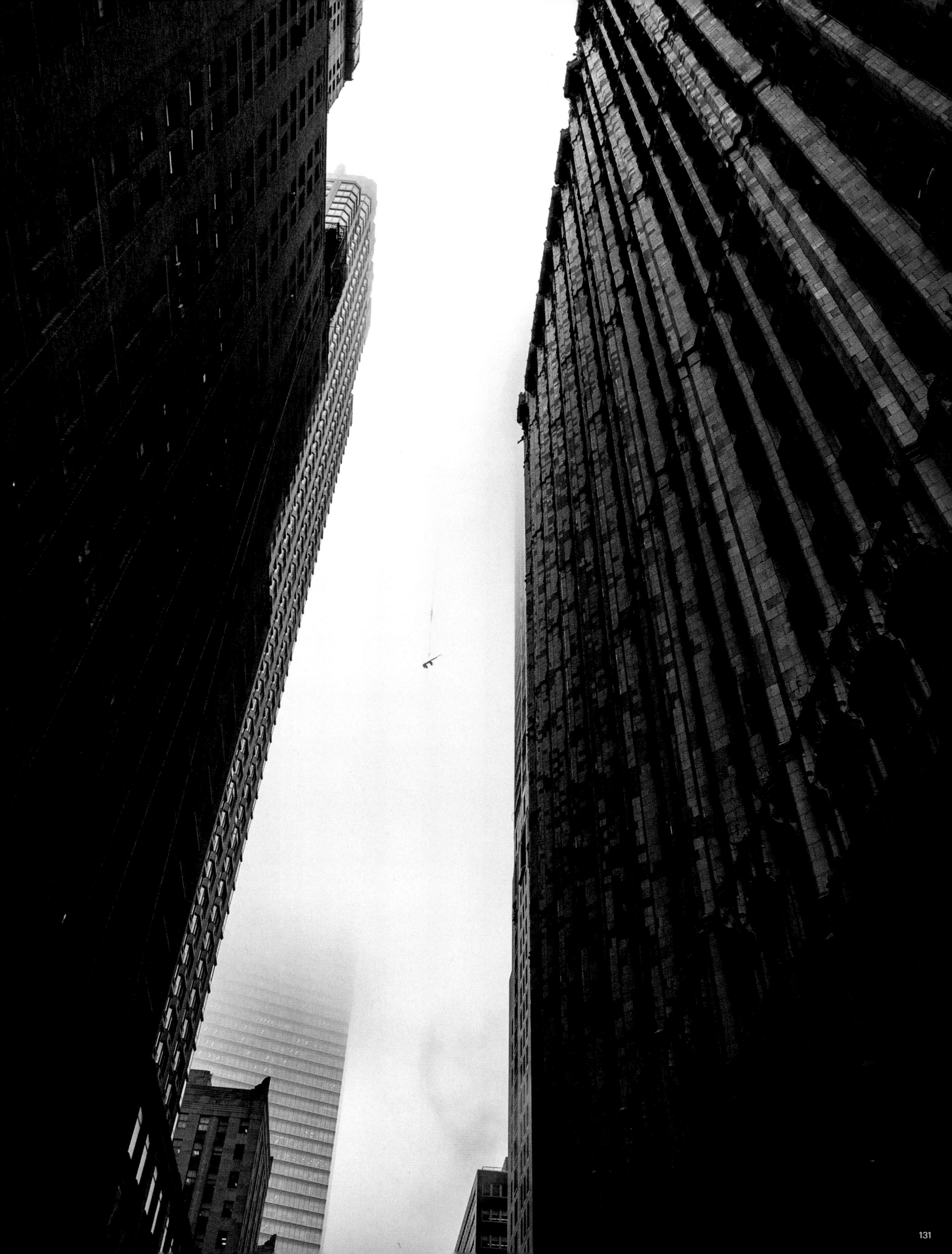

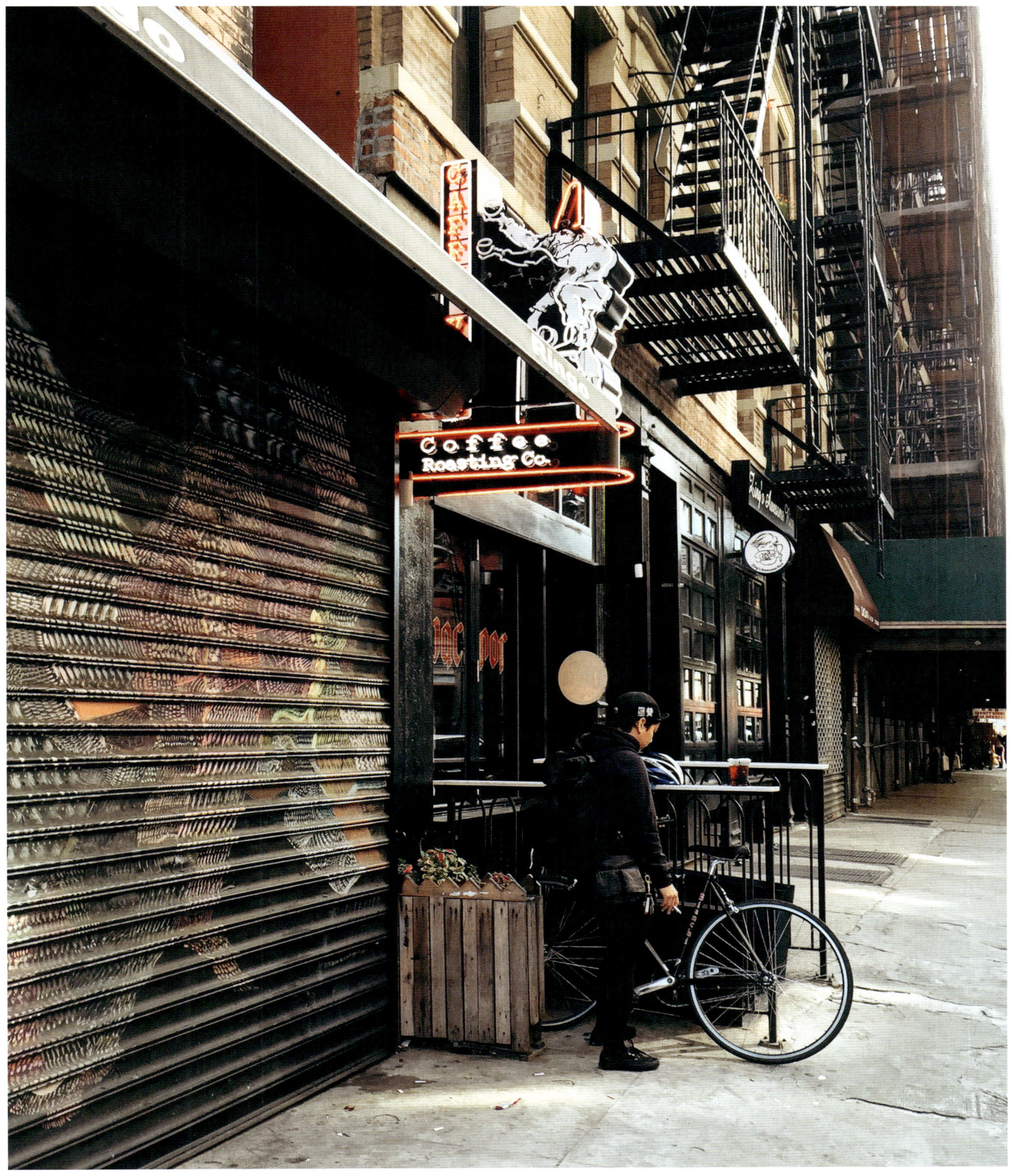

Ringo's Salon & Caffe Vita
Lower East Side, Manhattan
William Meier

Apotheke
Chinatown, Manhattan
Cindy Sung -

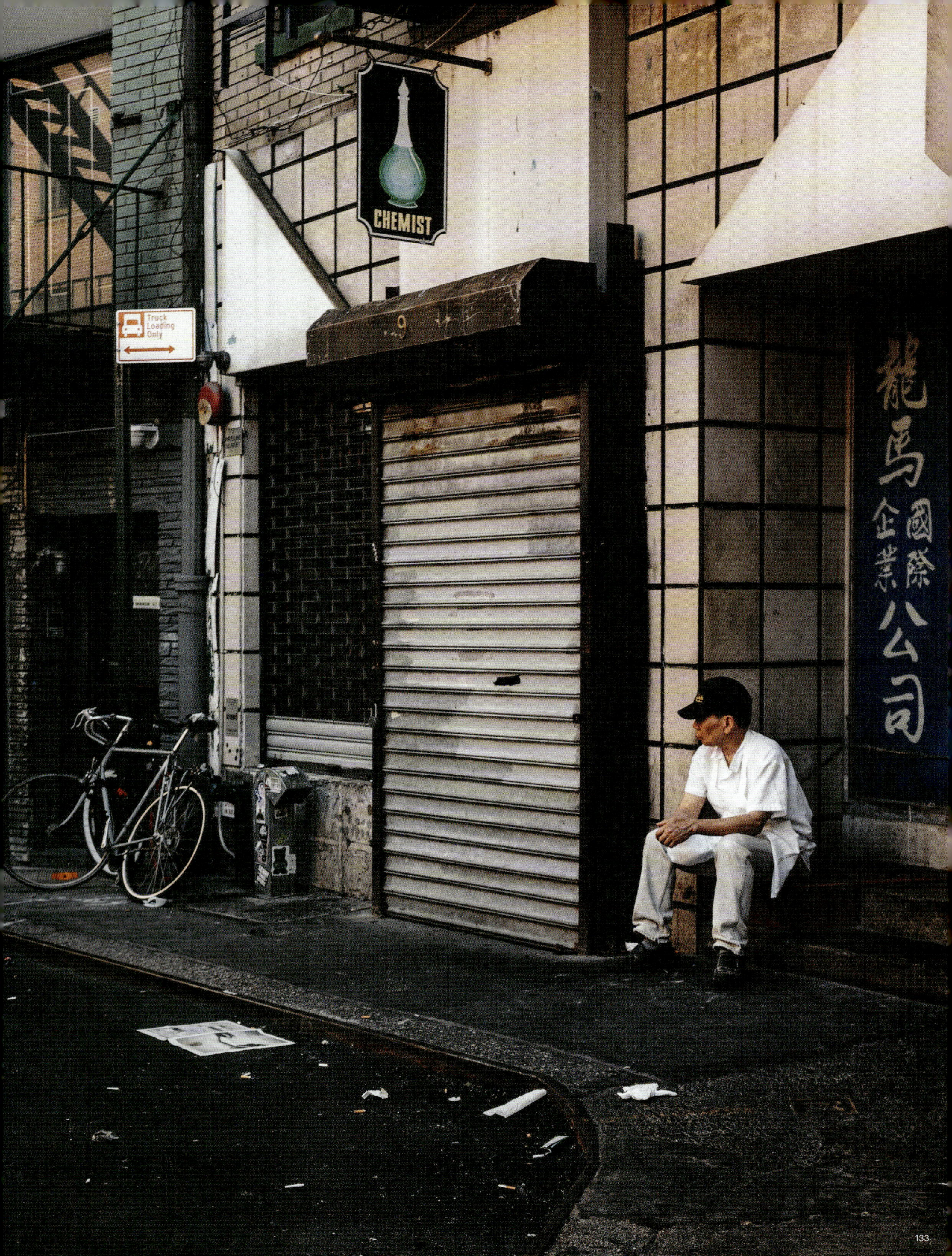
CHEMIST
Truck
Loading
Only
9
龍馬國際企業公司

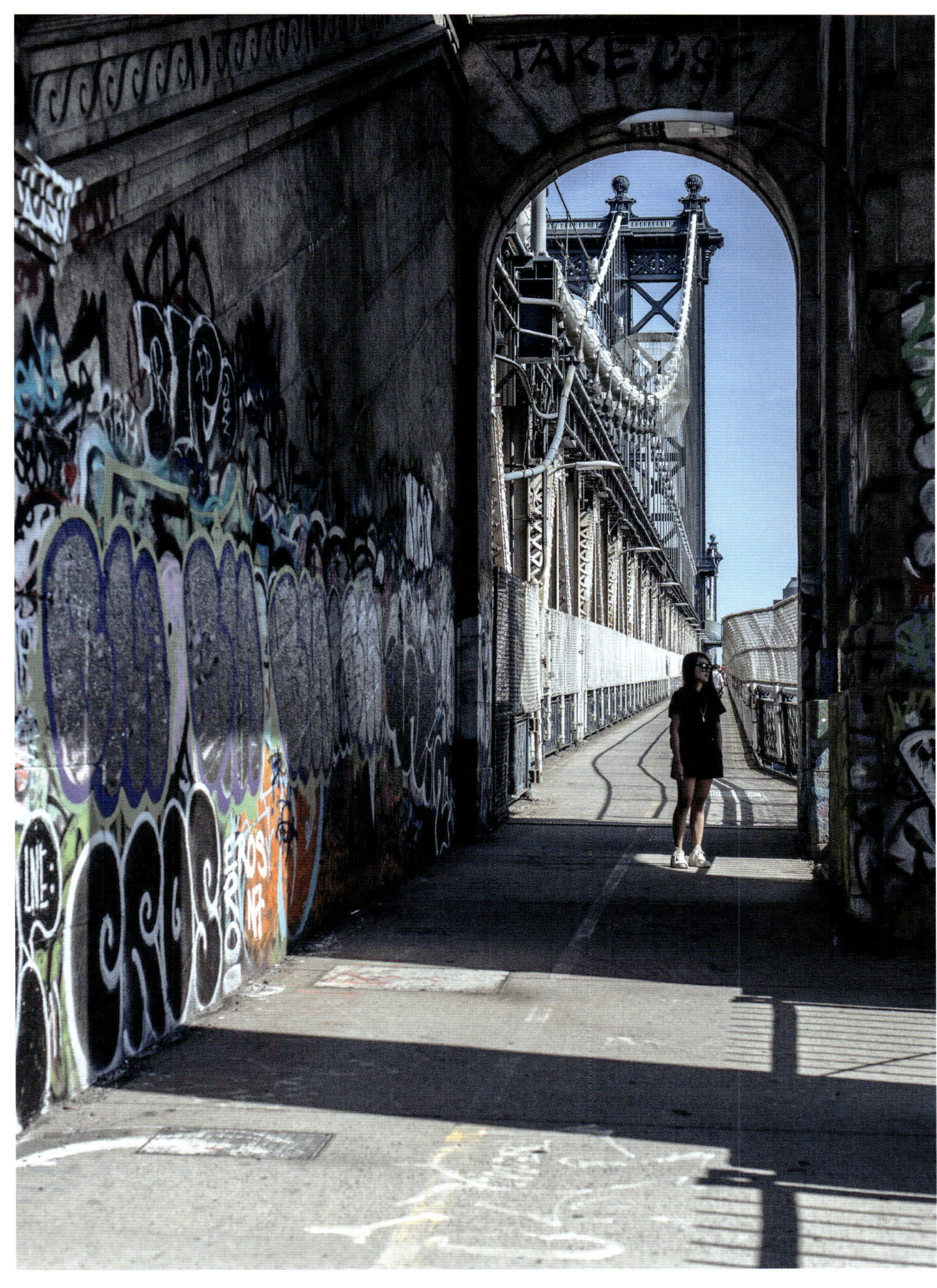

The Manhattan Bridge
Two Bridges, Manhattan
Jennifer Bin

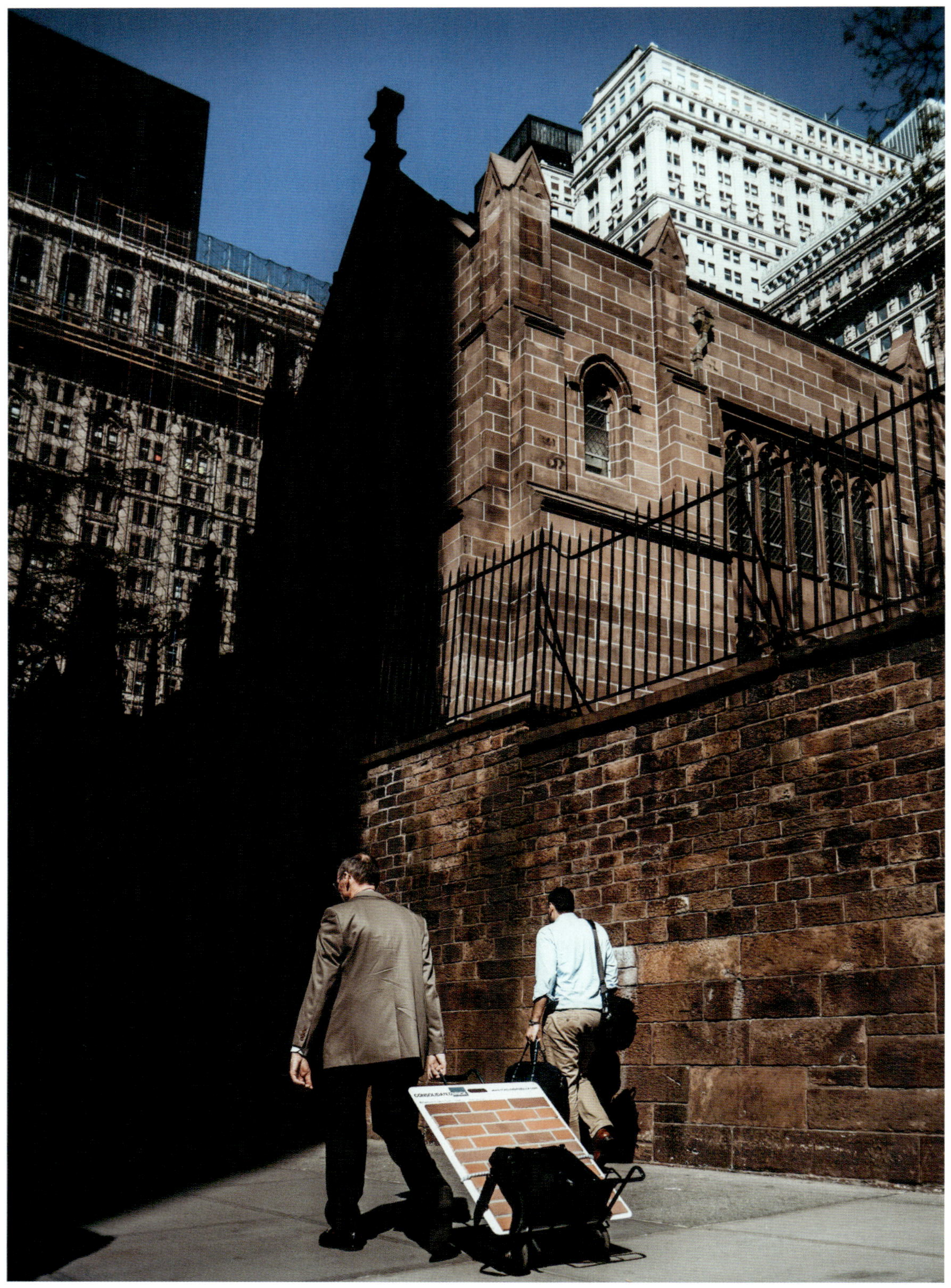

Manhattan
Stijn Hoekstra

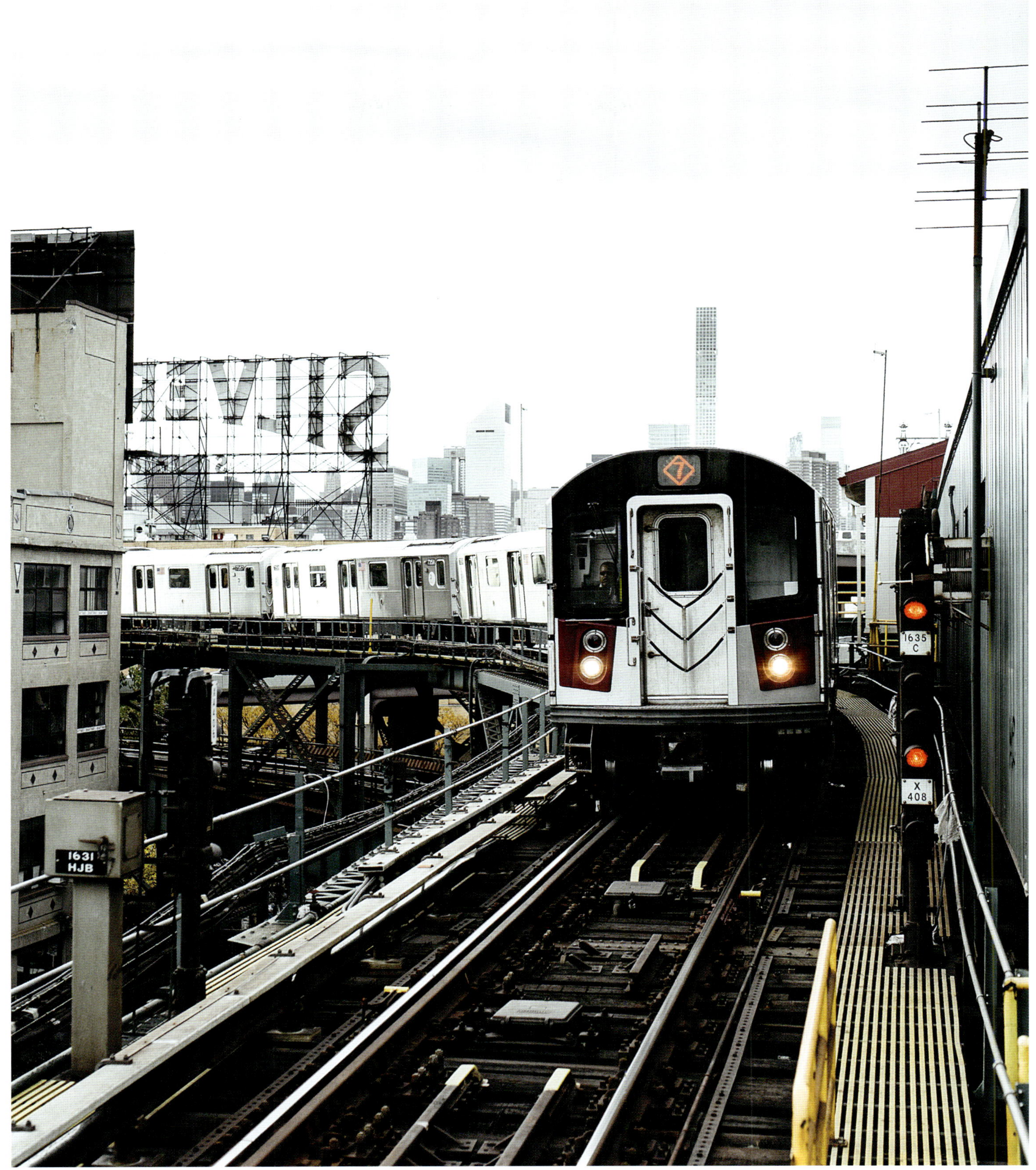

Queensboro Plaza Subway Station
Hunters Point, Queens
Ollie Nordh

The Manhattan Bridge
Two Bridges, Manhattan
Hal Haines –

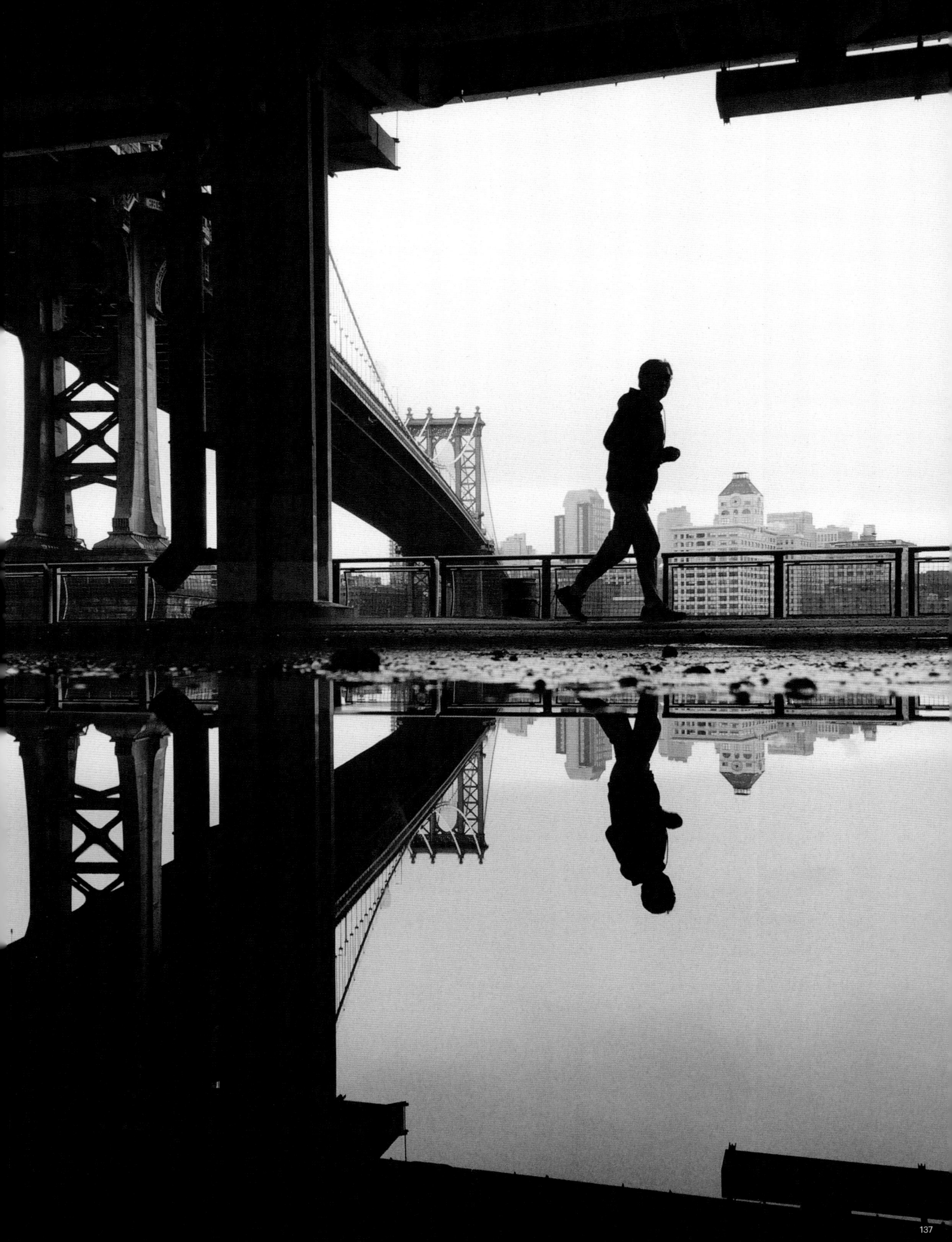

I live in the absolute best city in the world; it's hard not to love it.

—Edgar Santana

Central Park, Manhattan
William Meier

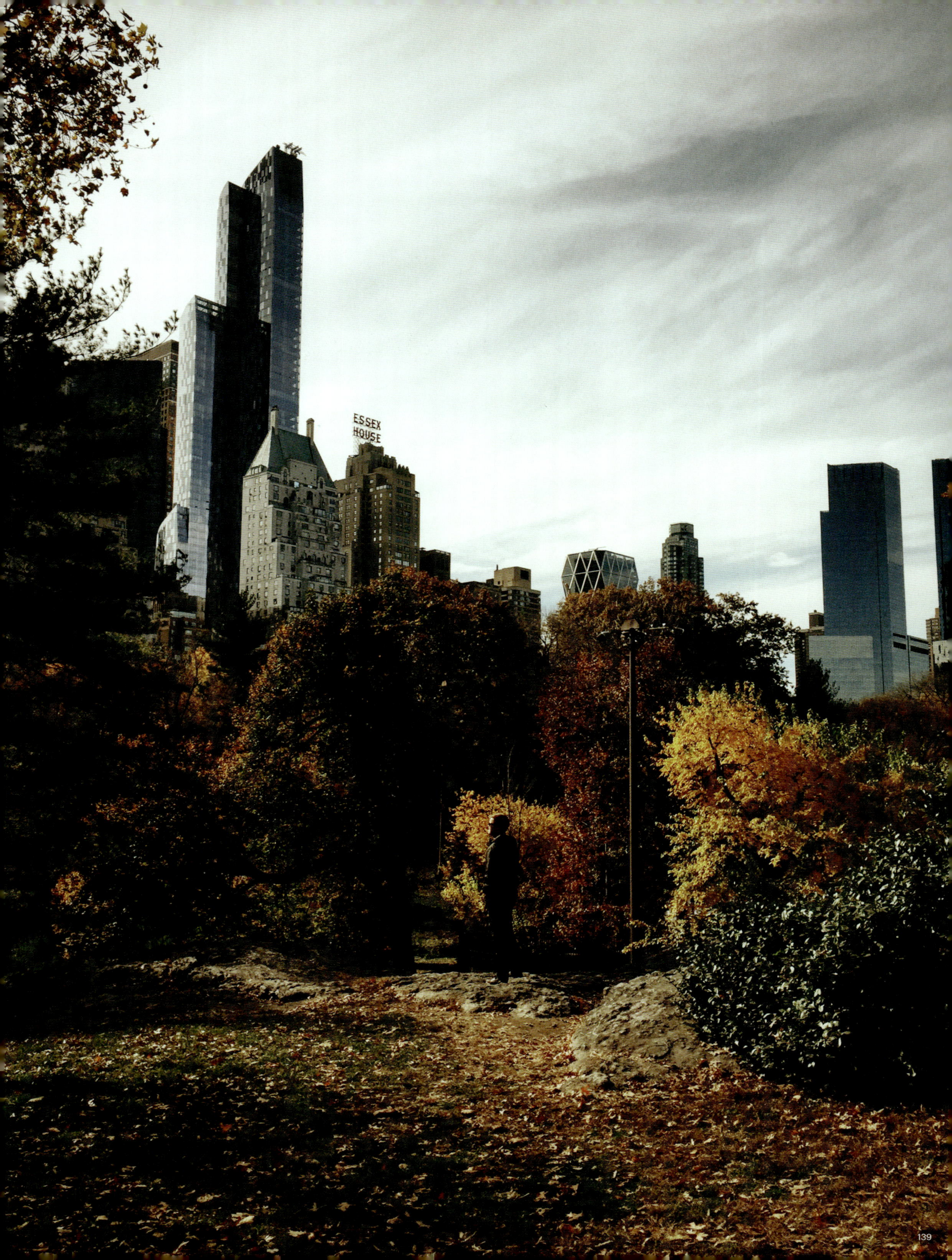
ESSEX
HOUSE

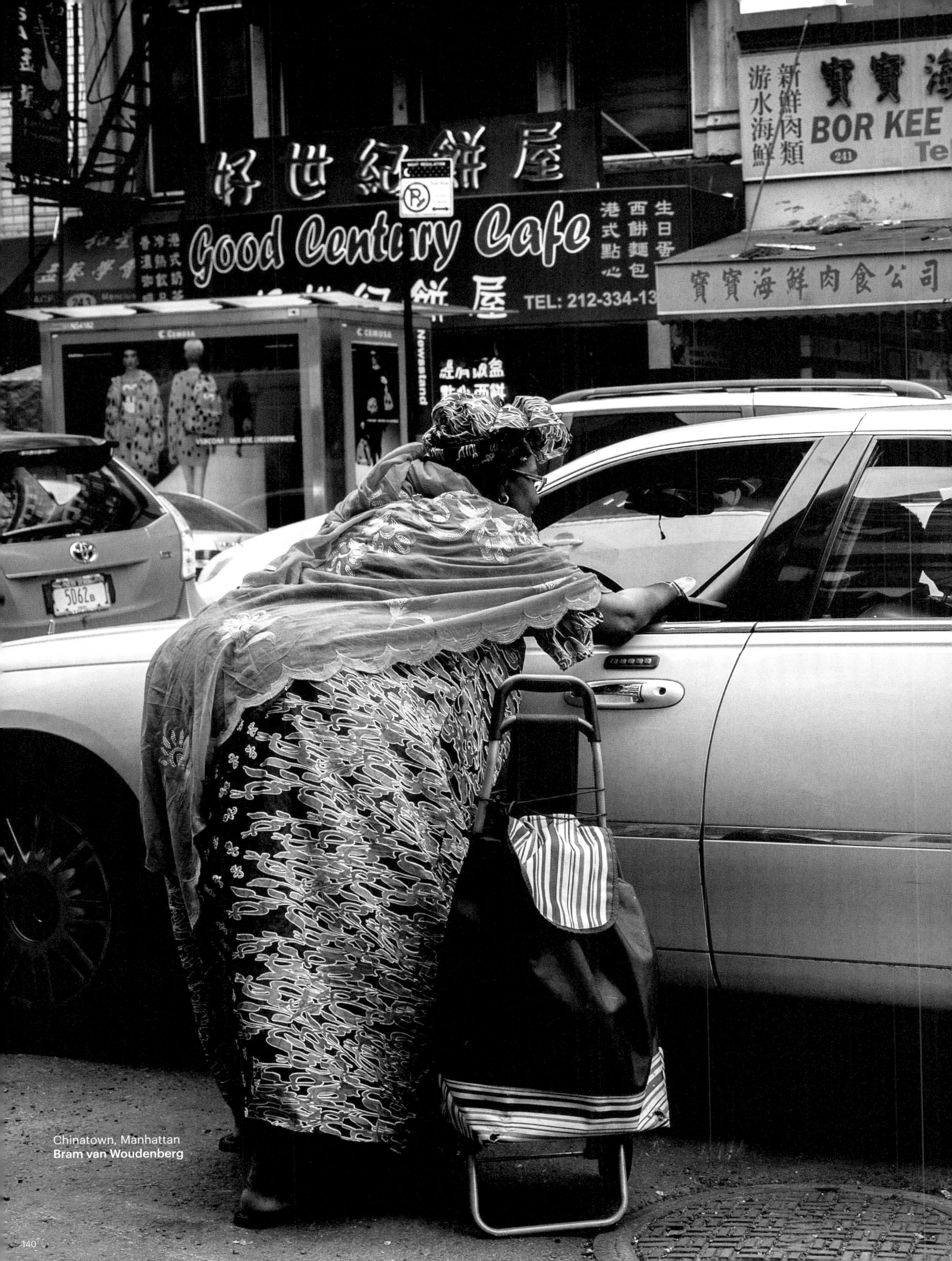

Chinatown, Manhattan
Bram van Woudenberg

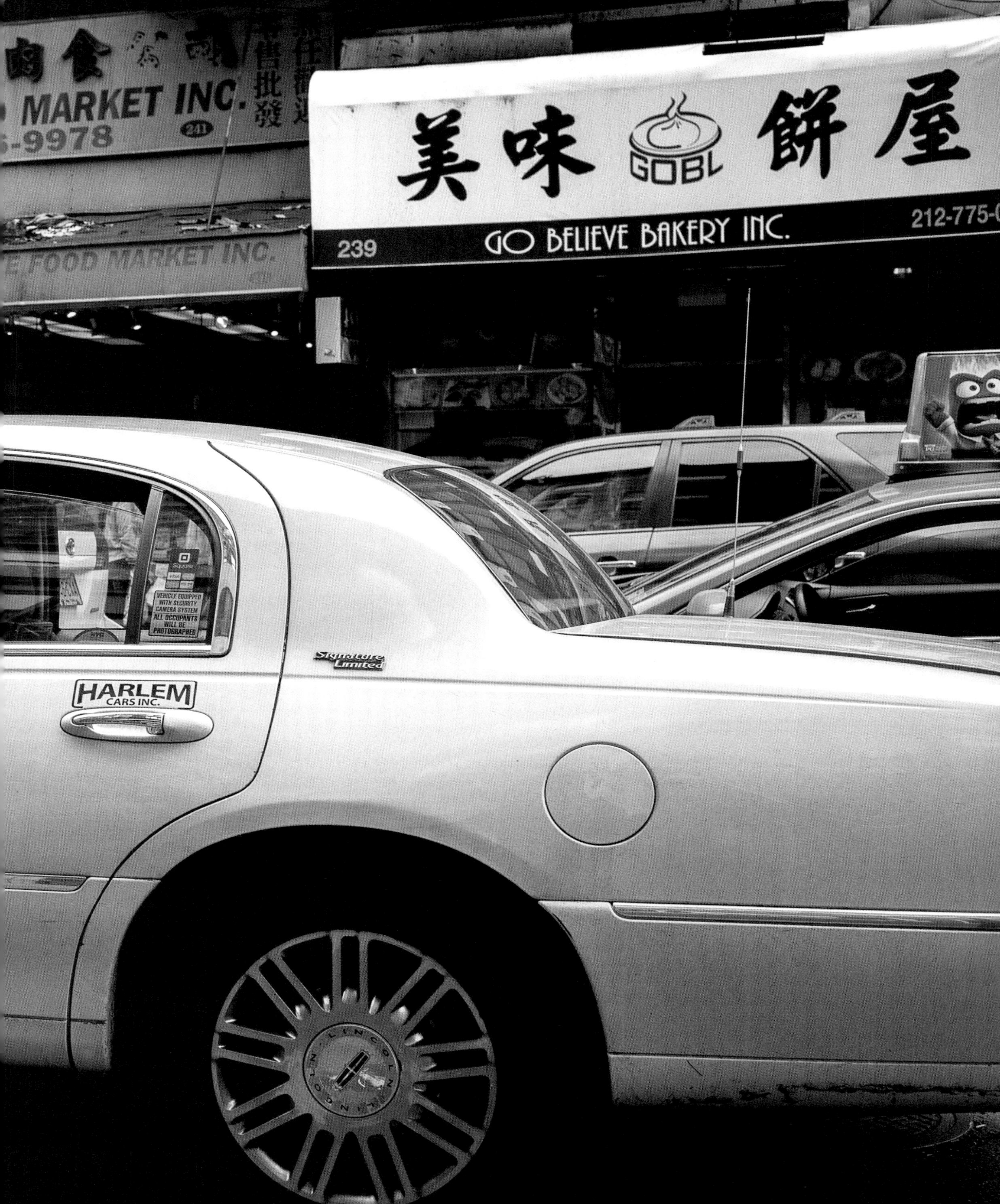
MARKET INC.
-9978
241
E FOOD MARKET INC.
美味
GOBL
餅屋
239
GO BELIEVE BAKERY INC.
212-775-0
VEHICLE EQUIPPED WITH SECURITY CAMERA SYSTEM
ALL OCCUPANTS WILL BE PHOTOGRAPHED
Signature Limited
HARLEM
CARS INC.
LINCOLN

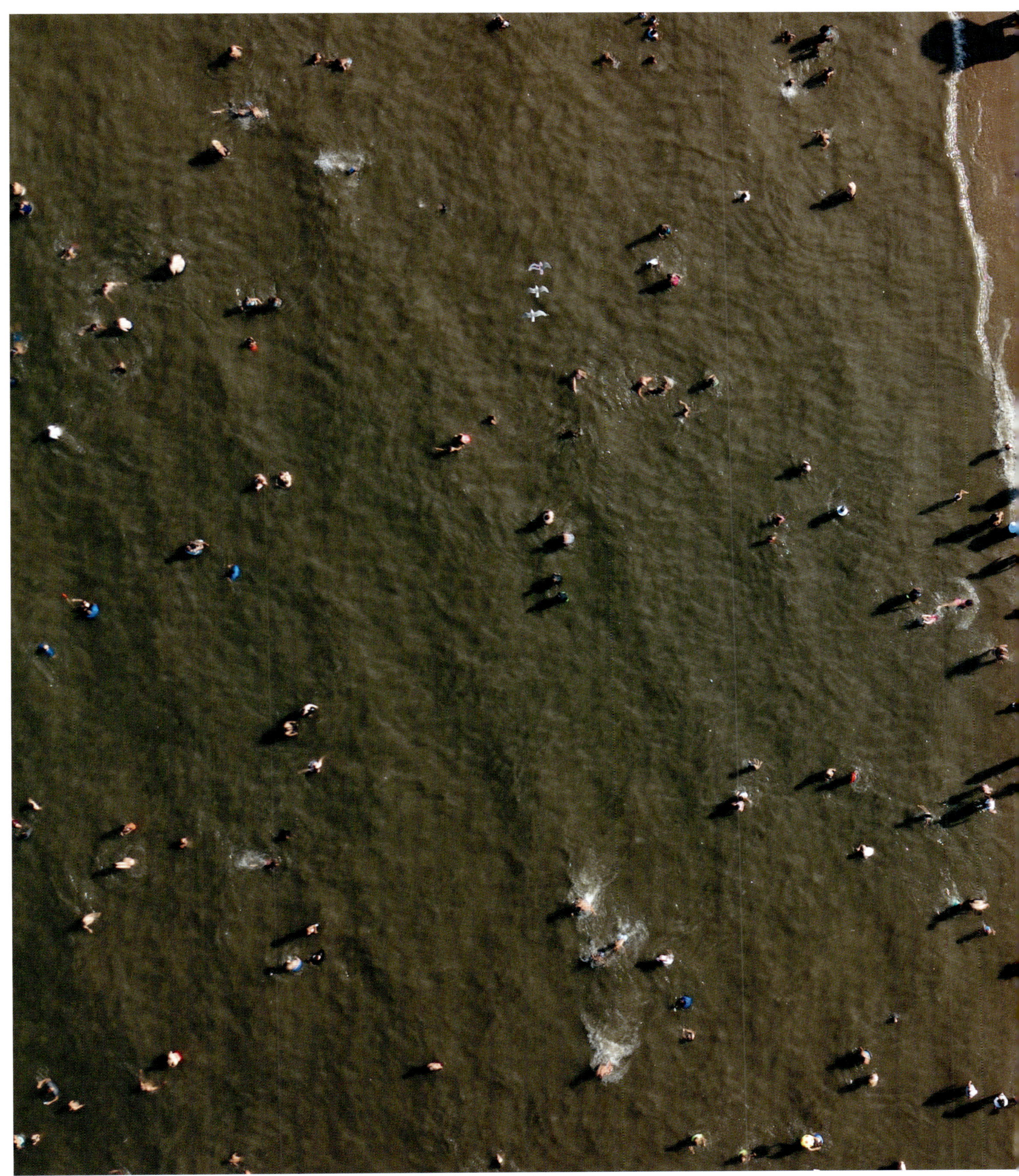

Orchard Beach
The Bronx
Alex Rivera

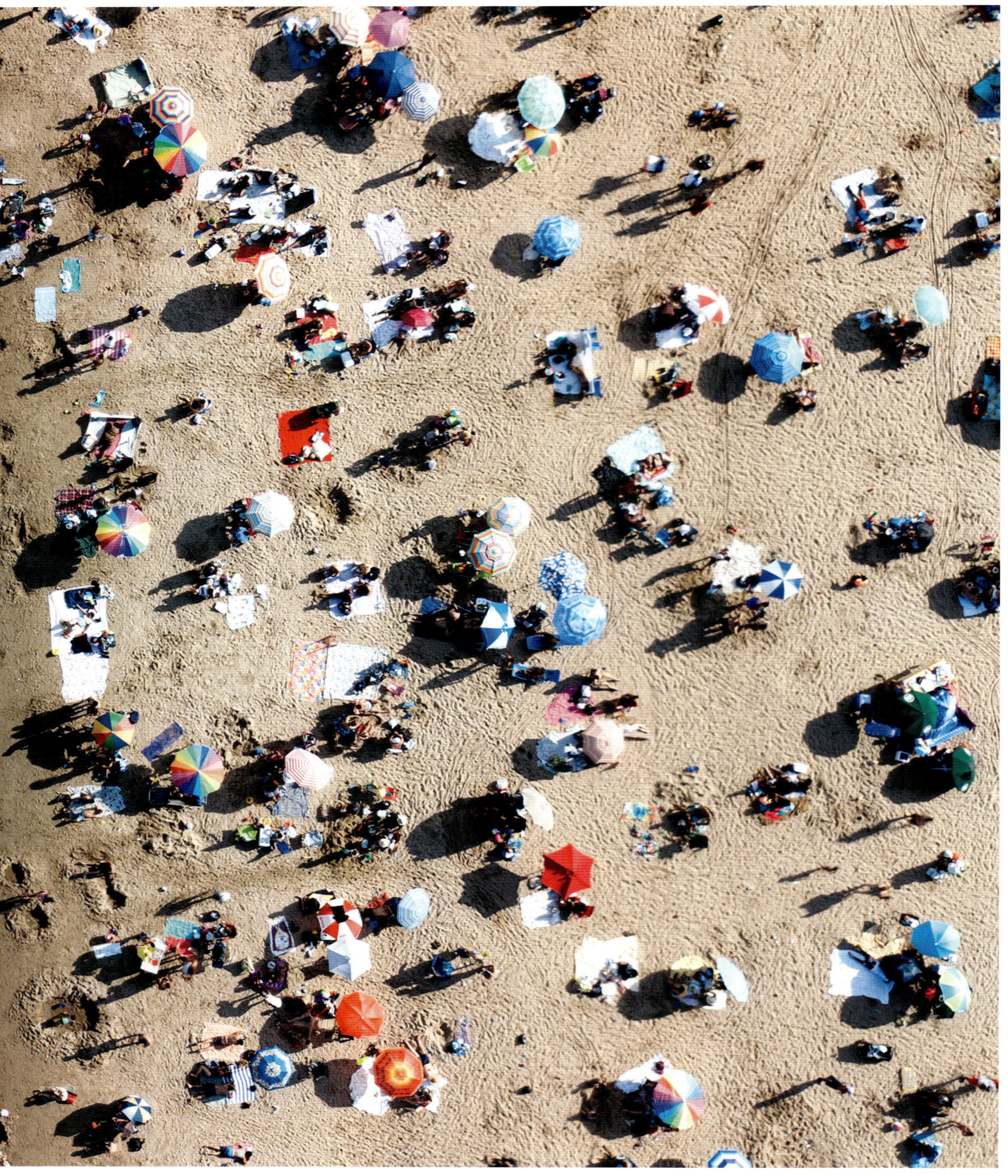

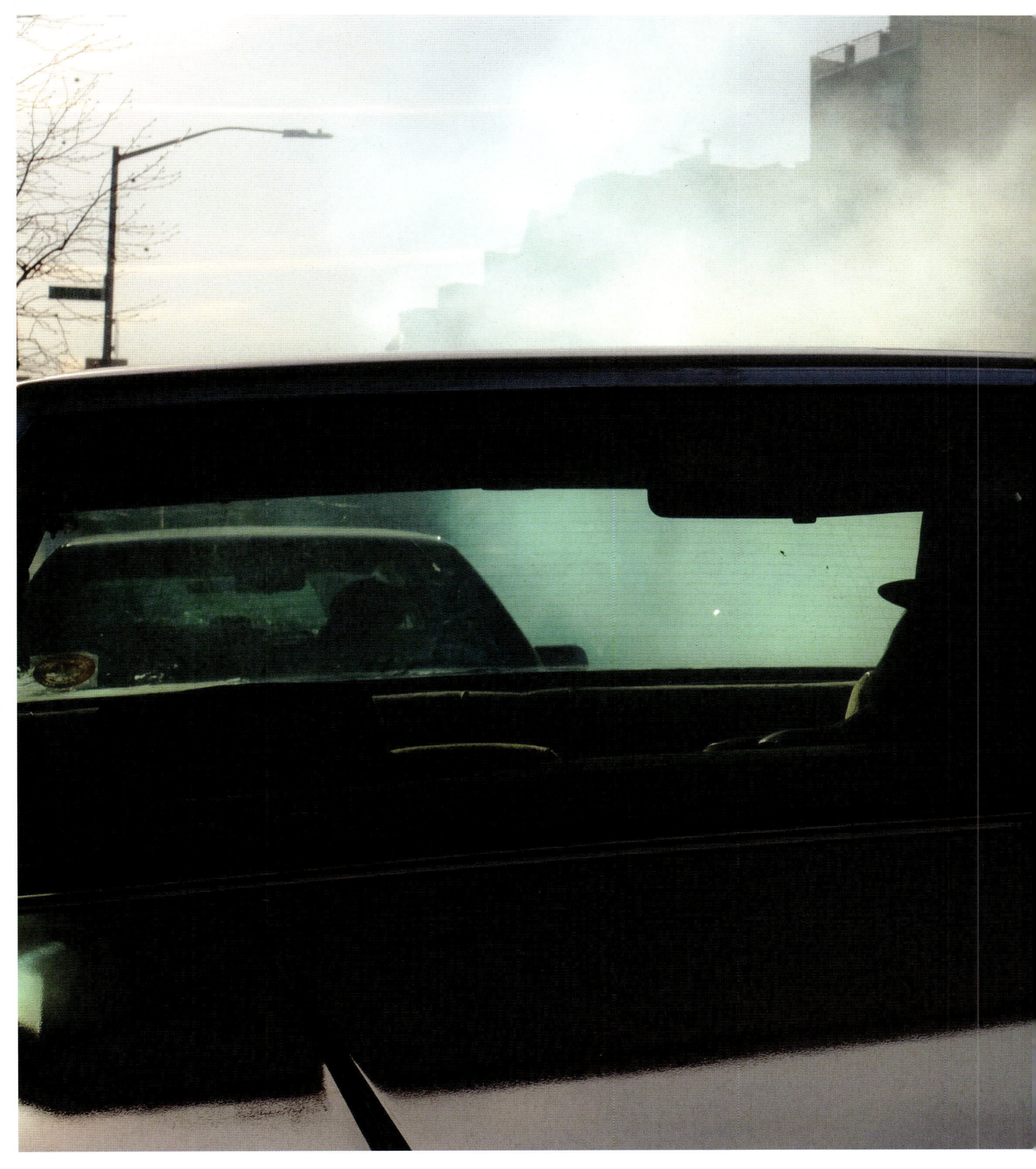

Brooklyn
Vincent Peone

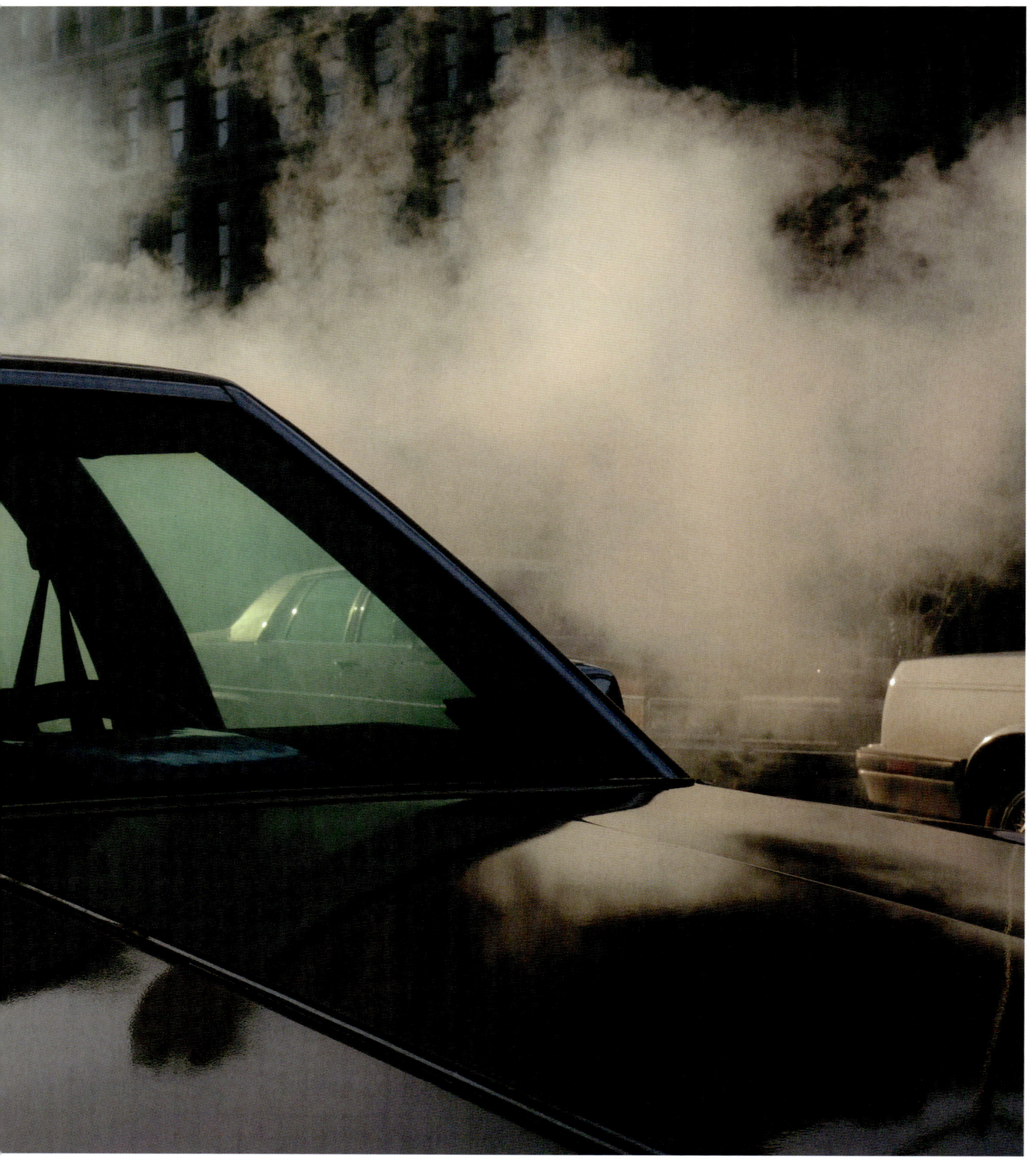

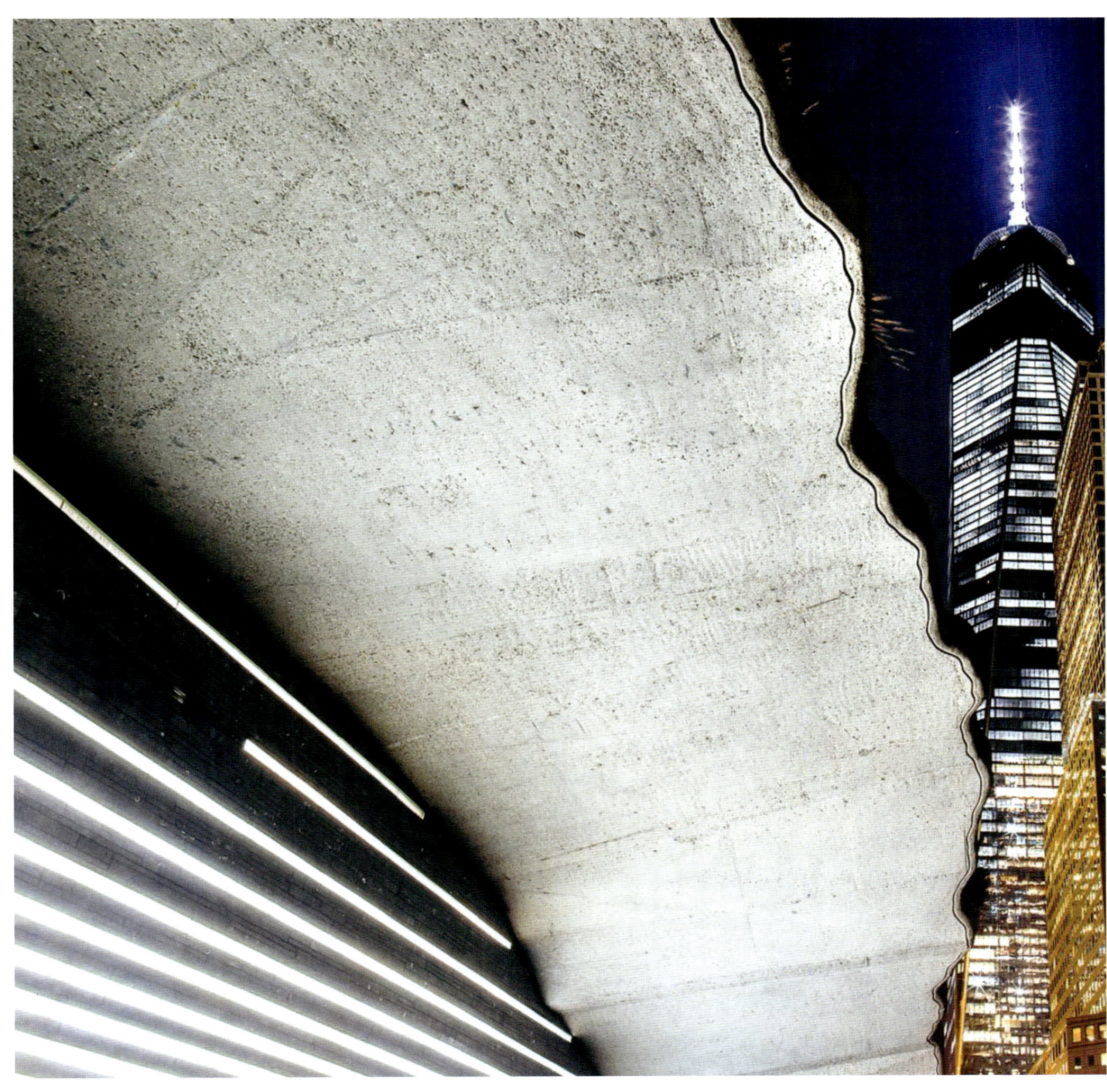

One World Trade Center
Financial District, Manhattan
Demilade Balogun

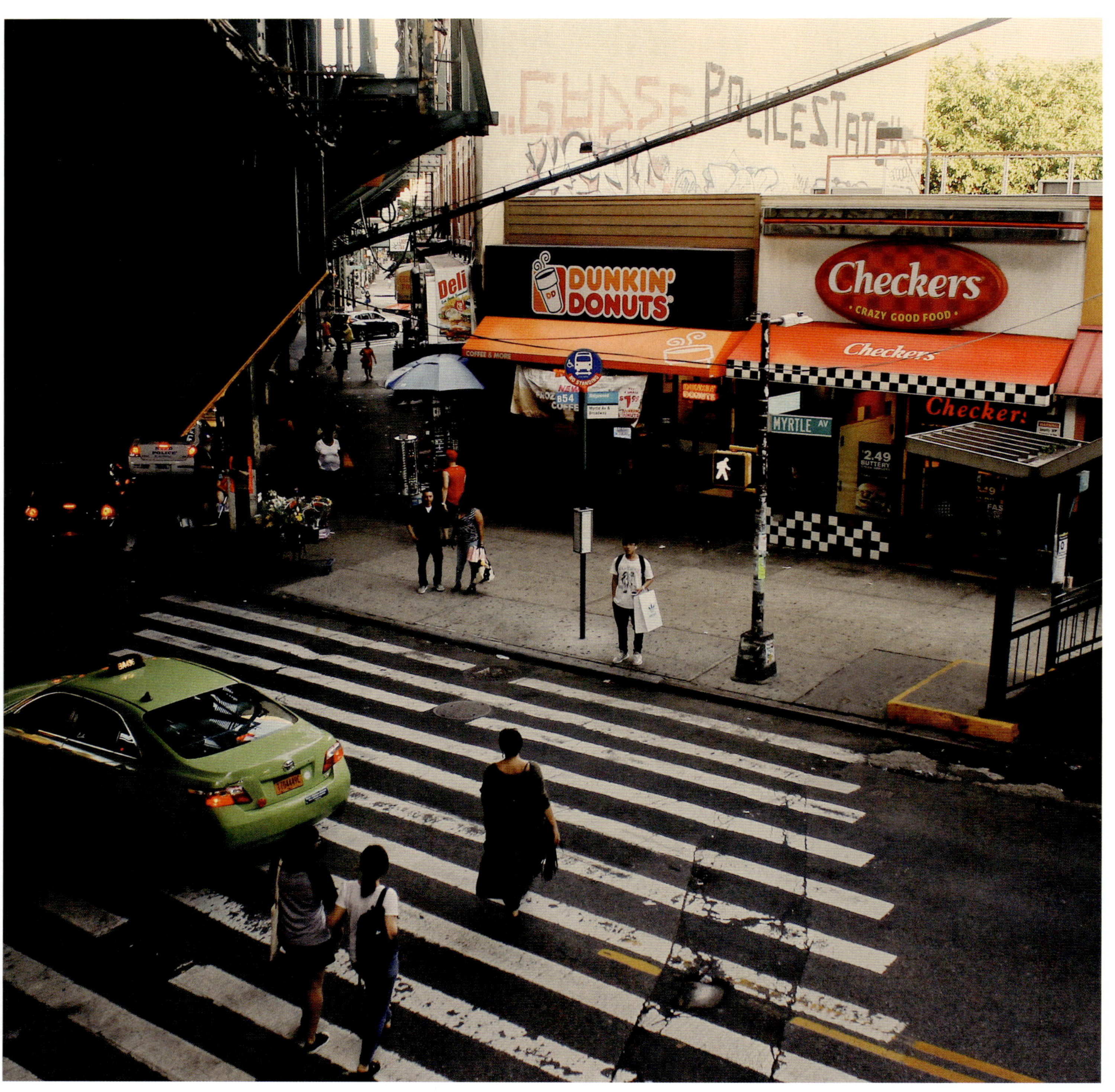

Bushwick, Brooklyn
Darius Hertzog

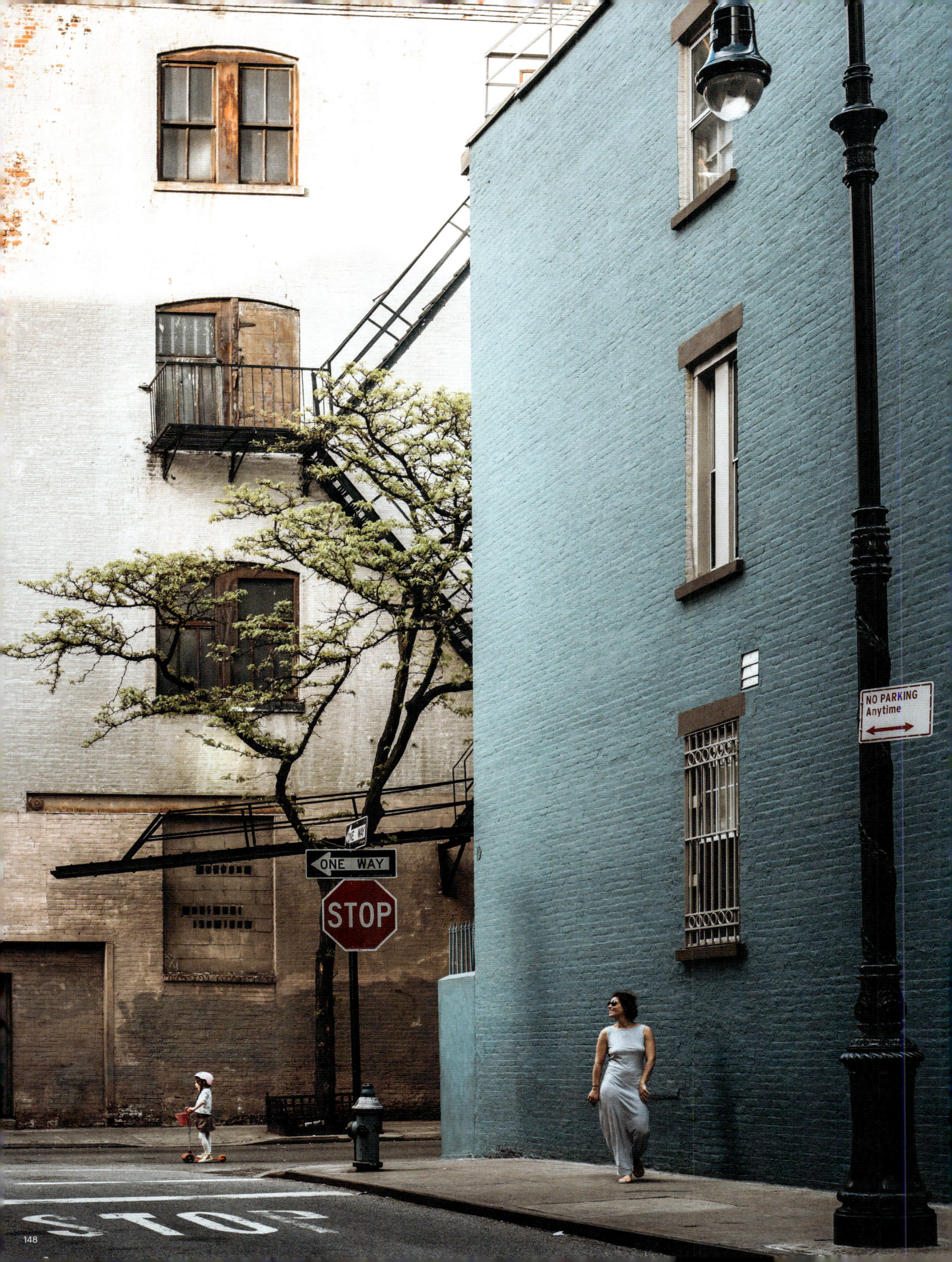
ONE WAY
STOP
NO PARKING
Anytime
STOP

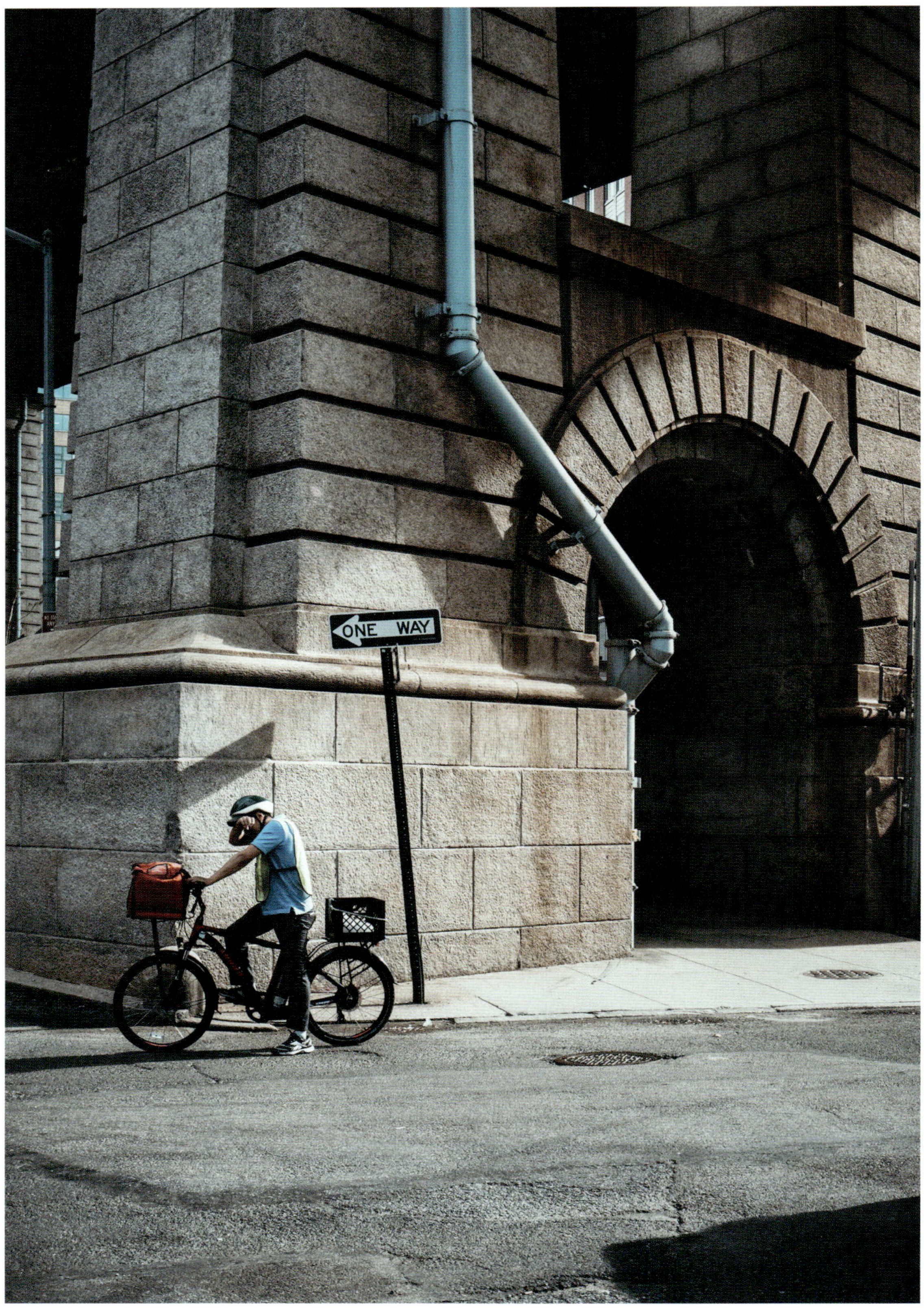

Greenwich Village, Manhattan
Stijn Hoekstra

The Brooklyn Bridge
Dumbo, Brooklyn
Stijn Hoekstra

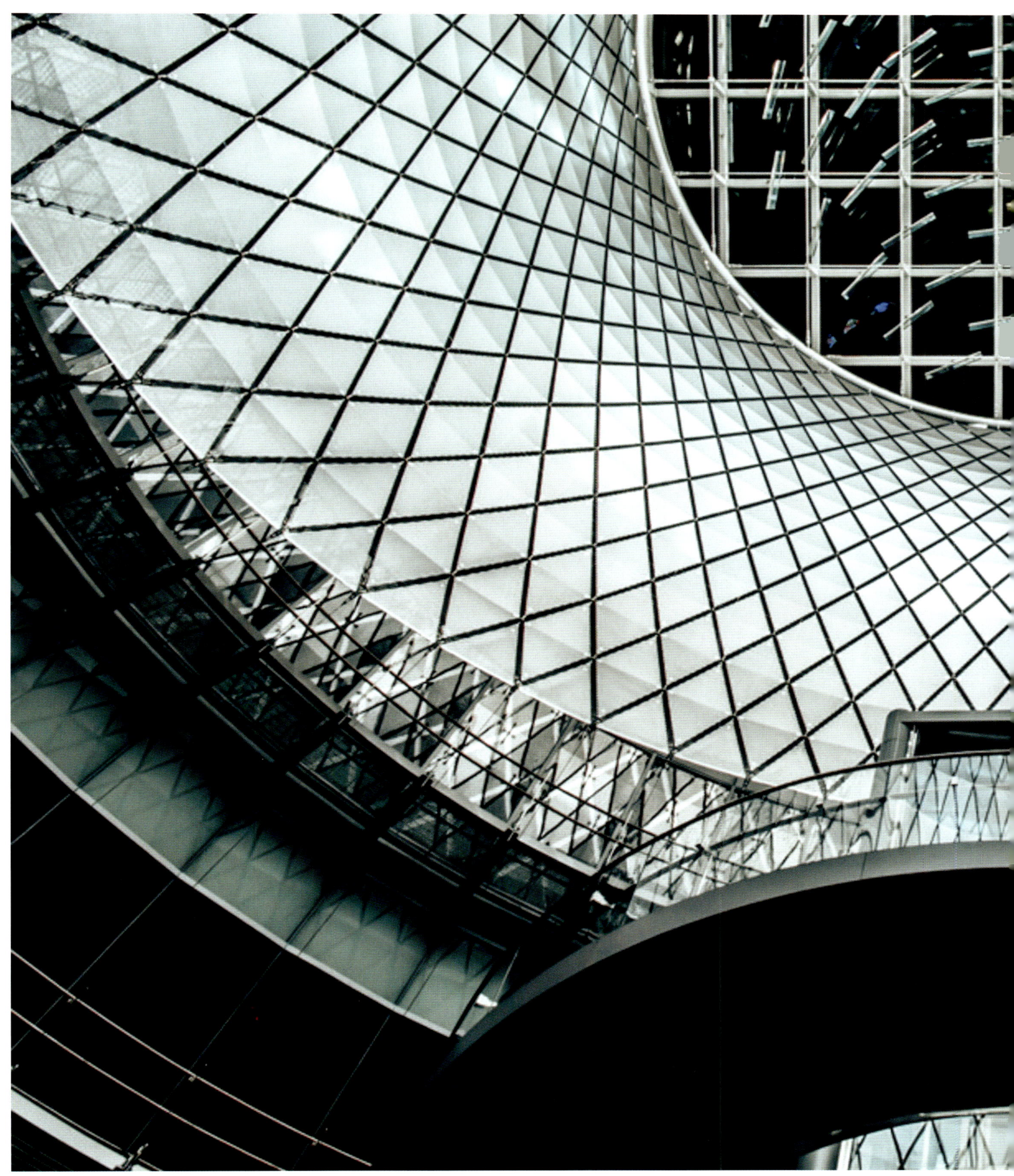

The Fulton Center
Financial District, Manhattan
Demilade Balogun

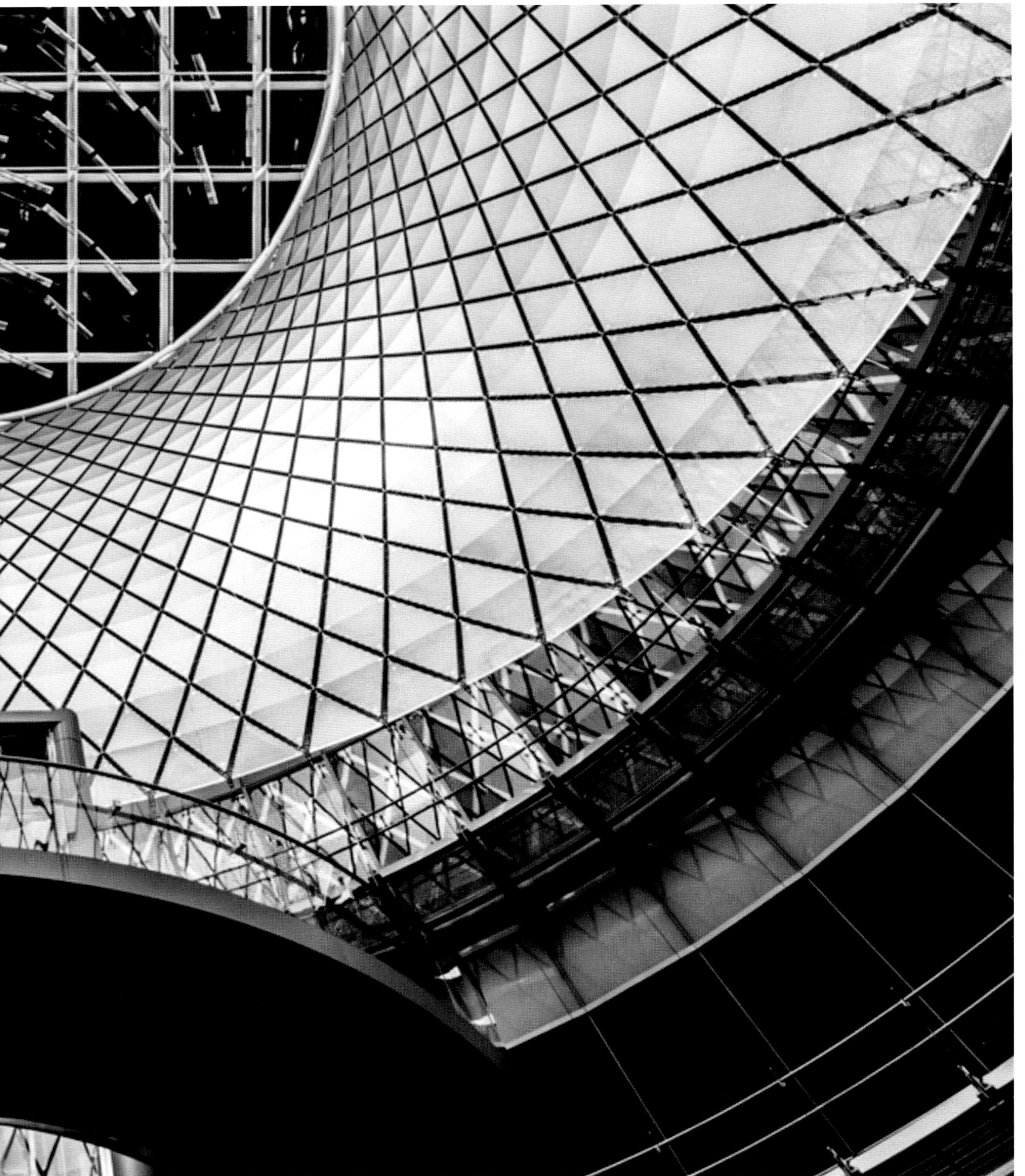

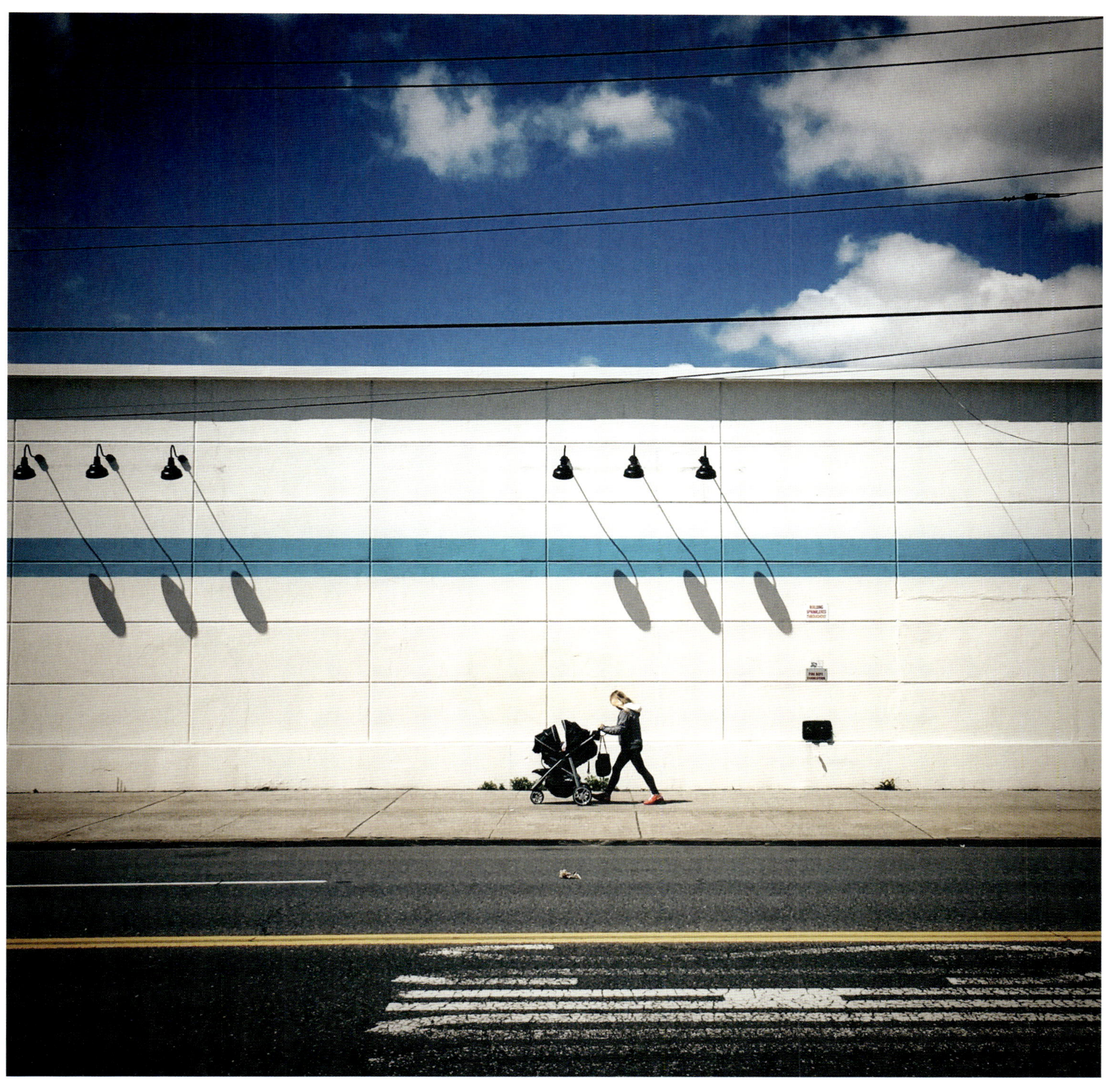

Throggs Neck, The Bronx
Edgar Santana

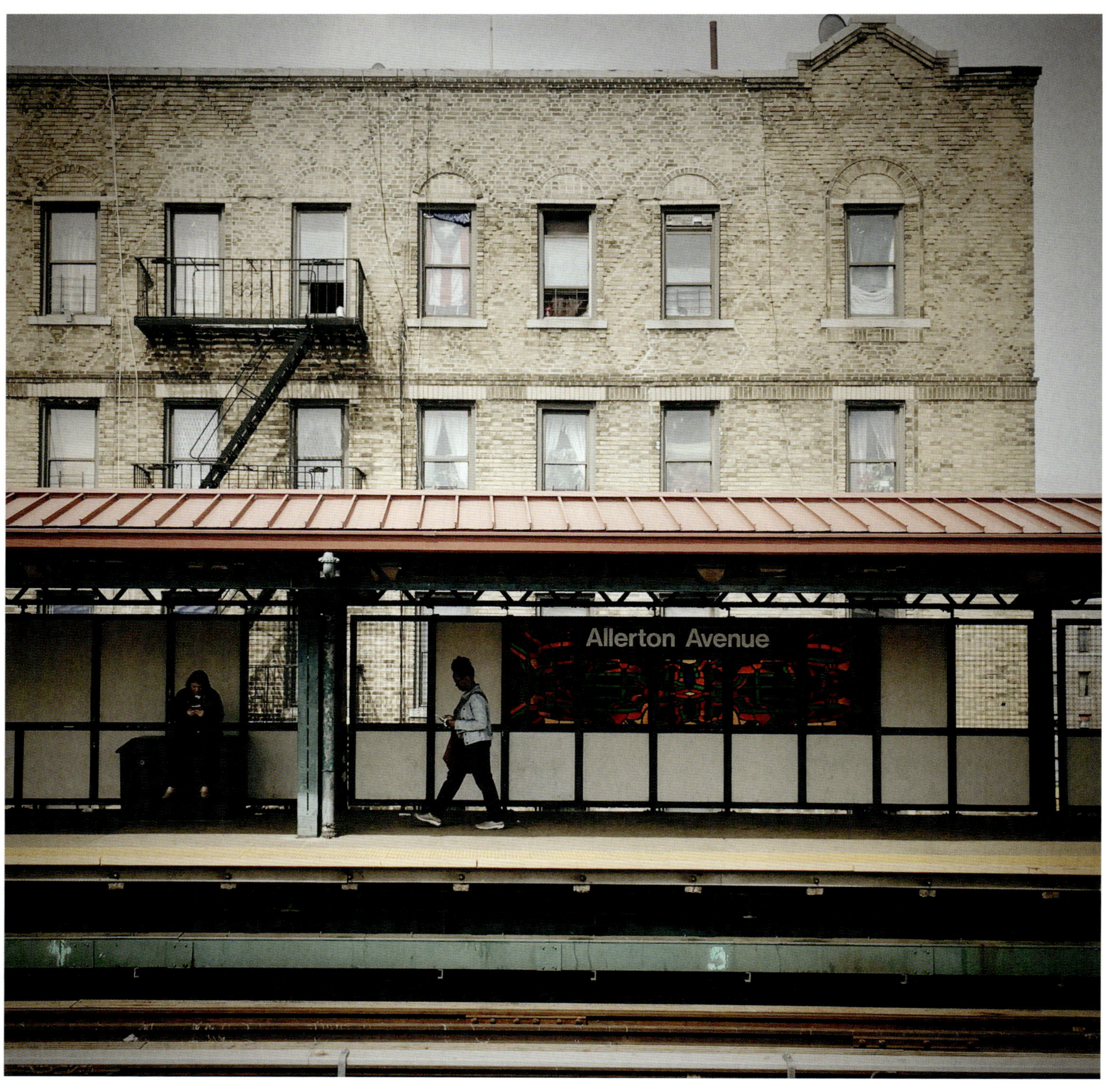

Allerton Avenue Subway Station
Bronxdale, The Bronx
Edgar Santana

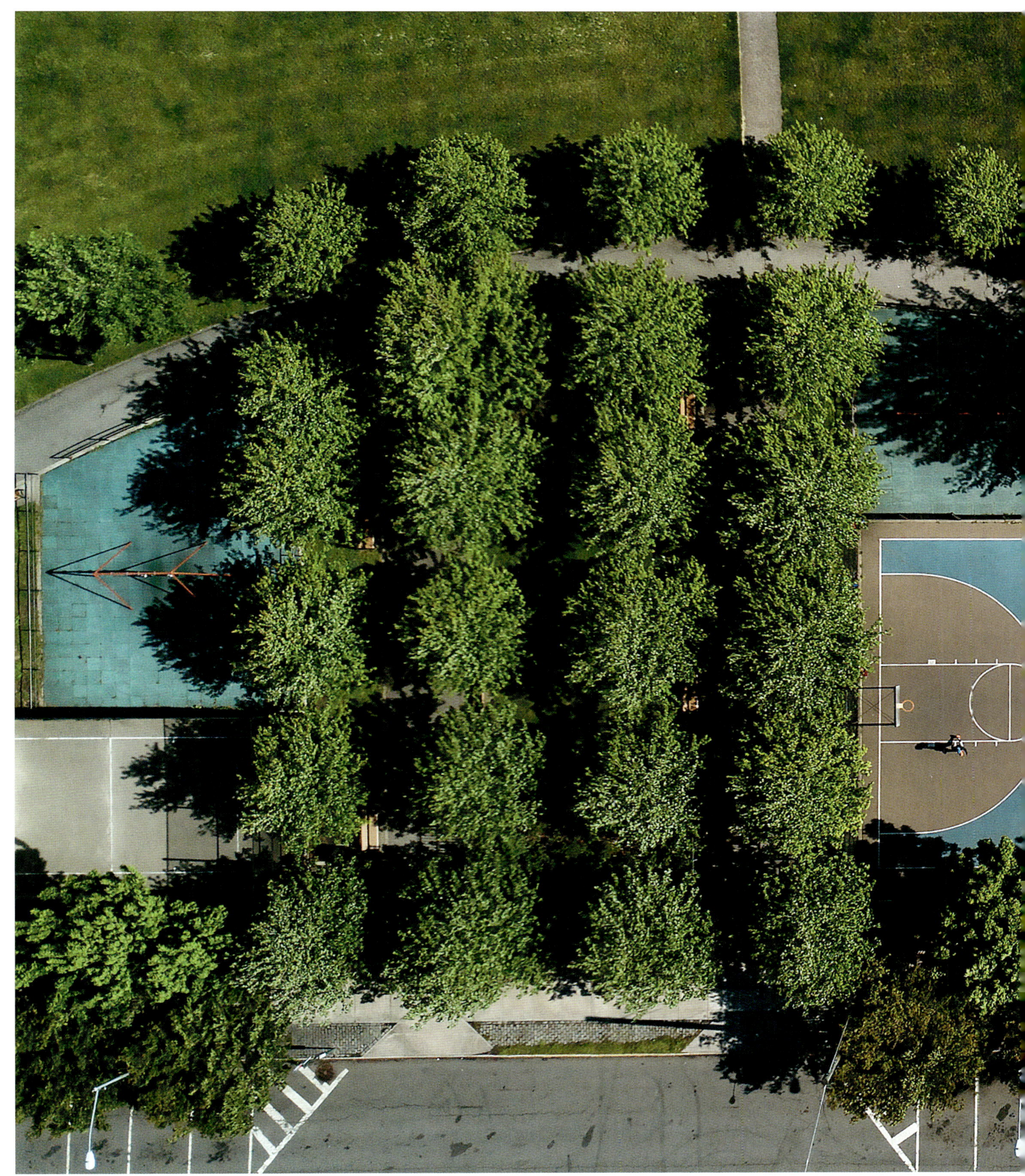

Barretto Point Park Basketball Court
Hunts Point, The Bronx
Alex Rivera

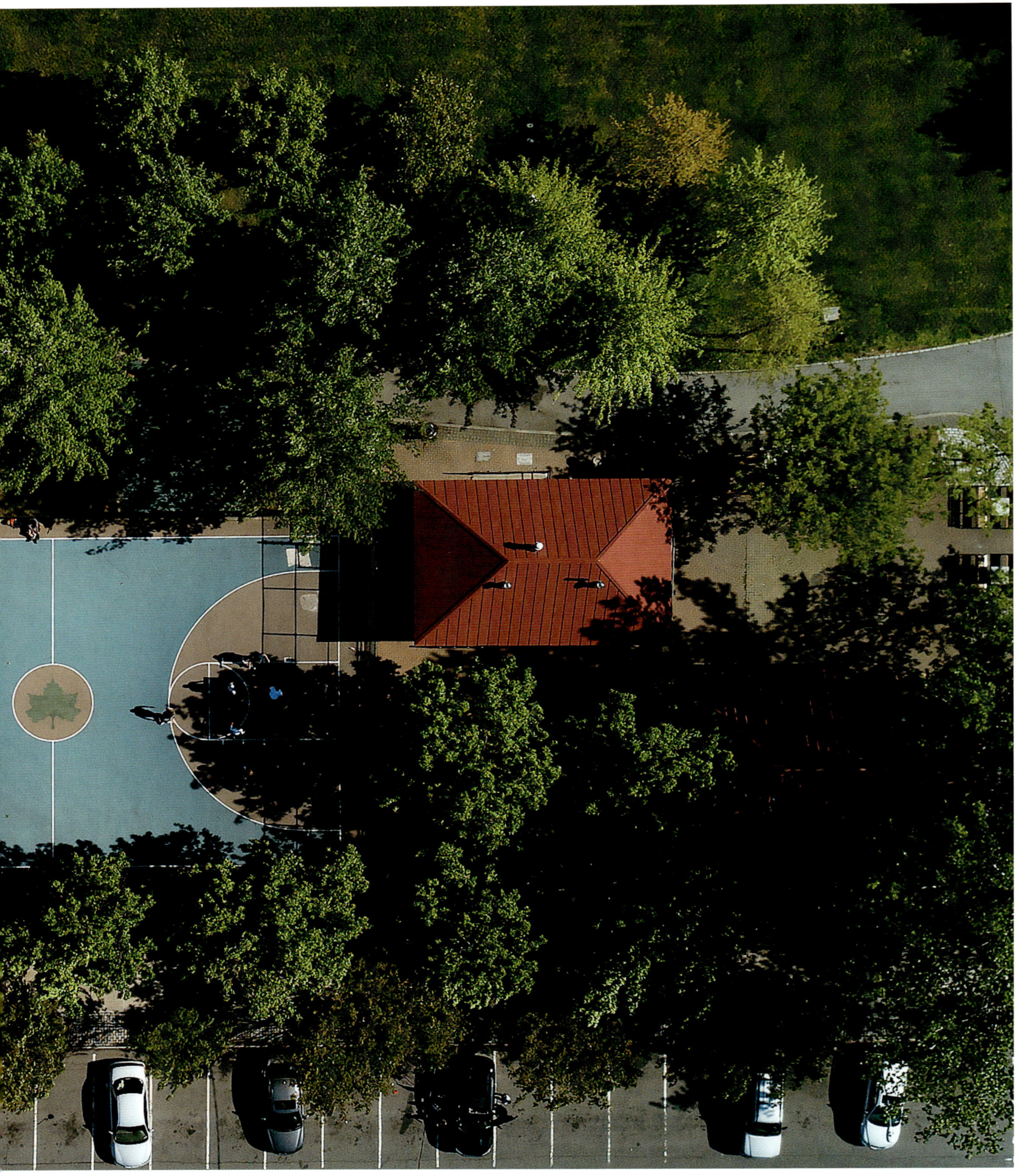

Gay Street
West Village, Manhattan
Nazly Kasim

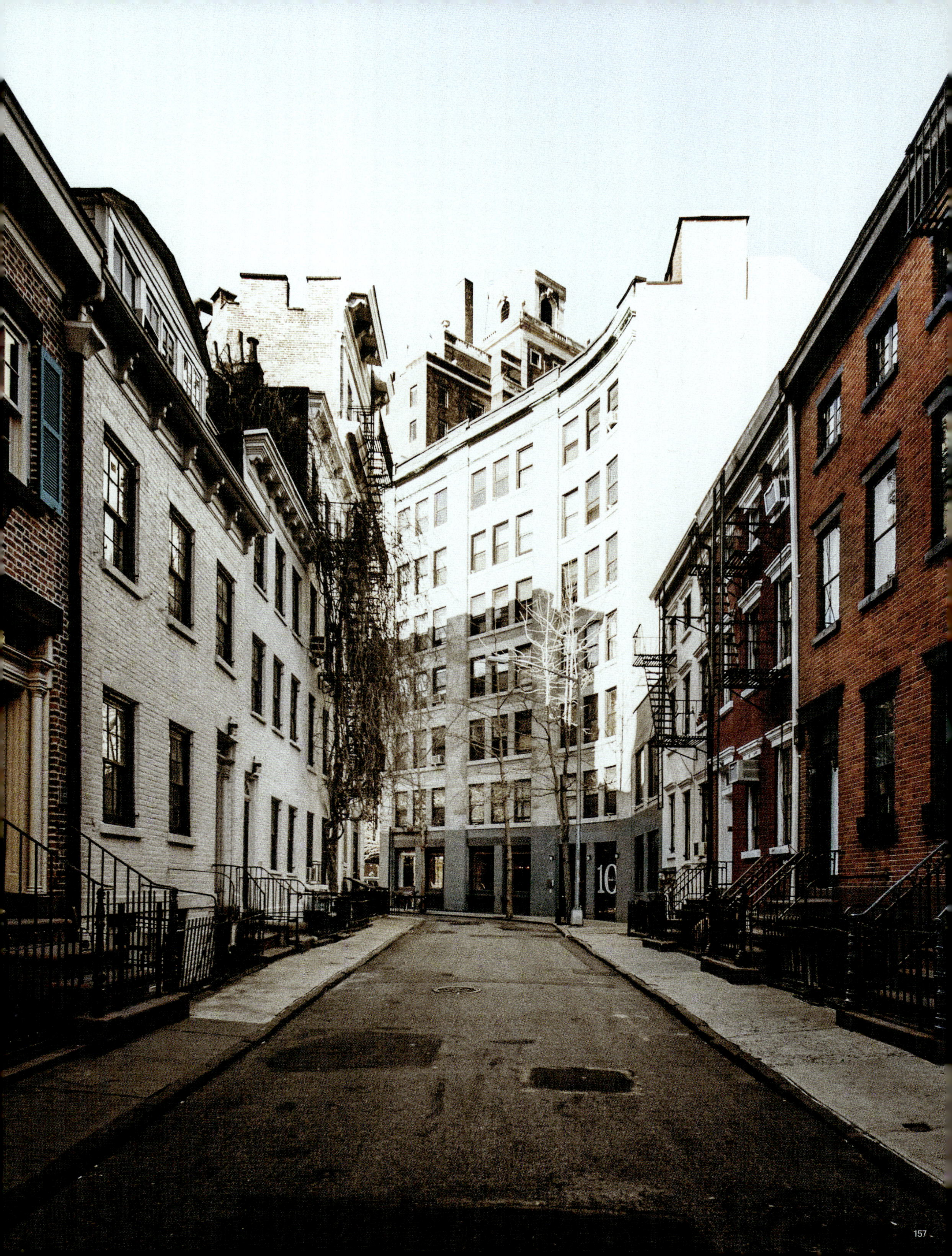
10

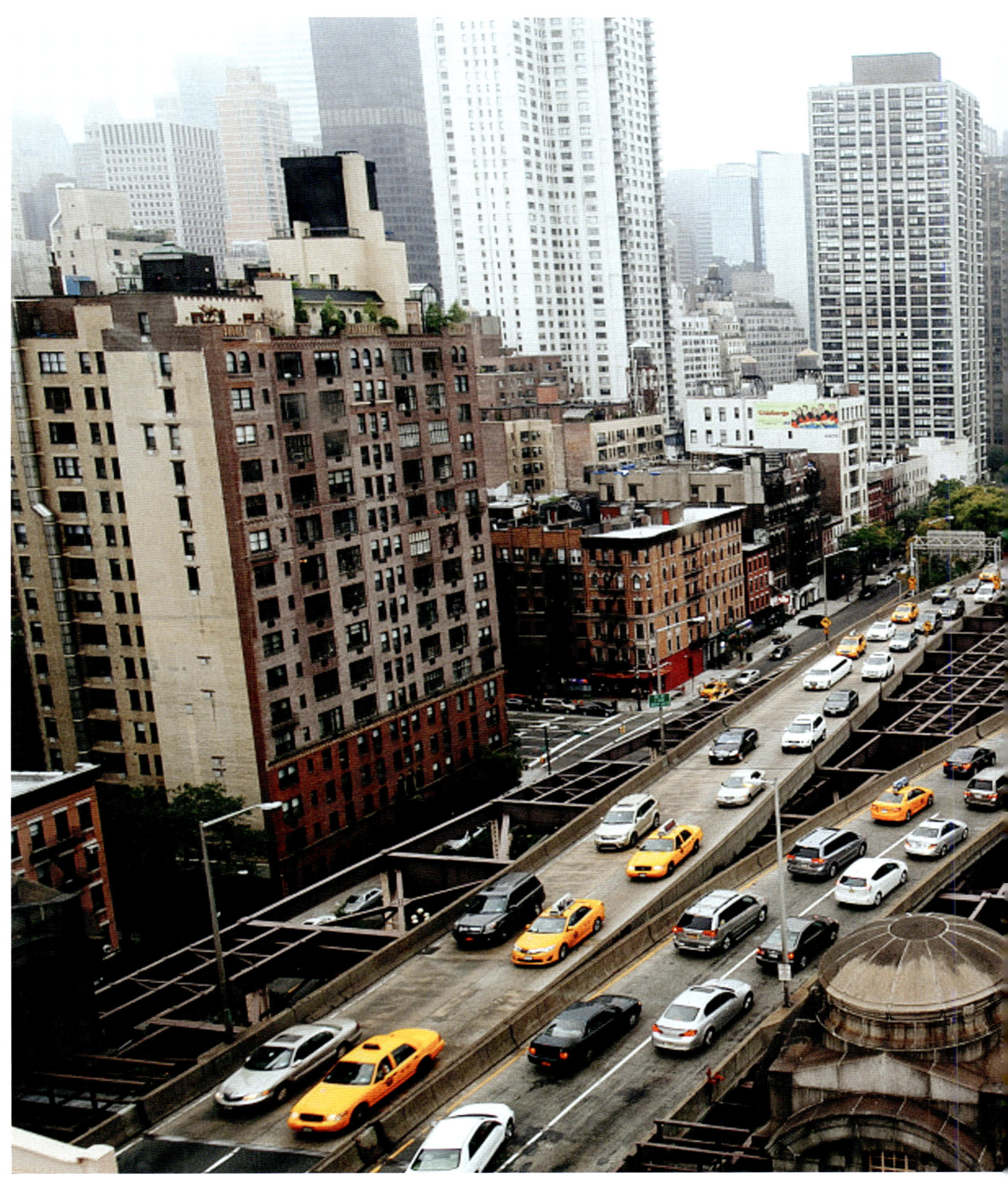

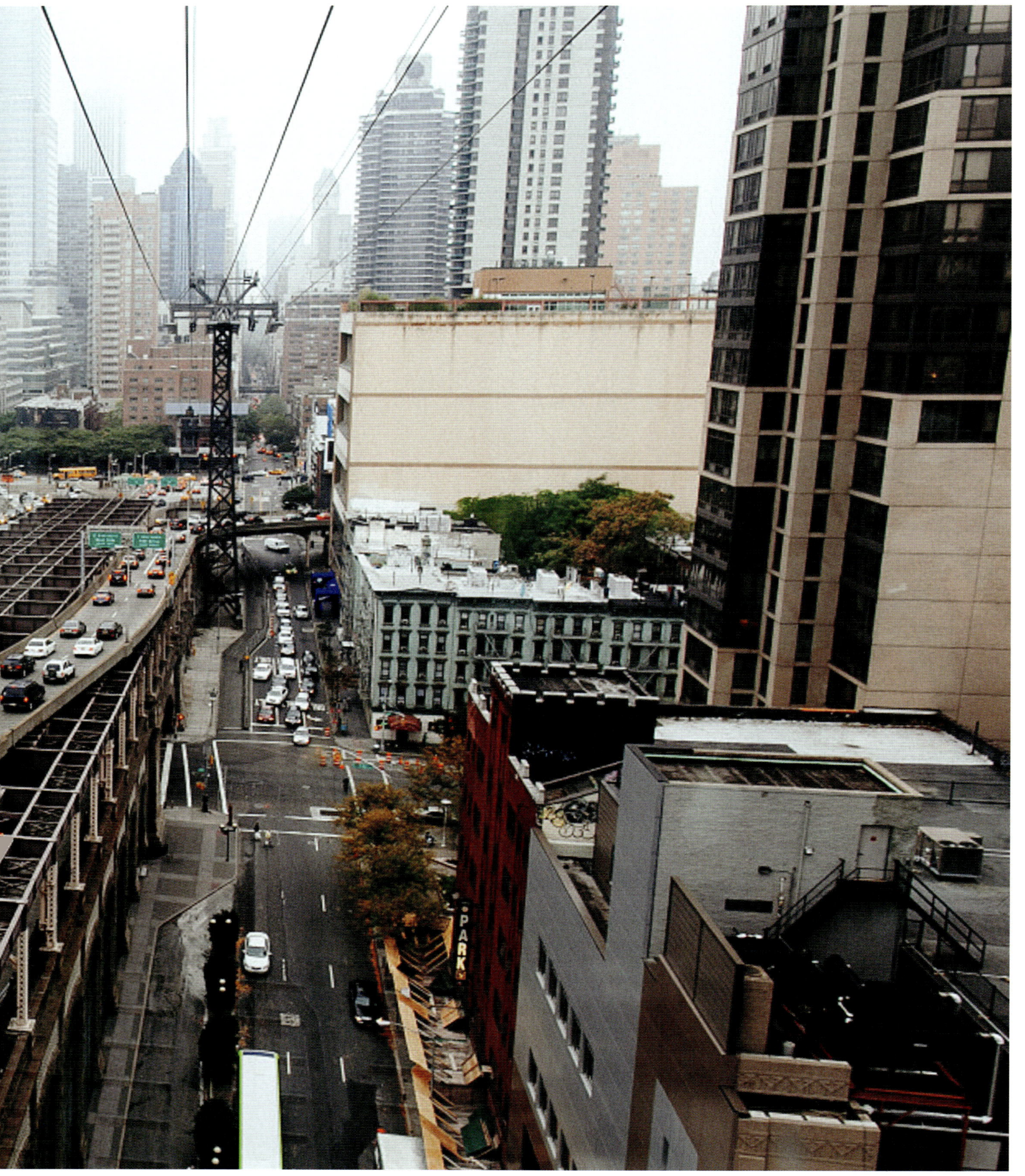

Ed Koch Queensboro Bridge & Tramway Plaza
Upper East Side, Manhattan
Demilade Balogun

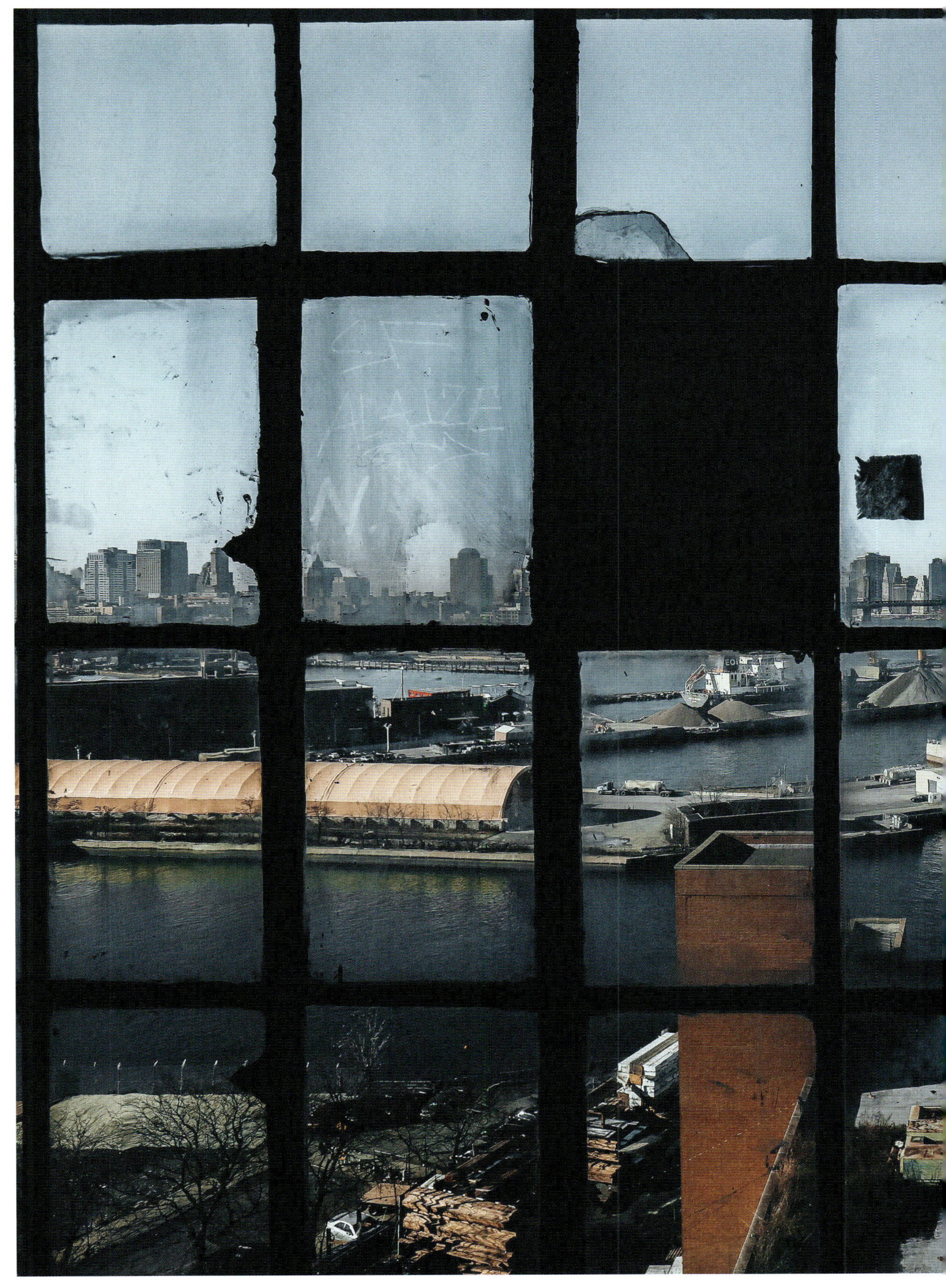

Brooklyn Navy Yard
Brooklyn
Pie Aerts

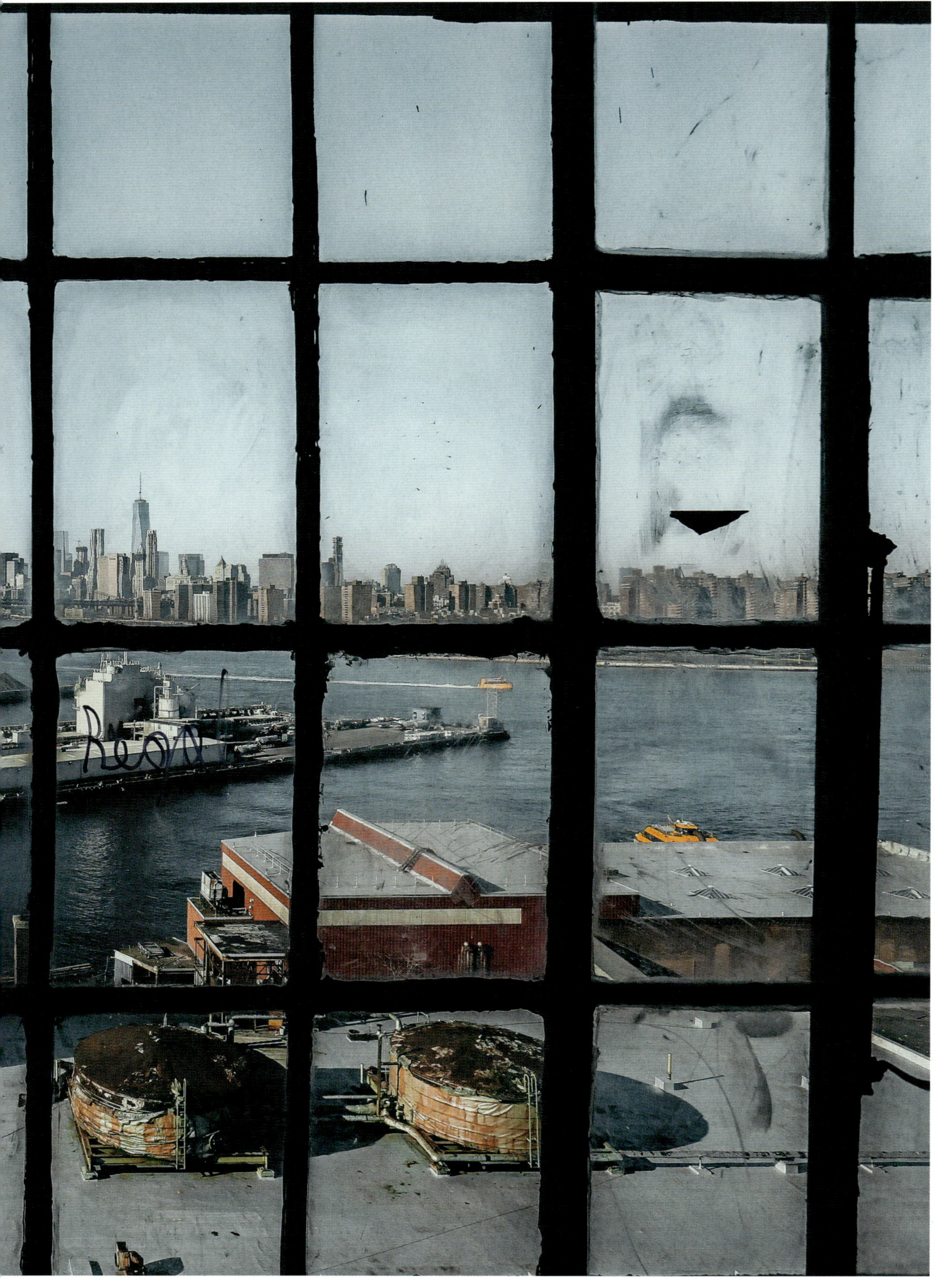

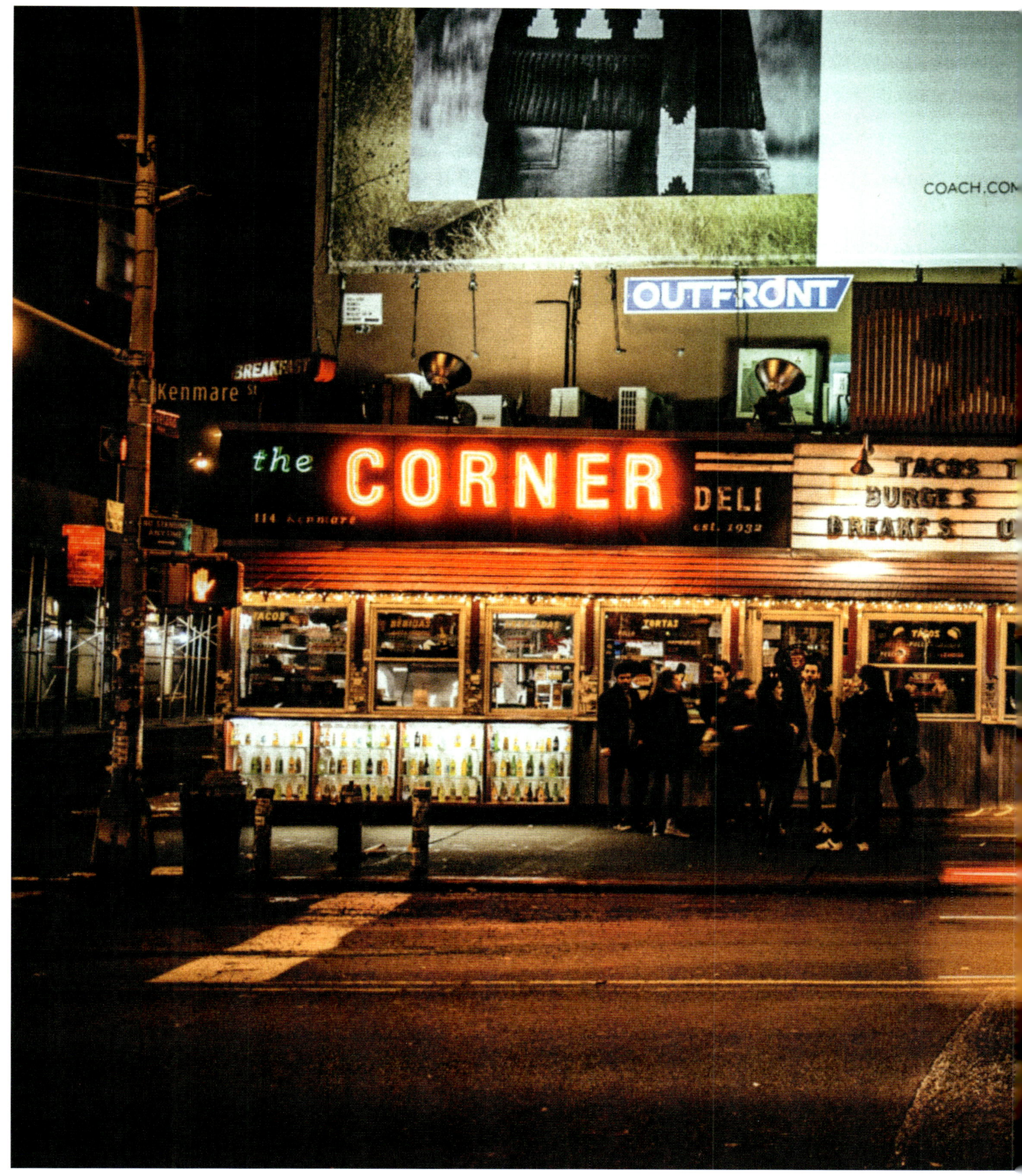

The Corner Deli
Nolita, Manhattan
Wil Suárez

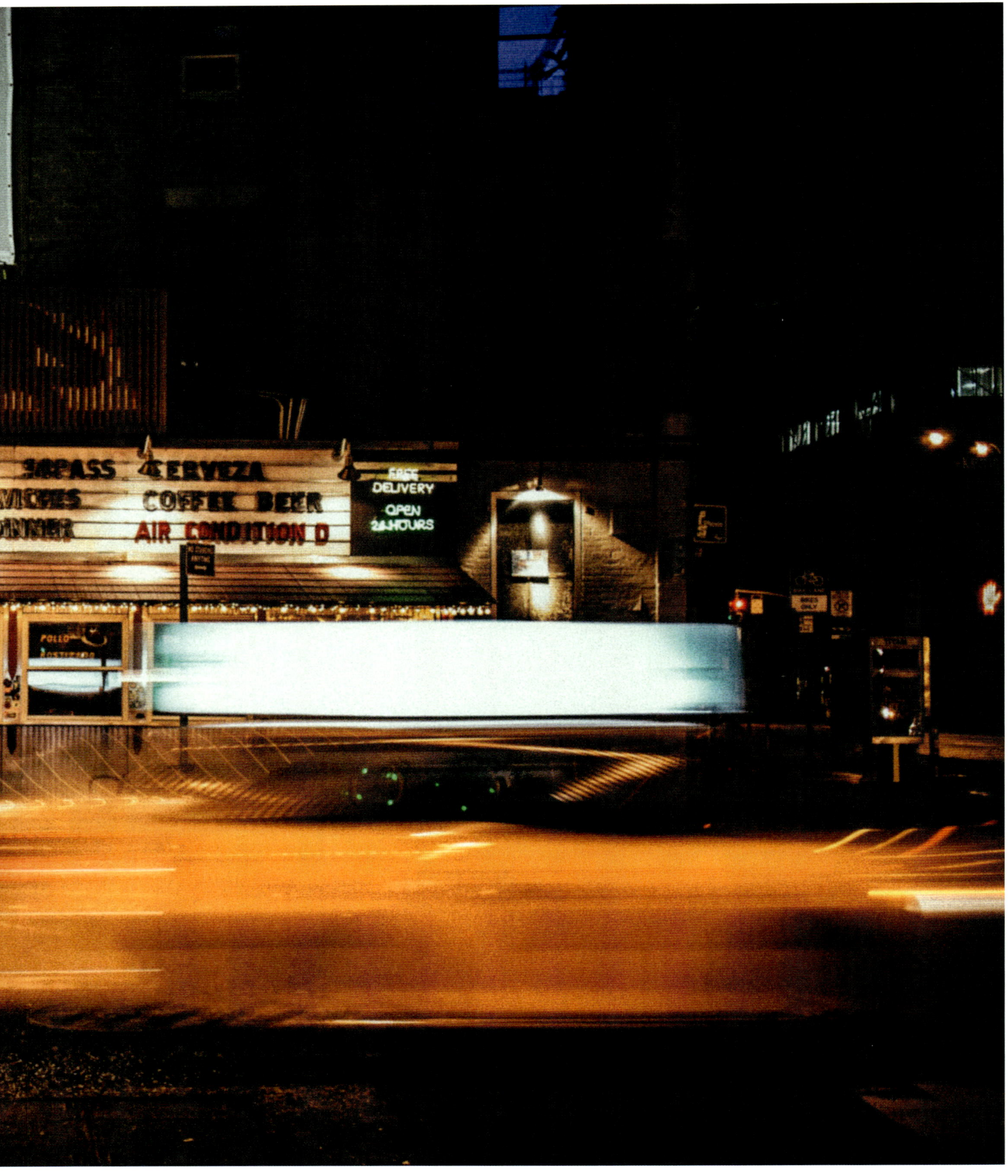
COFFEE BEER
AIR CONDITION D
DELIVERY
OPEN
24 HOURS

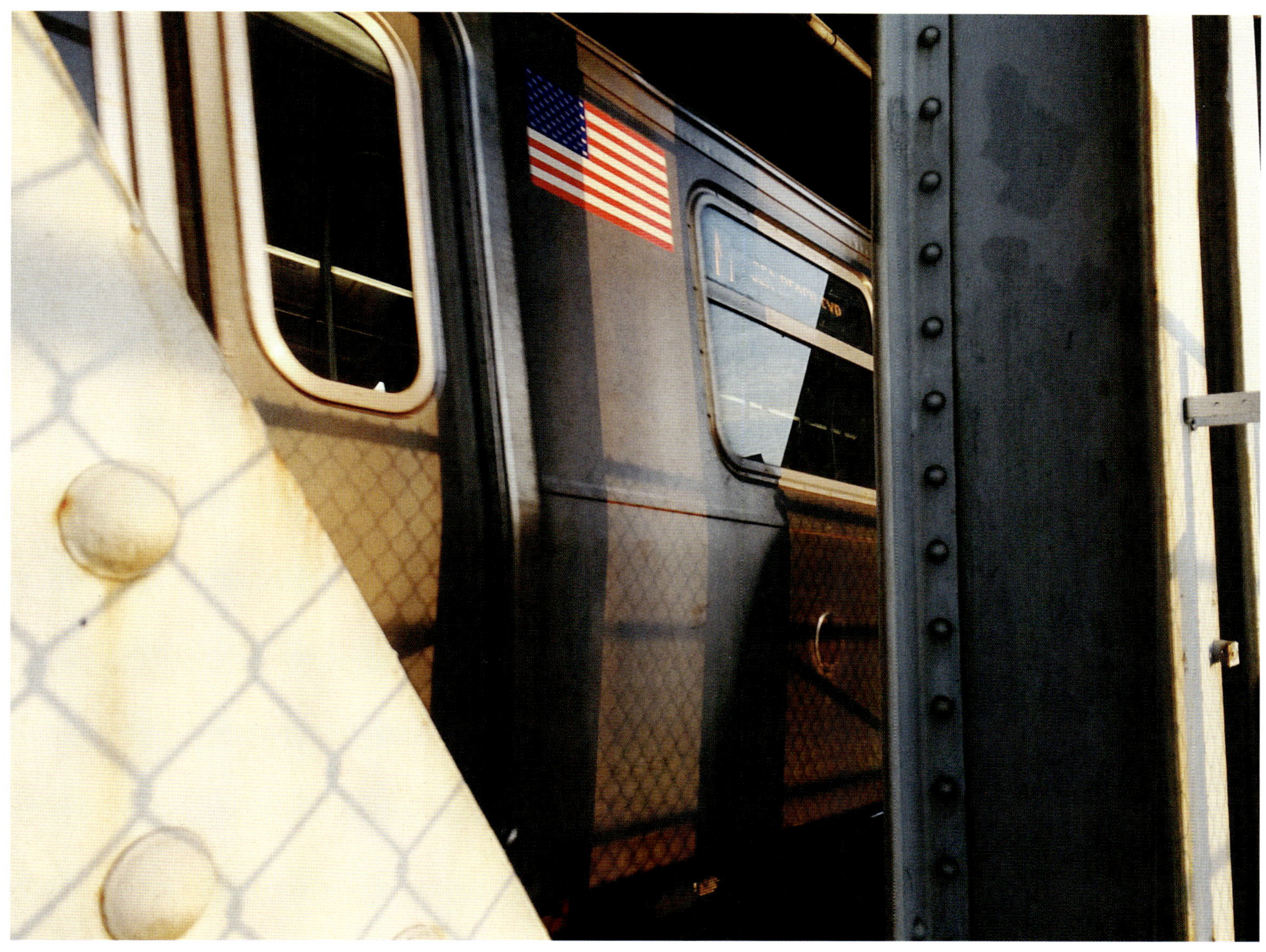

New York City Subway
Hal Haines

Manhattan
Lucas Hornsby –

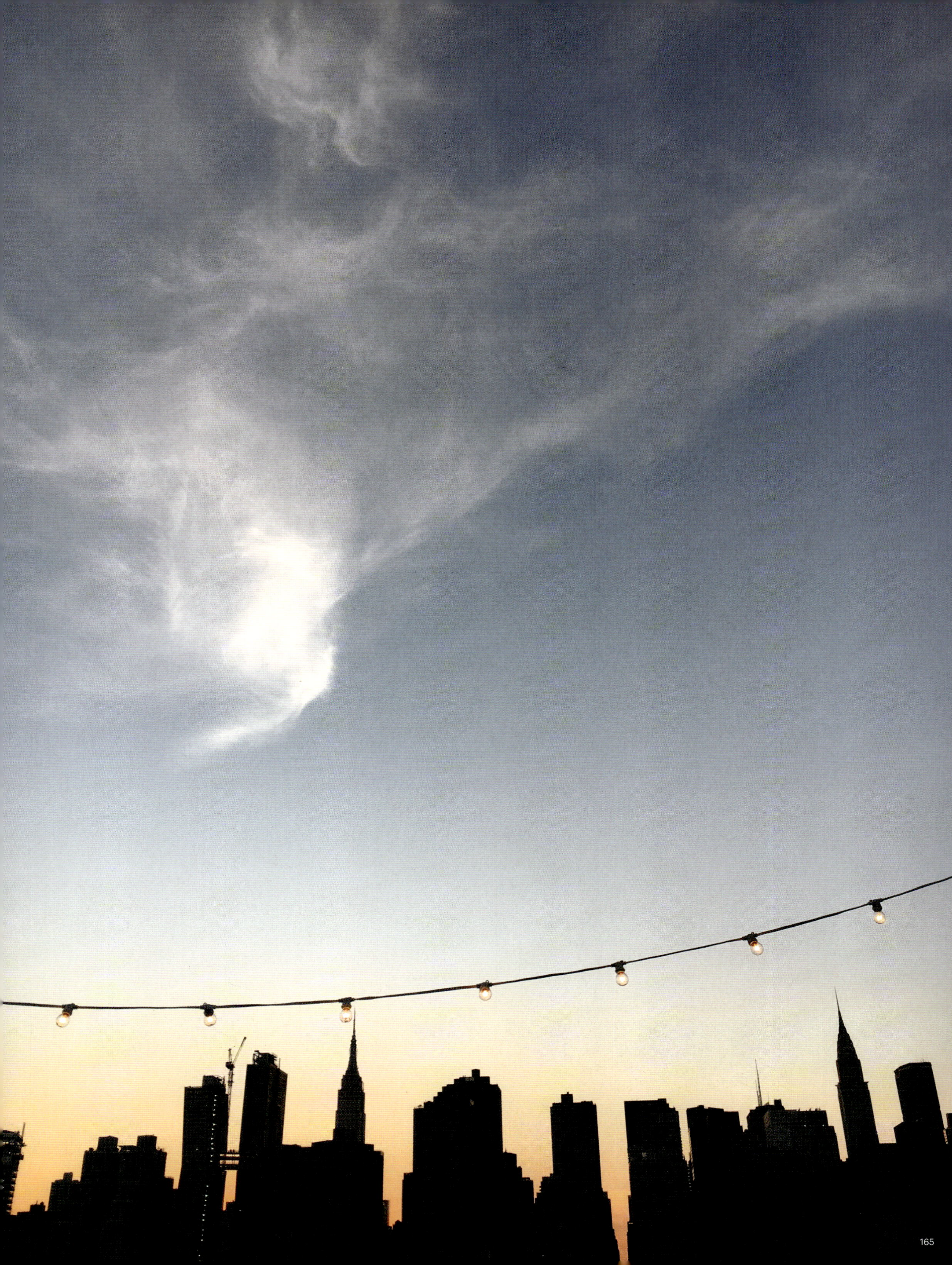

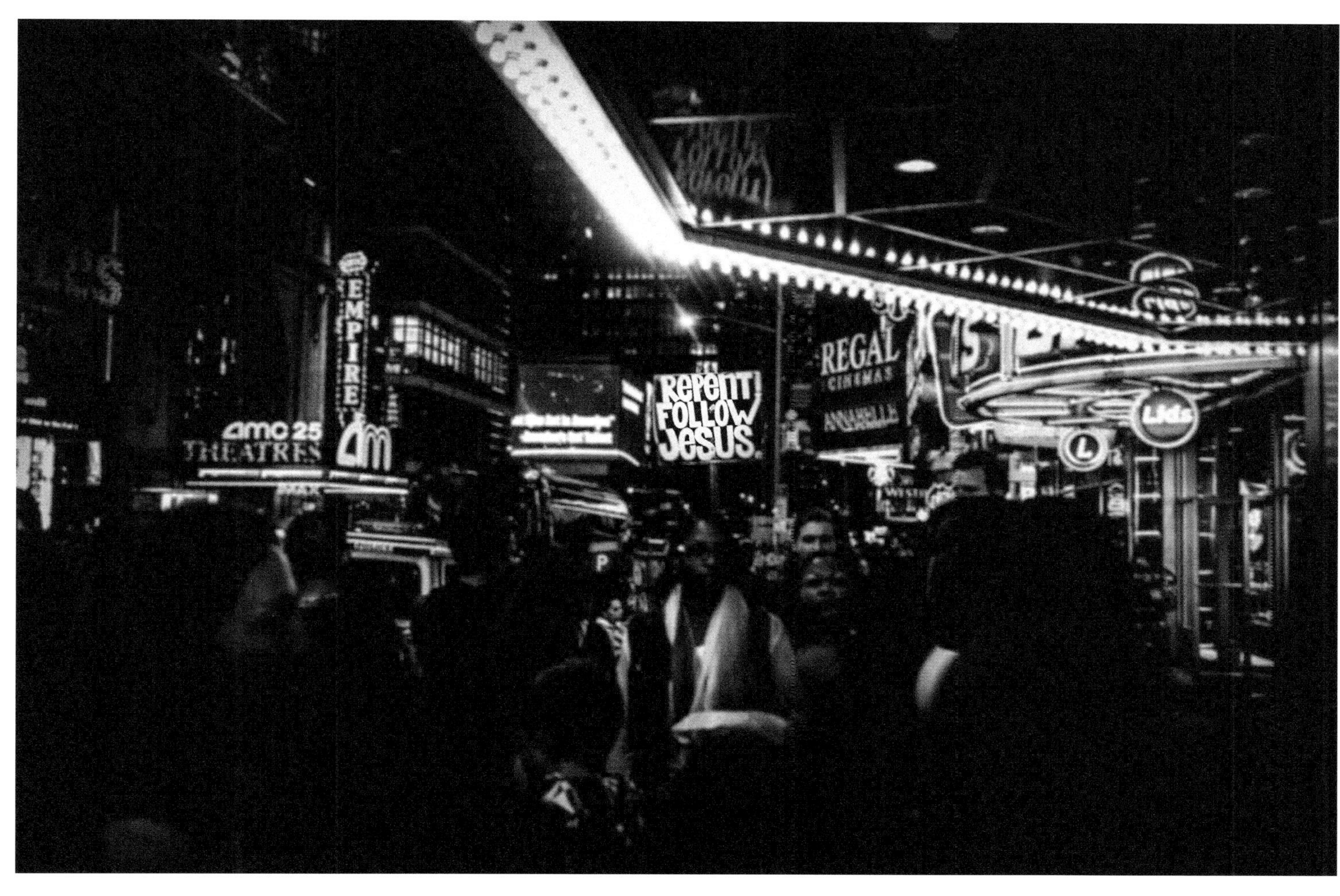

Theater District, Manhattan
Wil Suárez

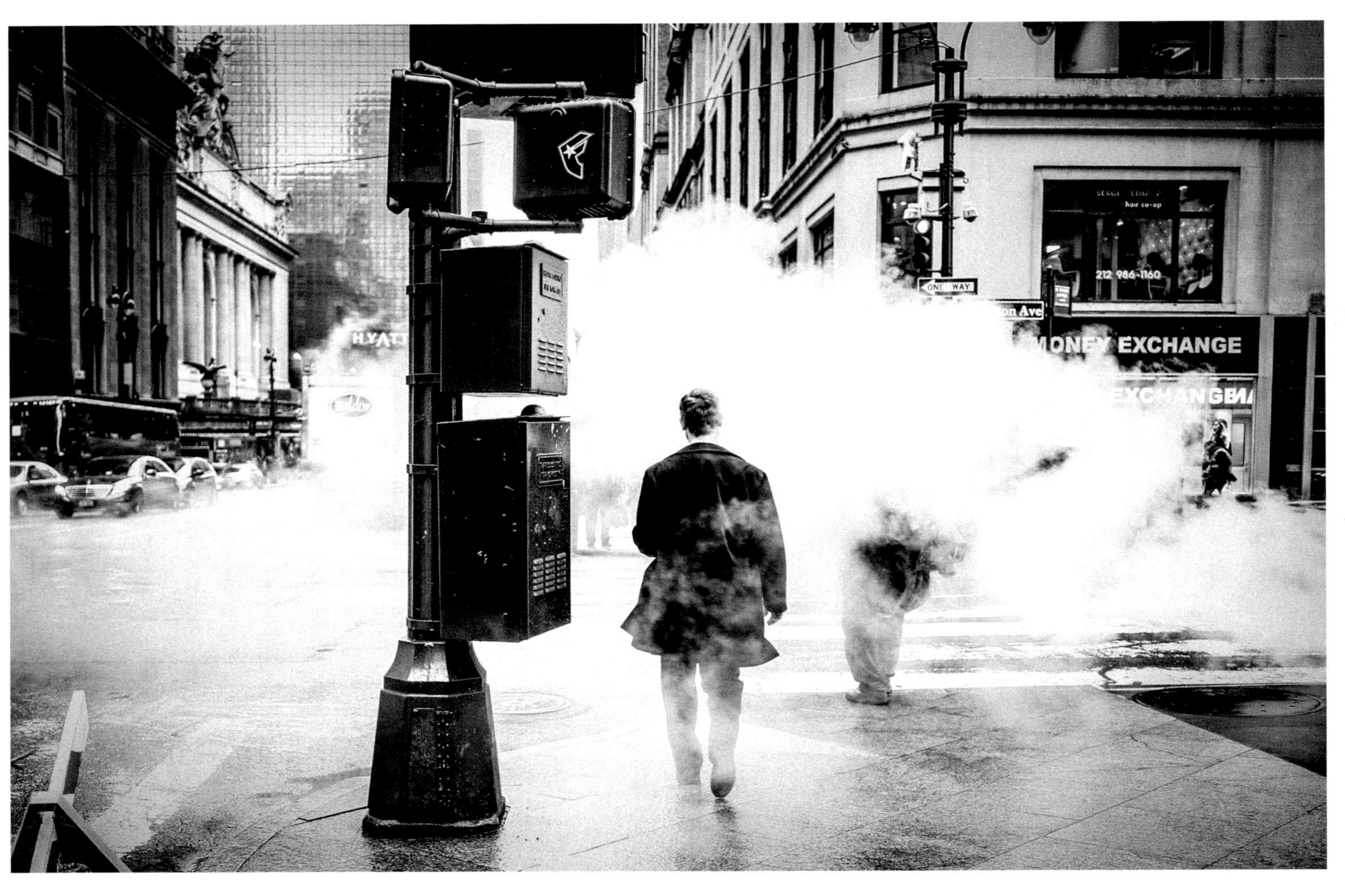

Murray Hill, Manhattan
Wil Suárez

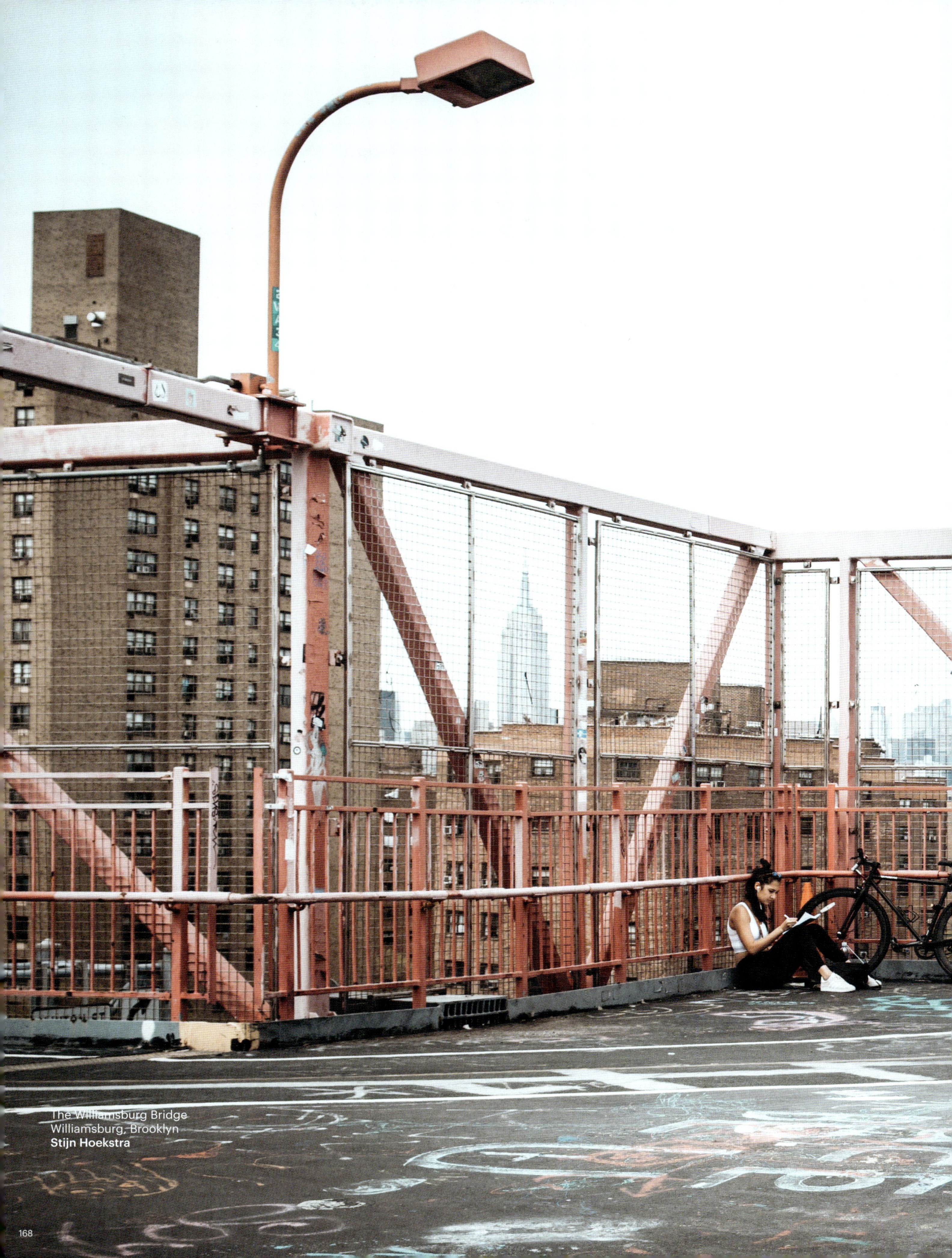

The Williamsburg Bridge
Williamsburg, Brooklyn
Stijn Hoekstra

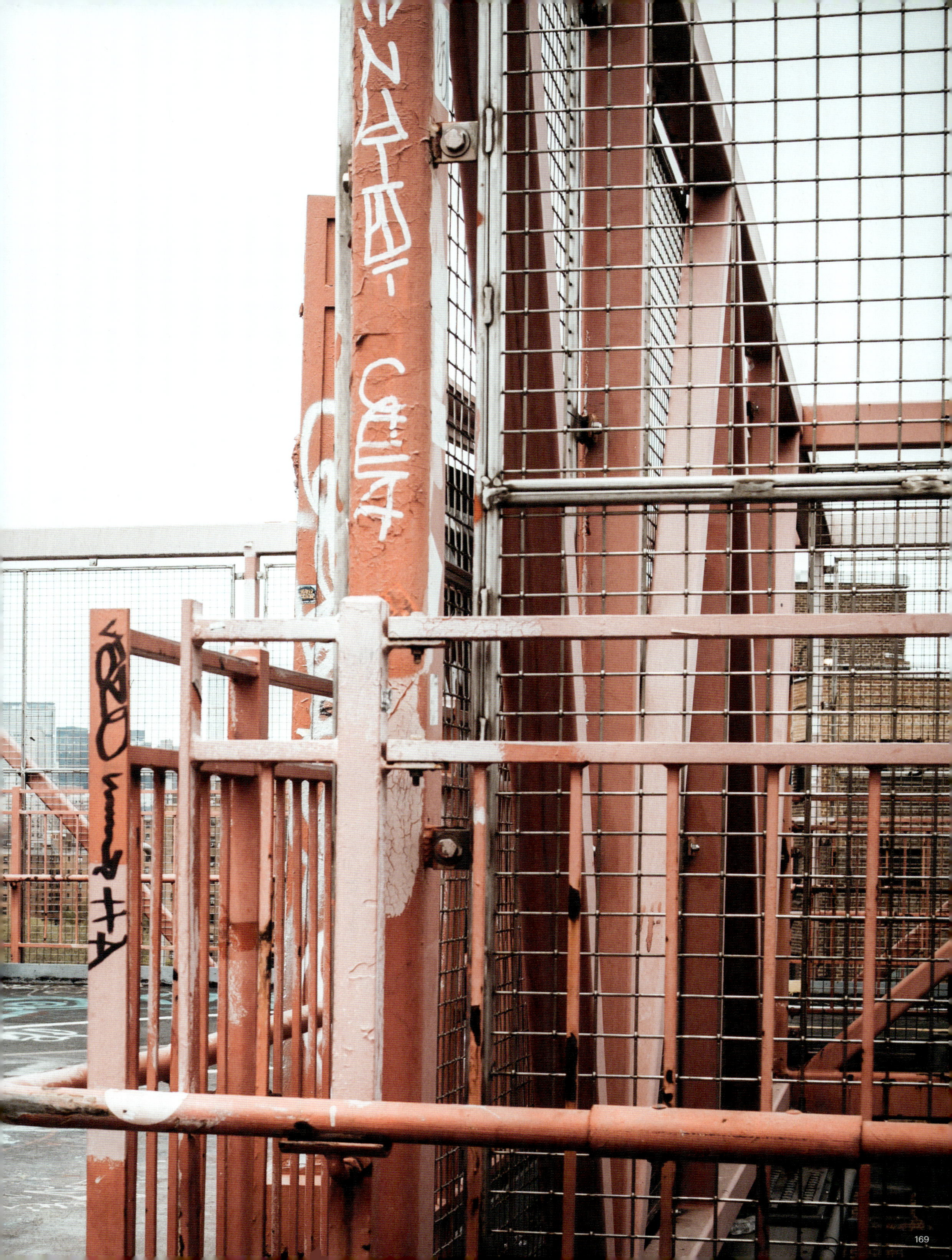

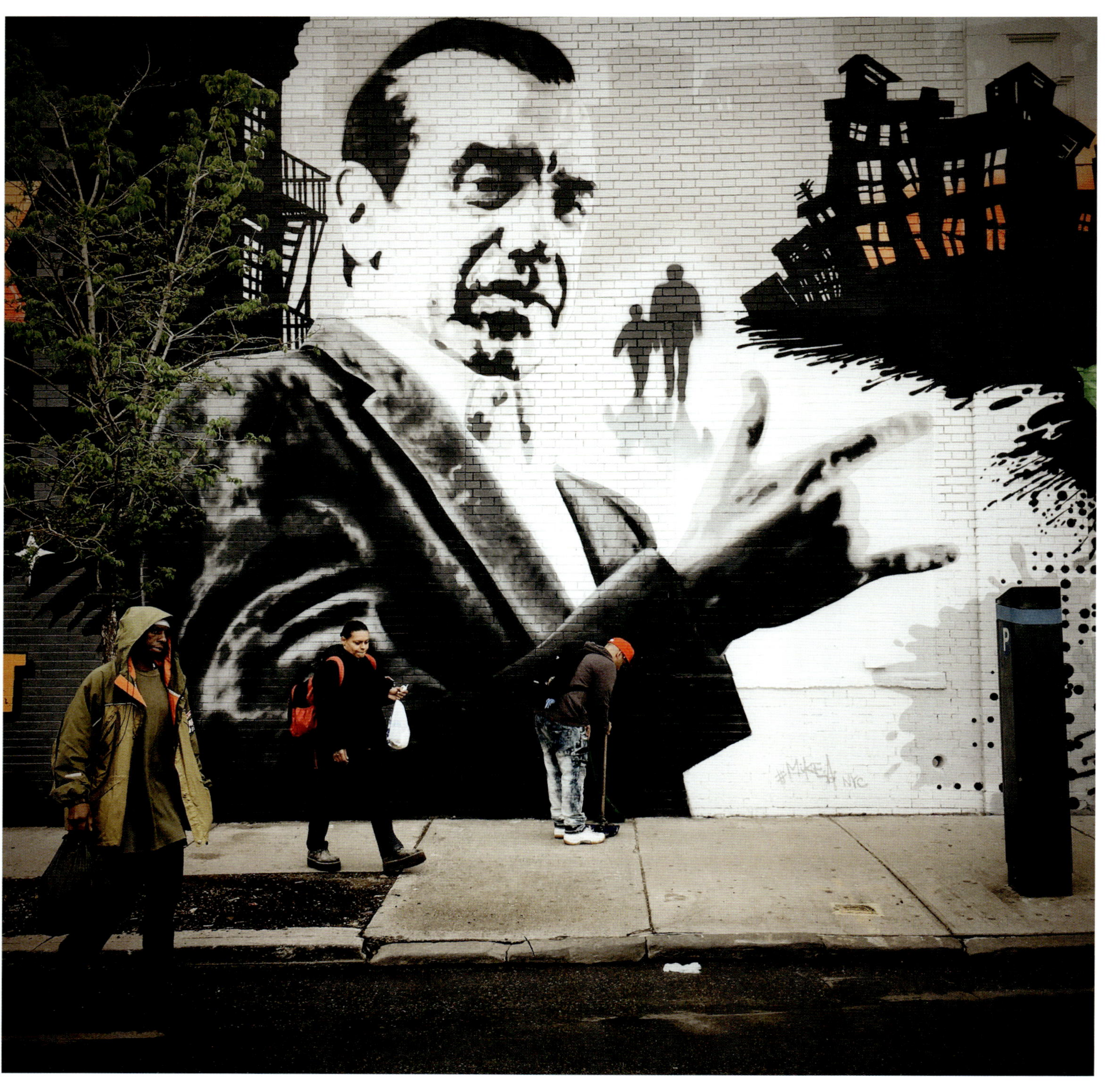

"A Bronx Tale" ft. Chazz Palminteri
Belmont, The Bronx
Edgar Santana

Casey Tang

hometown Santa Maria, California, USA
IG handle @casey.tang

To Casey Tang, New York is the center of the world. "It's where our culture is constantly shaped and molded," he says. "You can feel the city's ripples from anywhere. Also, there's always a clock ticking in everyone's minds there. Every minute in New York is precious. People usually don't waste time on what isn't important."

Social media exposed Casey to the wide variety of styles and talent in the world of photography. "It showed me I also had a unique story to tell," he says. In New York, though, you can't just point your camera and shoot, unless you want to take the same picture as everybody else. "Good photography has a balance of familiarity and newness with the viewer," Casey says. "A lot of the best photos are good because they're a new take on a place or thing that the viewer has seen before. This allows the viewer to bring their own history into the experience of viewing the photo. You need to put your own spin on it and tell your own story. Sometimes perfect moments only last a few seconds. You have to be ready for when they come."

Influenced by graphic design and abstract art, Casey's constantly looking for unique perspectives. "I use a wide-angle lens quite a bit, which allows me to get some really interesting reflection shots. It's all about spotting the reflective surface that's near you. Sometimes it's a puddle, a glass window, or the body of a black car." Casey is always aiming for symmetry and balance when he shoots. "And I want the viewer to feel a bit of a thrill when they see my photos, so I usually try to convey a sense of scale and vastness. It usually takes a little imagination and some risk."

Für Casey Tang ist New York das Zentrum der Welt. „Es ist der Ort, an dem unsere Kultur ständig geformt und gestaltet wird", sagt er. „Überall fühlt man die Vibrationen, die von der Stadt ausgehen. Außerdem tickt dort bei allen Menschen ständig eine Uhr im Kopf. Jede Minute ist in New York kostbar. Die Leute verschwenden in der Regel keine Zeit an Dinge, die nicht wichtig sind."

Über die sozialen Medien lernte Casey die große Vielfalt an Stilen und Talenten in der Welt der Fotografie kennen. „Das zeigte mir, dass auch ich eine einmalige Geschichte zu erzählen hatte", erklärt er. In New York kann man allerdings nicht einfach mit der Kamera drauflos knipsen, wenn man nicht das gleiche Bild wie alle anderen machen will. „Gute Fotografie wahrt eine Balance zwischen Vertrautheit und Neuem", erläutert Casey. „Viele der besten Fotos sind deshalb herausragend, weil sie eine neue Herangehensweise an Orte oder Sachen, die die meisten Menschen schon einmal gesehen haben, aufzeigen. So können sie ihre persönlichen Erfahrungen in die Betrachtungsweise eines Fotos einbringen. Man muss seinen eigenen Dreh finden, eine eigene Story erzählen. Manchmal dauern perfekte Momente nur ein paar Sekunden und man sollte bereit sein, wenn sie kommen."

Beeinflusst von Grafikdesign und abstrakter Kunst, sucht Casey ständig nach einzigartigen Perspektiven. „Ich benutze ziemlich oft ein Weitwinkelobjektiv, das mir erlaubt, wirklich interessante Aufnahmen von Spiegelungen zu machen. Dabei geht es darum, eine reflektierende Oberfläche in der unmittelbaren Umgebung zu entdecken. Manchmal ist es eine Pfütze, manchmal ein Fenster oder die Karosserie eines schwarzen Autos." Casey zielt beim Fotografieren immer auf Symmetrie und Balance ab. „Und ich möchte, dass die Betrachter meiner Fotos einen kleinen Thrill erleben, deshalb versuche ich meistens, ein Gefühl von Größe und Weite zu vermitteln. Oft braucht es dafür ein wenig Fantasie und ein gewisses Risiko."

Pour Casey Tang, New York est le centre du monde. « C'est là qu'en permanence, notre culture se façonne et se forge », déclare-t-il. « Partout, nous pouvons sentir les ondes de la ville. Il y a aussi le passage du temps qui est sans cesse présent dans l'esprit de chacun ici. Chaque minute à New York est précieuse. On ne gaspille généralement pas le temps pour ce qui n'est pas important ». Les réseaux sociaux offrent à Casey l'accès à une grande diversité de styles et de talents issus du monde la photographie. « Ils m'ont également permis de comprendre que j'avais une histoire unique à raconter », affirme-t-il. A New York, cependant, impossible de se contenter de pointer son appareil pour capturer une image, à moins de vouloir prendre le même cliché que tout le monde. « Une grande photographie se caractérise par un équilibre entre ce qui est familier et ce qui est nouveau pour le spectateur », constate Casey. « Nombre des meilleures photographies sont réussies parce qu'elles proposent un regard nouveau sur un lieu ou une chose que le spectateur a vus auparavant. Ce qui permet à ce dernier d'introduire sa propre histoire dans l'expérience qui consiste à regarder l'image. Il est nécessaire d'y intégrer son interprétation personnelle, de raconter sa propre histoire. Les instants parfaits ne durent parfois que quelques secondes. Il faut être prêt lorsqu'ils se produisent ».

Influencé par le graphisme et l'art abstrait, Casey est sans cesse en quête de points de vue uniques. « Je recours souvent au grand angle qui me permet d'obtenir des images de reflets. L'idée, c'est de remarquer les surfaces réfléchissantes qui sont autour de nous. Il s'agit parfois d'une flaque d'eau, d'une vitre ou encore, de la carrosserie noire d'une voiture ». Lorsqu'il photographie, Casey recherche systématiquement la symétrie et l'équilibre. « Je veux aussi que le spectateur éprouve une sorte de frisson en regardant mes images, donc, je m'efforce généralement de véhiculer une sensation d'échelle et de grandeur. Ce qui suppose toujours un peu d'imagination et une forme de risque ».

The Grabler Building
Tribeca, Manhattan
Casey Tang

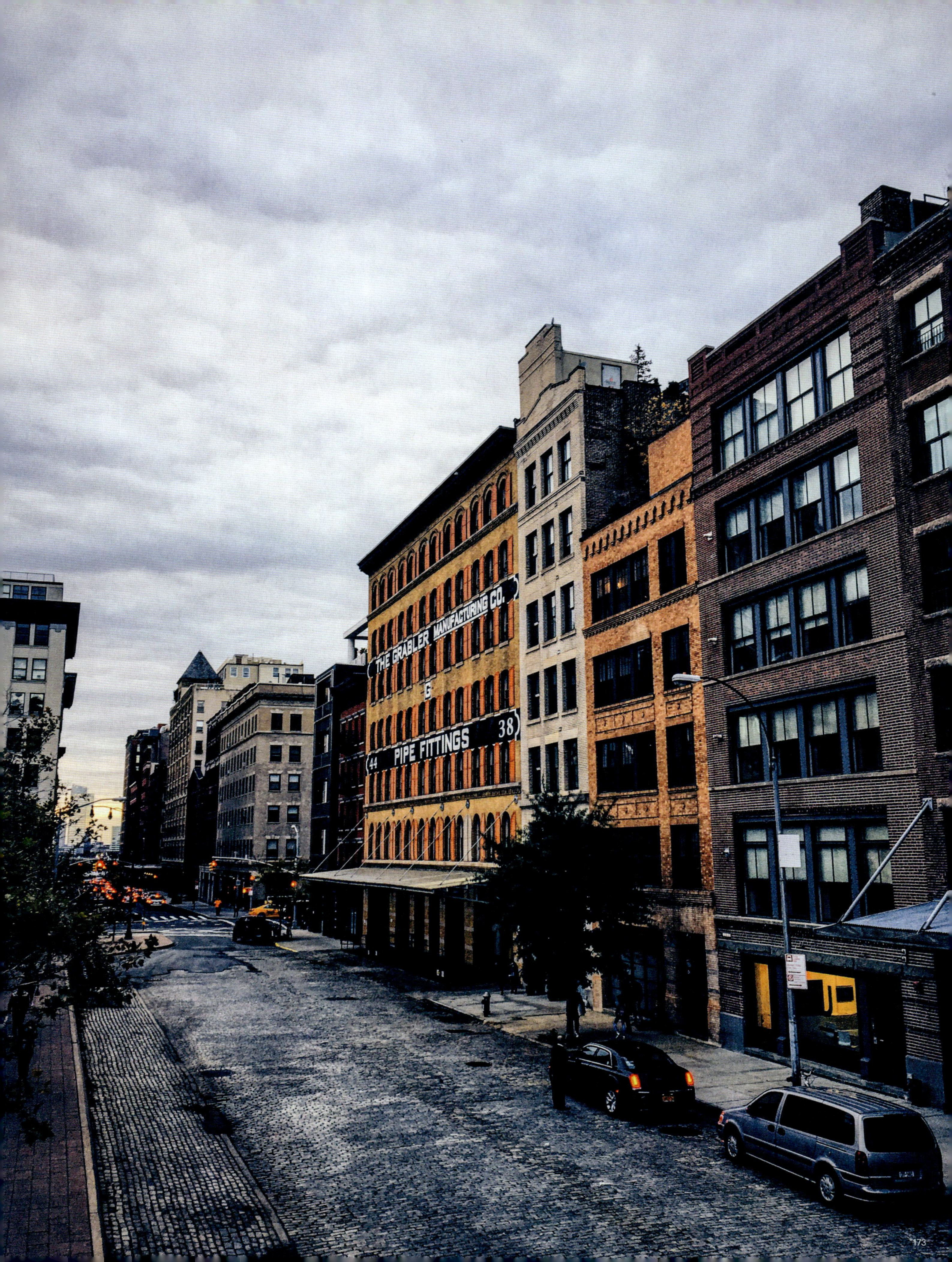

THE GRABLER MANUFACTURING CO.
G
44 PIPE FITTINGS 38

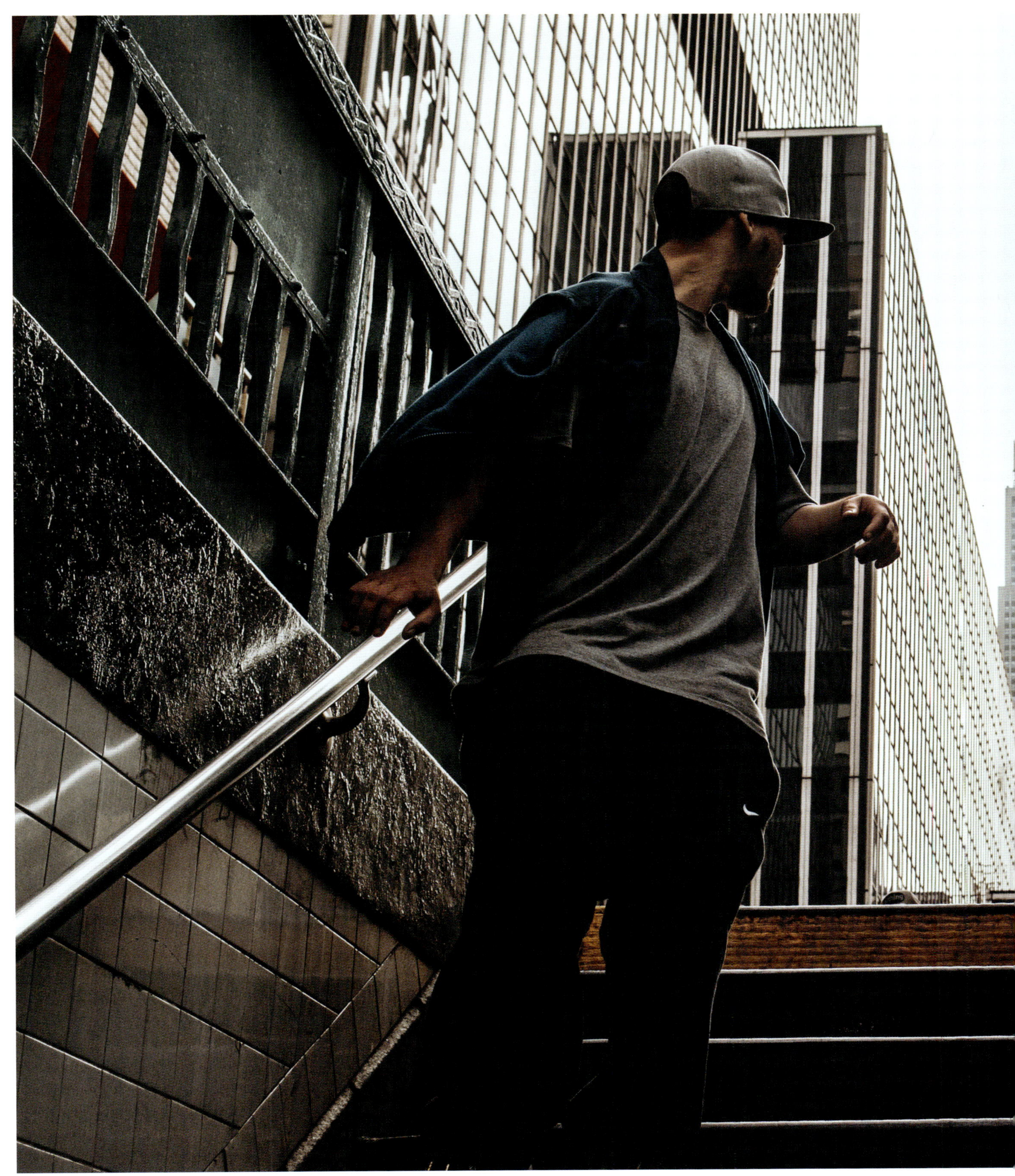

The Empire State Building
Manhattan
Stijn Hoekstra

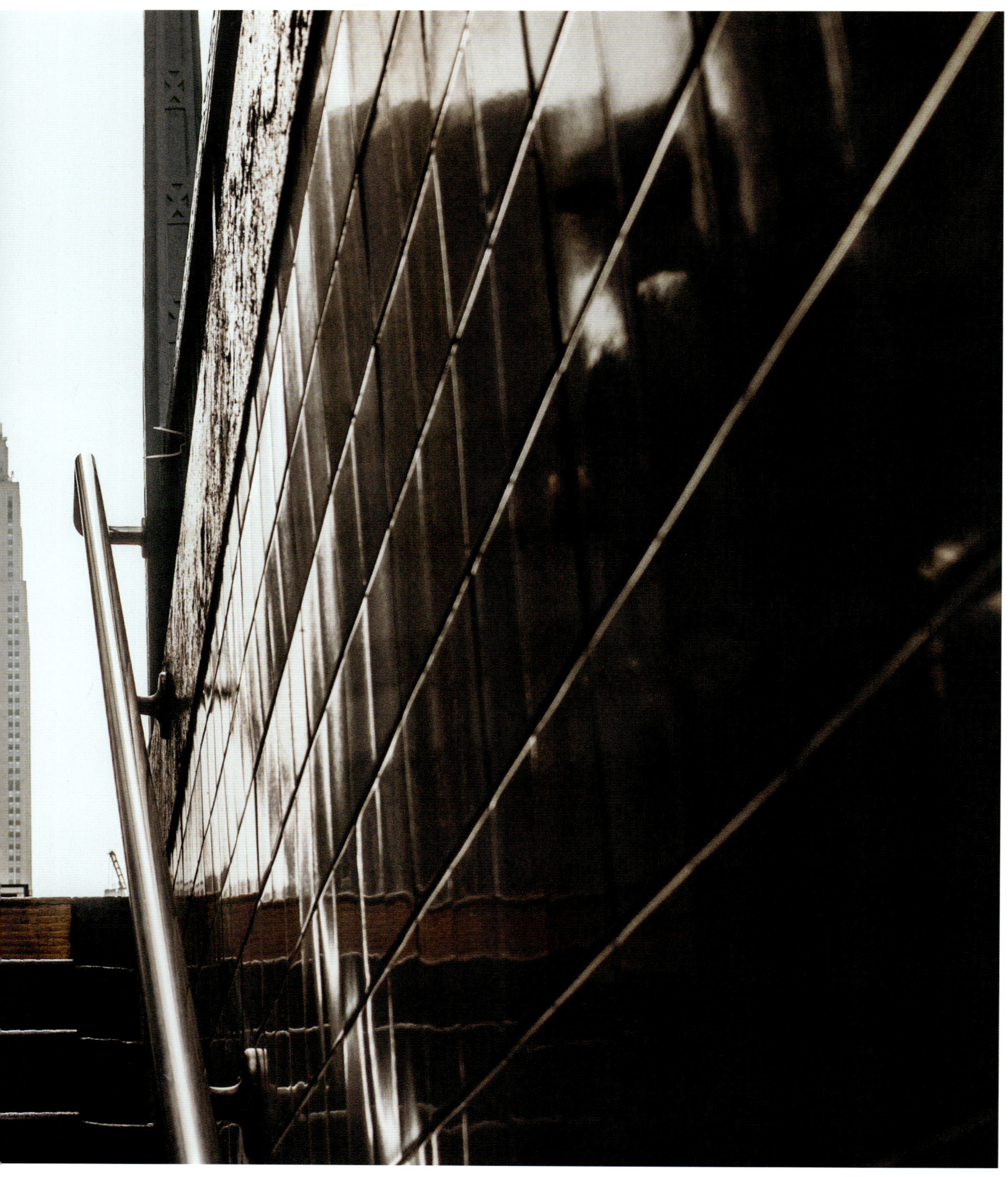

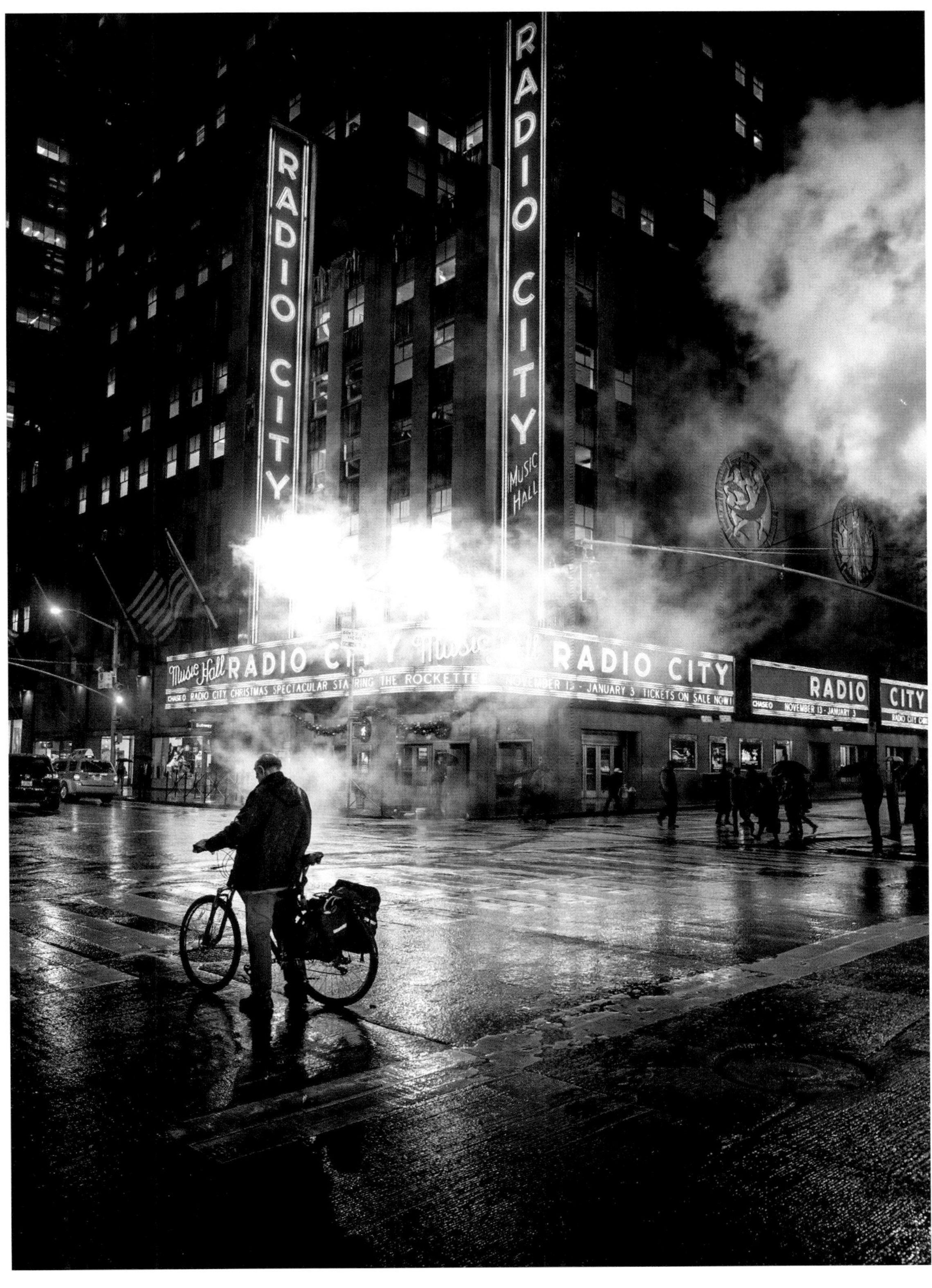

Radio City Music Hall
Theater District, Manhattan
Jason Peterson

Grand Central Station
Midtown East, Manhattan
Jason Peterson

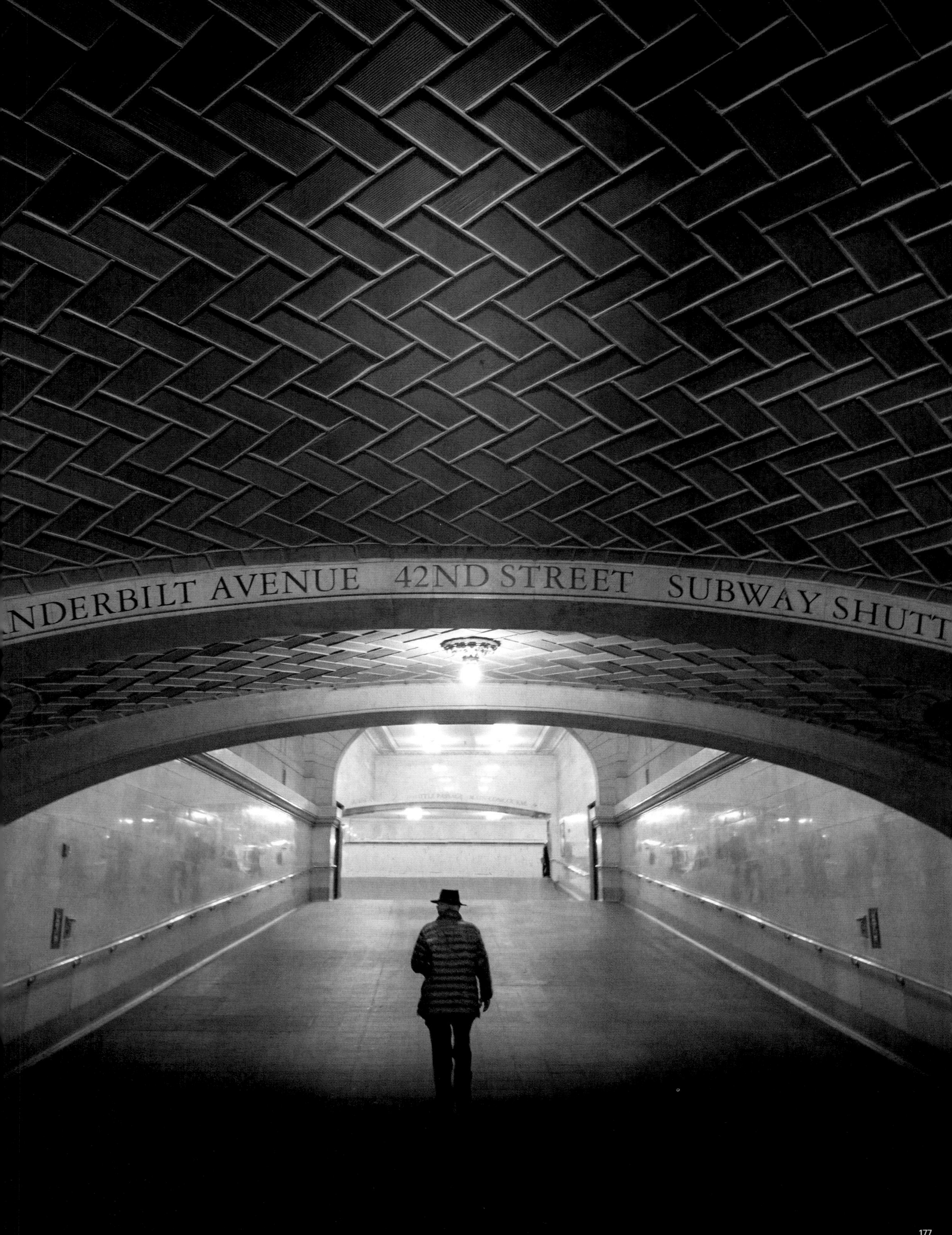
NDERBILT AVENUE 42ND STREET SUBWAY SHUTT

New York City has an amazing ethnic diversity, a unique social fabric that shapes its society.

—Joost Bastmeijer

South Bronx, The Bronx
Dondre Green

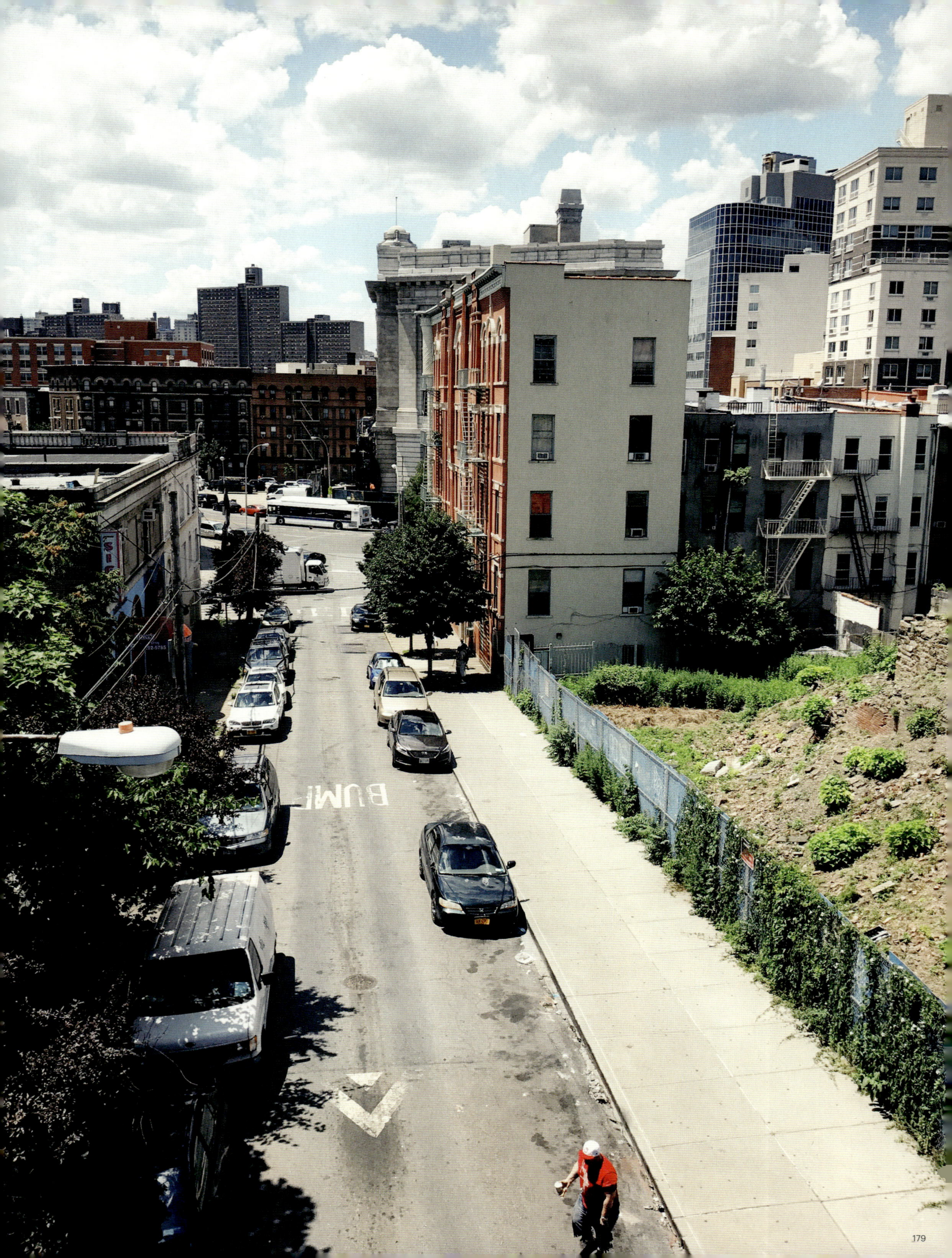

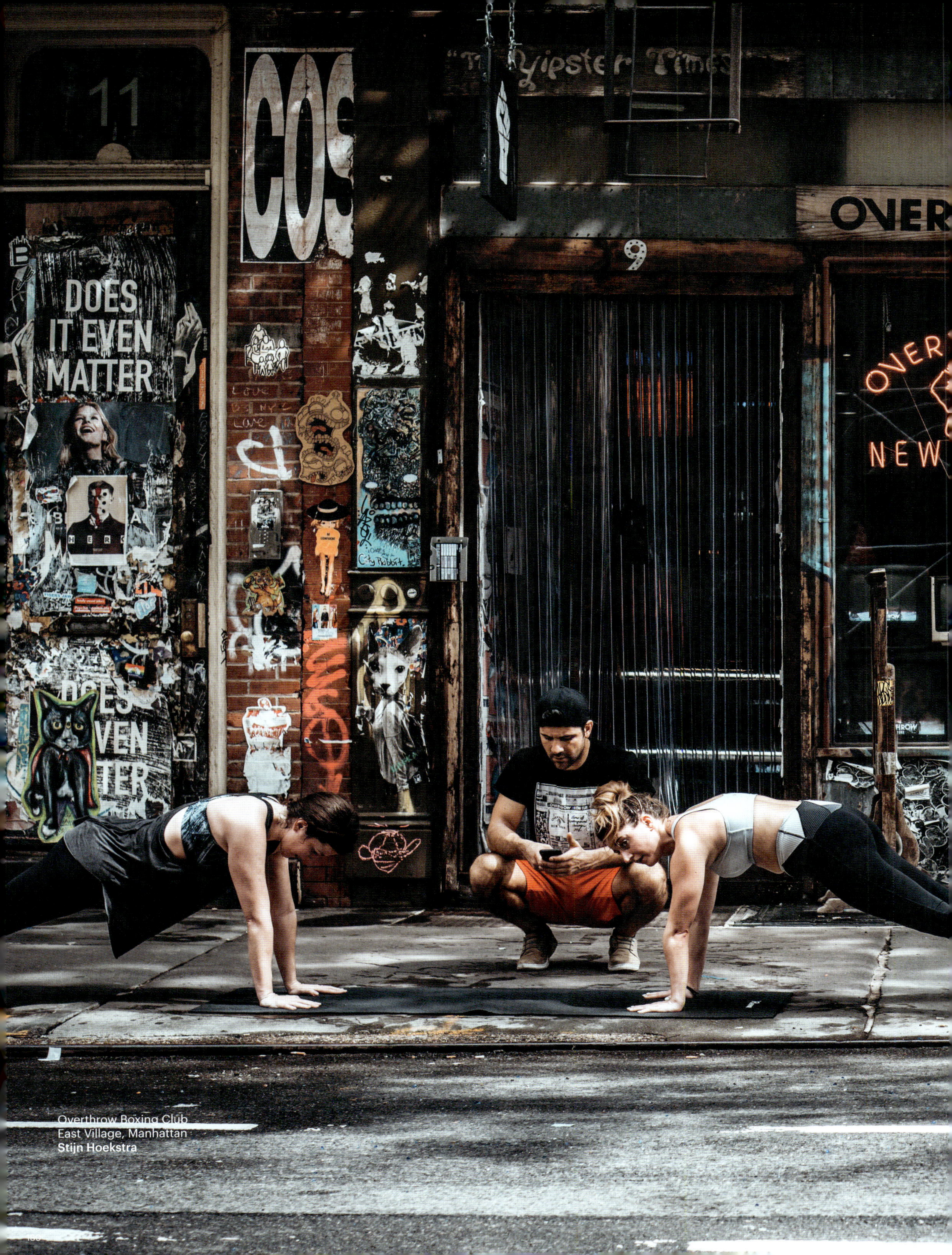

Overthrow Boxing Club
East Village, Manhattan
Stijn Hoekstra

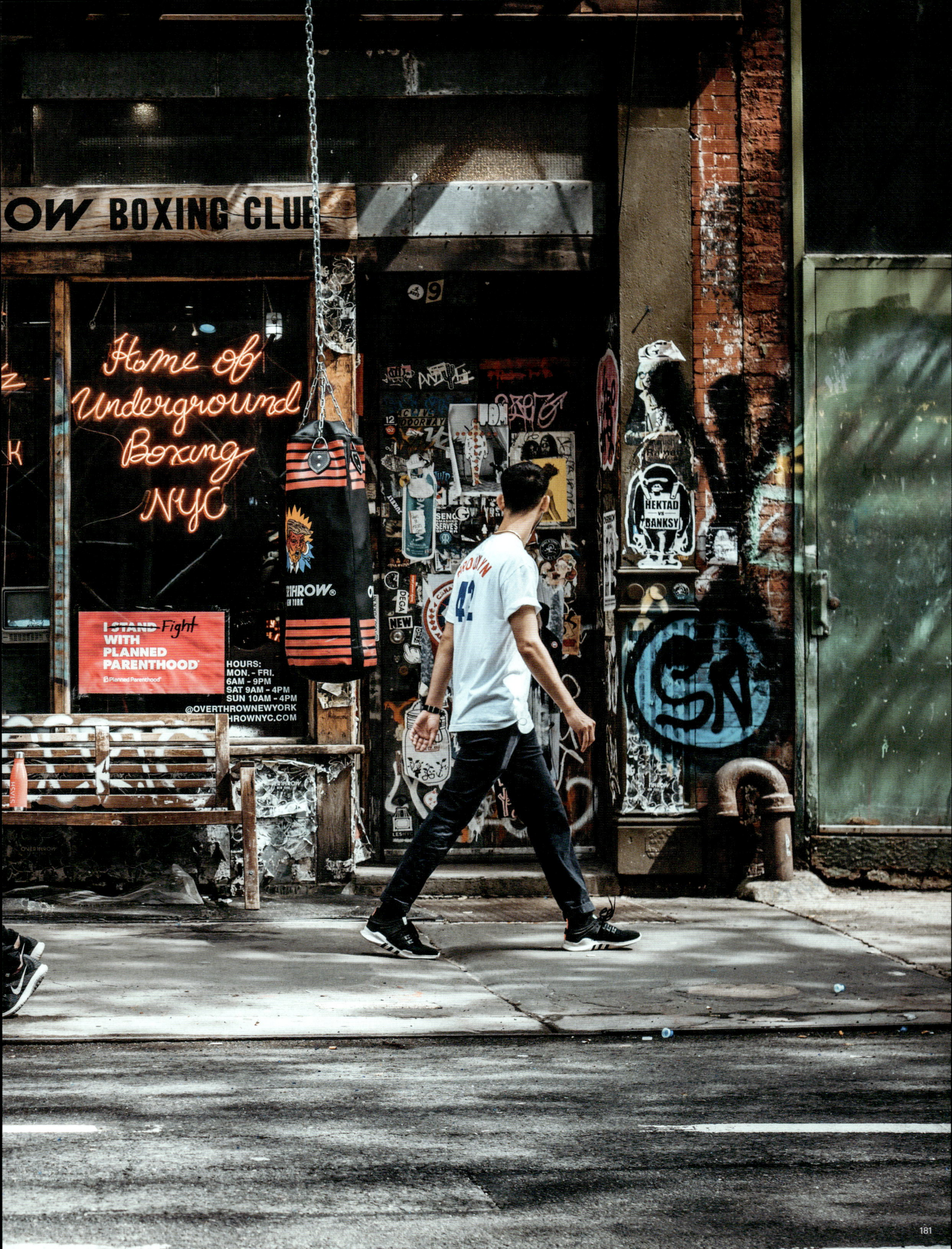
OW BOXING CLUB
Home of Underground Boxing NYC
I STAND Fight WITH PLANNED PARENTHOOD
Planned Parenthood
HOURS:
MON. - FRI.
6AM - 9PM
SAT 9AM - 4PM
SUN 10AM - 4PM
@OVERTHROWNEWYORK
HROWNYC.COM
HEKTAD vs BANKSY

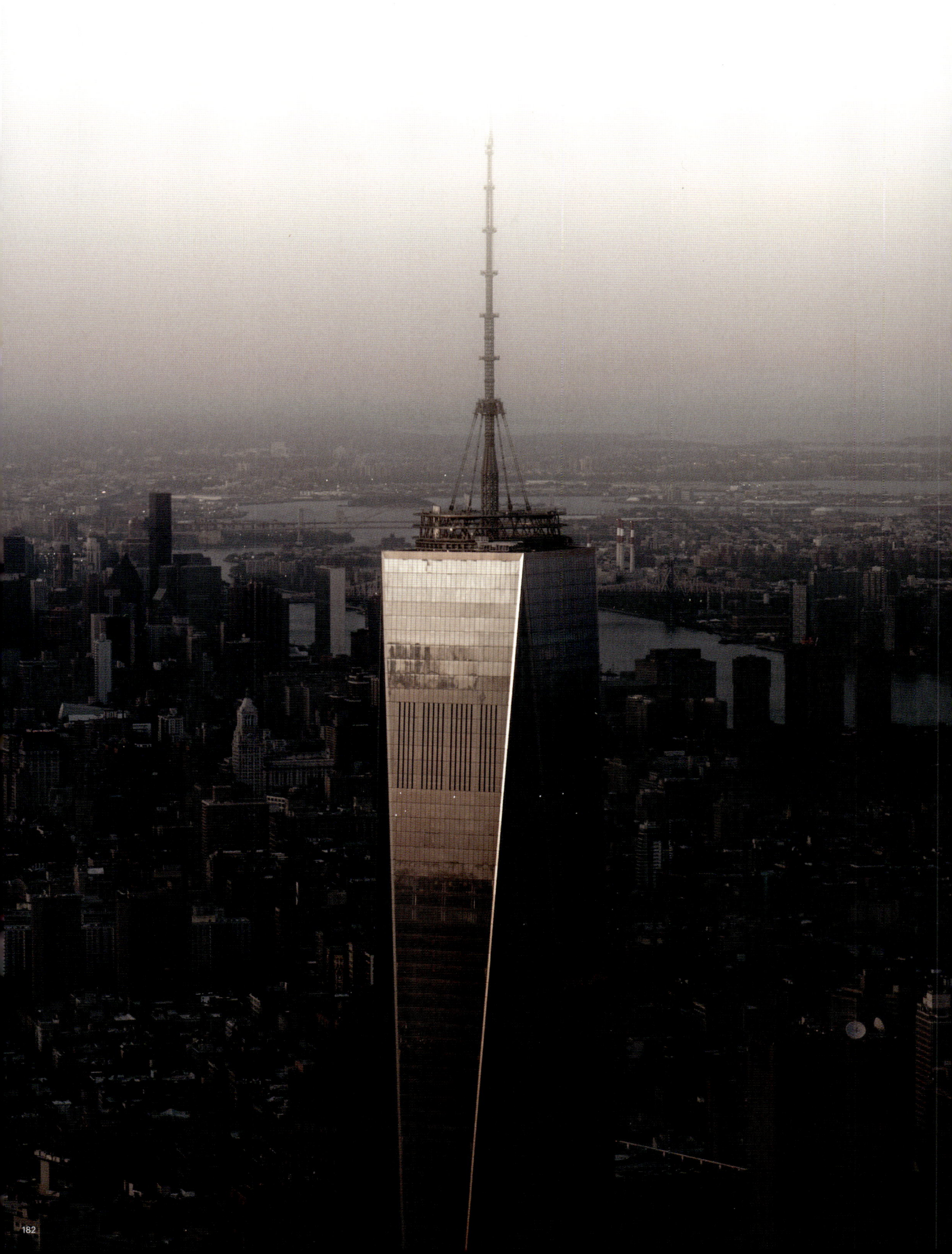

One World Trade Center
Financial District, Manhattan
– **Jason Peterson**

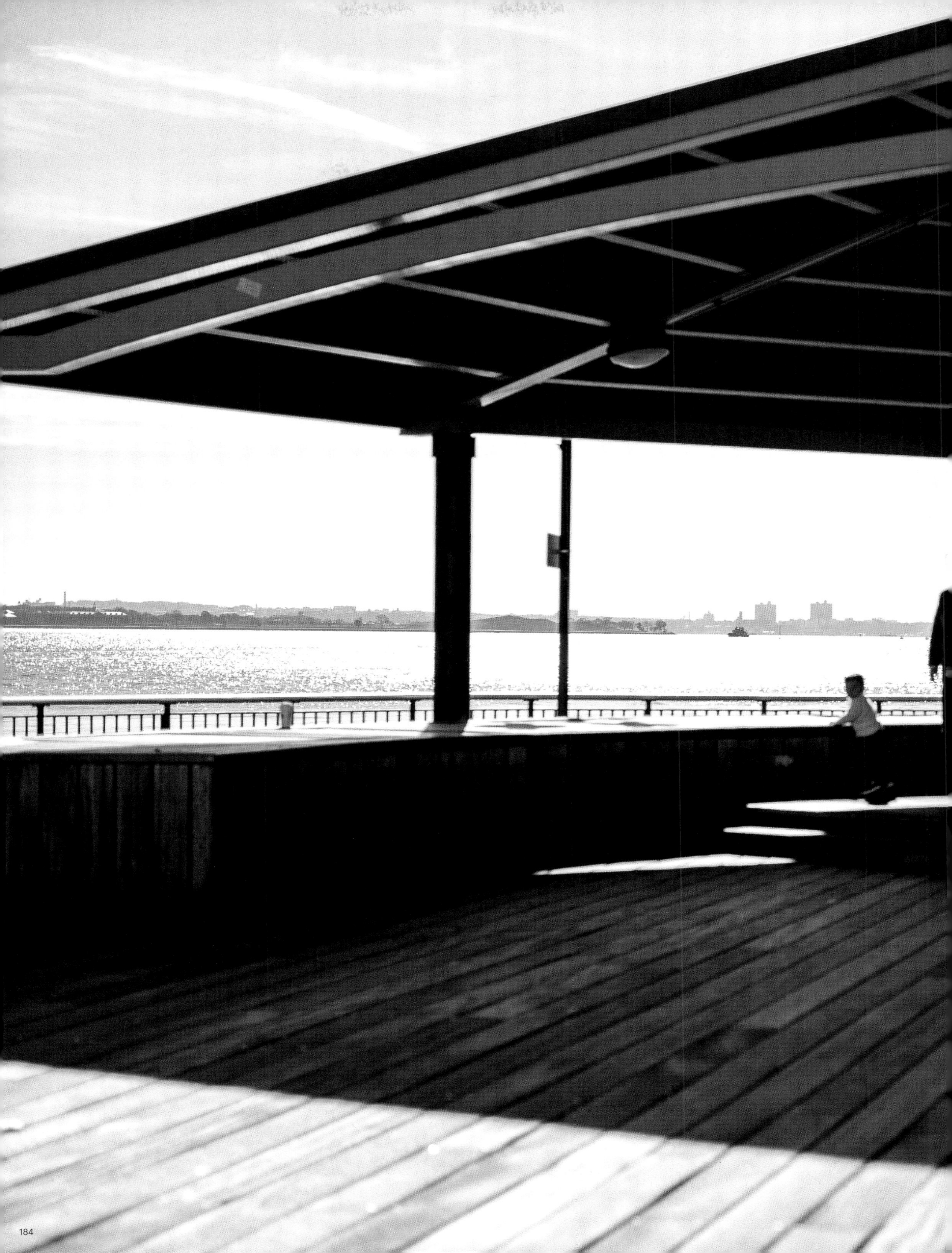

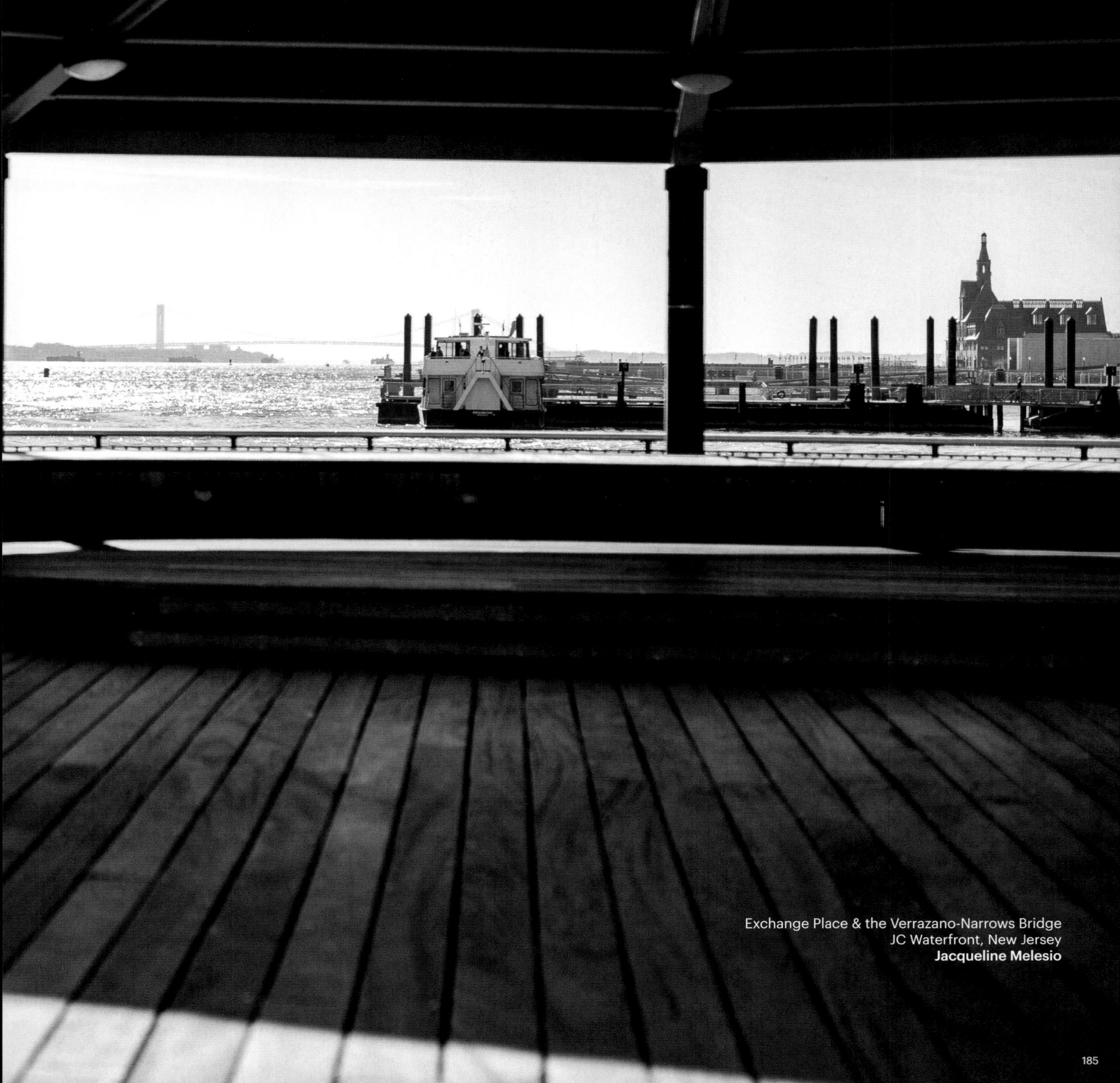

Exchange Place & the Verrazano-Narrows Bridge
JC Waterfront, New Jersey
Jacqueline Melesio

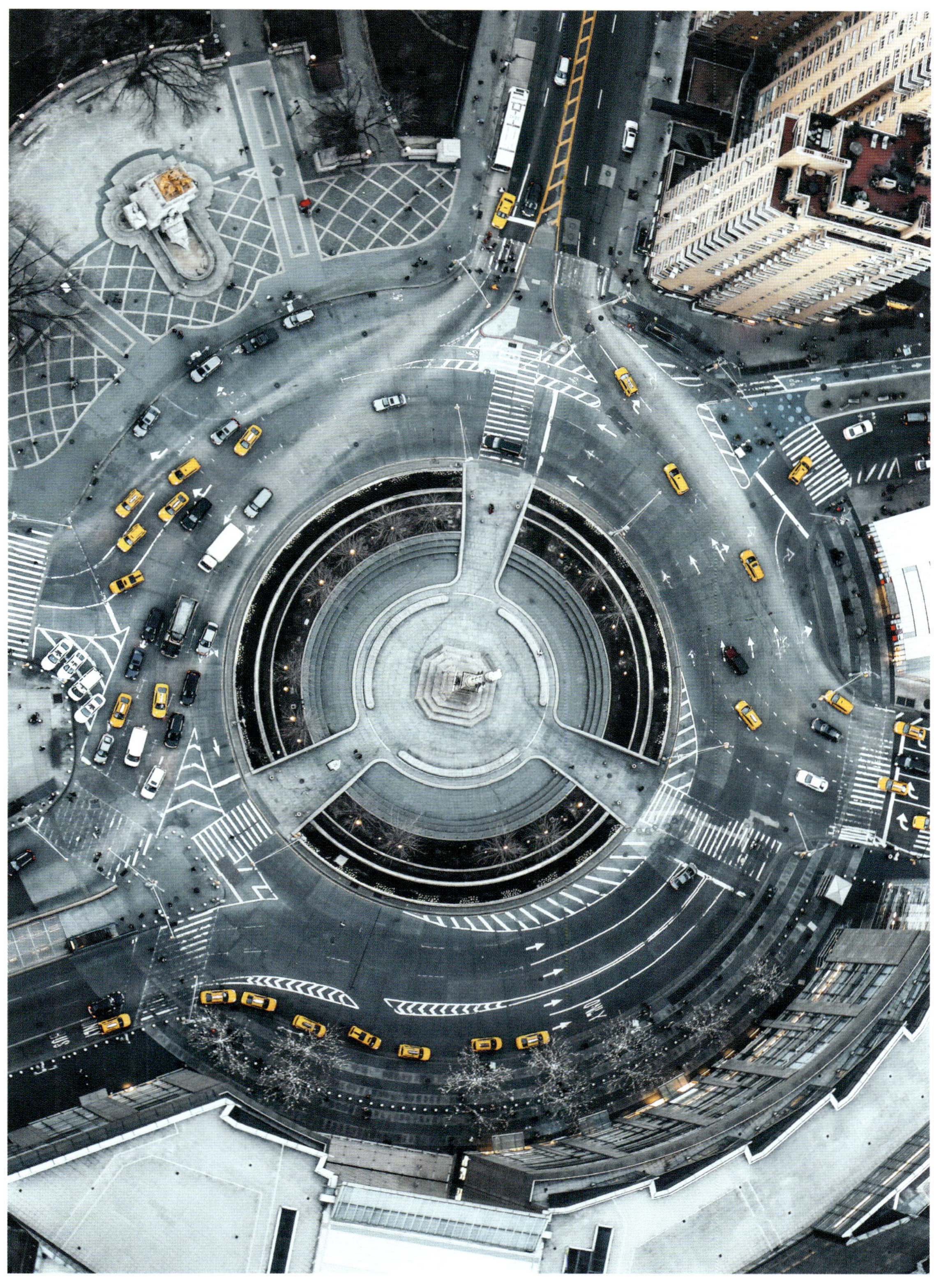

Columbus Circle
Lincoln Square, Manhattan
Pie Aerts

The Manhattan Bridge
Brooklyn
Pie Aerts —

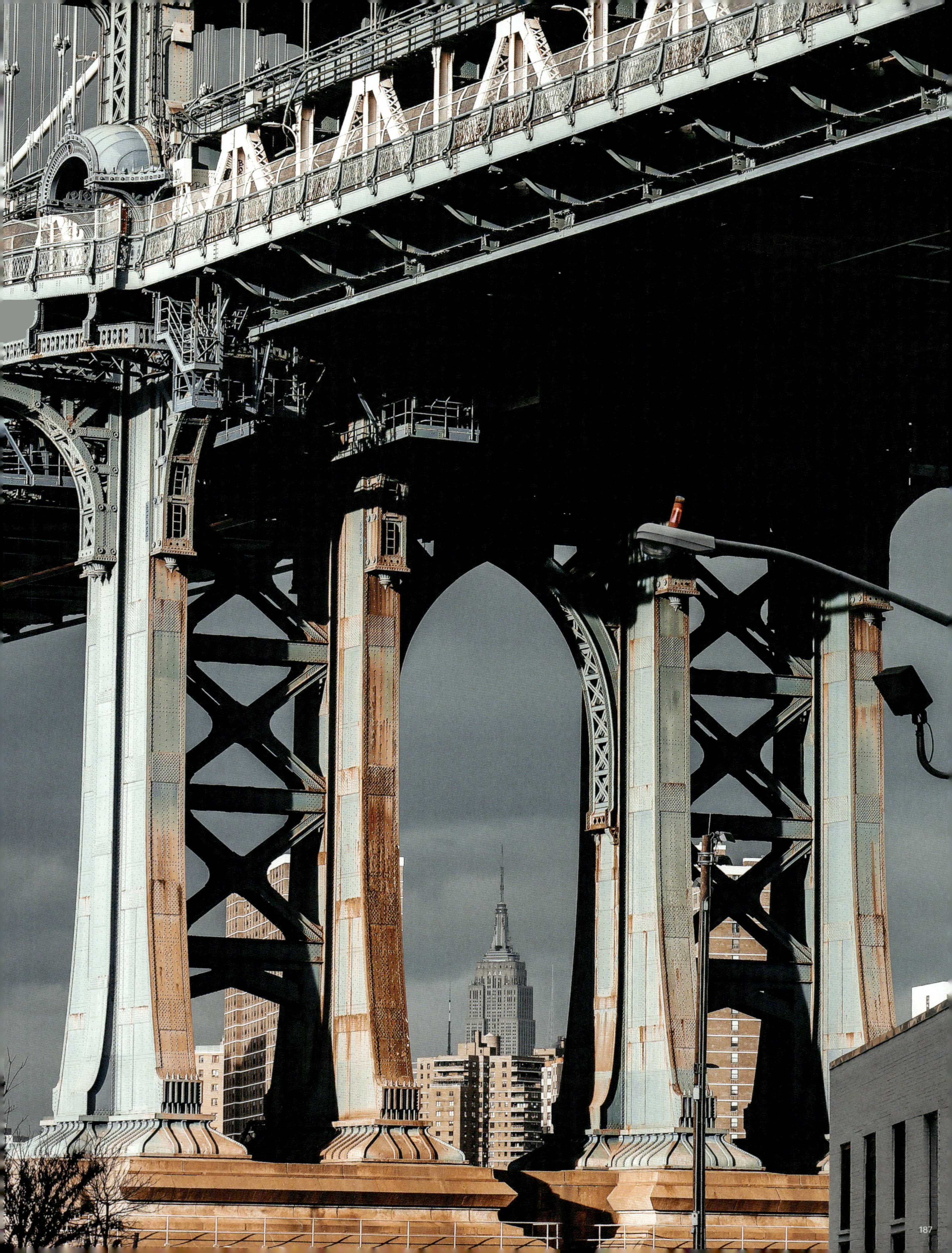

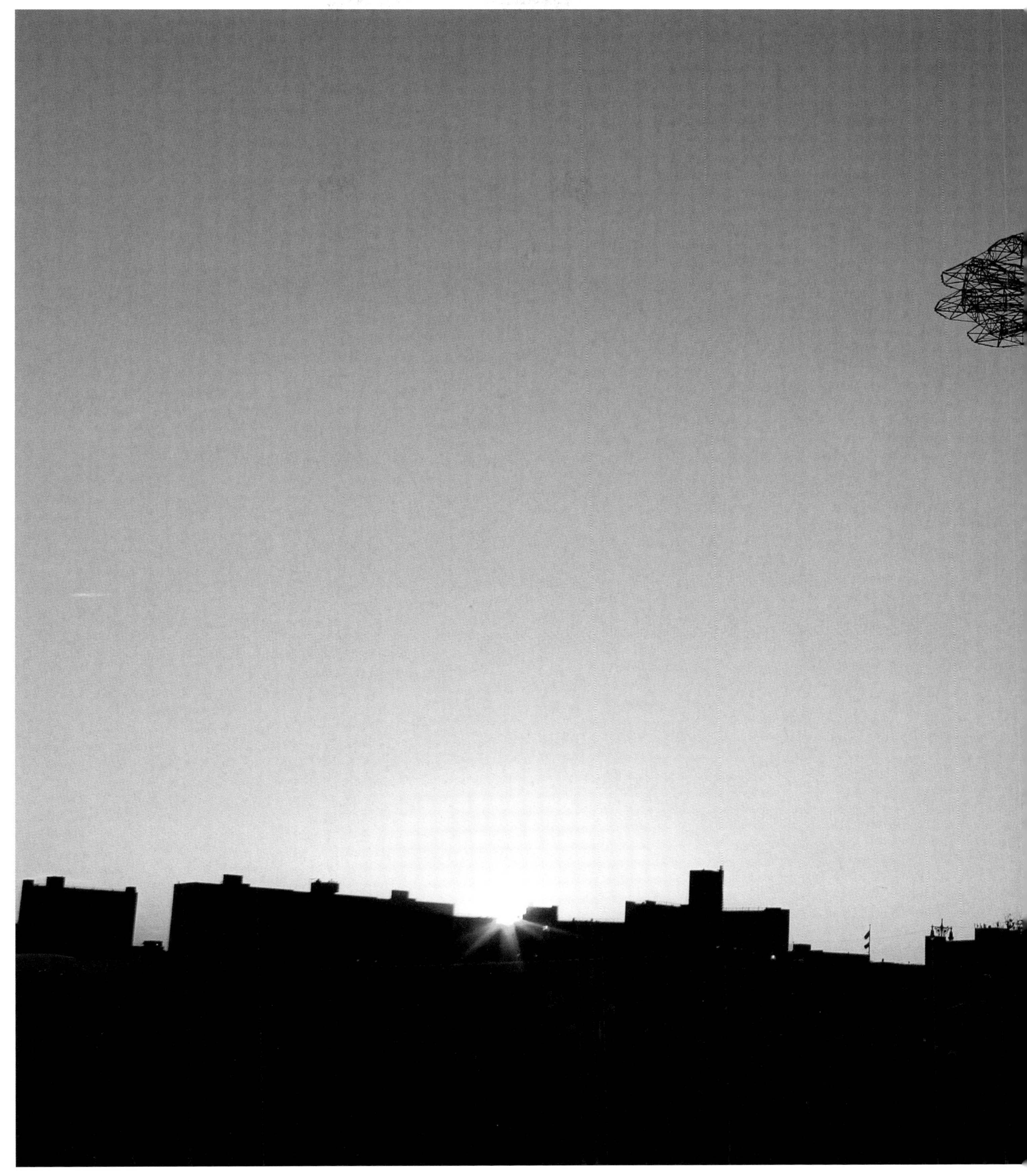

The Parachute Jump
Coney Island, Brooklyn
Rafia Afsar

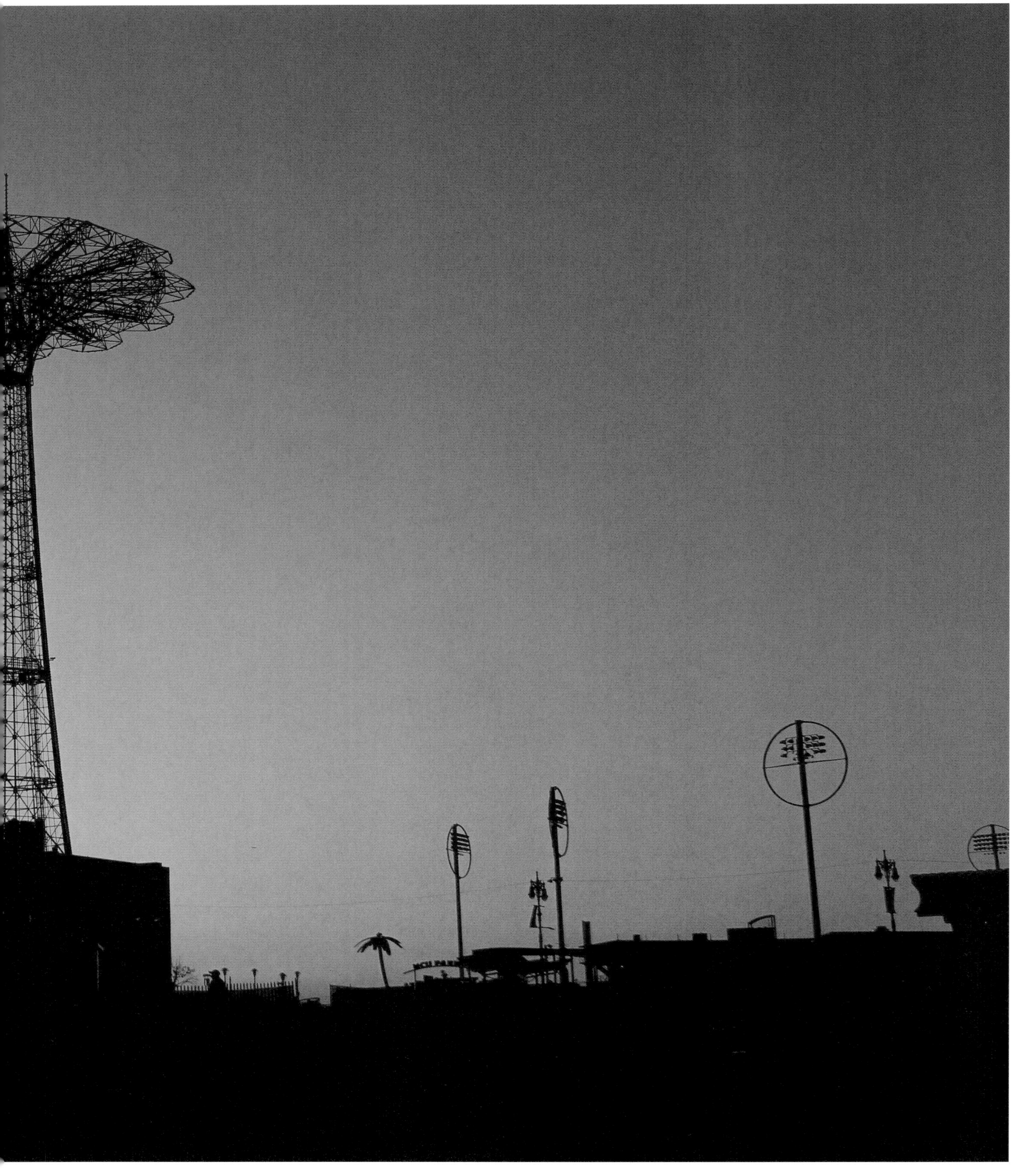

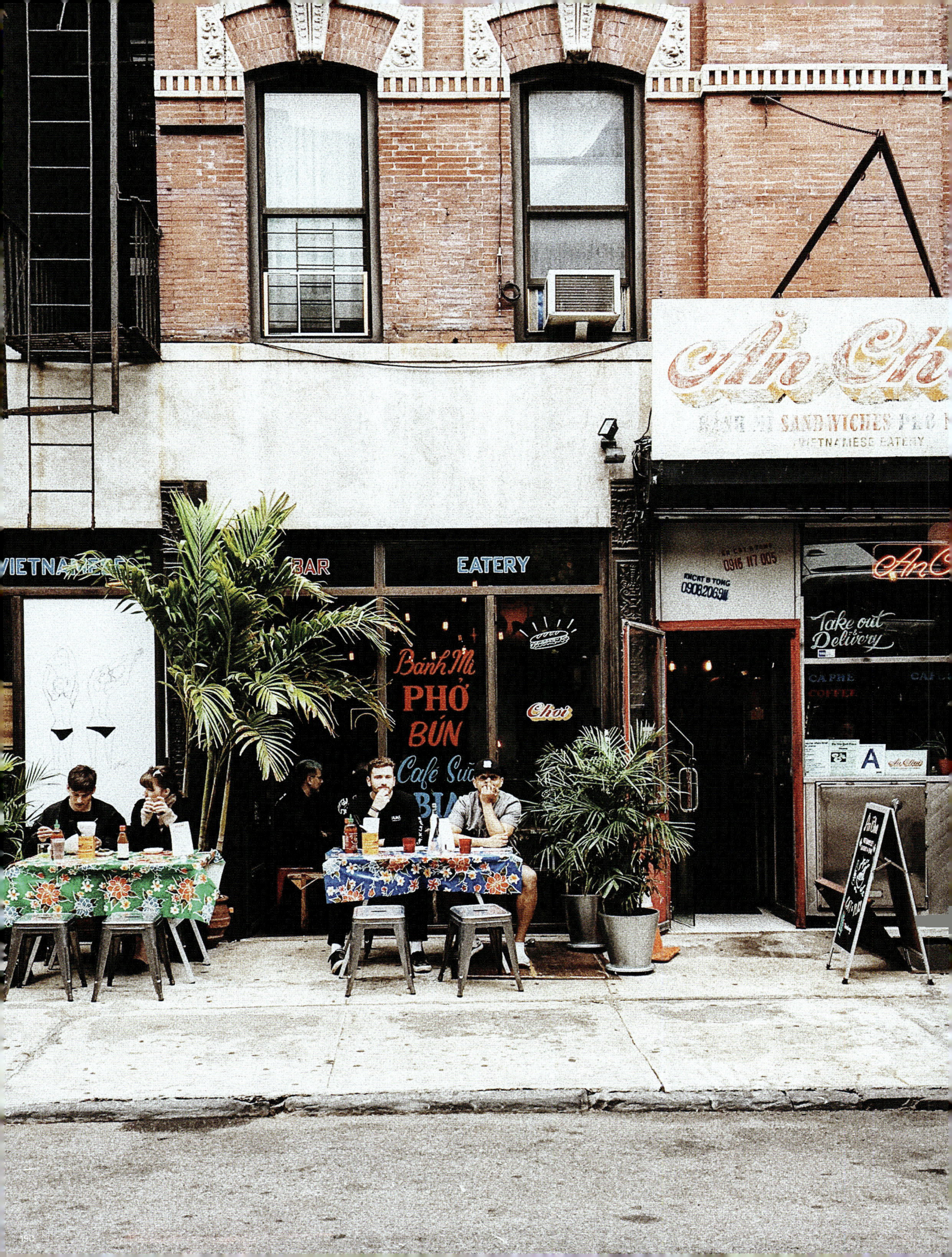
VIETNAMESE EATERY
BAR
EATERY
Bánh Mì
PHỞ
BÚN
Take out
Delivery
0916 117 005
09082069

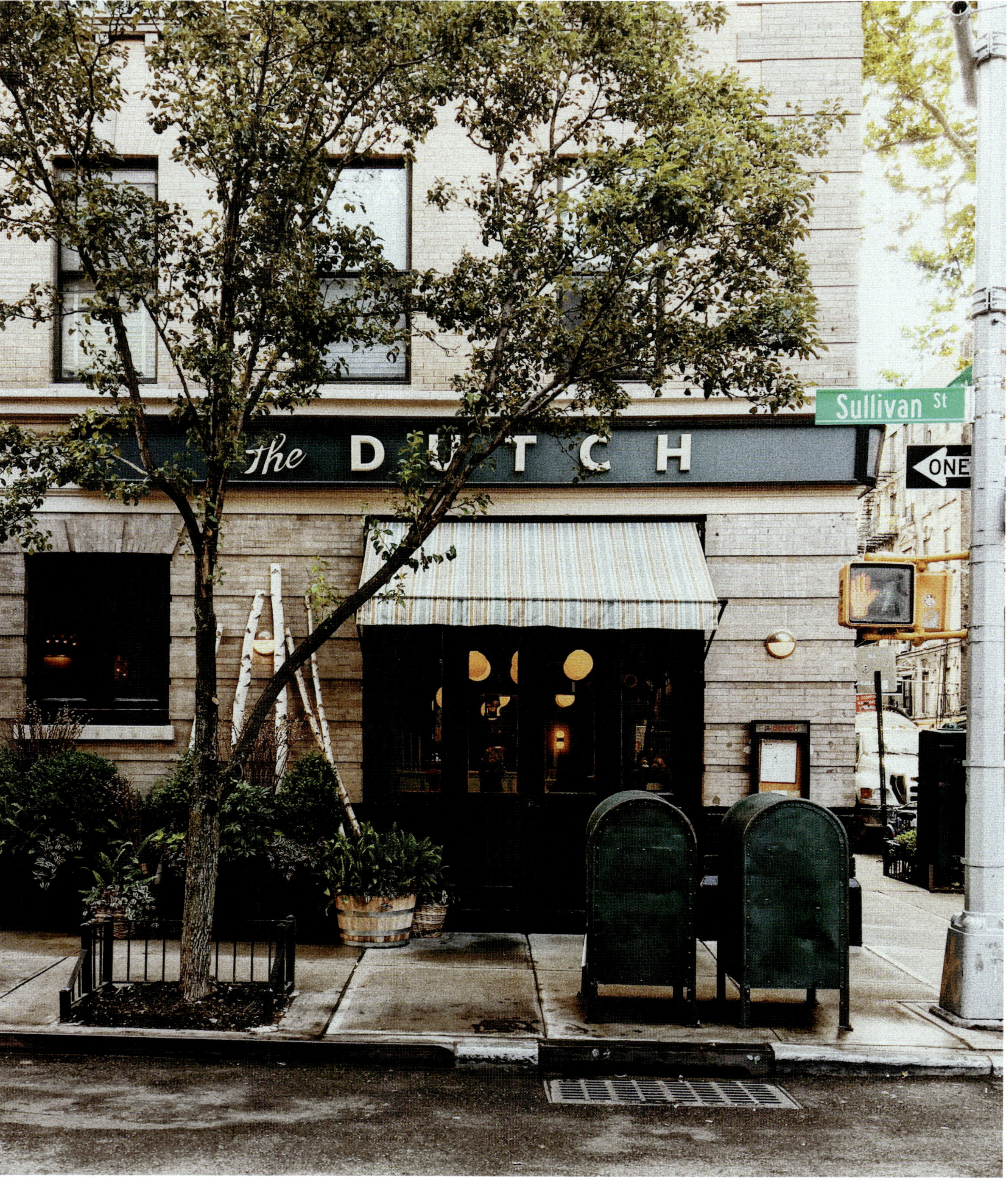

Lower East Side, Manhattan
Nazly Kasim

The Dutch
SoHo, Manhattan
Nazly Kasim

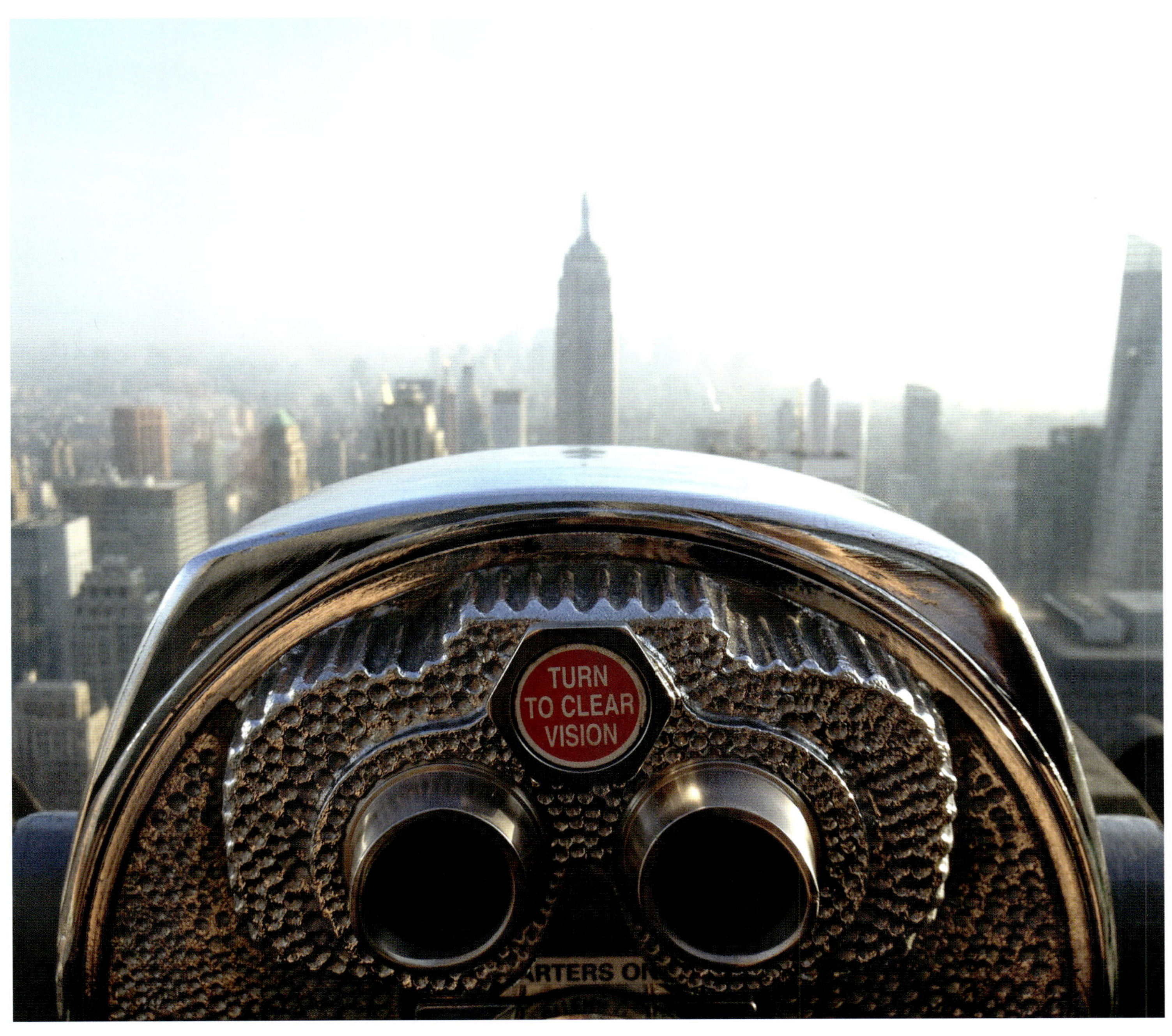

Rockefeller Center
Theater District, Manhattan
Patrick Janelle

DeSalvio Playground
Nolita, Manhattan
Lucas Vocos -

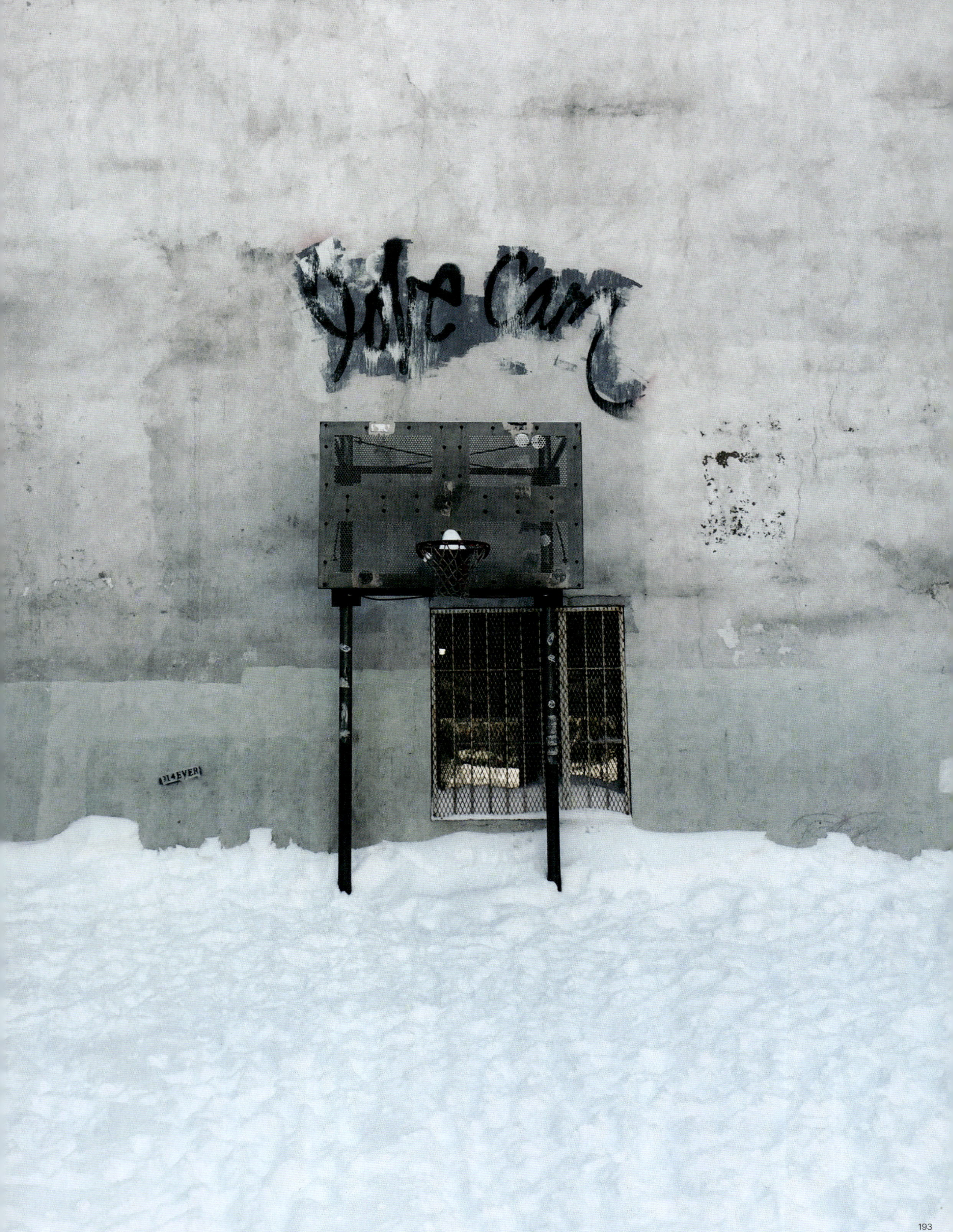

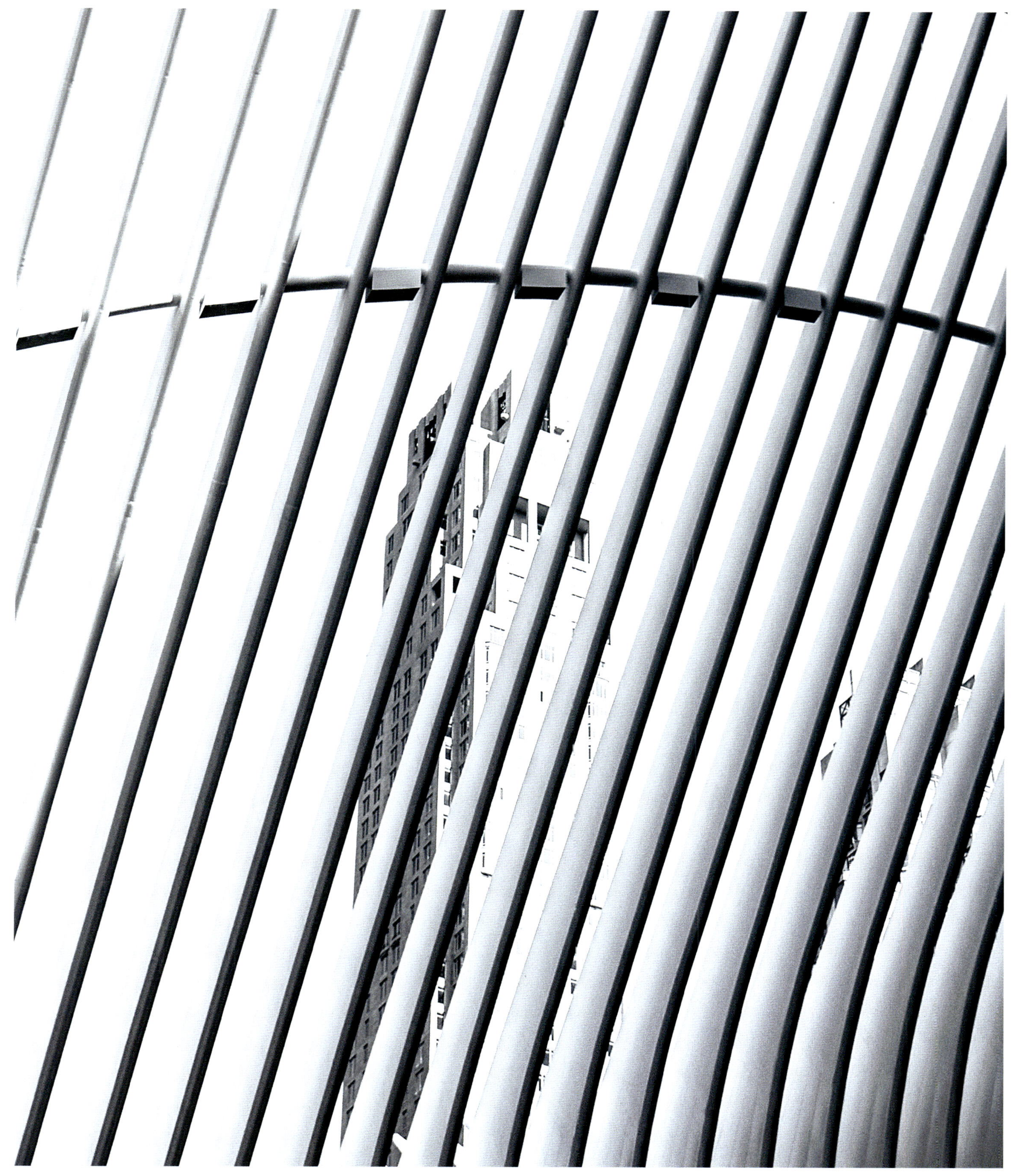

The Oculus
World Trade Center, Manhattan
Casey Tang

Manhattan
Michael Young –

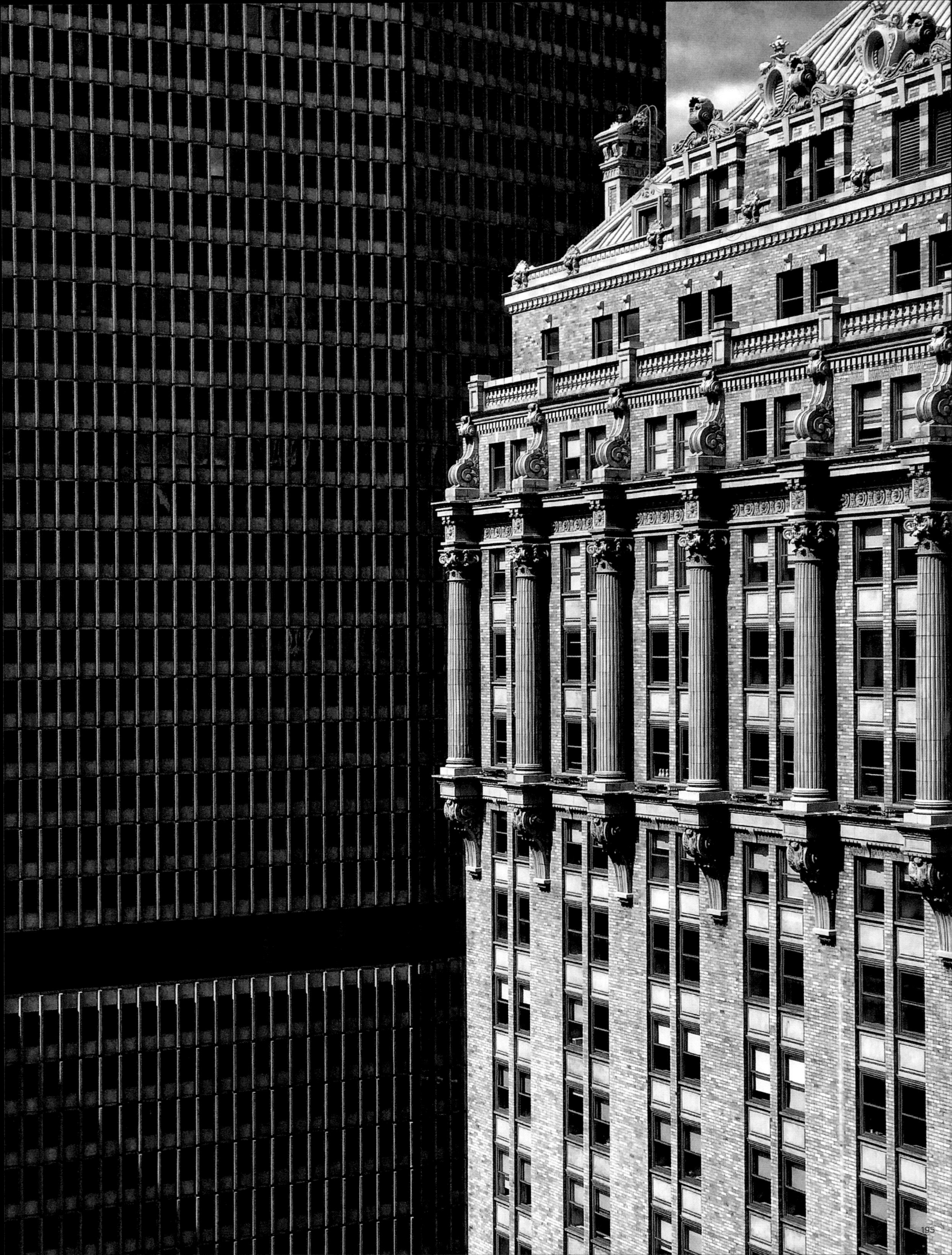

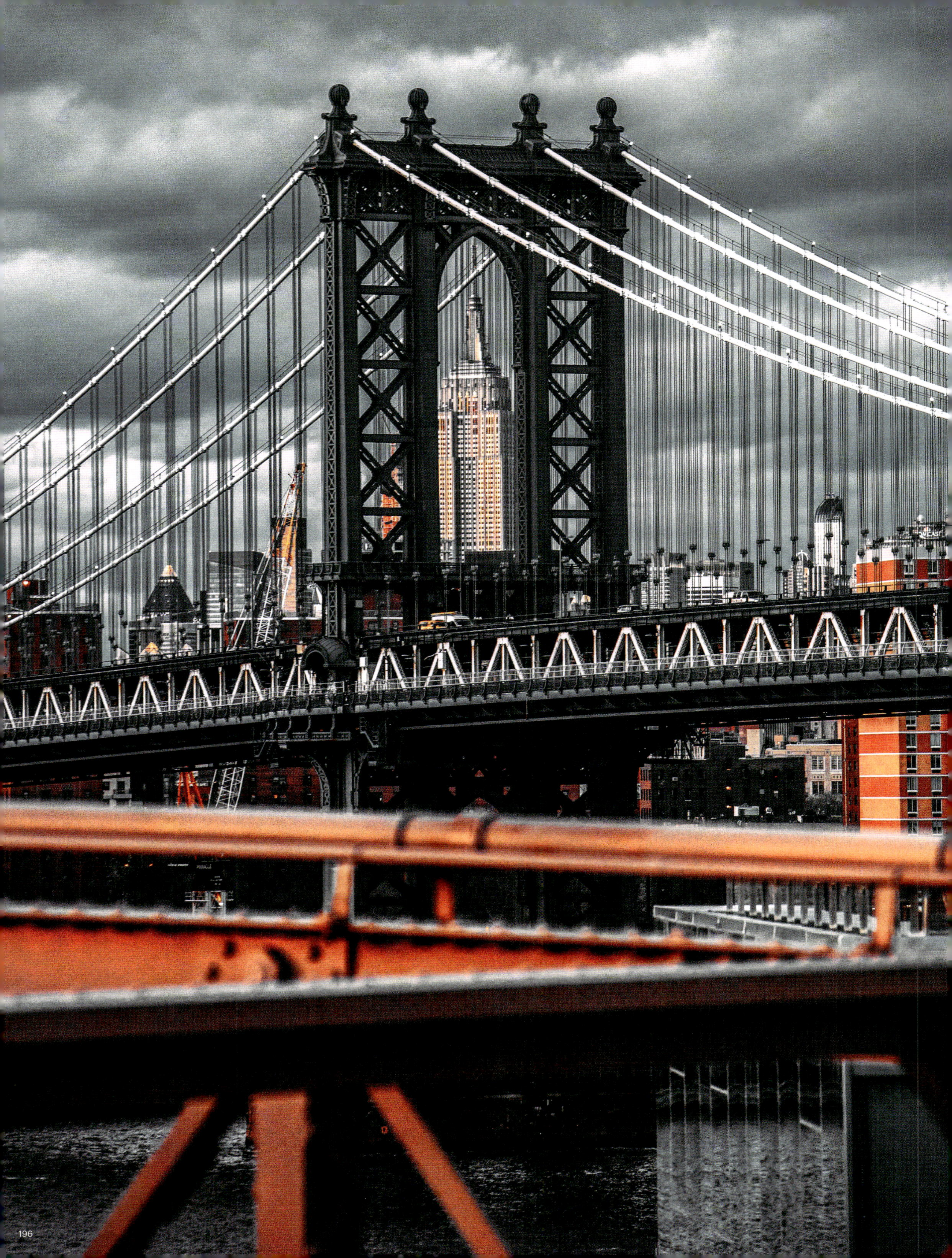

The hardest part is wanting to capture it all.

—Wil Suárez

The Manhattan Bridge
Dumbo, Brooklyn
Jones Crow

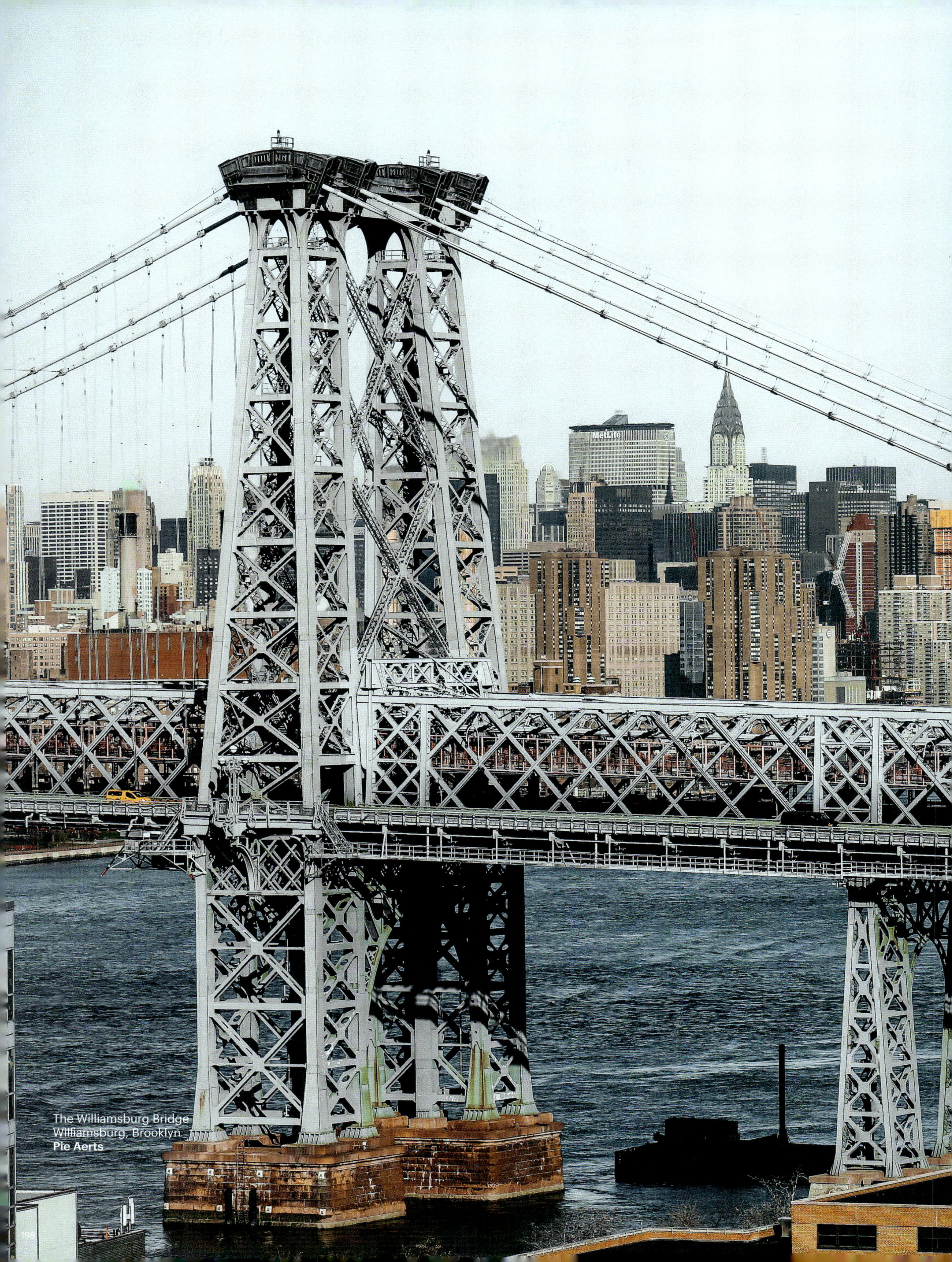

The Williamsburg Bridge
Williamsburg, Brooklyn
Pie Aerts

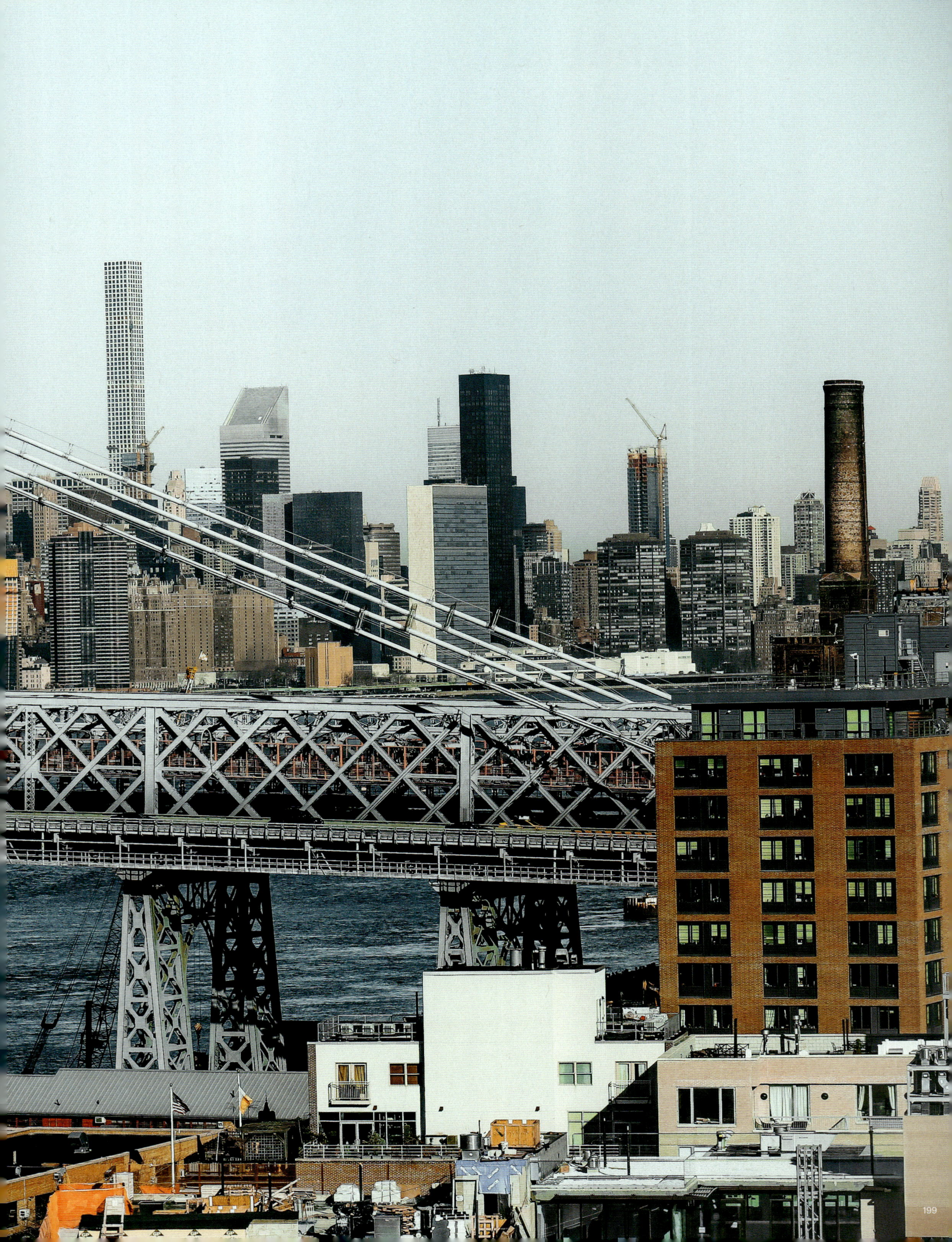

Wesley Verhoeve

hometown New York City, New York, USA
IG handle @wesleyverhoeve

"My relationship with New York City is the cliché love-hate one," says Wesley Verhoeve, who moved to "the most amazing and at times the most infuriating city" in 2003. "The creative energy and drive feels unparalleled," he explains, "and it's very easy to meet people and find your community. There is a constant influx of newcomers who bring interesting perspectives and unique voices. At the same time, this constant change can also be found in the fact that the city is a never-ending construction site, often replacing interesting old buildings with boring new ones."

With his father being a photographer, Wesley spent much of his childhood in galleries and his father's darkroom. His fascination with New York City also stems from his childhood, as he was a big fan of Spider-Man comic books and 80s and 90s hip-hop music. "Even though I grew up in a small rural town, I felt right at home in this big crazy city from the first moment."

In 2000, he took his first picture of New York, on a short trip in the middle of a snow storm. "I had a small film camera. I took the ferry with my girlfriend and I took a picture of her with the Twin Towers in the background." As an introverted person, Wesley prefers being behind a camera. "I'd often rather notice, observe, and capture." He soon became aware of the fact that New York City is always changing, and therefore there are always new angles to find. "It's a never-ending story. When I had this realization, I decided I wanted to be a better New Yorker and started taking a half-day off here and there, just to walk around the city and take photos."

„Meine Beziehung zu New York City ist die klischeehafte Hassliebe", sagt Wesley Verhoeve, der 2003 in die „erstaunlichste und manchmal empörendste aller Städte" gezogen ist. „Die kreative Energie und Dynamik hier ist unvergleichlich", berichtet er, „und es ist sehr einfach, Leute kennenzulernen und eine Gemeinschaft zu finden. Es gibt einen ständigen Zustrom von Neuankömmlingen, die interessante Blickwinkel und unverwechselbare Stimmen mitbringen. Gleichzeitig zeigt sich dieser stete Wandel auch in der Tatsache, dass die Stadt eine unaufhörliche Baustelle ist, die interessante alte Gebäude oft durch langweilige neue ersetzt."

Schon sein Vater war Fotograf, und Wesley verbrachte einen Großteil seiner Kindheit in Galerien und in der Dunkelkammer seines Vaters. Auch seine Faszination für New York City stammt aus Kinderzeiten, denn er war ein großer Fan von Spiderman-Comics und der Hip-Hop-Musik der 1980er und 1990er. „Ich bin zwar in einer ländlichen Kleinstadt aufgewachsen, aber ich fühlte mich vom ersten Augenblick an vollkommen zu Hause in dieser großen, verrückten Stadt."

Im Jahr 2000 nahm er sein erstes Foto von New York auf, bei einem Kurztrip während eines Schneesturms. „Ich hatte eine kleine analoge Kamera dabei. Ich nahm die Fähre mit meiner Freundin und machte ein Foto von ihr, mit den Twin Towers im Hintergrund." Als introvertierter Mensch zieht Wesley es vor, hinter der Kamera zu stehen. „Oft ist es mir lieber, etwas zu bemerken, zu beobachten und einzufangen." Bald wurde ihm bewusst, dass sich New York City ständig verändert und dass es daher immer neue Betrachtungsweisen gibt. „Es ist eine unendliche Geschichte. Als ich das erkannt hatte, beschloss ich, ein besserer New Yorker zu werden und nehme mir seitdem hin und wieder einen halben Tag frei, um einfach in der Stadt herumzulaufen und Fotos zu machen."

« Mon rapport à New York relève typiquement d'une relation amour-haine », explique Wesley Verhoeve qui s'est installé en 2003 dans « la plus étonnante, et parfois la plus exaspérante, des villes ». Et de poursuivre : « l'énergie et l'impulsion créative y sont inégalées. Et il est extrêmement facile d'y faire des rencontres, d'y trouver sa communauté. Il y a un afflux constant et massif de nouveaux-venus qui apportent des points de vue intéressants, des voix uniques. Simultanément, à ce changement permanent fait écho le chantier perpétuel qu'est la ville où des édifices anciens sont remplacés par de nouveaux bâtiments, ennuyeux ».

Wesley, dont le père était photographe, a passé une grande partie de son enfance à fréquenter des galeries, aussi bien que la chambre noire où officiait son père. De son enfance aussi, et des bandes dessinées de Spider Man ou de la musique hip-hop des années 1980, 1990, et dont il était fan, vient la fascination qu'il éprouve pour New York. « Quoique j'aie grandi dans une petite ville rurale, je me suis senti chez moi dès le premier instant dans cette ville folle ».

C'est en 2000 qu'il prend sa première photographie, lors d'une tempête de neige. « J'avais un petit appareil. J'ai photographié ma petite amie sur le ferry, avec les Twin Towers à l'arrière-plan ». De nature plutôt introvertie, Wesley préfère se dissimuler derrière un appareil photo. « Ce que j'aime le plus, c'est remarquer, observer, saisir ». Rapidement, il prend conscience du changement constant qui s'opère à New York, et donc, des points de vue nouveaux qu'il faut découvrir. « C'est une histoire sans fin. Lorsque j'en ai pris conscience, j'ai décidé d'être plus proche de ma ville et j'ai commencé à garder des demi-journées, ici ou là, pour déambuler dans la ville et prendre des photographies ».

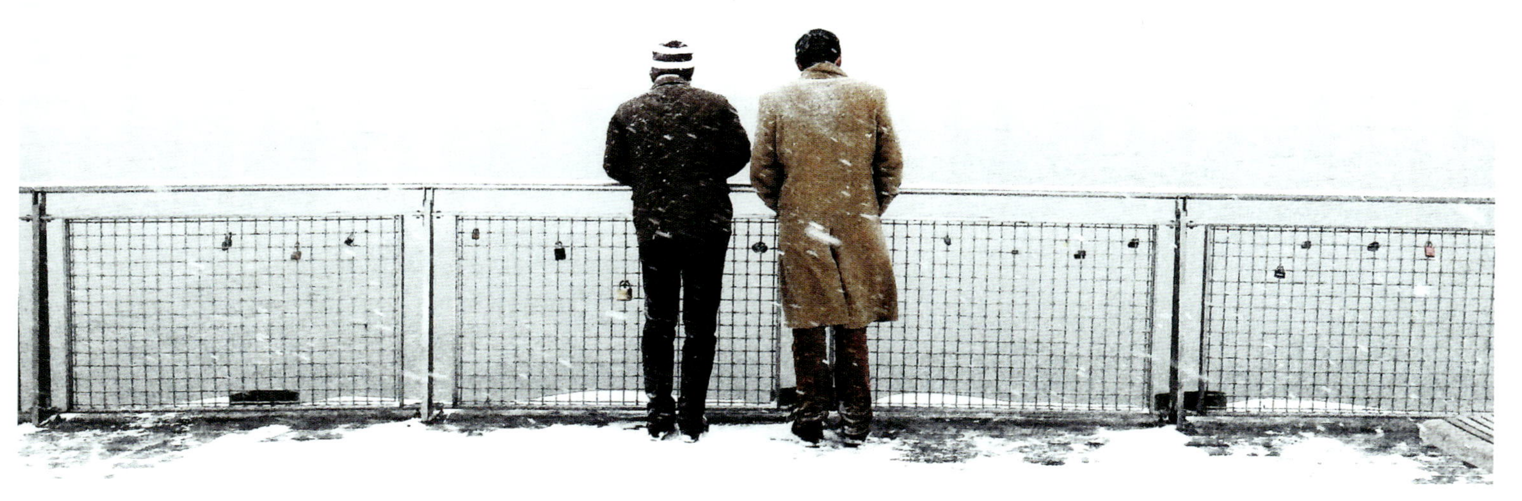

Green Point, Brooklyn
Wesley Verhoeve

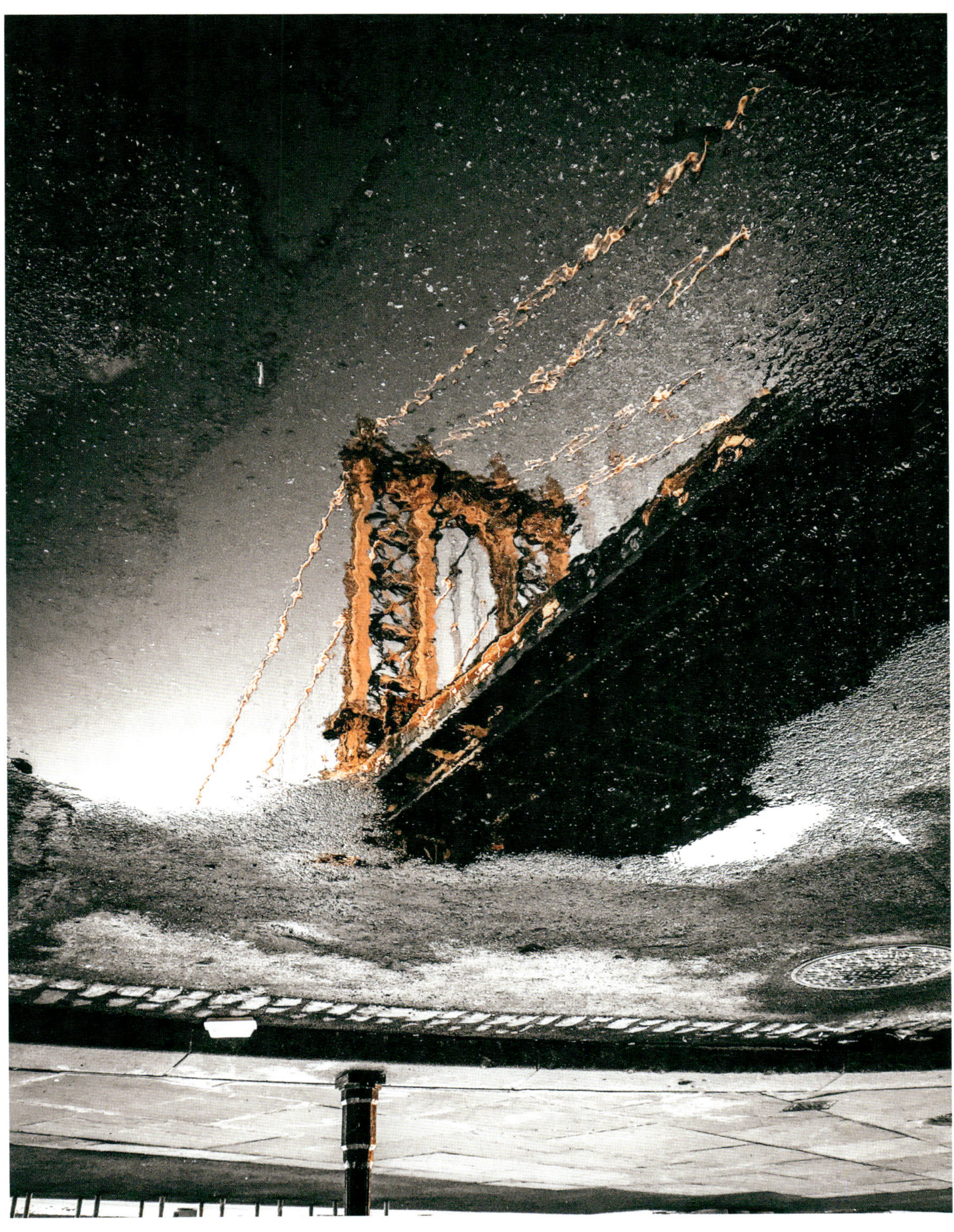

The Manhattan Bridge
Brooklyn
Neal Kumar

Chinatown, Manhattan
Neal Kumar –

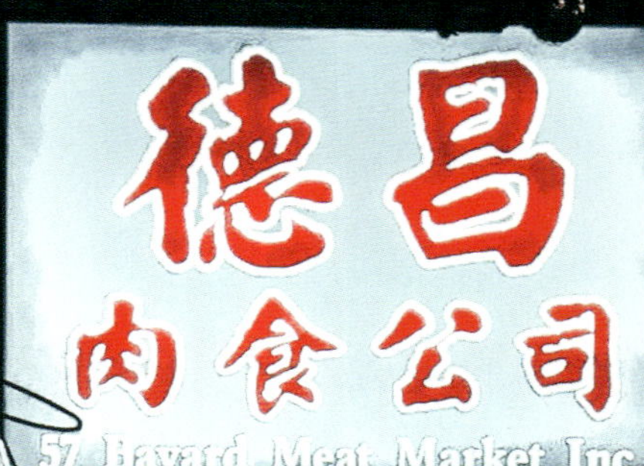
德昌
肉食公司
57 Bayard Meat Market Inc.

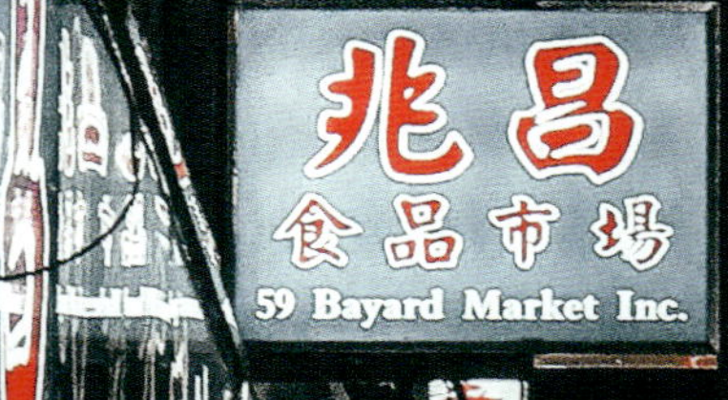
兆昌
食品市場
59 Bayard Market Inc.

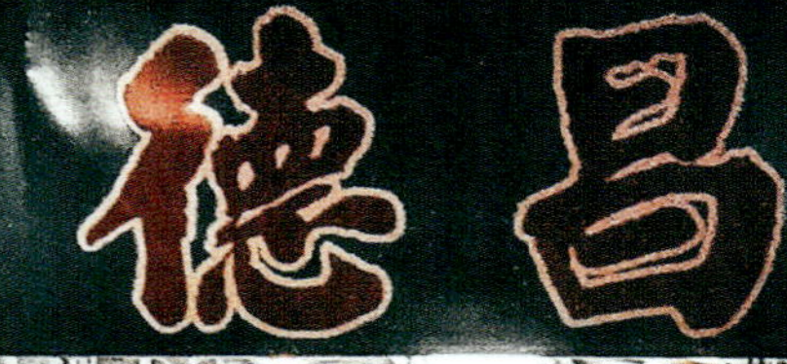
德昌

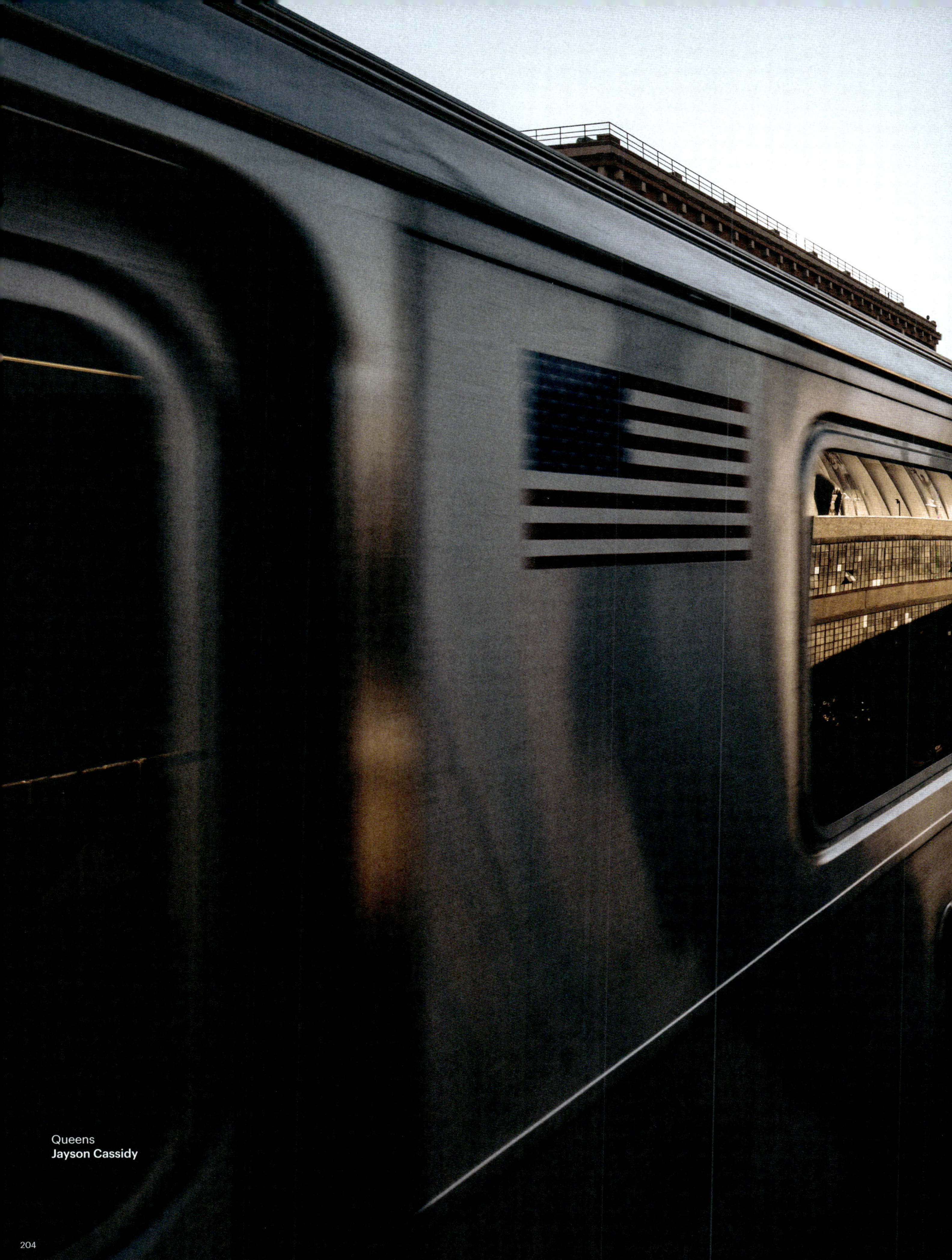

Queens
Jayson Cassidy

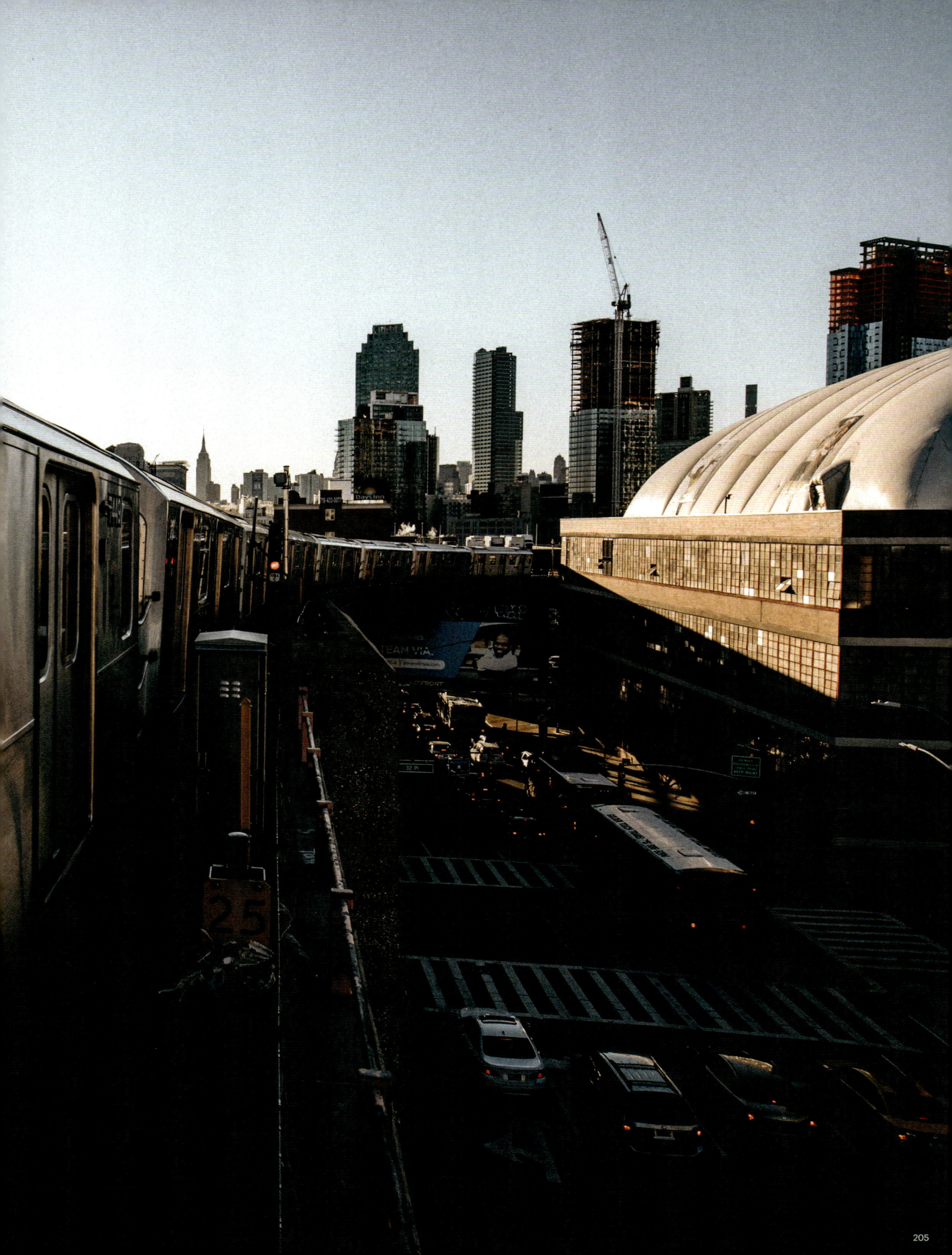
TEAM VIA.
25

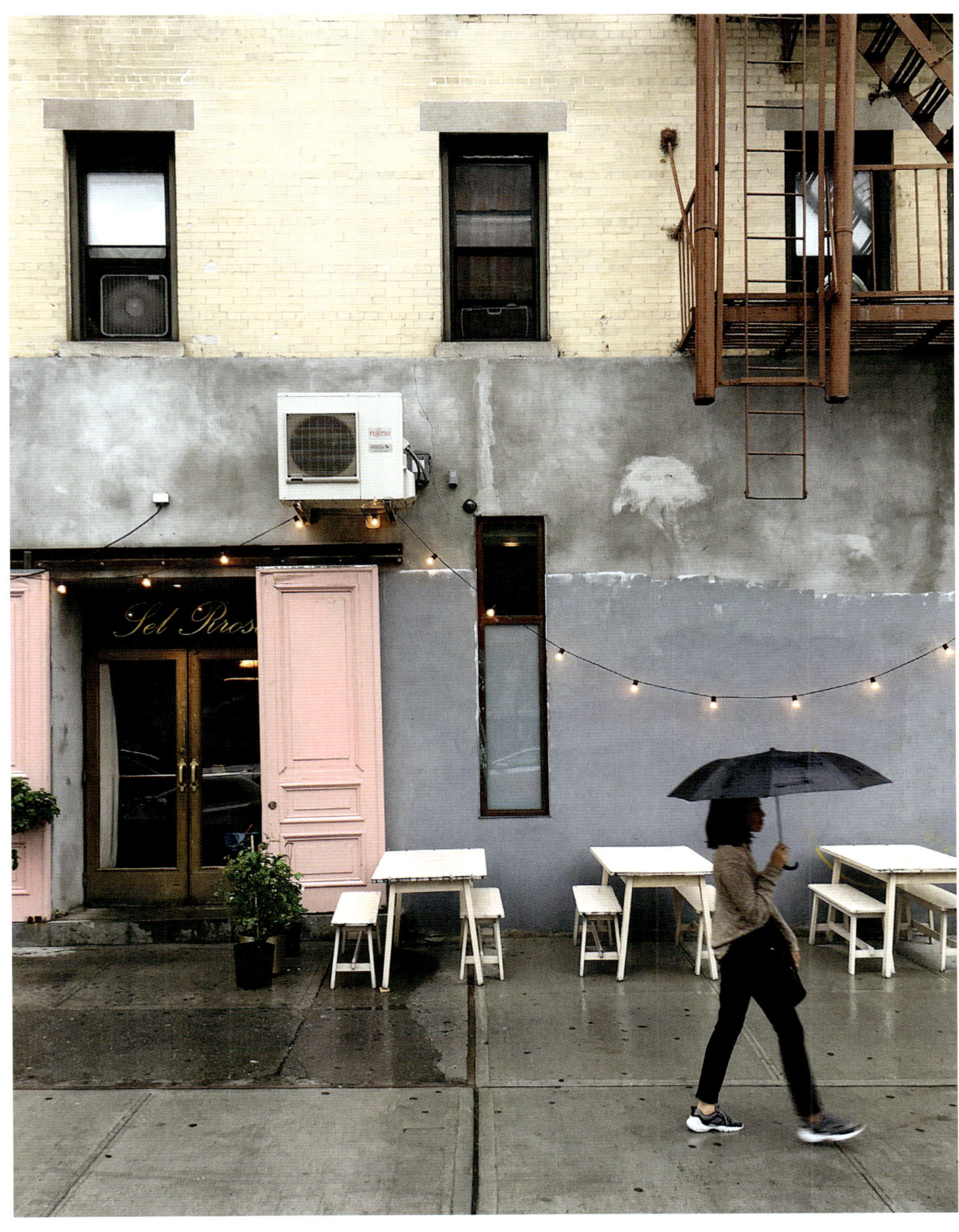

Sel Rrose
Nolita, Manhattan
Steven Fingar

Little Prince
SoHo, Manhattan
Steven Fingar →

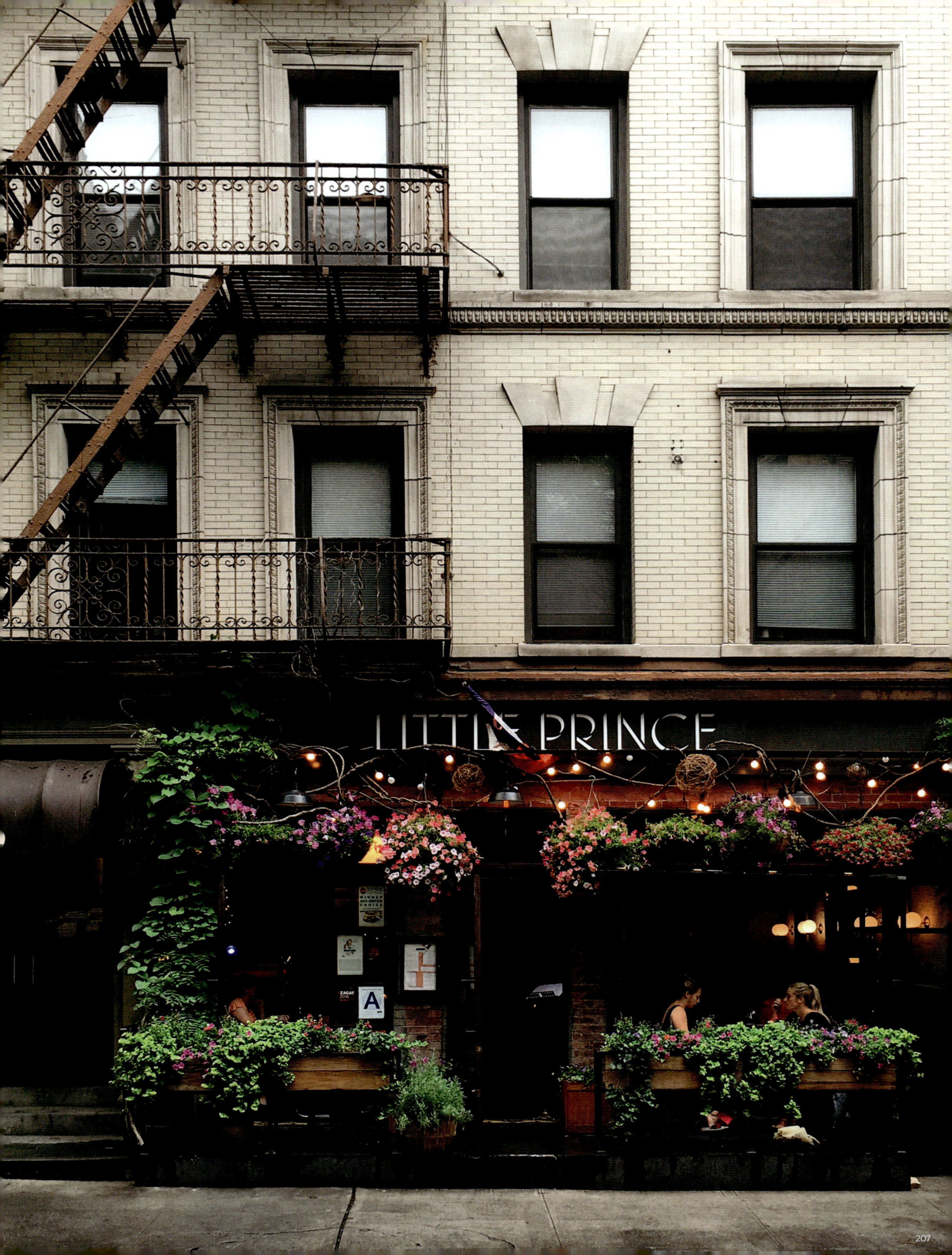
LITTLE PRINCE

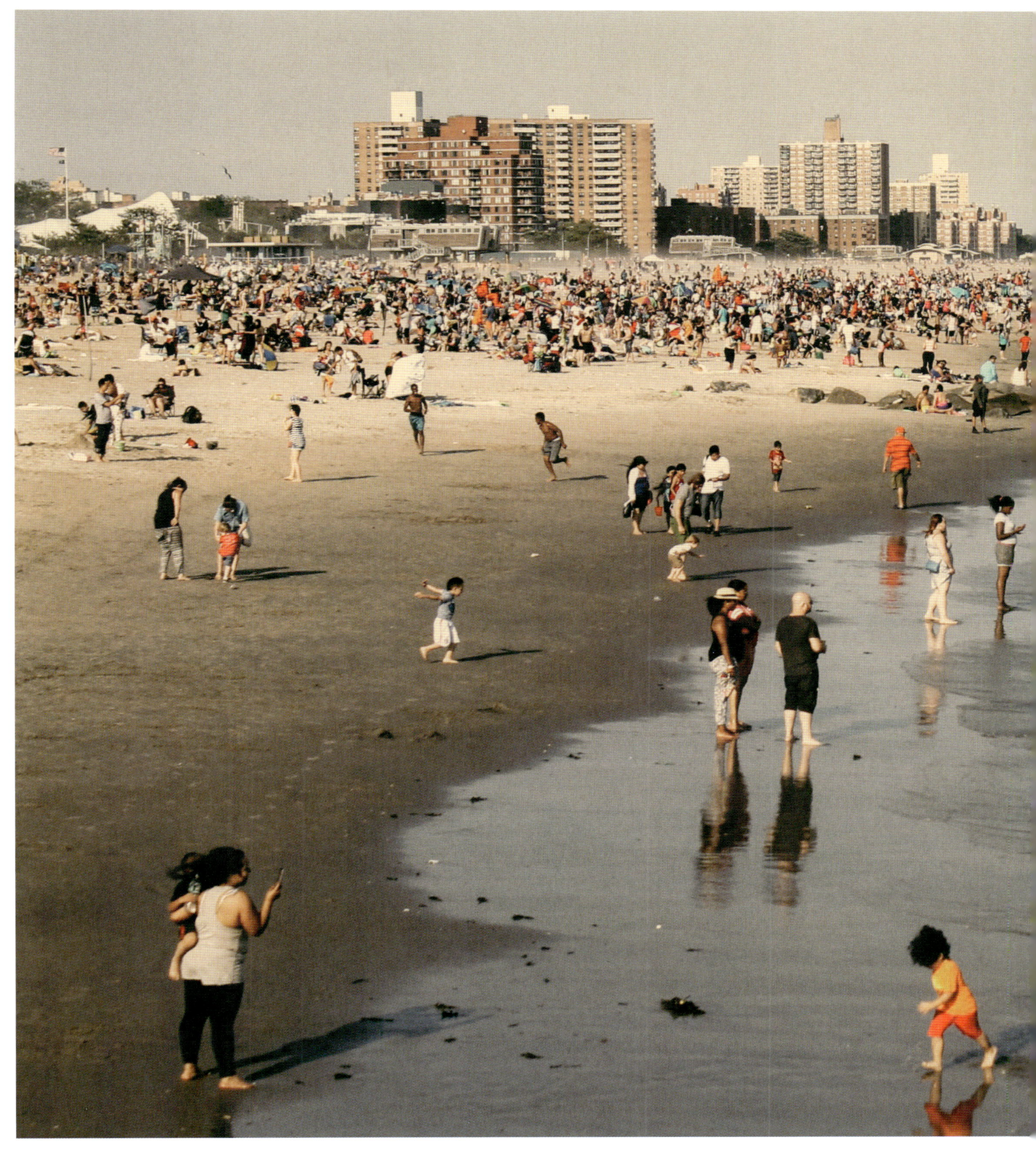

Brighton Beach, Brooklyn
Darius Hertzog

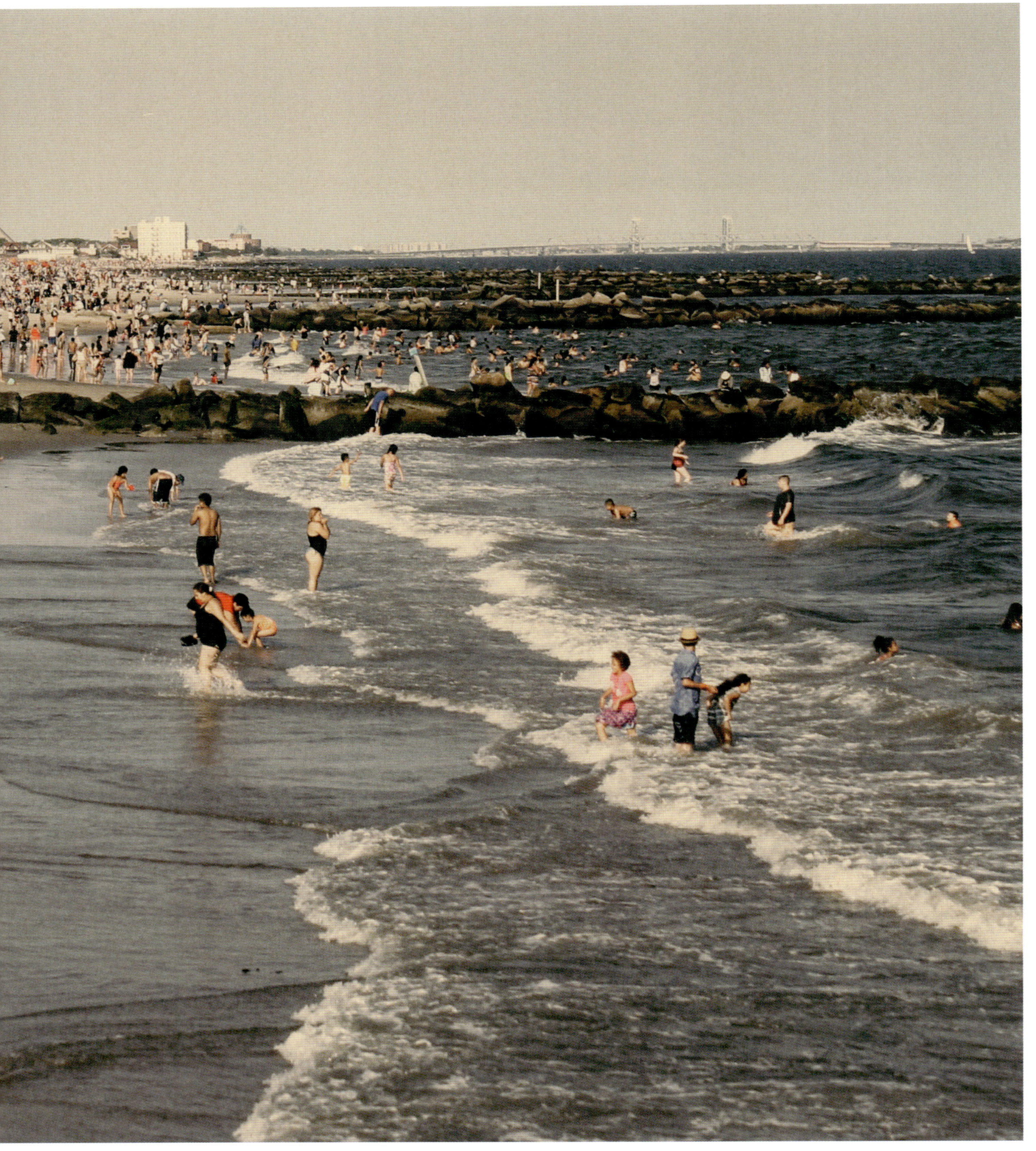

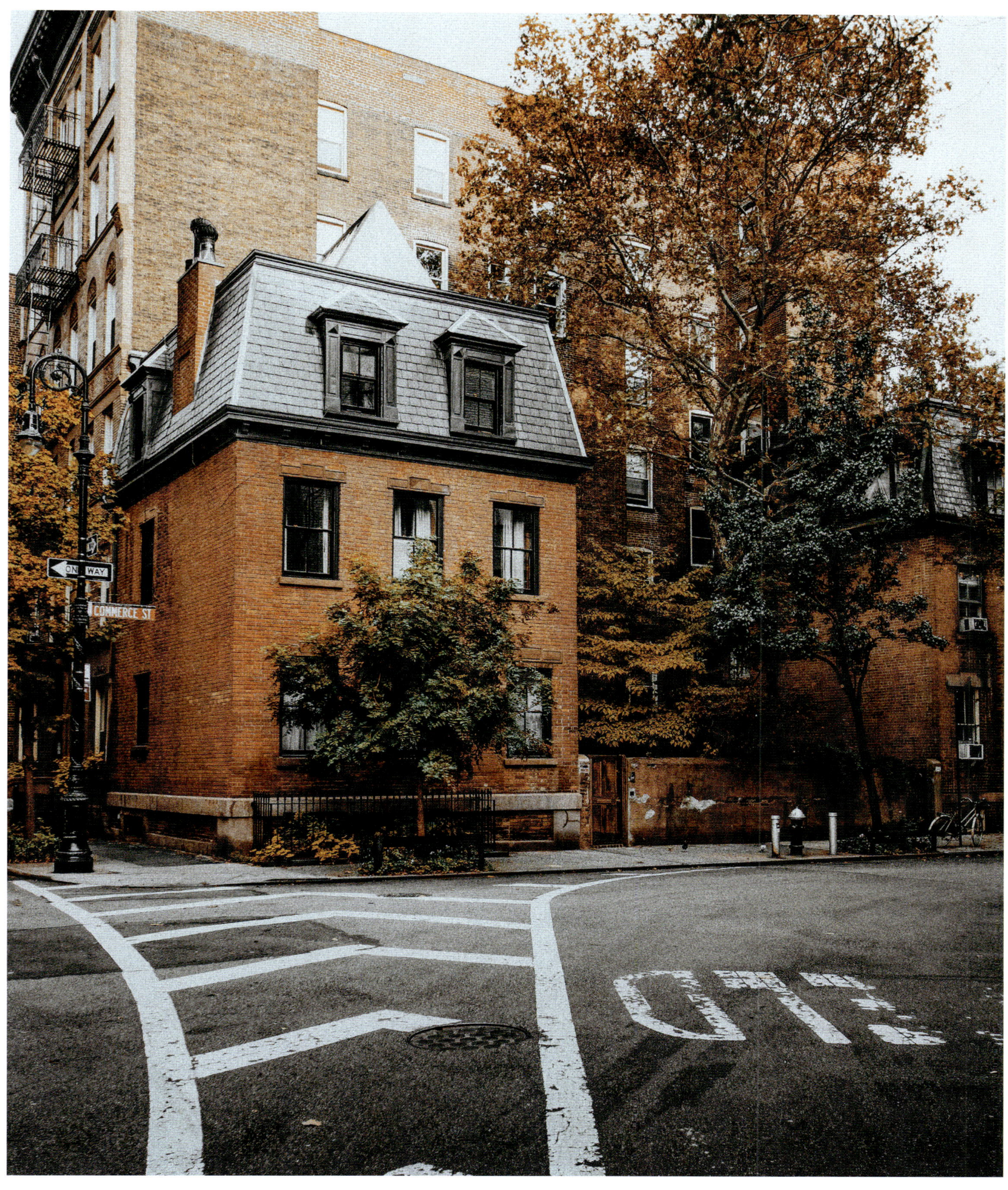

Greenwich Village, Manhattan
Nazly Kasim

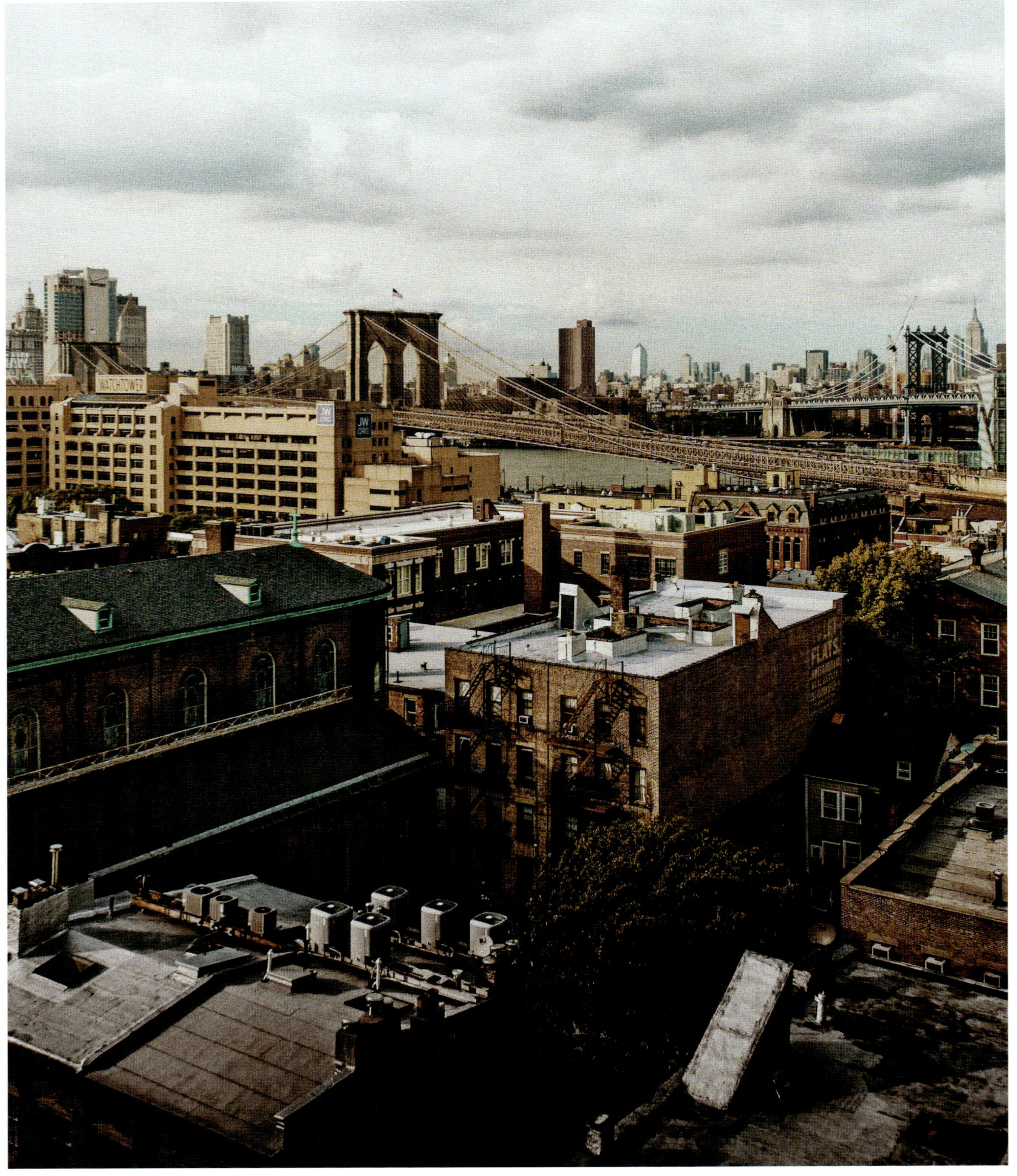

Brooklyn Heights, Brooklyn
Nazly Kasim

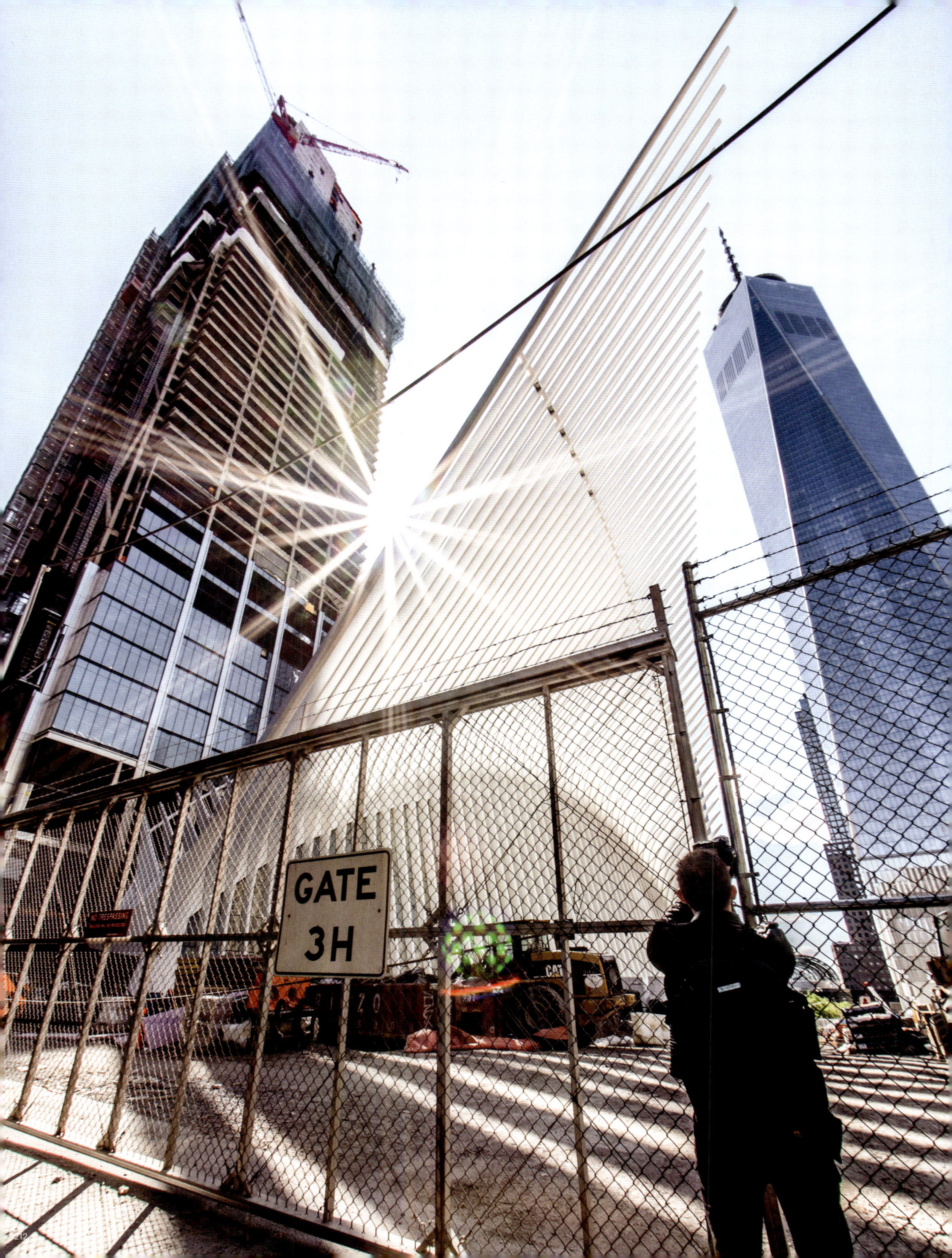
GATE
3H

The Oculus
World Trade Center, Manhattan
Ivan Meneses

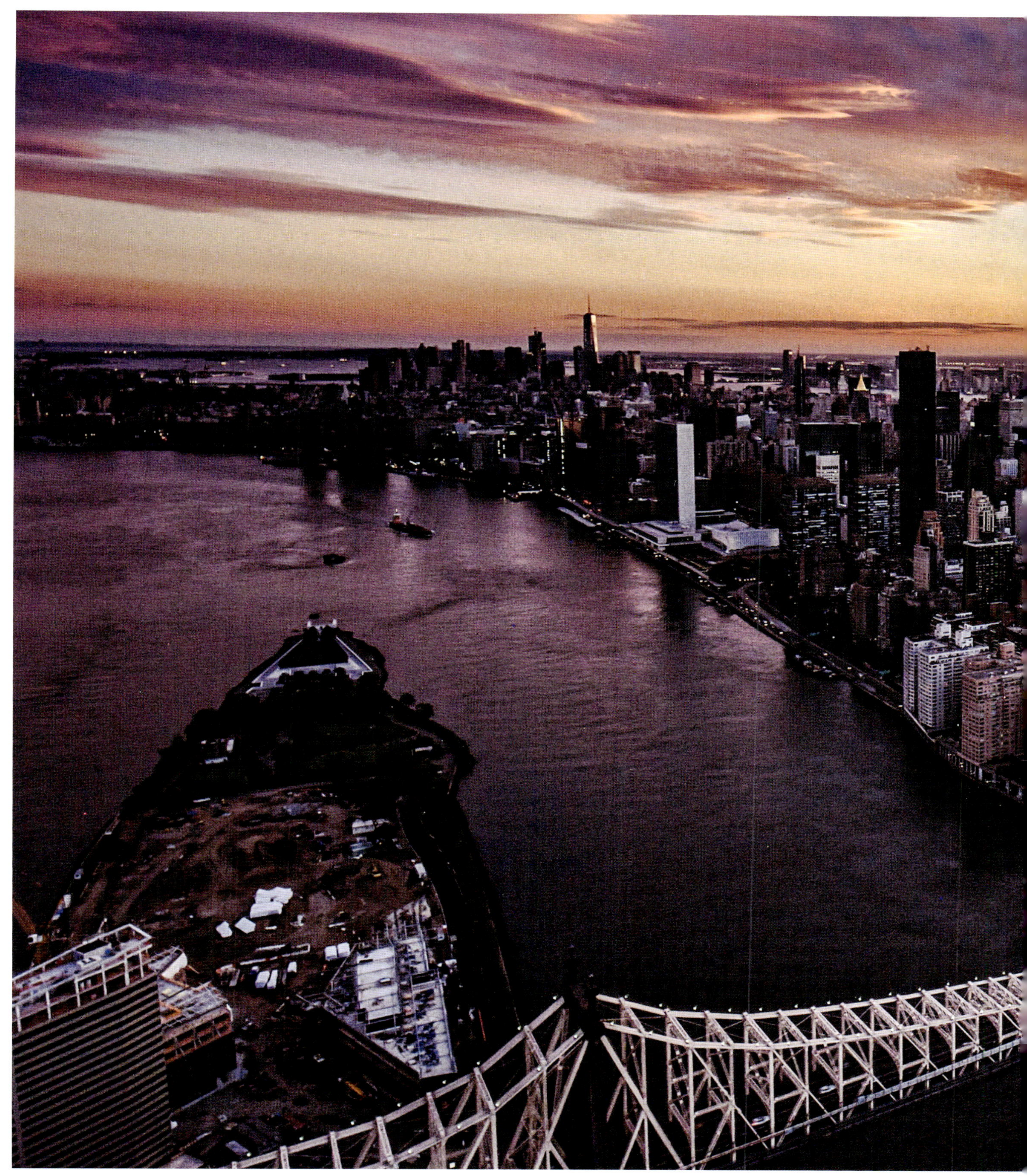

Roosevelt Island, the Ed Koch Queensboro Bridge & Manhattan
Bryan Dumas

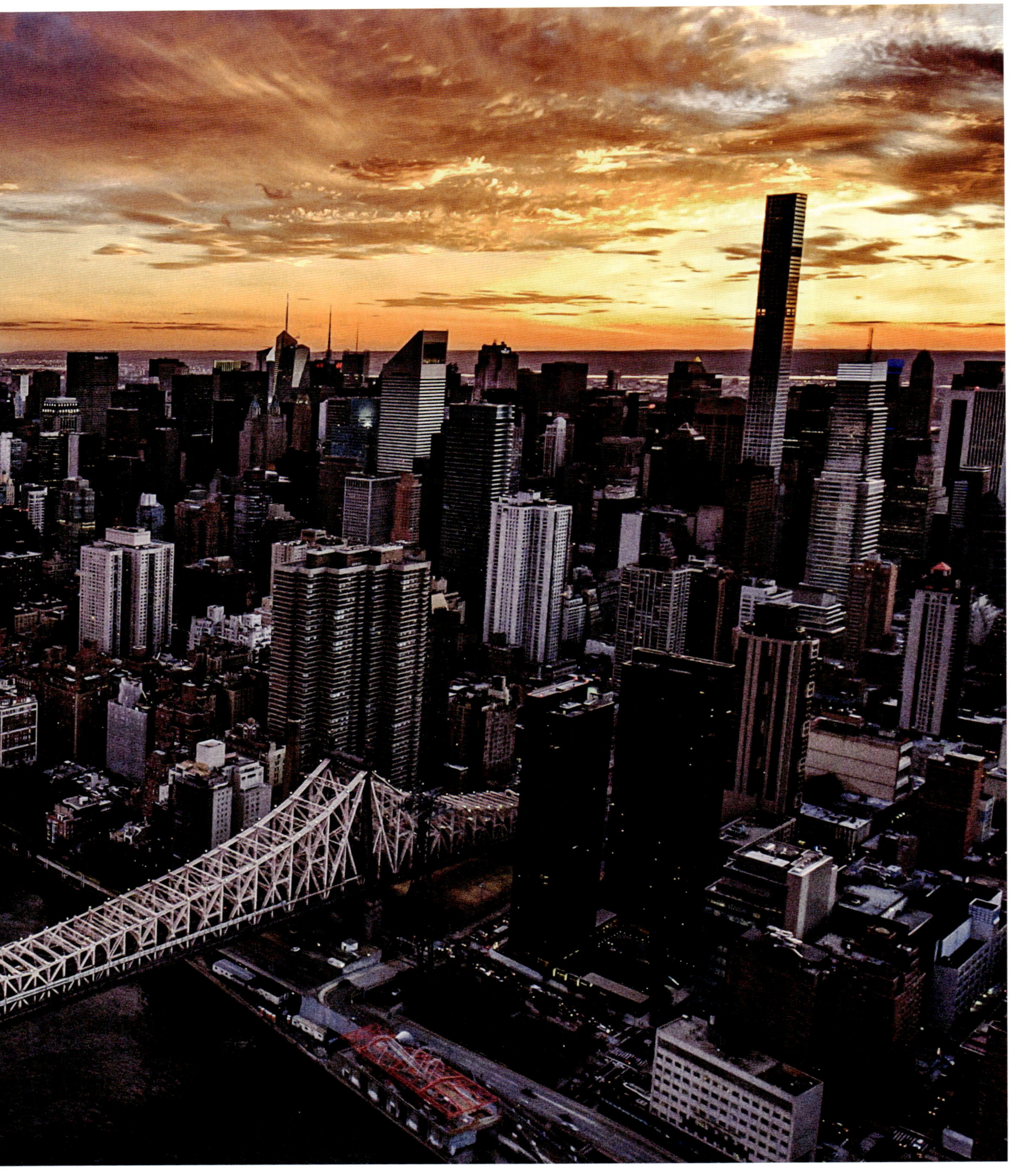

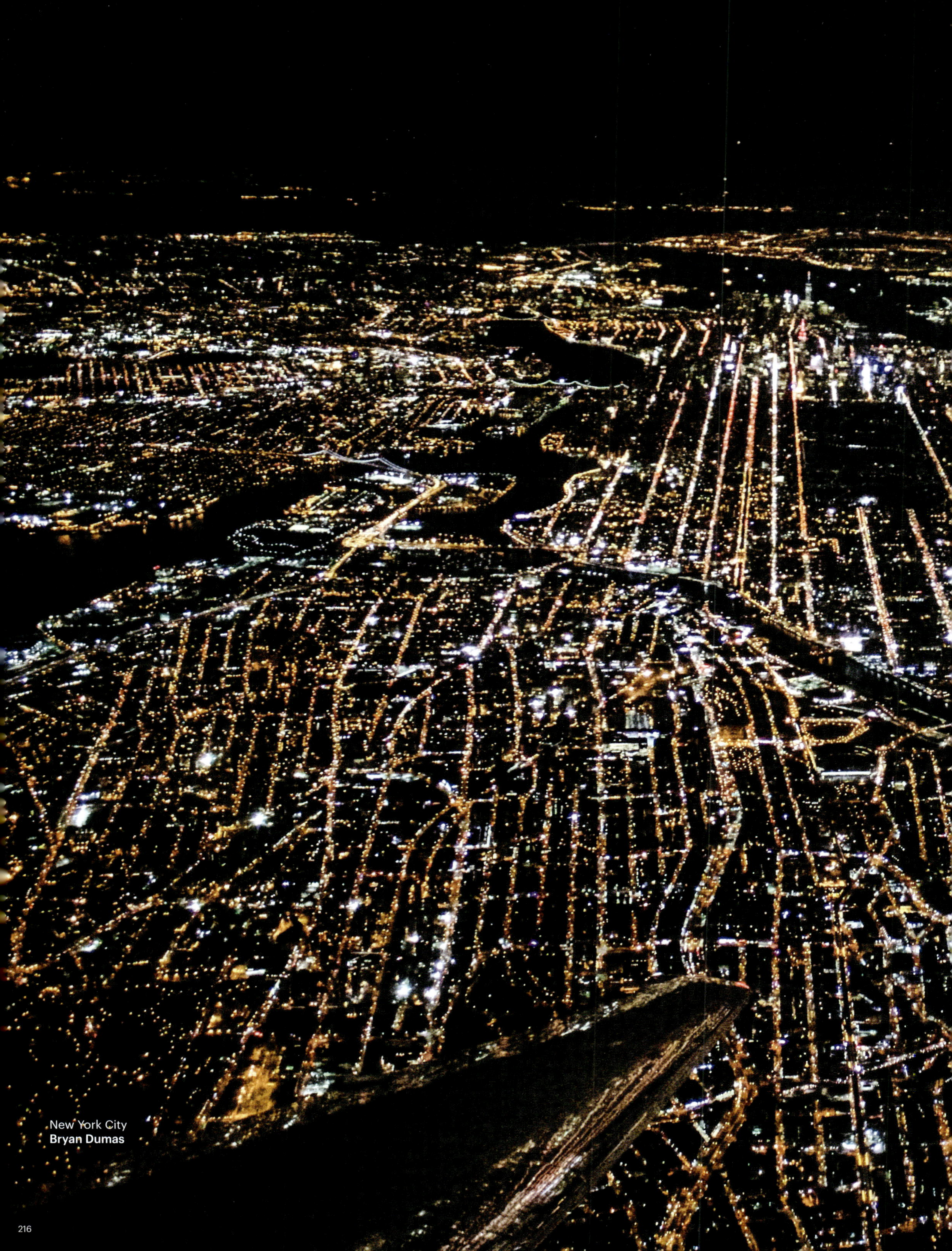

New York City
Bryan Dumas

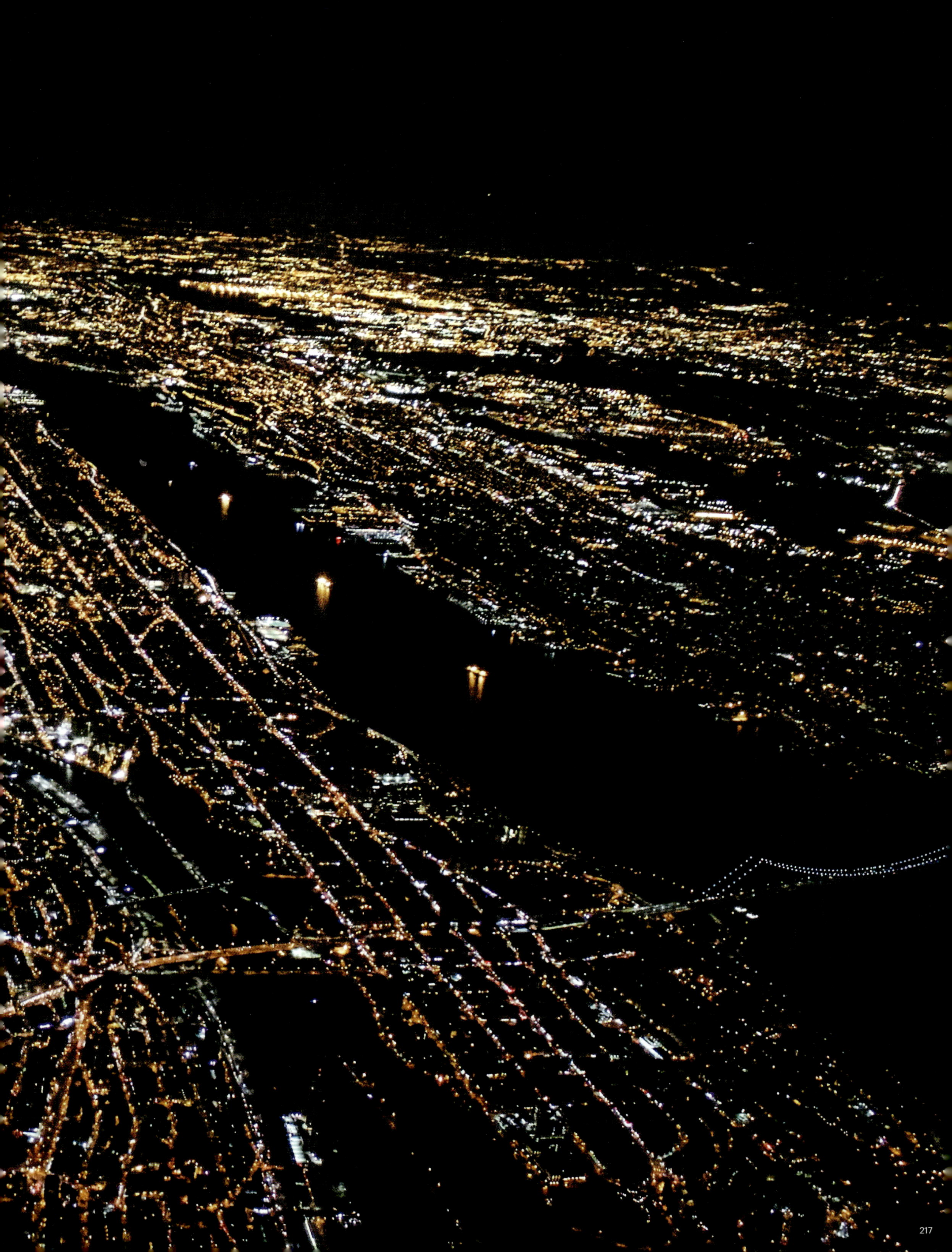

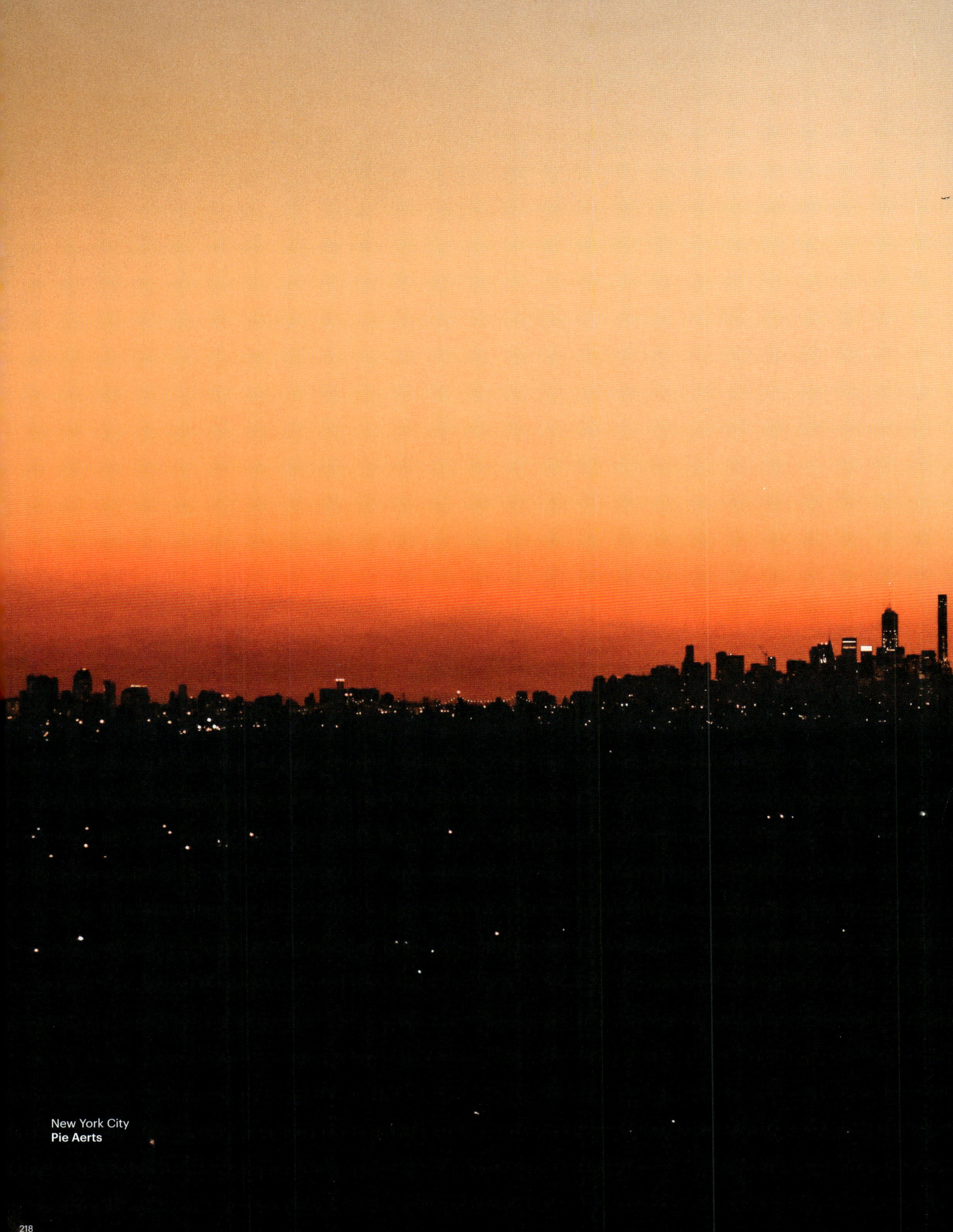

New York City
Pie Aerts

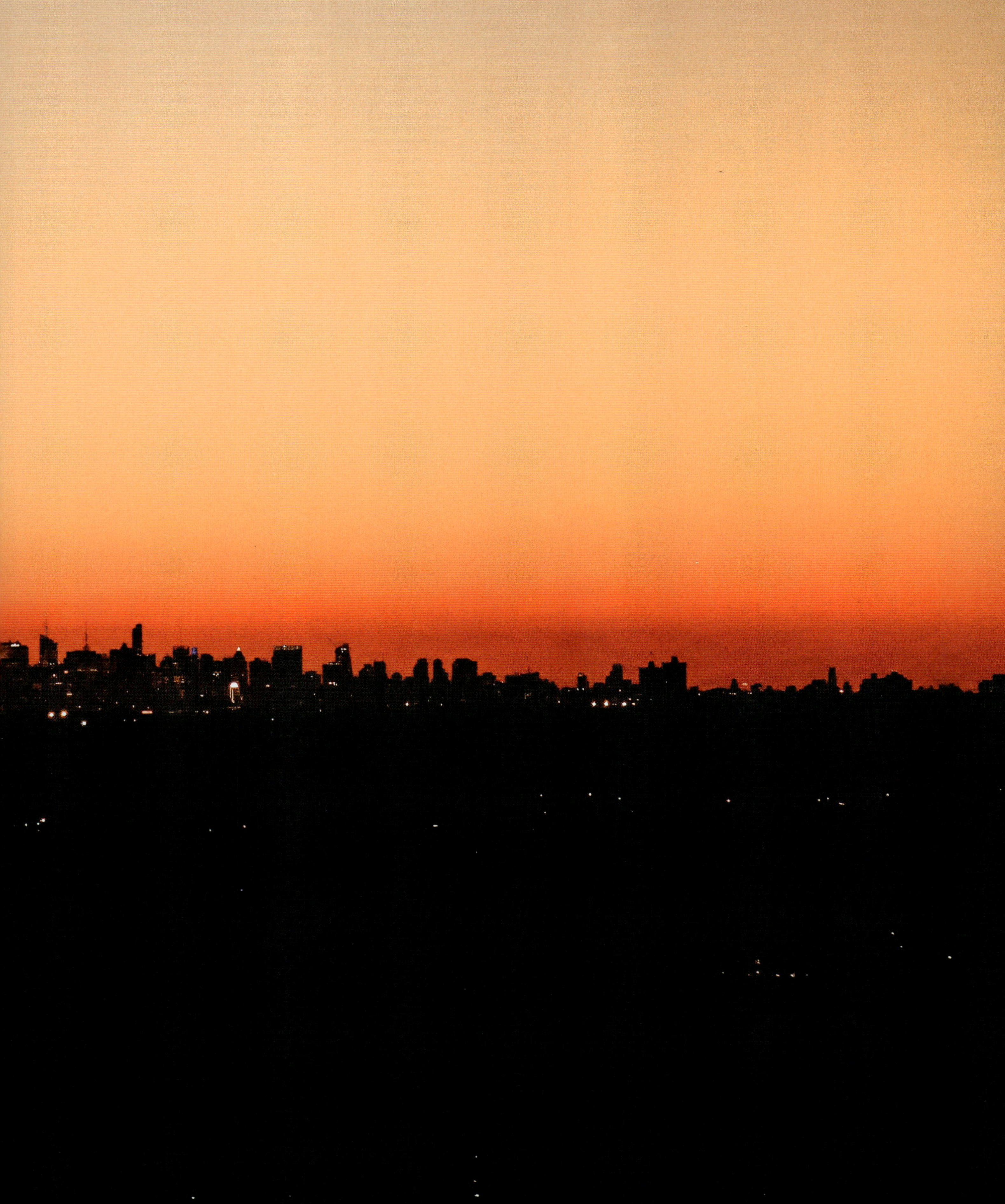

Photographers index a/z

Alex Rivera
@thebronxer

Alexis Le Bagousse
@alexlebag

Bram van Woudenberg
@bramvanwoudenberg

Bryan Dumas
@b_dumas

Casey Tang
@casey.tang

Charissa Fay
@charissa_fay

Cindy Sung
@fartatoes

Darius Hertzog
@abrooklynsoul

Demilade Balogun
@sirroyston

Dondre Green
@dondregreen

Edgar Santana
@esantana

Eelco Roos
@croyable

Emile Almekinders
@emilealmekinders

Hal Haines
@hal_ellis_davis

Ivan Meneses
@ai.visuals

Ivan Wong
@ivvnwong

Jacqueline Melesio
@by_jaxx

Jared Blake
@imnotjaredblake

Jason Peterson
@jasonmpeterson

Jayson Cassidy
@jayson.cassidy

Jennifer Bin
@jenniferbin

Jones Crow
@jonescrow

Lucas Hornsby
@lucas_whitaker

Lucas Vocos
@lucasvocos

Michael Young
@mgyoungphotography

Mikel van den Boogaard

Miklas Manneke
@miklasmanneke

Nazly Kasim
@cainite_

Neal Kumar
@nealkumar

Ollie Nordh
@ollienordh

Patrick Janelle
@aguynamedpatrick

Peter Wu
@peterjwu

Pie Aerts
@pie_aerts

Rafia Afsar
@rafsiaa

Steven Fingar
@stevenfingar

Stijn Hoekstra
@stijnhoekstra

Vincent Peone
@vincentpeone

Wesley Verhoeve
@wesleyverhoeve

Wil Suárez
@wsuarez

William Meier
@williameier

Imprint

Streets of New York – MENDO

First published in 2018 at
teNeues Media Verlag GmbH & Co. KG, Kempen

Edited and written by MENDO *mendo.nl*
Publisher: Gunifort Uwambaga, MENDO
Creative Director: Joost Albronda, MENDO
Editorial Coordination: Joost Bastmeijer, MENDO
Copy: Joost Bastmeijer, MENDO

Published by gestalten, Berlin 2025

Editorial Management by Stephanie Rebel, gestalten
Production by Sandra Jansen-Dorn, gestalten
Color separation by Robert Kuhlendahl, gestalten
Copy editing & proofreading: Cheryl Redmond
Translation: Alice Boucher (French); Sofia Blind (German)

ISBN 978-3-96171-695-1

1st printing, 2025

Printed in the Czech Republic by PBtisk a.s.

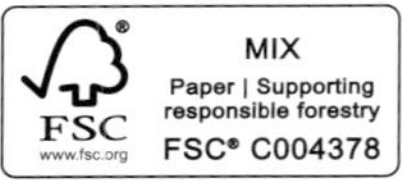

For more information and
to order books, please visit
www.teneues.com and www.gestalten.com

Die Gestalten Verlag GmbH & Co. KG
Mariannenstrasse 9–10
10999 Berlin, Germany
hello@gestalten.com

Düsseldorf Office
Waldenburger Straße 13
41564 Kaarst, Germany
verlag@teneues.com

teNeues Press Department
press@gestalten.com

Bibliographic information published by the Deutsche Nationalbibliothek. The Deutsche Nationalbibliothek lists this publication in the Deutsche Nationalbibliografie; detailed bibliographic data is available online at www.dnb.de

https://instagram.com/teneuespublishing

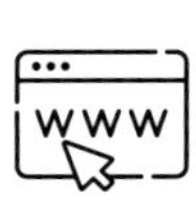

www.teneues.com

streets of new york

teNeues | MENDO